CW01499084

A History of Music in the Czech Lands

In a collection of essays from prominent music scholars both in the Czech Republic and abroad, this book provides a nuanced overview of major topics connected to the history of musical culture in the Czech lands (Bohemia, Moravia, and Silesia) from the Middle Ages to the present. Whereas most previous English-language musicological scholarship on the Czech lands focused solely on music that was understood as ethnically Czech, this book also considers musical cultures of non-Czech groups that lived, and sometimes still live, in the geographical area, most importantly people of German, Jewish, and Romani backgrounds. Spanning over a thousand years, this book combines innovative approaches to present fresh perspectives on a complicated musical tradition. This is the first overview of music in the Czech lands to offer such an inclusive view of the region's musical developments.

MARTIN NEDBAL is Professor of Musicology at the University of Kansas. He has authored two monographs: *Morality and Viennese Opera in the Age of Mozart and Beethoven* (2017) and *Mozart's Operas and National Politics: Canon Formation in Prague from 1791 to the Present* (2023).

KELLY ST. PIERRE is Professor of Musicology at Wichita State University. She has authored numerous publications, including a monograph on Bedřich Smetana (2017). Her newest research, exploring trauma and memory in Czech folksong scholarship, has been supported by a Fulbright Grant and by Prague's Center for Theoretical Studies.

HANA VLHOVÁ-WÖRNER is a Czech musicologist. She has widely published on Czech medieval music, with focus on liturgical poetry and fifteenth-century vernacular chant. She is author of the four-volume edition of tropes *Repertorium Troporum Bohemiae Medii Aevi* and general co-editor of the critical edition of the Jistebnice Kancionál.

A History of Music in the Czech Lands

Edited by

MARTIN NEDBAL
University of Kansas

KELLY ST. PIERRE
Wichita State University and Center for Theoretical Studies, Prague

HANA VLHOVÁ-WÖRNER
Masaryk Institute and Archives, Czech Academy of Sciences, Prague

CAMBRIDGE
UNIVERSITY PRESS

Shaftesbury Road, Cambridge CB2 8EA, United Kingdom

One Liberty Plaza, 20th Floor, New York, NY 10006, USA

477 Williamstown Road, Port Melbourne, VIC 3207, Australia

314–321, 3rd Floor, Plot 3, Splendor Forum, Jasola District Centre,
New Delhi – 110025, India

103 Penang Road, #05–06/07, Visioncrest Commercial, Singapore 238467

Cambridge University Press is part of Cambridge University Press & Assessment,
a department of the University of Cambridge.

We share the University's mission to contribute to society through the pursuit of
education, learning and research at the highest international levels of excellence.

www.cambridge.org
Information on this title: www.cambridge.org/9781009168656

DOI: 10.1017/9781009168663

First published 2025

A catalogue record for this publication is available from the British Library

Library of Congress Cataloging-in-Publication Data
Names: Nedbal, Martin, editor. | St. Pierre, Kelly, editor. | Vlhová-Wörner, Hana, editor.
Title: A history of music in the Czech lands / edited by Martin Nedbal, Kelly St. Pierre, Hana
Vlhová-Wörner.
Description: [1.] | New York : Cambridge University Press, 2025. | Includes bibliographical
references and index.
Identifiers: LCCN 2025004222 | ISBN 9781009168656 (hardback) | ISBN 9781009168670
(paperback) | ISBN 9781009168663 (ebook)
Subjects: LCSH: Music – Czech Republic – History and criticism. | Jews – Czech Republic –
Music – History and criticism. | Romanies – Czech Republic – Music – History and criticism. |
Germans – Czech Republic – Music – History and criticism.
Classification: LCC ML247 .H57 2025 | DDC 780.9437–dc23/eng/20250220
LC record available at https://lccn.loc.gov/2025004222

ISBN 978-1-009-16865-6 Hardback

For EU product safety concerns, contact us at Calle de José Abascal, 56, 1°, 28003 Madrid, Spain, or
email eugpsr@cambridge.org

Contents

Chapters marked * were translated from Czech, German, or Slovak by
    Martin Nedbal
The chapter marked + was translated from Czech by Hana Vlhová-
    Wörner and Martin Nedbal

Figures

Tables

Musical Examples

Contributors

MICHAEL BECKERMAN is Carroll and Milton Petrie Professor of Music at New York University and has published widely on Czech music. He has received honorary doctorates from Palacký and Masaryk Universities in the Czech Republic.

JAN BLÜML is Assistant Professor, Department of Musicology, Palacký University Olomouc. His main academic interest lies in the history of popular music in East Central Europe with special emphasis on music in the former Czechoslovakia. He is co-editor of the monograph *Popular Music in Communist and Post-Communist Europe* (Peter Lang, 2019).

MIRIAM BLÜMLOVÁ received her PhD in musicology from Palacký University Olomouc in 2018. She is the author (under the name Hasíková) of a monograph on interwar musical theater in Olomouc (Palacký University, 2016) and co-author of a monograph on the history of ballet in Olomouc (Palacký University, 2016).

EVA BRANDA is an Instructor at the Faculty of Music, Wilfrid Laurier University. She holds a PhD in musicology (University of Toronto). With special attention to Dvořák, her work focuses on genre and reception in the late nineteenth century. Her articles have appeared in *Music & Letters, Journal of the Royal Musical Association, Cambridge Opera Journal, Nineteenth-Century Music Review*, and *Acta Musicologica*.

ALEŠ BŘEZINA has been the director of the Bohuslav Martinů Institute in Prague since 1994. As chairman of the Martinů Complete Edition, he won the Best Edition award from the German Music Publishers Association in 2016 and the Czech Science Forum Foundation award in 2020. Additionally, he writes music for film, TV, and theater.

ANJA BUNZEL works at the Institute of Art History, Czech Academy of Sciences. She is the author of *The Songs of Johanna Kinkel: Genesis, Reception, Context* (Boydell, 2020) and co-edited *Musical Salon Culture in the Long Nineteenth Century* (with Natasha Loges, Boydell, 2019) and *Women in Nineteenth-Century Czech Musical Culture* (Routledge, 2024).

CHRISTOPHER CAMPO-BOWEN is Assistant Professor of Musicology at Virginia Tech and holds a PhD in musicology from UNC Chapel Hill. His research explores how opera intersects with race and ethnicity, gender, and politics in various historical contexts. He is the author of *Visions of the Village: Ruralness, Identity, and Czech Opera* (OUP 2025).

GEOFFREY CHEW is Emeritus Professor of Music at Royal Holloway, University of London. He specializes in Czech music and literature; he has published many articles and chapters in monographs, and translations of Czech literature, including *Beyond the World of Men: Women's Fiction at the Czech Fin de Siècle*. In 2018, he received a Leoš Janáček Medal for his contributions to Czech culture, especially Janáček research.

TEREZA HAVELKOVÁ is Assistant Professor at the Institute of Musicology, Charles University. She is the author of *Opera as Hypermedium: Meaning-Making, Immediacy, and the Politics of Perception* (OUP, 2021), and co-editor of the special issue "Sounding Corporeality" of *Theatre Research International* 46.2. She is the convenor of the Music Theatre Working Group of the International Federation for Theatre Research.

ERIKA SUPRIA HONISCH is Associate Professor of Critical Music Studies, Stony Brook University. She has published widely on music and pluralism in early modern Central Europe, and collaborated with ensembles that include Schola Antiqua and the Newberry Consort. She currently sits on the editorial boards of the *Journal of the American Musicological Society* and the *Yale Journal of Music and Religion*.

MARTIN HORYNA is a musicologist and Associate Professor at the University of South Bohemia, České Budějovice. His research focuses on issues of music and music theory, musical life, and the intersection of confessionalism and music in Bohemia between the fourteenth and seventeenth centuries. He has published eleven monographs together with numerous studies.

JAKUB HRŮŠA is Chief Conductor of the Bamberg Symphony and Music Director of The Royal Opera, Covent Garden. He collaborates with the world's greatest orchestras and opera companies, and is the 2023 Opus Klassik Conductor of the Year. His many other accolades include the Antonín Dvořák Prize awarded by the Czech Republic's Academy of Classical Music.

ZUZANA JURKOVÁ is the chair of the Anthropological Studies and Ethnomusicology programs at Charles University's Faculty of

Humanities. She focuses on Romani music (*Romani Musicians in the Twenty-First Century*, FHS, 2018) and urban ethnomusicology (*Prague Soundscapes*, Karolinum, 2014). She has been awarded numerous grants, including the Fulbright Research Fellowship.

Jiří Kopecký is the Musicology Department chair at Palacký University in Olomouc. His research focuses on the history of musical culture in the nineteenth-century Czech lands and the life and works of Zdeněk Fibich.

Matěj Kratochvíl is a researcher at the Institute of Ethnology, Czech Academy of Sciences. His main interests include the revival of traditional folk music, historical sound recordings, and digital humanities. His recent book (*Vy havíři umouněný, co vy z toho máte…*; Etnologický ústav, 2022) analyzes Czechoslovak folk-music research under communism.

Lenka Křupková is an associate professor at the Department of Musicology, Palacký University in Olomouc. Her main areas of research interest are Czech music of the nineteenth and twentieth centuries (particularly the work of Vítězslav Novák, Leoš Janáček, Josef Suk, and J. B. Foerster), music theatre, sociology of music, music and politics.

Brian S. Locke holds the position of Professor of Musicology at Western Illinois University. His publications include *Opera and Ideology in Prague: Polemics and Practice at the National Theatre, 1900–1938* (Rochester, 2006) and a critical edition of Otakar Zich's polytonal 1922 opera, *Vina* (Guilt; A-R Editions, 2014).

Judith Mabary is Associate Professor of Musicology at the University of Missouri, Columbia. Her research centers on Czech music of the nineteenth century. Her book *Contextualizing Melodrama in the Czech Lands in Concert and on Stage* was released in 2021 by Routledge. She is presently working on a monograph provisionally titled *Jeannette Meyer Thurber as Patron and Interpreneur: Making America's Music*.

Martin Nedbal is Professor of Musicology at the University of Kansas. He is the author of two monographs: *Mozart's Operas and National Politics: Canon Formation in Prague from 1791 to the Present* (CUP, 2023) and *Viennese Opera and Morality in the Age of Mozart and Beethoven* (Routledge, 2017).

Marc Niubo is Associate Professor of Musicology at Charles University in Prague. His research focuses on Italian opera and sacred music in the seventeenth and eighteenth centuries. His habilitation thesis was published by Karolinum in 2022.

JANA PERUTKOVÁ is Professor of Musicology at Masaryk University. Her research focuses on eighteenth-century music, aristocratic patronage, Italian opera, and oratorio. She participates in research projects in both the Czech Republic and Austria. She is the author of *Der glorreiche Nahmen Adami. Johann Adam Graf von Questenberg (1678–1752) als Förderer der italienischen Oper in Mähren* (Vienna: Hollitzer Verlag, 2015).

KELLY ST. PIERRE is Professor of Musicology at the College of Fine Arts, Wichita State University. She has authored numerous publications in addition to her monograph on *Bedřich Smetana* (2017). She was awarded both a Fulbright Grant (2019–20) and position at the Center for Theoretical Studies in Prague (2020–23) in support of her newest research, which explores trauma and memory in Czech folksong scholarship.

KAREL ŠIMA studied history and anthropology at Charles University. He has done research in social history and higher education studies. His interests include a range of topics from public festivities and rituals to higher education policy. He is currently working on a book on public festivities in the nineteenth-century Czech lands.

JANICE B. STOCKIGT is Associate Professor (Honorary) at the University of Melbourne. Her interests include Dresden court musicians (1720–65), Czech, and Australian topics. Apart from her prize-winning monograph *Jan Dismas Zelenka* (2000, 2018), she publishes widely, including articles in *Bach-Jahrbuch*, *Bach Perspectives*, *Clavibus unitis*, *Eighteenth-Century Music*, *Händel Jahrbuch*, *Hudební věda*, *Musicology Australia*, *Royal Musical Association Research Chronicles*, and *Studi vivaldiani*.

VIKTOR VELEK is a Czech musicologist. His research focuses on music and spirituality, Czech music in the "long" nineteenth century, musical migration, and the musical culture of Slavic minorities in Vienna between 1840 and 1945.

HANA VLHOVÁ -WÖRNER is a Czech musicologist at the Masaryk Institute and Archives, Czech Academy of Sciences, Prague. She has widely published on Czech medieval music, with focus on liturgical poetry and fifteenth-century vernacular chant. She is author of the four-volume edition of tropes *Repertorium Troporum Bohemiae Medii Aevi* and general co-editor of the critical edition of the Jistebnice Kancionál.

DAVID VONDRÁČEK is a postdoctoral researcher at the Czech Academy of Sciences, Institute of Art History with specialization in Czech modernist and popular music. He holds a doctoral degree from Ludwig-Maximilians-Universität Munich. His dissertation, *Jaroslav Ježek zwischen Avantgarde und Jazz*, was published by Allitera in 2021.

JIŘÍ ZAHRÁDKA is Associate Professor at the Institute of Musicology, Masaryk University. He has authored numerous books about Leoš Janáček, including *The Story of Janáček's Jenůfa* (2021), which received the 2022 Presto Music Award. He serves as the chief editor of Janáček's correspondence and has prepared critical editions of Janáček's works for Universal Edition, Henle Verlag, and Editio Bärenreiter.

MILOŠ ZAPLETAL is Assistant Professor at the Institute of Historical Sciences, Silesian University, Opava. He has written forty studies and two books, dealing mainly with Czech music of the nineteenth and twentieth centuries. He has also contributed to *The Routledge Companion to Applied Musicology* and is currently completing a monograph on British pop music between 1978 and 1982.

VLADIMÍR ZVARA is Associate Professor at the Department of Musicology, Comenius University, Bratislava. His research focuses on music and opera in Central Europe in the nineteenth and twentieth centuries. He has studied in Prague, Basel, and Vienna and taught at the universities in Bayreuth and Prague. He has also worked as an opera dramaturge at the Slovak National Theater, in Austria and Switzerland.

Acknowledgments

First and foremost, we would like to thank all the contributors to this volume for delivering their chapters in a timely fashion and responding to our queries; it has been a pleasure working with them. We also want to thank the project's advisory board: Michael Beckerman, Geoffrey Chew, and Jana Perutková. They have provided invaluable assistance in shaping the initial structure of the book.

The editing of the chapters translated from Czech was facilitated with the assistance of two University of Kansas students, Sara McClure and Matthew Anderson. Their work was funded by the University of Kansas General Research Fund and by the Faculty Development Award at Wichita State University, College of Fine Arts. Additionally, funding for Kelly St. Pierre's editorial work on the book was provided by the Czech Science Foundation (GAČR) under the research project, "The Second Sense: Sound, Hearing, and Nature in Czech Modernity" (20-30516Y).

We are also thankful to the Ministry of Culture of the Czech Republic for funding the typesetting of the musical examples through the Year of Czech Music and Smetana200 projects (www.rokceskehudby.cz). This funding was made possible through the efforts of Aleš Březina. We also extend our thanks to Lívia Posádková Krátka for her work in typesetting the examples.

We are grateful to several institutions for providing the images that appear in this volume: Bohuslav Martinů Center in Polička, the Brown University Library, Bayerische Staatsbibliothek, Niedersächsische Staats- und Universitätsbibliothek Göttingen, Archiv Národního divadla, Národní knihovna České republiky, Národní muzeum, Památník Terezín, Severočeské divadlo v Ústí nad Labem, and Státní okresní archiv Teplice.

A special word of thanks goes to Kate Brett who initially suggested this ambitious project and saw it through completion.

As this book was being prepared for delivery to the publisher, we were devastated to learn of the tragic death of our colleague Lenka Hlávková. We dedicate this book to her memory.

Introduction

MARTIN NEDBAL, KELLY ST. PIERRE, AND HANA VLHOVÁ-WÖRNER

The editors of this volume view the many challenges of its title as an opportunity, not a problem. Although musical cultures that could be understood as "Czech" makes up a significant portion of this book, the volume does not exclusively focus on supposedly "Czech" music.[1] Additionally, the regions often referred to as "Czech lands" acquired many titles in various languages throughout history and sometimes held radically different meanings, including "the Czech Republic," "Czechia," "Bohemia, Moravia, and Silesia," "Čechy, Morava, a Slezsko," "Böhmen, Mähren, und Schlesien," and "the Bohemian crownlands," among other possibilities. In his landmark essay "Where is Central Europe?", historian Lonnie Johnson explains that even seemingly neutral descriptions of geographic spaces like these are actually deeply subjective and unstable, redefined time and time again by notions of religion, empire, monarchy, kingdom, ethnicity, race, region, sub-region, ordinal direction, nation, state, historical narratives, victimhood, belonging, "otherness," culture, homogeny, democracy, exclusion, and genocide.[2] And while this list is in no way exhaustive, its challenges are only intensified by the possibilities of combination and negation: notions of a multiethnic monarchy, for example, or heterogeneous post-communist nation. That is, Johnson reminds us that even at the level of geography, understandings of boundaries are not stable; instead, they are stories. And these stories, just like supposed "histories" themselves, are always cultivated, curated, and, by extension, incomplete and partial.

In connection with the so-called "Czech lands," one often encounters "histories" that focus on a Slavic people who arrived in the territory of the present-day Czech Republic in the sixth century. They coexisted with other peoples, including Germans, Jews, and Roma, though not always peacefully. One of the regions where the Slavic "proto-Czechs" settled had

---

[1] As Michael Beckerman points out in his "In Search of Czechness in Music," notions of "Czech" music are unstable and primarily reflect a mode of listening and reception, rather than a musical style. See his discussion in *19th-Century Music* 10 (1986): 61–73.

[2] Lonnie R. Johnson, "Introduction: Where is Central Europe?," in *Central Europe: Enemies, Neighbors, and Friends* (New York: Oxford University Press, 2011), 3–12.

previously been called Bohemia by Roman writers, named after the Celtic tribe of the Boii that once inhabited the area. Many historical accounts also discuss how rulers in Prague ascended to become Bohemian kings and gain control over surrounding regions, which eventually formed the Bohemian crownlands. Many of these territories are part of the present-day Czech Republic, which was not established until 1993. One significant aspect of the Bohemian monarchy is the perception that many of the kings were outsiders. This was particularly true for members of the Habsburg dynasty, who held the Bohemian throne from 1526 to 1918. They incorporated the Bohemian crownlands into a multinational empire ruled from Vienna, but sometimes also from Prague. Another important narrative thread concerns the complex relationship between the "Czech lands" and the "German lands," represented by various political entities, such as the Holy Roman Empire, the German Empire, and Nazi Germany. Equally significant are the narratives involving the eastern neighbors and their interactions with the Czech lands, especially regarding the creation of Czechoslovakia in 1918 and its incorporation into the Soviet bloc between 1948 and 1989. As Johnson reminds us, these narratives are unstable and constantly evolving, shaped by those who construct them.

Altogether, the layers of storytelling and social constructs embedded in any music history, including *A History of Music in the Czech Lands*, make presenting unified metanarratives (or, indeed, worse, "master narratives") impossible.[3] This circumstance also creates the opportunity to explore notions of "Czech" music from a plurality of viewpoints, which is the position the editors of this volume embraced; we encouraged targeted examinations in our directives to individual chapter authors, rather than attempts at comprehensiveness. On the most basic level, this strategy means that readers will find that each contributor defines the "Czech lands" as applicable to their own discussions. More largely, this strategy extended to the researchers themselves as well as the methods they employ. Both Anglo-American and Czech scholars are represented in this volume, and among the researchers whose affiliations lie within today's Czech Republic, both wider regions as well as its major capitals are represented. Seventeen of the book's thirty authors originally submitted their chapters in Czech; one of these chapters (Chapter 3) was translated into English by Martin Nedbal and Hana Vlhová-Wörner, and sixteen chapters (Chapters 2, 6, 7, 10, 14, 17, 19, 20, 24, 25, 27–32) were translated by

---

[3] Richard Taruskin, "The History of What?" in *Oxford History of Western Music*, vol. 1 (New York: Oxford University Press, 2005), xxiii.

Martin Nedbal. This mix of Anglophone and Czech authors along with the breadth of methodologies they practice fostered a fascinating dialogue between sometimes distinct approaches to musicological research. As the following chapters show, many authors focused on close readings and interpretive studies concerning a limited number of sources, whereas others pursued more general narratives with an emphasis on at least partial overviews.

This makes *A History of Music in the Czech Lands* the first resource of its kind available in English. At the same time, at least three earlier publications to some extent prefigure *A History of Music in the Czech Lands*: the 1936 volume *Geschichte der Musik in der Tschechoslowakischen Republik*, the 1971 *Hudba* ("Music") from the series *Československá vlastivěda* ("Czechoslovak Homeland Studies"), and the collection *Hudba v českých dějinách* ("Music in Czech History"), first published in 1983.[4] Still, there are significant distinctions between the present book and these earlier projects, extending beyond their languages and years of publication. The 1936 book mainly focuses on the nineteenth and early twentieth centuries. Although the other two books are more even in their breadth of inquiry, the 1971 one does not go beyond 1965, and the 1983 one concludes in 1948. The authors of the earlier publications, furthermore, wrote distinct chronological segments in the style of an encyclopedia, and their histories are focused on separating the developments of "Czech," "Slovak," and "German" music.

Our volume, like the earlier publications, is largely chronological but covers a broader span of time and engages with a larger variety of identities. It starts from the earliest notated music documents – Latin chant for the liturgy and Czech religious songs (discussed in Chapters 1 and 2) – and extends to discussions of and perspectives by musicians associated with musical cultures in the present-day Czech Republic, including the frontman of a Romani popular band (Jan "Jenda" Dužda – Chapter 25), a contemporary Czech female composer (Sylvie Bodorová – Chapter 31), and globally renowned star conductor (Jakub Hrůša – Chapter 32). Several chapters delve into musical activities undertaken by those who migrated from the Bohemian lands to Saxony (Chapter 8), North America (Chapter 22), and Slovakia (Chapter 30). Although most chapters touch on the multicultural and diverse aspects of the musical history in what is

---

[4] Vladimír Helfert and Erich Steinhard, *Geschichte der Musik in der Tschechoslowakischen Republik* (Prague: Orbis, 1936); *Československá vlastivěda*, part 9, vol. 3, *Hudba* (Prague: Horizont, 1971); and Vladimír Lébl, ed., *Hudba v českých dějinách: od středověku do nové doby* (Prague: Supraphon, 1983).

now the Czech Republic, several contributions focus on topics that are not exclusively Czech. These topics include Jewish music (Chapter 21), music and race studies (Chapter 23), Romani music (Chapter 25), and German musicians and institutions (Chapters 9 and 12). Several chapters also explore topics that became the subject of serious musicological enquiry only in recent decades, including female musicians (Chapters 11 and 31), colonialism (Chapter 26), jazz and cabaret music (Chapter 27), rock music (Chapter 28), and film music (Chapter 29). Although we avoided dedicating whole chapters to single composers in general, we made an exception for Leoš Janáček (Chapter 19), whose operatic works have gained global recognition for their gripping yet highly individualistic portrayals of human psychology, making Janáček, according to the Operabase statistics, one of the twenty most performed opera composers in the world.[5]

The chapters are divided into three large chronological groups. Part I, "Before 1800," contains eight chapters, focusing on various aspects of sacred and secular music in the Bohemian crownlands from the early Middle Ages, through the Hussite Wars, the reign of Emperor Rudolf II, to the Catholic Reformation. Part II, "The 'Long' Nineteenth Century," features nine chapters focusing on various genres, institutions, and ideologies associated with musical practices during the period in which the modern Czech nationhood was defined. Part III, "The Twentieth Century and Beyond," contains fifteen chapters that follow the developments of both classical and popular music.

Though our volume is organized chronologically and is divided into three Parts, we imagine these structures a means to an end – a framework for considering a multiplicity of perspectives, rather than an attempt to reinforce metanarratives or periodization. Indeed, our hope is that this volume offers a beginning, rather than an end, definitive statement; that its pages inspire inquiry and encourage further conversation among thinkers, musicians, students, and scholars alike.

---

[5] Operabase Statistics, www.operabase.com/statistics/en, accessed January 22, 2024.

PART I

Before 1800

1 | Medieval Traditions of Plainchant in Bohemia

HANA VLHOVÁ-WÖRNER

The visitors of Prague today, as they stroll through the city, are enchanted by countless architectural gems from the Middle Ages. Most of these architectural monuments are connected with the period of Charles IV (1346–78) and his son and successor Wenceslas IV (1378–1419) of the House of Luxembourg. The visitors start their walk at the Gothic Cathedral of St. Vitus, Wenceslas and Adalbert (Vojtěch), whose construction began in 1348, shortly after Prague bishopric (founded 973) was elevated to an archbishopric in 1344. They cross the river through the Charles Bridge (finished c. 1400) and enter the historical Old Town with its narrow winding streets and numerous churches and monasteries hidden behind the walls. On their way to the Old Town Square that is dominated by the Gothic Church of the Mother of God before Týn (c. 1380), they usually turn right to visit the Bethlehem Chapel (founded 1391), where Master Jan Hus, one of Luther's main forerunners in his reformist ideas, once preached. The first stroll can be conveniently finished in a cozy restaurant near the main Prague university building, the so-called "Karolinum" (from its Latin designation *collegium Carolinum*, that is, Charles's College), the main seat of the Prague university studies established in 1348.

What remains hidden from visitors to these architectural monuments today is that these spaces cultivated its specific musical repertory in the Late Middle Ages, each of them memorable in its own way. The rich variety of genres and styles documented in countless medieval music manuscripts – in many cases beautifully decorated books of monumental dimensions – is impressive. Not least because most compositions are monophonic and could be simply designated as "chant" or "monophonic songs." Unlike other contemporary cultural centers, where composers were already focusing on polyphonic works in the style of *ars nova*, Prague authors remained remarkably long faithful to the monophonic idiom. Some of them exploited the

This study was written as part of the project *Old Myths, New Facts. Czech Lands in Center of 15th-Century Music Development* of the Czech Science Foundation 19–28306-X, joint project of the Masaryk Institute and Archives, Czech Academy of Sciences, Prague and the Faculty of Arts, Charles University, Prague. The author would like to thank Dr. Rhianydd Hallas (Prague) and Professor Kelly St. Pierre (Wichita State University) for improving the English text.

symbolic value of Roman chant, paying tribute to its century-long tradition; others experimented with traditional forms and melodic styles; and still others strived to create a genuine "Czech" Roman chant and install Czech as an emancipated liturgical language. Parallel to these developments, local authors started to make use of vernacular songs for their distinct ability to convey ideas that may not be consistent with the Church doctrine of that time. All these traditions will be presented in the following paragraphs, which should provide a view behind the walls of the architectural monuments that still stand today: St. Vitus's Cathedral, Prague parish churches, and the Bethlehem Chapel.

The Conservative St. Vitus's Cathedral and Chants by the Archbishop Jan of Jenštejn

The roots of the unusually prominent position of the monophonic idiom in Bohemia prevailing until the early modern period is closely connected to the political program of Emperor Charles IV and the liturgy practiced in St. Vitus's Cathedral. In the second half of the fourteenth century, it became the space of an unprecedentedly flamboyant liturgical service. More than 200 clerics, ministers, boy choristers, and other servants attended to daily liturgical performance here. Emperor Charles IV himself generously supported the liturgical service, providing funds for clergy and making impressive donations, such as the "autograph" (as he believed) of the Gospel of St. Mark that he acquired in Venice. Some precious artifacts are today presented to visitors of St. Vitus's Treasury near the cathedral.[1]

Charles strived to establish Prague as a new Rome and make it the center of the Christian world of its time.[2] The liturgy of St. Vitus's Cathedral should align with this vision, especially in preserving and cultivating a distinctly conservative repertory that was not to be contaminated by uncontrolled additions. The legend about Pope Gregory the Great (d. 604) as the author of liturgical chant (hence called "Gregorian" chant) was revived and acknowledged in many ways. Pope Gregory was depicted in liturgical books, and a short, ancient piece of music, the prologue *Gregorius presul* that celebrated the pope's merits in the establishing liturgical chant in the first millennium, was solemnly proclaimed in the cathedral at the beginning of each Church

---

[1] The manuscript, today dated to the sixth century, is preserved in the Prague Archiv Pražského hradu, fond Knihovna pražské metropolitní kapituly u sv. Víta, shelfmark Cim 1.

[2] Kateřina Kubínová, *Imitatio Romae – Karel IV. a Řím* (Prague: Artefactum, 2006).

year.[3] In the 1360s, prevailingly conservative and even partly outdated Prague liturgical repertory was newly codified in a set of nine monumental and splendidly decorated chant books, donated by the Prague Archbishop Arnošt of Pardubice (Arnošt z Pardubic, 1344–64).[4] The volumes, displayed on pulpits, were to impress visitors of the cathedral and proclaim that the space preserved the "authentic" music tradition, which was meanwhile "lost" in many other places of medieval Europe. Their authority was obviously overwhelming. Some scribes of the new liturgical books went so far as to be reluctant to incorporate new repertory for the Feast of Corpus Christi during the following decades, even as new chants flourished within other churches of the Prague diocese, because, as one of them stated, its performance was not "approved" by papal authority.[5] That is, in the setting of a modern Gothic Cathedral building, equipped with countless new art objects, the music constituted the link to the past, acknowledged in the daily liturgy and not open to the creative output of contemporary authors.

The third Prague Archbishop Jan of Jenštejn (Jan z Jenštejna, in office 1378–97) and his chant compositions make a rare exception to the overall orthodox milieu. From his position, he was even able to introduce chants that were literally disapproved by the papal (Roman) curia, not only to St. Vitus's Cathedral, but also in the Prague diocese. His personality and output deserve much attention, not least because his career provides extremely colorful insight into the fate of a prominent chant author in the period of the Papal Schism (1378–1417). Today, Jenštejn is known as a main initiator in introducing the Feast of the Visitation of the Virgin Mary (*Visitatio beatae Mariae virginis in montanis*, 1386 in Prague; 1389 for the whole Church) into the Church calendar. He was also, however, a skilled poet and composer. As a highly educated prelate (he studied at the universities of Padua, Bologna, Montpellier, and Paris), he was also fully involved in the political negotiations to end the double-papacy, and his poetic and musical output is closely connected to this major political crisis.[6]

As Jenštejn later recounted in his letter to the Roman Pope Urban (1378–89), his inspiration for the introduction of the Feast of the Visitation came

---

[3] See David R. Holeton, Milena Bílková, and Hana Vlhová-Wörner, "The Trope Gregorius presul meritis in Bohemian Traditions," in *The Bohemian Reformation and Religious Practice*, vol. 6, ed. Zdeněk V. David and David R. Holeton (Prague: Czech Academy of Sciences, 2007), 215–46.

[4] Studies devoted to the collection and its repertory are included in the volume *Miscellanea musicologica* 37 (Prague: Univerzita Karlova, 2003).

[5] Hana Vlhová, "Die Fronleichnamsmesse in Böhmen: ein Beitrag zur spätmittelalterlichen Choraltradition," *Schweizer Jahrbuch für Musikwissenschaft. Neue Folge* 16 (1996): 13–36.

[6] On Jenštejn and his political career, see Michael van Dussen, *From England to Bohemia: Heresy and Communication in the Late Middle Ages* (New York: Cambridge University Press, 2012).

from an apocalyptic dream, in which the Virgin Mary appeared as the only source of consolation in the dramatic state of a fatally divided Church. Jenštejn accompanied his request to the Roman Curia to establish the new feast with a comprehensive set of chants for the Office and Mass, which he compiled partly on his own, and partly – as discovered only recently – with the help of his collaborator Mikuláš Rakovník.[7] The following several-years process is rather extraordinary in the history of plainchant: Jenštejn's pieces were subjected in Rome to a detailed analysis by a jury of nearly forty prelates with regard to their theological correctness and poetic quality. The jury reproached the submitted repertory for its deficiencies in the verse structure and the vocabulary. The Roman Curia finally prescribed in 1389 another set of chants (the rhymed office *Accedunt laudes* of Adam Easton) as obligatory for the Roman liturgy. Despite the papal verdict, not Easton's, but Jenštejn's chants became part of the Prague repertory and quickly spread in Bohemia and neighboring territories. To accomplish this, Jenštejn employed the efficient mechanism established already by his predecessors: an "approved" model with a full set of chants and texts was available in the archbishop's office, where the clergy of the entire diocese were to obtain a copy.

Jenštejn's work is extremely wide-ranging, including some twenty sequences[8] and other Mass chants, two dozen songs and two complete sets of chants for two Marian feasts (in addition to the Visitation of the Virgin Mary, one office for the Feast of Our Lady of the Snows): this makes him one of the most prolific ever medieval chant authors.[9] His sequences and *Alleluia* chants for the Feast of the Visitation of the Virgin Mary became particularly popular. They perfectly complemented the visual representations of the biblical "visitation" scene popular at that time, in which the pregnant Mary visits her relative and mother of John the Baptist, Aunt Elizabeth, in the mountains. His pieces are designed both as narratives and prayers to the Virgin Mary, and so in singing or listening to them, the believers both "learn" and "bow."

---

[7] The genesis and character of the Jenštejn Officium is described in Rhianydd Hallas, "Two Rhymed Offices Composed for the Feast of the Visitation of the Blessed Virgin Mary: Comparative Study and Critical Edition" (PhD diss., Bangor University and Charles University, Prague, 2021).

[8] The sequence repertory from Czech sources is available in the database Hana Vlhová-Wörner, ed., *Codicologica et Hymnologica Bohemica – Index Sequentiarum Bohemiae Medii Aevi*, www .hymnologica.cz, accessed November 21, 2023. The preservation of Jenštejn's sequences in European sources is recorded in the database *Cantus Index*, cantusindex.org, accessed November 21, 2023.

[9] The texts attributed to Jan of Jenštejn were published in *Analecta hymnica medii aevi* 48, ed. Guido Maria Dreves and Clemens Blume (Leipzig: Reisland, 1905), 421–51.

This can be illustrated by the pair of *Alleluia O Maria, mater Christi* and the sequence *Illibata mente sana*, in which Jenštejn concealed his name in the form of an acrostic (in the initial letters of each stanza) IOHANNES. Unlike the *Alleluia* chants of the earlier period, which generally drew on texts, Jenštejn's *O Maria, mater Christi* is a short poetic work with regular verse consisting of eight syllables and rhymes at the end of each verse:

O Maria, mater Christi,	O Mary, mother of Christ,
montana que adisti,	who came to the mountains,
et cognatam visitasti,	to visit a relative,
consilii mater casti.	out of a blameless motive.
Audi nos, dulcis et pia,	Hear us, sweet and holy,
natum nobis concilia.	reconcile us to your Son.

The biblical scene is only briefly mentioned in the text. Instead, the petition to the Virgin Mary to intercede with the divine Son (the two final lines) are dominant here, and the invocation "Audi nos" ("Hear us") makes it a direct prayer to the Virgin Mary (see Example 1.1).[10]

The sequence *Illibata menta sana* that immediately followed in the liturgy describes the key scene of the visitation in more detail. The text is outlined as a lively dialogue between two pregnant women and incorporates Mary's famous exclamation of the *Magnificat*, the beginning of the biblical canticle, which was sung daily at the end of Vespers.[11] Of course, only those educated in Latin could grasp the close parallel between the artistic and musical-literary depictions. But a sensitive listener would recognize a subtle link to the sequences to other female saints, which employed the same melody or used similar musical phrases.[12]

New Repertory of Churches Outside Cathedral and Chants Attributed to Záviš

While the cathedral watched carefully over their orthodox liturgy, the situation developed differently in the parish churches, in Prague and

---

[10] For the edition, see Karlheinz Schlager, ed., *Alleluia-Melodien II: ab 1100*, Monumenta monodica medii aevi, vol. 7 (Kassel: Bärenreiter, 1987), 258–60.

[11] See the text and music edition in Andrea Kovács, *Monuments of Medieval Liturgical Poetry in Hungary. Sequences – Critical Edition of Melodies*, Musica Sacra Hungarica 1 (Budapest: Argumentum, 2017), 228.

[12] Sequences *Margaritam preciosam* for St. Margaret that use the same melody (edited in Kovács, *Monuments of Medieval Liturgical Poetry*, 225–26) or *Gens fidelis iocundetur* for St. Dorothea that move in the same (Phrygian) mode and employ similar musical phrases (edited in Kovács, *Monuments of Medieval Liturgical Poetry*, 232–33).

Example 1.1: *Alleluia O Maria, mater Christi*, attributed to the Archbishop Jan of Jenštejn.

other wealthy cities alike. Parish churches were financially supported by rich citizens, who also increasingly intervened in the shaping of liturgical services and selection of music repertory. While laymen were more and more actively involved in the liturgical performance – such as in the St. Egidius (Jiljí) church in the Old Town, where they could sing lamentations during *Triduum* from the mid-fourteenth century – they also sponsored new votive ceremonies that gained in popularity: the morning Marian Masses and the evening "Salve," which were salutation

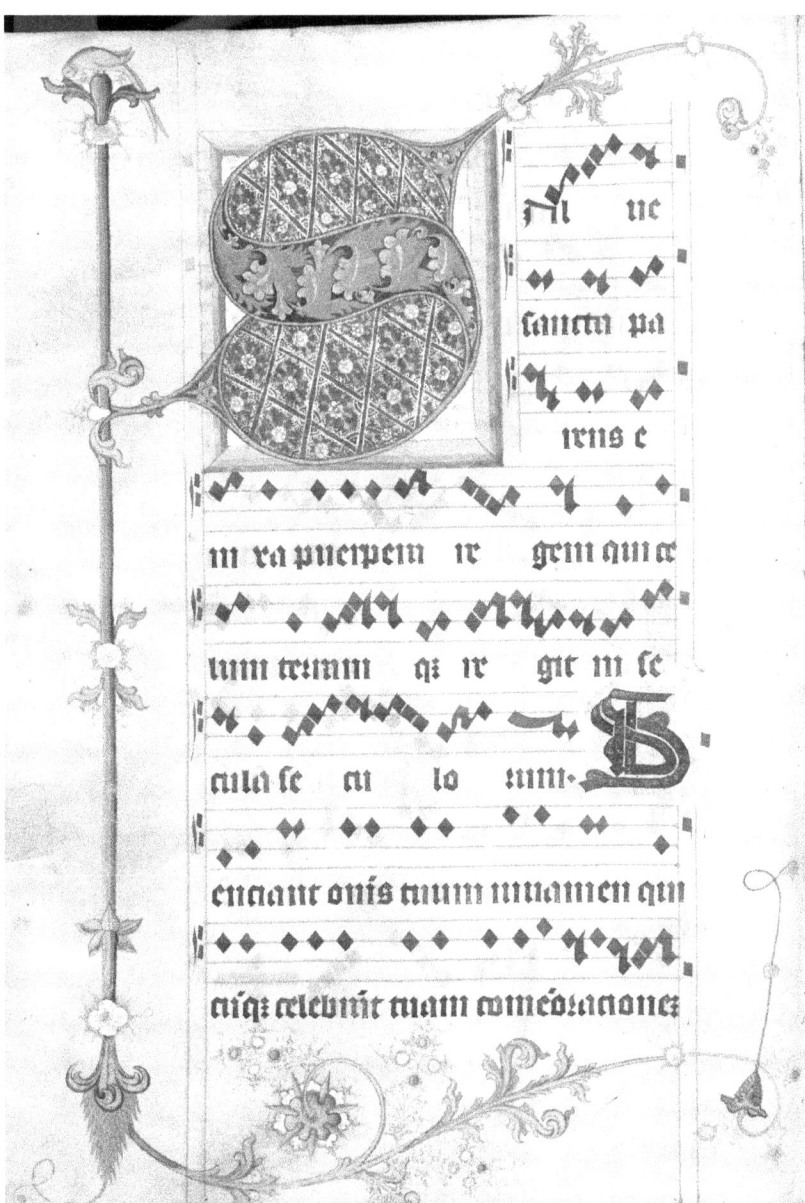

Figure 1.1: The beginning of the votive Marian Mass *Salve, sancta parens* from the Prague Gradual from the end of the fourteenth century. Prague, Knihovna Národního muzea, shelfmark XII A 1, fol. 33v. Reproduced by permission.

services to the Virgin Mary (see Figure 1.1 with the opening page of the Marian Mass *Salve, regina* from the Prague Gradual from the end of the fourteenth century).

Morning votive devotions in particular became almost the norm during this period. They became the forerunners of the famous so-called Rorate Masses, which were performed during Advent and became extremely popular in the following centuries. This tradition persists to this day in some churches, including the Church of the Mother of God before Týn on the Prague Old Town Square (see Chapters 3 and 8).

Marian devotions had a fundamental effect on the formation of the spiritual world for believers. They were complex rituals, combining visual sensation (the contemplation of images or statues) with simple gestures (bowing, kneeling) and perceiving sounds and music tailored to the event (ringing bells and singing). Rich citizens often spared no expense to embellish these devotions with special musical repertory. It is therefore not surprising that music manuscripts of that time incorporate abundantly new chant pieces, mostly for the Virgin Mary. Many of them demonstrate individual styles and partly also forms that differ from "traditional" Roman chant.

A special interest in the Marian repertory in Bohemia around 1400 has been repeatedly thematized in Czech music historiography, which emphasized the individual "musical languagues" employed by contemporary composers. In all surveys of Czech music history (which almost stubbornly ignore the extensive work of Jan of Jenštejn), a composer with the name "Záviš" emerges from the anonymity of many casual authors of that time.[13] Chants attributed to Záviš are today considered the epitome of chant composition of the period, and the designation "Závišovské" ("of Záviš," rendering his name as an adjective) refers to a certain type of melody popularly used at this time.

Who was Záviš, actually? His identity is still a matter of speculation. Most often, he is associated with Záviš of Zapy, a highly educated prelate and lawyer who studied around 1400 at the universities of Prague, Padua, and Rome.[14] Not too many chants are attributed to him, but they accurately capture the atmosphere of the urban milieu, in which the votive services and private devotional culture of the parish liturgy flourished. The versatility of his perhaps best-known Latin chant, *O Maria, mater Christi* ("O Mary, Mother of God") illustrates the situation excellently.

---

[13] Vladimír Helfert and Erich Steinhard, *Die Musik in der Tschechoslovakischen Republik*, 2nd ed. (Prague: Orbis, 1936), 13; *Československá vlastivěda*, part 9, vol. 3, *Hudba* (Prague: Horizont, 1971), 42; Jaromír Černý, "Středověk," in *Hudba v českých dějinách: od středověku do nové doby*, ed. Vladimír Lébl (Prague: Supraphon, 1983), 56 and 61.

[14] On the personality and work of Záviš, see most recently Hana Vlhová-Wörner, "Záviš, autor liturgické poezie 14. století," *Hudební věda* 3–4 (2007): 229–60.

The piece could be used either in the Mass as an *Alleluia* (the word "Alleluia" added to its opening), or as a "verse" or "lai" (a long, monophonic, structured piece) in Marian votive services. It was also translated into the vernacular, responding to the growing importance of the Czech language in religious and spiritual life among the Czech population. The vernacular version *O Maria, matko milostivá* could be heard during private devotions, or used simply when "singing for pleasure."[15] Záviš, however, did not only compose chant for liturgy and devotion. Today, he is best known for his vernacular song *Jižť mne vše radost ostává* ("All My Joy Is Leaving Me"), labeled in contemporary sources fittingly as "Zawissonis cantio de amore mundali" ("Záviš's Song on Mundane Love"). It is a beautiful piece of love poetry, possibly inspired by the work of Frauenlob, who was one of the leading Minnesang authors from the late thirteenth and early fourteenth century, and its melody shares similar passages with *O Maria, mater Christi*.[16]

Záviš's chant pieces are not isolated from the contemporary Marian liturgical poetry cultivated in wider Central Europe. A parallel with thencontemporary visual art, especially the countless images and sculptures of Madonna and her child – the so-called "beautiful Madonnas" – can also be drawn to his pieces. The text of *O Maria, mater Christi* praises, as do many other songs and prayers, Mary's exclusive position in salvation history in the chain of epithets "consolatrix" ("comforter"), "adiutrix" ("helper"), "restauratrix" ("restorer"), "amatrix" ("lover"), "curatrix" ("curator"), and "relevatrix" ("nurturer").

The melody also strives to be "beautiful" and employs many characteristics of liturgical compositions in Bohemia and the surrounding regions during the late Middle Ages, including those of Jan of Jenštejn (see the beginning included in Example 1.2): especially the use of the Phrygian (E) mode; melodic ornaments ("loops") around the notes E or B; and a strikingly expressive melodic line full of melismas (melodic embellishments), in which major jumps are no exception.[17] Strophic interpolations in the simple rhythmic pattern short-long (the so-called *cantus fractus*) are

[15] Jaromír Černý, ed., *Historical Anthology of Music in the Bohemian Lands (up to ca 1530)* (Prague: KLP, 2005), 82–83.

[16] His work includes the verse *O Maria, mater Christi*, the Kyrie with the trope *Inmense conditor poli*, and one may perhaps include the Gloria, which forms a pair with the Kyrie. For the Kyrie and Gloria editions see Hana Vlhová-Wörner, *Repertorium troporum Bohemiae medii aevi 2. Tropi ad Kyrie eleison et Gloria in excelsis deo* (Prague: Bärenreiter, 2006), 124–25, 160–63, 202, and 238–40.

[17] See Gábor Kiss, "The 'Liedhafte E-Melodik'," *Studia Musicologica Academiae Scientiarum Hungaricae* 40 (1999): 315–24.

Example 1.2: Verse-Lai *O Maria, mater Christi*, attributed to the composer known as Záviš.

the most characteristic component of longer pieces of that time. Their text complements the main piece, while the music forms an interesting contrast within a monophonic idiom.[18]

Unlike Jenštejn's liturgical chants, which aspired to the position of "permanent" – in the sense of prescribed, or obligatory – chant repertory

---

[18] *The cantus fractus* repertoire is the subject of two monothematic issues of the *Journal of the Alamire Foundation* 14/2 (2022) and 15/1 (2023), guest editors Rhianydd Hallas and Hana Vlhová-Wörner.

of the Prague diocese, Záviš's and many similar compositions of that time stood for free selection. Judging from their inclusion in various (non-liturgical) collections with selected repertory, they were particularly popular among vocally skilled clerics without permanent positions, who could be hired for singing votive services. Additionally, the sections with *cantus fractus*, which appear in many pieces, point to the possible participation of children, typically pupils from the adjacent parish school. Sources from various parts of Europe refer to this specific performance practice as an effective tool for early education.[19]

Bethlehem Chapel, Jan Hus, and the Use of Vernacular Songs

Bethlehem Chapel in Prague's Old Town was a special place from its very beginning. Today's visitors are attracted by the inscriptions of texts and songs on the walls – partly authentic, partly created in the twentieth century – that witness the Chapel's involvement at the beginning of the fifteenth century in many key moments that led to the outbreak of the Hussite Wars. From its foundation in 1391, Bethlehem Chapel was devoted almost exclusively to public preaching. In 1402, Jan Hus (c. 1372–1415) was appointed preacher at the Chapel.[20] His teaching became a magnet for a large number of listeners – some sources speak of gatherings of up to 3,000 – coming from all of society's stratas, from the common people to high-ranking nobility. Hus's preaching was connected closely to ongoing debates among the Prague intellectual elite, commenting on the critical state of the Church and advocating for frequent communion of the Corpus Christi by the faithful. During Advent and Lent, Marian morning Mass was practiced in Bethlehem Chapel, similar to other town churches. In 1403, Hus introduced the daily celebration of the Eucharist, while his close friend, the theologian and university professor Jakoubek of Stříbro (Jakoubek ze Stříbra, Jacobellus de Misa), began developing his idea to serve not only Christ's Body, but also His Blood to the laity.[21] In 1412, Hus was forced to leave the Chapel for the countryside, and his future fate is well

---

[19] Giulia Gabrielli, "*Cantus fractus* in South Tyrolean Medieval Manuscripts," *Journal of the Alamire Foundation* 15/1 (2023): 53–66.

[20] On the personality of Jan Hus, cf. František Šmahel and Ota Pavlíček, eds., *A Companion to Jan Hus* (Boston: Brill, 2015).

[21] Serving the chalice to the laity, that is the communion of both species (*sub utraque*), was first practiced by Jakoubek of Stříbro in 1414 in the Church of St. Martin in the Wall in Prague's Old Town as early as 1414. That is, more than five hundred years before the Catholic Church allowed this practice after the Second Vatican Council in the 1960s. See also Chapter 3 in this volume.

known: he was summoned to the Council of Constance, which condemned him as a heretic to death at the stake (1415).

Hus's preaching career at Bethlehem Chapel is associated with the growing importance of a new musical repertory: the use of monophonic vernacular songs. Vernacular songs were a truly special medium. Not just a "schola" of selected singers, but a full gathering could participate in their performance. Songs were typically inserted between the opening reading from scripture that introduced the main topic and the sermon itself. This was a practice already known in Prague, established, for example, several decades earlier in the Church of the Mother of God before Týn by one of Hus's predecessors, the preacher Konrad of Waldhausen (d. 1369). Their performance was, however, not always associated with pure religious experience. An infamous incident in Prague's history happened during Easter of 1389, when Jews were murdered and their houses burned down in Prague after the evening sermon. A contemporary commentary depicts the event vividly, noting that the Prague citizens killed Jews, with the song *Buoh všemohúcí* on their lips.[22]

The psychology of the moment, in which Hus's moral and often critical preachings were closely intertwined with the community's singing, cannot be overstated today. The performance of vernacular songs was a special experience of unity in faith, language, and shared history. Such moments contributed greatly to the formation of the idea of the "chosen" Czech nation nourished during the Hussite Wars in the following decades, in which Hussites waged their holy war against the whole of Christian Europe.

Hus's written sermons specifically mention four vernacular songs intoned by the gathered community. Unsurprisingly, all were well known in Prague around 1400 (see also Chapter 2). The song *Hospodine, pomiluj ny* ("Lord, Have Mercy upon Us") was most often selected, one of the oldest Czech literary and musical monuments, whose origins date back to the second half of the tenth century; that is, to the very beginning of the existence of the Prague diocese and Czech state (see Example 1.3 and Figure 1.2 with the oldest notated inscription of the song from 1473).[23] From the early Middle Ages, the song was intoned on important state occasions and in the four-teenth century became a staple part of the coronation order of Czech kings. Similarly, visitors to Bethlehem Chapel were familiar with the song *Svatý Václave* ("Saint Wenceslas"), a prayer to the patron saint of the Czech lands

---

[22] See František Mužík, "Christ ist erstanden – Buóh všemohúcí," *Miscellanea musicologica* 21–23 (1970): 7–45.

[23] Černý, *Anthology*, nos. 1, 3.

Figure 1.2: The oldest notated inscription (1473) of the song *Hospodine, pomiluj ny*, from the Prague Gradual from the end of the fourteenth century. Prague, Knihovna Národního muzea, shelfmark XII A 1, fol. 219v. Reproduced by permission.

St. Wenceslas and, in the context of Charles IV's ideology, its "heir" (see Example 1.4). It could be intoned more than during the two feasts dedicated to St. Wenceslas, the "passio" (September 28) and "translatio" (March 4). Two remaining songs mentioned in Hus's sermons were dedicated to Christ's passion and resurrection. The first of them, *Jezu Kriste, ščedrý*

Example 1.3: Czech vernacular song *Hospodine, pomiluj ny* ("Lord, Have Mercy upon Us"). English: Lord, have mercy upon us, Jesus Christ, have mercy upon us! Savior of the whole world, save us! And hear, Lord, our voices: Give us all, Lord, abundance and peace on earth! Kyrie eleison, Kyrie eleison, Kyrie eleison!

Example 1.4: Czech vernacular song *Svatý Václave* ("Saint Wenceslas"). English: 1. Saint Wenceslas, Duke of the Bohemian land, our Prince, pray for us to God, to the Holy Spirit! Kyrie eleison! 2. The heavenly Kingdom is beautiful, blessed is he who gets there, help us and banish all evil. 3. We ask for your help, have mercy on us, comfort the sad, banish all evil, saint Wenceslas! Kyrie eleison.

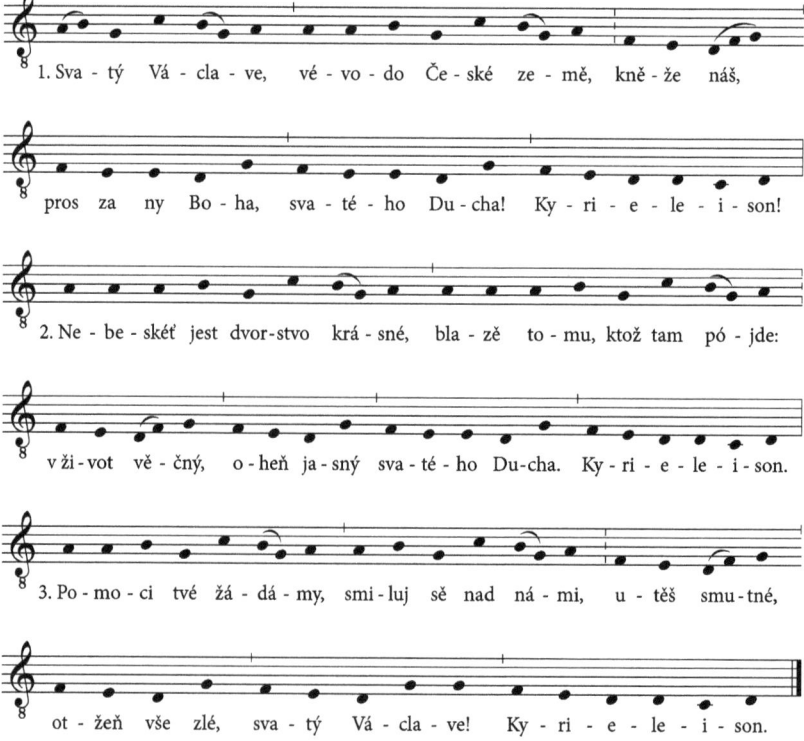

Example 1.5: Czech vernacular song *Jezu Kriste, ščedrý kněže* ("Jesus Christ, O Bounteous Priest"), first stanza. English: Jesus Christ, o bounteous priest, who with the Father and the Spirit is one God, all your bounty is ours. Kyrie eleison. (Fifteenth-century version: from your grace.)

(a) Fourteenth-century version

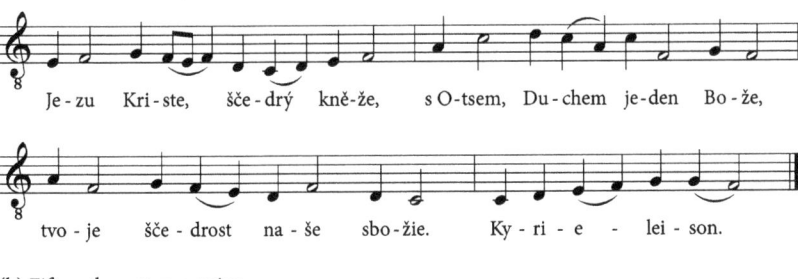

(b) Fifteenth-century version

kněže ("Jesus Christ, O Bounteous Priest"), was in the later tradition attributed to Hus himself (see Example 1.5, version b).[24] The second, *Buoh všemohúcí* ("God Almighty"),[25] was the Czech equivalent of the famous German song *Christ ist erstanden*, known to the German-speaking population of Bohemia (see Example 1.6). Historical documents give evidence that in Prague it was possible to perform this song simultaneously in both vernacular languages – Czech and German – while the preacher joined in with its Latin version, *Christus surrexit*.

The popularity of these vernacular sacred songs was not limited to Bethlehem Chapel and had spread from the last decades of the fourteenth century in both churches and monasteries. Some of the songs apparently also found their way even into the liturgy. In 1408, the Prague archbishop felt it necessary to ban the singing of "new songs" ("novas cantilenas") in the liturgy on pain of punishment, with the exception of the four songs Hus specifically invited to be performed at Bethlehem Chapel.[26] The archbishop's

---

[24] Černý, *Anthology*, nos. 47, 78–79.   [25] Černý, *Anthology*, nos. 46, 77–78.

[26] Jaroslav V. Polc and Zdeňka Hledíková, *Prague Synods and Councils of the Pre-Hussite Era* (Prague: Karolinum, 2002), 286.

Example 1.6: Czech vernacular song *Buoh všemohúcí* ("God Almighty"), first stanza. English: God almighty is risen from the dead awaited. Let us praise God with joy, as the Scripture calls, Kyrie eleison!

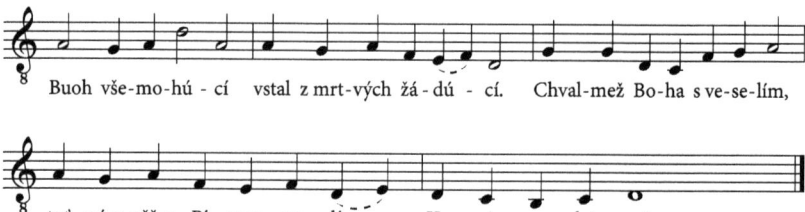

prohibition obviously came to nothing. Several dozen vernacular sacred songs were known already by 1410, some of which were adapted by reform churches in Bohemia during the following decades (see Chapter 3).[27] In the 1420s, Hussite authors further increased the repertory of vernacular songs, understanding well the power of communal singing in the vernacular. They used this well-established medium as an effective communication tool to disseminate the crucial ideas of Hussite theologians, such as Communion of both Bread and Wine and/or the Communion of Infants.

"Sacred Chant," Parish Liturgy, and Vernacular Language: The Birth of the Czech Vernacular Liturgy

The authority of sacred Roman chant, the laymen's interest in participating in the liturgy, and the practice of singing in the vernacular – all three of these aspects came together in Prague in the unique project of creating a vernacular liturgy for the Hussite parish church in the 1420s. Some historians suggested that this project may have originated directly in Bethlehem Chapel, the epicenter of reformist ideas. Hus, however, never sought to introduce the vernacular liturgy during his time there. He seems to have been as reticent about this serious departure from the centuries-old tradition of the Roman Church as he was about taking communion *sub utraque*. The Czech vernacular liturgy is very likely an achievement of the Prague intellectual elite with connections to the Prague university and to the Emmaus Monastery in the New Town of Prague, that cultivated from 1348 a "Slavonic" liturgy.

---

[27] Manuscript 42 in the library of the monastery in Vyšší Brod from 1410.

Probably in an extremely short time, a translation of the liturgical repertory for the Mass and the Office was conducted, most probably from the early 1420s or even shortly before. It is difficult to get an accurate picture of the whole project today because sources with Hussite content were systematically destroyed in Bohemia during recatholicization (see Chapter 5). Our knowledge today relies on a single codex that miraculously escaped destruction – the so-called *Jistebnický kancionál* ("Jistebnice Kancionál") from the 1420s or early 1430s, discovered by accident in the town Jistebnice (South Bohemia) in 1874.[28] Thanks to this discovery, it is possible to get a fairly accurate idea of what Czech vernacular liturgy intended to be and how it was created. The main scheme was to establish a vernacular Roman liturgy that would be a full equivalent to the Latin liturgy. Therefore, the Mass and the Office still preserve the main outline of the Roman liturgy. The Latin texts were translated as faithfully as possible into the vernacular. Authors of the Czech version usually treated the traditional ("Roman") chant melodies with the same purist approach. Major deviations from their Latin melodies rarely occurred, and mostly only in places where they were necessary for the differing length (syllables or full words) of both languages.

Despite this purist approach, the authors retained the license to adapt the liturgy to the ideology of the Hussite Church. This can be demonstrated in particular in the chants for one of the central festivities, the Feast of Corpus Christi. For example, the antiphon *Ego sum panis vivus*, famous from countless settings from the Renaissance even to today, draws its Latin text from the St. John Gospel, where Christ says: "Ego sum panis vivus, qui de caelo descendi, si quis manducaverit ex hoc pane, vivet in eternum" ("I am the living bread that came down from Heaven; whoever eats of this bread will live forever"). However, in the Hussite version, which is based on one of the following verses of John's Gospel, the translation is expanded to include the phrase, "whoever will eat of this bread *and drink of the chalice* will live forever" (emphasis mine), thus introducing the motif of receiving the chalice as a condition of salvation into the Hussite liturgy.[29] The motif of the chalice appears repeatedly in chant pieces and in vernacular songs recorded in the manuscript. It is powerfully expressed in the original Czech

---

[28] For a new edition of the manuscript with accompanying studies, see David Holeton and Hana Vlhová-Wörner, eds., *Jistebnický kancionál: MS. Prague, National Museum Library, II C 7: Critical Edition*, vol. 1, *Graduale* (Brno: Marek, 2005); and Hana Vlhová-Wörner, ed., *Jistebnický kancionál: MS. Prague, National Museum Library, II C 7: Critical Edition*, vol. 2, *Cantionale* (Chomutov: Marek, 2019).

[29] John, 6:52 and 6:55.

sequence *Abychme hodně pamatovali večeře božie slavnost* ("That We Might Remember Worthily the Celebration of God's Supper"). The lengthy chant that depicts the scene of the Last Supper is concluded with two stanzas that summon the believers to receive the chalice: "Aspoň kalich spasitedlý od tebe [Kriste] připravený v náboženství píme" ("Let us reverently drink the chalice of salvation which you [Christ] have prepared"). At this moment, the Hussite author resorted to a musical device proven already by the composer Záviš's generation: rhythmic singing (*cantus fractus*). The smooth chant melody changes into a rhythmically organized tune, and its strong expression adds to the significance of this key moment in the period of the early Reformation.[30]

Conclusion

All of these repertoires – the traditional Roman chant, the characteristic late medieval chants, sacred songs, and later also the vernacular chant – existed literally side by side in the first decades of the fifteenth century. The immediate proximity of two musical idioms, strictly orthodox Latin chant and vernacular service, is fascinating. They normally stand apart in sacred music historical surveys, the first having roots in the culture of the first millennium, the other associated with the Reformation period of the sixteenth century. Above all of these ideological concepts, however, remains a common denominator relevant to further music development in Bohemia: the fascination with supposedly "beautiful" melodies and the popularity of communal singing in the Czech language.

---

[30] See Hana Vlhová-Wörner, "Cantus fractus in Pre-Hussite Bohemia: Lost Repertories and Reconstruction Challenges," *Journal of the Alamire Foundation* 15/1 (2023): 11–31.

2 | Medieval Music and Czech National Identity

VIKTOR VELEK

This chapter explores how five medieval religious songs with Czech texts transformed into prominent musical signifiers of national identity in the nineteenth century. These songs have largely retained their ideological significance into the present. The following pages focus on the songs *Hospodine, pomiluj ny* ("Lord, Have Mercy upon Us," see Example 1.3), *Buoh všemohúcí* ("God Almighty," see Example 1.6), *Svatý Václave* ("Saint Wenceslas," see Example 1.4), *Jezu Kriste, ščedrý kněže* ("Jesus Christ, O Bounteous Priest," see Example 1.5), and *Ktož jsú boží bojovníci* ("You Who Are the Warriors of God," see Example 2.1). These samples of medieval sacred music gradually shed their predominantly religious functions to become prominent symbols of Czechness in music. As such, they have been discussed by generations of Czech musicologists and critics. These songs reflect both medieval and modern Czech cultural history. In the nineteenth century, incorporating these songs into new works was associated with the rise of Czech nationalism, illustrating how modern ethnocentric Czech identity is rooted in ancient traditions dating back to the Middle Ages.

Nationalistic Appropriations of the Middle Ages

Nineteenth-century Czech composers used references to a wide range of iconic medieval sites, characters, and events to signal Czechness in their works. These included historically significant cities, such as Prague and Tábor, a city built to become the center of the Hussite movement in the fifteenth century; iconic buildings, such as St. Vitus's Cathedral and the Charles Bridge; various royal castles, such as Vyšehrad, Karlštejn, and Zvíkov; famous battle sites, such as the Vítkov Hill in Prague, where the Hussites defeated papal crusaders in 1420; and prominent historical figures, such as the fourteenth-century Holy Roman Emperor and Bohemian King Charles IV, the Hussite warrior Žižka, and the ninth-century Byzantine missionaries Cyril and Methodius, who brought Christianity to the Slavs.

This chapter was translated from Czech to English by Martin Nedbal.

Example 2.1: Hussite song *Ktož jsú boží bojovníci* ("You Who Are the Warriors of God"), first stanza. English: Verse – You who are the warriors of God and of his law, beg God for help and trust in him, that you will win with him the final victory. Verse – Christ warrants of your losses, he promises a hundred times more, if one lays down his life for him, he will have an eternal one, blessed is everyone who falls [in battle] for truth. Refrain – This lord commands [us] not to fear those who kill the body and commands to give up even one's life for the love of one's neighbor.

In choosing historical subjects for their works, Czech nineteenth-century artists emphasized those that were most clearly connected to current cultural and political conditions. This is clearly illustrated in those operas by Bedřich Smetana that were based on medieval themes. Smetana's *Braniboři v Čechách* ("The Brandenburgers in Bohemia") focuses on historical events from the thirteenth century that strongly resonated with the political struggle in the early 1860s, in which Czech elites pursued a greater degree of autonomy from the Austrian government and started to redefine their relationship to the Bohemian Germans on an ethnic principle.[1] By contrast, Smetana's *Libuše*, based on the myths about the founding of the city of Prague, reflects the

---

[1] See Martin Nedbal, "Smetana's *The Brandenburgers in Bohemia* and Czech Nationalism: A Historical Reevaluation," *Music and Politics* 14 (2020), https://doi.org/10.3998/mp.9460447.0014.102.

Czech elite's desire to preserve constructive modes of communication with Austrian imperial authorities and, at the same time, emphasizes the idea of Czech statehood. Musical works with historical subjects received notable recognition from audiences and were supported by various institutions in Prague, as illustrated in Count Harrach's competition for an opera based on Czech national history, announced in 1861 (see Chapter 10). Similarly, the festive laying of the foundations for the Czech National Theater in Prague in 1868 was dominated by performances of compositions with historical subjects, such as the arrangement of *Hospodine, pomiluj ny* by Josef Leopold Zvonař, Karel Šebor's opera *Drahomíra*, about the pagan mother of St. Wenceslas, and Smetana's opera *Dalibor*, portraying the tragic tale of a fifteenth-century knight who challenges the authority of a king. Intensifying the medievalist bent of the 1868 festival even further was the presentation of Josef Jiří Kolár's prologue *Věštba Libušina* ("Libuše's Prophecy").[2]

Another common way in which Czech composers constructed what they considered Czech national sound was the use of medieval songs. Medieval songs therefore had similar significance to folksongs and to musical references to old-Slavonic and Slavic music.[3] As Jiří Fukač has pointed out, the use of famous medieval songs as musical signifiers of national values represented a continuation of the tradition of quoting folksongs in works by Smetana, Dvořák, Janáček, and Novák.[4] As nationalistic tensions between Czechs and Germans in the Czech lands intensified in the late nineteenth and early twentieth centuries, the use of medieval songs in musical compositions became so controversial as to become subject to censorship. For example, during both world wars, the use of *Svatý Václave* was restricted by the imperial Austrian and later German occupational authorities.[5] During World War I, Austrian authorities considered performances of the song nationalistic provocations, and during World War II, the song contradicted the view of the Nazi authorities and their Czech collaborators that St. Wenceslas was the first Czech to acknowledge the political subordination of the Czechs to the Germans. The use of the Hussite song *Ktož jsú boží bojovníci* was part of the nationalist interest in the Hussite movement, which nineteenth-century Czech historians considered the most glorious moment

[2] The 1868 festivities are described in Servác Heller, *Slavnost položení základního kamene k národnímu divadlu* (Prague: Grégr, 1869).

[3] Marta Ottlová and Milan Pospíšil, "Idea slovanské hudby," in Zdeněk Hojda, Marta Ottlová, and Roman Prahl, eds., *Slavme slavně slávu Slávóv slavných. Slovanství a česká kultura 19. století* (Prague: KLP, 2006), 172–83.

[4] Jiří Fukač, "Citace," in *Slovník české hudební kultury*, ed. Petr Macek (Prague: Supraphon, 1997), 107.

[5] Viktor Velek, "The Saint Wenceslas Tradition during the Time of the Swastika," *Czech Music Quarterly* 1 (2015): 29–39.

of Czech national history.[6] During periods of governmental restrictions of Czech nationalist sentiments, such as between 1939 and 1945, composers still used the song's melody but often applied either augmentation or diminution, or left out individual segments, to make their reliance on this musical symbol of Czechness more discreet. By contrast, references to the Hussite movement were intensely promoted and encouraged after the 1948 Communist Coup.[7] Communist ideologues viewed the totalitarian regime as a successor of the medieval Hussite movement and used the Hussites' social agenda to legitimize the 1948 communist takeover of power.

The Origin and Historical Development of Nationalized Medieval Songs

The reason why certain medieval songs were prioritized over others was often connected to their original extra-musical and extra-liturgical significance. Many of these songs had been associated with prominent figures of Bohemian history since the Middle Ages (see also Chapter 1). *Hospodine, pomiluj ny* was ascribed to St. Adalbert of Prague (c. 956–97), the second Bishop of Prague and a martyred missionary to the Hungarians, Poles, and Prussians, who became one of the patron saints of the Czech lands and Poland. *Jezu Kriste, ščedrý kněže* was ascribed to the religious reformer Jan Hus starting in the fifteenth century. *Buoh všemohúcí* is the Czech equivalent to the German song *Christ ist erstanden*, and performances of the song were associated with the prominent late fourteenth-century Prague preacher Konrad of Waldhausen, considered one of the predecessors of Hus. *Ktož jsú boží bojovníci* was also associated with a prominent medieval figure: the Hussite warrior Jan Žižka (see Example 2.1). Some of these songs also had significant political functions already in the Middle Ages. *Hospodine, pomiluj ny*, for example, was sung during elections and coronations of Bohemian kings, and *Jezu Kriste, ščedrý kněže* has been for centuries sung during graduation ceremonies at Prague's Charles University, founded in 1348. Thus, these songs were for generations understood as symbols of the Bohemian state and Bohemian institutions and sometimes also as national heritage.[8]

---

[6] Jaromír Černý, ed., *Historical Anthology of Music in the Bohemian Lands (up to ca 1530)* (Prague: KLP, 2005), 3, 76–79, 167, 168.

[7] Viktor Velek, "V záři rudého kalicha aneb Jan Hus a husitství v hudbě 50. let 20. století," *Opus Musicum* 55/2 (2022): 6–19.

[8] Viktor Velek, "Die St. Wenzelsche Musiktradition von ihrem Anfang bis 1848" (PhD diss., University of Vienna, 2008).

The traditional symbolic significance of the five songs became one of the main reasons so many composers used them in their works starting in the nineteenth century. The songs' importance was tied to other aspects of the nineteenth-century Czech national movement. Initially, between the 1830s and 1860s, scholars were mainly interested in establishing and editing the songs' original texts and melodies, as well as researching their authorship, original functions, and the linguistic evolutions.[9] One of the first Bohemian commentators to view the four pre-Hussite songs together with the Hussite song *Ktož jsú boží bojovníci* as particularly iconic and unique was the German-Bohemian musicologist August Wilhelm Ambros.[10] Viewing the four pre-Hussite songs as important developed in Czech literary studies, for example in the work of Josef Jireček.[11] Subsequently, notions of these songs' significance also appear in early musicological studies.[12]

In the 1860s, the interest in the songs ceased to be merely academic. Composers started to produce polyphonic settings of these songs for newly established male choral societies. Initially, these settings most often drew on *Hospodine, pomiluj ny* and *Svatý Václave*, which had remained in liturgical use. The Hussite song *Ktož jsú boží bojovníci*, rediscovered in the late eighteenth century, soon rose in prominence as well. Initially regarded as a literary rather than a musical monument, it gradually supplanted compositions whose texts were either musical forgeries (such as the so-called "Hussite Song" with the incipit *Těšme se blahou nadějí*) or poems with themes from Czech medieval times. Another group of inauthentic works that were influential at first and gradually fell out of use were those based on poetic texts drawn from the famous early nineteenth-century forgeries of allegedly medieval poetry, the Dvůr Králové (Queen's Court) and the Zelená

---

[9] John Bowring, ed., *Cheskian Anthology: Being a History of the Poetical Literature of Bohemia with Translated Specimens* (London: Rowland Hunter, 1832); Karel Jaromír Erben, ed., *Výbor z literatury české* (Prague: Řivnáč, 1845); Josef Leopold Zvonař, ed., *Hudební památky české. Výbor krásných zpěvů českých, církevních i světských pro smíšený i mužský sbor v původní skladbě i v novém upravení s průvodem piana i bez průvodu z rozličných zpěvníků staročeských*, 4 vols. (Prague: Kober, 1862–1864).

[10] August Wilhelm Ambros, *Geschichte der Music*, vol. 3 (Breslau: Leuckart, 1868), 418–19; see also Petr Vít, "A. W. Ambros und seine Beziehung zur Geschichte der Musik in Böhmen und der tschechischen Musik," in *Colloquium Česká hudba. Problémy a metody hudební historiografie*, ed. Rudolf Pečman (Brno: Mezinárodní hudební festival, 1974), 118–19.

[11] Josef Jireček, *Dějiny literatury české* (Prague: Tempský, 1876), 120.

[12] For a general study, see Karel Konrád, *Dějiny posvátného zpěvu staročeského od 15. věku do zrušení literátských bratrstev*, vol. 1, *XV. věk a dějiny literátských bratrstev* (Prague: Dědictví sv. Prokopa, 1893); see also Otakar Hostinský, "Musik in Böhmen," in *Die österreichisch-ungarische Monarchie in Wort und Bild. Böhmen*, vol. 2 (Vienna: Kaiserlich-königliche Hof- und Staatsdruckerei, 1896), 1–7.

Hora (Green Mountain) Manuscripts – the importance of these manuscripts had diminished already in the nineteenth century, although their status as forgeries was only proven in the twentieth century.[13]

Historical and linguistic research combined with nineteenth-century nationalism and historicism to imbue the medieval songs with a symbolic value, thus allowing the emerging Czech national community to postulate links between the imagined past and the present. These notions led to a widespread use of these historical songs in modern music, giving rise to a unique phenomenon in the development of Czech culture. The compositions drawing from these songs also reflect different socio-political events affecting Czech society's development, particularly those events connected to the "fateful eights" – years that ended with number eight and significantly changed the course of Czech history, such as 1918 (the establishment of Czechoslovakia), 1938 (the occupation of Czechoslovak borderlands by Nazi Germany), 1948 (the Communist Coup), and 1968 (the invasion of Czechoslovakia by Warsaw Pact armies).

There are hundreds of compositions featuring quotes from medieval sacred songs, many of which are now "iconic," such as the Hussite-themed conclusion to Smetana's *Má vlast* (where *Ktož jsú boží bojovníci* makes an appearance in the fifth and sixth movements, *Tábor*, and *Blaník*). Other examples include Dvořák's *Husitská overtura* ("Hussite Overture") and Josef Suk's *Meditace na svatováclavský chorál* ("Meditation on *Svatý Václave*"). The list of composers drawing on these songs also comprises Karel Šebor (1843–1903), Karel Bendl (1838–1907), Leoš Janáček (1854–1928), Zdeněk Fibich (1850–1900), Josef Bohuslav Foerster (1859–1951), Otakar Jeremiáš (1892–1932), Vítězslav Novák (1870–1949), Miloslav Kabeláč (1908–79), Svatopluk Havelka (1925–2009), Petr Eben (1929–2007), Jiří Laburda (b. 1931), and many others. The following sections explore modern uses of each of the five medieval songs in greater detail.

Hospodine, pomiluj ny as a Symbol of Czech Musical Origins

In examining the ideological significance of *Hospodine, pomiluj ny*, one notices a pattern: compositions that incorporate this song usually do not react to dramatic events in national history, unlike the works that make use

---

[13] See Dalibor Dobiáš, *The Forged Dvůr Králové and Zelená Hora Manuscripts* (Prague: CAS, 2019); Jitka Ludvová, "Hankovy padělky v české hudbě," *Hudební věda* 27 (1990): 299–319; Jitka Ludvová, "Hudební motivy Hankových padělků," *Hudební věda* 25 (1988): 293–309.

of *Ktož jsú boží bojovníci* and *Svatý Václave*. This distinction may have to do with the fact that *Hospodine, pomiluj ny* does not depict and call for "courage" and "combativeness" from the Czech nation. However, works based on the song reflect other aspects of Czech cultural history, especially the cult and national significance of St. Adalbert.

The first modern transcriptions and harmonizations of *Hospodine, pomiluj ny* appear in early nineteenth-century collections of organ accompaniments for religious songs,[14] in Zvonař's historical edition of music,[15] in Bendl's collection of communal songs,[16] and Bohuslav Jeremiáš's book for school youth.[17] Harmonization approaches were common in the late nineteenth and early twentieth centuries. Leoš Janáček used this approach in his 1896 cantata-like composition *Hospodine*, likely created in connection to the 900th anniversary of St. Adalbert's death in 1897. Similar harmonizations also appear in Josef Cyril Sychra's 1922 mixed chorus *Gospodi pomiluj ny* and Václav Dobiáš's male chorus *Gospodi, pomiluj ny!*, written in reaction to the end of World War II in 1944–45.

Dvořák's 1886 oratorio *Svatá Ludmila* ("St. Ludmila") represents the first and influential example of incorporating the song into a large-scale modern composition. In the oratorio, *Hospodine, pomiluj ny*, stands out as an archaic musical element and thus enhances the semblance of historical authenticity in the work's conclusion. Similarly, Vítězslav Novák incorporated *Hospodine, pomiluj ny* into his opera *Karlštejn*, Op. 50, which was composed during the first years of World War I (1915–16). Novák juxtaposes *Hospodine, pomiluj ny* with *Svatý Václave*, thus creating a recurring musical idea that Czech musicologist Vladimír Lébl has called the "Czech motive."[18] Several critics strongly opposed the use of both songs as "unorganic" and "contradictory."[19] Because *Hospodine, pomiluj ny* was ascribed to St. Adalbert of Prague, furthermore, the song is also featured in numerous compositions dedicated to the saint's legacy. Novák also used the song in his 1929 oratorio *Svatý Václav*, emulating Dvořák's *Svatá Ludmila*.

---

[14] For example, Josef Foerster, *Katolický varhaník / Der katholische Organist* (Prague: Jana Hoffmanna vdova, 1860), 101.

[15] Josef Leopold Zvonař, *Hudební památky české*, vol. 1 (Prague: I. L. Kober, 1862), 2.

[16] Karel Bendl, *Hospodine, pomiluj ny! Mužský sbor ve dvojí úpravě dle starého a dle Kobrova vydání složil Karel Bendl*, autograph manuscript, Prague, Czech Museum of Music, shelfmark I D 8.

[17] Bohuslav Jeremiáš, *Pobožnost jinoha studujícího. III. část, sbory* (Písek: Theodor Kopecký, 1896), 66.

[18] Vladimír Lébl, *Vítězslav Novák. Život a dílo* (Prague: ČSAV, 1964), 183.

[19] Most prominent among these critics was musicologist Zdeněk Nejedlý who wrote a separate study of the opera. Zdeněk Nejedlý, *Vítězslava Nováka "Karlštejn"* (Prague: Hudební knihovna časopisu Smetana, 1916).

The 950th anniversary of St. Adalbert in 1947 led to the creation of new compositions dedicated to the saint, but the composers did not make as extensive use of *Hospodine, pomiluj ny* as in previous generations. Some of these, predominantly choral, compositions were completed by Adolf Kramenič (1889–1953), Jan Nepomuk Boháč (1888–1968), Josef Blatný (1891–1980), and Otto Albert Tichý (1890–1973). Many of these works were published by the Committee for St. Adalbert's Millennium, and the committee also published some older compositions.

Many more compositions dedicated to St. Adalbert were written between 1947 and the millennial anniversary in 1997. Future research will reveal how many of these works incorporate *Hospodine, pomiluj ny*. For example, the oratorio *Svatý Vojtěch* (1970–73) by Jitka Snížková-Škrhová (1924–89) has never been published and remains in autograph, and it is therefore unclear whether it makes use of *Hospodine, pomiluj ny*. Several well-known Czech composers of the second half of the twentieth century, by contrast, clearly used the song. Miloslav Kabeláč (1908–79) included *Hospodine, pomiluj ny* in Part 2 of his pathbreaking electroacoustic work *E fontibus Bohemicis / 6 obrazů z českých letokruhů* ("From Bohemian Sources / Six Images from Czech Tree Rings," 1965–72), Op. 55. Kabeláč also features the song prominently in *Proměny chorálu Hospodine pomiluj ny* ("The Transformations of *Hospodine, pomiluj ny*," 1974–78), Op. 57, for large mixed chorus, solo baritone, male chorus, and a solo higher female voice (Op. 58 is a 1979 arrangement with solo piano). Another well-known and highly effective late twentieth-century composition that uses the song is the 1969 symphonic movement for three trumpets and orchestra *Vox clamantis* by Petr Eben (1929–2007).

Many compositions that make use of *Hospodine, pomiluj ny* were created in connection to St. Adalbert's 1997 millennial anniversary. Most of these compositions are choral, including those by Jan Hanuš (1915–2004), Antonín Tučapský (1928–2014), Petr Eben, Petr Řezníček (1938–2019), Jan Bernátek (b. 1950), and Pavel Helebrand (b. 1960). Helebrand's 1996 *Mystérium cesty sv. Vojtěcha* ("The Mystery of St. Adalbert's Journey") combines choral passages, including those based on *Hospodine, pomiluj ny* and the Polish song *Bogurodzica*, with instrumental passages performed by replicas of medieval instruments to create a unique, transnational musical representation of the Middle Ages. In connection to Helebrand's use of *Bogurodzica*, it is appropriate to point out that St. Adalbert has a strong cult in Poland, and that many Polish composers have commemorated him in their works, which are mostly unknown in the Czech lands. Another recent composition based on the song is Lukáš Matoušek's (b. 1943) *Viderunt omnes fines millennii* for chamber orchestra from 1998–99. The work synthesizes *Hospodine, pomiluj ny* and Pérotin's four-part organum *Viderunt omnes*, and the late twentieth-century combination of the tenth-century chant with the polyphonic composition that likely dates from the late twelfth century bears characteristics of postmodern polystylism.

Svatý Václave and Ideological Struggles over the Legacy of a Regional Saint

Soon after his violent death in 935 and canonization in the following decades, Wenceslas I, Duke of Bohemia, became the patron saint of the Bohemian state, but his significance was overshadowed by other figures in various periods.[20] In the eighteenth century, the attempts at radical recatholicization in the Czech lands led to the canonization of John of Nepomuk (Jan Nepomucký), and his cult acquired greater symbolic value than that of St. Wenceslas (on St. Wenceslas in the seventeenth century, see Chapter 4). In the nineteenth and twentieth centuries, Czech composers and critics emphasized the veneration of Jan Hus, and references to St. Wenceslas were frowned upon. Such sentiments dominate Bohumír Štědroň's discussion of Zdeněk Fibich's opera *Blaník* from the 1870s, which takes place during the enforced recatholicization in Bohemia in 1623. Štědroň was bothered that to depict the suffering of the prosecuted Czech Protestants, Fibich did not reference *Ktož jsú boží bojovníci* and cited only *Svatý Václave*, which Štědroň considered archaic and contrary to Fibich's otherwise "progressive" style.[21] At the same time, however, the cult of St. Wenceslas was also appropriated by the Czech national movement in the second half of the nineteenth century, which affected the ways in which both the Czechs and German Bohemians viewed the patron saint. German Bohemians felt increasingly alienated from St. Wenceslas whom they understood as an anti-German, ethnocentric symbol of the Czech domin-ation of the Bohemian lands. However, although many German Bohemians

---

[20] For the history of the reception of *Svatý Václave*, see Jan[?] Veselka, "Idea svatováclavská v české hudbě," in *Svatý Václav ve filmu českého tisku v září 1940*, ed. Jan Křiklava (Prague: Křiklava, 1940), 53.

[21] Bohumír Štědroň, "Husitské náměty v české a světové hudbě," *Časopis Národního muzea* (1953): 77. The opera does reference the Hussite song, albeit only in subtle ways that went unnoticed for a long time. See Viktor Velek, "Searching for a Programme, Searching for an Identity, or the Association and the Struggle between the Saint Wenceslas and Hus-Hussite Traditions in Czech Music of the Second Half of the 19th Century," *Musicologica Olomucensia* 33 (2021): 374–408.

ridiculed St. Wenceslas during this period, others continued to venerate him as a patron saint of their homeland. During the same period, Czech approaches to St. Wenceslas were conflicted, as pro-Habsburg, conservative Czech Catholics tried to defend St. Wenceslas's legacy against both German Bohemians and those Czechs who viewed the saint as an anachronistic symbol of the Catholic Church and the Habsburg monarchy.[22]

The song *Svatý Václave* is one of dozens of sacred songs dedicated to St. Wenceslas, but it is certainly the most famous one. As such, it has undergone numerous arrangements and has been quoted many times. Musical appropriations of *Svatý Václave* have produced hundreds of compositions with diverse instrumentation, form, and function. The song is frequently encountered in the realm of popular music, such as in the 1990 song *Neopouštěj nás (Svatý Václave)* ("Don't abandon us [St. Wenceslas]") by Czech singer-songwriter Petr Skoumal. For many Czech composers abroad, the song represented a connection to the homeland. For example, Antonín Tučapský emigrated from Czechoslovakia to Great Britain in 1975, and in 1983, he composed his solo cello piece *Meditation*, based on *Svatý Václave*. Composers also often turned to the song in moments of either personal or national crisis, emphasizing the phrase "Nedej zahynout nám ni budoucím" ("Do not let us or our descendants perish"). František Smetana's *Meditace na chorál sv. Václava* ("Meditation on the St. Wenceslas Chorale") responded to both types of crises, as the composer wrote it during his imprisonment by the communist regime soon after the 1948 coup (the work was completed in the Pankrác Prison in Prague on June 6, 1949) – Smetana later emigrated to the United States and worked at Virginia Commonwealth University.

Jezu Kriste, ščedrý kněže and the Hussite Tradition

The text and music of this song has been well known since the nineteenth century thanks to the extensive research concerning Jan Hus, to whom the piece was ascribed.[23] The song was also published in many nineteenth-century collections, recorded throughout the twentieth century, and featured in novelistic literature on the Hussite period, for example in the works of late nineteenth- and early twentieth-century Czech novelist Alois

---

[22] See, for example, Josef Kalousek, *Obrana knížete Václava Svatého proti smyšlenkám a křivým úsudkům o jeho povaze* (Prague: Bursík a Kohout, 1872).

[23] See David R. Holeton and Hana Vlhová-Wörner, "A Remarkable Witness to the Feast of Saint Jan Hus," *The Bohemian Reformation and Religious Practice* 7 (2009): 156–84.

Jirásek. Performances of the song also accompanied many important events of modern Czech history. In the memoirs of the politician Václav Benda, we find an account of an anti-communist demonstration at a 1988 procession celebrating St. Agnes of Bohemia, during which the participants replaced a newly composed song that had been approved by the authorities with *Jezu Kriste, ščedrý kněže*.[24] The song was featured at the funeral of Cardinal František Tomášek, a prominent Catholic official who was persecuted by the communist regime, on August 12, 1993,[25] and it was sung by participants of the Hussite Conference in the Vatican in 2000 at the arrival of Pope John Paul II – the pope later expressed remorse about the cruel death of Jan Hus at the stake in 1415. Czech politician Petr Pithart noted that "the pope was radiant, catching both the melody and the words, and then he gave a speech to us."[26]

Composers started to use the song at a relatively late date. František Zdeněk Skuherský's late nineteenth-century arrangement of the song for voice and organ was followed by Miroslav Krejčí's arrangement for the same ensemble.[27] Zdeněk Nejedlý's musicological research inspired composer Hubert Doležil's arrangement for male choir during World War I.[28] The song gained strength during World War II, both in its original form and as a quote in Ladislav Vycpálek's extensive cantata *České requiem: smrt a spasení* ("Czech Requiem: Death and Salvation"), Op. 24, completed in 1940, for choir, soloists, and orchestra/piano.[29] An immediate response to the approaching end of the war was also Josef Plavec's *12 variací na chorál "Jezu Kriste, ščedrý kněže"* ("Twelve Variations on the Chorale *Jezu Kriste, ščedrý kněže*") for organ from 1945 (published 1948).

The communist interpretations of the Hussite legacy as folk-like, anti-elitist, and anti-German were reflected in a series of artistic works incorporating *Jezu Kriste, ščedrý kněže*, such as Vítězslav Novák's stage music for František Rychlík's 1949 play *Žižka*, which also features the Hussite war song *Slyšte rytieři boží* ("Hark, Soldiers of God").[30] At the same time, spiritually inclined composers returned to the song, including Jaromír Urbanec in a 1953 choral arrangement.[31] The song is also the basis for

---

[24] Václav Benda, *Noční kádrový dotazník a jiné boje* (Prague: Agite, 2009), 42.

[25] Jan Hartmann, ed., *Kardinál Tomášek. Generál bez vojska* (Prague: Vyšehrad, 2003), 175.

[26] Petr Pithart and Martin T. Zikmund, *Ptám se, tedy jsem. Rozhovor* (Prague: Portál, 2010), 270.

[27] For Skuherský, see *27 staročeských chorálů* (Prague: Urbánek, 1887); for Krejčí, see *Čtyři staročeské písně duchovní* (Kutná Hora: Česká hudba, 1934).

[28] *Staročeské duchovní zpěvy 14. a 15. století* (Prague: Melantrich, 1917).

[29] Jaroslav Smolka, *Ladislav Vycpálek: tvůrčí vývoj* (Prague: SNKLHU, 1960), 179–99.

[30] Vladimír Lébl, *Vítězslav Novák. Život a dílo* (Prague: ČSAV, 1964), 285–90.

[31] K. V. Štěpka, ed., *Staročeské zpěvy duchovní* (Prague: Blahoslav, 1953).

the first part of Ladislav Vycpálek's 1950 orchestral cycle *Vzhůru, srdce! Dvě variační fantasie na chrámové písně doby* ("Upward, Heart! Two Variation Fantasies on Church Songs of the Time"), Op. 30,[32] which also quotes *Svatý Václave* to express internal resistance to the beginning of the communist terror.[33] The song was also used in 1998 by Vladimír Svatoš in his *Fantazie na chorál "Jezu Kriste, sčedrý kněže* ("Fantasy on the Chorale *Jezu Kriste, sčedrý kněže*") for organ. The song is also featured in the 1999 opera *Johann Hus* by the Sudeten German composer Widmar Hader and in the 2005 oratorio *Jan Hus* by Richard Pachman.

Buoh všemohúcí – A Song Appreciated Only in the Twentieth Century

Nineteenth-century composers paid only marginal attention to *Buoh všemohúcí*, a renowned medieval Easter song. Composers' interest in using the tune in their works was tied to the song's status as an important medieval work (as one of the four vernacular songs that were allowed to be performed in church – see Chapter 1), but the song did not necessarily possess the political symbolism of the other prominent Czech medieval songs. One of the first arrangements of the song, by Hubert Doležil, appeared only in 1917 and was based on Zdeněk Nejedlý's recently pub-lished transcription.[34] Another choral arrangement was created by Adolf Cmíral in the 1950s as part of a historical anthology.[35] In the 1950s, composers started to use the song more extensively in instrumental works. In 1950, Vycpálek incorporated it, together with *Jezu Kriste, sčedrý kněže*, in his orchestral work *Vzhůru, srdce!*, Op. 30 (see above). The song was made even more visible in Petr Eben's Brass Quintet from the late 1960s. Eben was likely drawn to the archaic nature of the original song as opposed to any specific political symbolism, as in a later memoir, he claimed that for the piece he chose a "distantly archaic [idiom] . . . as if the sound of the instruments reached out to me across many centuries from the top of a Gothic tower."[36] Jiří Laburda also worked with the song several

---

[32] Ladislav Vycpálek, *Vzhůru srdce. Dvě variační fantasie na chrámové písně doby: Jesu Kriste, sčedrý kněže – Buóh všemohúcí* (Prague: Hudební matice, 1950).

[33] Tomáš Židek, "Polyfonie v dílech J. B. Foerstera a jeho současníků" (PhD diss., HAMU, Prague, 2014).

[34] Hubert Doležil, *Staročeské duchovní zpěvy 14. a 15. století. Dle transkripcí Zdenka Nejedlého pro čtyřhlasý sbor mužský* (Prague: Melantrich, 1917), 1.

[35] Adolf Cmíral, *Staročeské zpěvy duchovní* (Prague: Blahoslav, 1953), 3.

[36] Eva Vítová, *Petr Eben. Sedm zamyšlení nad životem a dílem* (Prague: Baronet, 2004), 273.

times. For example, he set it polyphonically in the second part, titled *Svědkové minulosti* ("The Witnesses of the Past"), of his 1989 five-part *Sonata da chiesa* for brass quintet and organ. In Laburda's 1993 *Canto Pasquale* for trumpet and organ, however, Czech nationalism becomes more prominent: the composition's commission called for the use of the German Easter chorale *Christ ist erstanden*. Since the two songs share the same melody, Laburda fulfilled the commission requirements but also brought in a specifically Czech element (*Buoh všemohúcí*) into the work. The song also represents one of many historical quotations used in Widmar Hader's opera *Johann Hus*, specifically in the second scene of the first act, which takes place in the Bethlehem Chapel in Prague, the main venue for Hus's sermons (see Chapter 1).

Ktož jsú boží bojovníci as a Symbol of National Protest and Victory

The elevation of *Ktož jsú boží bojovníci* to the status of an iconic medieval composition, often integrated into modern works, can be attributed to its unique exhibition of national characteristics connected to wartime activities. Unlike the four pre-Hussite medieval songs, *Ktož jsú boží bojovníci* is not a prayer in the broader sense but a musically arranged set of militaristic rules. The distinctiveness has led to its use in compositions representing protest or expressing hopes for victory. In contrast to the other four medieval songs, the use of and familiarity with *Ktož jsú boží bojovníci* in the Czech lands was suppressed during the recatholicization in the seventeenth and eighteenth centuries. During the nineteenth century, Bohemian critics and musicologists embraced the idea that *Ktož jsú boží bojovníci* and *Svatý Václave* represented the two primary medieval symbols of Czech identity. Although Smetana was not the first to incorporate the Hussite song into his works, its exposure in the symphonic cycle *Má vlast* and the opera *Libuše* significantly influenced later composers. Also, the programmatic description that Smetana added to the final portion of the cycle contributed to the symbolic value of *Ktož jsú boží bojovníci*:

Blaník Hill. You, who are the warriors of God! On the basis of this melody (this Hussite principle), the resurrection of the Czech nation will take root, future happiness and glory, the composition and the entire cycle [Má] Vlast concludes with the victorious hymn in the form of a march.

Blaník. Kdož jste boží bojovníci! Na podkladě této melodie (tohoto husitského principu) se vyvine vzkříšení národa českého, budoucí štěstí a sláva, kterým vítězným hymnem v podobě pochodu skladba skončí a tak celá řada symfonických básní [Má] Vlast.[37]

Ktož jsú boží bojovníci was predominantly used by Czech composers, but it also found place in the 1939 work *Concerto funebre* by German composer Karl Hartmann, who wrote it to protest against the occupation of Bohemia and Moravia by Nazi Germany. The most famous use of the song in the context of protest music, however, is in Karel Husa's 1969 programmatic work for symphonic band *Music for Prague 1968*, created in response to the invasion of Czechoslovakia by Warsaw Pact armies. Similarly, the song is incorporated into the 2009 *Requiem for Jan Palach* by Welsh composer Daffy Bullock, commemorating a Prague university student who committed suicide by self-immolation in protest against the 1968 invasion. The song, furthermore, was used in a number of film scores from the communist period, such as the "Hussite trilogy" from 1954–55 *Jan Hus*, *Jan Žižka*, and *Proti všem* ("Against Everyone"), music Jiří Srnka, direction Otakar Vávra; and in stage music, such as *Jan Žižka*, 1948, music Vítězslav Novák, direction František Rachlík. In the late 1980s, Czech rock musicians used the song to express anti-communist sentiments, such as in the 1988 punk version of *Kdož jsú Boží bojovníci* by Visací zámek. The punk rockers from Visací zámek view themselves as the "warriors of God," fighting for civil liberties.

Conclusion

This chapter presented the reception of prominent medieval songs from various perspectives. For many centuries, these songs have mirrored social and political developments in the Czech lands. In particular, the reception of these songs delineates the shift in the predominant modes of community identification among the inhabitants of what is now the Czech lands from a focus on religion, region, and the state to one centered on language and ethnicity. The widespread practice of repurposing these songs in later compositions gained prominence in the nineteenth century and continues until the present day. The incorporation of these ancient Czech songs in newer composition remains, and undoubtedly will continue to be, an important technique through which Czech composers infuse their works with national identity.

---

[37] Vladimír Helfert, *Bedřich Smetana* (Brno: Nový lid, 1924), 62.

3 | Liturgical Music of the Bohemian Reformation

MARTIN HORYNA

On July 6, 1415, the Council of Constance (1414–18), convened to end the Great Schism (1378–1418), condemned Jan Hus, a Prague priest and leader of the reform movement in Bohemia, to death at the stake. Prior to this, Hus, an important teacher and former rector of the Prague university (established in 1348), gained popularity for his vernacular preaching in the Bethlehem Chapel in Prague's Old Town (see Chapter 1). His calls for Church reforms and passionate defense of John Wycliffe's writings, denounced as heretical by the Church, led to a conflict with the Church hierarchy. Despite the Church's attempt to erase Hus's name from memory through his ignominious death, he became a symbol of resistance to the official Roman Church and inspired countless followers from all ranks of society. These followers called themselves "Hussites" and venerated Hus as a martyr and saint.[1] Subsequently, the tensions in the Kingdom of the Bohemian Crown escalated into an open military conflict between the Hussites and the Roman Church, supported by the Holy Roman Empire. The conflict resulted in a wide destruction of church buildings and furnishings, including organs. The ensuing Hussite Wars (1419–34) transformed the political, social, and religious situation in the Bohemian Kingdom, laying the groundwork for the first European Reformation, a century before the reformation movements of the early sixteenth century.[2]

   After the wars, the Council of Basel (1431–49) acknowledged the legal coexistence of the Roman Catholic Church (*sub una*) and the Utraquist Church (*sub utraque*) in Bohemia.[3] The radical Hussites advocated for

---

This chapter was translated from Czech to English by Hana Vlhová-Wörner and Martin Nedbal.

[1] See David R. Holeton, "The Celebration of Jan Hus in the Life of the Churches," *Studia Liturgica* 35 (2005): 32–59; David R. Holeton and Hana Vlhová-Wörner, "A Remarkable Witness to the Feast of Saint Jan Hus," *The Bohemian Reformation and Religious Practice* 7 (2009): 156–84; David R. Holeton, Pavel Kolář, and Eliška Baťová, "Liturgy, Sacramental Theology, and Music," in *A Companion to the Hussites*, ed. Michael van Dussen and Pavel Soukup (Leiden: Brill, 2020).

[2] Zdeněk V. David, *Finding the Middle Way: The Utraquists' Liberal Challenge to Rome and Luther* (Washington D.C.: Woodrow Wilson Center Press, 2003).

[3] Utraquists, or "Calixtins": the chalice was a symbol of Communion *sub utraque specie* (of Body and Blood) not only to priests, but also to the laity. The majority of the Czech-speaking population declared its support to Utraquism during this period. Some towns, however, as well as some members of the Czech aristocracy and territories on the borders remained Catholic.

the introduction of vernacular worship, that would be understandable to the laity.[4] Another radical change, the secularization of Church property, made the Church dependent on the decisions of the laity, which contributed to a reshaping of the liturgy and liturgical repertory. The newly established religious tolerance did not apply to the radical Hussites, who formed the so-called Unity of Brethren in 1457. Members of the Unity sought protection on the estates of tolerant noble families. In 1478, the so-called "Lower Consistory" was established at the university college (*Collegium Carolinum*) in Prague, to which all Hussite parish churches in Bohemia were subordinated. Finally, in 1485, an agreement called the Religious Peace of Kutná Hora brought an end to the ongoing religious conflicts, creating conditions for a relatively tolerant religious environment that lasted until the defeat of the Bohemian anti-Habsburg uprising at the Battle of the White Mountain in 1621. Yet, religious stability remained elusive in the sixteenth century, as the German-speaking population in border regions started to embrace Lutheranism,[5] and the Unity of Brethren incorporated many tenets of Calvinism. The Utraquist Church never agreed on a unified religious doctrine, which led to the coexistence of many individual factions that were difficult to distinguish from one another. The ideals of the German Reformation played an increasingly significant role in the sixteenth century. In particular, the non-Catholic population of Moravia that declared their affiliation with the (Lutheran) Augsburg Confession.

In the sphere of the liturgical chant cultivated by the Czech-speaking non-Catholic population, we encounter an unbroken development of genuinely Czech repertories in various denominations: Czech (vernacular) chant, along with Czech strophic songs (*cantiones*), became a staple part of characteristic songbooks, so-called cantionals (*kancionály*). Sixteenth-century vernacular chant differed from the first vernacular repertory created for the Hussite Church in the early fifteenth century (see Chapter 1). The vernacular texts used in plainchant were not faithful translations but rather longer paraphrases of the original Latin words, while their melodies,

---

[4]   David R. Holeton, "Bohemia Speaking to God: The Search for a National Liturgical Expression," in *Public Communication in European Reformation. Artistic and other Media in Central Europe 1380–1620*, ed. Milena Bartlová and Michal Šroněk (Prague: Artefactum, 2007), 103–32.

[5]   The predominantly German-speaking population of the Bohemian borderlands adopted religious practices from neighboring German regions. At the same time, many important composers of the Lutheran repertory were active in Bohemia, such as Nicolaus Herman (1500–61) and Johannes Mathesius (1504–65) in Jáchymov (St. Joachimsthal), and Balthasar Harzer-Resinarius (c. 1485–1544), the author of polyphonic elaborations of German Reformation songs, in Česká Lípa (Böhmisch Leipa).

based on the Roman chant, proceeded syllabically. Although the repertory gradually responded to various stimuli, it was never fully replaced until around 1620, and the rich tradition of Czech-language liturgical music persisted into the following decades (see Chapter 5).

Institutional Background of Liturgical Music

The secularization of Church property left the Church financially strained, grappling not only with a shortage of priests but also relying on the active involvement of laymen in liturgy, including the performance of chant. In line with a growing trend that had appeared already in the pre-Hussite period, parish schools took on a central role in cultivating the repertory for worship.[6] School choirs, led by school cantors, often comprised musically gifted students from poor families, for whom engaging in music performance was a means to fund further education, potentially paving the way to a financially secured career of a priest. School regulations from this era typically lack specific details about the curriculum, but they are quite precise when outlining the singing responsibilities of both schoolteachers and pupils, along with details about their compensation.

The primary responsibility of the parish school centered around singing at the morning Marian Mass, known as *matura*, and at the afternoon Vespers. On Sunday and major feasts of the Church year, students from wealthy town families would join in. Some of these students would later use their experience by becoming members of literary brotherhoods (*Fraternitates litteratorum* in Latin, *Litteratenbruderschaften* in German), ensembles of wealthy citizens dedicated to cultivating monophonic and polyphonic repertories in town churches. These lay societies, fashioned after religious fraternities, recruited members from educated townspeople who had graduated from local schools, earning them the designation "literary," or *literáti* in Czech. Students from less privileged families received a substantial part of their income from occasional payments for singing at funerals, weddings, and town council meetings. In essence, the school faculty, including school masters (*rector, magister scholae*), cantors, assistants (referred to as *kumpáni* in Czech, *adstantes, adiuvantes* in Latin), and choristers (*pauperi* – poor students, young students, and *cantores*) played an indispensable role in musical performances for both the Church and the town council. As a result, they received additional financial support from

---

[6] Martin Horyna, "Vícehlasá hudba v Čechách v 15. a 16. století a její interpreti," *Hudební věda* 43 (2006): 117–34.

both the parish church and the city.[7] The same duties (Mass and Vespers) were prescribed for the organist, a professional musician, who usually played *alternatim* to the monophonic or even polyphonic performances of the students. Some towns also employed small ensembles of professional brass players, especially from the second half of the sixteenth century onward. These musicians regularly performed motets from the town hall towers and supported church choir singers on feast days.

Around 1490, shortly after the 1485 Religious Peace of Kutná Hora, literary brotherhoods were established in both Utraquist and Roman Catholic towns. Voluntarily taking on various responsibilities in public worship, such as morning Masses (*maturae*) on Sundays and feast days and the Rorate morning Masses in Advent, members of the literary brotherhoods often played a crucial role as Church patrons. They provided valuable financial support, including the procurement of chant books used by school choristers. The musical culture of literary brotherhoods was characterized by remarkably luxurious graduals, often written on high-quality parchment, and richly decorated with illuminations.[8] Both parish school ensembles and literary brotherhoods were selective institutions requiring members to undergo preparation through education and practice. This preparation involved the ability to read and accurately interpret music notation and the skills to perform polyphonic music, based on both advanced interpretation skills and the knowledge of sometimes complicated notation.

A different music tradition was cultivated in the radical Hussite Church and later in the Unity of Brethren and the Calvinist Church. Their ideal centered around communal singing of songs, where the whole congregation participated. While communal singing was practiced by various Reformation Churches, it gained prominence primarily in the more radical denominations that rejected ostentation and ornamentation. As evidenced in contemporary music documents, the traditional repertory of the Roman Church was never entirely abandoned by both the Hussite Church and the Unity of the Brethren (see below). In some denominations, communal singing became an important part of the church repertory, but it never replaced the traditional role of the church choir, which continued to cultivate chant and polyphony integral to the Roman liturgy in Bohemia.

---

[7] In a broader context, the institution of the parish school choir is similar to the so-called "Kantorei" in the Protestant part of Germany.

[8] Barry Graham, *Bohemian and Moravian Graduals (1420–1620)* (Turnhout: Brepols, 2007); and Ema Součková, *Výzdoba hudebních rukopisů Jana Táborského z Klokotské Hory* (Prague: Academia, 2019).

Language of Worship

The shift to communal singing in reformed Churches was closely tied to the language used in worship. Instead of the "universal" Latin language, which was incomprehensible to uneducated believers, the emphasis was on using the vernacular (Czech) language. A key source of the Czech vernacular liturgy from the period around the Hussite Wars is the so-called *Jistebnický kancionál* ("Jistebnice Kancionál") from the 1420s or early 1430s, which includes fourteen polyphonic compositions, Czech vernacular chants for the Mass and the Office, and around ninety Czech spiritual songs (see Chapter 1 and Example 1.5b, with the fifteenth-century version of the song *Jezu Kriste, ščědrý kněže*, as recorded in the *Jistebnický kancionál*).[9] Although spiritual songs, a genre well-suited for communal performance, are part of the *Jistebnický kancionál*'s repertory, they by no means dominate it. Polyphonic pieces were not intended for congregation performance. The manuscript likely reflects the use of vernacular liturgy in a parish church in which the school cantor and students participated in liturgical singing. The call for the use of vernacular language in liturgy did not automatically lead to communal singing being equally promoted in this period. The linguistic aspect remained more crucial, as evident not only in the *Jistebnický kancionál* repertory but also in many Czech graduals from the second half of the sixteenth century. In churches where the quality of music performance took precedence over the experience of communal singing, trained singers, either those from school choirs or literary brotherhoods, played a decisive role.

Despite the development of Czech vernacular liturgy during the Hussite period, most Utraquist graduals from the early era of the literary brotherhoods compiled around 1500 feature Latin repertory. Yet, the notion of singing in the vernacular persisted, and a significant surge in new translations of the Mass repertory, including sacred songs and polyphonic pieces, occurred after 1540. During this period, these translations were acquired for literary brotherhoods that now preferred singing in Czech.[10] Chant pieces that included shorter or longer

---

[9] David Holeton and Hana Vlhová-Wörner, eds., *Jistebnický kancionál: MS. Prague, National Museum Library, II C 7: Critical Edition*, vol. 1, *Graduale* (Brno: Marek, 2005); and Hana Vlhová-Wörner, ed., *Jistebnický kancionál: MS. Prague, National Museum Library, II C 7: Critical Edition*, vol. 2, *Cantionale* (Chomutov: Marek, 2019).

[10] Eliška Baťová, *Kolínský kancionál z roku 1517 a bratrský zpěv na počátku 16. století* (Prague: KLP, 2011); and Eliška Baťová, "Opomíjený pramen husitského zpěvu doby poděbradské a repertoár cantiones hebdomadae sanctae," *Hudební věda* 51 (2014): 229–76.

melismas (ornamental embellishments) were set to new texts and typically attached to purely syllabic melodies.[11] Utraquist churches, with
a longstanding tradition of involving school choirs and literary brotherhoods in Latin singing during worship, continued to use Latin for
specific music repertory, such as Office chants, Mass Ordinary chants,
and motets – whether composed by Czech authors or imported. In
printed cantionals, however, the vernacular language clearly dominated,
be it Czech or German, in prints catering to German-speaking members
of the Unity of Brethren. Latin texts still appeared in prints specifically
intended for schools.

Books for Worship

The structure of worship in the Bohemian reformed Churches closely
mirrored that of the Roman Church, with minimal deviation from the
Roman liturgy, except in regions affected by more radical forms of
reformation. Consequently, the outline and content of chant books followed the model of the Roman Church. The Mass repertory was included
in graduals featuring forms and melodies similar to those that were part
of the chant repertory of the Prague diocese before the Hussite Wars.
These graduals supplemented the Mass Proper chants with sequences,
tropes, and, in some cases, spiritual songs and archaic polyphony. The
number of manuscripts containing repertory for the Office (antiphonals,
hymnals) is relatively small, which does not mean, however, that the
community did not engage in liturgical singing during the Office hours,
particularly during Vespers and Matins on major feasts. Vespers and
Matins were performed primarily by school choirs. Other important
music sources from this period have been preserved, such as manuscript
and printed collections of polyphonic compositions and books containing liturgy for the Advent morning Masses (*Rorátníky*), which included
supplementary repertory.

   A quintessential songbook associated with the music of the
Reformation is the cantional (*kancionál* in Czech, *Kantional* in
German). Comprising mostly spiritual songs (*cantiones*), cantionals
had an extraordinary social impact, thanks to their use of the then-
modern technology of print. The oldest printed Czech cantional, likely
from a Utraquist milieu, was published as early as 1501. The highpoint of

---

[11] Jiří Žůrek, ed., *Graduale Bohemorum. Proprium sanctorum* (Prague: Krystal OP, 2011).

cantional production, both in terms of content and typographic sophistication, was achieved in prints released for the Unity of Brethren.[12] The public outreach potential of the new media inspired other Churches, including the Catholic Church, to produce their own printed cantionals. Some cantionals mirrored the size, format, and content of Latin chant books, with repertory selection akin to the modern *Liber usualis*, containing music for the Mass and selected Office hours for the most important feasts of the Church year.[13] In addition to spiritual songs, cantionals featured numerous vernacular chant pieces (antiphons, introits, Kyrie eleison, sequences, and hymns). Melodies of their core repertory drew on pre-Hussite and Hussite traditions while also reflecting mutual exchange with song melodies from the German Reformation. The most intensive adoption and translation of songs from the German Reformation occurred between 1540 and 1560.[14] Typically, the repertory of most cantionals was less denomination-specific, contrary to what one would expect in a historical period marked by heated theological disputes and political struggles. The prologues often proclaimed supraconfessionalism, attempting to appeal to members of other denominations. In addition to notated music books, several Czech and Latin elaborations of the Book of Psalms were compiled in Bohemia between 1570 and 1620. Some were intended for metric recitation in the style of a humanistic ode. The most successful among them was the Czech translation of the Geneva Psalter by the Bohemian Brethren priest Jiřík Strejc (1587). Among the approximately twenty music editions up to 1620, distinctions can be made between prints by the Union of Brethren and Prague editors. Two editions (1596, 1618) included four-part settings by French composer Claude Goudimel (1514–72), performed by school choirs.

---

[12] Notated editions of cantionals for the Unity of Czech Brethren were published in 1541, 1561, 1564, 1576, 1581, 1594, 1598, 1615, and 1618. German notated editions were published in 1531, 1544, 1566, 1606, 1639, and in several later exile reeditions; the edition from 1661 was revised by Jan Ámos Komenský (Comenius).

[13] The largest of Czech cantional prints, *Písně chvál Božských* ("Songs of Divine Praise"), compiled and published in 1602/1606 by Tobiáš Závorka Lipenský, contains 1,260 chants and songs (of which 822 with music) and the entire Psalter. The cantional was compiled for Moravian Lutherans and was commonly used in the Utraquist milieu. Further related to the contents of the cantional is the *Pravidlo služebností církevních* ("The Rule of Church Services") from 1607, an agenda for priests containing all the necessary liturgical texts and other sung parts. See Jan Kouba, *Slovník staročeských hymnografů (13.–18. století)* (Prague: Etnologický ústav AVČR, 2017), 475–86.

[14] Jan Kouba, "Německé vlivy v české písni 16. století," *Miscellanea musicologica* 27–28 (1975): 117–71.

Music in Worship

There are some common features connecting music in worship across various denominations of the Czech Reformation. These include the preservation of elements of the pre-Hussite tradition, the retention of certain repertory removed from Catholic worship at the Council of Trent (1545–63) in some chant books, and the presence of links to earlier traditions in some sources from the late sixteenth and early seventeenth centuries. Detailed information about the music repertory and its role in worship is typically found in the so-called *Agenda* (a book with service instructions), chant book indices, rubrics (in both manuscript and printed cantionals), and other chant books. Sometimes, insights can also be gleaned from the songs themselves.[15] Detailed instructions for the inclusion of music in worship were published in the Cantional (1602/ 1606) and *Agenda* (1607) compiled by Tobiáš Závorka (1553–1611). The main services are scheduled for Sundays and feast days, followed by less important services on other days of the week, known as "ferial services." The *proprium de sanctis*, a cycle of feasts dedicated to saints during the Church year, is mostly reduced to the veneration of saints from the New Testament (apostles, evangelists) and Bohemian patron saints, especially St. Wenceslas, and includes Hussite martyrs Jan Hus and his follower Jerome of Prague (Jeroným Pražský), who was burned at the stake at the Council of Constance in 1416.

Závorka designates the different festive ceremonies according to the time of day for which they were scheduled: "At Dawn," "In the Morning," "High Mass," "After Lunch," "Vespers," and "Salve." The following description of these ceremonies provides insight into the context of the music repertory cultivated in this period.

The "At Dawn" ceremony was celebrated on major feast days. Originally a night service known as the Vigil, by the late Middle Ages it had often been moved to other times, typically in the morning. According to Závorka, the structure was as follows: beginning with the opening chant (*Adiutorium nostrum*) and the invitatory chant (*Venite, exultemus*), the central and longest part, known as the Nocturn, comprised three psalms with their antiphons and hymns, three lessons from the Gospel, and a responsory or hymn after each lesson. The service concluded with Benedicamus Domino and the hymn *Te Deum laudamus*.

---

[15] See Martin Horyna, "Česká reformace a hudba. Studie o bohoslužebném zpěvu českých nekatolických církví v období 1420–1620," *Hudební věda* 48 (2011): 5–40.

The "In the Morning" ceremony, also known as the "Morning" or "Morning Sermon," originally began as a morning Marian Mass in the pre-Hussite period and included the popular Rorate Mass during Advent (see Chapter 1). By the late sixteenth century, it evolved into a full Mass with a homily, canon, and a Communion, though sometimes likely without consecration. It could be celebrated in Latin or the vernacular, with the school choir or literary brotherhood performing all the chants and responses to the priest. In the Mass Proper, spiritual songs occasionally substituted some chants, and for the Mass Ordinary, only the Kyrie, Gloria, and Credo remained as staple components of the celebration. The Sanctus and Agnus Dei were not prescribed, as the second half of the Mass was significantly shortened. The so-called *Preces*, a later development of the *prima hora*, celebrated in medieval monasteries and collegiate churches in the morning hours, could be performed instead of the "In the Morning" ceremony. Its name corresponds to its main content, which consists of supplications (Latin: *praeces*) to God. In this context, a characteristic cycle of prayers (Our Father, Hail Mary, Creed, and the Decalogue) was established, sometimes sung to the same melody.

The "High Mass," also known as *summa*, short for *summa missa*, served as the main service on Sundays and feast days, closely adhering to the structure of the Roman Mass. However, individual liturgical chants, such as Gloria and Credo, could be replaced by strophic paraphrases, spiritual songs, and motets.

A crucial question arises concerning who was responsible for the music performance and the selection of the repertory. Literary brotherhoods documents often emphasize that the *literáti* were only obliged to perform the "In the Morning" ceremony. This might explain why some parts of the Mass Ordinary, such as the Sanctus and Agnus Dei, were recited by the priest rather than being performed by the literary brotherhoods.

The "After Lunch" ceremony, also known as the "Catechism," took place on Sunday afternoons and involved the instruction of children in catechism. These sessions were scheduled from Easter to the sixth Sunday after the feast of Holy Trinity, covering a span of fourteen to fifteen Sundays. Závorka prescribes the inclusion of two spiritual songs during these sessions.

Vespers stood out as one of the ceremonies frequently celebrated in public. In towns with Catholic parishes, Vespers were performed daily, featuring the participation of school choirs and organists. On feast days, the repertory in these churches included polyphonic hymns, psalms, and the Magnificat.[16]

---

[16] Martin Horyna, ed., *XXII hymni quatuor et quinque vocum (1540–1600)* (České Budějovice: Státní vědecká knihovna, 2000).

There is abundant information on Vespers performance in Utraquist Churches, suggesting that in the Utraquist Church, too, this service constituted a staple part of regular worship, complete with polyphony performed by school choirs. Like the liturgy of the Roman Church, the Vespers service comprised a series of antiphons and psalms (typically two to five), hymns, a Magnificat, and concluded with Benedicamus Domino. Both vernacular and Latin chants were interspersed with stanzas of spiritual songs.

Finally, "Salve," also known as "Complete," was an evening service held during the Lenten period and on days commemorating the deceased. This ceremony consisted of antiphons and hymns.

Typical for non-Catholic parish churches were regular gatherings with sermons on Wednesdays and Fridays, commonly referred to as "weekday sermons," in which spiritual songs and litanies were performed.

Sources, Transformations, and Durability of the Music Repertory

The core of the music repertory for the service after the Hussite Wars still clung to the traditional Roman Latin chant, supplemented by sequences, tropes, Latin *cantiones*, late medieval polyphony, and Czech vernacular songs, cultivated in the Prague diocese even before the Hussite period (see Chapter 1). The intensive composition of vernacular songs, a central genre in the Reformation period, could therefore draw upon earlier traditions. The composition of *cantiones* and polyphonic motets persisted throughout the Hussite Wars and extended into the fifteenth and sixteenth centuries.[17] Both Latin and vernacular chants appear abundantly in the printed cantionals. Franco-Flemish polyphony represented a certain novelty and started to appear in Bohemian sources around the mid-fifteenth century.[18] It was not accepted everywhere and was limited to specific music collections of literary brotherhoods from around 1500. Some historians inaccurately label this phenomenon as "development retardation," although it was a deliberate rejection of modern polyphony.[19] This attitude is even more obvious in

---

[17] Jaromír Černý, ed., *Moteti medii aevi* (Prague: Supraphon, 1989); Jaromír Černý, ed., *Historical Anthology of Music in the Bohemian Lands (up to ca 1530)* (Prague: KLP, 2005).

[18] Paweł Gancarczyk, "The Dating and Chronology of the Strahov Codex," *Hudební věda* 43 (2006): 135–45; Lenka Hlávková, "Behind the Stage: Some Thoughts on the Codex Speciálník and the Reception of the Polyphony in late 15th-Century Prague," *Early Music* 37 (2009): 37–48.

[19] See Jaromír Černý, "Středověký vícehlas v českých zemích," *Miscellanea musicologica* 27–28 (1975): 15.

the sources of literary brotherhoods from 1540–70. The archaic polyphony continuously cultivated by literary brotherhoods in the Utraquist Church retained its vitality until the early seventeenth century. In the Central-European context, this is not an isolated anachronism. Late medieval polyphony persisted in educational settings across Central Europe until the first half of the sixteenth century, and afterwards, it was adopted by the literary brotherhoods. It experienced a revival once again in Scandinavia in the late sixteenth century.[20]

After 1570, there was a significant surge in interest in modern polyphony within literary brotherhoods. This sparked a relatively substantial output of approximately two generations of composers, some of whom are identifiable by name.[21] Characteristic of their work are compositions scored *ad voces aequales* ("for equal voices," in this case for male voices only), with a particular emphasis on genres suitable for the liturgy of the Mass, including parts of the Mass Ordinary and the Mass Proper, motets, and the Tenorlied genre. The compositions by Clemens non Papa and his contemporaries served as a stylistic model for this group of works.

Unlike literary brotherhoods, school choirs had access to high boys' voices and were not restricted by the range of *ad voces aequales*. This allowed them to draw on the extensive contemporary production of motets and Masses, of both domestic and foreign origin. Alongside manuscript and printed collections of international repertories, there was a flow of simpler polyphonic compositions found in the prints *Veteres ac piae cantiones* ("Old and Devotional Songs"), a 1561 Catholic chant book influential in Protestant circles, and *Libellus elementarius* ("Alphabet Book") from 1569, as well as several manuscripts, such as the 1610 *Prachatický kancionál* ("Prachatice Cantional").[22] This collection, aside from songs, featured simple polyphonic pieces set to texts from the Mass and the Office. Around 1590, the practice of double choirs gained popularity in Bohemia.[23]

---

[20] Timo Mäkinen, *Die aus frühen böhmischen Quellen überlieferten Piae cantiones-Melodien* (Jyväskylä: Jyväskylän Yliopistoyhdistys, 1964); Martin Horyna, "Die Kompositionen von Peter Wilhelmi von Graudenz als Teil der spätmittelalterlichen Polyfonie-Tradition in Mitteleuropa und insbesondere im Böhmen des 15. und 16. Jahrhunderts," *Hudební věda* 40 (2003), 291–328.

[21] Jaromír Černý, ed., *Hudba české renesance* (Prague: SNTL, 1982); Martin Horyna, ed., *Jan Trojan Turnovský: Opera musica* (České Budějovice: Státní vědecká knihovna, 2002); Martin Horyna, ed., *Officium in Nativitate Domini* (Prague: Národní knihovna České republiky, 2009).

[22] Martin Horyna, ed., *Prachatický kancionál (1610): cantilenae piae 4, 5, 6 et 8 vocum* (České Budějovice: Jihočeská univerzita, 2005).

[23] Petr Daněk and Martin Horyna, eds., *The Double-Choir Motets of Rudolphine Prague. An Anthology of Eight-Voice Motets from Bohemian Manuscripts and Prints*, vol. 1 (Prague: KLP, 2020).

The Legacy of the Non-Catholic Repertory after 1620

The defeat of the Bohemian Revolt in the Battle of the White Mountain near Prague in 1620 and the subsequent recatholicization following the introduction of Revised Land Ordinance (*Verneuerte Landesordnung*) in 1627–28 led to the eradication of non-Catholic worship in Bohemia and Moravia. Non-Catholic hymnbooks faced censorship, and some were confiscated and destroyed. However, lavishly illuminated Utraquist graduals have been preserved relatively well. In these, folios containing chants dedicated to Jan Hus and chants with references to the Communion *sub utraque* and the Chalice were intentionally torn out.

The musical culture from the previous era did not vanish entirely. Singing in Czech remained a regular part of Catholic worship. The monophonic songs and chant, as well as the polyphonic repertory recorded in school cantionals, retained their vibrancy, and were commonly incorporated into manuscript and printed chant books at least until the end of the seventeenth century. In some towns, literary brotherhoods endured until the second half of the eighteenth century. In 1785, Emperor Joseph II (r. 1780–90) abolished all religious brotherhoods including literary brotherhoods, and most of their music collections were destroyed during subsequent secularization, with only a small remnant surviving to the present. Our understanding of the Bohemian Reformation polyphony, particularly that recorded in partbooks, is today affected by these losses.

The feudal subjects had no option but to convert to Catholicism, while non-Catholic freemen were allowed to emigrate. It was mainly the non-Catholic nobility, clergy, and intellectuals who chose to leave the country. In exile, the hymnographic activity of Czech non-Catholics continued well into the eighteenth century, serving the needs of exile communities and, to some extent, those in Bohemia and Moravia who remained secret non-Catholics. Two figures, Jan Amos Komenský (Johann Amos Comenius, 1592–1670) and Jiří Třanovský (Georgius Tranoscius, 1592–1637), played pivotal roles in shaping the definitive form of Czech non-Catholic music repertory recorded in hymnbooks in exile.[24]

Komenský left behind a vast literary legacy, and his relationship to music is evident in several areas. As a poetry theorist, he favored quantitative as opposed to qualitative metric prosody and considered the humanist ode to

---

[24] It was not until 1781 that Emperor Joseph II issued The Patent of Toleration, which allowed certain non-Catholic denominations in the monarchy, specifically the Augsburg, Helvetic (Calvinism), and Orthodox ones.

be its ideal musical counterpart. Building on the contributions of earlier figures, Komenský translated a portion of the Psalter in metrical prosody in Czech. As an education specialist, he emphasized the role of music in the early education of children, viewing their natural inclination for musical expression as a vital aspect. According to Komenský, children could learn the simplest chants at the age of five or six, progress to singing in their mother tongue with knowledge of notation at city schools (ages six to twelve), and finally, in Latin schools (ages twelve to eighteen), delve into a deeper understanding of music theory, integrated into the teaching of the seven liberal arts.[25] Komenský's pedagogical concept did not mandate students to sing in the Church, aligning with other contemporary humanist school reform proposals. Concurrently, the prevailing practice allowed gifted but poor students to join the education system in connection to Church singing. Although Komenský acknowledged the utility of playing instruments, he rejected dancing and secular music. Starting in the 1620s, he contemplated a new form of the cantional for the Unity of the Brethren and created his own spiritual songs (one such song is provided in Example 3.1). From 1628, he lived permanently in exile, and the limited conditions for the functioning of the Unity of Brethren in the diaspora influenced Komenský's decisions about the cantional's contents. The multi-confessional character and typographically luxurious execution of previous editions of cantionals, especially the editions of 1541, 1564, and 1615, featuring a large number of songs and chant pieces, were not suitable for the scattered remnants of the Unity of the Brethren. Therefore, the definitive version of Komenský's *Kancyonál* ("Cantional"), published in Amsterdam in 1659, appeared in a compact pocket format.[26] It included the complete Psalter with melodies from the Genevan Psalter and a collection of 456 other chants, consisting of a reduced number of chant pieces and spiritual songs, alongside 146 new songs. The total number of texts composed and translated by Komenský himself is estimated at 148. Two years later, in 1661, Komenský published in Amsterdam the German cantional *Kirchen- Haus- und Hertzens-Musica*.[27]

Simultaneously, another cantional, titled *Cithara Sanctorum*, by Komenský's contemporary Třanovský was published in exile and garnered an even greater response. Třanovský went into emigration as early as 1626 and worked from 1628 in various places in Slovakia (then Upper Hungary),

---

[25] *Johannis Amos Comenii Opera omnia*, vol. 11, ed. Bohuslav Havránek (Prague: Academia, 1973).

[26] Petr Daněk, and Jiří K. Kroupa, eds., *Jan Amos Komenský, Kancyonál. Faksimile vydání z roku 1659 (Amsterdam, Christoffel Cunradus)* (Prague: KLP, 2018).

[27] This was a reedition of the 1639 German Brethren Cantional (see n. 12).

Example 3.1: Jan Amos Komenský's Czech translation of the German Lutheran song *Auf meinen lieben Gott* as *V Bohu já skládám svém*, published in the 1659 Amsterdam *Kancyonál*. English: In my only God I place my hope, he can relieve me of misery, he will handle danger. His hand is mighty, protecting from all evil.

where non-Catholic denominations continued to be tolerated. *Cithara Sanctorum*, his magnum opus, was first published in 1636 in Levoča in eastern Slovakia, containing over 400 songs, with melodies accompanying 160 of them. Třanovský continued the tradition of Moravian Lutherans (including Tobiáš Závorka and others); about half of the songs were drawn from the Czech tradition, while the rest consisted of his original lyrics and translations. The dissemination of *Cithara Sanctorum* was remarkable; it had seen at least ten publications by 1711, was identified as a Cantional of the Slovak Evangelical Church and endured as such for three and a half centuries, being published in over two hundred editions.[28]

Conclusion

The Czech Reformation was unique in some of its manifestations. It preceded the main Reformation wave of the early 1500s by a century. One of its distinctive features was the creation of its own repertory, with the most striking part being vernacular (Czech) songs and paraphrased chant in the vernacular. Throughout the sixteenth century, the song repertory was enriched by adopting elements from the Lutheran German song

---

[28] Jiří Třanovský, *Sborník k 300. výročí kancionálu Cithara Sanctorum* (Bratislava: Učená společnost Šafaříkova, 1936).

traditions (in mutual exchange) and from the radical Reformation, such as the Geneva Psalter. The first printed Bohemian cantional was published as early as 1501, and certain printed cantionals, especially those produced by the Unity of Brethren, stand out as pinnacles of the cantional production in terms of both scope and typographic sophistication, even in an international context. The polyphonic repertory, persisting well into the sixteenth century, retained some aspects of late medieval style. The conservatism of the bourgeois milieu, from which the singing activity of the lay literary fraternities emerged, was evident in both the acquisition of expensive manuscript graduals and the character of the newer polyphonic music from the second half of the sixteenth century tailored for this milieu.

Despite the defeat of the Bohemian Revolt in 1620, leading to the prohibition of non-Catholic worship in Bohemia and Moravia, the practice of singing in Czech during liturgy continued to be tolerated within Catholic worship (see Chapter 5). Several songs have endured as a consistent part of the Church repertory up to the present day. Cantionals for non-Catholic denominations were published in exile after 1620. Some of their repertory was reintroduced in Bohemia after the legalization of non-Catholic denominations in 1781 or later, during the twentieth century, as part of historicizing reforms of various denominations' liturgical music.

4 | Music at Rudolf II's Court in Prague

ERIKA SUPRIA HONISCH

Arrivals, 1583

The three-dozen singers, composers, and instrumentalists employed by Rudolf II, Holy Roman Emperor and King of Bohemia, arrived in Prague from Vienna in the early 1580s to find that their new home already had plenty of musicians.[1] Brotherhoods of musical laymen, proud of their ability to sing from notation, called themselves *literati* in Latin (*literáti* in Czech) and sang plainsong and polyphony in urban churches on Sundays and feast days, and daily during Advent (see Chapter 3). Quotidian liturgical needs were met by choirs of schoolboys who sang at morning Mass and Vespers, their service helping cover the costs of their education. Civic trumpeters played from the tower of the Old Town Hall.[2] Schoolteachers and the many learned men associated with Charles University delighted in canons, settings of metrical texts and neo-Latin aphorisms, and other displays of musical and literary erudition. Jewish ensembles, although vulnerable to anti-Jewish decrees, mob violence, and expulsion, provided instrumental music for dancing and other lay entertainments.[3] They also sang polyphony at royal entries, where their performance of fealty to king and emperor positioned their community as integrable into, if not integral to, the body politic.[4] Cultivated amateurs enthusiastically collected music books and took up the lute, viol, and keyboard instruments.[5]

---

[1] Rudolf II was emperor from 1576–1612, and King of Bohemia from 1575–1611. An excellent history of this period is Jaroslav Pánek, "The Czech Estates in the Habsburg Monarchy (1526–1620)," in *A History of the Czech Lands* (Prague: Karolinum, 2009), 191–229.

[2] Jan Baťa's work on musical culture in Prague's Old Town is indispensable: see, among others, Jan Baťa, "Hudba a hudební kultura na Starém Městě pražském 1526–1620" (PhD diss., Charles University, Prague, 2011).

[3] Jews were expelled in 1541 and 1557, and petitions to the emperor for their expulsion continued. The situation stabilized somewhat under Rudolf II; see Pánek, "The Czech Estates," 218.

[4] On Jewish participation in the royal entries of 1527 and 1558, see Jan Baťa, "Praga festivans: Music Played during the Prague Festivities of 1527 and 1558," *Historie-Otázky-Problémy* 2 (2015): 250 and 256–57.

[5] On lutenists specifically, see Emil Vogl, "Lautenisten der böhmischen Spätrenaissance," *Die Musikforschung* 18 (1965): 281–90.

Although Rudolf II was not the first emperor to make the Bohemian capital his home – the Prague-born Emperor Charles IV of the Luxembourg dynasty had resided there in the fourteenth century – he was the first Habsburg emperor to choose it for his residence. Rudolf's musicians sought to please their melancholic employer, whose education at the court of his uncle Philip II had left him (in the words of Elizabeth I's unimpressed ambassador) "extreemely Spaniolated," and whose cultural touchstones and creative enthusiasms bore little resemblance to those of his new subjects.[6] Foreign and Catholic, his singers and instrumentalists were in many respects interlopers.[7] They wrote music for a chapel whose religious practices were at odds with those of the local population: of the city's three dozen churches, all but the cathedral and four monastery churches were Utraquist, and Lutheran sympathies were widespread. The imperial musicians conversed in Italian, Dutch, Spanish, German, and French, while the majority of Prague's inhabitants communicated in Czech. This warranted comment. Records of a lawsuit between the imperial chamber musician Mauro Sinibaldi and the architect he hired to build his Malá Strana (Lesser Town) house indicate that the quarreling parties spoke to each other entirely in Italian.[8] The court's most prominent composer, the Flemish Chapelmaster Philippe de Monte (1521–1603), went so far as to claim that he was unable to speak even German – an astonishing disclosure, given his long service to the Austrian Habsburgs, and surely an inconvenience given the size and prominence of Prague's German-speaking minority.[9]

Yet by the time the emperor died, compositions connected to his musical interlopers could be heard not just in Prague, but in institutional and domestic settings all across Bohemia and Moravia.[10] Mass settings,

---

[6] Robert James Weston Evans, *Rudolf II and His World: A Study in Intellectual History* (Oxford: Clarendon Press, 1984), 122.

[7] Older studies of Rudolf II's musical personnel are superseded by Michaela Žáčková Rossi, *The Musicians at the Court of Rudolf II: The Musical Entourage of Rudolf II (1576–1612) Reconstructed from the Imperial Accounting Ledgers* (Prague: KLP, 2017).

[8] Gustav Pazaurek, "Beiträge zu einer Geschichte der Musik in Böhmen," *Mitteilungen des Vereins für Geschichte der Deutschen in Böhmen* 23 (1884): 284, citing documents in Prague, Archiv hlavního města Prahy, shelfmark cod. 1126 fol. B 11 v.

[9] Philippe de Monte, letter dated February 17, 1588, quoted in Richard Wistreich, "Philippe de Monte: New Autobiographical Documents," *Early Music History* 25 (2006): 294.

[10] The study of Rudolfine compositions has been hampered by a lack of modern editions; even the Philippe de Monte *Opera Omnia* remains incomplete. Through the efforts of the Czech members of the Musica Rudolphina study group, however, more repertory has become accessible; see http://www.bibemus.org/musicarudolphina/stranky/publikace_en.html, accessed July 6, 2023. Editions of Sales's music by Thomas Engel and Michael Steiner-

motets, madrigals, Lieder, and *canzonette* by Rudolf II's musicians traveled via local nobles or court officials to places such as Český Krumlov (Krumau), Prostějov (Proßnitz), and Kutná Hora (Kuttenberg) and beyond: to Olomouc (Olmütz), Zábrdovice (Obrowitz), Rajhrad (Groß Raigern), Jihlava (Iglau), Uherské Hradiště (Ungarisch Hradisch), among others.[11] Indeed, manuscripts compiled by Czech users are sometimes the sole extant sources for Rudolfine compositions. A six-voice setting by Monte of the Lamentations of Jeremiah, for instance, is known only from a set of manuscript partbooks originally owned by a lawyer named Václav Kristian of Greifenfels (d. 1606), and from a contemporary inventory of the collections of Moravian nobleman Karl I of Liechtenstein (1569–1627).[12] Likewise, the earliest known copy of the motet *Dies est laetitiae* by the imperial organist and composer Carolus Luython (1557–1620) – not printed until 1629 – is found in a binder's volume owned by the poet Jiří Carolides (1569–1612). Outfitted with a celebratory Czech text, *Nastal nám den veselý* ("A Happy Day Has Come for Us"), it entered the repertory of the *literati*.[13]

The spread of Rudolfine music across the Czech musical landscape was largely due to the prestige of the imperial court and the rhizomatic influence of the resurgent Catholic Church in Bohemia and Moravia.[14] But its propagation also depended on local tastes and practices: the aspirational cosmopolitanism of the region's nobles and townspeople, and the Utraquist cultivation of polyphony in worship and education. It hinged, too, on the enterprising efforts of musicians such as the imperial tenor Franz Sales (1540?–99), whose polyphonic prints are representative both of the stylistic range of Rudolfine music and the individualized nature of its circulation.

Schweißgut for *Musikedition Tirol* are available at https://musikedition.musikland-tirol.at/, accessed July 6, 2023.

[11] On extant music prints, see Petr Daněk, *Historické tisky vokální polyfonie, rané monodie, hudební teorie a instrumentální hudby v českých zemích do roku 1630* (Prague: KLP, 2015).

[12] Greifenfels's music books are presently held at New York University's Fales Library as "The Sabbateni Collection of Renaissance Music Manuscripts," Mss. 239; on their complicated provenance, see Petr Daněk, "On the Fate of the Collection of Bohemian Musical Prints and Manuscripts in the Sabbateni Collection New York," *Czech Music Quarterly* 2022, no. 1: 16–19. On Liechtenstein's inventory, see Vladimír Maňas, "Music in Moravia circa 1600," in Gerold Gruber, ed., *Zur Geschichte und Aufführungspraxis der Musik des 16.-18. Jahrhunderts in Mittel- und Osteuropa* (Bratislava: Accentus Musicalis, 2013), 105.

[13] Marta Vaculínová and Petr Daněk, "*Vita ceu harmonia*: Jiří Carolides: A Poet and Composer between the Imperial Court and the New Town of Prague," *Musicalia* 1–2 (2022): 23. Carolides's manuscript is held in the National Library of the Czech Republic, shelfmark Se 1137.

[14] Erika Supria Honisch, "Music In-Between: Sacred Songs in Bohemia, 1517–1618," in *Renaissance Music in the Slavic World*, ed. Vasco Zara and Marco Gurrieri (Turnhout: Brepols, 2019), 209–59.

With ambition and canny pragmatism in the face of an indifferent employer, Sales and other imperial musicians composed polyphony that had local appeal. In Bohemia's fertile ground, their music was more than an offshoot of court culture, reproducing Habsburg ideology and Catholic doctrine: it was whatever people made of it. Sounding in the multi-lingual, multi-confessional capital of a multi-lingual, multi-confessional kingdom, its meanings were contingent on who was singing, who was listening, and where, and when, and to what end.

Musical Employees

Rudolf II's music establishment was the largest the Bohemian royal court had seen, surpassing that of his uncle Archduke Ferdinand of Tyrol, who resided in Prague as governor from 1551 to 1567, and comparable in size to the Wittelsbach chapel in Munich.[15] The musicians were organized following a scheme typical of early modern courts: singers and organists formed the Chapel (*Capelnpartey*), brass and wind players, as well as drummers, were employed in the Stables (*Stallpartey*), and a select few singers and instrumentalists were designated chamber musicians (*Cammer musici*). A handful of musicians were given more prestigious titles which, in principle, opened up the possibility for advancement at court. On discovering that the chamber musician Odd'Antonio Budi was born a gentleman, for instance, Monte arranged for him to be appointed as *gentilhuomo di casa* ("court servant").[16]

The Chapel was dissolved and reconstituted with each new Habsburg sovereign, but Rudolf retained many of his father's musicians, chief among them Monte, snagging musicians from other Habsburg courts if the opportunity presented itself. His ensemble comprised choirboys (primarily Flemish), discantists (castrati, typically from Spain, and falsettists), altos, tenors, basses, and organists. The fleet of support workers included the calcant (bellows operator), organ tuner, copyist, and tutors *in litteris* and *in musica* for the choirboys. The Chapel as a whole was overseen by the imperial Almoner Jacobus Chimarrhaeus (1542–1614), an amateur musician himself. His musical affiliations were captured by the poet Carolides, who deftly rearranged

---

[15] On Archduke Ferdinand II's chapel, established in 1564, see Jan Bat'a, "Ferdinand of Tyrol and the Music Culture in Renaissance Prague," *Wissenschaftliches Jahrbuch der Tiroler Landesmuseen* 5 (2012): 20.

[16] Wistreich, "Philippe de Monte," 271.

the letters "IACOBUS CHIMARRHEUS" to produce the anagram: "Ubi chorus, hic ars mea" – roughly, "Where the chorus is, is my skill."[17]

The four or five imperial chaplains were expected to be musically competent, able at minimum to sing in services, but often capable of more. Those known to compose include Giovanni Battista Galeno (who joined the imperial chapel after stints at the Habsburg courts in Graz and Brussels); Vincenzo Neriti, whose Magnificats and *canzonette* were well-received both north and south of the Alps; and Jacobus de Kerle (1531/2–91), famous for his *Preces speciales* (Venice, 1562), which had informed discussions of music at the Council of Trent. Kerle spent his final years in Prague and had a collection of motets printed by the local printer Georgius Nigrinus in 1585.[18] Like other imperial musicians, some of the chaplains participated in activities at the Jesuit College. The imperial chaplain and alto Zachiaras Zanotti sang Mass there in 1609, for instance.[19]

Few locals would have had occasion to hear the Chapel musicians perform as a group, since they sang primarily up at Prague Castle in the cathedral and All Saints Chapel, and only now and again in the Old Town at the Franciscan Church of St. James. But few could have avoided hearing the imperial trumpets and drums reverberating in Prague's public spaces during religious processions and royal and civic entries. In what must have been one of the more memorable entries of Rudolf II's reign, the 1609 procession welcoming the Ottoman ambassador from the Buda Pashalik, imperial trumpeters and drummers rode on horseback at the head of a group of Bohemian nobles (see Figure 4.1), their sounds juxtaposed with those of Prague's civic trumpeters and Turkish musicians playing shawms (*zūrnā*) and drums elsewhere in the procession.[20]

For coronations and announcements of military victories, fanfares – coupled with church bells and gunfire – extended the acoustic arena of the royal complex to include the city below. When news came in 1593 of an imperial victory over Ottoman forces in Hungary, for example, the emperor conveyed the news to Prague's inhabitants via the joyous volleys (*frewden*

---

[17] Jiří Carolides, *Farrago Symbolica Sententiosa* (Prague, 1597), fol. K4 r.

[18] Jacobus de Kerle, *Selectiorum aliquot modulorum, qui in sacris templis . . . decantari solent* (Prague, 1585).

[19] Emilian Trolda, "Jesuité a Hudba," *Cyril* 66 (1940): 74.

[20] Erika Supria Honisch, "Encounters with Music in Rudolf II's Prague," *Austrian History Yearbook* 52 (2021): 68–69; and Kateřina Horníčková and Michael Šroněk, "Staging Oriental Delegations at the Habsburg Court in Prague (1600–1610)," *Culture & History Journal* 11 (2022): https://doi.org/10.3989/chdj.2022.019.

Figure 4.1: The Imperial Trumpeters depicted in Samuel Suchuduller, *Ankunft und Einzug der Tyrkgischen Potschafften wie sy allhier zu Prag den XII October Anno 1609. . .* (n.p. [1610?]). Anne S. K. Brown Military Collection, Brown University Library. Reproduced by permission.

schüß) of seventeen artillery pieces fired from the Summer Palace, and a *Te Deum* punctuated by the sounds of kettledrums and trumpet blasts.[21]

The imperial "trumpeters" comprised both the field musicians who played fanfares and signals, and a complement of what were elsewhere termed "musical trumpeters" (a category including trombonists and cornettists), which augmented vocal polyphony and performed sinfonias, ricercars, intradas, and other instrumental genres as circumstance and ceremonial demanded. The 1597 Intradas by the trumpeter Alessandro Orologio (1551–1633), suitable for performance on "all kinds of musical instruments," give a sense of the energetic and sonorous style.[22] Falling in

[21] Hieronymus Ortelius, *Chronologia oder Historische beschreibung aller Kriegsemporungen vnd belägerungen der Stätt vnd Vestungen, . . . biß auff gegenwertige Zeitt . . .* (Nuremberg, 1602), fol. 58v.

[22] Alessandro Orologio, *Intradae . . . quarum in omni genere instrumentorum musicorum usus esse potest* (Helmstedt, 1597).

two or three short sections, they are characterized by short phrases and shifts between declamatory homophony and passages in a fluid, lightly imitative style.

The most influential brass and wind players were Italian, and shaped regional performance practice through their instruction. The rosters of apprentices (*Trommetter Lehrjung*) and full-fledged trumpeters in the imperial ensemble trace their impact, suggesting an increase in Czech and German members over time.[23] A representative example is Marcus Štastný – who served as an apprentice of Luca Zigotta in the early 1590s, and entered the *Stallpartey* in 1596. Štastný testified in 1603 before the Old Town Court at inheritance proceedings connected to the deceased wife of his landlord Václav Trubka of Roviny (Václav Trubka z Rovin) precisely the sort of archival trace indicative of local roots.[24]

The region's Italophile aristocracy opened up other avenues for contact and influence: in the 1590s, for instance, Petr Vok of Rožmberk (Petr Vok z Rožmberka, 1539–1611), scion of a venerable Bohemian noble family, hired the imperial trumpeter Luca Zigotta to teach six youths.[25] He likely did so in hopes of populating the ensemble his brother Vilém had established at Český Krumlov in 1552 after a formative six-month trip to Italy. Around the same time, Zigotta sent music and musical instruments to the nobleman Ladislav Velen of Žerotín (Ladislav Velen ze Žerotína, 1579–1638), whose cultural interests were shaped by studies abroad that took him to Padua and Siena.[26] In 1606, Karl of Liechtenstein paid an imperial musician referred to in the records as "Petr Kapaun" to sing and play the lute at one of his Moravian residences.[27] This *cappone* (castrato) was probably Pietro di Nagera, an imperial discantist.[28]

The performing capabilities of Rudolf's chamber musicians were known to those outside court circles only by reputation. Nobles, courtiers, and visiting diplomats did get to hear them, however, and they were listeners whose opinions mattered. In what was probably a typical

---

[23] Žáčková Rossi, *The Musicians*, xxiii.

[24] See the entries on "Marx Stiasni," in Žáčková Rossi, *The Musicians*, 172–73 and 197. On the inheritance proceedings, see Pazaurek, *Beiträge*, 284, and Baťa, "Hudba a hudební kultura," 101. On Trubka of Roviny's significant musical inclinations, see Jan Baťa, "*Quod laudat praesens, omnis mirabitur aetas*: Graduál Trubky z Rovin, jeho repertoár a evropský kontext," in *Littera Nigro Scripta Manet: In honorem Jaromír Černý*, ed. Jan Baťa, Jiří Kroupa, and Lenka Mráčková (Prague: KLP, 2009), 126–52.

[25] Petr Daněk, "Rudolfinian Prague as a Musical Center in its Time," *Die Tonkunst* 6 (2012): 317.

[26] Daněk, "Rudolfinian Prague," 317.   [27] Maňas, "Music in Moravia," 104.

[28] See the entries on Nagera (Nasera) in Žáčková Rossi, *The Musicians*, 24–25 and 132–33.

scenario, a French diplomat heard imperial musicians perform during a meal with Marquis Francesco Gonzaga of Castiglione on a summer evening in 1600. Impressed, he singled out a viol player for particular praise.[29] In an image of the banquet celebrating Rudolf II's 1585 induction into the Order of the Golden Fleece, we see the musicians singing and playing instruments, their "stattliche, herrliche Music" praised by the official chronicler in the same terms as the splendid displays of food (*herrliches Shawessen*) (see Figure 4.2).[30]

Little is known about the duties of chamber musicians beyond their obligation to entertain the emperor in his chambers, and to perform at banquets, masques, and other court diversions. They tended to live in Hradčany or Malá Strana, close to work and presumably available to serve on a moment's notice.[31] Sinibaldi, a celebrated Cremonese viol player, was recruited specifically as a chamber musician, as was his wife, Marta – scouted by Monte in Mechelen in 1570 for her ability to sing, and play the lute and virginals.[32] Other chamber musicians included the brothers Carlo and Giovanni Paolo Ardesi and "trumpeter" Marc Antonio Mosto, one member of a musical family from Udine whose service to the court spanned multiple generations.

Even the most effusive reports say nothing specific about what the chamber musicians performed, but there was no shortage of available repertory. Madrigals – for example the four-voice settings by the Ardesi brothers (both viol players) printed in 1597 – lent themselves well to instrumental performance.[33] Monte was extraordinarily productive in the genre: with over 1,000 madrigals to his name, he wrote more than anyone else.[34] Evidence for their instrumental performance comes from Monte himself. He writes in the dedication of his fifteenth book of madrigals for five voices

---

[29] François-Georges Pariset, "Pierre Bergeron à Prague (1600)," in *Relations artistiques entre les Pays-Bas et l'Italie dans la Renaissance: Études dédiées à Suzanne Sulzberger*, ed. N. Dacos (Brussels: Institut historique belge de Rome, 1980), 191–92.

[30] Paul Zehendtner von Zehendtgrub, *Ordenliche Beschreibung mit was stattlichen Ceremonien und Zierlichkeiten, die Röm[ische] Kay[serliche] May[estät], ... den Ordens deß Guldin Flüß ... empfangen und angenommen* (Dillingen, 1587), 114. See also Jan Baťa, "Remarks on the Festivities of the Order of the Golden Fleece in Prague (1585)," *Musicologia Brunensia* 51 (2016): 25–35.

[31] Scott Lee Edwards, "Repertory Migration in the Czech Crown Lands, 1570–1630" (PhD diss., University of California, Berkeley, 2012), 94–95.

[32] Robert Lindell, "Marta gentil che'l cor m'ha morto: Eine unbekannte Kammermusikerin am Hof Maximilians II.," *Musicologica austriaca* 7 (1987): 59.

[33] Carlo Ardesi, *Il Primo Libro de Madrigal a quattro voci* (Venice, 1597).

[34] Brian Mann, *The Secular Madrigals of Filippo di Monte, 1521–1603* (Ann Arbor: UMI Research Press, 1983) offers a helpful stylistic overview.

Figure 4.2: The Imperial Musicians at the 1585 Golden Fleece Banquet in Prague, depicted in Paul Zehendtner von Zehendtgrub, *Ordenliche Beschreibung mit was stattlichen Ceremonien . . . die Röm. Kay. May. . . . den Orden deß Guldin Flüß in disem 85. Jahr zu Prag . . . empfangen vnd angenommen* (Dillingen: Mayer, 1587). Bayerische Staatsbibliothek München, shelfmark 4 J.publ.g. 168 [114a]; urn.nbn:de:bvb:12-bsb10163025-6. Reproduced by permission.

(Venice, 1592) that given how much the papal nuncio Camillo Caetano had enjoyed their performance on viols some months earlier he could not help but issue them under the protective shadow of his illustrious name.

The archlute intabulations of Pietro Paolo Melli (1579–1623) open a window onto the array of enthusiasts attracted to music cultivated at the Habsburg court, although they date from the reign of Rudolf's brother Matthias (r. 1612–19).[35] They comprise musical portraits of sorts named after specific individuals, many of whom had been active at the Rudolfine court: a Prelude subtitled *Il Bransuico* ("The Braunschweig") is for Duke Heinrich Julius, while the *Alemana detta la Capona* ("Allemande named 'the Castrato'") is a nod to Pietro di Nagera.[36] Among the women

---

[35] Pietro Paolo Melli, *Intavolatura di liuto attiorbato*, vols. 2 and 3 (Venice, 1616).
[36] Žáčková Rossi, *The Musicians*, 132–33.

honored in the prints is the powerful widow of imperial Burgrave Vilém of Rožmberk (Vilém z Rožmberka), Polyxena of Pernštejn (Polyxena z Pernštejna, 1566–1642), to whom Melli dedicated divisions (*passaggi*) on Palestrina's madrigal *Vestiva i colli*.

Listening in Prague

Many of the emperor's musicians composed, but only a few were obligated to: Monte, as Chapelmaster; Luython, who was named *Hofkomponist* at Monte's death in 1603; and the series of Vice-Chapelmasters – Alard du Gaucquier, Jacob Regnart, Camillo Zanotti, and Orologio – each of whom was a well-established composer by the time he was named to the position.[37] The rest, like the entrepreneurial Sales, composed speculatively, in hopes of securing bonus payments from the emperor, in addition to whatever could be recouped in sales of self-funded prints and contributions from well-heeled dedicatees. A great deal of what the imperial musicians composed is cast in a supra-regional style, suited to a Europe-wide market. Monte is representative of this tendency: his many madrigal and motet prints, all issued in Venice, respond to music-stylistic developments and literary and devotional trends (for example the popularity of Guarini's poetry, the emergence of the spiritual madrigal, the canzonetta craze) in Italy and Germany.[38] It is symptomatic of their interest in a broader market that neither he nor other court composers took up the most obvious feature of local polyphony: scoring *ad aequales* for the literary brotherhoods (that is, voices that share the same range, facilitating performance by adult men, see Chapter 3). But Rudolf's composers were nevertheless listening to the city around them, and some – notably those who chose to have their music printed in Prague – incorporated regional practices or elements of the local soundscape into their compositions.

The title of Luython's *Popularis anni jubilus* (Prague, 1588) foregrounds its regional character, explaining its exuberant contents as the musical celebration of the "people's year."[39] The Latin texts, by Prague

---

[37] On Luython's career trajectory, see Žáčková Rossi, *The Musicians*, 114–16.

[38] On Monte's spiritual madrigals, see Daniele Filippi, "'Ask the Jesuits to Send Verses from Rome': The Society's Networks and the European Dissemination of Devotional Music," in *Exploring Jesuit Distinctiveness: Interdisciplinary Perspectives on Ways of Proceeding within the Society of Jesus*, ed. Robert Aleksander Maryks (Leiden: Brill, 2016), 62–80.

[39] Erika Supria Honisch, "Drowning Winter, Burning Bones, Singing Songs: Representations of Popular Devotion in a Central European Motet Cycle," *Journal of Musicology* 34 (2017): 559–609.

cathedral canon Jiří Pontanus, a native of Most (Brüx), allude to such characteristically Bohemian traditions as the drowning of the goddess Morana to mark the end of winter. Arranged as a cycle from New Year's Day to Christmas, the six-voice settings chart the changing seasons in a noisy countryside – where insects buzz during the *dies caniculares* (the languorous "dog days" of summer) and geese honk to mark St. Martin's Day. Each half of the Christmas lullaby *Salve beate infantule* ends with a lilting setting of the word "Bruneya" – a regionalism evoking the practice of *Kindlwiegen*, when the Christian faithful rocked the Infant Jesus to sleep. Sales's *Missa Exultandi tempus est* (Munich, 1598) also evokes the practice: both it and the motet (also by Sales) on which it is modeled refer audibly to *Resonet in laudibus*, a tune that circulated in Bohemia as *Hajej můj andílku* and *Joseph lieber Joseph mein* and commonly underpinned the Austro-Bohemian Christmas pastorella of the seventeenth and eighteenth centuries.[40]

Court musicians and their autochthonous counterparts captured Central Europe's polyglot disposition in the "quodlibet": a polyphonic hodgepodge of passages in Latin, Italian, German, and Czech, taken from genres serious and light, sacred and bawdy. The vigorous syllabic declamation and disruptive style (if not the ribald texts) of these musical patchworks found their way into the liturgy via the three *Missae quodlibeticae* that conclude Luython's first book of Masses (Prague, 1609).[41] Quodlibets and other raucous pieces are anthologized in the *Musicalischer Zeitvertreiber* (Nuremberg, 1609), probably compiled by Luython and Nicolaus Zangius (c. 1570–c. 1618), imperial *Hofdiener* and chapelmaster to Karl of Liechtenstein.[42] Among its contents is a composition entitled *Judenschul* ("Synagogue").[43] Purporting to represent Jewish worship, a distinctive feature of the Prague soundscape, its chaotic setting of fragmentary Hebrew and Italian phrases gives dehumanizing voice to widespread Christian stereotypes of Jews as noisy and disordered (see also Chapter 21).

Locals were listening to their city too, of course. A 1598 four-language dictionary by the Czech printer and polymath Daniel Adam of Veleslavín

---

[40] Geoffrey Chew, "The Christmas Pastorella in Austria, Bohemia, and Moravia" (PhD diss., University of Manchester, 1968), 53–74.

[41] Carolus Luython, *Liber primus missarum* (Prague, 1609).

[42] Scott Edwards, "'Is There No One Here Who Speaks to Me?' Performing Ethnic Encounter in Bohemia and Moravia at the Turn of the 17th Century," *Diasporas* 26 (2015): 17–34, and online at https://doi.org/10.4000/diasporas.402, accessed March 3, 2023.

[43] No. 27 in *Musicalischer Zeitvertreiber ... mit 4. 5. 6. 7. vnd 8. stimmen componirt* (Nuremberg, 1609).

gives a sense of the terms available to describe the music they heard.[44] For Veleslavín, as for Helfrich Emmel, on whose German-Latin-Greek-French dictionary he modeled his *Nomenclator*, "music" is above all the "art of singing" ("ars canendi" or "umění zpěvu").[45] *Concinnitas* is "voices sounding together well" or in a pleasing way ("pěkné znění hlasu / Wollautung"), while dissonance is understood as voices in disarray ("nesrovnání hlasů / wans nicht zusammen stimmt") – and here the *Judenschul* comes to mind. Veleslavín's musicians include chapelmasters, choir directors, and singers, along with wind players ("pískač"), trumpeters ("trubač"), and fiddlers ("hudec"). He categorizes music according to function: "songs of praise" ("Píseň chvály"), "wedding songs" ("Píseň svatební"), and "sacred songs" ("Duchowní píseň"). "Prodrobování hlasu v zpěvu" is Veleslavín's take on *chroma*, which Emmel had translated simply as either "melody" or "the coloration of song."

Styles and Practices

The most useful music composed by imperial musicians was Latin-texted sacred music. Despite the emperor's retreat from formal religion after about 1585, His musicians kept writing Mass Ordinaries (mostly parody settings based on motets or madrigals), motets, and Psalm settings. The three volumes of Mass Proper settings by Sales (cantus firmus settings based on plainchant) issued by Nigrinus in the 1590s are late examples of a genre whose roots at the Habsburg court reach back to the *Choralis Constantinus*.[46] That Sales's settings were reprinted may reflect the Utraquist cultivation of "plenary Masses," that is, polyphonic settings of both the Proper and Ordinary, of which there are many instances by Czech composers such as Jiří Rychnovský (1545–1616).

Sales was the most entrepreneurial of the imperial composers, dispatching his prints to town councils and churches across the region. He

---

[44] Daniel Adam z Veleslavína, *Nomenclator Quadrilinguis, BoemicoLatinoGraecoGermanicus* (Prague, 1598), cols. 345–52.

[45] On the connection to Emmel's dictionary, see Helmut Glück et al., eds., *Deutsche Sprachbücher in Böhmen und Mähren vom 15. Jahrhundert bis 1918: Eine teilkommentierte Bibliographie* (Berlin: De Gruyter, 2011), 27.

[46] Franz Sales, *Tripartiti operis officiorum missalium, quibus introitus, alleluia et communiones*, vols. 1–3 (Prague, 1596, 1594, and 1596). Only a 1596 edition of the first volume survives, and is likely a reprint.

was also in some respects the most original. While organs were ubiqui-
tous in Catholic and Utraquist contexts, Sales's prints are unusual in
specifying when and how the organ was to be used. In the prefatory
materials to his *Missa Exultandi tempus est*, he likens the interaction of
voices and organ to a dialogue, and uses symbols to indicate precisely
when the organ is to play.[47] In his 1593 motet setting the text of the
Easter sequence *Victimae paschali laudes* the effect is explicitly dramatic. Sales's instructions for the use of the organ (brought in for the
final celebratory verset, *Scimus Christus surrexisse*), placement of
singers, and distribution of the text between the tutti and a trio of
boy soloists (representing the three Marys) dressed in white, result in
a musical mini-drama akin to the *sepolcro* cultivated at later Habsburg
courts.[48]

Sales's skill at using voices alone for dramatic effect is evident in
the preceding motet, *Maria Magdalena stans ad monumentum*, which
dramatizes the moment when Mary Magdalene encounters the resur-
rected Christ, who asks her why she weeps. Sales gives Christ's voice
the rich, warm texture of six-voice polyphony. Magdalene's response
comes faintly in the upper voices: "Lord? Lord?" ("Domine,
Domine"), the spacing rendering her voice frail and hollow (see
Example 4.1).

But Bohemians wanted music for entertainment too, and savvy
imperial composers participated in the fashion for vernacular part-
song in the 1580s and 1590s. Jacob Regnart's *Lieder* were early best-
sellers, as were the Nuremberg reprints of Orazio Vecchi's *canzonette*.
Vecchi's writing transformed the way Orologio and Monte
approached the madrigal, and may have charmed even the emperor
himself: in 1604, Vecchi was courted as a successor to Monte as
imperial chapelmaster.[49]

Andiamo a dormire ("Let's Go to Sleep!"), a playfully raunchy three-
voice canzonetta *alla napolitana* by Sales (Prague, 1597), gives a sense of
the genre's charm.[50] The speaker urges his coachman homeward, com-
plaining in suggestive terms that his beloved has no use for his song and
will only open her door for money:

---

[47] Franz Sales, *Patrocinium musices in Natalem Domini … Mutetum … et Missa …* (Munich, 1598), fol. A ii r.

[48] Discantus partbook, fol. C iiij v.   [49] Edwards, "Repertory Migration," 82.

[50] Franz Sales, *Canzonette, Vilanelle et Neapolitane, per cantar' et sonare con il liuto et altri simili istromenti* (Prague, 1598). The text appears in *Opera nuova dove si contiene Vilanelle, Canzoni, e Ciciliane* (Mantua, 1590?; reprint, Milan, 1595).

Example 4.1: Franz Sales, *Maria Magdalena stans ad monumentum* (secunda pars), mm. 17–27 and 33–42.

Example 4.1: (cont.)

Andiamo à dormire	Let's go to bed
Poi che madonna non ci vuol aprire	Because my lady doesn't want to open the door
E volto altrove tien' il suo pensiero	And her thoughts are turned the other way –
Sù, sù tocca cocchiero	Hurry up, up, coachman!
Vuole altro che canzon,	She wants something other than a song,
Basso, Tenor, Falset e Semiton,	Bass, Tenor, Falsetto and Semitone,
Bisogna ritrovar altro mestiero,	We need to find another job –
Sù, sù tocca cocchiero	Hurry up, up, coachman!
Il canto puoco vale,	Singing is worth little,
Bussa lo piè se vuoi salir le scale,	Tap your foot if you want to climb the stairs,
E'l borsel non haver voto ò leggiero,	And your wallet should be neither empty nor light –
Sù, sù tocca cocchiero	Hurry up, up, coachman!
Ogn'altra cosa è vana,	Everything else is useless,
L'oglio sol di moneta unger risana,	Only the salve of money heals
L'aspra passion d'amor crudel, e fiero,	The bitter passion of cruel and ferocious love
Sù, sù tocca cocchiero	Hurry up, up, coachman!

In Sales's strophic, sectional setting, the characteristic homorhythmic texture projects the text clearly. Each verse concludes with a refrain on "Sù, sù," the bass springing to life only to tumble downwards in an ungainly sequence of descending thirds (Example 4.2).

The continuing popularity of such Italianate musical trifles among the region's noble dilettantes is attested by Joachim Lange's three-voice *Neue kurzweilige Lieder* (Prague, 1606), dedicated to Vilém Slavata (then Burgrave of Karlštejn) and a similar collection by Nicolaus Zangius (Vienna, 1611), dedicated to Jan Diviš of Žerotín (Jan Diviš ze Žerotína, 1575–1616), whom Zangius lauds as a *Musophilus* (lover of the Muses). Hackneyed praise, to be sure, especially given the context, but expressed in terms the emperor himself would have encouraged.

Departures and Returns

With Rudolf's death in 1612, his musical institutions were disbanded. His successor Matthias preferred to live in Vienna and was not interested in retaining his brother's personnel. With a few exceptions (Luython among them), the Rudolfine musicians dispersed, taking their music with them – to Spain, Italy, the Low Countries, Germany, Poland. One itinerant, Caspar Vincent, had sung in the chapel as a choirboy in 1597 and probably trained as an organist with Luython. It was likely through

Example 4.2: Franz Sales, *Andiam'a dormire.*

Vincent that Luython's motets, along with motets by Monte, Orologio, Zangius, and Tiburzio Massaino, entered the enormously successful *Promptuarii musici* anthologies (Strasbourg, 1611–14 and 1617), which Vincent compiled with a Speyer schoolteacher and furnished with a *bassus ad organum*. A set was purchased by the choir director Nicholaus Dionysius of Doubrovín for use at the Lutheran Church of the Holy Savior, constructed in Prague between 1611 and 1614, and so the music found its way back to the city where it first sounded.

The books used by the imperial chapel do not survive, but Rudolf's musicians left plenty of music behind, in prints and in manuscripts compiled by Czech users. In such ad hoc anthologies, motets by imperial composers keep company with the polyphony of Czech composers like Rychnovský and Pavel Spongopaeus Jistebnický, but also surface in forms that diverge from their printed versions – as with two Luython motets copied into partbooks used by the Rokycany literary brotherhood near Plzeň.[51] That these recensions were probably reworkings by the composer himself is a reminder that – uniquely during the reign of Rudolf II – home-grown imperial music reached deep into the Czech crown lands to be cultivated anew, shedding the constraints of Habsburg dynastic piety and Catholic triumphalism along the way.[52]

[51] Kateřina Maýrová, Stephanie Schlagel, and Hana Hrachová, *Rokycanská hudební sbírka: Katalog franko-nizozemských duchovních skladeb dochovaných v nejstarší vrstvě repertoáru* (Prague: Národní muzeum, 2016).

[52] Jan Bilwachs, "Die Konkordanzen der Carl Luythons Motetten *Bellum insigne* und *Festa dies hodie*," *Musicologica Brunensia* 51 (2016): 37–45.

5 | Music in the Catholic Reformation
of Seventeenth-Century Bohemia

GEOFFREY CHEW

The Historical Background

The music of seventeenth-century Bohemia, the age of the Baroque, represents an amazing achievement, for its foundations were laid during the Thirty Years' War, a time of catastrophic upheaval. That war began in 1618 with the Defenestration of Prague, a pseudo-medieval "tragi-comic charade" when three Catholic envoys were thrown from a window in Prague Castle by rebellious Protestant noblemen.[1] Frederick, the Protestant Elector Palatine, crowned King of Bohemia in 1619, had to flee ignominiously in 1620 after the defeat of his army at the Battle of the White Mountain near Prague by the Catholic forces of the Habsburg Emperor, Ferdinand II. The war spread through Europe, reducing towns and peasantry to poverty, and costing many lives. Nevertheless, Ferdinand II, and Ferdinand III, who succeeded him in 1637, reinforced the status of their court musicians, giving them preferential treatment and continuing to devote enormous sums to music, even during the war.[2]

With the Peace of Westphalia, signed in 1648, the war came to a sluggish end, and an end was also put to Protestant hopes in Bohemia and Moravia. Ferdinand II, a fanatical Catholic, regarded Protestantism as simple disloyalty, and quickly enforced Catholic public worship, extinguishing religious pluralism.[3] There is still debate as to the complete success of the conversion of Bohemia and Moravia to Catholicism, even by the following century,

---

[1] R. J. W. Evans, *The Making of the Habsburg Monarchy, 1550–1700* (Oxford: Clarendon Press, 1979), 66.

[2] Richard Taruskin still maintains the opposite in his history of "Western music": "Rebuilding of the impoverished German courts and their cultural establishments could only begin after the signing of the Peace of Westphalia" (*Music in the Seventeenth and Eighteenth Centuries* (New York: Oxford University Press, 2009), 68). But Ferdinand "neither dissolved his chapel nor reduced its size; on the contrary, his huge *Kapelle* was virtually without rival in early seventeenth-century Europe": see Steven Saunders, "The Hapsburg Court of Ferdinand II and the *Messa, Magnificat et Iubilate Deo a sette chori concertati con le trombe* (1621) of Giovanni Valentini," *Journal of the American Musicological Society* 44 (1991): 362.

[3] In Hungary (including Slovakia), pockets of Protestantism survived, even though Ferdinand was also King of Hungary.

and the authorities were probably slack in enforcing religious conformity among the peasantry unless money was involved in disputes. But the religious orders worked hard to deepen Catholic piety, and preferment for nobility and clergy depended on public loyalty. Some 150,000 people, including educated Protestants and many of the aristocracy, were forced into exile, and had their property confiscated. Many incomers received aristocratic titles and lands; leading composers, too, could hope to be promoted to the nobility.

For later Czech patriots chafing under Austrian rule, the period seemed in retrospect one of *temno*, "darkness," with Czech culture suppressed by the Habsburgs for three centuries before rising in a wonderful Renaissance in the *národní obrození*, the nineteenth-century Czech National Revival.[4] The status of the Czech language was indeed weakened, but, though Prague was now merely a provincial capital, both Czech- and German-speaking musicians were active in cultivating ensemble music, secular and sacred, dance music, solo and chamber music for strings, solo continuo song, and keyboard and lute music.[5]

Moreover, patronage, and music, crossed political borders. There was cultural interchange between Bavaria and the Habsburg lands, despite rivalry between the two. Bohemian musicians, such as the composer Jan Dismas Zelenka, later worked outside Bohemia while retaining connections to Prague (see Chapter 8). And there may have been a key relationship between the independent prince-archbishopric of Salzburg and the Bohemian Lands: Heinrich Biber, with Adam Michna one of the two greatest seventeenth-century Bohemian composers, spent much of his career in Salzburg, while continuing to supply music to the court at Kroměříž (Kremsier) in Moravia, where he had previously worked, and his colleague Georg Muffat, who came to Salzburg from Prague, claimed to have been the first to introduce the French style of Lully to Bohemia

---

[4] *Temno: historický obraz* ("Darkness: A Historical Picture," 1913–15) was a historical novel by Alois Jirásek, popular during World War I. Jirásek's historical interpretation was later taken up by the Stalinist ideologue Zdeněk Nejedlý and the Baroque specialist Jan Racek, and became orthodoxy during the communist period. See Geoffrey Chew, "Jan Racek, Zdeněk Nejedlý and the Construction of Czech Music History after the Second World War," in *The Phoney Peace: Power and Culture in Central Europe 1945–49*, ed. Robert B. Pynsent (London: School of Slavonic and East European Studies/University College London, 2000), 346–58.

[5] Jiří Sehnal's extensive and indispensable work on the period in Bohemia and Moravia is summarized in his *Adam Michna of Otradovice – Composer* (Olomouc: Palacký University, 2016), 8–25. See also his overview in "Pobělohorská doba (1620–1740)," in *Hudba v českých dějinách: Od středověku do nové doby*, ed. Vladimír Lébl (2nd ed., Prague: Supraphon, 1989), 147–215; and see Robert G. Rawson, *Bohemian Baroque* (Woodbridge: Boydell & Brewer, 2013).

and then to Salzburg.[6] These and other cross-border contacts of this period cannot be neglected.[7]

However, this essay will avoid conflating the entire period between 1600 and 1750 or later into an undifferentiated "Baroque." This will allow some focus on several of the fundamental changes in musical structure that took place during this period in Bohemia, notably in solo devotional music. These changes resulted in part from the introduction of new Italian and French styles – and ultimately by the establishment of the modern so-called "common-practice" system of tonality (especially in non-liturgical music). Some compositions continued to appear in collections ordered according to eightfold or twelvefold systems of modes, linked with plainchant psalmody or (supposedly) with Greek antiquity.[8] And émigré Czech Protestant cantionals (hymnals) continued to give a large place to older Lutheran melodies, which are often thought modal (see Chapter 3).[9] But common-practice tonality cannot best be understood as having evolved from modality, however defined.[10] Nor can the "characteristic tonalities" that emerged during the century,[11] some of which are illustrated in the music examples below; the topic deserves further research.

The *pietas austriaca*: A Model for Competitive Piety

The strengthening of court music during the 1640s, and especially of sacred music, at a time when the war seemed to be turning against the Habsburgs,

---

[6] Muffat spent time in Paris and also in Rome, where he encountered Corelli at first hand in the early 1680s. He was a pioneer in publishing Corellian sonatas in Central Europe (*Armonico tributo*, Salzburg, 1682), and possibly in introducing the French style to Bohemia. See Heinrich Rietsch, ed., *Georg Muffat: Florilegium primum*, Denkmäler der Tonkunst in Österreich 1/2 (Vienna: Universal Edition, 1919), 10.

[7] Two of the seventeenth-century Prince-Archbishops of Salzburg, though not Bohemian-born, belonged to the aristocratic Thun und Hohenstein family, which had Bohemian branches.

[8] See the documentation of "modal cycles" in Frans Wiering, *The Language of the Modes: Studies in the History of Polyphonic Modality* (London: Taylor and Francis, 2015).

[9] Notably the Protestant Czech cantionals of Georgius Tranoscius (Jiří Třanovský, *Cithara sanctorum*, Leutschau (Lőcse, Levoča), 1636) and Jan Amos Comenius (Komenský, *Kancyonál*, Amsterdam, 1659).

[10] Scholarly debate on modality and tonality is summarized in Wiering, *The Language of the Modes*, and in Megan Kaes Long, *Hearing Homophony: Tonal Expectation at the Turn of the Seventeenth Century* (New York: Oxford University Press, 2020). See also Charles E. Brewer, *The Instrumental Music of Schmeltzer, Biber, Muffat and Their Contemporaries* (New York: Routledge, 2016), especially Chapter 1.

[11] The term is borrowed from Megan Kaes Long, "Characteristic Tonality in the 'Balletti' of Gastoldi, Morley, and Hassler," *Journal of Music Theory* 59 (2015): 235–71.

served to refashion the public image of the emperor, following the so-called *pietas austriaca*, as "a pious, protective father looking out for his citizens under the care of God," and, especially, of the Virgin Mary.[12] This "style of piety" reached its peak after 1650; incorporating ideas from Bavaria, it was particular to the ruling dynasty. And it provided a model to be emulated by other rich noblemen, prelates, and religious orders, who could compete in demonstrating the depth of their Catholic piety and their dynastic loyalty. Few could match Prince-Bishop Karl Liechtenstein-Castelcorno, of the powerful diocese of Olomouc (Olmütz), with his establishment at Kroměříž (Kremsier).[13] Yet the prince-archbishop of Salzburg was able to headhunt Heinrich Biber in 1670 and steal his services from Liechtenstein, to the latter's considerable annoyance.[14]

The *pietas austriaca* was projected especially in ceremonial liturgical music, whose vibrancy (together with that of intimate devotional music) was characteristic of Bohemia and Austria. This liturgical music has usually been viewed through the lens of a binary opposition between a reactionary *stile antico* and a progressive *stile moderno*. But this interpretation is inadequate even as a simplification. Noel O'Regan identifies four compositional approaches to liturgical music of the period: (1) cultivating continuity with the past, particularly through imitation and parody (understood in their contemporary sense of "reworking," often with the aim of paying homage);[15] (2) scoring for two or more choirs; (3) scoring for small numbers of solo singers, with instrumental accompaniment, often for heightened emotional expression; (4) juxtaposing multichoral settings with sections for soloists and purely instrumental sections, in a combination of (2) and (3) deploying all available forces, not necessarily for sheer impact, but in order to build a constantly changing "kaleidoscope" of textures.[16]

---

[12] The classic discussion of the *pietas austriaca* is Anna Coreth, *Pietas austriaca* (Vienna: Verlag für Geschichte und Politik, 1959, 2nd ed., 1982), in English as *Pietas austriaca* (West Lafayette, IN: Purdue University Press, 2004).

[13] Liechtenstein was fabulously rich (by the late seventeenth century the Liechtenstein family owned some 20 percent of all the peasant families in Moravia), with ambitions of independence that also brought him into conflict with the Jesuits.

[14] Biber was sent to buy violins, but absconded to Salzburg, without permission but evidently with the archbishop's approval. Liechtenstein did not fully acquiesce in his departure until 1676.

[15] There is an extensive literature on this subject: see especially Thomas M. Greene, *The Light in Troy: Imitation and Discovery in Renaissance Poetry* (New Haven: Yale University Press, 1982); and the distinctions drawn between three "classes" and three "versions" of Renaissance imitation in G. W. Pigman III, "Versions of Imitation in the Renaissance," *Renaissance Quarterly* 33 (1980): 1–32.

[16] Noel O'Regan, "The Church Triumphant: Music in the Liturgy," in *The Cambridge History of Seventeenth-Century Music*, ed. John Butt and Tim Carter (New York: Cambridge University Press, 2005), 283–323 (this classification at pp. 292–95).

And, far from excluding local cults, the *pietas austriaca* encouraged them in Bohemia, including that of Wenceslas (the Czech patron saint), in a *pietas bohemica* integrating the ancient Bohemian royal line into a history of Habsburg rule (on St. Wenceslas, see also Chapter 2).[17] Contrasting examples are the *Missa sancti Wenceslai* by Adam Michna of Otradovice (Adam Michna z Otradovic, c. 1600–76) and the *Requiem Claudiae imperatricis* by Philipp Jacob Rittler (c. 1637–90), both probably intended for the cathedral of St. Wenceslas at Olomouc.[18] Michna's Mass, with a "joyful" ensemble of two trumpets, six string parts, and six voices (SSATTB, both soli and tutti), may have celebrated the rebuilding of the cathedral in 1661; Rittler's *Requiem*, commemorating the death in Vienna in 1676 of Claudia Felicitas, second wife of Leopold I, has a "mournful" ensemble of four trombones, four string parts, and five voices (SATTB). Both feature large homophonic tuttis, instrumental sonatas, and some limited chromaticism and dissonance in duets of soloists. But a much larger Mass setting also exemplifying the fourth of O'Regan's categories, possibly the largest ever, is Biber's *Missa Salisburgensis*, with two eight-voice choirs and multiple choirs of instruments, probably for the 1,100th anniversary of the archbishopric of Salzburg in 1682.[19]

The Religious Orders

For Austria and Bohemia, this was virtually a Jesuit century. Founded in 1540 by St. Ignatius Loyola (1491–1556), highly centralized and energetic, the Jesuits soon adopted education as their primary mission. Ferdinand I summoned them to Vienna in 1554 and to Prague in 1556; under Ferdinand II they were providing elite Latin education for the aristocracy besides undertaking missionary work among the rural poor.

The order's missionary activities extended worldwide in the Spanish and Portuguese empires, with the martyrdom in Asia of Francis Xavier (1506–52,

---

[17] See Marie-Elizabeth Ducreux, "Emperors, Kingdoms, Territories: Multiple Versions of the 'Pietas Austriaca'?," *The Catholic Historical Review* 97, no. 2 (2011): 276–304. Veneration of St. Wenceslas had been encouraged by the Jesuits from the 1650s; the supposed legitimacy of the Habsburgs through their connection with St. Wenceslas was still the subject of Zelenka's *Sub olea pacis*, a three-act Latin school drama with interpolated music, in 1723.

[18] Editions: Jiří Sehnal, ed., *Adam Václav Michna z Otradovic: Missa sancti Wenceslai*, Musica antiqua bohemica II/1 (Prague: Supraphon, 1984); Jiří Sehnal et al., eds., *Philippus Jacobus Rittler: Requiem Claudiae imperatricis* (Olomouc: MusicOl, 1998).

[19] Formerly believed to have been composed by Orazio Benevoli. See Eric Thomas Chafe, *The Church Music of Heinrich Biber* (Ann Arbor: UMI Research Press, 1987), chapters 2 and 3, and esp. pp. 63–66.

canonized in 1622) as their model.[20] This quasi-colonialism encouraged the preservation of very diverse non-Catholic traditions, provided they could be set to work for Catholic devotions. In Bohemia these included ancient pagan literature and local traditions of vernacular sacred song, and translation and adaptation played a substantial part in literary and musical production.

Their culture was consequently diverse, though unified in dependence on the order's "Spiritual Exercises," codified by St. Ignatius. In these exercises in prayer and discernment, biblical scenes are imaginatively recreated in affective detail, and lead to a conscious "decision" to submit to God's will. They underlie the greatest achievements of the period in Czech literature – the lyrical songs, hagiographic translations, and non-moralizing reflective prose of Friedrich Bridel, and the sacred poetry of the rich townsman Adam Michna – a repertory later drawn on by nineteenth-century Romantic poets.[21]

The pattern also emerges in Latin "school plays" with music, and especially in theatricalized paraliturgical devotions, some using vernacular texts, for seasons such as Holy Week and Christmas.[22] One such was the Christmas *pastorella*, developed for non-elite audiences mainly in the eighteenth century, usually projecting a "rustic" style and often with a vernacular text. Pastorellas drew on traditional "crib-rocking," lullaby-singing, Christmas plays, and classicizing pastoral poetry.[23] Some seventeenth-century pieces may represent precursors of the genre, including a Christmas offertory, *Venite ocyus*, by Schmelzer, and a quasi-dramatic *Serenada*, by Pavel Vejvanovský (c. 1633–93), both from the Kroměříž collection.[24]

---

[20] Bohemian Jesuits thought the Marianas Islands particularly prestigious, because particularly dangerous, and competed to be sent there. Augustin Strobach (1646–84), from Iglau (Jihlava), was a Jesuit missionary there and was martyred by the Chamorro: see Ulrike Strasser, "Copies with Souls," *Journal of Jesuit Studies* 2 (2015): 558–85; and David R. M. Irving, "Jesuits and Music in Guam and the Marianas, 1668–1769," in *Changing Hearts*, ed. Yasmin Haskell and Raphaële Garrod (Leiden: Brill, 2019), 211–34. Later globetrotters included Martin Dobrizhoffer (1717–91), active in Paraguay, from Friedberg (Frymburk) near Český Krumlov.

[21] It has been suggested that Baroque features remained central in Czech culture for centuries: see Robert B. Pynsent, "The Baroque Continuum of Czech Literature," *The Slavonic and East European Review* 62 (1984): 321–43.

[22] Holy Week devotions included the specifically Viennese genre of the *sepolcro*, for which sepulchres were constructed: see especially Robert L. Kendrick, *Fruits of the Cross* (Oakland, CA: University of California Press, 2019).

[23] On pastorellas, see Rawson, *Bohemian Baroque*, 107–43; Jiří Berkovec, *České pastorely* (Prague: Supraphon, 1987). Inventories show that vernacular pastorellas existed outside aristocratic courts before 1700; these may have been numerous.

[24] On the Schmelzer piece, see Brewer, *The Instrumental Music*, 95–106; on the Vejvanovský piece, which quotes a Christmas lullaby (later known in Czech or German as *Hajej můj andílku*, or *Heidi pupeidi*), see Rawson, *Bohemian Baroque*, 117–18.

Another useful survival was the centuries-old Bohemian tradition of literary brotherhoods, or confraternities, which also existed in other territories, notably Bavaria. These were religious associations of laymen, providing mutual support and meeting regularly to sing vernacular devotional songs (see also Chapters 3 and 4).[25] These were tolerated, and indeed new confraternities were established, centering on the cults of the Virgin Mary and the Eucharist.

Of new religious orders, Piarists competed with Jesuits (and other religious orders) in providing the lower orders of society with vernacular education, which often included music.[26] They were fully established as an order in 1621, and in 1631 Cardinal Franz von Dietrichstein, governor of Moravia, summoned them to Mikulov (Nikolsburg), notorious for its heretics; this was the earliest Piarist foundation outside Italy.[27] A later Piarist foundation at Ostrov nad Ohří (Schlackenwerth) in western Bohemia provided education and employment for the composer Johann Caspar Ferdinand Fischer (1656–1746), whose works include liturgical compositions and orchestral and keyboard suites; some of the themes in his organ works were adopted by J. S. Bach in the *Wohltemperiertes Clavier* (see Chapter 7).

Vernacular Song

Developments in solo song in this period contributed to raising the status of both German and Czech as languages for poetry, and the lively tradition of vernacular song may have represented one of the most important stimuli for the further development of Czech music. This took place partly through the adoption of models from Italy, rather than in the development of earlier native traditions such as the Tenorlied. These new Italian models included light genres of homophonic strophic canzonettas, such as the *balletti* of Giovanni Gastoldi, which became sensationally popular across Europe from the 1590s.[28] And their potential was reinforced with the innovations

---

[25] The "literary brotherhoods" have often been thought to be specifically Czech, but were widespread: see Jiří Mikulec, *Barokní náboženská bratrstva v Čechách* (Prague: Lidové noviny, 2000); and Vladimír Maňas, 'Hudební aktivity náboženských korporací na Moravě v raném novověku' (PhD diss., Masaryk University, Brno, 2008). Maňas compares Czech confraternities with others beyond Bohemia, but comparative work still remains to be done, especially for Bavaria.

[26] See Alberto Tanturri, "Ordres et congrégations enseignants à l'époque de la Contre-Réforme: Barnabites, Somasques, Scolopes," *Revue historique* 313 (2011): 811–52, on the "Scolopes" (that is, Piarists), including their relationships with the Jesuits and their later history, though omitting any mention of music in their curriculum (pp. 837–50).

[27] On the Mikulov Piarists between 1631 and 1648, see Miguel Ángel Asiain García, 'Calasanz y Nikolsburg,' *Analecta calasanctiana* 61 (2020): 11–232.

[28] These are the subject of Long's *Hearing Homophony*.

of the poet Gabriello Chiabrera, replacing traditional Italian versification with "short, novel metres and often symmetrical internal rhyme schemes [that] ... were natural aids to musical organization."[29] Indeed Massimo Ossi has argued that Monteverdi's Chiabrera settings in his *Scherzi musicali* (1607) are the real exemplifications of the composer's *seconda pratica*.[30] Even with traditional seven- and eleven-syllable lines, such Italian poetry demanded a new approach to text-setting, and its short repeated, or balanced, phrases effectively generated musical form and a cadence-oriented sense of tonality. Its characteristics were not entirely effaced in translation, even in German and English, where Italian syllabic setting was replaced with accentual text-setting, nor in Czech, though accentual setting was not recognized in Czech at this period (see also Chapter 10).[31]

An early adaptation of a *balletto* of this period in German and Czech is *Victoriosi duces* (1626), a contrafactum of Gastoldi's *Amor vittorioso*, given new political texts in four languages, celebrating Catholic victories in the (Thirty Years') war, and also alternative devotional texts in Czech and Latin (Example 5.1). It refers to the Battle of the White Mountain and also to the later Catholic victory at Lutter am Barenberge (1626). In this and subsequent examples, I preserve the original spelling for the German texts but modernize the Czech spelling and punctuation. The original is from Gastoldi's *Balletti a cinque voci* (Venice: Ricciardo Amadino, 1591); Jan Sixt of Lerchenfels (Jan Sixt z Lerchenfelsu, also known as Joannes Sixtus a Lerchenfels), provost of the collegiate church at Litoměřice (Leitmeritz), published the contrafactum in his *Laus, honor, virtus, gloria, triumphus et victoria* (Litoměřice: Sixt z Lerchenfelsu, 1626). Sixt replaces the "fa la" nonsense-syllable refrain with a more warlike "bidi bidi bom." The verse retains the traditional seven-syllable lines of the Italian original in all the translations, with rough success in terms of accentual stress.

A related strand in vernacular song is provided by those cantionals in which texts and music follow the formal principles of canzonettas, though not necessarily their light style. Two which were translated into Czech will

[29] Barbara Russano Hanning, "Chiabrera, Gabriello," *Grove Music Online*, www-oxfordmusiconline-com.www2.lib.ku.edu/grovemusic/view/10.1093/gmo/9781561592630.001.0001/omo-9781561592630-e-0000005560. See also Silke Leopold, "Chiabrera und die Monodie: Die Entwicklung der Arie," *Studi musicali* 10 (1981): 75–106.

[30] Massimo Ossi, "Claudio Monteverdi's 'Ordine novo, bello et gustevole,'" *Journal of the American Musicological Society* 45 (1992): 261–304.

[31] Text-setting following the quantity of syllables in Czech, or "časomíra" (literally, "measurement of time"), as in the classical languages, was an inheritance from Renaissance humanism. It is still advocated by Comenius, from exile, in the lengthy introduction to his cantional of 1659, but is irreconcilable with the Italian-derived canzonetta style.

Example 5.1: Contrafactum of a Gastoldi *balletto*, from Sixt z Lerchenfelsu, *Laus, honor, virtus, gloria* (1626); additional Latin devotional texts omitted.

Vic	- to - ri - o - si	du	- ces,	con	- ce - le - bra	- te	lu	- ces!
Sol	- dá - ti se	hej	- bej	- te,	a	Čech-ům po	- koj	dej	- te!
Frisch	frö - lich ihr	Sol	- da	- ten,	last	sie - den und	auch	bra	- ten!
Voi	che ve - nist'	ar	- ma	- ti,	o	for - ti miei	sol	- da	- ti!
Ví	- těz - i - tel - i	své	- mu,	Kris	- tu Pá - nu	mi	- lé	- mu!
Vy	- kup - i - tel - i	své	- mu,	Kris	- tu Pá - nu	mi	- lé	- mu!

Ves - trae nunc vic - to - ri - ae,	bi - di	bi - di	bi - di	bom.
By - dy by - dy by - dy	bom,	by - dy	by - dy	by - dy	bom.
Bi - di bi - di bi - di	bom,	bi - di	bi - di	bi - di	bom.
Bi - di bi - di bi - di	bom,	bi - di	bi - di	bi - di	bom.
Ple - sej vše - cko stvo - ře - ní,	neb je - ho sva - té rá - ny...
Ple - sej vše - cko stvo - ře - ní,	neb je - ho na - ro - ze - ní...

be briefly considered here: in these, all or some of the hymns (usually ordered according to the liturgical year) are grouped as unified Ignatian devotional cycles of continuo songs, a very distinctive seventeenth-century Bohemian genre. Both the literary and the musical style are modernized, using fashionable motifs such as echo and dialogue, both well suited to the canzonetta form. One is the German Jesuit Friedrich Spee's *Trutz Nachtigal*, probably written in the 1620s, which proclaims itself a pioneer in the use of the German language.[32] The other is the monumental *Epithalamium Marianum*, perhaps the principal literary and musical achievement of the Bavarian priest Johannes Khuen (first published in the 1630s).[33]

Spee's *Trutz Nachtigal* was translated in the *Zdoroslavíček* of Felix Kadlinský, another Jesuit (Prague, 1665), with added music (melody and

---

[32] Friedrich Spee von Langenfeld, *Trutz Nachtigal* (Cologne: Wilhelm Friessem, 1649), published posthumously, but probably in circulation much earlier.

[33] Johannes Khuen, *Epithalamium Marianum* (Munich: Niclas Hainrich, 1638, with further editions, some enlarged). Khuen, educated by Jesuits, may have intended the *Epithalamium* for Franciscan nuns in Munich. See Alexander J. Fisher, "Sound and the Spaces of Devotion," in his *Music, Piety, and Propaganda* (New York: Oxford University Press, 2014), 105–89, esp. pp. 135–37.

continuo).[34] It includes a sequence of elegant poems whose female narrator, identified as the Bride of Christ, wanders in an idyllic landscape seeking her lover. Example 5.2 is a stanza from one of these. The overall AAB form is subdivided into strongly marked four- and two-measure phrases, reinforced by rhymes in the text and half-closes and full closes in the music, with descending melodic sequences, strongly cadence-oriented, in the B section. The poem centers on the repetitions and deformations of echoes from caves, and hence their meaning in prayer (but in a characteristically Baroque tone of semi-comic playfulness); these coincide precisely with the full cadences concluding the A and B sections ("verborgen/verborgen" and "Namen/Amen," respectively, in the German).

Khuen's *Epithalamium* comprises a cycle of twelve songs each comprising twelve stanzas, with melodies.[35] Khuen extends Spee's theme in representing the mystical marriage of the soul with Christ, including female characters from scripture and classical antiquity, and casting some of the poems in dialogue form. The *Epithalamium* provided a direct model for one of the most impressive monuments of the Czech Baroque, the *Loutna česká* ("The Bohemian Lute," 1653) of Adam Michna. Michna's version, while retaining the same number of songs and much of Khuen's imagery, improves on Khuen's original: the very varied poetry and music are simplified along lines inherited from canzonettas, and elaborate instrumental ritornelli are added. The final song is the lament of the Foolish Virgins consigned to outer darkness in the Gospel parable, whose emotional impact is greatly intensified by its placing (for Khuen, far less tellingly, it precedes a final moralizing song about the struggle between flesh and spirit). It dwells on the Meditation on Hell of St. Ignatius's Spiritual Exercises, using each of the five senses to depict the "length, breadth and depth" of hell, and the agony of the damned.[36] For the ritornello, Michna reduces the elaborate figuration of the previous ritornelli to a slow triple-meter dance, abruptly replacing the violins of earlier ritornelli with a solemn trio of "viole" over a continuo bass, which also accompany the sung stanzas.[37] Example 5.3 shows the ritornello and the first stanza.

---

[34] Felix Kadlinský, *Zdoroslavíček* (Prague: Staropražská kolej, 1665). Modern edition: Milan Kopecký, ed., *Zdoroslavíček Felixe Kadlinského* (Brno: Universita J. E. Purkyně, Filosofická fakulta, 1971). The word "zdoroslavíček" might be translated "counter-nightingale" – songs which with their Catholic message defy the beauty of the bird's song.

[35] The number "twelve" is evidently chosen for theological reasons.

[36] The Spiritual Exercises are divided into the four notional "weeks" of an extended retreat; the Meditation on Hell is the fifth exercise concluding the first "week."

[37] Final serious, cathartic, instrumental sections in slow triple meter are known also in Italian music of the seventeenth century. Their effect is paralleled, perhaps coincidentally, in some final movements and final sections by such composers as Beethoven and Janáček.

Example 5.2: Spee, *Trutz Nachtigal* / Kadlinský, *Zdoroslavíček*, song 4: *Die Gesponß Jesu spielt im Waldt mit einer Echo oder Widerschall / Nevěsta Ježíšova má svou kratochvíli v háji s echo aneb s hlaholem* ("The Bride of Christ Makes Sport with an Echo in the Woods"), stanza 11; the "echoed" words are in bold type.

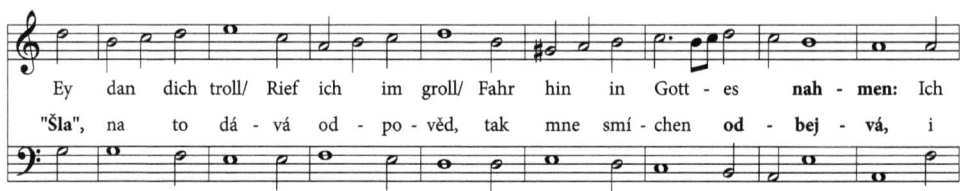

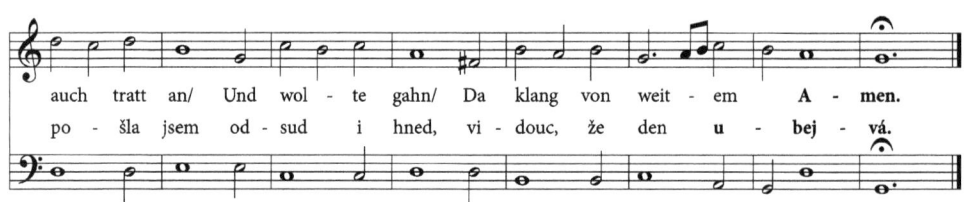

Recreational Music

Recreational music at this period catered for the tastes of the wealthy, with a sharp division between the repertory which they played themselves and that which their professional employees played to them. Lute music for such amateurs, in particular, was often not technically taxing, and usually reflected French style, in marked contrast to public sacred music (on this repertory, see Chapter 7).

But recreational music at the highest level was often designed to evoke *meraviglia*, "marveling." The "marvelous" is most evident in the virtuoso music for bowed string instruments, with rapid passagework, multiple stops, and high registers, composed by Heinrich Biber and his putative teacher at the Viennese court, Johann Heinrich Schmelzer. Some such music was comic or grotesque, accompanying Carnival events to entertain the aristocracy;

Example 5.3: Michna, *Loutna česká*, final song, ritornello and stanza 1 ("O tragic slumber! It has caused us to waste time that was so precious, to miss a feast that was so pleasant! Open the doors! There is danger in this game!").

some was devotional. Some of it imitates natural sounds, such as bird calls, battle scenes, and depictions of the peasantry, including evocations of rustic music;[38] and these "programmatic" pieces are perhaps best understood as fanciful "imitations and illusions of nature that could simultaneously be appreciated as products of human ingenuity," in a *stylus phantasticus* for audiences who valued such ingenuity.[39] They are comparable with machines in theaters, or automata in formal gardens, powered by running water, reproducing bird-calls and other natural phenomena.[40]

Also comparable was scordatura in string instruments – the "mistuning" of the open strings to create sonorous virtuoso effects otherwise unobtainable, to appeal to the taste of cognoscenti. This reached its peak in the *Rosenkranzsonaten* ("Mystery Sonatas") of Biber (c. 1674) – a devotional cycle of fifteen sonatas for solo violin, following the fifteen Mysteries of the Rosary, concluding with a passacaglia for the Guardian Angel. The unique manuscript in which the set is preserved, dedicated to his employer, Archbishop Maximilian Gandolph von Khuenberg, is itself an example of material culture, inscribing its incomprehensible scordatura notation in a lavish presentation volume.[41] Each sonata requires a different tuning, allowing special effects such as the imitation of a trumpet in the twelfth sonata, and the set is a compendium of the unusual timbres and figuration possible in scordatura through virtuoso double and multiple stopping.[42]

Figure 5.1 illustrates Biber's scordatura notation, from the final seventh "Partia" (suite) from his *Harmonia artificioso-ariosa* (1696), with the first of two violas d'amore tuned to C-minor chords, with Example 5.4 representing the equivalent in normal notation. These trios, late masterpieces, avoid the showiness of the solo violin sonatas in favor of rich virtuoso polyphony, and

---

[38] Examples are Biber's ensemble sonata *Pauern Kirchfartt genandt* (c. 1673), his *Battalia* (1673), and his *Sonata representativa* (c. 1669) for solo violin, with imitations of nightingale, cuckoo, frog, etc.

[39] See Philip Steadman, *Renaissance Fun: The Machines behind the Scenes* (London: UCL Press, 2021), 6. Such imitations have sometimes been used as evidence of folk music for which there is no other surviving evidence. The term "stylus phantasticus" came in the eighteenth century to mean an improvisatory style, but in the seventeenth century it probably referred to a composing style rooted in imaginative "genius." See Brewer, *The Instrumental Music*, especially chapters 1 and 5.

[40] A partial survival of such a garden is the water garden (*Wasserspiele*) at the Hellbrunn palace in Salzburg, originally laid out in 1613.

[41] Munich, Bavarian State Library, Mus. Mss. 4123; facsimile: Manfred Hermann Schmid, ed., *Rosenkranz-Sonaten, Bayerische Staatsbibliothek, Mus. Mss. 4123*, Denkmäler der Musik in Salzburg 14 (Munich: Strube, 2008).

[42] On the Lamento from the sixth sonata, see Christian Berger, "Musikalische Formbildung im Spannungsfeld nationaler Traditionen des 17. Jahrhunderts," *Acta Musicologica* 64 (1992): 17–29.

Figure 5.1: Biber, *Harmonia artificioso-ariosa* (1696), first viola d'amore part, opening of Partia VII in scordatura notation, with the tuning ('Accord') indicated in normal notation. Göttingen, Niedersächsische Staats- und Universitätsbibliothek, shelfmark 4° Mus VI, 1070: Viol 2 RARA. Reproduced by permission.

the final "arietta," variations on a ground bass, rounds off the set in a slow triple-meter dance, whose explosion into more rapid figuration, before a solemn, quiet close, is comparable in its cathartic effect to that of Michna's final song from the *Loutna česká*.

Conclusion

Seventeenth-century music in Bohemia and Moravia was no mere curtain-raiser to the achievements of the following century, but a glance ahead will be in order. By 1775 it had become a commonplace that the Bohemians were "the most musical people of Germany, or, perhaps, of all Europe," in the words of Charles Burney.[43] (He is often said to have described Bohemia as the "conservatory of Europe," but this phrase is probably a recent invention.[44]) And a decade later, C. F. D. Schubart echoed him, ascribing that pre-eminence to the patronage of Emperor Joseph I (1705–11), who, Schubart thought, had brought the musicians of Bohemia to such a pitch that "none of [Joseph's] provinces, perhaps none in the whole of Germany, outshone Bohemia in music."[45]

In fact, by the time of Burney and Schubart, Bohemia and Moravia were producing far too many musicians for local needs. The appetite of the great landowners for elaborate music, in simple parish churches as well as in aristocratic courts, had led rural people to regard education in music as a recipe for success. And the religious orders also encouraged this: the Hospitallers of St. John of God (Barmherzige Brüder in German,

---

[43] Charles Burney, *The Present State of Music in Germany, the Netherlands, and United Provinces* (2nd ed., London: T. Becket and others, 1775), 3.

[44] See Mikuláš Bek, *Konzervatoř Evropy?: K sociologii české hudebnosti* (Prague: KLP, 2003).

[45] Ludwig Schubart, ed., *Christ. Fried. Dan. Schubart's Ideen zu einer Ästhetik der Tonkunst* [1784–5] (Vienna: Degen, 1806), 74–75.

Example 5.4: Biber, *Harmonia artificioso-ariosa* (1696), extract from Figure 5.1 in normal notation.

Milosrdní bratři in Czech), a lay order, established at Valtice (Feldsberg) as early as 1603, for example, expected the brothers to have a knowledge of music as well as of medicinal herbs. So it is not surprising that, in Burney's words, "not only in every large town [in Bohemia], but in all villages, where there is a reading and writing school, children of both sexes" were taught music.[46] Nor is it surprising that talented Bohemian musicians came to feel the need to emigrate in great numbers in search of employment.[47]

Schubart also mentioned a distinctive Bohemian taste, "approach[ing] the comic," that had been established in the eighteenth century, and which has sometimes been taken to cement a special affinity between Mozart and Bohemia.[48] Schubart may have had in mind the "tuneful" style of such composers as F. X. Brixi (1732–71), with its roots possibly in the "rustic" style of pastorellas. However that may be, in viewing this comic style essentially as a precursor of the Classical music of his own time, he would have felt no need to look back before the establishment of common-practice tonality. But modern listeners may be able to tune their ears to those earlier styles and recognize the wonderful mastery in a repertory without which Viennese and Bohemian Classicism could never have come about.

[46] Burney, *The Present State of Music*, 4.

[47] This "emigration" has an extensive literature; for a recent more general treatment of the subject, see Edita Štěříková, *Více sluší poslouchati Boha než lidí* (Prague: Kalich–Exulant, 2015).

[48] *Christ. Fried. Dan. Schubart's Ideen*, 75. Much of the older Czech secondary literature represents Prague as sympathetic to Mozart and Vienna as opposed to him, especially referring to the success of the premiere of *Le Nozze di Figaro* in Prague in 1786.

6 | Music in Bohemian Royal Coronations and Opera in Prague in the Seventeenth and Eighteenth Centuries

MARC NIUBO

It is ironic that the most famous opera to be composed for a royal coronation, Mozart's *La clemenza di Tito*, celebrates a monarch who became the King of Bohemia unexpectedly and ruled for less than two years. Although Leopold II's ascension to the Bohemian throne followed standard procedures in a situation when the previous monarch had died childless, his coronation was by no means certain (his predecessors Joseph I and II, for example, had never held a coronation in Prague). In addition to Leopold's coronation, all other Bohemian coronations that took place in the seventeenth and eighteenth centuries reflected both the immediate political context and more general cultural and historical trends, such as the role of music in court ceremonies and the relationship between Bohemian and Viennese musical practices. This chapter does not aim at an exhaustive treatment of this topic but sketches out the relationship between coronation music and musical and operatic developments in Prague in general.

The defeat of the Bohemian anti-Habsburg uprising in 1620 had an enormous impact on the later political and cultural history of the Bohemian crownlands. The victorious King Ferdinand II decreed several laws, including the 1627 Renewed Land Ordinance (German: *Verneuerte Landesordnung*; Czech: *Obnovené zřízení zemské*), which made it illegal to practice any religion outside of Catholicism and transformed what until then was an elective monarchy into a hereditary one, thus strengthening the power of the Habsburg dynasty. The changing constitutional framework also influenced the nature of the coronation ceremony, which was no longer conditioned by the election of the new king by the Bohemian estates. Bohemian coronations, however, did not become mere ceremonial endorsements of the Habsburg monarchs' absolutist powers but were still understood as an important acknowledgement of both the Bohemian kingdom's autonomy and the new monarch's legitimacy.[1] During the ceremony in Prague Castle's St. Vitus's

---

This chapter was translated from Czech to English by Martin Nedbal.
[1] Klaas Van Gelder, "Eighteenth- and Nineteenth-Century Coronations and Inaugurations in the Habsburg Monarchy. Why do They Matter?" in *More than Mere Spectacles: Coronations and Inaugurations in the Habsburg Monarchy during the Eighteenth and Nineteenth Centuries*, ed.

Cathedral, the new king promised to uphold various rights and privileges, and the other attendees then declared obedience to the king.[2] The coronation regulations included several symbolic acts that framed the bestowal of the crown in the cathedral, such as the festive entrance into the city of Prague with the presentation of the keys to the city, the homage to the new king by the Bohemian estates, and the coronation feast.[3]

Music and sound in general played an important role in most of the coronation ceremonies. Music was particularly prominent in the special coronation liturgy, which was mostly based on the 1347 statutes of Emperor Charles IV but partially changed in the ensuing centuries.[4] Although specific works presented at coronations are unknown in most cases, starting in the seventeenth century, the sacred ceremonies combined portions that were recited, sung in chant, and presented in the concertato style.[5] The hymn *Te Deum* was the most prominent of the concertato works; it was presented in the middle of the liturgical ceremony, at the moment of enthronement. Significant moments of the coronation ceremony and the surrounding festivities were marked and announced to the entire city by gun and cannon fire, church bells, trumpet calls, and drumbeats. The coronation day began between six and seven in the morning with the ringing of the Zikmund, the largest bell in St. Vitus's Cathedral. The bells tolled again during the arrival of the monarch into the cathedral, which was also marked by trumpet calls and drumbeats. After the *Te Deum*, the bells tolled for the third time, and the first round of shots was fired from the cannons, accompanied by trumpet calls and drumbeats all over the city. The sound productions were repeated during the liturgical Elevation of the Host and at the conclusion of the Mass. Trumpet calls and drumbeats also accompanied most of the monarch's movements in the cathedral, which enhanced the monarch's dignity and the importance of the religious ceremony in general. Music also played an important role in the welcome Mass (which included a *Te Deum*) on the day of the monarch's arrival to the city and in the Mass preceding the homage by the estates, which took place in the Assembly Hall of Prague Castle's Royal Palace. The liturgical ceremonies were accompanied by both Vienna court and local

---

Klaas van Gelder (New York: Berghahn, 2021), 11–38; and Jiří Hrbek, *České barokní korunovace* (Prague: NLN, 2010), 28–35.

[2] For texts of the various declarations, see Zdeněk Veselý, *Dějiny českého státu v dokumentech* (Prague: Harvardské Fondy, 1994), 178.

[3] Hrbek, *České barokní korunovace*, 71–110.   [4] Hrbek, *České barokní korunovace*, 67–71.

[5] W. F. Riedel, *Kirchenmusik am Hofe Karls VI. (1711–1740)* (Munich: Katzbichler, 1977); Marc Niubo and Kateřina Bobková-Valentová, "Hudba a divadlo," in *Panovnický majestát. Habsburkové jako čeští králové*, ed. Jiří Hrbek (Prague: NLN, 2021), 141–47.

cathedral musicians, and until the 1791 coronation the ensuing feast was likely accompanied by court musicians only.

Seventeenth-Century Coronations

After 1620, Bohemian monarchs rarely visited Prague, and visits of the entire court were even rarer because they were expensive both for the monarch and the city. During occasional visits, the court pursued activities that were supposed to be as similar as possible to those in Vienna, and some of these activities involved music, as was the case with church services, pilgrimages, balls, and theater and opera performances attended by the sovereign and members of the royal family. Opera also started to be featured during Habsburg coronations, which was rather unusual for European coronations at the time. The use of opera was connected to the Habsburgs' cultural orientation toward Italy, which was strengthened by Ferdinand II's 1622 marriage to Eleonore Gonzaga from Mantua. One of the oldest operas presented at the Habsburg court was *La transformatione di Calisto* (libretto by Cesare Gonzaga di Guastalla; music by an unknown composer), the performance of which took place in Prague on November 27, 1627, as part of the coronation festivities for Ferdinand III and his stepmother Eleonore Gonzaga.[6] No operas were performed at the 1646 coronation of Ferdinand IV and the 1656 coronation of his brother Leopold I, but on both occasions the royal guests attended Jesuit plays with music.[7] During the long reign of the music-loving Leopold I (1657–1705), opera became a regular feature of court festivities and acquired the status of the most prestigious artform. Numerous musical and theatrical performances, including operas, were thus also performed during Leopold's court visit to Prague in 1679–80.[8]

---

[6] Historians usually consider the anonymous work with the generic title "Commedia, che doveva rappresentarsi" ("A comedy that was to be performed"), presented during the 1622 coronation of Eleonore Gonzaga as the queen of Hungary in Sopron (Ödenburg), the oldest opera associated with the Habsburg court. See Herbert Seifert, *Die Oper am Wiener Kaiserhof* (Tutzing: Schneider 1985), 432; and Herbert Seifert, *Die Oper am Wiener Kaiserhof im 17. Jahrhundert, Ergänzungen und Korrekturen des Autors zum Spielpan 1622–1705 (Stand 2010)*, http://www.donjuanarchiv.at/fileadmin/DJA/Forschung/Zentraleuropa/Opern-_und_ Theaterrepertoire/Forschungsliteratur_online/Seifert/Seifert_1985_Appendix_2010.pdf, accessed June 12, 2023.

[7] Niubo and Bobková-Valentová, "Hudba a divadlo," 174.

[8] Marc Niubo, "Leopold I. a hudba císařského dvora," in *Barokní Praha – Barokní Čechie*, ed. Olga Fejtová (Prague: Scriptorium, 2004), 91–131.

The "Pragmatic" Coronation of 1723

The first eighteenth-century coronation was that of Charles VI and his wife Elisabeth Christine in 1723. The coronation was a reaction to the instability of the Habsburg's holdings in Central Europe. After the premature death of his brother Joseph I, Charles VI had to relinquish the claims to the Spanish throne and used the 1711 imperial coronation in Frankfurt and his 1712 Hungarian coronation to consolidate his position in the Holy Roman Empire and in the monarchy's eastern provinces. The Bohemian coronation followed in 1723, likely in connection to the interest in bolstering the acceptance of the 1713 Pragmatic Sanction, which made it possible for his daughters to inherit the Habsburg hereditary lands undivided. The 1723 coronation was also significant in terms of domestic politics because it emphasized Charles VI's power and thus also the significance of the Bohemian crownlands within the Holy Roman Empire.[9] The documents concerning the initial discussions about the possibility of a Bohemian coronation in the Bohemian chancellery in Vienna in 1721 also show that the coronation was viewed as emphasizing the unity and indivisibility of the Bohemian crownlands.[10]

Although the 1723 coronation took place in September, the Habsburg court resided in Prague since June, and thus the Bohemian capital became the site of many secular and sacred festivities. These festivities reached a highpoint in late summer with the premiere of the opera *Costanza e Fortezza*, directed by composer Antonio Caldara, who took over from the opera's composer Johann Joseph Fux, who had fallen ill. Pietro Pariati's libretto is based on the history of the early Roman republic, telling the tale of an unsuccessful attempt by the last Roman king, Tarquinius, and his ally, the ruler of the Etruscans, Porsenna, to subjugate Rome. The text allegorically celebrates not only the coronations of Charles and his wife but also the queen's birthday on August 28. Throughout the opera, and particularly in the original concluding *licenza*, the queen is associated with Vesta, the Roman goddess of the hearth. Allegorical references to Charles VI, by contrast, are less obvious – he could be linked either to Jupiter or the Roman consul Pubblio.[11] At the same time, the virtues of constancy and strength are represented as Charles VI's personal

---

[9] Štěpán Vácha et al., *Karel VI. & Alžběta Kristýna: Česká korunovace 1723* (Prague: Paseka, 2009), 26–27.

[10] Vácha, *Karel VI.*, 50–51.

[11] A variant of the *licenza* that celebrates Charles can be found in one of the manuscript copies of the opera (Vienna, Österreichische Nationalbibliothek, Musiksammlung, Mus. HS. 17266). See also, Vácha, *Karel VI.*, 159 and 167.

motto, referenced in the opera's title. They are presented as traditional Roman values in the libretto and are further emphasized in the ballet between the acts. The plot could also be understood as a political allegory for the recent marriage between Joseph I's daughters and the sons of Saxon and Bavarian rulers, warning them of the dangers of imperial ambitions. The last scene of *Costanza e Fortezza* may be a subtle critique of these weddings and their political symbolism in that it depicts how Pubblio offers peace to the Etruscans but refuses to allow his daughter Valeria to be married to Porsenna because Roman laws prohibit the marriage of Roman women to foreigners. Pubblio, furthermore, addresses Porsenna with the words "In tua man sta la pace, e sta la guerra" ("In your hands there is peace and war"), which can be understood as a warning to Saxony and Bavaria to abstain from actions that would lead to a conflict with the Habsburgs. The allegory of the opera was therefore not only about the political situation in Prague, which is associated with the operatic Rome in the *licenza*, but also about the situation in the Habsburg lands in general.[12] The allegorical meanings of the opera must have been understood not only by the Habsburg courtiers and foreign guests but also by the broader public in Prague, as illustrated in the extensive discussion in the only Czech newspaper of the time.[13]

Fux's opera was in many ways a typical *festa teatrale*, a large festive work with an emphasis on spectacle. A wooden open-air theater was built next to the Prague Castle stables according to a design by Giuseppe Galli-Bibiena.[14] The proscenium was dominated by two tall towers that accommodated two ensembles of trumpeters; the orchestra and chorus had over 200 members. The opera also featured an unusually high number of choruses and contrapuntal textures, both of which fit the acoustics of the space and reflected the conservative tastes of Charles VI. The exact number of attendees is unknown, but since there were two performances (on August 28 and September 2) and the auditorium was quite large, several thousand people could have seen the production. Whereas the opera featured court artists and local and international guests (including Johann Joachim Quantz), another work produced during the imperial visit to Prague, the serenata *Il giorno felice* by court composer Giuseppe Porsile, had a chamber character and was presented by amateur (predominantly aristocratic) performers to celebrate the queen and the long-awaited, but ultimately unfruitful, conception of a male heir.[15]

---

[12] [Giovanni Pariati], *Costanza e Fortezza* (Vienna: Ghelen, 1723), 49, 51–52; Vácha, *Karel VI.*, 158–68.

[13] *Pražské poštovské noviny* (August 31, 1723). Partially cited in Vácha, *Karel VI.*, 55.

[14] Vácha, *Karel VI.*, 139.   [15] Vácha, *Karel VI.*, 213–15.

Highly successful was also the performance of the musical play *Sub olea pacis et palma virtutis conspicua orbi regia Bohemiae corona – Melodrama de Sancto Wenceslao* ("Under the Olive of Peace and Palm of Virtue Remarkable Bohemian Royal Crown – Melodrama of St. Wenceslas"), produced by Prague's Jesuits. The term "melodrama" refers to the fact that the work combined spoken and sung sections, which was typical for Latin school plays. The text was by Matheus Zill, experienced Jesuit playwright and rhetoric teacher in Prague, and the music (with the exception of the ballets) was by Jan Dismas Zelenka, who had resided in Dresden since 1710 but kept in touch with Bohemia (see Chapter 9).[16] Unlike the court productions, which do not stress Bohemian symbols, the Jesuit drama celebrates the connections between the Bohemian kingdom and the Habsburg dynasty. St. Wenceslas, the main protagonist of the work's first two acts, was often used to legitimize the Habsburg claims on the Bohemian crown during the Baroque period.[17] That is why *Sub olea pacis* foregrounds the relationship between the Habsburgs and the Přemyslids, the first Bohemian royal dynasty, of which St. Wenceslas was a member. If the Jesuit commissioners of the work are to be believed, the first performance of *Sub olea pacis* was received with exceptional enthusiasm both by the royal couple and by other prominent spectators.[18] Zelenka's score is more modern in style than Fux's *Costanza e Fortezza*, particularly in its virtuoso solo parts, which may have been the reason why some audience members preferred the Jesuit play to the court opera and called for a repeat performance of the play.[19]

The act of placing the crown on the monarch's head took place during a coronation Mass in St. Vitus's Cathedral on September 5. The Mass featured Fux's *Te Deum* in C Major (K. 270), but it is unclear what other liturgical music was performed during the Mass. At the same time, the coronation festivities incited an interest in the sacred works of Fux, Caldara, and other Viennese composers in Prague, as illustrated in some church music collections.[20]

---

[16] These contacts are illustrated by the presence of many sacred compositions by Bohemian authors in Zelenka's private collection together with the fact that many works by Zelenka were copied and performed in Bohemia. During his stay in Prague in 1723, furthermore, Zelenka composed his most extensive works. See Janice B. Stockigt, *Jan Dismas Zelenka (1679–1745)* (Prague: Vyšehrad, 2018), 166.

[17] Jiří Hrbek and Jiří Mikulec, "Království jako dědictví," in Hrbek, *Panovnický majestát*, 38–42.

[18] Stockigt, *Jan Dismas Zelenka*, 172–73.   [19] Stockigt, *Jan Dismas Zelenka*, 173.

[20] This trend is prominent in the music collection of St. Vitus's Cathedral although it was not preserved in entirety. Jiří Štefan, *Ecclesia Metropolitana Pragensis Catalogus Collectionis Operum Artis Musicae*, 2 vols. (Prague: Supraphon, 1983–85).

The events of 1723 piqued the interest of Bohemian aristocrats and religious authorities in Viennese music, which was generally more influential in Moravia than Bohemia. But the Bohemian nobility also cultivated contacts with other musical centers, such as Venice, Rome, Naples, and Dresden. These contacts led to an increasing interest in Italian opera in Prague. Soon after the coronation, the opera company of Antonio Maria Peruzzi came to Bohemia under the protection of Count Franz Anton von Sporck (see Chapter 7).[21] Peruzzi was later replaced by Antonio Denzio who organized regular public performances of Italian opera, including works by Antonio Vivaldi, in Prague between 1724 and 1735. To gain greater support from the Prague public, in 1734 Denzio produced the patriotic pasticcio *Praga nascente di Libussa e Primislao* ("Prague Founded by Libussa and Primislao") based on a myth about the founding of the Přemyslid dynasty and the city of Prague. The ancient myth is clearly influenced by contemporaneous politics: although the Přemyslid rulers did not gain royal status until much later, the opera concludes with the royal coronation of Primislao, the dynasty's founder, and a prophecy by Primislao's wife Libussa, in which Denzio included a celebration of Charles VI and a foretelling about the birth of a male heir.[22] Although this *licenza* was quite exceptional in Prague's musical culture of the time, it did not save Denzio from bankruptcy and incarceration.[23]

Maria Theresa's Conciliatory Coronation of 1743

The 1743 coronation of Charles VI's daughter Maria Theresa took place under radically changed circumstances. Disregarding their promise to respect the Pragmatic Sanction, European monarchs started the War of the Austrian Succession after Charles VI's death in 1740. A coalition of French, Saxon, and Bavarian troops temporarily occupied Prague in 1741, and Bavarian elector Charles Albert was proclaimed the King of Bohemia. Maria Theresa eventually regained control over most of the Habsburg hereditary lands and organized a coronation in Prague in 1743 to legitimize her control over the region. Although it followed the basic scenario from

---

[21] Daniel E. Freeman, *The Opera Theater of Count Franz Anton von Sporck in Prague* (New York: Pendragon Press, 1992), 17–50.

[22] [Antonio Denzio], *Praga nascente da Libussa e Primislao* (Prague: Kamenitzky, 1734), 71–76; Jana Spáčilová, "Zpracování pověsti o Libuši v barokní opeře," *Musicologica Brunensia* 57 (2022): 85–113.

[23] Freeman, *The Opera Theater*, 65.

before – the festive entrance into the city, the homage by the estates, the coronation Mass and feast – the 1743 coronation was strongly affected by the preceding events. The city and its surroundings were damaged by the war, some members of the Bohemian estates were under investigation for their support of Charles Albert, and the Habsburg court was in partial mourning for the death of Charles VI's sister, Archduchess Maria Magdalena. Although the punishments for Charles Albert's Bohemian supporters were mild,[24] they did affect the 1743 coronation. For example, Maria Theresa was crowned by the Olomouc (Olmütz) bishop because the Prague archbishop was under house arrest and was banned from executing his duties.[25] The warfare also influenced the music content of the 1743 festivities. For example, Maria Theresa ordered an extra *Te Deum*, including the cannon fire, to be performed shortly before the beginning of the coronation to express gratitude for the victory of Habsburg troops in the Battle of Simbach.[26]

In terms of courtly festivities, the most prominent difference between the 1723 and 1743 coronations was the opera *La Semiramide riconosciuta*, performed on May 12 in a small theater that was built in the castle gardens in 1680. The opera's production was entrusted to Viennese impresario and court dancer Joseph Carl Selliers.[27] The opera used an earlier text by Pietro Metastasio (first set to music in 1729), which was significantly altered, but it is unknown who adapted the text. Also unknown are the names of the composer and the performers. The solo arias were reduced and substituted to such an extent that scholars now view the resulting work as a *pasticcio*, a genre in which Selliers specialized during that period.[28] Selliers's choice of subject was fitting: Semiramide is an Assyrian queen who rules in disguise; when her identity is revealed, she wants to abdicate, but the assembled people call her the rightful monarch. The scene in which Semiramide is crowned and glorified is filled with political symbolism. The work concluded with a ballet (music by Ignaz Holzbauer; choreography by court dancer Franz Hilverding), which functioned as the concluding *licenza*, in which a portrait of Semiramide is crowned with a starry garland by the figure of Gloria in heaven. *La Semiramide* was performed for about three

[24] Eduard Maur, *12. 5. 1743. Korunovace na usmířenou* (Prague: Havran, 2003), 92.

[25] Maur, *Korunovace*, 92.

[26] Rudolph Khevenhuller-Metsch and Hans Schlitter, eds., *Aus der Zeit Maria Theresias. Tagebuch des Fursten Johann Josef Khevenhuller-Metsch*, vol. 1 (Vienna: Holzhauser, 1907), 145.

[27] Khevenhuller-Metsch and Schlitter, *Aus der Zeit Maria Theresias*, 146.

[28] See Milada Jonášová, "*Semiramide riconosciuta*. Eine Oper zur Prager Krönung Maria Theresias 1743," *Studien zur Musikwissenschaft* 55 (2009): 53–120; and Niubo and Bobková-Valentová, "Hudba a divadlo," 164–66.

weeks in alternation with other unknown (German) plays and was followed by *Barsene*, another *pasticcio*, which Maria Theresa attended unofficially.[29]

To celebrate the coronation, Prague Jesuits produced a Latin allegorical musical play based on the Old Testament story of Judith in their Old Town college.[30] The libretto was by Ferdinand Silbermann, professor of rhetoric, and consisted of a prologue; three acts, which depicted Holofernes's camp and Judith's victorious return to Betulia; and an epilogue, in which Maria Theresa was celebrated as a present-day personification of the biblical heroine. The musical numbers by Josef Sehling, composer and violinist at St. Vitus's Cathedral, are no longer extant, nor are the dances, choreographed by Prague dancing master Clemens Antonius Zeidler. The production must have been spectacular considering that it involved 150 performers (including twenty-five solo roles), most of which were students at the Jesuit college. Sehling's student Johann (Joseph?) Preissler appeared in the title role and was richly rewarded by Maria Theresa.[31] The coronation festivities also incorporated specifically Bohemian aspects, particularly in connection to the feast of St. John of Nepomuk (Jan Nepomucký) on May 16 – the cult of this Bohemian saint was also greatly supported by the Habsburgs. The most attractive musical component of the festivities associated with the feast of St. John of Nepomuk was the popular water festival on the Vltava River. It was organized by the order of Canons Regulars of the Penitence of the Blessed Martyrs on the eve of the feast day. Before the beginning of the 1743 water festival, the freshly crowned Maria Theresa arrived on a decorated boat accompanied by six trumpet choirs and general jubilations from the people. The queen brought her own retinue and the court musicians, who likely joined the Prague musicians in the performance of the St. John litanies and a *Regina coeli* during the festival.[32]

[29] Khevenhuller-Metsch and Schlitter, *Aus der Zeit Maria Theresias*, 154; Elisabeth Grossegger, *Theater, Feste und Feiern zur Zeit Maria Theresias. Nach den Tagebucheintragungen des Fürsten Johann Joseph Khevenhüller-Metsch, Obersthofmeister der Kaiserin. Eine Dokumentation* (Vienna: Österreichische Akademie der Wissenschaften, 1987), 14.

[30] Milada Jonášová, "Judith—ein Jesuitendrama zur Krönung Maria Theresias 1743 in Prag," in *Bohemia Jesuitica*, vol. 2, ed. P. Čemus and Richard Čemus (Prague: Karolinum, 2010), 1041–51.

[31] G. J. Dlabacz, *Allgemeines historisches Künstler-Lexikon für Böhmen und zum Theil auch für Mähren und Schlesien*, vol. 3 (Prague: Haase, 1815), 507–8; Jonášová, "Judith," 1048.

[32] The St. Jan Nepomucký water festivals took place between 1715 and 1781. The music (consisting of a Concentus, litanies, and a *Regina coeli*) was usually supplied by prominent Prague composers or the order's music directors. The composer of the music presented in 1743 was Jan Rohn. See Vladimír Novák and Ludmila Mašlanová, *Musicae navales pragenses* (Prague: Národní knihovna, 1993), 129–41.

The Intensification of Bohemian Patriotism in the Coronations of 1791 and 1792

The coronation of Leopold II in 1791 reflected the social and political changes of the previous decades, changes that also affected the music featured at the event. Bohemian elites had high expectations from Leopold, viewed all over Europe as "a philosopher on the throne."[33] The radical reforms by Leopold's older brother Joseph II, including the centralization of the Habsburg lands' administration and the Germanization of the Bohemian lands, incited a strong opposition in the form of regional patriotism. Bohemian aristocrats hoped that at least some of the rights and privileges taken away from them in the centralizing campaigns of the previous decades would be restored.[34] Leopold was a savvy tactician and managed to reach a compromise agreement with the Bohemian nobility: he did not increase the Bohemian estates' political privileges but called off both his predecessor's tax and land reforms, which were disadvantageous for the nobility, and some of the Germanizing measures. Leopold was also aware of the symbolic importance of the coronation ceremony and agreed, unlike his brother, to be crowned as the Bohemian king, though he called for economic pragmatism in the organization of the Prague festivities.[35]

Whereas the coronations of 1723 and 1743 featured operatic performances mostly produced by Viennese personnel at the expense of the court, the coronation opera of 1791 involved Prague-based artists and other personnel to a greater extent and was entirely financed by the Bohemian estates. The subject of the coronation opera was chosen by the Bohemian estates, and the performance was commissioned from Domenico Guardasoni's Italian opera company, which had close ties to Prague. Guardasoni took over the Prague-based company from Pasquale Bondini in 1787, who had established it in 1781.[36] Among the greatest and most successful achievements of the company were the production of Mozart's

---

[33] Adam Wandruzska, *Leopold II: Erzherzog von Österreich, Grossherzog von Toskana, König von Ungarn und Böhmen, Römischer Kaiser*, 2 vols. (Vienna: Herold, 1963–65), 7–8.

[34] Pavel Bělina, Jiří Kaše, and Jan P. Kučera, *Velké dějiny zemí koruny české*, vol. 8 (Prague: Paseka 2001), 126–28.

[35] Hugh Agnew, "Ambiguities of Ritual: Dynastic Loyalty, Patriotism and Nationalism in the Last Three Royal Coronations in Bohemia," *Bohemia* 41 (2000): 7–9; and Jiří Beránek, "K otázce hudební složky českých korunovačních slavností v roce 1791," *Miscellanea Musicologica* 30 (1983): 94–95.

[36] Marc Niubo, *Italská opera v mozartovské Praze* (Prague: Karolinum, 2022), 32–39.

Le nozze di Figaro in 1786 and the commission and production of *Don Giovanni* in 1787.[37] Although they left Prague for Warsaw in 1789, Guardasoni and his troupe returned in the spring of 1791, possibly in connection to the upcoming coronation. The final decision about the inclusion of an opera into the festivities came relatively late and depended on the participation of Leopold's wife Maria Louisa in the coronation.[38] Although the final decision about Maria Louisa's participation was not made until August 3, 1791, the Bohemian estates had signed a contract with Guardasoni about the production of a coronation opera on July 8, 1791.[39] The contract shows that the estates were interested in securing first-class performers, new stage sets, and a new musical setting either of a new libretto or one based on Metastasio's *La clemenza di Tito*.

It was Metastasio's *Tito* that was chosen in the end. The character of the magnanimous and compassionate sovereign who manages to pardon his opponents was an ideal choice for a coronation opera. Leopold, further-more, was often compared to Roman emperor Titus by his contemporaries,[40] and the work's plot also resonated with Leopold's per-sonal motto "pietate et concordia" ("by piety and concord"). The text was arranged according to contemporaneous tastes by Caterino Mazzolà, Dresden court poet, who also temporarily served at the Viennese court between late spring and July 1791. Mazzolà made the libretto more dra-matic by transforming the revolt against Titus into a new finale, thus possibly accentuating the fears of a revolution incited by recent events in France.[41] We can only speculate to what extent the Enlightenment parable about a magnanimous sovereign strengthened the Prague audience's belief in Leopold as a guarantor of peace and stability. For the musical setting,

[37]   *Don Giovanni* was also at one point connected to Habsburg imperial politics; the opera's premiere was planned as an homage to Archduchess Maria Theresa during her trip from Vienna to Dresden with her new husband Anthony of Saxony. This episode does not mean, however, that *Don Giovanni* should be considered "one of festive commissions" by the Viennese court, as has been argued by Ian Woodfield. Instead, the planned use of the opera as a celebratory work may have represented an attempt by Guardasoni (as well as Da Ponte and Mozart) to use every opportunity to publicize their new work. Ian Woodfield, *Performing Operas for Mozart* (New York: Cambridge University Press, 2012), 79.

[38]   Walter Brauneis, "Mozarts KV 621: Eine Krönungsoper in 18 Tagen? Der 3. August 1791 als *terminus ante quem* für die Composition von *La clemenza di Tito*," in *Klang-Quellen: Festschrift für Ernst Hintermaier zum 65. Geburtstag. Symposionsbericht*, ed. Lars E. Laubhold and Gerhard Walterskirchen (Munich: Strube, 2010), 235–51 (238).

[39]   Magnus Tessing Schneider and Ruth Tatlow, eds., *Mozart's La clemenza di Tito: Reappraisal* (Stockholm: Stockholm University Press, 2018), 7–9.

[40]   John A. Rice, *W. A. Mozart: La clemenza di Tito* (New York: Cambridge University Press, 1991), 12–13.

[41]   Rice, *W. A. Mozart*, 10–11, 41–44.

Guardasoni initially approached Antonio Salieri, who turned him down, possibly because he was in disgrace at the court at the time.[42] That is when Mozart stepped in and composed *La clemenza di Tito* in what was most likely a very short period of a few weeks – the premiere of the opera took place on the day of the king's coronation, September 6, 1791.

The 1791 coronation festivities featured an abundance of other music. Although he rejected the commission for the coronation opera, Salieri came to Prague and directed the music at several festive services, including his own *Te Deum*; compositions by Leopold Hoffmann, music director at St. Stephen's in Vienna; and by Johann Anton Koželuh, music director at Prague's St. Vitus's Cathedral.[43] One of the highpoints of the coronation festivities was the grand ball, which took place in the Estates Theater on the queen's coronation day (September 12). The opening part featured a performance of Leopold Koželuh's cantata *Heil dem Monarchen* ("Hail to the Monarch"), based on the text of Prague's university professor August Gottlieb Meissner. Leopold Koželuh, cousin of St. Vitus's music director Johann Anton, was likely chosen as the composer to be featured at the ball because of his Bohemian origin. The intensifying patriotic sentiments among the Bohemian elites may also explain why Koželuh's cantata was initially accepted more enthusiastically than Mozart's *Tito*.[44] In the following decade, however, *Tito* became associated with a Bohemian patriotic cult of Mozart as much as with the adulation of the Habsburg dynasty, which may have contributed to its popularity in Prague during this period – not only was the work performed often in the Estates Theater but it was also adapted as sacred music for numerous local churches.[45]

The unexpected death of Leopold II in March 1792 hastened his son Francis's ascension, marked by three coronations in one year: as Hungarian king in Buda (on June 6), as the Holy Roman Emperor in Frankfurt (on July 14), and as Bohemian king in Prague (on August 9). The quick succession of coronations had to do with the international situation: on

---

[42] John A. Rice *Antonio Salieri and Viennese opera* (Chicago: University of Chicago Press, 1998), 505–6; Sergio Durante, "The Chronology of *La clemenza di Tito* Reconsidered," *Music & Letters* 80 (1999): 566–67.

[43] David Black, "Mozart and the Practice of Sacred Music," (PhD diss., Harvard University, 2007), 230 and 277; Niubo and Bobková-Valentová, "Hudba a divadlo," 147.

[44] Beránek, "K otázce hudební složky," 95–96, 106–7.

[45] Marc Niubo, *The People of Prague Pay Homage to Me* (Prague: Národní knihovna, 2006); Michaela Freemanová, "Bohemia in the Early 19th Century. The Second Life of Wolfgang Amadeus Mozart," *Hudební věda* 50 (2013): 83–102; and Martin Nedbal, *Mozart's Operas and National Politics: Canon Formation in Prague from 1791 to the Present* (New York: Cambridge University Press, 2023), chapter 4, 143–84.

April 20, the French national assembly declared war against Francis, and the monarch had to consolidate his power quickly. The imperial and Bohemian coronations were marked by reduced spending, due to Francis's unexpected ascension so soon after the coronations of his predecessor and the war. The Prague coronation excluded some of the previously customary ceremonies, but the monarch still entered the city under jubilations of the assembled crowds, was accompanied by the usual cannonade and church bells, and participated in the homages by the estates. The music of the ceremonies was once again directed by Salieri, but instead of an opera, a historical play was staged in the Estates Theater at Francis's coronation. Additionally, an open-air folk festival (*Volkfest*), including a series of choral songs with orchestra and folk dances, was arranged on the day of the coronation of Francis's wife Maria Theresa. The choruses were composed and directed by Prague composer Vincenz Maschek (Vincenc Mašek).[46] Both events featured the Czech language but each for different reasons. Prague's Patriotic Theater company presented the play *Povýšení českého knížectví na království* ("The Elevation of the Czech Princedom to Kingdom"), a translation of a German work originally intended for the coronation of Leopold II.[47] The reason why the troupe, which usually performed in both Czech and German, chose to perform in Czech may have been that most of its German actors participated in the summer season in Karlovy Vary (Karlsbad) at the time of the coronation.[48] The use of the Czech language and newly commissioned "folk" compositions in the festival, which was opened to a broad public, thus contrasting with the more exclusive theatrical productions in earlier coronations, point to an intensifying interest of the Bohemian elites in engaging the working classes in the adoration of the young monarch and in instilling patriotic sentiments in them in order to prevent the spread of revolutionary ideals from France. The last eighteenth-century Bohemian coronation and its musical component therefore reflect contemporaneous political upheavals in Europe, which ultimately shattered crowned heads and their coronations.

---

[46] Jiří Mikuláš, "Dožínky v Bubenči roku 1792 jako plenérová inscenace s hudbou Vinzenze Maschka," *Divadelní revue* 23 (2012): 49–73.

[47] Heinrich Ferdinand Möller, *Wladislaw II. böhmischer Herzog, dann König* (Prague: Schönfeld–Meissner, 1791).

[48] Alena Jakubcová, "Václav Thám, Heinrich Ferdinand Möller a pražská korunovace knížete Vladislava II. K problematice korunovačních her v repertoátu Vlastenského divadla," in *Post tenebras spero lucem. Duchovní tvář českého a moravského osvícenství*, ed. Jaroslav Lorman and Daniela Tinková (Prague: Casablanca, 2008), 326–40.

7 | Aristocratic Patronage of Music in the Bohemian Crownlands: A Series of Vignettes

JANA PERUTKOVÁ

From the seventeenth until the early nineteenth centuries, the aristocracy had a strong influence on musical developments in Europe. In the Bohemian crownlands, aristocratic patronage of music became particularly significant after the Habsburg dynasty moved the royal court permanently to Vienna in the early seventeenth century. To compensate for the lack of courtly musical activities, many Bohemian aristocrats established private musical ensembles following the Thirty Years' War.[1] These ensembles performed during meals provided dance music, and were used during various festive occasions, such as name day and birthday celebrations. Occasionally, the ensembles performed during church services as well.

The size and composition of these ensembles depended on a particular noble family's interests and financial means.[2] Support for musical activities could stretch across generations or be associated with a single music-loving individual. Musicians also often traveled with their patrons to various country estates, to the regional capitals, or to Vienna, the imperial metropolis. These ensemble activities peaked after 1730, but in the late 1700s, many of them were transformed into wind harmonies, their smaller size becoming desirable among noble patrons for aesthetic and economic reasons. In Austrian Silesia, however, larger ensembles were established only in the late 1700s. By the early nineteenth century, aristocratic patronage focused predominantly on salon music and initiated the emergence of public institutions. Already in earlier decades, furthermore, aristocratic patronage was a major resource for musically inclined youth to receive education.[3] Noble families also often procured music and funded musical activities of local and parish churches and some religious orders.

---

[1] Jiří Sehnal, "Der Einfluß der Hofmusikkapelle auf das Musikleben in Böhmen und Mähren," in *Die Wiener Hofmusikkapelle III. Gibt es einen Stil der Hofmusikkapelle?*, ed. Hartmut Krones et al. (Vienna: Böhlau, 2011), 175–93.

[2] Václav Kapsa, "Šlechtické kapely v českých zemích doby baroka: staré a nové otázky jejich zkoumání," *Clavibus unitis* 3 (2014): 177–82.

[3] Tomislav Volek, "Böhmische Schlosskapellen des 18. Jahrhunderts und der europäische musikalische Kontext," in *Mozart, die italienische Oper und das Musikleben im Königreich Böhmen*, vol. 2, ed. Milada Jonášová and Matthias Pernerstorfer (Vienna: Hollitzer, 2016), 693–702.

Researchers of aristocratic patronage in the Bohemian crownlands often deal with limited resources. Collections of music-related materials (musical scores, librettos, music inventories) are rarely preserved in their entirety.[4] Information about musical activities can also be found in aristocratic financial records, employee instructions, correspondence, and in documents from some non-aristocratic archives, such as those of various state and Church authorities. In exploring seventeenth- and eighteenth-century aristocratic music patronage, nineteenth- and twentieth-century Czech historians tended to focus on the ethnically and linguistically defined Czech nation – a concept that did not exist in the early modern period when national and other communities were defined by region, not language and ethnicity (for example, the inhabitants of Bohemia identified as Bohemian rather than Czech).[5] Nineteenth- and twentieth-century music historians also focused primarily on "truly Czech" composers and generally ignored composers of cosmopolitan background, especially those from primarily German-speaking regions. In the early twentieth century, Czech musicologist Vladimír Helfert went against these trends and explored eighteenth-century aristocratic musical cultures.[6] The methods he used in his studies of musical life in Jaroměřice (Jarmeritz) influenced his followers, such as Jiří Sehnal and Tomislav Volek, and later also Václav Kapsa, Jana Spáčilová, Vladimír Maňas, and the author of this chapter.

The following sections explore some general characteristics together with a few unique aspects of the aristocratic musical establishments that existed in the Bohemian crownlands from the late 1600s to the early 1800s.[7] My overview is neither exhaustive nor chronological but focuses on a few music-loving aristocrats, their diverse approaches to music patronage, and their motivations for supporting music and musicians.

---

[4] For a catalogue of one of the few aristocratic music collections that have been preserved in entirety, see Eliška Šedivá, *Catalogus collectionis operum artis musicae comitis Clam-Gallas* (Prague: Národní knihovna, 2018).

[5] Jiří Kubeš, "Vyšší šlechta z českých zemí v letech 1650–1750. Úvod do tématu," in *Vyšší šlechta v českých zemích v období baroka (1650–1750). Biogramy vybraných šlechticů a edice typických pramenů*, ed. Jiří Kubeš (Pardubice: Univerzita Pardubice, 2007), 9–33.

[6] Vladimír Helfert, *Hudební barok na českých zámcích. Jaroměřice za hraběte Jana Adama z Questenberku* (Prague: Česká akademie císaře Františka Josefa pro vědy, slovesnost a umění, 1916); Petr Slouka, "Jaroměřické monografie Vladimíra Helferta jako vzor pro výzkum opery ve střední Evropě v první polovině 18. století," *Musicologica Brunensia* 50 (2015): 87–100.

[7] See for example Vladimír Lébl, ed., *Hudba v českých dějinách: od středověku do nové doby* (Prague: Supraphon, 1989), 149–293.

Aristocratic Patronage and Bohemian Musical Migration

The boom of aristocratic music ensembles in the early eighteenth century was one reason why, in later decades, the Bohemian crownlands became a major supplier of instrumentalists for other European regions. Starting in the late seventeenth century, subjects and employees of Bohemian nobles could sometimes gain a position and be promoted more easily when they obtained musical education and demonstrated good music skills.[8] For example, in 1762 Joseph Adam von Schwarzenberg issued a decree stating that musically accomplished subjects were to be given preferential treatment in his household.[9] Although these court musicians often had other responsibilities besides music, many of them became highly accomplished performers.

Aristocratic patronage of music had its limits. Following the ravages of the Thirty Years' War, many Bohemian aristocratic families spent large sums renovating their residences. This was one reason why they could not pay their house musicians as much as some of their counterparts in other regions, particularly in Germany.[10] Unlike in Germany, furthermore, where aristocratic music ensembles were often considered state institutions (due to Germany's political disunity), Bohemian music ensembles were purely private aristocratic endeavors, and thus their financial backing was more limited. It is understandable that many subjects of Bohemian nobility migrated to large European cities and other major cultural centers to gain larger benefits from the music education they received in their homeland (some aspects of this process are discussed in Chapter 8).

Some Bohemian aristocrats also had connections and possessions in other countries and could therefore support local composers both in Bohemia and elsewhere. This was the case of Johann Caspar Ferdinand Fischer (1656–1746), whom the first Bach biographer Johann Nikolaus Forkel considered one of the best composers for keyboard of his day.[11] Fischer was born in western Bohemian Krásno (Schönfeld) and started his career as the music director for the Sachsen-Lauenburg family in western

---

[8] Václav Kapsa, "Hofmusici a lokajové. K postavení hudebníka na šlechtickém dvoře v Čechách první poloviny 18. století," *Theatrum historiae* 9 (2011): 241–55.

[9] Martin Voříšek, "Kapela schwarzenberské gardy v Českém Krumlově" (PhD diss., Masaryk University, Brno, 2008).

[10] Samantha Owens, Barbara Reul, and Janice Stockigt, *Music in German Courts, 1715–1760: Changing Artistic Priorities* (Rochester, NY: Boydell & Brewer, 2011).

[11] Johann Nikolaus Forkel, *Über Johann Sebastian Bachs Leben, Kunst und Kunstwerke* (Leipzig: Hoffmeister und Kühnel, 1802), 5.

Bohemian Ostrov nad Ohří (Schlackenwerth). Fischer's employer Sibylla Augusta von Sachsen-Lauenburg (1675–1733) married Ludwig Wilhelm von Baden (1655–1707), a famous imperial commander in the wars against the Ottoman Empire, and in 1715 Fischer followed her to Rastatt, Germany, where he became the Baden court music director. Fischer's 1702 collection *Ariadne musica* contains preludes and fugues in twenty keys and therefore prefigures J. S. Bach's *Wohltemperiertes Clavier*.

Princely Families and Their Musical Interests

Some of the most prominent patrons of music in the Bohemian crownlands came from the ranks of the higher nobility, such as the princely families Lobkowitz, Schwarzenberg, and Liechtenstein. The musical interests of the Lobkowitz family were particularly diverse and included collecting musical works, organizing music performances, supporting prominent composers, and personal music-making. The enormous Lobkowitz music collection, mostly preserved to the present day, was initiated by Ferdinand August von Lobkowitz (1655–1715). His music collection included French music, which was unusual because most Bohemian aristocracy followed the Habsburg court's focus on Italian music. Ferdinand August's son, Philipp Hyacinth (1680–1734), together with his second wife Anna Wilhelmina, primarily collected lute music. Both Philipp Hyacinth and Anna Wilhelmina were accomplished lutenists and composed their own music for the instrument. Philipp Hyacinth's son and successor, Ferdinand Philipp (1724–84), inherited his parents' musical aptitudes; he composed at least one symphony with Carl Philipp Emanuel Bach, and Charles Burney praised his compositions. The most well-known Lobkowitz patron of music was Ferdinand Philipp's son, Franz Joseph Maximilian (1772–1816), whose sumptuous support of music likely contributed to his financial ruin. Franz Joseph Maximilian was an important patron of Ludwig van Beethoven and retained in his service composers Anton Wranitzky, Antonio Cartellieri, and Johann Joseph Rössler. He also participated in the development of Czech-language musical culture, such as when he had Haydn's oratorio *The Creation* translated into Czech and performed in 1805.

Musical activities in south Bohemian Krumlov (Krumau) during the rule of the Eggenberg and Schwarzenberg families were similarly rich. The Eggenbergs founded a Baroque theater in Krumlov sometime before 1686. The theater was to be used again under Adam Franz von Schwarzenberg (1680–1732) for the performance of Antonio Caldara's opera *L'asilo d'Amore* during the visit of Emperor Charles VI in 1732. However, before the performance could take place, the emperor accidentally shot Schwarzenberg while hunting, and the prince died a few days later. Schwarzenberg's son, Joseph Adam (1722–82), continued to produce operas in Krumlov. He was particularly interested in Italian *opera buffa* and French *opéra-comique*. In the 1760s, the prince initiated a renovation of the Baroque theater, which was based on the designs of the imperial court's architect Giuseppe Galli-Bibiena. The theater has been preserved in its original state, including the orchestra pit with music stands, the stage with machinery, and the collection of decorations and costumes, making it one of the most intact Baroque theater buildings in the world. Joseph Adam had other musical interests as well: he was an accomplished cello player and founded a wind ensemble of eight players, which for some time employed famous Viennese oboe player Georg Triebensee and composer Johann Nepomuk Vent.

The Liechtensteins were another princely family that supported music for generations. Although they spent most of their time in Vienna, they also owned several estates in Moravia and Austrian Silesia: Lednice (Eisgrub), Valtice (Feldsberg), and Opava (Troppau). Various generations of the family were associated with the development of instrumental ensemble music. In a testament for his successor, Karl Eusebius (1611–84) wrote an extensive passage about music, which details not only music's function in court representation but also the use and characteristics of musical instruments – his preferred musical medium was a mixed, vocal-instrumental, twelve-member ensemble.[12] In the early eighteenth century, Anton Florian (1656–1721) sponsored a much larger, thirty-member ensemble. A few decades later in 1789, Alois I Joseph (1759–1805) founded a famous twelve-member wind ensemble – although the size was the same as that of Karl Eusebius's group, the instruments and music performed were radically different. Two years later, in 1791, Alois I Joseph also created a "Türkische Banda" ("Turkish band"), which had the character of a military band, and established a new theater in his summer estate, Valtice.

The Musical Patronage of the Olomouc Bishops

The central Moravian city of Olomouc (Olmütz) became the seat of a diocese in 1063, and the Olomouc bishops (and, starting in 1777,

---

[12] Vladimír Maňas, "'. . . viell fürsten halten ein Musica'. Musik und Musiker am Hofe der Fürsten von Liechtenstein im 17. Jahrhundert," *Studia historica Brunensia* 64 (2017): 189–215.

archbishops) operated with a relatively large budget, substantial portions of which were often devoted to music. Similar to other aristocratic music establishments in the Bohemian crownlands, the music ensembles of the Olomouc bishops had no official institutional function; they were purely private and therefore linked to the bishops' personal tastes. At the same time, Olomouc bishops devoted significant resources to the music in the Olomouc cathedral, which was the center of ecclesiastical administration of large parts of Moravia and at times Silesia as well. Olomouc bishops also promoted music education in the region: the Piarist seminaries in Kroměříž (Kremsier) and Bílá Voda (Weisswasser) were particularly important for the training of performers.[13]

Some of the Olomouc bishops became prominent sponsors of internationally known composers and established large instrumental ensembles. Franz von Dietrichstein (1570–1636), also a cardinal and the governor of Moravia, spent several years in his youth in Rome, where he befriended Pope Clement VIII and became acquainted with early Baroque musical idioms. He imported these to Moravia, partially thanks to composer Giovanni Battista Alouisi (1600–65), his music director and secretary in south Moravian Mikulov (Nikolsburg).[14] Another musically inclined bishop, Karl Liechtenstein-Castelcorno (1624–95), established a renowned ensemble in his Kroměříž castle. The bishop's music director, copyist, and trumpeter was Pavel Vejvanovský, whose compositions together with the works he copied (including many by imperial court composers from Vienna), form the basis of the large and unique historical music collection in Kroměříž.[15] Another prominent composer who served Liechtenstein-Castelcorno was Heinrich Franz Ignaz Biber.[16] Biber only stayed with the bishop for two years before escaping, without permission, to Salzburg. As compensation for his departure and to gain his release from servitude, Biber was required to send autographs of his compositions to the bishop, which became an invaluable part of the Kroměříž music archive. In the late eighteenth century, the

---

[13] Jiří Sehnal, "Die adeligen Musikkapellen im 17. und 18. Jahrhundert in Mähren," in *Studies in Music History presented to H. C. Robbins Landon on his Seventieth Birthday*, ed. Otto Biba and David Wyn Jones (London: Thames and Hudson, 1996), 195–217, 265–70.

[14] See Lucie Brázdová, *Hudba a kardinál Dietrichstein 1599–1636* (Olomouc: Univerzita Palackého 2012); and Eduard Tomaštík, "Giovanni Battista Alouisi – život a dílo" (PhD diss., Masaryk University, Brno, 2013).

[15] Jiří Sehnal, *Pavel Vejvanovský and the Kroměříž Music Collection. Perspectives on seventeenth-century Music in Moravia* (Olomouc: Univerzita Palackého, 2008).

[16] Jiří Sehnal, "Heinrich Bibers Beziehungen zu Kremsier," in *De editione musices: Festschrift Gerhard Croll zum 65. Geburtstag*, ed. Wolfgang Gratzer and Andrea Lindmayr (Laaber: Laaber-Verlag, 1992), 315–27.

tradition of Olomouc musical patronage continued with Leopold Egk von Hungersbach (1696–1760) and Maximilian von Hamilton (1714–76), both of whom employed Anton Neumann as their music director. Neumann was the author of highly expressive music.[17] In 1769, he received the prestigious post of music director of the Olomouc cathedral. One of Neumann's late eighteenth-century successors in the post was composer Josef Puschmann. In the early nineteenth century, Archduke Rudolph of Austria (1788–1831) continued the tradition of Olomouc music patronage in his support of Ludwig van Beethoven.

Active Musicianship

Many of the aristocrats mentioned above were themselves active musicians, as instrumental and vocal performance was a common part of noble education. This education often included a grand tour of European countries, which sometimes exposed young aristocrats to cosmopolitan musical styles.[18] Several Bohemian aristocrats reached the level of the most famous professionals. For example, Johann Anton Losy von Losinthal (1650–1721) was a famous lute player and composed more than 200 compositions for the instrument.[19] Prague count Johann Hubert Hartig (1671–1741) was a well-known keyboard player whose skills were noted in Johann Joachim Quantz's autobiography.[20] Hartig bought the first historically recorded piano in the Bohemian crownlands, an instrument from Bartolomeo Cristofori's Florence workshop.[21] Hartig also patronized performances of oratorios and other church compositions by Italian composers, some of whom he was personally acquainted with, in various Prague churches. He was also a patron of the Prague *Musical-Academie*, one of the first public concert series in Europe. It organized performances for the nobility and the middle class, at least between 1713 and 1717, and possibly longer.[22]

---

[17] Marek Čermák, "Anton Neumann. Nové poznatky k životním osudům a tvorbě zapomenutého skladatele, houslisty a kapelníka," *Musicologica Olomucensia* 30 (2019): 131–52.

[18] See, for example, Jiří Kubeš, *Náročné dospívání urozených. Kavalírské cesty české a rakouské šlechty (1620–1750)* (Pelhřimov: NTP, 2013).

[19] Jan Čižmář, ed., *Acta Losyana: sborník příspěvků k odkazu Jana Antonína Losyho a jeho rodu* (Prague: Česká loutnová společnost, 2021).

[20] On the Hartig family, see Gottfried Johann Dlabacz, *Allgemeines historisches Künstler-Lexikon für Böhmen und zum Theil auch für Mähren und Schlesien* (Prague: Gottlieb Haase, 1815), 565–68.

[21] Petr Koukal, "Byl v Čechách Cristoforiho klavír?," *Opus musicum* 44 (2012): 6–13.

[22] Václav Kapsa and Claire Mádl, "Weiss, the Hartigs, and the Prague Music Academy – Research into the 'Profound Silence' Left by a 'Pope of Music,'" *Journal of the Lute Society of America* 33 (2000): 47–74.

Antonio Vivaldi in Bohemia and Moravia

Antonio Vivaldi found many admirers among Bohemian and Moravian nobility. One of his most prominent Bohemian patrons was Count Wenzel Morzin (1675–1737), whose purely instrumental ensemble was unusual because it employed solely professional musicians.[23] In the 1720s, Morzin hired Vivaldi as his honorary music director, with a regular salary and the title "maestro di musica in Italia." Vivaldi dedicated his 1725 collection of twelve violin concertos, *Il cimento dell'armonia e dell'invetione* ("The Contest between Harmony and Invention"), which includes *The Four Seasons*, to Morzin. Vivaldi also served as a music agent for Morzin, procuring music for the Bohemian count in Italy. Additionally, Vivaldi composed several concertos and trio sonatas for the Wrtby family, and several Moravian families supported him as well. Joseph Johann Adam von Liechtenstein (1690–1732), son of the previously mentioned Anton Florian, made Vivaldi an honorary music director.[24] The composer also had contact with south Moravian noblemen Tommaso Vinciguerra Collalto et San Salvatore (1710–69) from Brtnice (Pirnitz) and Johann Adam von Questenberg (1678–1752) from Jaroměřice (see below).[25]

Aristocratic Opera Productions

Opera was an important component of aristocratic musical patronage in the Bohemian crownlands. There was a marked difference, however, between operatic activities in Bohemia and those in Moravia and Austrian Silesia. Whereas in Bohemia, operatic productions in private aristocratic residences were irregular and most Bohemian aristocrats mainly supported opera companies in Prague, Moravian and Silesian nobility sponsored performances of operas and oratorios in their castles more frequently, likely due to both their personal interests and their proximity to the imperial court in Vienna.[26]

---

[23] Václav Kapsa, *Hudebníci hraběte Morzina* (Prague: Etnologický ústav AVČR, 2010); Václav Kapsa, "Account Books, Names and Music: Count Wenzel von Morzin's Virtuosissima Orchestra," *Early Music* 40 (2012): 605–20.

[24] Jóhannes Ágústsson, "Joseph Johann Adam of Liechtenstein, Patron of Vivaldi," *Studi Vivaldiani* 17 (2017): 3–77.

[25] Tomislav Volek, "Antonio Vivaldi a česká šlechta," *Opus musicum* 40 (2008): 4–9.

[26] Jana Spáčilová, "Počátky opery ve Slezsku – současný stav pramenů," *Musicologica Brunensia* 51 (2016): 157–70.

Following the 1723 coronation of Charles VI as the King of Bohemia, which was accompanied by numerous musical performances (see Chapter 6), several Bohemian aristocrats became interested in Italian opera. The first one was Franz Anton von Sporck (1662–1738), who opened his Prague palace to the Italian opera company of Antonio Denzio and Antonio Peruzzi from Venice in 1724. Sporck operated his own ensemble under the direction of Tobias Seemann, but he sometimes invited the Prague Italian company to his eastern Bohemian estate Kuks (Kukus) to enhance his prestige.[27] In the late eighteenth century, Italian opera was also performed in the Prague palace of the Thun-Hohenstein family.[28] And in 1783 another Bohemian aristocrat, Franz Anton von Nostitz-Rieneck (1725–94), built and temporarily operated a theater in Prague, originally called the Nostitz, later the Estates Theater (see Chapter 9).

Many Moravian aristocrats supported public opera performances in Brno (Brünn), particularly those produced by Angelo Mingotti between 1732 and 1736, but three Moravian noblemen focused on private opera productions. Olomouc bishop Wolfgang Hannibal von Schrattenbach (1660–1738) had operas performed in Kroměříž and Vyškov (Wischau) and produced oratorios in his palace in Brno.[29] For these productions, Schrattenbach employed both Italian musicians, including castratos, and Moravian artists, some of whom received musical training at Schrattenbach's expense. Another example of private opera theater existed in Holešov (Holeschau) under Franz Anton von Rottal (1690–1763): for the large operatic productions Rottal supplemented his own ensemble with the Brno opera company personnel.[30] Between 1736 and 1739, Rottal also employed composer Ignaz Holzbauer, who was later associated with the musical innovations of the Mannheim orchestra.

Musical endeavors in Austrian Silesia were similarly episodic and connected to specific individuals. An important patron of music and musicians was the Breslau bishop Philipp Gotthard Schaffgotsch (1716–95), who settled in the Jánský Vrch (Johannisberg) castle in the town of Javorník (Jauernig) after being exiled from what became Prussian Silesia during the

---

[27] Pavel Preis, *František Antonín Špork a barokní kultura v Čechách* (Prague: Paseka, 2003); Daniel E. Freeman, The *Opera Theater of Count Franz Anton von Sporck in Prague* (Stuyvesant, NY: Pendragon Press, 1992); Stanislav Bohadlo, "Questenberg a Sporck – oddělené a nezávislé barokní hudební subkultury na Moravě a v Čechách?," *Musicologica Brunensia* 46 (2011): 15–34.

[28] Marc Niubo, *Italská opera v mozartovské Praze* (Prague: Karolinum, 2022).

[29] Jana Spáčilová, *Hudba na dvoře olomouckého biskupa Schrattenbacha* (Olomouc: Univerzita Palackého, 2018).

[30] Kateřina Jurášková and Jana Spáčilová, *Italská opera na holešovském zámku v době Františka Antonína Rottala* (Holešov: Město Holešov, 2019).

War of the Austrian Succession (1740–48) due to his support of the Austrian empress Maria Theresa. Schaffgotsch brought together a semi-professional ensemble of about twenty musicians and hired composer Karl Ditters von Dittersdorf as his music director.[31] The ensemble's repertoire included numerous operas. One of Dittersdorf's students in Javorník was Wenzel Müller, later music director of Vienna's Leopoldstadt Theater and Prague's Estates Theater, and author of many famous *Singspiele*. Another Silesian patron of opera was Albert Joseph Hoditzky von Hoditz (1706–78), whose main seat was in Slezské Rudoltice (Rosswald), but whose estates lay in two different countries after the partition of Silesia between Austria and Prussia. In 1765, Hoditz put together a musical ensemble from his musically trained servants that also performed *opera buffa*.[32] After the death of his wife, Hoditz became involved with several singers from his ensemble, and his contemporaries talked about his "harem." Many of these singers were highly accomplished and later found employment in large European opera houses. Hoditz's castle in Slezské Rudoltice received important visitors, including Voltaire and Prussian King Frederick II. However, this sumptuous lifestyle eventually led to bankruptcy, forcing Hoditz to relocate to the Potsdam court of Frederick II and bringing the rich musical life in Slezské Rudoltice to an end in 1776.

Questenberg's Jaroměřice (Jarmeritz)

In the first half of the eighteenth century, the south Moravian town of Jaroměřice became one of the busiest musical centers in the Bohemian crownlands thanks to the musical interests of Johann Adam von Questenberg. Questenberg started his career as an official to the court of Emperor Charles VI but later channeled his energy into his own estates and musical interests. Questenberg was an accomplished lute player and composed music for the instrument. Despite his limited financial resources, Questenberg managed to organize a rich musical life in his palace in Vienna, in Jaroměřice, and in two other estates in Lower Austria and western Bohemia. Most prominent among these activities were performances of operas, congratulatory compositions, and oratorios. Questenberg adapted a hall in the Jaroměřice castle for opera performances, and in 1734 he also

---

[31] Jan Blüml and Jana Spáčilová, eds., *Carl Ditters von Dittersdorf – Contexts and Perspectives*, special issue of *Musicologica Olomucensia* 30 (December 2019).
[32] Milan Myška, *Hrabě Hodic a jeho svět: zámecká kultura ve Slezsku mezi barokem a osvícenstvím* (Ostrava: Ostravská Univerzita, 2011).

built an open-air auditorium in the castle gardens. These performances took place in Jaroměřice between 1722 and 1752, with a frequence comparable to that of professional companies in major cities. Questenberg was personally involved in the operatic productions; he discussed them with his employees and commented on them in writing.[33] Questenberg's daughter Maria Carolina, an accomplished keyboard player and student of the imperial composer Gottlieb Muffat, also contributed to some of the productions.

Questenberg's collection of music scores comprised works by over thirty composers, including the Bononcini brothers, Antonio Caldara, Johann Joseph Fux, Johann Adolf Hasse, Leonardo Vinci, Nicola Porpora, and Giovanni Battista Pergolesi.[34] Questenberg also obtained music by George Frideric Handel, who was otherwise not well known in the Habsburg lands. Questenberg's keen interest in the composer can be gleaned from the count's copy of the orchestral score of Handel's *Agrippina*, which contains the count's remarks about staging, notes on instrumentation, text revisions, and written-in names of characters. The count was also in contact with Vivaldi (see above) and Johann Sebastian Bach. He obtained most of his scores, up to ten different operas a year in the mid-1730s, from his aristocratic friends, composers, singers, booksellers, and members of religious orders. Particularly important for the acquisition of music materials were the artists of the Viennese Kärntnertortheater, especially impresario Franceso Borosini. When away from Vienna, the count received updates about Viennese theatrical life, including information from his educated and musically gifted *Hofmeister*, advisor, and confidant Georg Adam Hoffmann, about which operas were nearing production, which singers would appear in them, and the success newly produced works achieved. Hoffmann also bought copies of musical compositions, arranged for translations and printings of librettos, and negotiated with famous artists for Questenberg.

For opera performances, Questenberg used a private orchestra of about twenty musicians. At times, Questenberg tried to hire talented musicians from Moravia and Austria, but he never employed any Italians. Professional musicians from elsewhere, however, did not participate in the count's musical productions often, and the ensemble mainly consisted of Questenberg's employees and subjects, mostly from Jaroměřice. Local children received early compulsory music education, and some – especially girls – sang in the

---

[33] Jana Perutková, *Der glorreiche Nahmen Adami. Johann Adam Graf von Questenberg (1678–1752) als Förderer der italienischen Oper in Mähren* (Vienna: Hollitzer, 2015).

[34] Václav Kapsa, Jana Perutková, and Jana Spáčilová, "Some Remarks on the Relationship of Bohemian Aristocracy to Italian Music at the Time of Pergolesi," *Studi pergolesiani – Pergolesi Studies* 8 (2012): 313–41.

count's ensemble. Most of Questenberg's musicians served in multiple roles. For example, Franz Petschner sang in opera productions, appeared in comedy performances, was active as a music director for the Servite Order, and assisted in a local school with the instruction of German. Questenberg's *Kapellmeister*, František Antonín Míča (Franz Anton Mitscha), son of a local organist, prepared and directed most of the count's music productions, often appeared in tenor roles, and composed numerous works for the count. Questenberg later acquired a second court composer, Carl Müller, originally the count's subject from western Bohemia.

Questenberg was unusually concerned about the well-being of his subjects and employees. For example, he paid for both food and music at the wedding of singer Catharina Geiger and comedy director Michael Walter.[35] He also provided health care for his musicians and other artists. For the inhabitants of Jaroměřice, most of whom were Czech speakers, Questenberg ordered Czech translations of German and Italian librettos so that they could understand the sung content. This practice was most common for oratorio performances in the Holy Sepulcher chapel during Holy Week. Furthermore, the count commissioned some original works in Czech, which was unique within eighteenth-century Bohemian crownlands.

Questenberg's concern about his personnel and the cultivation of Czech-language culture was linked to his philanthropy and Moravian patriotism. These sentiments can be found in Míča's 1730 Italian opera *L'origine di Jaromeriz in Moravia* ("The Origin of Jaroměřice in Moravia"), which emphasizes the unity of and peace in the Bohemian crownlands and constructs a link between Questenberg and the opera's main character and Jaroměřice founder, Gualtero. The mythological glorification of Questenberg in the operatic works he commissioned emulates, somewhat daringly, the allegorical celebrations of Emperor Charles VI in Metastasio's Viennese librettos.

Quenstenberg was also interested in sacred and instrumental music. His opera singers, including women, often performed in the Loreto chapel of the Jaroměřice monastery of the Servite Order. Additionally, Questenberg's ensemble performed numerous oratorios, not only in the Jaroměřice church of St. Margarete, but also in the Capuchin monasteries in Brno and Olomouc, and St. James's Church in Brno. Questenberg often used instrumental music to accompany public events. For example, he sometimes organized so-called "musicae navales" ("water music") in his Jaroměřice garden. During these events, musicians performed in boats floating in the local river for an audience gathered on the surrounding banks.

---

[35] See Perutková, *Der glorreiche Nahmen Adami*, 142.

The Beginnings of Musical Historicism

Only a few Moravian aristocrats continued to support opera productions and private ensembles in the early nineteenth century. The activities of Count Heinrich Wilhelm von Haugwitz (1770–1842) at his country estate in Náměšť (Namiescht) exemplify how early nineteenth-century aristocratic patronage differed from that in the eighteenth century.[36] Haugwitz prefigured the historicist interest in dead composers that became prominent in the nineteenth century. Under the influence of historical repertoire presented at Viennese concerts organized by Gottfried van Swieten in the 1780s, Haugwitz developed an interest in the works of Gluck, Handel, Caldara, and Fux. Among more recent composers, Haugwitz was interested in Johann Gottlieb Naumann and Mozart, and the count was also a friend of Antonio Salieri who dedicated his Requiem to Haugwitz, wrote a celebratory cantata for him, and visited Náměšť several times. In 1800, Haugwitz built a theater in Náměšť and hired an orchestra of thirty to forty players, which was unusually large for the period. Furthermore, the ensemble no longer consisted mainly of servants but also relied on teachers from the surrounding region. Haugwitz's ensemble performed up to three times a week, and admission was free, which was not common.

Aristocratic Women as Music Patrons

Many aristocratic women were involved in their fathers' and husbands' musical endeavors, but some also pursued musical patronage on their own. In the first half of the eighteenth century, Marie Gabriela Lazansky von Bukowa, née Czernin (1691–1758) was active both as a patron and a musician in the west Bohemian Manětín (Manetin). In her youth, she served as a lady-in-waiting at the Viennese court of Emperor Joseph I where she became known as a singer and keyboard player.[37] She continued her musical activities even after her marriage and the premature death of her husband. Her patronage focused on Mauritius Vogt, who dedicated his 1719 music theoretical treatise *Conclave thesauri magnae artis musicae* ("Chamber

---

[36] Martin Nedbal, "Heinrich Wilhelm Haugwitz and the Reception of Mozart's Operas in Early Nineteenth-Century Moravia," *Musicologica Brunensia* 56 (2021): 43–57; Marek Buš, ed., *Haugwitzové a hudba* (Náměšt nad Oslavou: Národní památkový ústav, 2003).

[37] Václav Kapsa, "Variace na manětínské téma – Marie Gabriela hraběnka Lažanská jako hudebnice," in *Cantantibus organis. Hudební kultura raného novověku ve středoevropských souvislostech. Ad honorem Jiří Sehnal* (Brno: Moravská zemská knihovna, 2016), 171–79.

Figure 7.1: Élisabeth Vigée Le Brun, *Sophie Fries, Future Countess Haugwitz, Playing a Lyre as Sappho* (c. 1794). Státní zámek Náměšť nad Oslavou. Reproduced by permission.

of Great Treasure of Musical Art") to Lazansky. Vogt also designed a new organ for the Manětín church and performed his compositions there after rehearsing them with local youths. Lazansky also employed composers Joseph Anton Planitzky and Gunther Jacob as tutors for her sons.

A dedicated patron of music in the early nineteenth century was Countess Sophie Fries (1769–1835), daughter of a Viennese banker who married the previously mentioned Heinrich Wilhelm Haugwitz. The marriage fell apart in 1802, and the countess moved to her Moravian castle of Nový Světlov (Swietlau), where she pursued her musical interests. She was a gifted harp player, and had a portrait made of herself with the harp by Élisabeth Vigée Le Brun, formerly the portrait painter of the French queen Marie Antoinette (Figure 7.1). The countess initiated numerous musical festivities and public concerts in Nový Světlov, which were attended both by local aristocrats and commoners. Her orchestra had up to forty-eight members – an unusually large size, modeled on the large music ensemble of her ex-husband.[38]

Bohemian Aristocracy and Nineteenth-Century Public Musical Culture

Aristocratic patronage in the Bohemian crownlands had many different forms and significantly contributed to the region's musical development. Although aristocratic patronage of music reflected the nobility's private interests, it also contributed to the exceptional musicality in the Bohemian lands, as noted by foreign commentators, including Charles Burney and Friedrich Reichardt. At the turn of the nineteenth century, this exceptional musicality was seen as waning, so Bohemian aristocrats initiated new types of music institutions. In 1808, several Bohemian noblemen called for the establishment of the Association for the Promotion of Music in Bohemia (Verein zur Beförderung der Tonkunst in Böhmen), which would support accomplished orchestral performers and provide for the education of young musicians. The society was founded in 1810 with the support of over fifty aristocrats and was instrumental in the establishment of the Prague Conservatory in 1811. Bohemian nobility therefore stood at the beginnings of some of the main institutions of public and, later, also national forms of nineteenth-century musical culture.

---

[38] Jiří Sehnal and Jiří Vysloužil, *Dějiny hudby na Moravě. Vlastivěda moravská* (Brno: Muzejní a vlastivědná společnost, 2001), 127.

8 | "il'y aura six enfants de Choeur ou Clercs": The Bohemian *Kapellknaben* Ensemble of Dresden's Catholic Court Church

JANICE B. STOCKIGT

> *I had frequently been told, that the Bohemians were the most musical people of Germany, or, perhaps, of all Europe; ... I crossed the whole kingdom of Bohemia, from south to north; and being very assiduous in my enquiries, how the common people learned music, I found out at length, that, not only in every large town, but in all villages, where there is a reading and writing school, children of both sexes are taught music.* (Charles Burney)[1]

The natural inquisitiveness of the distinguished English music historian Charles Burney (1726–1814) led him to visit various Bohemian village schools in September 1772 to observe the musical education of children. His admiration for the Mannheim-based Johann Stamitz (1717–57), the "celebrated Misliwiceck" (Italian-based Josef Mysliveček; 1737–81), for certain Viennese-based composers of the Classical era – including Florian Leopold Gassmann (1729–74) and Johann Baptist Wanhal (1739–1813), and the Berlin-based František (Franz) Benda (1709–86) – excited Burney's curiosity. This caused him to personally witness the role village schools played in the early training of Bohemian performers and composers. Moreover, almost all of these, and other expatriate composers from the Czech lands had been on a well-known course of advancement followed by young musicians, a pathway described later in the eighteenth century by Johann Ferdinand von Schönfeld (1750–1821) who observed that outstandingly talented boys of village schools might be taken to an establishment where musical training could continue. In translation, von Schönfeld wrote:

Here, he became acquainted with priests and friends of music who initially occupied him with only small bits and pieces such as, for example, musical copies or a violin part. Because monasteries, prelates, and recognized families were then known as protectors and patrons of music, an opportunity soon was found to

---

[1] Charles Burney, *The Present State of Music in Germany, the Netherlands and the United Provinces* (London, 1775), ed. P. Scholes as *Dr. Burney's Musical Tours in Europe*, 2 vols.; vol. 2 as *An Eighteenth-Century Musical Tour in Central Europe and the Netherlands* (New York: Oxford University Press, 1959), 131–32. Burney's visit to Bohemian schools included Havlíčkův Brod (Teutchenbrod), Čáslav (Czaslau), and Český Brod (Böhmisch-Brod).

secure a place for young artistic geniuses in an orchestra or *Kapelle*. . . . As Prague frequently is visited by foreigners, it often happened that skilled people moved to a different country, either through recommendation, or even through abduction, where they trained and made a career. So it happens that Bohemian musicians are to be found in all states, and they are sought and honored everywhere.

Er erlangte hier die Bekanntschaft mit Priestern und Freunden der Musik, die ihn anfänglich nur mit Kleinigkeiten beschäftigten, dergleichen musikalische Abschriften oder eine Violinstimme waren. Wie nun ehedem vorzüglich Klöster, Prälaten und ansehnliche Familien als Schützer und Beförderer der Tonkunst bekannt waren, so fand sich bald Gelegenheit, junge Künstlergenies in einem Orchester oder in einer Kapelle anzubringen. . . . Da Prag häufig von Fremden besucht wird; so geschah es oft, daß geschickte Leute entweder durch Empfehlung oder wohl gar durch Entführung in ein anderes Land kamen, wo sie sich ausbildeten und ein Glück machten, das der Vorzüglichkeit ihrer steigenden Kunstfertigkeiten angemessen war. Daher kömmt es, daß in allen Staaten böhmische Tonkünstler anzutreffen sind und daß sie überall gesucht und geehrt werden.[2]

Bohemian children and young men were among those who left their homeland to serve in the newly-established Catholic court church of Dresden, a development resulting from the conversion to Catholicism of the Saxon Elector Friedrich Augustus I (1670–1733).

After the death of Jan III Sobieski (1629–96), the Elector of Saxony was crowned King of Poland and Grand Duke of Lithuania in 1697. Due to various setbacks, however, it wasn't until 1709 that the sovereignty of the Saxon elector was firmly established when he became Augustus II ("der Starke"), King of Poland.[3] This development alarmed the Lutheran population of Saxony because the election of the Saxon elector was made possible due to his change of religion in 1697: only a Catholic could be eligible for election as King of Poland. The principal court of Augustus II, however, remained in Dresden which, under royal patronage, became a major cultural center of Europe served by many groups of musicians. Court ensembles included the *Hof-Italianische Opern-und Französische Comödien* (singers for Italian opera and a troupe of French actors, dancers, and musicians), *Trompeter*, the *Pohlnische Capell-Musici* (the king's travelling orchestra), the *Jagd-* and *Bock-Pfeiffer* ensembles,[4] numerous regimental *Hautboisten*

---

[2] Johann Ferdinand von Schönfeld, *Jahrbuch der Tonkunst von Wien und Prag* (Vienna, 1796; repr. 1976), "Musikalische Verfassung von Prag," I, 103–8 (105–6).

[3] This followed the Peace of Altranstädt (1706). Wolfgang Horn, *Die Dresdner Hofkirchenmusik 1720–1745: Studien zu ihren Voraussetzungen und ihrem Repertoire* (Kassel: Bärenreiter, 1987), 18–19, 21.

[4] These musicians are named in annual publications of the *Königl. Polnischer und Churfürstl. Sächsischer Hof- und Staats-Calender* (HStC) (Leipzig, 1728–29, 1730–33, 1734–57).

bands, even ensembles attached to households of Dresden-based nobles,[5] and these groups could be a conduit for a talented musician to the musical pinnacle of Dresden: the famed *Hofkapelle*. This pan-European ensemble included a succession of Bohemian singers and instrumentalists, as well as superb horn players: Johann Adalbert Fischer, Johann and Andreas Schindler, Johann Georg Knechtel, Anton Hampel, and Carl Haudeck.[6]

The dynastic ambitions of Augustus II were to be realized through his son and sole heir, Electoral Prince Friedrich Augustus II. In 1709, this twelve-year-old Lutheran prince (who later succeeded as Augustus III of Poland) secretly traveled to Prague's Clementinum college to meet his father, who had arrived via a different route. There, meetings were held and an Austrian Jesuit chaplain was appointed to instruct the prince. Also, a secret court of Bohemian Catholics was assembled to serve him in Dresden.[7] Were musicians among this court? At the end of his Grand Tour, between September 1717 and late in 1719, this prince was stationed in Vienna for eighteen months during which time he successfully pursued and then, in August 1719, he married the Austrian Archduchess, Maria Josepha (1699–1757), daughter of the late Emperor Joseph I (1678–1711). While in Vienna, the prince's court included two young Bohemian horn players, Johann Joseph Götzel (Goetzel) the elder, and Tobias Butz (Buz; Putz; d. 1760). Until the mid-1720s, both were attached to the household of the prince,[8] and each became a distinguished musician, Götzel as a solo vocal bass singer of the Dresden *Hofkapelle*, and Butz as a much-admired church composer, most of whose musical output is lost.[9]

[5] Szymon Paczkowski, "Christoph August von Wackerbarth (1662–1734) and His 'Cammer-Musique'," in *Music Migration in the Early Modern Age: Centres and Peripheries – People, Works, Styles, Paths of Dissemination and Influence*, ed. Jolanta Guzy-Pasiak and Aneta Markuszewska (Warsaw: Liber Pro Arte 2016), 109–26, http://www.ispan.pl/music-migration.pdf-17283.

[6] Thomas Heibert, "The Horn in Early Eighteenth-Century Dresden: The Players and Their Repertory" (PhD diss., University of Wisconsin-Madison, 1989), esp. chapters 1, 3, 4.

[7] Janice B. Stockigt and Jóhannes Ágústsson, "Reflections and Recent Findings on the Life and Music of Jan Dismas Zelenka (1679–1745)," *Clavibus unitis* 4 (2015), 9, https://www.acecs.cz/media/cu_2015_04.pdf.

[8] Janice B. Stockigt, *Jan Dismas Zelenka (1679–1745): A Bohemian Musician at the Court of Dresden* (New York: Oxford University Press, 2000), 50. Republished as *Jan Dismas Zelenka (1679–1745): Český Hudebník na Drážďanském Dvoře*, with new Introduction (Prague: Vyšehrad, 2018), 90.

[9] On Butz, a composition student of Zelenka, see Stockigt and Ágústsson, "Reflections and recent findings," 39. At the beginning of 1760 during the Seven Years' War when Dresden became a battleground, both Butz and his wife died. Augustus III was living in exile in Warsaw, and the Dresden court had sought refuge in Munich. Apart from one Mass now held in Dresden, Sächsische Landesbibliothek (shelfmark Mus. 2834-D-1), the chaos of 1760 in Dresden led to the loss of almost every work by Butz whose compositions, under normal circumstances, would have been purchased by the court.

Apart from the well-known migrations of important musicians from the Czech lands during the eighteenth century (see also Chapter 5), this chapter investigates a relatively unreported exodus of a succession of musically gifted Bohemian children and young men to serve in the royal Catholic court churches of Dresden and Leipzig, a migration made necessary due to the almost total lack of Catholic children in predominantly Lutheran Saxony at that time.[10]

*****

Following his change of religion in 1708, Augustus II founded a Catholic church in the renovated theater of the Dresden palace, while in 1710 a smaller Catholic chapel was established in the Pleißenberg castle of Leipzig. Each was open to the public, and each was dedicated to the Most Holy Trinity. Whereas Dresden's royal Catholic chapel possessed a musical establishment of Bohemian boys and young men from 1710, the more modest Leipzig chapel was served by a succession of talented young Bohemian organists following the completion of an organ in 1720. Three of these musicians, Augustin Uhlig, Joseph Tiederle, and Anton Harnisch, were moved to Dresden to serve the much more important Catholic church of the court.[11] Thus, it was Bohemian boys and young men who bore most of the musical duties in the newly established Catholic churches of Dresden and Leipzig. Two Bohemian composers, Jan Dismas Zelenka (1679–1745) and his student Tobias Butz (the former personal horn player in the court of the electoral prince), were involved with the music of this Dresden establishment, which was served by Jesuits from the Province of Bohemia. While many young musicians returned home for further studies when their voices broke, others remained to contribute to Dresden's musical life during an era of economic, cultural, and artistic splendor known as the "Augustan Age" (1697–1763), and beyond.

The Bohemian choristers and instrumentalists of Dresden's Catholic court church first are mentioned in an incomplete draft document which served as a blueprint for regulations to govern the practice of Catholicism in Lutheran Saxony. Titled "Memoire Pour L'eglise ou Chappelle Royale," the document was prepared early in 1708 by the confessor chosen by Augustus II, Fr. Maurizio Vota SJ (1629–1715),[12] who suggested that six young *clercs* skilled in music should serve the chaplains at the altar and sing

---

[10] Janice B. Stockigt, "The Organists of Leipzig's Royal Catholic Chapel: 1719–56," *Hudební věda* 53 (2016): 1–12.

[11] See their entries in Stockigt, "Organists of Leipzig's Catholic Chapel."

[12] Archivum Romanum Societatis Iesu (ARSI [I-Rar]), Fondo Vecchia Compagnia; Provinciae Bohemiae (Boh), 205/2. Fr. Vota had been the confessor to Augustus II's predecessor, Jan III Sobieski.

the music of the Mass and Vespers. The final royal decree, however, stated that another four instrumentalists and an organist would be required.[13] The *clercs* were to be under the direction of a Jesuit chaplain who would teach Latin and be responsible for the upbringing of the boys and young men who constituted what became known as the *Kapellknaben* institute. In Dresden they lived in the Jesuit house. At the conclusion of the school year in August or September when prizes were awarded, the Bohemian practice of an end-of-year performance of a stage play came to be given by the boys, sometimes in the presence of members of the Dresden court, after which the students returned to their Bohemian homes for an annual holiday.[14]

The first Music Prefect of the *Kapellknaben* was the secular priest and former Jesuit, Johannes Jungwirth (b. České Budějovice (Budweis); d. 1737) who came to Dresden from Teplice (Teplitz). Their first chaplain Fr. Elias Broggio SJ (1668–1737) came from an Italian family of the northern Bohemian town of Litoměřice (Leitmeritz). This priest made several trips to Bohemian villages seeking musicians for the small royal ensemble. On January 16, 1710, the first entry in the *Diarium* of the Dresden Jesuits named the musical personnel of the royal musical establishment:

[...] Father Jungwirt, Kapellmeister, who a few years ago was dismissed from the Society [...] Ignatius Hoffmann [from Děčín (Tetschen)] who taught the Trivium and was first violinist, and eight young musicians recruited in various places by Father Elias Broggio: Laurentius John [organist and teacher of Rhetoric], Joannes Walter, Josephus Müldner [violinist], Georgius Ibscher [tenor], Georgius Pohl, Joannes Georgius Kreibig [discantist], Antonius Angerer, Josephus Pusch.[15]

[...] R.D. Joannes Jungwirt Magister Capellae seu Musicae ante paucos annos a Societate dimissus [...] Dominus Ignatius Hofman qui Triviales informabat, et simul egit primum fidicinem, et octo Juvenes Musici variis locis opera Patris Eliae Broggio collecti, Laurentius John, Joannes Walter, Josephus Müldner, Georgius Ibscher, Georgius Pohl, Joannes Georgius Kreibig, Antonius Angerer, Josephus Pusch.

---

[13] ARSI (I-Rar), Boh 205/1: *"Dresda." Reglements du Roy pour l'Eglise et Chapelle Royale, ouverte aux Catholiques* (signed "Augustus Rex"). The Bohemian Jesuit college at Litoměřice, and the residence at Krupka (Graupen) are named as places of recruitment.

[14] Franz Paul Saft, *Der Neuaufbau der katholischen Kirche in Sachsen im 18. Jahrhundert* (Leipzig: St Benno, 1961), 59. On these plays, see Magdaléna Jacková, "The End of School Year on the Stage of Jesuit Schools in the Bohemian Province," *Acta Universitatis Carolinae Philologica* 2 – *Graecolatina Pragensia* 2 (2016): 125–35.

[15] *Jhs: Diarium seu Protocollum Missionis Societatis Jesu* [...]. 2 vols. (*Diarium.*) Excerpts published by Wolfgang Reich in *Zelenka-Studien II: Referate und Materialien der 2. Internationalen Fachkonferenz Jan Dismas Zelenka, Dresden und Prague 1995*, ed. W. Reich and G. Gatterman, Deutsche Musik im Osten, 12 (Sankt Augustin: Academia, 1997), 315–79. Engl. trans. by the late David Fairservice. *Diarium*, January 16, 1710.

Academic examinations were held annually. Some *Kapellknaben* then moved to Prague for further education. The Dresden Jesuits took great pride in the results they achieved, especially of those students who entered the Society of Jesus.[16] One reference only exists of a contract between a parent and the Jesuits: "Two copies of the contract by which the discant and the alto were taken on were made: One copy was given to Höger [the parent], the other kept here."[17] In the church, the *Kapellknaben* wore a cotta or tunicle,[18] but in public their uniform was expensive royal livery for which the court initially paid 400 Thaler.[19] Each boy received 100 Rthl. annually, and their organist was paid 200.[20]

The sacred repertoire performed by the *Kapellknaben* came from published sets of partbooks. Among the many examples held in Dresden today are volumes of Giovanni Battista Bassani's music for Vespers, Compline, and Requiems,[21] while seven Mass settings (1706) by Johann Christoph Anton Fiebig, a prelate from the Bohemian Cistercian monastery at Osek (Osseg), entered their repertoire.[22] In time, three court composers, Johann David Heinichen (1683–1729), Giovanni Alberto Ristori (1692–1753), and Zelenka, began to write, collect, and arrange a repertoire of sacred Catholic music suitable for performance by the Dresden *Hofkapelle* and for the *Kapellknaben*.[23] "Ordinary" Vespers psalm settings are among Zelenka's compositions for them,[24] as are four "Asperges" settings (ZWV 163), numerous Marian antiphons and hymns, a litany (ZWV 150) to be sung as they processed to the Marian shrine during their pilgrimage to Krupka (Graupen) in 1725, and arrangements of works by Palestrina for four-part choir (SATB), the usual

---

[16] Dresden *Kapellknaben* who entered the Society of Jesus included Laurentius John (*Diarium*, October 7, 1710), Casper Hegenwald, and Joseph Jähnel (*Diarium*, July 7, 1740), while Johannes Ipscher, Wenceslaus Zlatousty, and Jacob Cardona were to pursue studies in Prague (*Diarium*, September 19, 1710; September 8, 1727; September 15, 1729). Saft, *Der Neuaufbau der Katholische Kirche in Sachsen*, 60.

[17] *Diarium*, October 1, 1710.

[18] ARSI (I-Rar), Boh. 140, "Annuae Missionis Dresdensis ad annum 1725," 22.

[19] Moritz Fürstenau, *Zur Geschichte der Musik und des Theaters am Hofe zu Dresden* (Leipzig, Kuntze, 1862, repr. Leipzig, Peters 1971), vol. ii, 36.

[20] ARSI (I-Rar), Boh. 205/1, "Reglements [!] du Roy pour l'Eglise et Chapelle Royal [...]."

[21] Dresden, Sächsische Landesbibliothek, shelfmark Mus. 2114-D-1, -E-1, -E-2.

[22] Dresden, Sächsische Landesbibliothek, shelfmark Mus. 2368-D-1.

[23] The three tiers of sacred music practiced in chapels of the Viennese court – "Solemn," "Ordinary," and *a cappella* – were employed for the music of Dresden's Catholic court church. See Friedrich W. Riedel, *Kirchenmusik am Hofe Karls VI: (1711–1740)* (Munich and Salzburg: Katzbichler, 1977), "Die Liturgisch-Musikalische Struktur der Hofgottesdienste," 61 ff. Dresden's *Hofkapelle* members were mainly responsible for solemn and "Ordinary" music; the *Kapellknaben* performed the *a cappella* and some "Ordinary" repertoire, which was shorter, musically less elaborate, and less richly orchestrated than "solemn" music.

[24] Stockigt, *Jan Dismas Zelenka*, 212–25.

choral vocal scoring used by the royal choristers. Reports on music-making in the Jesuit house are frequent: for example, "…music which our domestic organist [Uhlig] composed" was performed on the name-day in 1728 of the Royal Confessor Heinrich Dassik.[25]

The most famous of the Bohemian *Kapellknaben* of Dresden undoubtedly was František Benda whose earliest music education was received in Benátky nad Jizerou (Benatek). His acceptance into the Jesuit College of St. Nicholas in the Lesser Town district of Prague followed. From there, Benda was recruited for Dresden by a student named Roscher, a candidate for the Society of Jesus, and apparently an agent of the Dresden Jesuits in their constant search for replacement discantists.[26] On September 15, 1721, Dresden's *Diarium* recorded Benda's arrival: "Joseph Roscher came today with a discantist from Prague. He also brought with him a tenor and another discantist to be auditioned." Two days later the *Diarium* reported: "Dominus Roscher was sent back with a discantist whom he had brought with him for audition. The Prague discantist [Benda] and the tenor were retained."[27] Benda became a leading singer of the *Kapellknaben* ensemble. His autobiography (which states that in Dresden he initially spoke Czech because he knew no German) reveals that *Kapellmeister* Heinichen composed a new setting of the Marian antiphon *Salve Regina* which Benda was to sing in the presence of royalty.[28] He also played viola and violin, claiming to have played Vivaldi violin concertos from memory. The *Diarium* recorded his departure on May 5, 1723: "Today the alto Franciscus Benda left us. Nothing would induce him to stay here."[29] Was Zelenka complicit in Benda's decision to leave? Perhaps Benda already was in Zelenka's mind to sing the role "Suspicio" in the Prague performance of Zelenka's highly successful work *Sub olea pacis: Melodrama de Sancto Wenceslao* (ZWV 175), commissioned by the Jesuits of the Clementinum college for performance before Charles VI and Elisabeth Christine in

---

[25] *Diarium*, July 15, 1728. "Augustin Uhlig" is the autograph signature in his petition to the Dresden court, 1733. Variations include Uhlich, Uhlick, Ulich, Ulick, and Ulig.

[26] *Diarium*, October 14, 1724: "Fr Jos. Roscher arrived at night, bringing an altist, his brother." This must be the Joseph Roscher who earlier brought Benda to Dresden from Prague.

[27] *Diarium*, September 17, 1721.

[28] František [Franz] Benda, [Autobiography] (Potsdam, 1763), ed. in *Neue Berliner Musikzeitung* 10 (1856). Engl. trans. by Paul Nettl as "Franz Benda's Autobiography," in *Forgotten Musicians* (New York; Greenwood Press, 1951), 204–45. In 1723, *Salve Regina* was sung between Compline on the Saturday before Trinity Sunday (May 22, 1723) until Friday before the first Sunday of Advent (November 28, 1723). Thus, Heinichen's setting would not have been performed by Benda.

[29] *Diarium*, May 5, 1723: "Hodie a nobis abivit Franciscus Benda altista, qui nulla ratione hic manere voluit."

September 1723 during their visit to Prague to be crowned King and Queen of Bohemia (see Chapter 6). The annual Clementinum report to Rome describes how the imperial couple complimented and praised the production, Zelenka's music (*moduli musici*) in particular.[30]

While many Bohemian parents were delighted with and actively sought the educational opportunities Dresden presented to their musical sons, the removal of Bohemian children to Saxony also caused anger. In February 1737, for example, Count Philip Joseph Kinsky began searching for students who were his subjects, threatening to imprison their parents. This fate touched the parents of Joseph Hancke, a discantist from Kamenický Šenov (Stein-Schönau), while in 1738, another discantist named Palme was sent home from Dresden when Count Kinsky began recalling all his subjects, including the Dresden *Kapellknabe*: "Indeed, the parents are to be imprisoned until their sons return," it was reported.[31]

Due to the decision of 1727 by a new Dresden superior, Fr. Franz Nonhardt SJ, the musical role of Dresden's *Kapellknaben* was augmented, and the ensemble began to grow both in size and importance.

At the beginning of the school year the number of young musicians was increased to amplify Marian devotions, and all Saturdays and ferial days preceding Marian feasts will be celebrated with litanies, the Exposition of the Blessed Sacrament … and finally, the Benediction of the congregation. The Rorate, which until now had been celebrated on Sundays and feast days, has now been extended to all ferial days of Advent (on Rorate, see Chapters 1 and 3).[32]

Sub initia Anni scolastici aucta juventute musica Marianum cultum ampliaturi Sabbata cuncta, idem feriae festa Mariana praecedentes habebunt, Litaniis, exposito in ciborio Sanctissimo […] Benedictio ad finem populo datur. Sed et Rorate, dominicis, festique hucusque habitum, extensum est ad omnes Adventûs ferias […]

Recruiting trips for young Bohemian musicians became less frequent when cantors and parents began bringing their musically talented children to Dresden. On May 6, 1728, Fr. Jungwirth, whose voice the Electoral Prince and Princess, Friedrich Augustus and Maria Josepha, could not tolerate,[33] was replaced by Fr. Johannes Frantze SJ (1695–1750) as Prefect of Music, a position he previously had held in Olomouc (Olmütz). The stay of Fr. Frantze, however, was to be short-lived: on February 16, 1729, a decision of the Jesuit Provincial

---

[30] Janice B. Stockigt and Jana Vojtešková, "Zpráva o návštěvě císaře Karla VI. s chotí v Klementinu v roce 1723," *Hudební věda* 4 (1992): 351–59.

[31] *Diarium*, November 30, 1738.

[32] ARSI (I-Rar), Boh 143, "Annuae Litterae Missionis Dresdensis ad annum 1727," 19.

[33] *Diarium*, December 30, 1722.

Head led to his departure for the Jesuit seminary in Prague where Fr. Frantze became the *Praefecto maior et musicorum*.[34] From about this time, Zelenka (whose position as court *Compositeur* was formalized in 1732 or 1733, and as *Kirchen-Composit*[*eur*] by 1735[35]) seems to have become more strongly associated with Dresden's *Kapellknaben*, directing their music and occasionally using some as copyists: "Descripsit [copied by] Josephus Kalousek. Anno 1731" is written by a *Kapellknabe* at the conclusion of a part for "Organo o' Violoncello" for Zelenka's performance materials of a *Litaniae Lauretanae* by Johann Antonín Reichenauer (c. 1694–1730).[36] Fr. Nonhardt's decision of 1727 saw the arrival of more Bohemian *Kapellknaben*, and although the *Diarium* names some, many remain anonymous. In July 1727, for example, the *Diarium* recorded the arrival of an un-named bass singer from Litoměřice, a violinist from Děčín, and four *Juvenes* (two were discantists) from unrecorded places. Auditions led to the acceptance of some, and rejection of others. In October 1729, two musicians from "Apostelberg" (possibly Postoloprty (Postelberg)), and three altos arrived, one from Děčín.

To the relatively sparse records of named Dresden-based *Kapellknaben*, the musicians who served between 1726 and 1732 may be identified by name. They were among those eligible to be buried in the Catholic cemetery of the Dresden court. The accompanying Table 8.1 names the *Kapellknaben* who held this privilege.[37] Several boys and young men apparently were related, the brothers Cardona,[38] Pfeiffer, Kalousek, Churfürst, and Wenzel, for example. Some musicians left voluntarily: Benda departed in 1723; two horn players left in 1732 (they soon were replaced when "Cantor Pumpe from Tetzen [Tetschen / Děčín] brought his two sons who are horn players"[39]); the altist Pompe (Pumpe), "a young man who is ignorant and addicted to freedom, ran

---

[34] ARSI (I-Rar), Boh 921: Bohemiae Catal. Brev. 1720–1742; Boh 51, Boh Cat. Trien. 1730.

[35] "Zelenka, Johann Dismas: *Compositeur.*" Published in the list "Die Königl. Capelle und Cammer-Musique," in *HStC*, 1733; as *Kirchen-Composit*[*eur*] in 1735.

[36] Preparation of performance materials for three works from the early 1730s suggest the involvement of members of the *Kapellknaben* ensemble: *Litaniae Lauretanae* by Reichenauer (Dresden, Sächsische Landesbibliothek, shelfmark Mus. 2494-D-3) and František Poppe (Dresden, Sächsische Landesbibliothek, shelfmark Mus. 3610-E-2a), and a Mass by Antonio Caldara: *Missa Quid mihi et tibi* (Dresden, Sächsische Landesbibliothek, shelfmark Mus. 2170-D-14).

[37] Following the accession of Electoral Prince Friedrich Augustus II as Elector of Saxony (1733) and coronation as King of Poland (1734), a public Catholic cemetery was established in Dresden. See Jóhannes Ágústsson and Janice B. Stockigt, "Records of Catholic Musicians, Actors and Dancers at the Court of Augustus II, 1723–32: The Establishment of a Catholic Cemetery in Dresden," *Royal Musical Association Research Chronicle* 45 (2014): 26–75. http://www.tandfonline.com/eprint/SbZwWFm2Gt3J4IjxbX6q/full. Jesuit chaplains and *Kapellknaben* first are listed in 1726. Note that Jesuit and court records contain many spelling variations of Bohemian towns and names of persons.

[38] The origin of the Cardona brothers is unknown.   [39] *Diarium*, July 17, 1733.

away." The Jesuits refused to take him back, despite his father's pleas.[40] Two deaths are recorded among the *Kapellknaben*. On October 3, 1731, the *Diarium* reported a Requiem being sung for the musician Lorenz Lange[r]; later, a young discantist, Joseph Sieber died of quinsy.[41] Occasionally, these Bohemian musicians traveled abroad: a foundation member of the *Kapellknaben*, Georg Pohl[e] went to Rome with the royal confessor, Fr. Vota SJ,[42] who was about to enter retirement. Others moved into households of Dresden court members: Anton Fridt was appointed as a valet and musician to the court of the "Most Eminent,"[43] and a *Kapellknabe* named Miller was taken into service by the renowned Dresden court male soprano, Ventura Rochetti ("Venturini").[44]

Table 8.1 *Kapellknaben* of the Dresden Catholic court church: 1726–32.

Name	Spelling variations	Place of origin	Role	1727	1728	1729	1730	1731	1732
Bernt, Johannes	Bernk		Bassoonist?					X	X
Bock, Hanspachio[45]			Violinist				X		
Cardona, Carolus				X	X				
Cardona, Jacobus				X	X	X			
Cardona, Petrus									
Churfürst, Johann		Rakonitz (Rakovník)	Discant-Altist	X	X				
Churfürst, Georgius	Kuhrfurst	Rakonitz	Discantist	X		X	X	X	X
Eiselt, Joseph			Violinist	X					
Frey, Wolffgang									
Jähnel, Joseph	Pähnel								X
Kalousek, Johannes	Kalongeck	Rakonitz				X			

---

[40] *Diarium*, July 7, 1732; July 17, 1732; November 11, 1735.
[41] ARSI (I-Rar), Boh 156, "Annuae literae Regiae Missionis Dresdensis ad annum 1737," 45–6. *Diarium*, January 2, 1738.
[42] *Diarium*, June 1, 1711.
[43] *Diarium*, January 31, 1720. Perhaps the "Most Eminent" refers to Cardinal Christian August of Saxe-Zeitz, cousin of Augustus II.
[44] *Diarium*, July 8, 1735.
[45] The violinist 'Hanspachio Bock (Pock?) is named only in the *Diarium*, September 23, 1730: "The violinist Hanspachio Bock returned."

Table 8.1 (cont.)

Name	Spelling variations	Place of origin	Role	1727	1728	1729	1730	1731	1732
Kalousek, Ignatius	Kalouvreck; Kulousak Kalouseick; Kolauseck	Rakonitz				X	X	X	X
Kalousek, Josephus	Kalouseick; Kolauseck	Rakonitz					X	X	X
Keinichen, Josephus						X			
Kurtzweil, Johann					X	X			
Kühnel, Georg		Markersdorf (Markvartice)?	Horn					X	
Langer, Laurentius							X	X	
Lufft, Christophorus					X				
Nohl, Adelbertus									
Pfeiffer, Adelbertus		Teplitz (Teplice)							
Pfeiffer, Jacob									
Pock, Leopoldus							X		
Pomps, Wenceslaus	Pombs	Tetschen (Děčín)	Horn			X	X	X	X
Pulz, Franciscus									X
Reimisch, Josephus							X	X	X
Ritzschel, Franciscus	Ritzel	Teplice	Vocal bass				X	X	X
Schürer, Georg[46]		Raudnitz (Roudnice nad Labem)?	Discantist						X
Sehan, Christophorus							X	X	X
Stelzig, Johannes									X

---

[46] *Diarium*, May 16, 1732: "A new discantist named Schürer arrived from Bohemia."

Table 8.1 (cont.)

Name	Spelling variations	Place of origin	Role	1727	1728	1729	1730	1731	1732
Tannenberger, Anton					X				
Tiederle, Joseph	Tiderle; Giderle		Violinist	X	X	X			
Thollkopff, Theod.	Thollhopff; Tollhopff		Altist		X				
Tolkopff, Thadeus								X	X
Uhlig, Augustinus	Uhlih; Uhlick; Ulick	[Výsluní]	Organist	X	X	X	X	X	X
Ullrich, Wenceslaus	Ulrich							X	X
Vatter, Antonius						X			
Wenzel, Joh. Michael					X	X	X	X	X
Wenzel, Leopoldus			Tenor			X	X	X	X
Zlatousty, Wenceslaus	Zladousty		Tenor	X					
TOTALS				**9**	**10**	**11**	**13**	**15**	**17**

On February 1, 1733, King Augustus II died in Warsaw. Almost immediately his son and successor (titled Augustus III following his coronation in January 1734) began to reorganize Dresden's musical forces, including the reduction of the now-greatly expanded music ensemble of the royal chapel. On July 27, 1733, the *Diarium* reported that all but six of the seventeen *Kapellknaben* were to be dismissed. Their role in the church would be taken by the newly arrived Italian castrati (the *Virtuosi*) who had been selected and trained in Italy for the revival of Dresden's opera. This led the Father Superior, Michael Gruber SJ, to conclude the annual letter to Rome with this lament:

One more thing before we close the annual letter: among the various changes made this year by the court one needs to be mentioned. The adolescents who live with us in our house and serve the royal chapel as choristers and musicians have been sent away, except for six who were kept on solely to assist the fathers and for chapel duties. The responsibility for performing music was then given to the King's musicians who, after the feast of the Nativity of the Blessed Virgin, began to frequent the choir on a regular basis. However, the King's *Virtuosi* repeatedly refrained from performing many *a cappella* works [exercitia choralia], which had been customary in previous years and omitted many things which, at other times, have served for public edification. Thus, no more Rorate [Masses] in Advent, which had here been a daily occurrence for the last few years; no more Asperges because, so they claim, they are never performed in Italy; At times there was no singing before the sermon because the new organist said that until, as he requested, another organist had been engaged for this purpose, he was not obliged to perform this; Requiems are no longer sung, except on the bidding, or with the permission of the court.[47]

Nobiscum cohabitantes domo, quâ vocibus, quâ instrumentis musicis Capellae Regiae inservientes adolescentes sint dimissi, sex modo exceptis ac nobiscum remanentibus, qui solum retinerentur ad Patrum Nostrorum obsequia, simul et Capellae Servitia. Musica peragenda deinceps Orchestrae Regiae demandata fuit, quae post Festum B. V. Nascentis constanter chorum frequentare coepit. Sed a plurimis per alios annos consuetis. Exercitiis choralibus se frequentius substraxerunt Virtuosi Regii ... Ita omissa sunt sub Adventum Dominicum Rorate ... quotidiana Omissa sunt Asperges ... aliquot etiam vicibus cantus ante Concionem omissus ... Requiem nullum decantatur amplius, nisi jussu vel aulae consensu.

*****

It is not surprising that following the dismissal of the *Kapellknaben* the six boys retained for chapel duties at Dresden's Catholic court church were the best musicians. Although the ensemble gradually was re-established under the much-admired teacher, Anton Harnisch, never again did it reach its former strength. Nevertheless, over the following years young Bohemian musicians continued to serve in the great *Hofkirche* which, in 1751, replaced the original Catholic court church.[48] In 1769–70 seven of the nine *Kapellknaben* came from Bohemia.[49] Annual published membership lists in the *Hof-und Staats-Calender* demonstrate that members of the *Hofkapelle* included several former *Kapellknaben*: the vocal bass Franciscus Ritszchel, violinists Uhlig, Tiederle,[50] and Hancke (who also served with the *Pohlnische Capell-Musici*).[51] In 1748, Johann Georg Schürer (c. 1720–86), a Bohemian discantist who arrived in Dresden on June 16, 1732, joined Butz as a Dresden court "Kirchen Composit,"[52] while Schürer's colleague, the former altist and organist Joseph Schuster (father of the famed composer of the same name), and the former

---

[47] ARSI (I-Rar), Boh 150, "Annuae Literae Missionis Dresdensis ad Annum 1733," 34.
[48] The *Hofkirche*. Now the Kathedrale Sanctissimae Trinitatis, Dresden.
[49] Saft, *Der Neuaufbau der katholischen Kirche in Sachsen*, 56.   [50] HStC, 1757.
[51] Alina Żórawska-Witkowska, *Muzyka na polskim dworze Augusta III* (Lublin: Wydawnictwo Muzyczne Polihymnia, 2012), chapter 5, "Kapela Polska," 158–207.
[52] "Catalogo (Thematico) [sic] della Musica di Chiesa (catholica [sic] in Dresda) composta Da diversi Autori – secondo l'Alfabetto 1765." Staatsbibliothek zu Berlin, Stiftung Preußischer Kulturbesitz, Musikabteilung, shelfmark Mus. ms. theor. Kat. 186.

horn player in the court of the electoral prince, Johann Joseph Götzel, now were vocal soloists of the *Hofkapelle*.

In 1765, after the Seven Years' War when the musicians of Dresden's court ensemble, now renamed the *Capell- und Cammer-Musique*, re-assembled, many familiar names continued to appear in published lists. They included the church composers Schürer who, in 1765, supervised the removal and cataloguing of the important collection of sacred music from Maria Josepha's apartments to Dresden's new Catholic *Hofkirche*, and Schuster, Uhlig (now the Instrument Inspector of the *Hofkapelle*[53]), as well as family members of the next generation: the principal flautist was "Franc.[iscus] Josef Götzel" (son of Johann Joseph), and violinists Simon Uhlig (son of Augustin) and Johann Eiselt (son of Joseph). The *Corni da Caccia* players were the Bohemian-born Anton Hampel and Carl Haudeck. Thus, the annual migration of young Bohemian musicians that began in 1710 led to exceptional contributions to the musical life of Dresden, and to a *Hofkapelle* that was to become a pre-eminent orchestra: the Dresdner *Staatskapelle*.

[53] *HStC*, 1765: "Ulich, August: Violinist, Instrument-Insp.," 60, 63.

PART II

The "Long" Nineteenth Century

9 | Bohemian Public Music Institutions and National Politics

MARTIN NEDBAL

The Rudolfinum is not only one of Prague's two main concert halls and the seat of the Czech Philharmonic, but also a symbol of the close links between Bohemian cultural institutions and political ideologies. The building was financed by the Böhmische Sparkasse (Bohemian Savings Bank) and completed in 1885. The building's name refers both to Crown Prince Rudolph of Austria, son of Emperor Franz Joseph I and heir to the throne until his suicide in 1889, and to sixteenth-century Emperor Rudolf II. The dedication to the crown prince reflected the Sparkasse's allegiance to the Habsburg dynasty, and the reference to Rudolf II emphasized the cultural autonomy of Bohemia because the Habsburg emperor chose Prague as his residence and transformed the city into a center of late Renaissance culture and science (see Chapter 4). The Sparkasse's visionary director Wenzel Worowka, who initiated the Rudolfinum's construction, therefore acted on a patriotic belief in Bohemia's cultural autonomy within the Habsburg empire.

But Bohemian patriotism and the Habsburgs' role in Bohemia's history became contentious in late nineteenth-century Prague, where many Bohemians identified as either Czechs or Germans. Despite its patriotic background, the Rudolfinum was heavily criticized in the Czech press as not pro-Czech enough and pandering to German national interests. The report in the Czech journal *Národní listy* on the festive opening on February 7, 1885, decried that the event was attended mainly by Germans, that Czech was not spoken at all, and that foreign performers were featured.[1] Despite the nationalistic, anti-German objections, however, the Rudolfinum became an important site of Czech music and helped shape the Czech symphonic canon. Already the opening concert, for example, featured Antonín Dvořák's second *Slavonic Rhapsody*. The Rudolfinum also hosted occasional Slavic music concerts put on by Czech organizations.[2] On January 4, 1896, furthermore, the inaugural concert of

---

[1] *Národní listy*, February 8, 1885.
[2] On these concerts, see Vladimír Lébl and Jitka Ludvová, "Pražské orchestrální koncerty v letech 1860–1895," *Hudební věda* 17 (1980): 132–33.

the Czech Philharmonic took place in the Rudolfinum; it was conducted by Antonín Dvořák and focused on his works. But the orchestra eventually abandoned the Rudolfinum, citing its Germanness.[3]

German commentators emphasized the Rudolfinum's presumed German character in 1919 and 1920, when the government of the newly created Czechoslovakia decided to use the building as the seat of the parliament. During the first session of the parliament in the refurbished building, for example, some German deputies claimed that the building was German and was stolen.[4] The alleged link between the Rudolfinum and Germanness also led to a costly reconstruction back to a concert hall during the Nazi occupation in 1940–41.[5] The politicization of the Rudolfinum is also illustrated by the famous episode during the Nazi occupation when German authorities removed the statue of Mendelssohn from the Rudolfinum's roof and planned to replace it with a statue of Bruckner.[6]

Most Bohemian public music institutions have been affected by the region's complex political history. This chapter focuses on the politicization of public music institutions dedicated to opera (both opera theaters and opera companies) and symphonic music (both concert halls and the ensembles that perform in them).[7] To avoid Pragocentrism, I also explore music history in the north Bohemian spa town Teplice (Teplitz), a sought-after summer resort that hosted prominent Central European politicians and artists, including Ludwig van Beethoven and Richard Wagner. Unlike Prague, furthermore, Teplice remained a predominantly German-speaking city until the forced removal of the German population from the Czech lands after World War II. In both cities, musical institutions transformed according to their inhabitants' social and political preferences, and musical works of the past entered the artistic canon in connection to patriotic and national agendas.

---

[3] Lébl and Ludvová, "Pražské orchestrální koncerty," 106.

[4] Michal Novotný, "Poslanecká sněmovna v Rudolfinu" in *Chrám umění Rudolfinum*, ed. Jakub Bachtík, Lukáš Duchek, and Jakub Jareš (Prague: Česká filharmonie, 2020), 281–322 (284).

[5] See Michal Novotný, "Rudolfinum v moci nacistů" in *Chrám umění Rudolfinum*, 323–66.

[6] Paradoxically, in the 1870s Czech commentators complained that the statues were by German and Austrian sculptors and did not include any Czech composers. See Jindřich Vybíral, "Koncepce, soutěž a výstavba Rudolfina" in *Chrám umění Rudolfinum*, 67–142 (101). In his famous 1958 novel *Mendelssohn je na střeše* ("Mendelssohn Is on the Roof"), Czech Jewish writer Jiří Weil mixes fact and fiction when he has Reinhard Heydrich request the removal of Mendelssohn's statue (although the statue was removed only several months after Heydrich's assassination), and the workers, confused by the lack of name tags, briefly consider taking down the statue of Wagner because of its "Jewish" nose (although Wagner is not among the composers displayed in the Rudolfinum). See Novotný, "Rudolfinum v moci nacistů," 324.

[7] A helpful resource for mid-nineteenth-century concert life in Prague is the database Prague Concert Life, 1850–1881, https://prague-concerts.info, accessed March 22, 2024.

The Estates Theater and Bohemian Patriotism

One of Prague's first public music institutions was Bohemia's first "national" theater, presently called the Estates Theater. Built by Count Franz Anton Nostitz-Rieneck and opened in 1783, the theater was modeled on Joseph II's National Theater, operating in the Vienna Burgtheater since 1776. The creation of the Vienna national theater was the result of a lengthy process in which Viennese intellectuals and administrators embraced the concept of theater that was no longer simply a site of courtly representation or popular entertainment, but rather an institution through which the state edified large segments of the population by presenting vernacular works considered politically and socially appropriate.[8] Social conditions specific to Bohemia distinguished the Prague theater from its Viennese model. The main issue was the conflicted nature of national and regional identities that the theater was supposed to represent. In the 1780s, many educated consumers of literate culture in Prague considered German their primary language. However, most Bohemians spoke Czech. The clash between the Bohemian population's linguistic variety and the emerging concept of Germanocentric patriotism is reflected in the inscription on the main facade of the new building: "Patriae et musis" ("To the Fatherland and the Muses"). Although for the next decades, the theater was considered a predominantly German-language institution, Count Nostitz chose a motto in Latin, the language many educated Bohemians viewed as the chief literary language prior to Habsburg centralization and Germanization efforts of the mid-eighteenth century. Nostitz certainly considered German the primary language of the enlightened Bohemian theater, and in a 1782 proclamation he stated that the theater would allow its Bohemian audiences to demonstrate that they did not "feel any less German blood in their veins" ("weniger deutsches Blut in unseren Adern fühlen") than other inhabitants of the "German hereditary lands" ("deutsche Erbländer").[9] At the same time, Nostitz allowed the theater to perform in any language that fit the desires of the nobility and the public (thus not excluding the possibility of Czech performances, which indeed commenced in 1785). As a result, the theater became a center of not only German, but also Italian and Czech opera. Besides world premieres of Mozart's *Don Giovanni* and

[8] This process is discussed in Martin Nedbal, *Morality and Viennese Opera in the Age of Mozart and Beethoven* (New York: Routledge, 2017).
[9] Cited in Oscar Teuber, *Geschichte des Prager Theaters* (Prague: Haase, 1883–88), 3 vols., vol. 2, 95.

La clemenza di Tito, the theater hosted premiere productions of works by Bohemian composers, including German and Czech operas by Wenzel Johann Tomaschek (Václav Jan Tomášek), Franz Skraup (František Škroup), and Johann Friedrich Kittl.

Prague's Opera Houses and the Rise of Czech and German Nationalism

In the early nineteenth century, Czech intellectuals sought to negate, at least rhetorically, Czech culture's connections to and dependence on German culture, and the establishment of an independent Czech theater therefore became a major goal. Until the 1860s, Czech operas were mostly performed at the Estates Theater, where the German repertoire reigned supreme, and Czech performances therefore usually took place on Sunday and holiday afternoons. Lengthy operatic works had to be shortened to allow the preparation and timely beginning of evening German performances. Initially, such practices reflected the reality that most Czech speakers came from the working class and did not have enough spare time on weekdays. As more members of the elite identified as Czech, however, the continuing relegation of Czech performances to non-workday afternoons acquired the character of a Germanocentric bias against Czech culture as plebeian and inferior. From 1844 on, Czech elites called for and collected funds for the construction of an independent Czech theater in Prague. Before the collected finances could support the construction of a monumental theater, the national leaders decided to build a temporary stage, the Provisional Theater, which opened in 1862.

In response to Czech emancipation, Bohemians who identified with the German language and culture gradually abandoned Bohemian patriotic sentiments (that viewed Czech-language culture as a significant part of Bohemian culture while taking for granted the superiority of German culture) and aligned with German national views.[10] This also meant that many Bohemian Germans became increasingly antagonistic to the Czech cultural movement. One example of these shifting sensibilities can be found in the writings of Franz Balthasar Ulm, who contributed, under the acronym "V.", to Prague's German-language journal *Bohemia* between 1849 and 1881. In 1850, Ulm, a German writer, reviewed a Czech

---

[10] This process is also discussed in Gary B. Cohen, *The Politics of Ethnic Survival: Germans in Prague, 1861–1914*, 2nd rev. ed. (West Lafayette, IN: Purdue University Press, 2006).

production of *Die Zauberflöte* at the Estates Theater and raised what seem like sincere concerns about the state of the Czech opera company in Prague.[11] Ulm claims, for example, that the performance was heavily attended although the main roles were sung by singers who did not speak Czech, and the production did not offer any new decorations, costumes, or even complete staging. Ulm also expresses support for Czech opera productions in a difficult time (the difficulties were related to the anti-nationalist reaction by the Austrian authorities to the revolutions of 1848–49) and urges critics to tamp down their criticism of Czech performances in an attempt not to endanger their very existence.[12] A similarly supportive attitude is still apparent in Ulm's review of the Czech *Zauberflöte* performed on December 1, 1861.[13] Although it was written a mere two months later, Ulm's review of the next Czech *Zauberflöte* performance (on January 25, 1862) exudes a more critical stance toward the Czech opera company, and this changed attitude likely had to do with the plan, announced on January 21, 1862, to build the Provisional Theater, which angered many Prague supporters of the German theater who feared that the competition of two opera companies would weaken the German company at the Estates Theater.[14] Although he found Czech performances admirable and on a par with German productions in earlier reviews, Ulm now stresses that the Czech opera company is dependent on the German ensemble and complains that the quality of the Czech performance is below that of German performances. The "low" quality of the Czech *Zauberflöte* is a particularly sore issue, Ulm claims, since the Czech company is now receiving a state subvention of 300 gulden, which the Bohemian government approved for performances of Czech operas in the fall of 1861.[15] Thus, in his earlier evaluations of the Czech performances of *Die Zauberflöte*, Ulm expressed a somewhat patronizing but generally supportive view, not dissimilar from German reviews of Czech performances published between the late eighteenth and mid-nineteenth centuries. But once the Czech theater sought to make itself independent, Ulm became more spiteful and irritable – a transformation that was to intensify within Prague's German community in the following decades.

---

[11] *Bohemia*, December 12, 1850.

[12] The difficulties faced by supporters of Czech performances in Prague are described in Teuber, *Geschichte*, vol. 3, 571–73.

[13] *Bohemia*, December 3, 1861.

[14] *Bohemia*, January 25, 1862. On the German opposition to an independent Czech theater in Prague, see Teuber, *Geschichte*, vol. 3, 577–78.

[15] On the subvention, see Teuber, *Geschichte*, vol. 3, 576.

German Bohemian fears of the rise of Czech culture intensified by the 1880s, as is clearly illustrated in Oscar Teuber's *Geschichte des Prager Theaters*, published in three volumes between 1883 and 1888. In the study, Teuber mainly focuses on the history of German theater in Prague. In the third volume, published in 1888, Teuber points out he did not feel it was his task to provide "an exhaustive depiction" ("eine erschöpfende Darstellung") of the history of Czech theater and that his book presents "naturally and in the first place" ("selbstverständlich und in erster Linie") the history of German theater in Prague, "which has always remained in the closest intimate relationship with the great German world of theater [despite] its exposed [geographical] location" ("das sich auf exponirtem Posten stets in innigster Verbindung mit der grossen deutschen Bühnenwelt erhalten").[16] The feeling of a threat from Czech culture is prominent in the second volume's preface (published in 1885), where Teuber claims that the history of Prague's German theater deserves attention "particularly today, when it struggles for survival under unfavorable social and national circumstances and under the threat of powerful competition from the Slavic cultural institution, that originated only recently and drew most of its inspiration from [German theater]" ("gerade heute, wo sie unter ungünstigen socialen und nationalen Verhältnissen, bedroht von der mächtigen Concurrenz einer neu erstandenen und im Grunde doch aus ihr hervorgewachsenen Kulturanstalt, den Kampf um ihr Dasein kämpft").[17] In the 1885 volume, Teuber's fear about the status of German culture in Prague was likely affected by the second opening of the Czech National Theater in 1883 (the theater first opened in 1881 but burned down a few months later). The lavishly decorated building not only dwarfed the Provisional Theater but also made more prominent the space shortage and outdatedness of the old Estates Theater, which was used exclusively by the German company after the Czech company split in 1862. Prague's German community had sought to build a new German theater in the Bohemian capital since the 1870s, but the construction took place only between 1886 and 1888, primarily thanks to private donations, not state support, which was refused by the Czech-dominated regional government, as Teuber does not forget to emphasize.[18] The New German Theater (Neues deutsches Theater) eventually opened on January 5, 1888, with Wagner's *Die Meistersinger*, a fitting festive counterpart to Smetana's *Libuše*, which inaugurated both the 1881 and 1883 completions of the National

---

[16] Teuber, *Geschichte*, vol. 3, 18.   [17] Teuber, *Geschichte*, vol. 2, x–xi.
[18] Teuber, *Geschichte*, vol. 3, 835–41.

Theater. The two opera houses continued to operate in competition and cooperation until 1945, when the New German Theater was taken over by Czech revolutionaries and has operated as a Czech institution ever since (the Estates Theater was occupied by a Czech mob and incorporated into the National Theater in 1920).

The Municipal House and Czech Cultural Politics in the Early Twentieth Century

The involvement of cultural institutions with national politics further intensified in the early twentieth century as illustrated in the history of the second major concert hall in Prague, located in the Municipal House (Obecní dům). The building was initiated by the Czech civic organization Municipal Union (Měšťanská beseda), which looked for new spaces to host social and cultural activities of the Czech public in Prague. Eventually the Prague city council, seeking to represent and promote Czech social and cultural life, agreed to finance the design and construction, which took place between 1905 and 1911. The concept of the building was strongly anti-German, as its location was close to the German House and Casino and the main German boulevard of the city, the Na příkopě (Am Graben) Street. Music was not a component of the building's initial concept, but eventually a plan for a large concert hall was included at the suggestion of Czech composer and conductor Oskar Nedbal.[19] After the building's completion, the new concert hall became the main seat of the Czech Philharmonic, partially since the Rudolfinum continued to be viewed as German and somehow anti-Czech. The distinction from the "German" Rudolfinum is emphasized in the contrasting decorations of the Municipal House concert hall. Whereas the Rudolfinum features classicizing motives, which the founders likely thought of as appropriate and neutral but Czech nationalists perceived as ignoring the interests of Prague's Czech population, the Municipal House hall is dominated by Ladislav Šaloun's sculptural representations of Dvořák's *Slavonic Dances* and Smetana's *Vyšehrad*; the balconies, furthermore, are decorated by medallions of composers considered either ethnic Czechs or somehow linked to Czechness (this strongly contrasts with the choice of composer statues on the roof of the

---

[19] Hana Svatošová, "Maják českosti Prahy nebo Dům u zakopaných miliónů?: Idea a koncepce Obecního domu" in *Město a jeho dům: Kapitoly ze stoleté historie Obecního domu hlavního města Prahy (1901–2001)*, ed. Hana Svatošová and Václav Ledvinka (Prague: Obecní dům, 2002), 75–96 (88).

Rudolfinum). According to official policies, the interior of the building was closed to German organizations and the use of German was banned.[20] That the ban was taken seriously is obvious from the fact that in 1933 the Czechoslovak Mozart Society (which was officially bilingual) was fined for using a Czech and German booklet to accompany a Czech Philharmonic concert featuring German conductor Gustav Brecher conducting the music of Haydn, Mozart, and Beethoven.[21]

Public Music Institutions, Local Patriotism, and German Nationalism in Teplice

Teplice represents a fascinating counterpart to the development of music institutions in Prague: Teplice's institutions were initiated by aristocratic patronage and later relied on public support, though this transformation proceeded at a different pace than in Prague (see also Chapter 12). The shift to public sponsorship in Teplice was accompanied by an intensification of patriotic rhetoric, which nevertheless did not reach the same nationalistic ferociousness as in Prague. Musical productions in Teplice were for a long time sponsored by the local nobility, the house of Clary-Aldringen. The first public performances took place in the Garden House, built by architect Christian Lagler for Franz Wenzel Clary-Aldringen in 1732. Franz Wenzel's son Johann Nepomuk built a theater next to his Teplice castle; the theater opened in 1789 and hosted theatrical companies that performed plays and opera performances for the local population and the spa guests, mostly in the summer months.[22] The first historically documented troupe to perform in the theater was Prague's Patriotic Theater company under the leadership of Anton Grams. Grams led the company in 1795–97 and then again from 1799 until approximately late 1802; during Grams's second stint as a theater director, his company visited Teplice in the summers of 1801 and 1802, performing both spoken plays and German operas, including Mozart's *Die Zauberflöte*.[23] Numerous other theater companies performed in the Clary-Aldringen theater in the following decades, most

---

[20] Václav Ledvinka, "Politika a Obecní dům v průběhu století," in *Město a jeho dům*, 225–44 (229).

[21] Jan Škoda, "Život Prahy v Obecním domě v letech 1912–1948," in *Město a jeho dům*, 143–67 (156–57).

[22] For an overview of the castle theater's history, see Jana Michlová, *Zámecké divadlo v Teplicích: Divadelní cedule ve sbírce knihovny muzea*, 2nd rev. ed. (Teplice: Regionální muzeum v Teplicích, 2014).

[23] Michlová, *Zámecké divadlo v Teplicích*, 8.

prominently Johann August Stöger's company from Prague's Estates Theater in 1835, the year when Teplice hosted a meeting of Austrian Emperor Ferdinand I, Russian Tsar Nicolas I, and Prussian King Friedrich Wilhelm III.[24]

Teplice also became a center of orchestral music, which was more independent of aristocratic patronage than opera. One of the earliest discussions of instrumental music production in Teplice appears in 1802's *Allmanach für die Badegäste zu Teplitz*, the first such printed prospect for spa guests, which continued to appear annually in the following decades. The *Allmanach* points out that "music by wind instruments" ("eine Musik von blasenden Instrumenten") was performed in a local park daily, and that every Wednesday the Clary-Aldringen theater hosted "musical concerts" ("musikalische Konzerte").[25] Earlier than in Prague, Teplice representatives also strived to establish a regular orchestra supported from public funds. Debates about the orchestra's organization took place in the late 1820s and the 1830s, and on April 14, 1838, the regional governor's office in Litoměřice (Leitmeritz) decreed that Teplice should have a public orchestra partially financed from fees collected from spa guests.[26] The negotiations about the proportion of spa fees provided for the salaries for the orchestral musicians involved Teplice mayor Joseph Wolfram, himself a notable composer (see Chapter 12).[27] In late 1838 and early 1839, Wolfram wrote two letters to Litoměřice authorities arguing for an increase in the musicians' pay. Despite initial financial difficulties, the orchestra continued to be very active in the following decades and even received occasional praise from critics, such as an 1840 anonymous correspondent of the Prague journal *Bohemia*:[28]

I have found the music in Teplice so splendid that I need to say a few words to you about it. There is an orchestra here that could match those in some capital cities; the rare case has often occurred here that the audience demanded the repeat of overtures. . . . Many artists from abroad have confirmed that the orchestra is very accomplished and accommodating in accompanying.

Die Musik habe ich in Teplitz so trefflich gefunden, dass ich Ihnen noch einige Worte darüber sagen muss. Es ist hier ein Orchester, das manchen hauptstädtischen nicht nachzustehen braucht; öfter hat sich hier das Seltene

---

[24] Michlová, *Zámecké divadlo v Teplicích*, 6.

[25] *Allmanach für die Badegäste zu Teplitz, auf das Jahr 1802* (Prague: Gerzabek, [1802]), 78 and 80.

[26] Roman Dietz and Lenka Přibylová, *Severočeská filharmonie Teplice: Historie a současnost* (Teplice: Severočeská filharmonie Teplice, 2018), 25.

[27] Dietz and Přibylová, *Severočeská filharmonie*, 28–29.   [28] *Bohemia*, September 18, 1840.

ereignet, dass das Publikum die Wiederholung von Ouverturen verlangte. . . .
Mancher fremder Künstler hat bestätigt, wie fein und nachgiebig dies Orchester
begleitet.

Both the Teplice theater and orchestra continued to rely on the Clary-
Aldringen castle theater as the principal venue until the early 1870s. In
May 1874, the new Teplice municipal theater opened thanks to funds from
the city, which also operated and financed the now fully public institution
(with the exception of the 1876–77 season, when the city leased the theater to
a private company).[29] The municipal theater had ambitious opera programming – in the first few months of operation until the end of 1874, the
company produced twenty operas, starting with Weber's *Der Freischütz*.
The Teplice orchestra came to serve as the theater orchestra as well, and its
symphonic repertoire gradually became both standardized and historicizing,
as illustrated by the "historical concert of the Teplice spa orchestra" ("historische Konzert der Teplitzer Curkapelle") on July 8, 1883. The music director
Carl Peters led the orchestra in the performance of works by Handel, Bach,
Gluck, Haydn, Mozart, Beethoven, Weber, Meyerbeer, Rossini, Schubert,
Schumann, Mendelssohn, Verdi, Gounod, and Wagner.[30] The historicist
and canonizing orientation of the spa orchestra becomes more prominent
under the directors Karl Wosahlo (1886–98) and Franz Zeischka (1898–
1906). Among Wosahlo's most celebrated achievements was the 1886 revival
of Andreas Romberg's 1809 choral setting of Schiller's poem *Das Lied von
der Glocke*.[31] Zeischka continued the historicist trend, for example by programming all of Beethoven's symphonies in his first season, but he also
invited famous contemporaneous composers, such as Felix Weingartner and
Richard Strauss, to present their works.[32]

Similar to the developments in Prague, the emergence of modern public
music institutions in Teplice had ideological and political overtones. At the
same time, because Teplice was a regional spa and predominantly German-
speaking, the use of music institutions for political purposes was not as
intense and aggressive as in Prague. In the early nineteenth century, the
activities of music institutions resonated with various forms of Bohemian
patriotism. Thus, the only documented production of Mozart's *La clemenza di Tito* (as *Titus der Gütige*) in nineteenth-century Teplice was, just as

---

[29] For the theater's early history and repertoire, see Dana Pospíchalová, *První městské divadlo
v Teplicích v letech 1874–1878 aneb pýcha města a jeho obyvatel* (Ústí nad Labem: Univerzita
J. E. Purkyně, 2005).

[30] For the entire program, see Dietz and Přibylová, *Severočeská filharmonie*, 37.

[31] For a review, see *Teplitz-Schönauer Anzeiger*, April 24, 1886.

[32] Dietz and Přibylová, *Severočeská filharmonie*, 40–45.

in Prague, linked to pro-Habsburg patriotism. The performance, on August 30, 1821, commemorated the 1813 Battle of Chlumec (Kulm), in which the coalition of Austria, Prussia, and Russia defeated the French.[33] In the following decades, various commentators connected Teplice music institutions to Bohemian patriotism more explicitly. The 1831 *Teplitzer Almanach* points out that many of the musicians active in the city are graduates of the Prague Conservatory, which supplies performers for most cities inland and abroad, thus reflecting the fact that Prague is "the true seat of the arts" ("der eigentliche Sitz der Künste") and Bohemia possesses "a populous troop of Apollo's sons and daughters" ("ein zahlreiches Heer von Söhnen und Töchtern Apollo" (on the Prague Conservatory, see Chapter 17).[34] The anonymous author of the 1840 letter about Teplice in *Bohemia* expresses similar sentiments when he writes that the Teplice music director Karl Schmit and the members of his orchestra are Bohemian natives and mostly students of the Prague Conservatory, which confirms the old saying that "Bohemia is the land of music" ("Böhmen ist das Land der Musik"). A more regional form of patriotism was the cultivation of the memory of Joseph Wolfram. An expression of these sentiments appears in a review of the Teplice Men's Chorus concert on March 18, 1887, in which the critic calls for the revival of Wolfram's music, especially excerpts from his opera *Die Normannen in Sicilien*, in the next season and presents this wish as coming from "numerous music friends" ("viele Musikfreunde").[35]

German nationalist sentiments become associated with Teplice culture in the late nineteenth century. For example, the reviewer of Peters's 1883 "historical" concert claims: "How proud can we Germans be of the development of music, the most German of arts!" ("Wie stolz können wir Deutschen auf die Entwicklung der deutschesten der Künste, der Musik, sein!").[36] German-Bohemian commentators also attempted to incorporate Teplice into general developments of German music. An example of these tendencies is Alois John's 1890 article "Richard Wagner in deutsch-böhmischen Bädern" (Richard Wagner in the German-Bohemian Spas) about the composer's visits to Teplice in 1834 (when working on *Das Liebesverbot*), 1842 (when sketching *Tannhäuser*), and 1843, and to another Bohemian spa, Mariánské Lázně (Marienbad), in 1845 (when

---

[33] The performance is documented in a theater poster, preserved in the Teplice Museum. See Michlová, *Zámecké divadlo v Teplicích*, 84.

[34] *Teplitz im Jahre 1830 oder: Almanach für die Teplitzer Kurgäste auf das Jahr 1831* (Prague: Gerzabek, 1831), 16–17.

[35] *Teplitz-Schönauer Anzeiger*, March 23, 1887.   [36] *Teplitz-Schönauer Anzeiger*, July 11, 1883.

sketching the plots of *Lohengrin* and *Die Meistersinger von Nürnberg*).[37] John claims that it was the people, nature, and folk culture in the region around Teplice and Mariánské Lázně that inspired Wagner's works. Even before Wagner, John asserts, western Bohemia, which he views as a purely German region, inspired the German operas *Hans Heiling* and *Der Freischütz*:[38]

Bohemia is the homeland of both [operas], the pleasant valley of the Eger [Ohře] river with its weather-beaten rocks, the bleak loftiness of the Böhmerwald [Šumava], the Angel [Úhlava] river valley, east of the Osser [Ostrý] hills. That is the backdrop for the Wolf's Glen [scene,] in which free bullets are cast, which led to a trial in the nearby town of Taus [Domažlice], the records of which were used in Weber's opera.

Beider Heimat ist Böhmen, das anmutige Thal der Eger in seinem verwitterten Felsgestein und die düstere Erhabenheit des Böhmerwaldes, das Thal der Angel, östlich vom Ossagebirge. Da ist der Schauplatz der "Wolfsschlucht," wo die Freikugeln gegossen wurden, welche zu einem im nahen Städchen Taus geführten Processe führten, dessen Acten zu Webers Tondichtung benützt wurden.

Thus, the choice of *Der Freischütz* as the first opera to be performed in the new municipal theater in 1874 and of *Die Meistersinger* as the inaugural work for the second Teplice theater, constructed after the fire of the first and completed in 1924, must have resonated with national and patriotic sentiments specific to north Bohemian Germans. Also, the widely publicized 1912 Teplice production of Siegfried Wagner's opera *Banadietrich*, the first performance of which was attended by the composer himself, had both nationalistic and regional connotations. The opera was based, as a Teplice newspaper commentator signed E. Wisshaupt pointed out, on a north Bohemian German legend from the Varnsdorf (Warnsdorf) region, which was one of the reasons why the writer exhorted his Teplice compatriots to be "truly national and unselfish regarding our holy German art" ("auf dem Gebiete unserer heiligen deutschen Kunst wirklich national und selbstlos") and greet the opera and its author "warmly and with thankful feelings" ("warm und mit dankbaren Gefühlen").[39]

Czech music became prominent in Teplice only in the 1920s, after the creation of Czechoslovakia, when the Czech minority was allowed to use the theater on certain days. In the 1930s, moreover, the German ensemble

---

[37] *Teplitz-Schönauer Anzeiger*, March 22, 29, and April 5, 1890.
[38] *Teplitz-Schönauer Anzeiger*, March 22, 1890.
[39] *Teplitz-Schönauer Anzeiger*, September 2, 1911.

performed German adaptations of Czech operas, starting with Dvořák's *Rusalka* on January 9, 1931. A watershed in the history of Teplice public music institutions came in 1945 when most German citizens were forcefully expelled. The Teplice theater became an exclusively Czech institution and reopened with a performance of Smetana's *Prodaná nevěsta* ("The Bartered Bride") on June 24, 1945. It took several years for the symphonic orchestra to form once again, and the first concert of the new Czech ensemble took place only in 1948.

Similar to Prague, public music institutions in Teplice reflected the changing social and political situation in Bohemia throughout the nineteenth and early twentieth centuries. Both cities developed institutions devoted to opera and symphonic music in connection to the rise of patriotic sentiments in the late eighteenth century, and these institutions embraced sharp nationalistic viewpoints throughout the nineteenth century. Both Czech and German institutions also gradually transformed into musical museums devoted to reverent presentations of supposedly timeless "masterworks" and thus significantly contributed to the construction of operatic and symphonic canons. The tension between Czechs and Bohemian Germans came to a violent cataclysm during the Nazi occupation, which eventually led to a complete destruction of German music institutions in what became exclusively Czech lands. Only in the last few decades have Czech public institutions begun to uncover and re-evaluate the multicultural heritage of the country, as reflected, for example, in the return of the bust of Mozart to the facade of Prague's former New German Theater (now State Opera) in 2020 and in the revival of Wolfram's once famous opera *Bergmönch* at the 2022 Beethoven Festival in Teplice.

10 | The Emergence of a Czech National Opera
Tradition in the Nineteenth Century

JIŘÍ KOPECKÝ

The core works of what is considered the Czech national opera tradition
were created in the late nineteenth century, a time when Czech cultural and
political elites were shaping modern Czech identity and cultural institutions.
These works were, and still mostly are, viewed as both establishing national
values and representing the Czech nation internationally. Throughout
Central Europe, and particularly in the Habsburg lands, opera became an
important tool for expressing the political interests of various national
groups. This chapter explores the formation of the Czech operatic tradition
by focusing on three aspects: the connection between opera and the establishment of the modern Czech language and poetry; the search for suitable
subjects that would both incorporate national viewpoints and attract Czech
and non-Czech audiences; and the ways in which Czech librettists and
composers both familiarized themselves with the conventions of various
operatic types and approached them from unique perspectives.

Czech Becomes an Operatic Language

The first opera performances in Czech took place in the eighteenth century,
though most of these events were rather isolated. Among the most widely
discussed eighteenth-century operatic performance in Czech was the 1794
production of Mozart's *Die Zauberflöte* in a translation by Václav Thám
(Wenzel Tham), presented at the Patriotic Theater in Prague. The production
coincided with the attempts by some Bohemian intellectuals to prevent the
complete disappearance of Czech language and culture due to the
Germanization processes initiated by the Habsburg government's centralization policies under Maria Theresa and Joseph II. An expression of these
attempts is František Martin Pelcl's (Franz Martin Pelzl) 1793 speech delivered
at his appointment as the first professor of the Czech language at the Prague

This chapter was translated from Czech to English by Martin Nedbal.

Funding for this study was provided by the Czech Science Foundation (GAČR) under the
project "Libuše Sings. Musico-Dramatic Adaptations of the Mythological Subject in Central
European Culture between the Seventeenth and Twentieth Centuries" (20-14534S).

university, titled "Akademische Antrittsrede über den Nutzen und Wichtigkeit der Böhmischen Sprache" ("Academic Appointment Speech about the Need for and Importance of the Czech Language") – the speech was delivered in German because Czech was not a language used in universities then.[1] In regard to future developments of Czech opera, the most significant part of Pelcl's speech was his point about the superior musicality of the Czech language and Czech speakers:

...Czechs have delicate ears, and that is also the source of their musical talent. Music teachers are certain that they advance more rapidly with Czech-speaking pupils than others. It has also been noted that there are more musicians in Czech villages than in German villages.

...der Böhme [hat] ein sehr delikates Ohr ... und daher rührt auch sein Talent für die Musik. Die Musikmeister versichern, dass sie mit einem Schkolar, der böhmisch spricht, in weniger Zeit weiter, als mit einem andern kommen. Man bemerkt auch, dass es in den böhmischen Ortschaften weit mehr Musikanten giebt, als in deutschen.

The most important incentive for creating Czech-language operas came in the 1820s, when Prague's Estates Theater initiated regular Czech performances. At first, most operas performed in Czech were adaptations of foreign works. First came the Czech adaptation of Joseph Weigl's *Die Schweizerfamilie*, which was performed on December 28, 1823. Other important works of the Central European repertoire followed, including *Der Freischütz* in 1824 and *Don Giovanni* in 1825. Czech operatic adaptations from the 1820s were not exact translations of the original works and often aimed at making the plot more relatable to Czech audiences. In his Czech adaptation of *Die Schweizerfamilie*, for example, Karel Simeon Macháček initially wanted to transfer the plot to Slovakia and call the work "Tatranská rodina" ("A Family from the Tatra Mountains") but then merely transferred the plot from Germany to Bohemia.[2] Similarly, in his Czech adaptation of *Der Freischütz*, Jan Nepomuk Štěpánek, also known as the author of the first Czech translation of *Don Giovanni*, changed the main protagonists' names from Max and Agathe to Liborin and Lidunka, thus making the opera more appealing to the Czech public.[3]

---

[1] See the facsimile of the document in "František Martin Pelcl: Akademická nástupní řeč o užitečnosti a důležitosti češtiny," ed. Dušan Šlosar and Miloš Štědroň, in *Sborník prací Filozofické fakulty brněnské univerzity*, H, Řada hudebněvědná 37–38 (1988): [67]–94 (80).

[2] Milan Pospíšil, *Švýcarská rodina v Praze. Opera a její libreto / Die Schweizerfamilie in Prag. Die Oper und ihr Libretto* (Prague: Divadelní ústav, 2021), 62–63.

[3] For the poster of the first performance, see Stanislav Jareš and Tomislav Volek, *Dějiny české hudby v obrazech od nejstarších památek do vybudování Národního divadla* (Prague: Supraphon, 1977), unpaginated, no. 319.

These adaptations of pre-existing works laid the foundation for original Czech operas, several of which were premiered in the 1820s and 1830s, starting with *Dráteník* ("The Tinker"), by František Škroup (music) and Josef Krasoslav Chmelenský (libretto), in 1826. The opera's simple love story was imbued with national elements particularly in the figure of the tinker, an itinerant worker from Slovakia who confirms the ideal of a friendship between the Czechs and the Slovaks when he sings that "Czechs and Slovaks are brothers" ("Slováku bratr Čech") in the second-act finale (No. 15). The other characters, too, engage in nationalist rhetoric, such as in the second-act sextet (No. 14), where they sing: "Český hoch k němu dívčina česká, / Kdo lepšího co na světě zná?" ("Czech boy with a Czech girl, / Does anyone know anything better in the world?"). Škroup followed with two more operas set to librettos by Chmelenský. The most ambitious was *Libušin sňatek* ("Libuše's Marriage") from 1835, which Škroup likely foresaw as a work that would be used during the 1836 Bohemian coronation of Ferdinand V, and possibly also the coronation of Franz Joseph I, which never took place. Because he postponed the premiere of the entire work, possibly in anticipation of having it accepted as a coronation opera, *Libušin sňatek* never became a Czech repertoire piece. Thus, apart from *Dráteník*, Škroup's most famous work is the song *Kde domov můj* ("Where Is My Home"), originally written for Josef Kajetán Tyl's 1834 musical play *Fidlovačka* and later used as the Czech national anthem.

With the translations and original librettos of the 1820s also came the need to figure out what kind of poetic language would be most appropriate for Czech opera. Czech librettists initially used two different metric systems: "syllabotonic," where poetic feet are determined by word accents, and *časomíra*, where poetic feet are determined by both accents and lengths of syllables (see also Chapter 5). Proponents of the *časomíra* system hoped to imitate the poetic meters of the ancient Greeks and differentiate their products from German poetry, which relied on the "syllabotonic" system and which some Czech writers, such as František Palacký and Pavel Josef Šafařík, therefore viewed as unmusical.[4] By the middle of the nineteenth century, most Czech writers came to the conclusion that *časomíra* relied on unnatural accentuation: Czech language places the heaviest emphasis on the first syllable of each word, but *časomíra* sometimes called for emphasizing other syllables, which makes it sound awkward to modern Czech

---

[4] See Martin Nedbal, "František Šír's First Czech Translation of Mozart's Final *Opera Buffa* and the Reception of *Così fan tutte* in Prague 1791–1831," *Divadelní revue* 27, no. 2 (Fall 2016): 63.

speakers. *Časomíra*, nevertheless, was the system used in many librettos set to music by František Škroup. In *Dráteník*, Škroup followed the *časomíra* principles by placing the elongated (but not necessarily accentuated) syllables on the downbeats. Although most of *Libušin sňatek* is set according to Chmelenský's *časomíra* text, Škroup abandoned the stiff poetic meters and used more declamatory inflections in Act 1, Scene 7 – the moment when Libuše prophesies to her retinue where her future husband, the founder of Bohemia's first royal dynasty, will be found.[5] Although this moment prefigures later operas, particularly Bedřich Smetana's *Libuše*, the awkwardness of the poetic language in the rest of the work likely contributed to the fact that this (and other Czech operas by Škroup) did not enter the repertoire of Czech companies that emerged during the liberalization of the 1860s. The lack of clarity about proper accentuation of operatic Czech also may have contributed, together with the reliance on antiquated Mozartian musical language, to the failure of composer Josef Leopold Zvonař to have his opera *Záboj* (composed 1859–62) produced at the first independent Czech theater institution, the Provisional Theater in the 1860s, despite the efforts of Smetana and the critic Jan Neruda to promote the work.

The initial fervor with which Czech writers produced opera librettos gradually died down. This, together with the controversies about the poetic system, the limited number of Czech performances, and the fact there were fewer elite Czech than German opera goers in Prague, led to a situation in which several Bohemian authors turned to German librettos. For example, Škroup set several German texts throughout his career. His most successful work was *Der Meergeuse* ("The Sea Gueux" – libretto by Carl Johann Hickel), which was positively received in Prague, was performed throughout the Habsburg lands, and had an enthusiastic reception in Rotterdam, where Škroup worked as opera director at the end of his life. Another prominent Bohemian composer of German operas was Johann Friedrich Kittl, who achieved his greatest success with *Bianca und Giuseppe oder die Franzosen vor Nizza* (premiered on February 19, 1848), based on a libretto by Richard Wagner, with whom Kittl collaborated during the composition process. The work is clearly inspired by Meyerbeer's *Les Huguenots* and takes place during the French Revolution, which made it timely when it premiered, just a few weeks before revolutions broke out in Central Europe.

---

[5] See Josef Plavec, *František Škroup* (Prague: Melantrich, 1941), VII–VIII (musical examples); and Michal Fránek and Jiří Kopecký, "Rukopisy královédvorský a zelenohorský a česká opera" in *Rukopisy královédvorský a zelenohorský v kultuře a umění*, vol. 2, ed. Dalibor Dobiáš (Prague: Academia, 2019), 940.

The march from the opera was used by the Prague revolutionary guard during the uprising of 1848. Because of the rising nationalistic tensions and the segregation of Prague's culture into Czech and German camps beginning in the 1860s, Škroup's and Kittl's operas and their activities as promoters of Wagner in the 1850s have been mostly overlooked by Czech critics and musicologists.

The "Declamation" Controversies

The 1860s were dominated by the activities of Smetana, whose works significantly influenced debates about the rhythm and accentuation of vocal lines in Czech opera, a topic Czech historians usually refer to as debates about declamation (*deklamace*). The sudden emergence of an independent Czech opera company in Prague (prior to the foundation of the Provisional Theater, Czech opera performances were much less frequent than German ones and were often limited to matinees and holidays) led to an intense demand for original Czech works, which Czech composers and librettists initially struggled to meet. Furthermore, their works became the subject of intense debates which also encompassed reactions to Wagnerian innovations.

For example, after the premiere of Karel Bendl's opera *Břetislav* in 1870, Prague critic August Wilhelm Ambros complained that the libretto did not present a "coherent drama" ("souvislé drama").[6] Bendl's librettist Eliška Krásnohorská reacted in an open letter where she explained that Czech composers and librettists were not yet ready for a systematic use of Wagner's methods.[7] At the same time, she identified with Wagnerian views when she wrote that "poets need to be musicians and musicians poets, only then will they create . . . a perfect musical drama" ("básník musí být hudebníkem a hudebník básníkem, jen pak utvoří . . . dokonalé drama hudební").[8] The passage in which Krásnohorská urges librettists to use words sparingly and thus allow composers to develop their talent resembles Wagner's concept of "sounding silence" ("das tönende Schweigen").[9]

---

[6] August Wilhelm Ambros, "První provozování Bendlovy opery 'Břetislav' dne 18. září 1870," *Hudební listy* 1 (1870): 243.

[7] Eliška Krásnohorská, "Český básník a hudební drama," *Hudební listy* 1 (1870): 298–99.

[8] Krásnohorská, "Český básník a hudební drama," 301.

[9] Wagner used the term in a letter to Mathilde Wesendonck from October 12, 1858. See *Richard Wagner an Mathilde Wesendonk [sic], Tagebuchblätter und Briefe 1853–1871* (Berlin: Alexander Duncker, 1904), 68.

Although the work of librettists was not highly valued at the time, Krásnohorská showed that preparing a libretto was a demanding task because "two words [of a librettist] have to express as much as ten words of a dramatist" ("u něho [libretisty] obsahovat musí dvě slova tolik, co u dramatika deset slov").[10] Krásnohorská also claimed that to create an effective "melodic speech" ("melodická mluva") librettists needed to "excise each verse that they could not sing to themselves; preferably, they should be singing while writing, either aloud or in their minds, either famous melodies or such that they imagine at the moment" ("vyškrtne každý verš, jejž sám zazpívat nedovede; nejlépe, pak-li při psaní již zpívá, buď hlasitě neb v duchu, buď známé melodie nebo takové, jaké právě ve fantazii zrodí").[11] This idea resonates with what Smetana describes in an 1880 letter to his friend Josef Srb-Debrnov, where he claims that when he composes he walks around the room and enunciates the text until the words change to music.[12] In an 1871 series of articles, titled "O české deklamaci hudební" ("On Czech Musical Declamation"), Krásnohorská used excerpts from Smetana's *Prodaná nevěsta* ("The Bartered Bride") to illustrate incorrect accentuations and explain the principles of what she viewed as proper musical declamation in Czech.

Example 10.1 illustrates Smetana's faulty accentuation in the vocal line of Mařenka in Act 1 of *Prodaná nevěsta*. The musical setting of the first phrase contains several accents on syllables that are not accentuated in Czech. The unnatural accentuations are in **bold**: "Kdybych se co tak**ové**ho o tobě do**vě**děla" ("If I found out something like that about you"). The first part of the second phrase is accentuated naturally: "Krutou pomstychtivou zlobou" ("A fierce, vengeful spite"). However, another incorrect accent appears in the second part: "na tě bych za**ne**vřela" ("I would conceive for you"). Despite the faulty accentuation, Smetana's music is appealing and folk-like because the composer set words with multiple syllables to repeated pitches, which is a common trope in Czech folksongs.

Despite initial misunderstandings, Krásnohorská eventually became Smetana's exclusive librettist. Their first work, *Hubička* ("The Kiss" – premiered in 1876), allowed Smetana to regain favor with Czech audiences, after they had become discouraged by his previous works, *Dalibor* (1868) and *Dvě vdovy* ("The Two Widows" – 1874). Critics viewed *Hubička*'s main protagonist (Vendulka) as a close relative of the main character of

---

[10] Krásnohorská, "Český básník a hudební drama," 309.
[11] Krásnohorská, "Český básník a hudební drama," 309.
[12] Karel Teige, ed., *Dopisy Smetanovy* (Prague: Urbánek, 1896), 104.

Example 10.1: Mařenka's outburst of jealousy in *Prodaná nevěsta*, act 1, scene 2, mm. 522–30.

Smetana's most popular opera *Prodaná nevěsta* (Mařenka). At the same time, in *Hubička*, Smetana had already applied natural accentuation in Czech; he had fully mastered command of Czech declamation in *Libuše* (1869–72).

Krásnohorská's views about Czech musical accentuation were developed by late nineteenth-century Czech aesthetician Otakar Hostinský, who in his 1882 essay "O české deklamaci hudební" ("On Czech Musical Declamation"), published in the music journal *Dalibor*, presented a system of matching accents and lengths of syllables to the position and lengths of notes in measures.[13] Hostinský used the theory in his collaboration with Zdeněk Fibich, for whom he wrote the libretto to the 1884 opera *Nevěsta messinská* ("The Bride of Messina"). Fibich set the libretto according to the principles of "proper" declamation as defined by Hostinský. Hostinský's principles were used in music criticism as well. Hostinský's

---

[13] Otakar Hostinský, "O české deklamaci hudební," in *Hostinský: O hudbě*, ed. Miloslav Nedbal (Prague: Státní hudební nakladatelství, 1961), 257–97.

pupils Zdeněk Nejedlý and Otakar Zich, for example, ridiculed the operas of Antonín Dvořák for faulty declamation.[14] At the same time, Hostinský's views were also subjected to criticism by Leoš Janáček. Janáček claimed that Hostinský's essay diverts Czech opera away "from Slavonic national music" ("od slovanské národní hudby") and that what Hostinský deems "fully natural" according to his declamation principles is not always "pleasing" ("hezké").[15]

It took another decade before Czech composers got used to the strict declamation rules and managed to muster enough creative freedom to use the operatic Czech to effectively depict characters and situations in their works. One work that features both a natural accentuation of the sung text and an expert psychological characterization of the main protagonists is Fibich's 1895 *Bouře* ("The Tempest").[16] Janáček, too, developed a highly expressive method of accentuating Czech texts. In his operas, he combined his knowledge of contemporaneous operatic works by other authors with his interest in folksongs and his concept of "speech tunelets" (see Chapter 21) to create sensitive and expressive characterizations of human psychology. In act 1 of *Jenůfa*, the opera's eponymous heroine tries to calm down Laca, her lover's brother who has feelings for her, with the phrase "Potom tě mají mít rády" ("How could they like you [if you are like this]"), set to a melody that uses natural accentuation and has a calming quality (see Example 10.2).

In their attempts at proper musical settings of Czech texts, Czech composers were also drawing on Czech translations of foreign works for spoken theater, particularly Shakespeare's plays. Although Smetana did not finish his opera *Viola*, based on Shakespeare's *Twelfth Night*, later composers produced several works based on Shakespeare's dramas: in 1892 Karel Weis set the complete libretto to *Viola* that Smetana had not finished; Fibich based his 1895 *Bouře* on *The Tempest*; and Josef Bohuslav Foerster based his 1905 *Jessika* on *The Merchant of Venice*. Fibich's *Nevěsta messinská*, furthermore, was based on a shortened translation of Schiller's play *Die Braut von Messina* and thus went beyond the genre of so-called *Literaturoper*, which used a pre-existing work's subject but a newly written libretto and represented one of the first examples of

---

[14] In his study of the ideological campaign against Dvořák in the early twentieth century, Antonín Srba pointed out that most Czech composers had difficulty following the rules of proper declamation. See Antonín Srba, *Boj proti Dvořákovi* (Prague: Lidové družstvo, 1914), 71.

[15] Leoš Janáček, "Slovanstvo ve svých zpěvech," in *Leoš Janáček. Folkloristické dílo*, series 1, vol. 3-1, ed. Jarmila Procházková, Marta Toncrová, and Jiří Vysloužil (Brno: Editio Janáček, 2009), 1–8 (8). Originally published in *Hudební listy* 3, no. 10 (March 1, 1887): 73–78.

[16] See Jiří Kopecký, "Fibich's Path to Success in Prague's National Theater," in *Czech Music Around 1900*, ed. Lenka Křupková, Jiří Kopecký et al. (Hillsdale, NY: Pendragon Press, 2017), 145–66.

Example 10.2: Leoš Janáček, *Jenůfa*, act 1, scene 1.

operas that set theatrical texts directly. The sensitivity of Czech composers to operatic language is also illustrated in works such as Janáček's *Jenůfa* (see Chapter 21), based directly on the text to a play by Gabriela Preissová; in Fibich's experiments with melodrama (works with spoken text with orchestral accompaniment) in his trilogy *Hippodamie*, completed around 1890; and in Jaroslav Čelanský's 1897 opera *Kamilla*. Also in the late nineteenth century, Czech translations of foreign operas represented a significant aspect of the operatic repertoire. Numerous Czech critics considered Wagner's works untranslatable, but Václav Juda Novotný proved otherwise in his accomplished translations of *Lohengrin* (premiered in the National Theater in 1885), *Tannhäuser* (premiered in Plzeň (Pilsen) in 1888), and *Die Meistersinger von Nürnberg* (premiered in 1894 in the National Theater).

The Subjects for Czech Operas

The links between the emerging Czech opera tradition and national politics meant that Czech librettists and composers focused on subjects that were connected to the Czech lands and the Slavic world in general. Operas setting German and Italian librettos did not become a part of the Czech theater and were sometimes deliberately ignored. Besides the previously mentioned German works by Škroup and Kittl, other non-Czech operas created by composers active in the Czech lands were works by Italians settled in Prague (Giovanni Battista Gordigiani and Luigi Ricci), Czech-Italian composer Ladislav Zavertal, and Bendl's 1884 dramma lirico *Gina*.[17] Karel Weis's 1901 *Der polnische Jude*, first performed in German and based on a libretto by Victor Léon, caused controversy because the composer offered it to Prague's New German Theater after it was rejected by the National Theater. The opera then achieved an unprecedented success on international stages but was mostly ignored by the Czech public.

Works inspired by foreign literature encountered similar challenges. Although critics appreciated the efforts to engage the Czech public with such themes, operas of this nature were usually not received enthusiastically. This pattern held true for operas with Slavic themes, exemplified by Bendl's *Černohorci* ("The Montenegrins"), Dvořák's *Vanda* and *Dimitrij*, and Fibich's *Pád Arkuna* ("The Fall of Arcona"). Among the most extensive works based on foreign literature that saw infrequent performances were Škroup's German opera *Columbus*,[18] Fibich's *Hedy* (premiered 1896), adapted from Byron's *Don Juan*, and Dvořák's *Armida* (premiered 1904), based on Tasso's *Gerusalemme liberata*.[19] Only works based on Shakespeare's plays (see above) had a better reception. Czech audience tastes are also reflected in the reception history of Smetana's *Dvě vdovy*, based on a French comedy by Jean Pierre Mallefille. Whereas the first version (1874) failed, the second (1878) enjoyed success, likely because Smetana added characters and music inspired by Czech folk traditions (see also Chapter 13). The reception of operas with exotic subjects posed some challenges as well. Despite often being well received by audiences, they faced harsh criticism in the press. This is evident in Bendl's *Lejla*, set in Spain and first performed in 1868, and Josef Richard Rozkošný's veristic *Stoja* from 1894, set in Bosnia and Hercegovina.

The most typical and successful Czech operas were based on local topics, which invited the use of ancient chorales, folk-like elements, and

[17] Marta Ottlová and Milan Pospíšil, "Italská opera v kontextu české národní opery," *Miscellanea musicologica* 23 (1992): 53.

[18] Smetana tried to produce the work in the 1860s but was unsuccessful although the work's German libretto was not yet viewed negatively at that time. See Plavec, *František Škroup*, 391.

[19] Veronika Vejvodová, "'Jsem šťasten, že po tak dlouhém odpočinku opět mohu pracovati na tom, co já chci a ne, co chtějí jiní.' Ke genezi Dvořákovy Armidy," *Opus musicum* 47, no. 4 (2015): 36–57.

traditional Czech dances, such as polkas and furiants. Among the most famous works with folk themes are Smetana's 1866 *Prodaná nevěsta*, Vilém Blodek's 1867 *V studni* ("In the Well"), Bendl's 1874 *Starý ženich* ("The Old Bridegroom"), Dvořák's 1874 *Tvrdé palice* ("The Stubborn Lovers") and 1877 *Šelma sedlák* ("The Cunning Peasant"), Šebor's 1879 *Zmařená svatba* ("The Frustrated Wedding"), and Janáček's 1904 *Jenůfa*. Czech composers also created numerous historical operas, in which they often imbued historical settings with national mythologizing. Several operas touched on the fifteenth-century Hussite Wars. Fibich presented a positive view of the Hussites in his magical opera *Blaník* (1881), and the Hussites also appear in one of the tableaus at the end of Smetana's *Libuše*, in which the eponymous heroine prophesies major events of Czech history. A more somber approach to the Hussites appears in Bendl's 1892 tragic opera *Dítě tábora* ("The Child of the Encampment"). Other source materials for Czech historical operas were the Queen's Court and Green Mountain manuscripts, allegedly medieval documents containing Czech poetry that proved to be nineteenth-century forgeries. Two different operas, for example, were based on the story of Záboj, a mythological Czech hero who fought an invading foreign army. Záboj's story presented in the forged manuscripts contains scenes of singing to the accompaniment of a mythical lyre-like instrument, the *varyto*. As a result, both Záboj operas (Josef Leopold Zvonař's from the 1860s and Emanuel Chvála's from the early 1900s) make extensive use of the harp and unusual harmonies to illustrate the "ancient" instrument. The *varyto* also inspired the opening of Smetana's symphonic poem *Vyšehrad*.

Another prominent thematic group of Czech operas were those based on fairy tales. One of the most successful works in this vein from the period of the Provisional Theater was Hřímalý's 1872 *Zakletý princ* ("The Enchanted Prince"). The most prolific composer of fairy-tale operas was initially Rozkošný with his 1871 *Svatojánské proudy* ("St. John's Currents") and 1885's *Popelka* ("Cinderella"). At the turn of the century, however, Antonín Dvořák's two fairy-tale operas, 1899's *Čert a Káča* ("Kate and the Devil") and 1901's *Rusalka*, came to dominate this segment of the operatic repertoire. Although both Rozkošný's *Svatojánské proudy* and Dvořák's *Rusalka* feature water nymphs, Rozkošný's work is more in line with the earlier tradition of folk magical plays, whereas Dvořák's depiction of a *Tristan*-like love death in *Rusalka*'s conclusion was based in more recent Wagnerian music drama and therefore more appealing to modern audiences.

The subjects of Czech operas were also influenced by several operatic competitions. The first, announced in 1861 by Bohemian Count Harrach, sought two types of operas by composers born in the Bohemian crown-lands. The first category drew inspiration from the history of the Bohemian crownlands, while the second focused on "the Czechoslavic national life in Bohemia, Moravia, and Silesia."[20] The requirement was for the music to possess a "truly national character" ("ráz v pravdě národní") and be grounded in "the dutiful study of Czechoslavic national songs" ("na pilném studiu prostonárodních nápěvů českoslovanských"). Comedic works were encouraged to incorporate national dances, and composers of historical works were advised to utilize "ancient chorales as themes of choruses" ("starožitné chorály co themata ve sborech"). Reflecting the nascent state of Czech opera in the early 1860s, only three operas were submitted by the competition deadline in 1863, more than two years after the initial call for submissions. The winner, Smetana's *Braniboři v Čechách* ("The Brandenburgers in Bohemia"), was announced after an awkwardly lengthy deliberation in 1866, several months after the opera's celebrated premiere. The next competition, tied to the planned completion of the National Theater and with the deadline set for 1880, introduced criteria similar to Harrach's. Smetana's *Libuše* emerged as the undisputed winner, and this time, the decision was made within a few months. The criteria for the next National Theater opera competition, announced in 1882 in con-nection to the theater's second opening (following the building's destruc-tion by fire in 1881), shifted focus from national and political considerations to artistic and practical ones:

The subject should be drawn from Czech history or at least be familiar to Czech audiences. The best works to be rewarded will fulfill certain aesthetic criteria, fill an entire evening, and fit the production requirements of the National Theater stage.

Látka má být čerpána z českých dějin nebo alespoň blízká českému obecenstvu. Oceněny budou nejlepší práce, které vyhoví určitým požadavkům estetickým, vyplní celý jeden večer a budou schopny provozu na jevišti Národního divadla.[21]

This time, seven operas were submitted by the January 1883 deadline, and the committee chose Fibich's *Nevěsta messinská*. The final nineteenth-century opera competition coincided with the 1895 Czechoslavic Ethnographic Exhibition. The exhibition's organizers and visitors sought subjects drawn "from Czech life, either contemporary or historical"

---

[20] Jan hrabě Harrach, "Vypsání cen za nejlepší dvě české opery a náležité k nim texty," *Dalibor* 4, no. 6 (February 20, 1861): 45.

[21] Iva Horová, "Operní konkursy, vypsané v souvislosti s otevřením Národního divadla v Praze," *Hudební věda* 27 (1990): 156.

("ze života českého a sice buď nynějšího nebo historického").[22] Karel Kovařovic's *Psohlavci* ("The Dogheads") was declared the winner, although two other submissions, Fibich's *Šárka* and Foerster's *Eva*, also found a place in the Czech repertoire.

National Appropriation of Foreign Operatic Types

Throughout the nineteenth century, Czech opera composers drew on conventions from other national traditions, infusing them with individualistic features. Italian opera held immense appeal for Czech audiences, and the conventions of both Italian comic and tragic operas heavily influenced Czech composers. In the 1830s, Škroup modeled *Libušin sňatek* on the *opera seria* style, and later Czech composers explored the style of Italian *bel canto*, often tailoring their compositions to specific singers. Smetana, for instance, wrote Tausendmark's lyrical arias in *Braniboři v Čechách* with baritone Josef Lev in mind; Dvořák arranged Marina's coloratura aria in *Dimitrij* for Marie Sittová; and Fibich composed Fernando's aria in *Bouře* for Vladislav Florjanský. Many Czech composers also relied on Italianate structures, such as multipartite forms and double arias, along with the use of coloratura in comic operas and in secondary roles of serious ones. Czech composers also embraced multi-sectional finales, though they regarded them as both an Italian innovation and a typical feature of Mozart's operas. The Italian influence gained further prominence with the Czech premieres of Verdi's *Otello* (1888) and *Falstaff* (1893). However, operas that openly embraced Italian models faced criticism for their supposedly simplistic use of the orchestra and reliance on outdated forms, as observed in Šebor's works. This criticism extended to later compositions, such as Hanuš Trnneček's *Andrea Crini*, premiered in 1900, and Janáček's *Jenůfa*. Moreover, composers of serious operas often modeled their works on French grand opera, as exemplified in Dvořák's *Dimitrij*.[23]

Genre and style in opera, along with the reliance on specific national traditions, became the subject of many critical debates. Czech journalist Jan Neruda advocated for Czech theaters to present a varied repertoire aimed at cultivating all segments of the national community. This approach was exemplified in the output of Smetana, all of whose operas are in a distinct

---

[22] *Dalibor* 17, no. 45 (November 23, 1895): 347.
[23] Jan Smaczny, "Grand Opera among the Czechs," in *The Cambridge Companion to Grand Opera*, ed. David Charlton (New York: Cambridge University Press, 2003), 366–82.

style: *Braniboři v Čechách* could be considered a variant of grand opera, *Prodaná nevěsta* and *Hubička* are comic operas depicting peasant life, *Dalibor* is a heroic opera, *Libuše* a festive historical opera, *Dvě vdovy* a comic opera portraying the middle classes, *Tajemství* ("The Secret") a lyric opera, and *Čertova stěna* ("The Devil's Wall") a romantic comedy. Another perspective on the appropriate styles and types for Czech operatic repertoire was presented by Hostinský. He believed that Czech opera should aspire to the highest standards, presenting complex and demanding artworks that would elevate the taste of Czech audiences. His 1871 essay "'Wagnerianismus' a česká národní opera" ("'Wagnerianism' and Czech National Opera" – published in *Hudební listy*) defended Smetana's tragic opera, which had been disparaged by one of the composer's critics, František Pivoda, as "Dalibor Wagner," implying an un-Czech imitation of Wagnerian procedures.[24] For Hostinský, the operatic ideal embodied a modern music drama with a prominent use of the orchestra, leitmotivic technique, and the avoidance of word repetition, arias, ensembles, and choruses that interrupted the plot. Hostinský's concepts eventually found expression in Fibich's *Nevěsta messinská*. Despite ongoing criticism from Pivoda, who continued to disparage Hostinský's approaches as late as 1881,[25] Czech composers remained drawn to Wagnerian techniques, especially after Wagner's late music dramas were produced in Prague in the late 1880s.[26] During this period, Czech composers began blending Wagnerian principles with other operatic styles and traditions. This approach also drew on similar combinations found in works by foreign composers that were produced in Prague, most importantly Verdi's *Otello* and *Falstaff*, operas by Tchaikovsky and Massenet, and Goldmark's *Die Königin von Saba*. The combinatory approaches from around the turn of the century are well represented in the operatic output by Dvořák, Fibich, and Janáček.

Much like Czech composers of tragic operas grappling with Wagner's influence, those working on national comedies steeped in folksongs and dances, set in a village milieu, found themselves in competition with Smetana's *Prodaná nevěsta*. Several Czech composers attempted, with some degree of success, to explore alternative avenues. They achieved this by adopting continuous musical structures, deviating from rural settings – such

---

[24] Reprinted as Otakar Hostinský, *Bedřich Smetana a jeho boj o moderní českou hudbu* (Prague: Jan Laichter, 1901).

[25] František Pivoda, *O hudbě Wagnerově* (Prague: J. Otto, 1881).

[26] On the productions of Wagner's works under director Angelo Neumann at the New German Theater in the late 1880s, see Jitka Ludvová, *Až k hořkému konci: Pražské německé divadlo 1845–1945* (Prague: Divadelní ústav, 2012), 143.

Example 10.3: Antonín Dvořák, *Rusalka*, act 3, mm. 1303–7.

U-mí - rám   šťas-ten,   u-mí - rám   ve tvém   ob - je-tí!

as in Bendl's *Karel Škréta* set in Italy – and opting for an aristocratic milieu as seen in Dvořák's *Jakobín* ("The Jacobin"). Both comic and serious operas gravitated toward a symmetrical structure, typically comprising three acts with the second serving as a contrast to the outer two. The need to attain balance and symmetry across an entire opera led to meticulous considerations of musical ideas recurring throughout the entire work. In *Rusalka*, Dvořák used leitmotifs to unify the individual acts. This is exemplified by the recurring progression of major chords with roots an augmented fourth apart that underlie Rusalka's demand to the Witch to make her a human in act 1: "Tvoje moudrost všechno tuší, dej mi lidské tělo, lidskou duši" ("Your wisdom senses everything, give me a human body [and] a human soul"). The same chords underlie the Prince's death in the last scene but in reversed order (D-flat major – G major): "Umírám šťasten, umírám ve tvém objetí" ("I die happy, I die in your arms"; see Example 10.3).[27]

The development of the Czech operatic repertoire was a lengthy and complex process. Numerous late nineteenth-century Czech composers struggled with the challenge of identifying suitable librettos that would appeal to both critics and diverse audience groups while being composed in a poetic language that avoided artificiality. Setting Czech texts to music presented a multitude of challenges, ranging from determining the proper accentuation to exploring how music could effectively convey the characters' psychology and emotions, as well as reflect Czech society and its values. Only the most persistent authors managed to overcome these obstacles and earn recognition for their work (most prominently Karel Weis, Otakar Ostrčil, and Jaromír Weinberger).

[27] See also David Beveridge, "A Rare Meeting of Minds in Kvapil's and Dvořák's *Rusalka*: The Background, the Artistic Result, and Response by the World of Opera," in Křupková and Kopecký et al., *Czech Music Around 1900*, 61–80.

11 | Women and Opera in the Czech Lands

JUDITH MABARY

During the long nineteenth century, opera in Bohemia expanded from a German-language repertoire to include translated and newly written works in Czech as part of the nationalist movement that spanned much of Europe. Within this context, composers and writers became largely identified, whether by choice or assignment, either with the practice that drew subject matter from Czech myths, legends, and folk traditions or with the philosophy that Bohemian culture should explore the artistic monuments of other parts of the world in a "Europeanization of the Czech intelligentsia."[1] The same can be said for the female writers and singers gaining prominence in opera during this period.

Without question, women were instrumental in advocating for social and cultural change. As Kelly St. Pierre has argued, maintaining a healthy home, where children were taught the Czech language, was a manner by which domestic life contributed to the nineteenth-century nationalist cause.[2] For those with the means and the time, charitable work to support humanitarian organizations and, in several cases, to found and manage such organizations, was also within the female sphere. Several of the women discussed in this chapter were, in fact, heavily involved as activists in the feminist movement and in the success of establishments directed to providing opportunities and improving conditions for working women.

An obvious venue open to women in the public sphere was the opera. Composers often had a specific singer in mind when they constructed a character. Nevertheless, renowned female singers could encounter social hostility as performing in the theater or the opera house was still viewed by many as no place for a lady. Presumably, only those with questionable morals would pursue such a career. Consequently, to achieve success in opera during the long nineteenth century, women needed not only an

---

[1] Arne Novák, *Czech Literature*, trans. Peter Kussi (Ann Arbor: Michigan Slavic Publications, 1986), 210.
[2] Kelly St. Pierre, "Singing Women and the 'Woman Question' in the Czech Lands," in *Women in Nineteenth-Century Czech Musical Culture*, ed. Anja Bunzel and Christopher Campo-Bowen (New York: Routledge, 2024), 191–203 (192).

159

exceptional voice and a high level of artistry but the ability to negotiate the political territory. The latter is also true for those entering the world of opera by writing its texts.

Librettists

In the nineteenth century, several female librettists working in Prague gained recognition as among the best of their time, even when compared to their male counterparts. Nevertheless, the opinion remained that the libretto was an inferior type of literary activity, secondary to poetry and large-scale narratives. Yet the truth is more complicated. There was, indeed, a greater percentage of women writing texts for Czech opera than for the long-standing traditions in Italy, Germany, and France. The Czech language was also undergoing a revival, having been superseded by German under Habsburg control. Consequently, no long lineage of authors writing in Czech existed; no sizable body of literature in the vernacular was available as a source for libretti. The campaign to create a Czech literary culture able to compete on the world stage without such pre-existing sources opened the field to both men and women who supported the national revival in the latter half of the nineteenth century. Among the earliest of the female writers was Božena Němcová with her *Babička* ("The Grandmother"), published in 1855, whose success left no doubt that women were capable of creating nationalist literature for the public sphere.

To achieve and maintain a respectable standing among writers overall, it was advantageous for female authors to have already been recognized for writing in other mediums before adding the opera libretto to their repertoire. It was also useful to be from the social class that produced influential cultural and/or political members, which allowed a young artist to become acquainted with and even respected by Prague's cultural elite. In addition to their activities in the feminist and nationalist movements, the women discussed in this section had accumulated the literary experience, or in the case of librettist Anežka Schulzová, had the family connections and extensive exposure to literature, to be capable collaborators with the likes of Smetana, Dvořák, and Fibich.[3]

---

[3] One might be tempted to regard Fibich's librettist, Anežka Schulzová, as one who was selected only because of her intimate relationship with the composer. While this may have been part of the equation, Schulzová was also well educated in literature, domestic and international, and produced translations of foreign works and literary criticism during her career.

Eliška Krásnohorská (b. Alžběta Pechová, 1847–1926)

While opportunities taken early in life may not determine one's future direction, for Alžběta Pechová they were decisive. Supported by her mother after her father's death, as well as an uncle, older brothers, and friends, Alžběta was educated more broadly than was typical for a female of her time. Her family's status also brought her into contact with important members of the Prague intelligentsia, notably composer Karel Bendl (1838–97), the recipient of one of her early librettos, and prominent writer Karolina Světlá (1839–99), whose mentorship enabled associations with feminist literary circles. As an adult, Pechová dedicated herself to the Czech National Revival and changed her name to Eliška Krásnohorská ("beautiful mountain"), after "her imaginary father, the knight of Krásná hora."[4]

To better understand Krásnohorská's impact on Czech culture, one must look outside the world of opera. While she devoted the greater portion of her career to writing and translation, she was also active in promoting education and opportunities for women. She held a leadership position in the Women's Industrial Society (Ženský výrobní spolek), founded in 1871, whose aim was to "alleviate poverty among the female population through educational programs"[5] and to enable women to be gainfully employed and self-sufficient.[6] In addition, her editorial management of *Ženské listy* ("Women's Pages") allowed her to alter its focus toward a liberalist philosophy.[7] Finally, educational equality was advanced in 1890 with her founding of Minerva, the first preparatory school for women in Bohemia.

When Krásnohorská began writing librettos in the 1860s, composers were relatively inexperienced in setting the Czech language. Significant to remedying the problem was her 1871 article "O české deklamaci hudební" ("On Czech Musical Declamation"), in which she also criticized Smetana's

---

[4] Libuše Heczková, "Eliška Krásnohorská," in *Biographical Dictionary of Women's Movements and Feminisms: Central, Eastern, and South Eastern Europe, 19th and 20th Centuries*, ed. Francisca de Haan, Krassimira Daskalová, and Anna Loutfi (Budapest: Central European University Press, 2006), 263.

[5] Heczková, "Eliška Krásnohorská," 263.

[6] See "Ženský výrobní spolek český (1871–1972)," *Knihy znovunalezené*, published September 14, 2016, http://www.knihyznovunalezene.eu/cs/vlastnici/zensky-vyrobni-spolek.html, accessed March 25, 2024. See also St. Pierre, "Singing Women" for a full investigation of the Americký klub dám (AKD), a contemporaneous organization whose goals overlapped with those of the Women's Industrial Society.

[7] For additional information on Krásnohorská's efforts to achieve equal rights for women, see Veronika Tardonová, "Eliška Krásnohorská a *Ženské listy* (1873–1926)" (Bachelor's thesis, University of Pardubice, 2009); and Oleksandra Gorbina Gats, "Eliška Krásnohorská a její zápas o ženskou emancipaci" (Bachelor's thesis, Charles University, Prague, 2010).

text-setting in *Prodaná nevěsta* ("The Bartered Bride" – see also Chapter 10). The eminent composer heeded her evaluation, revised his approach in *Libuše*, and "took considerable pains over [the setting of text] in his later operas."[8] Thus began a productive collaboration on three works completed between 1876 and 1882.[9]

Allowed unusual freedom in her role as Smetana's librettist, Krásnohorská selected the subject matter (with one exception, *Viola*) and exerted some authority over voice types, placement of ensembles, and dramatic structure.[10] While her writing attracted criticism from her peers, mainly for what they perceived as a lack of drama, Smetana found it contained the type of musicality he needed. "I have become attached to your verses and to the music I feel instinctively to be in them. I can find this nowhere else."[11] According to Tyrrell, they also contained "situations and relationships, which ... touched a deep vein in him and brought to the surface some of his most personal utterances."[12]

The collaboration between the two began in 1871 with plans for *Viola*, which remained incomplete despite several attempts. Other works intervened, notably the operas *Dvě vdovy* ("The Two Widows"), *Hubička* ("The Kiss"), *Tajemství* ("The Secret"), and *Čertova stěna* ("The Devil's Wall"), the last three to librettos by Krásnohorská and representing a shift to Czech subject matter, which Tyrrell assessed was more congenial to Smetana's librettist, who had been reluctant to continue work on the foreign-based *Viola*.[13]

Smetana's reliance on his librettist is evident in that he rarely changed the work she sent him; when he did request alterations, he often met with considerable resistance. Nevertheless, their partnership was successful overall, until creative differences on key elements of *Čertova stěna* threatened to drive them apart. For the latter, Krásnohorská envisioned a serious conflict between the Church and the Devil; Smetana, however, was convinced of a comic treatment. While his librettist acquiesced, Smetana reversed his opinion and replaced the comic element with characters of

---

[8] John Tyrrell, *Czech Opera* (New York: Cambridge University Press, 1988), 107. The article also impacted Dvořák in his setting of Czech text, who, like Smetana, had worked according to German models.

[9] Krásnohorská also wrote libretti for five operas by Karel Bendl (*Lejla*, *Žena Vršovcova*, *Břetislav*, *Karel Škréta*, and *Dítě Tábora*) and one by Zdeněk Fibich (*Blaník*).

[10] Tyrrell, *Czech Opera*, 107, 109.

[11] Mirko Očadlík, ed., *Eliška Krásnohorská – Bedřich Smetana: vzájemná korespondence* (Prague: Topič, 1940), 119–20, as translated in Brian Large, *Smetana* (New York: Praeger Publishers, 1970), 331.

[12] Tyrrell, *Czech Opera*, 108.   [13] Tyrrell, *Czech Opera*, 108.

greater depth. Acting as both composer and librettist, he discarded much of the text Krásnohorská had worked against natural inclinations to provide.[14] Tyrrell concludes that "[she] did not, of course, know the extent of Smetana's illness and the fact that his changes were made not because he preferred his own musico-dramatic designs and conventions but because he was physically no longer capable of carrying out hers."[15] Yet this behavior was an exception. Their usual compatible relationship was made so by the "music" Smetana found in her texts.

Marie Červinková-Riegrová (1854–94)

With the advantages of belonging to an upper-middle-class family, Marie Riegrová benefited from an education and social environment conducive to becoming a writer and translator. Her father, František Rieger, was a prominent politician instrumental in the Czech nationalist movement; her mother, Marie Riegrová-Palacká, daughter of renowned historian František Palacký, became an important force in advocating for the poor through establishing kindergartens and promoting education for young women. Growing up in such a progressive household, Marie also became an advocate for women and girls less fortunate. In fact, her ambitions and those of Krásnohorská were similar in that both championed the belief that women should be able to work outside the home; at the same time, they faced the "trivializations, biases, biting, and acidity against intellectual working women in general."[16] Undeterred, they each supported the National Revival and tailored their writing to fulfilling their patriotic duty.

As a writer and convinced she had no talent for poetry, Červinková-Riegrová pursued other genres including the opera libretto. She and her husband, Václav Ladislav Červinka, enjoyed writing small-scale operatic works early in their marriage. When she completed *Zmařená svatba* ("The Frustrated Wedding"), based on the French vaudeville *Le petit Pierre*, she intended that it be performed at Christmas for the family,[17] but its future lay elsewhere with composer Karel Šebor. Encouraged despite the resulting opera's poor reception, she sent her next libretto to Šebor as well. His slow

---

[14] Christopher Fifield, "Smetana and *The Devil's Wall*," *The Musical Times* 128, no. 1728 (February 1987): 79.

[15] Tyrrell, *Czech Opera*, 111.

[16] Gabriela Preissová to Marie Červinková-Riegrová, June 19, 1893, as translated in Emma Taylor Parker, "'The Librettist Wears Skirts': Female Librettists in 19th-Century Bohemia" (PhD diss., University of California, Santa Barbara, 2016), 11.

[17] Parker, "The Librettist Wears Skirts," 51.

response prompted her father to suggest she present it to Dvořák,[18] the result of which was *Dimitrij*, a successful collaboration for both, "with many characters, ensembles, and choral scenes: a rarity for Czech opera of the time."[19]

While working on this opera, requesting only minor changes to the dramatic text, Dvořák asked Červinková-Riegrová for a second libretto, this time on a comic subject. However, "the comic was … alien to [her] character, so she wrote a text [*Jakobín*] that was essentially serious, in which only the secondary persons represented the comic."[20] Although he received the libretto in 1883, Dvořák did not begin serious work on the music until late 1887. As with Smetana and *Viola*, his initial excitement about the text waned in the face of other engagements. It was not until he requested a new romantically themed libretto, and Červinková-Riegrová asked him to return her previous work, that he redirected his attention to *Jakobín* ("The Jacobin").[21]

While her work with Dvořák advanced her reputation as a librettist, Červinková-Riegrová retained her aspirations as writer and patriot, leading to her 1893 biography of mathematician, philosopher, and theologian Bernard Bolzano (1781–1848), paying particular attention to his influence on the Czech National Revival. Her historical writing extended to her own family as well, with biographical studies on her maternal grandfather, historian František Palacký (1885), her father (1890), and her mother (1892). Her career culminated in a series of short stories, thereby realizing her desire to write fiction.

At her mother's death in 1891, Červinková-Riegrová began to doubt the value of her literary career and assumed her mother's charitable work with the poor. She founded the organization "Protection," whose purpose was to "protect both morally and materially working girls, especially girls working outside the home and living in unfavorable conditions, and to provide work for poor girls and women."[22] Her efforts were cut short unexpectedly by her death in 1895 of a cerebral embolism.

---

[18] Tyrrell, *Czech Opera*, 117.
[19] Milan Kuna, "Dvořák's *Dimitrij*," *The Musical Times* 120, no. 1631 (January 1979): 23.
[20] Karel Stloukal, "Maria Červinková-Riegrová," in *Velké ženy české*, ed. Milena Doudová (Prague: X-Egem, 1997), 81.
[21] Jan Smaczny, "Dvořák, His Librettists, and the Working Libretto for *Armida*," *Music & Letters* 91 (2010): 559–60.
[22] Božena Augustinová, *Marie Červinková-Riegrová, Životopisný nástin* (Prague: Bursík & Kohout, 1897), 85.

Anežka Schulzová (1868–1905)

Working during the latter part of the nineteenth century, amid efforts to achieve gender equality, Anežka Schulzová seemed "very much the 'emancipated woman' of the day."[23] The oldest of nine children in an influential Prague family – her father, Ferdinand Schulz, a historian and literary critic – she was well educated with a broad knowledge of domestic and international literature, which served her well in her own endeavors in literary criticism and translating foreign works into Czech.

In terms of her opera librettos, she wrote only for Fibich, with whom she had studied piano and composition in her late teens. Their professional collaboration and simultaneous intimate relationship resulted in three operas: *Hedy* (based on Byron's *Don Juan*), 1896; *Šárka* (derived from versions of the Czech legend by Julius Zeyer and Jaroslav Vrchlický), 1897; and *Pád Arkuna* ("The Fall of Arkona," revealing Schulzová's interest in Danish sources), 1900. Her writings about Fibich reveal that their emotional bond was unquestionably intense; John Tyrrell alleged, in fact, that "her life disintegrated after [Fibich's] death ... she committed suicide a few years later at the age of thirty-seven."[24]

The association of Schulzová with Fibich's operas is already apparent in 1894 with *Bouře* ("The Tempest"), based on Shakespeare's *The Tempest*. Vrchlický's libretto shifts the central focus to the love between Fernando and Miranda, with whom Fibich and Schulzová identified.[25] The plots for their three collaborations also maximize the intense attraction between characters, mirroring the relationship between librettist and composer. In fact, musicologist Jaroslav Jiránek describes *Hedy* as Fibich's most erotic dramatic work.[26]

In 1877, Fibich set Krásnohorská's libretto on the Czech legend of Blaník; twenty years later he returned to a nationalist subject for *Šárka* (1897). The plot appealed to his new librettist as well, who "seemed to have a strong voice not only with regards to the libretto, plot, and the dramatic situation, but also – to a certain degree – the musical content."[27] In the well-known story, the title character and her band of female warriors are determined to seduce, then murder the armed men led by Ctirad.

---

[23] Gerald Abraham, *Slavonic and Romantic Music: Essays and Studies* (New York: St. Martin's Press, 1968), 72.

[24] Tyrrell, *Czech Opera*, 116.   [25] Tyrrell, *Czech Opera*, 115–16.

[26] Jaroslav Jiránek, *Zdeněk Fibich* (Prague: Státní hudební vydavatelství, 1963), 185.

[27] Barbora Gregusová, "Reconsidering Fibich's *Šárka*: Myth, Gender, and the Construction of a Nation" (MM thesis, University of New Mexico, Albuquerque, 2015), 107. Gregusová supports this assertion with excerpts from their correspondence.

Schulzová altered the plot so that Šárka falls in love and defends Ctirad instead. According to Gregusová, "Schulzová successfully fuses the political message of the historical myth and her personal love story."[28]

Pád Arkuna, Fibich's final collaboration with Schulzová as librettist and his last opera, was based on the actual siege of the temple fortress of Arkona by Danish forces in the 1160s.[29] The manager of Prague's National Theater, František Adolf Šubert, visited the region in the late 1890s and returned to Prague with a subject for a grand opera spectacle he envisioned would be written by Fibich.[30] Correspondence between Šubert and the librettist shows that "the idea of a single work consisting of two operas *Helga* and *Dargun* ... was Schulzová's."[31] Here, the intimacy between the composer and his considerably younger librettist is, according to Tyrrell, reflected in the passionate relationship between father (Dargun) and daughter (Helga).[32]

After Fibich's death in 1900, Schulzová completed two publications that preserved his memory: *Zdenko Fibich: eine musikalische Silhouette* (1900), under the pseudonym Carl Ludwig Richter, and "Zdenko Fibich: hrstka upomínek a intimních rysů," first appearing in installments in *Květy* in 1902, this time under her own name. Although her career as a librettist was confined to Fibich's operas, her impact on the composer was immortalized in the relationships created there.

Singers

With singers as with librettists, those with correspondingly distinguished careers, the reputation to draw an audience, and, of course, the ability to sing beautifully and create a believable character were more likely to attract the attention of established composers and impresarios. Nevertheless, singers could not restrict themselves to only Czech works, the availability of which was limited, and achieve a successful career. Consequently, singers who advocated for a Czech identity through their performances of Czech works also devoted much of their careers to mainstream opera, that is, primarily Italian and French. The performers highlighted here present two scenarios: (1) for Kateřina Kometová-Podhorská, the female

---

[28] Gregusová, "Reconsidering Fibich's *Šárka*," 109.

[29] Arkona was the temple of the Slavic war god Svantovít that was destroyed by invading Christian Danes in the mid-twelfth century when they attacked the island of Rügen.

[30] Jiří Kopecký, "Karl Goldmark and Czech National Opera," *Studia Musicologica* 57 (2016): 352.

[31] Kopecký, "Karl Goldmark," 353.   [32] Tyrrell, *Czech Opera*, 84–85.

opera performer who achieved success primarily in the Czech lands and neighboring countries, while negotiating the terrain between German and Czech theaters and nationalist politics, and (2) for Ema Destinnová and Jarmila Novotná, the performers whose activities abroad rewarded them with significant renown and the opportunity to introduce international audiences to the level of fine-art music and performance of which a small Central European country was capable. The responsibilities of those performing abroad were not limited to the opera stage and concert performances, however; they were also the ambassadors of Czech culture, representing the international artist and the Czech woman simultaneously.

Kateřina Kometová-Podhorská (1807–89)

With the guidance of singer Tekla Podleská-Batková, her foster daughter Kateřina Kometová began her career at the German Estates Theater in Prague at the age of twelve, filling the role of Nanette in Boieldieu's *Das Rothkäppchen* (November 28, 1819). As shown by Martin Nedbal, both, as products of their time, began their careers in the German theater but "gradually became icons of Czech national music."[33] In 1827, Kateřina Kometová married fellow singer Matyáš Podhorský.[34] Although she received offers from abroad, she remained at the Estates until 1849 when, after the death of her husband, she decided to leave the theater entirely.

The roles Kometová-Podhorská performed during her career encompassed a wide range of challenges, evidence of her exceptional instrument, and extended from the Queen of the Night in Mozart's *Die Zauberflöte* and the titular character in Bellini's *Norma* to Romeo in the German translation of Bellini's *I Capuleti e i Montecchi*. With the capabilities of a dramatic soprano as well as a coloratura, her voice has been described as "sonorous in the lows and bell-like in the highs."[35] Most of her roles, however, were from the Classic and early Romantic repertoire – Mozart and *bel canto* – diminishing her appeal as the romantic style progressed.

Along with her employment at the German Estates Theater, Kometová-Podhorská also appeared on the Czech stage in translated works, among

---

[33] Martin Nedbal, "Bohemian Divas and the Rise of Czech National Consciousness," in *Women in Nineteenth-Century Czech Musical Culture*, 17–32 (17).

[34] Podhorský was also employed by the Estates Theater, where he sang the first Don Giovanni as well as Vojtěch opposite Kometová as Růžena in the 1826 premiere of Škroup's *Dráteník*, designated as the first Czech opera produced in Bohemia.

[35] Adolf Scherl, "Kateřina Podhorská," in *Národní divadlo a jeho předchůdci*, ed. Vladimír Procházka (Prague: Academia, 1988), 377.

them the first performance of *Don Giovanni* in Czech (1825), in which she was cast as Donna Anna – a role she had also sung in German. During her lifetime, some believed she brought the Czech stage to a level that exceeded that of Prague's German opera.[36] Understandably, there were those who questioned her allegiance to the German theater while Czech advocates claimed her as a national artist. Such arguments, some intent on demeaning her very career, contributed, no doubt, to her retirement.[37] Along with describing the antagonistic behavior to which Kometová-Podhorská was subjected, it should nevertheless be noted that this was also a time in the creation of a national identity in which a Czech-born singer, engaged by the German Estates Theater, could, by performing a comparatively few roles in Czech, become a national symbol.

Ema Destinnová (1878–1930)

Born Emilie Pavlína Kittlová, Ema Destinnová changed her surname likely as a tribute to her voice teacher, Marie Loewe-Destinn, with whom she began studying at age thirteen. Encouraged by her affluent parents to pursue musical training, Destinnová first learned violin, then undertook singing with Loewe-Destinn and finally acting with the renowned Czech artist Otýlie Sklenařová-Malá through the National Theater drama school. In 1897, she auditioned for František Šubert, then director of the National Theater, but was dismissed, despite a warning from Emanuel Chvála that "such an excellent talent will not likely return to us."[38] She obtained a position in Berlin in 1898, after a brief stint in Dresden, and was featured in forty-three roles and over seven hundred performances. Her greatest triumph was as the title character in Strauss's *Salome* (1906) with the composer conducting.[39]

The height of her international career was spent at the Metropolitan Opera in New York, initiated by her appearance in *Aida* in November 1908, with Enrico Caruso opposite and Arturo Toscanini conducting. During her eight seasons at the Met – and as its most highly paid female singer – she

---

[36] Nedbal, "Bohemian Divas," 25.

[37] For additional detail on this portion of Kometová-Podhorská's career, see Nedbal, "Bohemian Divas," 25–26.

[38] Letter from Emanuel Chvála to F.A. Šubert, Prague, October 19, 1898, as quoted in Jiří Kopecký, "1892: The International Success of Smetana's *The Bartered Bride*," in *Czech Music around 1900*, ed. Lenka Křupková and Jiří Kopecký (Hillsdale, NY: Pendragon Press, 2017), 42.

[39] Karla Hartl, "Emmy Destinn (1878–1930)," *Women in Music*, The Kapralova Society, http://kapralova.org/EMMY.htm (accessed March 17, 2025).

appeared in several premieres, among them as Minnie with Caruso as Dick Johnson in Puccini's *La fanciulla del west*.

With the help of Gustav Mahler, Destinnová began her promotion of Czech opera at the Met in 1909 in the role of Mařenka in a German translation of Smetana's *Prodaná nevěsta* with Mahler conducting.[40] During this period, Destinnová also toured several major cities across the country and made regular guest appearances in Europe, popularizing selections from her Czech repertoire.

Although her musical contributions met with great success, her intense patriotism and identification with the resistance in Bohemia also made her a target. Her trip to Europe during the 1915–16 season essentially ended her career with the Metropolitan. Under police surveillance and refusing to perform for the Austro-Hungarian troops, she was placed under house arrest and confined to her estate at Stráž nad Nežárkou in southern Bohemia until the end of the war. Nonetheless, in 1917 she appeared at the National Theater in Smetana's *Libuše*, and "was welcomed as a symbol of national and cultural freedom," her performance delivered "as a patriot with an unconcealed anti-monarchist mindset."[41] When she returned to the Met in 1919, however, it was for only one season, her successes there quickly forgotten.

Jarmila Novotná (1907–94)

> Even [as a child], I loved to immerse myself in theater . . . As for singing, that inclination was with me from the time I was no more than three or four. When my [older] sister said her prayers, I sang mine. Indeed, whenever there was an opportunity, I sang.[42]

Thus begins Novotná's autobiography *My Life in Song*, reflecting the lifelong centrality of singing and acting that would characterize her professional career. As a child, she learned about the history and folk traditions of her homeland into which World War I would soon intrude. When the war ended, Bohemia, Moravia, and Slovakia were united with Tomáš Garrigue Masaryk as president, whose son Jan would become Novotná's great friend and supporter.

---

[40] For additional information on the 1909 performance of *Prodaná nevěsta*, see Martin Nedbal's "Czech-German Collaborations at the Metropolitan Opera in the Early Twentieth Century," *Journal of Austrian-American History* 6 (2022): 16–24.

[41] Jaromír Paclt, "Ema Destinnová," in *Národní divadlo a jeho předchůdci*, 72.

[42] Jarmila Novotná, *My Life in Song*, ed. William V. Madison (Lexington: University Press of Kentucky, 2018), 3.

As normalcy returned to Europe, Novotná continued her study and by her early teens had already learned the role of Mařenka in *Prodaná nevěsta*.[43] At age sixteen, she auditioned for Destinnová, which she identified much later as leading to a turning point in her life. Writing to opera scholar Roger Pines in 1993, Novotná revealed that "It was she who led me to appreciate Mozart's genius. She maintained that one who can sing Mozart can sing everything. . . . I am happy that I had her advice right in the beginning."[44]

When Novotná's vocal talent and the fact that she had conquered the role of Mařenka came to the attention of Otakar Ostrčil, then conductor at the National Theater, he offered her the lead in Smetana's opera. Novotná debuted in the role in June 1925; her professional career had begun.

With a voice described as versatile, light, clear, and virtuosic, along with her graceful appearance and acting skills, Novotná, "at home in any style,"[45] garnered contracts and accolades nationally and internationally. Her first long-term permanent residence was in Berlin (1929–33), followed by employment at the Vienna Staatsoper (1933–38). Her longest contract, however, was with New York's Metropolitan Opera (1939–59). The conductors with whom she worked and who sought out her talents were among the foremost of the time, namely Otto Klemperer, Václav Talich, Gustav Mahler, Erich Korngold, Leo Blech, George Szell, and Bruno Walter. But the person she admired most and with whom she formed a lasting friendship was Arturo Toscanini. The roster of leading men she appeared opposite is no less impressive, among them Jussi Bjorling, Ezio Pinza, Richard Tauber, and Enrico Caruso.

Unlike her predecessors discussed in this chapter, Novotná also appeared on film. Transferring her singing and acting abilities to the new medium, she performed most notably in *The Search* with Montgomery Clift and *The Great Caruso* opposite Mario Lanza. She was also featured on Broadway in 1944 in the title role of *Helen Goes to Troy* – Korngold's adaptation of Offenbach's *La belle Hélène* – directed by Max Reinhardt.

Despite her many successes on the international stage, Novotná never neglected her national origins. During World War II, she participated in numerous performances in the United States in support of her homeland. On the 1942 recording *Songs of Lidice*, accompanied on piano by her longtime friend Jan Masaryk, she sang the melodies she had learned in her youth. Her description of this repertoire conveys the importance she

---

[43] Novotná, *My Life in Song*, 5.

[44] Roger Pines, "Jarmila Novotna, Adele Leigh, and Sena Jurinac," *The Opera Quarterly* 20 (2004): 708.

[45] Jaromír Paclt, "Jarmila Novotná," in *Národní divadlo a jeho předchůdci*, 342–43.

assigned to it: "In the folksong is represented the purest expression of a people's soul, born in the moment when they needed an outlet for their emotion. . . . it speaks of every aspect and condition of daily life."[46]

At home or abroad, in the studio or on the stage, working as librettist or performer, the women featured here helped shape Czech cultural identity. Whether participating in national or international endeavors or attempting to strike a balance between the two, these artists contributed in no small measure to the literary and musical history of their birthplace and to its recognition as a significant presence on the opera stage.

---

[46] Jarmila Novotná, "The Folk Song," *The Music Journal* 6, no. 6 (1948): 16.

12 | Bohemian Salon Culture in 1820s and 1830s Teplice

ANJA BUNZEL

During the nineteenth century, the Bohemian spa town of Teplice (Teplitz) enjoyed an excellent reputation as not only a popular destination for recreation and medical cures but also a cultural center encouraging international exchange, enabling artistic inspiration, and offering first-class musical entertainment.[1] Situated a little less than one hundred kilometers north-west of Prague, it attracted many people from the neighboring areas longing for a break from the hectic and unhealthy city life they would face, for instance, in Berlin. Yet sociability in Teplice was by no means provincial. The Prussian king himself was one of the spa town's regular guests; he engaged in social interactions with locals and other visitors, and he attended high-quality music, theater, and dance performances. Crucial figures in placing Teplice on the Central European music-cultural map were the composer and pianist Joseph Wolfram (1789–1839), who became Teplice's mayor in 1824, and his wife Anna (life dates unknown, née Himmelfahrt), as well as the local Bohemian nobility, Karl Joseph von Clary-Aldringen (1777–1831) and his wife Marie Aloisie (1777–1864, née Chotek von Chotkow-Wognin).[2] Contemporary accounts show that the Clary-Aldringens' contribution to the cultural life of Teplice was primarily material and social in nature – they hosted gatherings of various sizes and opened their garden and theater to the public. Wolfram, on the other hand, rehearsed and performed with visiting singers, provided his own compositions for local entertainment, and acted as a mediator between visiting artists and the local nobility. Together with his wife he opened their home to artists wishing to study, rehearse, or meet like-minded people in an intimate musical environment.

Funding for this project was provided by the Czech Science Foundation (GAČR) under the research project, "Semi-Private Musical Practices in Prague, Vienna and Berlin (1815–1850): Musical Repertoire within the Socio-Cultural Context of the Time" (22-16531S).

[1] I refer to Teplice by its current Czech name, unless I quote original sources, in which the German name, "Teplitz" or "Töplitz," is used. For reasons of unification, in those cases, I always write "Teplitz."

[2] Sometimes Wolfram is also referred to as "Joseph Matthias Wolfram" (Josef Matyáš Wolfram) or Joseph Maria Wolfram. See Matouš Pavlis, "Život a dílo Josefa Matyáše Wolframa se zaměřením na operu Bergmönch" (Bachelor thesis, Charles University, Prague, 2020), 16–17.

Despite Teplice's international renown during the 1820s and 1830s, the town's significance as a cultural center has remained largely unexamined. While there is some literature on Wolfram as a composer, his music-cultural legacy is almost forgotten today, possibly because, as suggested by Tomáš Spurný, he did not set Czech texts and subjects to music.[3] Another reason why Wolfram's and Teplice's impacts on nineteenth-century Bohemian musical culture have not received much attention in musicological discourse is perhaps that a substantial part of the musical activities cultivated in the town were private and semi-private in nature. As is typical within the context of salon research, sources are relatively scarce. Therefore, reconstructing musical life in 1820s and 1830s Teplice may be time-consuming and will most certainly never result in an exhaustive and complete picture. Nevertheless, assembling this jigsaw of a few available private sources opens fascinating windows into unique musical perform-ances and important professional networks fostered in Teplice, which was indeed the most-visited spa town of Bohemia at the time and was some-times referred to as "the salon of Europe."[4]

Two figures whose private accounts attest to precisely this reputation of Teplice as a cultural meeting point of international renown are the singer Maschinka Schneider (1815–82) and the writer Karl August Varnhagen von Ense (1785–1858). Schneider stayed in Teplice from July 1 to July 12, 1834, on route from Prague to Dresden (Karl Joseph von Clary-Aldringen

---

[3] Tomáš Spurný, "Joseph Wolfram – ein deutschböhmischer Komponist zwischen Prag, Teplitz-Schönau, Dresden und Berlin zu Webers und Spohrs Zeit," in *Musikkulturelle Wechselbeziehungen zwischen Böhmen und Sachsen*, eds. Jörn Peter Hiekel and Elvira Werner (Saarbrücken: Pfau, 2007), 99.

[4] A journal article dated September 4, 1843, reveals that the 1843 season was less busy than the previous one, stating that since King Friedrich Wilhelm's death in 1840, Teplice has no longer been "the salon of Europe, the stage of high diplomacy" ("der Salon von Europa, der Sprachsaal der hohen Diplomatik"). *Ost und West: Blätter für Kunst, Literatur und geselliges Leben, Beiblätter*, no. 141 (September 4, 1843): 563. According to contemporary sources, Teplice was visited by more than 1,000 people annually from 1801 onwards, with few exceptions because of the war in 1805, 1809, and 1813. The number of foreign visitors increased gradually, with more than 2,500 guests in 1810 and 1811; and 2,600 guests in 1822, for instance. These figures do not include people who traveled through and only stayed for a few days, members of the lower classes, or servants of the visitors, so actual numbers would have been much higher. See Joseph Wolfram, *Kurze Notizen über Teplitz* (Teplice: Gerzabek, 1828), 10–11. The Teplice spa lists – printed lists of the spa guests' names, professions, hometowns, and addresses of residence during their stays – reveal a wealth of information on further visitors to the town, culturally engaged and otherwise. Spa lists are recorded for Teplice from 1806 to 1835. An excerpt of the list for 1823 is digitized and free to access, see Weimar, Herzogin Anna Amalia Bibliothek, Teplitzer Kur- und Badegästeliste für das Jahr 1823 (Prague: Gerzabek, 1823), https://haab-digital.klassik-stiftung.de/viewer/image/1760712361_1823000000/1/LOG_0003/, accessed January 23, 2024.

had already passed away); Varnhagen visited Teplice more than once during the first half of the nineteenth century and received regular updates on current affairs in Teplice from the Prussian king. Schneider's and Varnhagen's diaries are laden with references to private and semi-private social gatherings bringing together visiting artists with local and foreign members of the middle classes and nobility.[5]

Although, as this chapter shows, salon sociability was always strongly determined by matters of etiquette and expectations between hosts and attendees, boundaries often encountered in (more) public music-cultural spheres were loosened, if not dissolved, and all participants benefited personally from their involvement within this complex web of non- or semi-official engagements. Besides leisure and pleasure, they gained social prestige, power, and sometimes even financial income. They also found creative inspiration, tested their musical works, presented their performative skills, and made valuable professional contacts. Therefore, as I argue in this chapter, a musicological exploration of such non-metropolitan towns as Teplice contributes not only to the specialized field of salon research but also to our understanding of Bohemian musical culture and broader Central European cultural history. It is within this wider context that this chapter is situated. I approach the music-cultural and social phenomenon of salonesque sociability through a short discussion of different definitions of the salon, followed by a more elaborative exploration of Teplice's music culture during the 1820s and 1830s. Despite many intersections between the two circles and the activities of both protagonists, for better orientation, I focus this exploration first on the main hosts, the Clary-Aldringens, and then on the main mediator and musical practitioner, Wolfram.

Defining Salon Culture

With regard to Czech musical culture, the 1997 *Slovník české hudební kultury* ("Dictionary of Czech Musical Culture") raises the concern that the term "salon" has been used too broadly. Although many social gatherings at the turn of the nineteenth century were rooted in noble and wealthy middle-class

---

[5] Maschinka Schneider, diary, unpublished manuscript. Dresden, Historisches Archiv der Sächsischen Staatstheater, estate Franz Schubert, NL Franz Schubert 151, https://kalliope-verbund.info/isil?isil.id=DE-2602, accessed March 21, 2024. For Varnhagen, I refer to the diary published in Karl August Varnhagen von Ense, *Blätter aus der preußischen Geschichte*, 5 vols., ed. Ludmilla Assing (Leipzig: Brockhaus, 1868).

salons, most of these gatherings preferred domestic music-making to salon-type gatherings. Moreover, according to the entry, the Czech middle classes mostly favored forms of public musical activities closely connected with the development of the national communal life.[6] Rather than adhering to the historically defined French model of the "salon," where a female aristocratic host gathered a number of regular and occasional visitors on a *jour fixe*, current salon research, bringing together music, literary, and cultural studies, places more emphasis on the heterogeneous and ever-changing nature of salon culture. As a result, salon culture is now defined more widely as a communicative and creative process unfolding in regular social gatherings in the (semi-)private domain.[7]

In terms of the first half of the nineteenth century, and defining the salon more widely, several private and semi-private gatherings entertained by the Bohemian nobility fall quite comfortably under the umbrella of "salon culture," including the Clary-Aldringens in Teplice; the Clam-Gallases, Kinskys, Nostitzes, Elise von Schlik, and the Waldsteins in Prague; or the Lobkowitz family in Roudnice nad Labem (Raudnitz).[8] These families' extensive musical libraries as well as the frequency of their gatherings, the number of their attendees, their partly professional nature, and the networking opportunities they sometimes enabled exceed the intimate setting typically associated with domestic music-making. Furthermore, facets of public, semi-private, and private musical life merged, and participation in one sphere did not – and does not need to – automatically exclude

---

[6] Jiří Fukač and Jiří Vysloužil, eds., *Slovník české hudební kultury* (Prague: Supraphon, 1997), 807.

[7] On narrower definitions, see, in chronological order, *Meyers Großes Konversations-Lexikon* (Leipzig: Meyer, 1909), vol. 17, 479; Andreas Ballstaedt, "Salonmusik," in *Die Musik in Geschichte und Gegenwart*, ed. Ludwig Finscher, Sachteil 8 (Kassel: Bärenreiter, 1998), coll. 854–67. On wider definitions, see Anja Bunzel and Natasha Loges, "Introduction," in *Musical Salon Culture in the Long Nineteenth Century* (Woodbridge: Boydell, 2019), 2.

[8] On Clam-Gallas and Nostitz, see Tereza Esterlová, "Neznámý pramen v archivu Pražské konzervatoře: Komorní hudba v domě Františka Švestky (1842-1864)" (MA thesis, Charles University, Prague, 2014); on Kinsky, see Eliška Bastlová(-Šedivá), *Collectio operum musicalium quae in bibliotheca Kinsky adservantur* (Prague: Národní knihovna, 2013), 25-26; on Elise von Schlik, see Marta Ottlová and Milan Pospíšil, "Hudební salon a salonní hudba," in *Salony v české kultuře 19. století*, ed. Helena Lorenzová and Taťána Petrasová (Prague: KLP, 1999), 51; Milena Lenderová, "Eliška hraběnka Schliková, (panu profesoru Robertu Kvačkovi k 70. narozeninám)," *Listy starohradské kroniky* 25, no. 1 (2002): 7–12; Milena Lenderová, "Portrét hraběnky Elišky Šlikové," *Z Českého ráje a Podkrkonoší: vlastivědný sborník* (2010): 33–42; Jana Sekyrová, "Eliška Šliková: Život neprovdané hraběnky v první polovině 19. století" (MA thesis, České Budějovice, 2006); and Henrike Rost, "Reminiscences of Past Sounds: The Musical Autograph Album (1813–1852) of Elise Gräfin von Schlik," in *Women in Nineteenth-Century Czech Musical Culture: Apostles of a Brighter Future*, ed. Anja Bunzel and Christopher Campo-Bowen (New York: Routledge, 2024), 138–52; on Lobkowitz, see Olga Mojžíšová, "Hudba v Lobkovických sídlech a salonech," in *Salony v české kultuře 19. století*, 208–16.

participation in the other.[9] This can be seen, for instance, in the case of the Clary-Aldringens and Joseph Wolfram, who were among Teplice's "most prominent benefactors" ("vorzüglichsten Wohlthäter"), as an 1834 local guidebook called them.[10]

Karl Joseph and Marie Aloisie von Clary-Aldringen: Cultivating (Musical) Sociability

The (semi-)private musical climate created by Karl Joseph and Marie Aloisie von Clary-Aldringen provided visiting artists with an excellent opportunity to display their skills and qualities as performers before a distinguished international audience. At the same time, the Clary-Aldringens benefited from the stays of international artists, as they attracted further foreigners who came to Teplice specifically to meet both Bohemians and high-caliber artists. In 1827, for instance, it was reported that the Prussian king postponed his visit to Teplice so his stay would coincide with that of the German singer Henriette Sontag. Due to her engagement at the Königstädtische Theater in Berlin, Sontag's time off for travel was strictly tied to the theater season, and the king planned his departure according to her availability. He anticipated high-quality entertainment and first-class musical performance while Sontag was present. In contrast, during the previous year's stay, he regretted that sociability was quite boring, possibly also because no famous artists were around during his stay.[11] It was the combination of the local hosts' engagement and taste on the one hand, and their invited guests' music-cultural contributions on the other, that made Teplice sociability so enjoyable.

The Clary-Aldringens' gatherings varied in size, (musical) activities featured, and the level of intimacy and spontaneity. Sometimes dancing took place alongside singing and conversation; and sometimes the boundaries between the audience's consumption of art as observers

---

[9] A more general account of intersections between private, semi-private, and public musical engagement of members of the nobility and upper middle classes toward (and after) mid-century can be found in Anja Bunzel, "František Palacký's (Musical) Life with the 'Aristocrats': Private and Semi-Private Musical Sociability in Prague during the First Half of the Nineteenth Century," *Musicologica Austriaca* (2023), online: https://musau.org/parts/neue-article-page/view/158, accessed February 8, 2024.

[10] Andreas-Chrysogonus Eichler, *Teplitz und seine Umgebungen. Geschichtlich, topographisch, naturhistorisch, statistisch, medizinisch und mahlerisch. Ganz neu dargestellt*, 8th ed. (Prague: Gerzabek, 1834), 104.

[11] Eichler, *Teplitz und seine Umgebungen*, 247.

and/or active practitioners, between professionalism and amateurism were blurred. For instance, on August 26, 1822, Varnhagen noted a large gathering at the Clary-Aldringens', at which professional dancers were hired. Their performance was strictly separated from the social dancing that involved all participants of the society, the "ball itself." Varnhagen von Ense wrote:[12]

Big ball today at Clarys' in the castle. The dancers performed a number of pieces. This morning it was still uncertain whether the dancers would stay for the ball itself, and whether the society [*Gesellschaft*] would dance with them. It was said that they would go home immediately after their show dance. Count Pückler and Pitt Arnim, however, had declared early on that they would ask [the dancers] Mlle. Lemière and Mad. Hoguet, and that they would dance only with them. The dance began; the King, after leading the Clary ladies to the polonaise, led Mlle. Lemière, soon followed by Prince Clary and Count Zichy, and so it went on, the dancers were engaged with everything like the first ladies of the society.

Heute großer Ball bei Clary's auf dem Schlosse. Die Tänzerinnen führten einige Stücke auf. Noch heute Vormittags war es ungewiß, ob die Tänzerinnen zum Ball selbst bleiben, und ob die Gesellschaft mit ihnen tanzen würde. Es hieß, sie würden gleich nach ihrem Schautanze zu Hause fahren. Graf Pückler und Pitt Arnim hatten sich aber schon früh erklärt, sie würden Mlle. Lemière und Mad. Hoguet auffordern, und nur mit diesen tanzen. Der Tanz begann; der König, nachdem er die Clary'schen Damen zur Polonaise geführt, führte Mlle. Lemière, bald folgten ihm Fürst Clary und Graf Zichy, und so ging es weiter, die Tänzerinnen waren wie die ersten Damen der Gesellschaft bei Allem mit.

Here, it becomes clear that the dancers were first meant to partake in this gathering solely in their capacities as professionals, presenting rehearsed performances. They ended up staying and mingling with the society because they were actively integrated by other (high-ranking) participants, including the king. One needs to bear in mind that Varnhagen was keen to stress his own socializing with the king, a point he emphasized in many of his diary entries.[13] On one occasion, the king even danced with Varnhagen's wife, the famous Jewish Berlin salonnière Rahel Varnhagen (1771–1833, née Levin, later Robert).[14] Varnhagen's account, however, also attests to the high significance of etiquette and certain behaviors in these circles. While Varnhagen was not dependent on formal introductions and

---

[12] Varnhagen von Ense, *Blätter aus der preußischen Geschichte*, ii, 184.
[13] See, for instance, Varnhagen von Ense, *Blätter aus der preußischen Geschichte*, ii, 174, 178.
[14] Varnhagen von Ense, *Blätter aus der preußischen Geschichte*, ii, 183.

invitations due to his and his wife's social standing, the same did not hold true for most visiting artists, who typically belonged to the middle classes.

Schneider noted this aspect in her diary, which she used primarily to take precise record of her positive interactions with the noble circles.[15] Her accounts reveal that, for her, participation at the gatherings of the Clary-Aldringens was characterized by constant negotiation between accepting kind offers, using valuable opportunities, and avoiding embarrassment. On July 7, 1834, she was introduced to the noble couple and a few selected guests by the mayor Wolfram, observing that:

The society was not numerous but very selected and consisted of approximately 20 people, the main protagonists of whom were the princely family and noblewomen, prince Carl of Prussia and Prince Schwarzenberg. My first aria . . . was received well. During the first bars I could read the admiration in all faces, which proved to me that nobody had believed the small person capable of anything. Everyone seemed amazed. The second piece was the romance from Othello, which, too, seemed to please. Some songs and the grace aria . . . brought my victory. Everything was most lovely.

Die Gesellschaft war nicht zahlreich aber sehr gewählt und bestand ungefähr aus 20 Personen, unter denen die fürstliche Familie und Hofdamen, der Prinz Carl von Preußen und der Fürst Schwarzenberg die Hauptpersonen waren. Meine erste Arie . . . gefiel außerordentlich. Bei den ersten Takten las ich die Bewunderung auf allen Gesichtern, die mir bewies daß niemand der kleinen Person etwas zugetraut habe. Alles schien entzückt. Das zweite Musikstück war die Romanze aus Otello, die ebenfalls sehr zuzusprechen schien. Einige Lieder und die grace arie . . . brachten meinen Sieg. Alles war höchst liebenswürdig.[16]

Upon this successful introduction to the local nobility, featuring a rich palette of famous opera arias and less famous songs, Schneider was invited officially to perform at one of the Clary-Aldringens' larger gatherings. This performance imposed a considerable amount of stress on her. There was not enough time to rehearse, but she could not reject Marie Aloisie von

---

[15] Maschinka Schneider was the daughter of the Prussian Hofkapellmeister Georg Abraham Schneider (1770–1839) and the singer and actor Caroline Schneider (née Portmann, 1775–1850). She moved to Dresden in 1833, where, in 1837, she married the Konzertmeister Franz Schubert. For further biographical details, see Robert Eitner, "Schubert, Franz (Geiger)," in *Allgemeine Deutsche Biographie* (Leipzig: Duncker & Humblot, 1891), xxxii, 628. She was a celebrated singer of the time: see various mentions of Schneider in the print media, for instance, *Iris im Gebiete der Tonkunst* 1, no. 50 (December 14, 1832), and no. 51 (December 21, 1832). As she visited Teplice before her marriage, I refer to her by her maiden name.

[16] Maschinka Schneider, diary, unpublished manuscript, Dresden, Historisches Archiv der Sächsischen Staatstheater, estate Franz Schubert, NL Franz Schubert 151, July 7, 1834, https://kalliope-verbund.info/isil?isil.id=DE-2602, accessed March 21, 2024.

Clary-Aldringen's request due to courtesy, and also because she could not risk missing this opportunity.

In retrospect on this particular performance, Schneider expressed her great satisfaction, but she also remarked that she could have sung much better had Wolfram accompanied her more effectively – according to Schneider, Wolfram had not devoted enough energy and care to the rehearsals.[17] Here, the key role taken by Wolfram within the context of Teplice sociability becomes especially clear.[18] Wolfram himself emphasized in promotional materials on Teplice that visitors could come into closer contact with each other and with the local nobility at the Clary-Aldringens' castle and surrounding gardens.[19] In many cases, however, closer contact among the individual visitors and between them and the local nobility would not have been possible without Joseph and Anna Wolfram.

Joseph and Anna Wolfram: Interpersonal Mediation and Musical Composition

Wolfram acted as a mediator and guarantor of formal introductions between visiting artists and the local *haute volée*, and the Wolframs provided study and rehearsal space for visitors in their home, where they also hosted small spontaneous social gatherings.[20] Indeed, according to the historian and Wolfram's contemporary Bernhard Scheinpflug (1811–82), not a single artist, performer, composer, singer, or actor came to Teplice without introducing themselves to Wolfram.[21] Musical visitors to Wolfram include, besides the aforementioned Schneider, the Teplice citizens Taddäus Kozischek and Johann Kroh; the Czech historian, writer, and Wolfram's long-time friend

---

[17] Schneider, diary, July 3, 1834.

[18] For further biographical information on Wolfram, see Bernhard Scheinpflug, "Joseph Wolfram: eine biographische Skizze," *Mitteilungen des Vereines für Geschichte der Deutschen in Böhmen* 9 (1871): 120–26; *Allgemeine Theaterzeitung und Originalblatt für Kunst, Literatur, Musik, Mode und geselliges Leben* 26, no. 147 (July 23, 1833): 589–90 (589); *Berliner Allgemeine musikalische Zeitung* 3/42 (October 18, 1826): 338–40.

[19] Wolfram, *Kurze Notizen über Teplitz*, 8–9. He also stresses the good infrastructural links to Prague, Dresden, Karlovy Vary (Karlsbad), Litoměřice (Leitmeritz), Louny (Laun), and Slaný (Schlan).

[20] Schneider, diary, July 3, 1834.

[21] Scheinpflug, "Joseph Wolfram," 120–26. Scheinpflug's accounts arose from an autobiographical fragment by Wolfram, which ends, however, in 1819. Some excerpts of this autobiography were also reproduced in *Teplitzer Zeitung*, January 27, 1871. Scheinpflug complemented his biographical sketch by way of excerpts he took from conversations with Wolfram.

František Palacký; and the German singer Anna Milder.[22] Furthermore, Wolfram accompanied singers on the piano during spontaneous (and less spontaneous) performances. Sometimes his seemingly sloppy piano accompaniment may have disappointed, as, for instance, in Schneider's case (see above). However, it is possible that Wolfram viewed these engagements as accompanist as a side activity precisely in the spirit of salon culture, alongside a large variety of other official (and less spontaneous) musical commitments. Indirectly, these other commitments, for instance, the leadership of a string quartet and the foundation of the spa orchestra (*Kurorchester*), interacted with his activities in the private and semi-private spheres, as they grew out of his contacts nourished through private and semi-private music-making, and they also increased Teplice's popularity as a musically attractive destination.[23] Finally, Wolfram offered his own published and unpublished compositions for local entertainment purposes, and promoted Teplice as a popular destination for musical socializing through dedications and mentions of famous visitors in his published scores.

In return, Wolfram benefited from his own position as a key point of contact. Exchanging ideas with performers in their roles as renowned practitioners and critics, he made direct use of the presence of international stars stopping by in Teplice. In her diary, Schneider mentioned that when visiting Wolfram privately, he discussed his operas *Das Schloss Candra* and *Drakäna* with her, upon which she offered her perspective on the individual parts of each composition. She also sang in an opera performance at Wolfram's during her stay.[24] An autograph of a recitative and cavatina taken from *Das Schloss Candra* attests to Wolfram's thorough preparation and practical use of the piano reductions for salonesque performances (Figure 12.1). As was typical of salon culture, these semi-private performances enabled Wolfram to rehearse, test out, and showcase his compositions within more intimate settings. For instance, Palacký heard *Die*

---

[22] Scheinpflug, "Joseph Wolfram," 126; the Teplice artists are mentioned in the Christmas supplement of the *Teplitz-Schönauer Anzeiger*, December 25, 1927, Weihnachtsbeilage; Palacký is mentioned in František Keller, concert introduction, Státní oblastní archiv Plzeň, unpublished typescript, 4.

[23] Josef Günther, "Die Entwicklung des geistigen Lebens in Teplitz," *Sudetendeutsche Heimatgaue*, no. 36 (1924): 30. The article is included as a manuscript copy in the estate of František Keller, SOA Pilsen; Spurný, "Joseph Wolfram," 100. On the orchestra and its further development, see also Pavlis, "Život a dílo Josefa Matyáše Wolframa," 16; and Eliška Chaloupková, "Lázeňský hudební život v Teplicích" (Bachelor thesis, Charles University, Prague, 2012), 18 and 33.

[24] Schneider, diary, July 5, 1834. A number of guests were invited, and the performance was well-received, although it almost ended in a row, because Gasparo Spontini, who also stayed in Teplice at the time, showed up uninvited and Schneider did not like him.

Figure 12.1: Title page of Wolfram's piano score including a recitative and cavatina from the opera *Das Schloss Candra*. Státní okresní archiv Teplice. Reproduced by permission.

bezauberte Rose "at the piano" ("při klavíru") at Wolfram's on July 29, 1825, almost ten months before its Prague premiere on May 24, 1826.[25]

Although Wolfram's operas contributed to Teplice's positive musical reputation, as they (or parts of them) were performed there, Wolfram's Lieder were also relevant for Teplice sociability. Spontaneous performances and the (less spontaneous) creation of more or less personal musical souvenirs for guests were common practices during the nineteenth century. Songs would be performed in private, and as a way of acknowledging already-existing support and encouraging further performances elsewhere, dedications were made to the visiting singers. Four of Wolfram's Lieder publications are particularly telling in this regard. His second Lieder opus was dedicated to the singer Anna Milder

---

[25] Vojtěch J. Nováček, ed., *Františka Palackého korrespondence a zápisky* (Prague: Česká akademie císaře Františka Josefa, 1898–1911), vol. 1, 111. On the Prague performance, see *Františka Palackého korrespondence a zápisky*, 151. *Die bezauberte Rose* was one of Wolfram's most successful works; it received ample attention in the German-language press, for instance, Ludwig Rellstab, "Beurteilungen: Die bezauberte Rose," *Berliner allgemeine musikalische Zeitung* 5, no. 4 (January 23, 1828), 28–29; no. 5 (January 30, 1828), 36–38; no. 6 (February 6, 1828), 43–45; no. 7 (February 13, 1828), 51–52; no. 10 (March 5, 1826); and *Allgemeine Theaterzeitung und Originalblatt für Kunst, Literatur, Musik, Mode und geselliges Leben* 26, no. 147 (July 23, 1833): 590.

Figure 12.2: Title page of Wolfram's second Lieder opus with dedication to Anna Milder. Státní okresní archiv Teplice. Reproduced by permission.

"during her presence in Teplitz" ("während ihrer Anwesenheit in Teplitz", Figure 12.2).[26] It was published in 1826, but Varnhagen's diary reveals that Milder sang with great applause in Teplice as early as September 1822.[27] Perhaps it was during this or a different visit that Wolfram socialized with Milder. While we do not know whether precisely these songs published in Wolfram's second Lieder opus were performed by Milder (and where/when), the dedication points to Wolfram's and Milder's mutual inspiration when they met in Teplice. The second edition of the opus was published in 1829; its mere existence testifies to the popularity of the songs during the 1820s.

Wolfram's third Lieder collection was dedicated to Mathilde von Clary (1806–96), Karl Joseph and Marie Aloisie's daughter, thus clearly recognizing the Clarys' musical engagement and patronage in the town. In a similar spirit, Wolfram's dedication to Goethe of his fourth Lieder opus

---

[26] The score is also available in Staatsbibliothek zu Berlin, Stiftung Preußischer Kulturbesitz, Musikabteilung, shelfmark 55NA781.

[27] Varnhagen von Ense, *Blätter aus der preußischen Geschichte*, ii, 193. Regarding the publication date, see review "Vier Lieder, mit Begleitung des Pianoforte, komponiert von Joseph Wolfram," *Berliner allgemeine musikalische Zeitung* 3, no. 47 (November 22, 1826): 378–80.

served as a marketing tool in promoting Teplice sociability (and Wolfram's own compositions) through the prism of the famous poet's visits to the spa town.[28] Finally, Wolfram's sixth opus, titled *Erinnerung an Teplitz*, perhaps more than any other opus of Wolfram's, shows that Teplice salon culture was both cosmopolitan and local. Published in Dresden with Wilhelm Paul in 1834 – like many others of his opus numbers – it was dedicated to the German artist and patroness Ida von Lüttichau (1798–1856, née von Knobelsdorf), and includes settings of poetry by Wilhelm von Marsano and Ludwig Rellstab. The title, *Erinnerung an Teplitz*, connects the pieces unmistakably with the spa town even for everyone who was not present when they were conceived (or performed) there. As seen in Milder's and Goethe's cases (but also in the aforementioned example of Henriette Sontag), sometimes it was the visitors – not the hosts – who were the major attraction in Teplice and who had a large impact on the memories the individual guests would bring home from their stays in the spa town. Wolfram had a significant stake in welcoming these visiting artists, and making them feel at home within the local cultural circles.

Conclusion: Creating the Self, Creating Musical Salon Culture in Teplice

Wolfram was a prolific composer-musician, an engaged citizen of Teplice, and a committed mayor mediating between the local nobility and middle classes as well as foreign visitors of both social strata. He helped to create professional relationships between guests and locals by accompanying visiting singers on the piano, composing pieces suitable for private and semi-private performances in Teplice, and, with his wife, making their home available for study, rehearsals, and socializing. At the same time, Teplice would not have been as attractive a destination for visitors of all classes and with various cultural interests without the local nobility. Not only did the Clary-Aldringens contribute to Teplice's pleasant overall appearance – the castle had a garden and theater – but they also hosted social gatherings of various sizes and types, to which they invited the Prussian king, Bohemian and/or foreign nobility, and culturally engaged intellectuals and artists. In so doing, they provided both entertainment and valuable networking opportunities for the guests of the spa town. All

---

[28] On Goethe in Teplice, see, for instance, Eduard Petiška, *Goethe v Čechách a Čechy v Goethovi* (Prague: Martin, 1999).

participants of Teplice sociability benefited personally and in their own ways from this complex web of contacts, networks, and activities. The Prussian king and other visitors enjoyed the entertainment, made acquaintances, and/or found business (or romantic) partners; the Clary-Aldringens gained prestige, revenue, and socio-cultural power; Wolfram tested out his compositions through performance and increased his international renown as a composer through dedications to important cultural protagonists; and visiting musicians had the opportunity to showcase their skills before an international audience in a relatively intimate and personal, yet musically high-quality and demanding cultural setting. After all, salon culture, like many fully public musical spheres as opposed to private ones, was always about creating a sense of community and negotiating one's own position within that community.

It is precisely this combination of opportunities for locals and foreigners of different social strata, of socio-cultural negotiations between etiquette and courtesy, and of expectations between hosts and visitors, that defined salon culture during the first half of the nineteenth century. Considering the small size of Teplice as a town, the high degree of interaction among the individual Teplice locals in making sociability happen, and the different threads of artistic activity enabled by this sociability, one can, indeed, speak of Teplice metaphorically as *one* salon (as opposed to a town with many salons, like, for instance Vienna, Berlin, or Prague). In its own way, the salon culture of Teplice placed the spa town on the European map of highly attractive destinations for musicians and musically engaged intellectuals – not with a focus on public musical venues, local music publishers, and the sheer quantity of resident composers, music critics, first-class musicians, or other musical practitioners, but rather with regard to its dense and intense networking and performance opportunities involving both locals and internationals.

As the example of Teplice shows, in the salonesque arena, boundaries between large-scale and small-scale genres, private, semi-private, and public spaces, spontaneous and planned musical activities, and amateurism and professionalism are blurred. Responsibilities of the individual participants are not as clear-cut as in other – more institutionalized – settings: composers may act as performers, performers as critics, guests or hosts as performers and/or patrons, dedicatees and friends as inspiration, and so on. In terms of its sources, the obscurity of salon culture may be frustrating, as more often than not, one relies on chance finds and autobiographical documents, and one can never get an exhaustive picture but rather small windows into a complex phenomenon. However, this obscurity also encourages original perspectives on non-canonical protagonists, repertoire, and musical activities. While they may seem off the beaten track, these sources demonstrate how most musical protagonists of the time spent large parts of their everyday lives. Reconstructing these facets of musical life helps to understand the full diversity of – an often all-too-simplified – nineteenth-century musical culture and challenges insistent abridged assumptions surrounding aspects of cultural metropolitanism, cultural agency, identity, and creative inspiration.

13 | "The Very Bosom of our Nation": The Dialectic of Folk and Art Music in Bedřich Smetana's *Hubička* and *Dvě vdovy*

CHRISTOPHER CAMPO-BOWEN

It was on the occasion of the epochal 1895 Czechoslavic Ethnographic Exhibition that a particular scholar described folksong as "one of the most significant and simultaneously most noble expressions of the people's spiritual life" ("jeden z nejvýznačnějších a zároveň nejušlechtilejších projevů lidového života duševního").[1] This writer was none other than Otakar Hostinský, who effectively founded the discipline of Czech musicology (on Hostinský, see also Chapters 16, 18, and 23). Given the Herderian intellectual lineage that he and his fellow nineteenth-century Czech intellectuals shared, this comes as little surprise – Johann Gottfried von Herder's theories, especially the idea that the practices, customs, and music of the rural folk were key to the proper development of the nation, were widely read and accepted across Europe.[2] Hostinský's statement is nevertheless significant for two reasons. One, it concisely encapsulates the motivation behind almost a century of folksong collection, if not incipient ethnographic research, in the Czech lands of Bohemia and Moravia. Two, it helps explain why folk music was such a heavily contested term in Czech music history – in such a framework, to properly characterize and understand folk music was to comprehend the innermost aspects of the Czech self.

The nineteenth century in particular saw the rise of folk music as both a genre label and a repertoire of music to be drawn upon, emulated, and perpetuated. This was especially true in the case of art music for elite audiences, such as symphonies, string quartets, and operas. The distinction between folk music and art music has been the subject of critique for some time, however. Matthew Gelbart points out that the very concepts of "folk music" and "art music" are not only examples of invented traditions that fulfilled specific social purposes in the context of their creation. More

---

Unless otherwise indicated, all translations are my own.

[1] Otakar Hostinský, "Lidová píseň, hudba, tanec," in *Národopisná výstava českoslovanská v Praze 1895*, ed. Karel Kusáček et al. (Prague: J. Otto, 1895), 229.

[2] See William A. Wilson, "Herder, Folklore and Romantic Nationalism," *Journal of Popular Culture* 6, no. 4 (March 1973): 819–35.

importantly, they constitute a historically interdependent, dialectical binary pairing – one cannot be understood without the other.[3] Thus, to comprehend the situation of folk music in the nineteenth-century Czech lands, it is important also to understand the state of art music composition, and how these categories mutually informed and co-created one another.

In this chapter, I explore the relationship between Czech folk and art music through the case studies of Bedřich Smetana's operas *Dvě vdovy* ("The Two Widows," 1874, rev. 1877) and *Hubička* ("The Kiss," 1876). These operas, and the reception of Smetana's music more generally, were crucial components in the larger process of institutionalizing folk music as one of, if not the primary resource for musical nationalism in the toolbox of Czech composers. Ironically, Smetana only used one actual folk tune in the composition of both these operas – indicating the extent to which "folk music" was more of an idealized and imagined category for intellectuals than a corpus of melodies and texts. The effects of the idealization of folk inspiration linger down into the present, with popular descriptions of the three most famous Czech composers in the modern day (Smetana, Antonín Dvořák, and Leoš Janáček) invariably mentioning how these figures drew on folk music in composing their own works. If we are to appreciate the fullness of these composers' oeuvres in all their complexity, it behooves us to understand, and to dismantle wherever appropriate, the dominant narrative of Czech composers' reliance on folksong.

Polemics and Folk Music from *Dalibor* to *Dvě vdovy*

Smetana's relationship to the concept of folksong was a complicated one, and it became ever more mythologized as he was increasingly figured as the founding father of Czech music. One of the main inflection points in this process of canonization – arguably the single most significant shift in public and critical opinion about the composer – came in the middle years of the 1870s, when Smetana's operas *Dvě vdovy* and *Hubička* were composed and premiered. Though *Dvě vdovy* was the fifth opera he had composed, it was only the fourth that had reached the public, as the opera *Libuše*, composed between 1869 and 1872 but not premiered until 1881, was still being held for the opening of the National Theater. Smetana's enemies in the press had used this perceived lack of compositional output

---

[3] See Matthew Gelbart, *The Invention of "Folk Music" and "Art Music": Emerging Categories from Ossian to Wagner* (New York: Cambridge University Press, 2007), 6–9 and throughout.

as part of a larger campaign against the composer. This campaign contributed to his ouster as principal conductor of the Prague Provisional Theater, but it was the onset of Smetana's deafness in 1874 that ultimately made his role there untenable.[4] The anti-Smetana campaign in certain quarters of Prague's musical circles also relied on a long-established narrative of polemics against Smetana's perceived Wagnerianism.

These polemics in turn resonated with the concept of folksong. The Old Czech political party, with which Smetana antagonists like František Ladislav Rieger and František Pivoda were aligned, had adopted a platform that specifically opposed Wagnerian operatic techniques, advocating instead for folksong as the basis for national opera – if nothing else, an indication of the public importance of opera in nineteenth-century Prague.[5] The Young Czech political party, with which Smetana and his compatriots in the Artists' Union (Umělecká beseda) were aligned, held that Wagnerian opera could lead to a more progressive means of creating a Czech national operatic tradition, one that eschewed folksong as the basis for number opera in favor of through-composed, harmonically and motivically complex textures.

An oft-repeated anecdote from the memoirs of Josef Srb-Debrnov, a close friend of Smetana and promoter of his music, shows the stakes of this conflict over the place of folk music. Sometime shortly before the composition of Smetana's first opera *Braniboři v Čechách* ("The Brandenburgers in Bohemia," 1862–63), the Old Czech politician Rieger and the composer got into a debate at a party about the proper way to create a lighter opera that showcased the life of the Czech people. As the story goes, "[Smetana] thought he could make a success of it. Rieger objected that the basis for such an opera would have to be Czech folksongs; Smetana again opposed this, saying that in this way a medley of various songs, a kind of quodlibet would come into being, but not an artistic work with any continuity."[6] In Srb-Debrnov's telling, Smetana's resolution in opposing Rieger led directly to the composition of *Prodaná nevěsta* ("The Bartered Bride," 1866), a work that thematizes and dramatizes the lives of rural villagers, but does so without recourse to quoted folksongs. Whatever its

[4] For an overview of this period in the composer's life and its various periodical battles, see Brian Large, *Smetana* (London: Duckworth, 1970), 233–46.

[5] See Kelly St. Pierre, *Bedřich Smetana: Myth, Music, and Propaganda* (Rochester, NY: Rochester University Press, 2017), 9.

[6] Quoted in František Bartoš, ed., *Bedřich Smetana: Letters and Reminiscences*, trans. Daphne Rusbridge (Prague: Artia, 1955), 67. For more discussion of the political and social resonances of this story, see St. Pierre, *Bedřich Smetana*, 51–52.

actual veracity, this anecdote contributed to the canonization of Smetana by casting him as both political underdog and progressive musical prophet, whose principles would be vindicated by history.

Smetana's insistence on continuing with Wagnerian operatic construction in *Dalibor* (1868) and *Libuše* invited repeated accusations of insufficient devotion to the Czech national cause, if not effectively traitorous behavior in using Wagnerian aesthetics. Smetana and his friends fought against this charge in an increasingly nasty battle.[7] Hostinský took the lead in nuancing the Smetanian approach to Wagner so as to defuse the association, in part through an 1873 article about Smetana's opera *Dalibor*. Hostinský characterized Smetana, as Kelly St. Pierre puts it, as "a composer who had progressed beyond Wagner's own model" in his ability to develop Czech opera through reliance on the Czech language and Wagnerian compositional techniques like leitmotif.[8] More importantly, Hostinský also linked the idea of folk (*prostonárodní*) song to Wagnerian aesthetics and Smetana's compositional gifts. *Prostonárodní* is one of those bugbears of translation unique to the Czech language, and one which is particularly important in the context of folksong and Czech opera. Etymologically, the word is an amalgam of the words *prostý/prostě* ("simple/simply") and *národní* ("national"). It is frequently translated as "folk," but this misses some of the word's connotative slippage, which directly links the national with the imagined simplicity of rural life in the Czech context.

Hostinský singles out the melody to Dalibor's line "Ničím je mi život" in act 1 as an example of Smetana's gift for writing melodies with true folk character.[9] Because Smetana then applied Wagnerian motivic development to the melody, which according to Hostinský pervades almost the entire opera, so too does the whole operatic fabric echo this national, folk character. As a rebuttal to Smetana's Old Czech detractors, he added that "these kinds of folk melodies are not simply mechanically inserted into the score, but rather they grow out of it into a single, living organism, and thus

---

[7] A key account of the battle over *Dvě vdovy* can be found in John Clapham, "The Smetana-Pivoda Controversy," *Music & Letters* 52, no. 4 (October 1971): 353–64; more recent discussions of the polemics and their importance to subsequent historiography are given in Brian S. Locke, *Opera and Ideology in Prague: Polemics and Practice at the National Theater, 1900–1938* (Rochester, NY: University of Rochester Press, 2006), 22–29; and St. Pierre, *Bedřich Smetana*, 72–73.

[8] St. Pierre, *Bedřich Smetana*, 62.

[9] Before Hostinský, several Czech and German Bohemian critics looked for and "found" folk melodies in operas from periods before Smetana, including works by Gluck and Mozart. See Martin Nedbal, *Mozart's Operas and National Politics: Canon Formation in Prague from 1791 to the Present* (New York: Cambridge University Press, 2023), 70–78.

the folk character of the musical theme becomes permanent" ("nejsou pak jakési prostonárodní melodie jenom do partitury mechanicky vloženy, nýbrž srůstají s ní v jednotný, živý organismus a prostonárodní ráz hudebního příznaku stává se tak permanentním").[10] This is a clear example of the dialectical relationship between folk and art music, in that the category of "folk music" here gains a culturally significant and valuable presence in the realm of "art music," and at the same time the national value of this "art music" is assured through "folk" character – though, notably, not through the wholesale insertion of a pre-existing folk melody.

Given the climate of nationalist fervor and polemic surrounding *Dalibor* and *Libuše*, Smetana's decision to turn to a French salon comedy – *Les deux veuves*, known in Czech as *Dvě vdovy* – as the source for a new Czech opera might have seemed somewhat strange. Figures on both sides of the quarrel wished for a second *Prodaná nevěsta*, which had from its premiere been hailed (if only by a few at first) as a touchstone of national art. After announcing in early March 1873 that Smetana had recently begun composing *Dvě vdovy*, a writer from the journal *Hudební listy* expressed the hope that it would "turn out for him like his first [*sic*] work, *Prodaná nevěsta*" ("Kéž by se mu tak podařila, jako prvá jeho práce 'Prodaná nevěsta'").[11] In an 1882 letter to his friend and former student Ludevít Procházka, Smetana stated that *Dvě vdovy* had initially been "an attempt – when I had already proven myself in different operatic styles – as with *Braniboři v Čechách, Prodaná nevěsta, Dalibor*, and *Libuše* – also to write a noble salon opera, and I found no text more suitable than *Les deux veuves*" ("Byl to pokus – když jsem se už osvědčil v jiných genrech operního stylu – jako Braniboři, Prodaná nevěsta, Dalibor, Libuša – taky jednou v ušlechtilém salonním slohu napsat operu, a nenašel jsem žádný jiný textový podklad vhodnější, jako zrovna Dvě vdovy").[12] This 1852 French conversation play by Jean Pierre Félicien Mallefille that had been translated into Czech by Smetana's eventual librettist, Emanuel Züngel, premiered at Prague's Provisional Theater on August 25, 1868.[13] The salon setting of *Dvě vdovy* was explicitly intended to contribute to enriching the

---

[10] Otakar Hostinský, "Smetanův Dalibor," in his *Bedřich Smetana a jeho boj o moderní českou hudbu* (Prague: Laichter, 1901), 252–53.

[11] Hudební listy (March 6, 1873): 78.

[12] See Jan Löwenbach, *Bedřich Smetana a Dr Lud. Procházka: Vzájemná korrespondence* (Prague: Umělecká beseda, 1914), 81–82.

[13] For more on Mallefille and the history of his play, see Mirko Očadlík, introduction to *Dvě vdovy / Emanuel Züngel*, ed. Mirko Očadlík (Prague: Státní hudební vydavatelství, 1962), 5–9. The first version of the opera was very close to a direct translation of Mallefille, though some passages were changed.

range of the domestic repertoire of Prague's Provisional Theater, which in 1873 was still under his artistic and musical direction. As Smetana elaborates in his letter to Procházka, he "**purposely** wrote it with just such a textual basis and *musical style* for *our Czech theater*" ("kterou jsem pro *naše české divadlo* **schválně** v takové podložce textové a takovým *slohem hudebním* napsal").[14]

Dvě vdovy, which ultimately premiered on March 27, 1874, had a complicated history of revisions and productions. The first version from 1874 featured four main characters: the titular widows, Karolina and Anežka, the gamekeeper Mumlal, and the ardent suitor in love with Anežka, Ladislav. Aside from opening and closing choruses, the entirety of the two-act opera was concerned with the interaction of the four main characters and proceeded through a combination of prose dialogue and discrete musical numbers. The plot is simple: Ladislav is in love with Anežka, who still mourns her husband, and Karolina, happy to be free of her husband and in charge of the estate, contrives to get the two of them together. Karolina eventually succeeds while Mumlal provides comic relief throughout the piece.

In its general outlines *Dvě vdovy* closely followed the example of French conversation operas of the nineteenth century. Later commentators have proposed Fromental Halévy's opera *L'Éclair* (1835) and Daniel François Esprit Auber's *Le Domino noir* (1837) as possible models, since both were very popular in the latter half of the century and frequently performed in Prague.[15] Initial reactions to Smetana's opera were warm. The reviews tended to focus on two issues that would recur with other productions of *Dvě vdovy*. The first was general dissatisfaction with Züngel's libretto, which was considered weak and not equal to Smetana's music. The second was a tendency on the part of critics to ascribe a clearly Czech character to the music, though they were unspecific about how exactly Smetana had achieved this feat. It was precisely these two ideas – Smetana's decidedly Czech music and Züngel's weak libretto – that provided much of the justification for revisions, both by Smetana and other, later figures. At the time of the premiere, however, the elegance of the salon setting also received high praise, and through Smetana's music, the French salon was transformed into a Czech one, with explicitly Czech aristocrats engaging in the witty intrigues usually attributed to the nobility of other

---

[14] Emphases in the original. See Löwenbach, *Bedřich Smetana a Dr Lud. Procházka*, 81.

[15] See Vlasta Hrušková, "Bedřich Smetana: Dvě vdovy—Dramaturgická analýza opery" (master's thesis, Charles University, Prague, 1972), 34.

lands. Despite the positive reviews, the opera was only performed seven times in 1874 before disappearing from the repertoire. The strategy that Smetana and Züngel eventually adopted in an attempt to rescue *Dvě vdovy* – the inclusion of more music with a self-consciously Czech folk character – makes much more sense if we consider the reception of the opera that fell in the middle of their work on *Dvě vdovy*: *Hubička*.

"A Single Grand Folksong": Critical and Popular Acclaim for *Hubička*

Unlike every single one of Smetana's operas to this point, *Hubička* received a universally positive reception from the moment of its premiere and remains second only to *Prodaná nevěsta* in terms of popularity on Czech stages. Biographers have consistently marveled at the fact that Smetana could write such a fundamentally warm-hearted opera, along with the first two movements of the tone poem cycle *Má vlast*, while he was facing cruel personal attacks in the press, losing a financial lifeline through the Provisional Theater, and swiftly and painfully going deaf.[16] Despite growing public awareness of Smetana's travails and a building sympathy because of them, some intellectuals remained opposed to the composer and his aesthetic principles. One such figure was Petr Mužák, the husband of writer Karolina Světlá, whose novella Eliška Krásnohorská would transform into the libretto for *Hubička*. In her memoirs, the librettist described Mužák's dismissive attitude toward Smetana just before the intensification of their work on the new opera:

[Smetana] himself is just a henchman of Wagner and wants to Wagnerize, that is to Germanize our musical world, which was once so celebrated throughout the whole of Europe, as long as it was Czech. But now here at home? Is this even music? These people don't know how to create a mere song . . . as do many a goose herder!

On sám je jen nohsled Wagnera a chce powagnePřit, to jest poněmčit náš hudební svět, který býval tak slavný po celé Evropě, dokud byl český. Ale teď u nás? Je to nějaká hudba? Ti lidé nedovedou udělat písničku . . . ba jako dovede leckterá husopaska![17]

That such opposition effectively melted away in the face of *Hubička* is in large part a testament to the opera's differing character and musical means.

---

[16] For an extended account of this unfortunate narrative see Přemysl Pražák, *Smetanovy zpěvohry*, vol. 3, "*Dvě vdovy. Hubička. Tajemství*" (Prague: Vydavatelství za svobodu, 1948), 99–128.

[17] Quoted in Pražák, *Smetanovy zpěvohry*, 130.

Subtitled a "folk [*prostonárodní*] opera," the work concerns the travails of a peasant couple, Lukáš and Vendulka. The two, who have been in love since childhood, are now able to court one another after the death of Lukáš's wife, whom he was forced to marry by his family. Conflict is spawned when Vendulka refuses a kiss from Lukáš, worried that to accept might anger the ghost of Lukáš's departed wife, who still watches over his infant child. This leads to misunderstandings and recriminations, but with time to cool off and the support of their respective families, Lukáš and Vendulka are reconciled, and the opera ends with their joyful reunion, sealed by a kiss. In keeping with the light plot and character-study quality of the opera, Smetana largely eschewed Wagnerian symphonic structures and grandiose orchestral textures. However, most of the opera flows smoothly in a through-composed manner, with ariosos connecting individual scenes and sections of full-fledged song. This sense of musical continuity is more evocative of Smetana's Wagnerian past than of his practice in *Dvě vdovy*, which owed more to the tradition of light opera with spoken dialogue as connective tissue between more or less independent numbers.

In addition to the flowing yet uncomplicated lyricism of the opera's musical texture, *Hubička* contains the one instance of a direct folksong quotation in all of Smetana's operas – the Christmas pastorella lullaby *Hajej můj andílku* ("Sleep My Angel"), which Vendulka sings to Lukáš's infant child near the close of act 1.[18] This moment, which is immediately followed by a second lullaby, one of Smetana's own invention but that parallels the folksong example closely, was singled out by contemporary critics and later authors alike as one of the most beautiful and significant scenes in the opera. The initial impetus for this addition may well have been Krásnohorská's rather than Smetana's. She added the following note to the text of the lullaby in a working draft of the libretto: "Allow me to append (without further intent in regards to musical composition) a national lullaby from Erben's collection, the rhythm of which is the basis of the text of Vendulka's lullaby" ("Dovoluji si připojiti [bez dalšího úmyslu vzhledem k hudební komposici] národní ukolébavku ze sbírky Erbenovy, její rythmus je podkladem textu ukolébavky Vendulčiny").[19] Regarding the second lullaby, she added "the non-prosodic rhyme [here] intentionally mimics the rhythm of several national songs" ("neprosodický rým

---

[18] For a discussion of the Bohemian Christmas pastorella tradition and its connection to *Hajej můj andílku*, see Large, *Smetana*, 312–13.

[19] See Pražák, *Smetanovy zpěvohry*, 139.

napodoben úmyslně dle rythmu některých národních písní"). Karel Jaromír Erben was one of the most important figures in the first wave of folksong collection that marked the second phase of the National Revival, a direct outgrowth of the Herderian intellectual lineage of the movement.[20]

Folksong stood at the forefront of the mind of Ludevít Procházka, who was one of the loudest voices in support of Smetana's new opera immediately before and after *Hubička*'s premiere. The following passage, drawn from a feuilleton published on the day of the premiere (November 7, 1876) in the leading daily newspaper *Národní listy*, is emblematic of much of the reception of *Hubička*, if perhaps somewhat hyperbolic:

> *The entire opera is like a diamond jewel, composed from the most beautiful folksongs with admirable artfulness; indeed, the whole work is like one grand folksong.* These sounds, with which the composer adorned ... scenes from the life of our rural people, seemed as though they were taken directly from the very bosom of our nation.

> *Celá zpěvohra jest jakoby démantový šperk, s obdivuhodnou umělostí složený z nejkrásnějších národních písní, ba jest celá jako jedna veliká národní píseň.* Zvuky ty, jimiž skladatel přioděl ... výjev z života našeho lidu venkovského, vyňaty jsou jakoby přímo z samých ňader národa našeho.[21]

Among other things, this passage is notable for its use of the term *národní píseň*, which translates literally as "national song." This term is more often translated as "folksong," which is corroborated by the term's translation in German as *Volkslied*, and it recalls the characteristically Czech linguistic slippage that equates the national, *národní*, with the folk, *lidový* – in a sense, the term means both "folksong" and "national song" simultaneously.[22] Procházka's effusiveness in this passage is likely due in part to his status as one of Smetana's former piano students, and to his membership in the Artistic Union, which functioned as a key base of support for Smetana's operas and aesthetics. Indeed, we might read Procházka's insistence on the importance of folksong – he goes so far as to suggest that multiple folksongs were used in the creation of the opera, when in fact only one was explicitly used in such a way – as a way of reclaiming the genre from the Old Czech

---

[20] For more on Erben and the National Revival as it related to ethnographic activity and a concern with representations of the rural countryside, see Christopher Campo-Bowen, *Visions of the Village: Ruralness, Identity, and Czech Opera*, forthcoming from Oxford University Press.

[21] Ludevít Procházka, "Smetanova prostonárodní opera 'Hubička,'" *Národní listy*, November 7, 1876. Emphases in the original, but italics here were originally printed as spaced-out letters.

[22] For more on the slippage between these two terms, see Derek Sayer, *The Coasts of Bohemia* (Princeton, NJ: Princeton University Press, 1998), 119.

political faction, associated with figures like Pivoda, who opposed Smetana. The results of Procházka's rhetorical strategy were twofold. It not only helped normalize the composer's progressive Wagnerian tendencies as the best aesthetic path forward, but in uniting both sides of the argument, Smetana's student could effectively rob the opposition of their ammunition.

This gambit becomes clearer in the full review that Procházka published, again in *Národní listy*, three days later. After taking the opportunity to lambast Smetana's opponents for their previous criticisms of the composer, Procházka got down to business. The following extended passage is worth quoting in its entirety for the clarity with which it not only sets up Smetana as a uniquely creative artist, but also explicitly unites folk music and art music in the context of opera:

The folksong must be for us the starting point for all artistic creation, but it must not be a servile bond. It is a starting point where the creative imagination must rise above prosaic scenes of the life of peasant people, for whom the folksong, naive in its nature, is of course the most appropriate expression … Every scene, every character here is garbed in the vestments of folksong, and the whole seems as if it was skillfully woven from folksongs themselves. However, this is not a blind imitation, but rather a wholly free and independent reproduction of folksong, adapted to the dramatic situation; it is somehow only used as an artistic element from which the whole is built and culminates. Even though many numbers in this opera are fully closed in terms of form, the whole moves along in a unified, ever-growing flow, each scene develops naturally from the other, and all kinds of psychological relationship are indicated by those leitmotifs that maintain the living connection of the individual parts with one another.

Národní píseň sice musí býti u nás východištěm všeho tvoření uměleckého, nesmí však být otrockým poutem, kde tvůrčí fantasie povznésti se musí nad prostičké výjevy života lidu selského, jemuž národní píseň naivní svou povahou jest ovšem výrazem nejpřiměřenějším … Každý výjev, každá osoba zde přioděny jsou v roucho písně národní a celek zdá se, jako by byl uměle utkaný ze samých písní národních. Neníť to však slepé nápodobování, nýbrž zcela volná samostatná reprodukce písně národní, přizpůsobené situace dramatické; použito jí jaksi jen co prvku uměleckého, z něhož celek uměle se buduje a vrcholí. Jakkoliv v opeře té jsou mnohá čísla co do formy zcela zakončená, přec béře se celek jednotným, vždy rostoucím proudem, každý výjev vyvinuje se přirozeně z druhého, všeliké vztahy psychologické naznačeny jsou těmi že motivy příznačnými, jež udržuji živou souvislost jednotlivých části mezi sebou.[23]

---

[23] Ludevít Procházka, "Literatura a umění. Zpěvohra," *Národní listy*, November 10, 1876.

Procházka clearly describes Czech folksong as the font from which all musical creation must flow, but immediately hedges this by placing the creative skill of the composer in an even more important position. The centrality of Smetana as composer allows him in turn to draw on folksong as a resource but bend it to the needs of the drama, to weave it into a larger texture, and to use it to depict the changing psychology of the various characters. Procházka completes the connection to Wagner by conspicuously deploying the Czech term for leitmotif, *příznačný motiv*, effectively tying the success and aesthetic beauty of *Hubička* to Smetana's ability to synthesize folksong in a Wagnerian operatic context. As with Hostinský and *Dalibor*, such a line of reasoning implies the dialectic of folk and art music. The latter is more successful and more valuable when based on folksong, which comes to be recognized as such – however invented and idealized – through its incorporation into examples of art music like opera.

"A New Folksong": Revising *Dvě vdovy*

In the wake of his incontrovertible success with *Hubička*, and likely with an eye toward securing further performances of *Dvě vdovy*, Smetana made significant revisions to the opera in 1877 with the help of Züngel. These revisions included the replacement of all spoken dialogue with recitatives, a new finale for act 1, and a new introductory song for Ladislav at the opening of act 2. The second act now also featured a pair of additional "lower-class" characters, the peasant sweethearts Toník and Lidunka. Smetana himself was more explicit about the deliberately Czech character of this newly composed music; in a letter to Züngel, he described Ladislav's song as written in a fully national style and went on to say that "I myself can confirm that it is a *new folksong*" ("sám mohu tvrditi, že jest to nová národní píseň").[24] Smetana referred to it as a pendant to the lullaby from *Hubička*, which was also marked in that score as a *národní píseň*.

Smetana also described the new finale of act 1 and an additional trio for Toník, Lidunka, and Mumlal as composed "in the national style" ("v národním slohu").[25] The explicit connection of the national to the lower-class, rural characters in Smetana's new version was a clear instance of folk character, especially as communicated through song, applied to an opera otherwise

---

[24] Lev Zelenka-Lerando, *B. Smetana a E. Züngl Listy B. Smetany E. Zünglovi* (Nymburk: Tisk J. Pospíšila, 1903), 8.

[25] Zelenka-Lerando, *B. Smetana a E. Züngl*, 8; and Pražák, *Smetanovy zpěvohry*, 46–47.

focused on aristocratic intrigues. In a letter to Procházka from 1880, Smetana discussed the updated character of the revised opera in the course of reporting on a recent performance:

Dvě vdovy, which was again repeated several days ago with decided success, gave me an idea: would this opera not be the most suitable for introduction to foreign lands, namely on German stages? . . . In its new version the opera projects both a national and cosmopolitan character, and as you know, does so in a kind of salon tone.

Dvě vdovy, které se před několika dny zase opakovaly, a sice rozhodným úspěchem, mě daly myšlenku, jestli by tato opera nebyla nejvýhodnější k uvedení na cizinu a sice německém jevišti? . . . V novém přepracování má opera tato obojí ráz, národní a kosmopolitický, a tento docela jak Vám známo, v jakémsi salonním tonu.[26]

Smetana's emphasis here on cosmopolitanism and attracting foreign attention to his operas may seem unusual, given subsequent insistence by critics and scholars on the purely Czech character of *Dvě vdovy* (and all his other operas, for that matter). The addition of recitative to replace spoken dialogue brought *Dvě vdovy* more into line with full-fledged opera, rather than operetta or musical comedy. Smetana had performed a similar revision with *Prodaná nevěsta* for the same purpose – to help attract outside notice to the opera and enable its staging in places other than the Czech lands.[27]

Smetana's village folk and self-consciously nationalist additions garnered praise from critics when the new version was produced on March 15, 1878, but they did little to further endear the work as a whole to Czech audiences. Despite reports that numerous numbers from the revised opera had to be repeated at its premiere, there were only seventeen total performances of *Dvě vdovy* between 1878 and 1885. At that point, the opera disappeared from the repertoire until 1893. By contrast, *Prodaná nevěsta* enjoyed seventy-five performances during 1878–85, and *Hubička* forty-six, and both continue to be performed almost without interruption into the present.[28] Subsequent revisions in the early 1890s by Václav Juda Novotný, a translator, musician, and writer who had known Smetana personally, attempted to remedy *Dvě vdovy*'s unpopularity through a series of unusually drastic revisions, some of which further concentrated

---

[26] Löwenbach, *Vzájemná korespondence*, 37.

[27] See Přemysl Pražák, *Smetanova Prodaná nevěsta* (Prague: Lidová demokracie, 1962), 50.

[28] For an accounting of the number of performances of Smetana's operas from 1866 to 1893, see Otakar Hostinský, "Něco o osudech zpěvoher Smetanových," *Lumír* 21 (1893): 321.

the emphasis on rural and folk topics by grouping the numbers that drew on such material in the same act. While Novotný's efforts were initially successful, resulting in seven performances of the opera in 1893, these revisions ran afoul of the increasingly dogmatic attitude surrounding Smetana and the canon of his works, and Novotný's changes were eventually discarded in favor of Smetana's revised version in 1923.

The fact that the folk-like additions to *Dvě vdovy* did not end up helping the opera is, ultimately, somewhat beside the point. The more important idea is that such a strategy – increasing the amount of self-consciously *národní* or *prostonárodní* music – was seen as a valuable course of action through to the end of the nineteenth century, if not beyond. Folk music, or even just the implied influence of folk music in the work of the composer, could be used to improve art music in the form of opera. Art music, in turn, could be a way of giving voice to the imagined essence of the people through judicious use of folksong. Smetana, his operas, and their reception showcased this clearly, and were a crucial component of the larger process by which folk music became institutionalized as an integral part of the history of music in the Czech lands.

14 | Choral Music and Modernity in the Bohemian Crownlands in the Nineteenth Century

KAREL ŠIMA

Choral singing had an important role in the transformation of Central European societies from the premodern era to a modern social world. The social functions of choral singing shifted from serving premodern (predominantly Catholic) religious practices to contributing to the construction of modern secular identities (and modern states) based on social class, ethnicity, and gender. Communal singing was also influenced by the changes in social conditions for music, especially the shift away from aristocratic representation and patronage to the professionalization of the music industry, the emergence of music publishing, and emergence of the musical public as the main consumer of artworks. These transformations contributed to the mass appeal and impact of choral singing.

The increasing social importance of organized communal singing and its impact on nineteenth-century modernization processes have to do with emerging social conflicts and cultural innovations that choral singing both reflected and helped shape. These processes, however, cannot be understood as a simple replacement of "old" regimes with "new" ones. Throughout the nineteenth century, choral singing retained certain characteristics from earlier periods while introducing innovations that reflected social transformation and modernizing impulses of the time. One of the most important new characteristics of nineteenth-century choral singing was its involvement with the processes of identity formation, which accompanied the transformation from a world based on local communities and a rigid social stratification to a modern society based simultaneously on individualization and a collective identity.[1] These processes also impacted choral repertoires.

In this chapter, I trace the development of choral singing in the Bohemian lands. My periodization of this development is based on the work of Evžen Valový, author of a substantial study of modern Czech choral singing.[2] Valový ignored German-language choral activities in the

---

This chapter was translated from Czech to English by Martin Nedbal.

[1] On these processes in general, see Ryan Minor, *Choral Fantasies: Music, Festivity, and Nationhood in Nineteenth-Century Germany* (New York: Cambridge University Press, 2012).

[2] Evžen Valový, *Sborový zpěv v Čechách a na Moravě* (Brno: Univerzita J. E. Purkyně, 1972).

late nineteenth century and focused primarily on activities that he viewed as "progressive." In the following pages, by contrast, I focus on the links between choral singing and social phenomena for which the question of musical innovation and quality was often irrelevant. My overview starts with the period between the late 1700s and the 1830s, which was dominated by Enlightenment reforms of the Church and gradually intensifying attempts by aristocratic and urban elites to promote music education and what they viewed as "progress" in music. Civic choral societies started forming in the Bohemian lands in the 1840s, in connection to similar but much earlier activities in Germany, where civic choral societies appeared soon after the Napoleonic Wars. In the 1860s, choral societies played a central role in nationalization processes embraced by the increasingly influential middle class. The economic problems and political crises of the 1870s dampened these mass nationalization tendencies, so the Czech choral movement was not fully reconfigured on an ethnocentric principle until the late 1800s. At the same time, even at the end of the nineteenth century, most German-language choral societies retained regional, as opposed to ethnic, affinities developed in the 1860s. Furthermore, choral activities were heavily influenced by new types of social differentiation, particularly the emergence of the industrial working class, which eventually appropriated the cultural and musical practices of the bourgeoisie. During this period, choral activities were also affected by the contradictory impulses to view choral singing as a social activity on the one hand and, on the other hand, as an artistic endeavor striving for progress, profession-alization, musical quality, and competitiveness in an international context.

The End of the Old before the Beginning of the New

In the Bohemian crownlands, choral singing had traditionally been con-nected to church communities and ceremonies, in some cases since the Middle Ages. In the eighteenth century, this type of choral activity was often connected to so-called literary brotherhoods (see Chapter 3), which sometimes had the character of civic organizations. The activities of these organizations were strongly curtailed in the wake of the Josephine religious reforms, which were supposed to bring all religious activities under the supervision of the state. Joseph II disbanded these societies in a 1783 decree, and although some of them continued to be active, communal choral singing became largely detached from church practices. The first largely independent music organization in Prague was the Society for

Musicians' Widows and Orphans (Tonkünstler Witwen- und Waisen-Societät) which mainly focused on providing economic support for those in economic need and organized musical productions, including choral activities. A similar early example of a communal organization, albeit still connected to church practices, was the Cecilian Union (Jednota sv. Cecilie) founded in Ústí nad Orlicí (Wildenschwert) in 1803. Bohemian nobility channeled their Enlightenment interest in educating musicians into the Association for the Promotion of Music in Bohemia (Verein zur Beförderung der Tonkunst in Böhmen), founded in 1810 (see Chapter 7). In the following year, the Association opened the Prague Conservatory, which was modeled on the Paris music education system (see Chapter 17).[3] The Prague Conservatory focused on the instruction of instrumental performance at first and introduced vocal instruction five years later. The third prominent Prague musical institution, likewise rooted in the Bohemian nobility's Enlightenment viewpoints, was the Association of the Friends of Church Music in Bohemia (Verein der Kunstfreunde für Kirchenmusik in Böhmen), which provided education for church musicians. Lastly, the Prague Organ School, founded in 1830, provided education not only in organ but also in singing and directing church choirs.[4]

The development of choral singing was dependent not only on educational institutions but also the availability of modern repertoire, which included both church music and relatively easy yet expressive compositions for amateurs. *Liedertafel*, amateur male choirs relying predominantly on collective singing of four-part songs, became popular in Germany after the Napoleonic Wars and eventually became widespread in the Bohemian crownlands, first in German- and later also Czech-speaking communities.[5] This music was initially sung in private and semi-public settings of pubs and taverns, and it engaged amateurs in performing music that could express both everyday and intellectual concerns, thus laying the foundation for collective singing as identity formation.

Another institution that contributed to the development of organized choral culture was the Prague (Archduchess) Sophia Academy (Sophien-Akademie), founded in 1840, much later than similar institutions in

[3] Michaela Freemanová, "The Prague Conservatoire in the Context of Nineteenth-Century Bohemia," in *Musical Education in Europe (1770–1914). Compositional, Institutional, and Political Challenges*, vol. 2, ed. Michael Fend and Michael Noiray (Berlin: Berlin Wissenschafts-Verlag, 2005), 519–36.

[4] Michaela Freemanová, "In the Shadow of the Conservatoire: The Prague Organists College (1830–1889/1890)," *Hudební věda* 48 (2011): 369–92.

[5] Valový, *Sborový zpěv*, 30.

German-speaking regions. The Academy was modeled on Berlin institutions and was supposed to educate choral singers.[6] Although the Academy still relied on aristocratic patronage, its activities were mainly aimed at non-aristocratic circles and secular choral activities. Similar functions were also associated with the Prague Cecilian Union (Cäcilienverein), which aimed at performing significant vocal, and later also instrumental, works.[7] The Union's founder, Anton Apt, created an amateur choir to be led by a professional in studying compositions that were not too demanding. The Union therefore represented a type of institution that started appearing in many different places in the middle of the nineteenth century.

Increasing Social Relevance

The earliest known amateur singing organizations in the Bohemian Crownlands date to the 1840s, though some may have existed in the preceding decade. These developments first occurred in German-speaking communities in the Bohemian-German borderlands. The first documented male singing union appeared in Česká Lípa (Böhmische Leipa) in 1845, Frýdlant (Friedland), Jablonec (Gablonz), Krásná Lípa (Schönlinde), and Varnsdorf (Warnsdorf) in 1846, and in Liberec (Reichenberg) and Ústí nad Labem (Aussig) in 1847.[8] These dates are based on official permissions for these organizations granted by state authorities, and it is possible that unofficial singing unions appeared even sooner elsewhere. In Kutná Hora (Kuttenberg), a union was supposedly founded in 1846 but the official permit dates from 1856.[9] Several singing societies were also established in the revolutionary year 1848, such as the Svatopluk in Žďár nad Sázavou (Saar) and the Academic Male Singing Society (Akademischer Männergesangverein) in Prague, but most of them were disbanded due to the Austrian government's counter-revolutionary policies. In the 1850s, however, the imperial authorities approved the constitutions of many civic associations, including choral ones, predominantly in German-speaking regions. Some of these associations were established as bilingual (Czech and German), but most of them were modeled on

---

[6] Helena Matějčková, "Hudební produkce Žofínské akademie v letech 1841–1850," *Hudební věda* 48 (2011): 173–200.

[7] Martina Vídenová, "Cecilská jednota a Antonín Dvořák," *Hudební věda* 55 (2018): 321–34.

[8] Eva Drašarová, "Společenský život v Čechách v období neoabsolutismu," *Paginae Historiae. Sborník státního ústředního archivu v Praze* (1992): 128–69.

[9] Valový, *Sborový zpěv*, 39.

German societies and singing festivals held in Germany in the 1840s. The most prominent among these German-Bohemian societies was The First Teplitzer Male Singing Society (Der erste Teplitzer Männer-Gesangverein), which had its own flag and regularly participated in the town's public events.[10]

The greatest impulse for the establishment of singing societies came with the October Diploma of 1860, which transformed the Habsburg Empire into a constitutional monarchy. Although the law of assembly originally issued in 1852 did not change until 1867, the new constitutional system created incentive for founding choral societies. The societies established in the 1860s were based on their members' national and ethnic affinities; most of them were either exclusively Czech or German. Earlier bilingual organizations ceased to exist or were replaced by Czech or German ones. The singing society from central Bohemian Josefův Důl (Josephsthal) exemplifies these developments. The society was initiated in a series of singing events in the 1840s, and in 1854 a more official organization was created, but it was approved by authorities only in 1857.[11] The society focused on German repertoire at first and moved its seat to the close-by larger city of Mladá Boleslav (Jungbunzlau). In Mladá Boleslav, the society was bilingual at first, but later the Czech members prevailed, renaming the society Boleslav in 1863 and focusing on exclusively Czech nationalist activities. For example, in 1865 the society organized a festive consecration of its own flag, which was attended by many prominent figures of the Czech national movement, including Bedřich Smetana. One of the society's original founders, accountant František Částka, later returned to Josefův Důl and founded another society, which was once again bilingual, mainly because the new society's most prominent honorary member and financial sponsor could not speak Czech. In Prague, too, a male singing society was founded in 1859 and operated in both Czech and German for a few years.[12] The German speakers, however, founded a separate society in the 1860s, which from 1864 was directed by Eduard Tauwitz, a prominent figure of Prague's music scene, the last director of the Sophia Academy, and a long-time music director of the Estates Theater, where he, paradoxically, produced

[10] Jiřina Řeřichová, "Činnost prvního teplického mužského pěveckého spolku jako iniciátora Německého pěveckého svatu v Čechách," in *Spolkový život v Čecháh v 19. a na počátku 20. století* (Ústí nad Labem: Univerzita Jana Evangelisty Purkyně, 2005), 49–71.

[11] The history of the society is based on a letter that one of its founders, František Částka, sent to the Prague Hlahol in 1868. Prague, Archiv Zpěváckého spolku Hlahol, 1868, uncatalogued letter.

[12] Josef Srb and Ferdinand Tadra, eds., *Památník pražského Hlaholu. Na oslavu 25leté činnosti spolku* (Prague: Hlahol, 1886).

several Czech works in the 1850s. Tauwitz and his society later pursued and promoted the idea of Bohemia as part of larger Germany and represented Bohemian Germans at the pan-German congress of choral societies in Dresden in 1865.[13]

The number of Czech and German singing societies therefore increased significantly in the 1860s. In 1860 alone, seventeen Czech societies were founded, and more than fifty were established between 1863 and 1868.[14] In the late 1860s, Prague hosted some of the largest public events ever organized by ethnic Czechs, and the most prominent institutions that participated in these events were the gymnastic organization Sokol and the Prague singing society Hlahol. Hlahol was informally established in 1860 on the recommendation of Jan Ludevít Lukes, a lawyer and opera singer who had recently returned from travels abroad.[15] Lukes gained support from both the Prague music circles and Count Rudolf Thurn-Taxis, prominent patron of Czech arts, to create the society. Its membership grew quickly and included many university students as well as lawyers, government officials, artisans, merchants, and musicians; those interested in admission to the society were first tested in sight-singing, and many members were expelled during the first year.[16] Most singing societies were organized on similar principles, which they often consulted and shared among themselves. Each society had a director and a secretary elected by the members; many societies also had a separate music director who served as the main officer in smaller societies. There were at least three types of membership: honorary, which included prominent representatives of civic and aristocratic circles, powerful officials, and other notable public figures; active, which included exclusively male singers; and sustaining, consisting of those who merely paid membership fees. Local elite members did not have to be active singers to significantly influence the organization, finances, operations, and often also musical repertoire and activities of the societies. These societies were therefore not only musical but also social institutions that provided members with the opportunity to foster cultural and professional contacts with local elites, which was unique particularly in smaller towns.

---

[13] Josef Sobitschka, *Geschichte des Deutschen Sängerbundes in Böhmen 1864–1884* (Tetschen an der Elbe: Deutscher Sängerbund, 1884).

[14] Valový, *Sborový zpěv*, 47.

[15] The Hlahol society membership book lists Lukes as "brewer and artist" ("pivovarník a umělec") because he had also opened a brewery after his return to Prague. Prague, Archiv Zpěváckého spolku Hlahol, "Kniha přání zpěváckého spolku Hlahol v Praze, rok 1861."

[16] Prague, Archiv Zpěváckého spolku Hlahol, "Kniha přání zpěváckého spolku Hlahol v Praze, rok 1861."

These social functions also determined these societies' disposition toward gender. Throughout the nineteenth century, men were considered the sole participants in public life, and singing societies were therefore for a long time exclusively male. Only in the 1870s did calls for female choirs appear, and it was another decade before female sections of male singing societies were established.[17] Choral singing also represented an important activity of the first female emancipation societies, such as the American Ladies Club (Americký klub dam) in Prague and the music-oriented Vesna Society in Brno.[18] Published collections of works performed by these societies were important for later development of female singing societies, not necessarily because they promoted emancipation ideals but because they made music for female voices available.[19]

The social functions of choral societies also determined the content and nature of the events in which they participated. The most prominent among these were fairly regular public concerts that took place both indoors and outdoors. The Prague Hlahol, for example, gave concerts both in the hall on Žofín Island and in the open air on Střelecký Island. Hlahol members also favored evening parties, which often included refreshments and dancing. These events almost always included speeches that commented on current social issues and satirized various aspects of everyday life. Societies also organized end-of-the-year and carnival parties that focused on entertainment including both singing and comical sketches. Some societies organized excursions to historical sights outside the city for their members, where they would sometimes perform as well.

These internal activities were complemented by appearances at significant social events. In the 1860s, newly established singing societies held conventions, significant public events through which the societies could introduce themselves to the public and lay claim on public urban spaces, which Austrian state authorities no longer controlled as restrictively as in the previous decades. German societies organized their first convention, which included a singing contest, in Teplice in 1860.[20] The most active

---

[17] Karel Šima, Tomáš Kavka, and Hana Zimmerhaklová, "'By Means of Singing to the Heart, by Means of Heart to the Homeland': Choral Societies and the Nationalist Mobilization of Czechs in the Nineteenth Century," in Krisztina Lajosi and Andreas Stynen, eds., *Choral Societies and Nationalist Mobilization in Nineteenth-Century Europe* (Leiden: Brill, 2019), 187–205.

[18] Kelly St. Pierre, "Singing Women and the 'Woman Question' in the Czech Lands," in *Women in Nineteenth-Century Czech Musical Culture*, ed. Anja Bunzel and Christopher Campo-Bowen (New York: Routledge, 2024), 191–203.

[19] See St. Pierre, "Singing Women and the 'Women Question' in the Czech Lands."

[20] Wolfgang Pilz, "Die Tätigkeit des Trautenauer Männergesangvereines seit 1854 bis zu seiner Reformierung und Erweiterung zum Musik- und Gesangverein Harmonie 1869," in

Czech society was the Prague Hlahol, which organized its first convention on May 15, 1862, a time when people from the countryside came to Prague for the traditional pilgrimage to St. John of Nepomuk (Jan Nepomucký). The convention featured both a concert in Prague's New Town Theater, the city's largest stage, and a public lottery for the benefit of Zdeňka Havlíčková, the orphaned daughter of Karel Havlíček, a prominent Czech journalist and politician. Up to 900 singers from thirty-eight societies purportedly participated in the event, and when they launched into the performance of the folksong *Utonulá* ("The Drowned Woman"), arranged and directed by Moravian priest Pavel Křížkovský, Smetana supposedly said, "This is our music. This is Czech music."[21] Many commemorative publications from these societal events have a mythologizing character, but the conventions were complex social gatherings that gave traditional performative activities new meaning linked to ethnic identities based on language use.

Together with the Sokol and other gymnastics associations, Czech singing societies were heavily involved in several national festivals of the 1860s, for which they both provided musical accompaniment and represented the Czech nation as a civilized, socially unified, and modern civic community. In 1863, another round of singing festivals took place in Brno in connection to the millennial anniversary of the arrival of the Christian evangelists Cyril and Methodius. According to contemporaneous reports, by that year there were about one hundred Czech-language (Slavic) singing societies in the Bohemian crownlands.[22] The highpoint of singing societies' public prominence came in 1868, during the festive laying of the foundation stones for the National Theater in Prague. Karel Šebor's festive cantata for the festival was chosen in a competition and presented by a combined chorus of several thousand men from different societies immediately before the main political speech by Karel Sladkovský. After the consecration of the foundation stones, all participants joined the singing societies to perform the song *Kde domov můj* ("Where Is My Home"), considered the Czech national anthem. That choral societies engaged the wider public in performative acts of identification with the nation is also reflected in Hlahol's motto: "By means of singing to the heart, through the heart to the nation" ("Zpěvem k srdci, srdcem k vlasti").

Sborníček. Příspěvky muzea Podkrkonoší v Trutnově (Trutnov: Muzeum Podkrkonoší v Trutnově, 2005), 138.
[21] Valový, *Sborový zpěv*, 45.   [22] Valový, *Sborový zpěv*, 46.

The nationalization of Czech and German singing societies proceeded at a different pace. German societies appeared and consolidated much sooner under the influence of the choral movement in Germany. As early as 1864, twelve north Bohemian German societies formed the German Singing Union in Bohemia (Der Deutsche Sängerbund in Böhmen) on the initiative of the Teplice society under the leadership of Ernst Rohn.[23] The association joined the pan-German choral union in 1865, and although it went through a period of stagnation, it organized the first communal singing festival in Teplice in 1876. In 1878, the association's headquarters moved to Prague, and societies from all over Bohemia joined, so that it represented 118 societies by 1885. Similar organizations formed in Moravia (German Singing Union in Moravia (Deutscher Sängerbund in Mähren)) and Silesia (Silesian Singing Union (Schlesischer Sängerbund)). Czech societies developed rapidly in the 1860s but were less active in the 1870s, the same period during which German societies integrated into larger associations. Czech societies founded a central association in 1869, but it became truly active only in the 1890s, as explained below.

The singing societies' repertoire mostly reflected their social functions. In the early decades, sacred music was still prominent, as were performances in churches and at religious fairs. In the 1850s, however, this type of music moved to church societies and choirs.[24] Amateur singing societies later performed sacred music only at funerals of prominent people and when it was programmed as part of national celebrations. Both German liberals and Czech nationalists aimed at desacralizing choral singing, and secular songs became the most significant part of the repertoire. They viewed both folk and art songs as a democratic aspect of the singing movement, enticing wide-ranging participation. Whereas German-language societies drew on repertoire published in German lands, Czech-language choirs relied on translations of German materials and later also on national songbooks published in large numbers.[25] The Prague Hlahol published the first such songbook in 1861, and dozens of similar publications appeared in the following decades. These songbooks and simple four-part arrangements for male voices drawn from them formed the core repertory of the Czech choral societies, most of which included mainly untrained singers. Czech choral music was also published in shorter

[23] Sobitschka, *Geschichte des deutschen Sängerbundes*, 23.
[24] Drašarová, "Společenský život", 138.
[25] Josef Kotek, *Dějiny české populární hudby a zpěvu*, vol. 1 (Prague: Academia, 1994), 106. See also Bedřich Václavek and Robert Smetana, *Český národní zpěvník. Písně české společnosti 19. století* (Prague: Svoboda, 1949).

songbooks, prepared by professional and semi-professional musicians such as Jan Malát, Emanuel Meliš, František Pivoda, Jan Ludevít Procházka, and Josef Leopold Zvonař, and distributed throughout the network of societies. Simple songs were gradually complemented with more demanding compositions by contemporaneous composers such as Karel Bendl, Pavel Křížkovský, Arnošt Förchtgott-Tovačovský, Smetana, and Dvořák. Smetana served as Hlahol's music director between 1863 and 1865 and shifted its focus to more demanding music. This changed later when Hlahol came under the influence of the conservative Old Czech Party and Smetana embraced the ideas of the liberal Young Czech Party.[26] Czech singing societies performed only a few of Smetana's simpler choral compositions, such as the choral songs *Věno* ("The Dowry") and *Slavnostní sbor* ("Festive Chorus"), whereas works by the other composers mentioned above were more widely known. Although Dvořák had a close relationship to many choral societies,[27] he composed only large choral works, such as the oratorio *Svatá Ludmila* ("St. Ludmila") and the cantata *Svatební košile* ("Wedding Shirts"). Only his *Moravian Duets* and *Stabat Mater* (for special occasions) entered the mainstream repertoire of the Czech choral societies.[28] Many societies, however, included arrangements of choruses from Dvořák's operas in their repertoire.

The repertoire of late nineteenth-century singing societies also depended on whether they performed in regular concerts or for special occasions. Special concerts, including various national celebrations, often included hymns, such as *Kde domov můj* and *Hej Slované* ("Hey Slavs"), and ancient chorales, such as *Ktož jsú boží bojovníci* ("You Who Are Warriors of God"), *Svatý Václave* ("Saint Wenceslas"), and *Hospodine, pomiluj ny* ("Lord, Have Mercy upon Us," see also Chapters 1 and 2). In the German environment, the most important songs were *Die Wacht am Rhein*, *Was ist dem Deutschen Vaterland*, and *Das deutsche Lied* – these songs became truly prominent in the German repertoire later than the Czech hymns and chorales in the Czech repertoire, mirroring the delayed arrival of pan-German nationalism in Bohemia. Special performances also featured occasional works that reflected the nature of the celebration. Some works, for example, celebrated important figures of the national

---

[26] See Kelly St. Pierre, *Bedřich Smetana: Myth, Music, Propaganda* (Rochester, NY: University of Rochester Press, 2017), 47.

[27] Well documented are Dvořák's contacts with the society in Turnov, which was eventually named after him. Eva Mikanová, "Dvořákova hudba v Pojizeří v repertoáru místních a pražských umělců," *Z českého ráje a Podkrkonoší* 14 (2001): 162–73.

[28] Valový, *Sborový zpěv*, 27.

movement, such as Bendl's cantata *Tichému géniovi* ("To the Quiet Genius"), composed for and performed at the 1873 festive founding of the monument for Czech linguist Josef Jungmann.

During these events, contemporaneous commentators noted the social significance of choral singing. In his review of the 1864 convention of Czech choral societies, famous Czech journalist Jan Neruda complained that the opening concert should have been "more national" ("prostonárodnější") and that choral societies could have saved their display of "an artistic height" ("umělecká výše") for other occasions.[29] According to Neruda, public celebrations should present music that "would speak to everyone" ("aby ke každému mluvila") and be "more understandable to a large audience" ("velkému obecenstvu srozumitelnější"). The second concert was, according to Neruda, less demanding artistically, so "the monumental singing had a great effect on the excitement of all minds" ("mohutný zpěv účinkoval znamenitě k rozjaření veškerých myslí"). The alleged high artistic demands of the first concert were likely tied to the participation of Hlahol's director Smetana, whose ambitions did not exactly match the needs and interests of amateur singers.

Programs of regular concerts included speeches and declamations of patriotic poems as well as choral and solo works. The concerts from the 1860s, for example, often featured patriotic songs by local composers, such as the chorus *Na Prahu* ("To Prague") by Václav Jindřich Veit (Wenzel Heinrich Veit) and *Zpěv Čechů* ("Song of the Czechs") by Leopold Procházka.[30] Most concerts also included arrangements of folksongs, though these were often not a substantial part of the program and likely had a predominantly symbolic function. Choral works alternated with solo pieces and duets, mostly arrangements of patriotic songs. Also common were excerpts from popular operas, such as arias and choruses from works by Rossini, Meyerbeer, Donizetti, and Wagner, as well as Czech operas by Blodek and Smetana.

Sharpening of Boundaries

In the late nineteenth century, Czech and German choral societies were more closely bound to hierarchical, centralistic national organizations. In 1890, the Central Union of Choral Societies (Ústřední jednota zpěváckých

---

[29] *Národní listy*, May 18, 1864.

[30] This information is based on the concert programs preserved in Prague, Archiv Zpěváckého spolku Hlahol; and Prague, Archiv Umělecké besedy.

spolků) reactivated and started contributing to the development of individual groups.[31] Around 1900, both Czech and German unions introduced internal divisions into regional sub-organizations ("župy" in Czech, "Gäu" in German). These subdivisions were important for German-speaking participants, who lived in geographically isolated borderland regions and developed individual regional identities.[32]

The late nineteenth-century choral movement became even more massive with the emergence of workers' choruses.[33] These organizations started to appear in the 1870s and initially focused on simple monophonic singing and imitated the activities and repertoires of bourgeois choral societies. After the large-scale May Day celebrations of the 1890s, however, workers' choruses started to embrace more distinct repertoire and social functions. Composers such as Josef Krapka Náchodský in Prague and František Koprda Lysický in Brno composed choruses that addressed the concerns of the working classes and featured a specific musical idiom based on energetic expression and marching rhythms. These works were published in collections that were easily available to other workers' choruses thanks to cheap prices and distribution channels among the societies. The increasing number of workers' choruses led to the foundation of both Czech and German unions of workers' choral societies. Although these organizations were modeled on the earlier bourgeois institutions, their focus on social problems and the conflict between workers and employers foreshadowed some of the most crucial social issues of the twentieth century.

At the turn of the century, the centralization of amateur singing societies was complemented by initiatives to increase their singers' technical and artistic level. Because of these initiatives, some societies became more professionalized and aimed at musical productions that could compete internationally. Many other singing societies, by contrast, came to be viewed as leisure organizations that gradually lost their national significance. The highly publicized participation of the Plzeň Hlahol at a choral competition in Paris in 1900 illustrates the professionalization of the Czech choral movement. In 1896, one of the Plzeň society's members chose the most promising singers from among his colleagues, and the group spent four years learning the competition repertoire. The group was successful not only in the Paris competition but also in an international contest in

---

[31] Valový, *Sborový zpěv*, 63.
[32] Řeřichová, "Činnost prvního teplického mužského pěveckého spolku," 55.
[33] See Vladimír Gregor, *Dělnické pěvecké spolky. Na Ostravsku a v jiných průmyslových střediscích českých zemí* (Ostrava: Krajské nakladatelství, 1961). On the repertoire, see Vladimír Karbusický and Václav Pletka, *Dělnické písně*, 2 vols. (Prague: SNLKHU, 1958).

choral singing in Brussels, and as a result it split from the original society and established a new one, called Smetana. Similarly, choral associations of Bohemian and Moravian teachers focused on professional approaches to the study and performance of musical repertoire, and they quickly became internationally successful and well known.

Throughout the nineteenth century – particularly between the 1860s and 1880s – choral singing in the Bohemian crownlands transformed from an activity of local church choirs and aristocratic representation into an important vehicle for social change. The organization and repertoire of newly emerging civic choral societies mirrored the intensifying ethnic tensions between Czechs and Germans. Although German societies were established first, they embraced explicit nationalist attitudes only after Czech societies and often in reaction to heightened Czech nationalism. In the 1890s, working-class singing societies quickly proliferated and became emancipated from the bourgeois cultural codes. By the outset of the new century, the choral movement split into mass organizations with centralized structures based on ethnic and social distinctions, and more artistically ambitious choirs that wanted to represent their communities internationally.

15 | Symphonic Music in the Nineteenth-Century Czech Lands

EVA BRANDA

Introduction

In his analysis of Antonín Dvořák's Seventh Symphony (1884–85), Michael Beckerman observes a kind of "battle" between the two themes of the scherzo. The lilting melody introduced at the outset of the movement is disrupted by hemiola rhythms, prompting Beckerman to suggest that the material can be interpreted either as "delicately elfin or brutal" (see Example 15.1). He characterizes the passage as "a staged brawl between a furiant and a waltz, that is between the Czech and Viennese impulse in the composer's artistic personality."[1] This statement applies not only to Dvořák's scherzo, but it encapsulates one of the concerns at the forefront of symphonic composition in the Czech lands during the nineteenth century.

At this time, the symphony more broadly carried many connotations – seen both as the pinnacle of achievement in instrumental music owing to its lingering Beethovenian prestige and as an increasingly outdated genre to be set aside in favor of the more progressive symphonic poem. The latter view was promulgated by several of the most prominent critics active in Prague from the 1870s onward; yet, Czech composers continued to cultivate the symphony. In light of these ongoing debates, Czech symphonic works in the second half of the nineteenth century often straddle the border between the programmatic and the absolute, and the genre's inherent ambiguity – its status as an "unmarked" medium, in the eyes of aestheticians like Eduard Hanslick – made it especially pliable. Even more significantly, the symphony had uniquely German associations throughout the century, further tainting its imagined purity even in the absence of explicit extra-musical content. Branded as a "serious" genre, the symphony became an outlet for constructions of German national identity.[2] Given the centrality of the nationalist project in the Czech lands during this period, the perceived Germanness of the symphony did not always sit easy with the Czechs, making it a complicated

---

[1] Michael Beckerman, "Dvořák," in *The Nineteenth-Century Symphony*, ed. D. Kern Holoman (New York: Schirmer Books, 1996), 286.
[2] Mark Evan Bonds, *Music as Thought* (Princeton, NJ: Princeton University Press, 2006), 89.

Example 15.1: Antonín Dvořák, Seventh Symphony, third movement, mm. 1–17.

vehicle for expressions of the kind of patriotism that was expected from this generation of composers. This chapter examines the "symphony" as a genre and investigates how these dichotomies – of traditional vs. modern, abstract vs. concrete, and Czech/Slavic vs. Viennese/German – played out specifically within a Czech context.

"The Most German of Musical Genres"

The symphony's supposed "Germanness" was deeply entrenched in the nineteenth century. The notion is evident as early as 1824 in the writing of critic Adolph Bernhard Marx, who asserts that "the more light-minded nations, for example, the French and the Italians, have never produced anything substantial in the entire genre [of the symphony] ... they have fallen far behind the Germans, for whom the symphony is characteristic."[3] The weightiness of the symphony – and by extension, German music in general – is implicit in Marx's comment. Elsewhere, Marx is even more direct, calling the symphony "virtually the exclusive property of the Germans."[4] Robert Schumann saw the genre in a similar way: "when the German talks of symphonies, he means Beethoven; the two names are for him one and indivisible; his joy, his pride. As Italy has its Naples, France its revolution, England its navigation, so Germany has its Beethoven symphonies."[5]

The reasons why Germans lay claim to the symphony are far too complex to be discussed at any length here, though some brief contextualization is in order. At a time when Germany was not yet united politically, a great deal of emphasis was placed on culture (*Kultur*) as a means of creating national identity.[6] Though opera was more prestigious, Germans could not justify claims of exclusivity in this realm, owing to its strong Italian connections. Choral music was not held in very high regard because of its association with amateur music-making,[7] leaving instrumental music for the taking. The symphony proved to be a particularly suitable genre for inciting feelings of national pride in the Germans, since it ranked high in the estimation of the early Romantics. Its aesthetic superiority had been established in German criticism; in his well-known review of Beethoven's Fifth Symphony from 1813, E. T. A. Hoffmann had famously labeled instrumental music as the most "purely romantic" of all arts.[8] Such statements were also backed by a strong Austro-German symphonic tradition; the contributions of the First Viennese School to this genre were quickly

---

[3] A. B. Marx, "Korrespondenz, Berlin, den 13. Dezember 1824," *Berliner allgemeine musikalische Zeitung* 1 (1824): 444; Sanna Pederson, "On the Task of the Music Historian: The Myth of the Symphony after Beethoven," *Repercussions* 2, no. 2 (1993): 17.

[4] A. B. Marx, "Korrespondenz: Berlin, den 28. April," *Berliner allgemeine musikalische Zeitung* 1 (1824):163; Sanna Pederson, "A. B. Marx, Berlin Concert Life, and German National Identity," *19th-Century Music* 18 (1994): 96.

[5] Robert Schumann, *Music and Musicians: Essays and Criticism*, trans. Fanny Raymond Ritter (Freeport: Books for Libraries, 1972), 38; originally published in "Neue Symphonien für Orchester," *Neue Zeitschrift für Musik* 11, no. 1 (1839): 1.

[6] Pederson, "On the Task of the Music Historian," 12–14.

[7] Barbara Eichner, *History in Mighty Sounds: Musical Constructions of German National Identity, 1848–1914* (Woodbridge: Boydell & Brewer, 2012), 229–72.

[8] E. T. A. Hoffmann, "Beethoven's Instrumental Music," in *E. T. A. Hoffmann's Musical Writings: Kreisleriana, The Poet and the Composer, Music Criticism*, ed. David Charlton, trans. Martyn Clarke (Cambridge: Cambridge University Press, 2003), 236; originally published in *Zeitung für die elegante Welt* 13 (1813).

becoming staples in concert halls throughout Europe. This meant that, when approaching the symphony in the nineteenth century, Czech composers needed to confront its German reputation and grapple with the baggage that it carried.

The symphony was, in fact, somewhat of a neglected genre among the Czechs during the early Romantic period. Jan Smaczny manages to compile a respectable list of Bohemian composers who wrote symphonies at that time;[9] however, their works hardly constitute a unified tradition. Like their eighteenth-century predecessors, some of these composers sought positions in German-speaking Europe. For example, Jan Václav Voříšek (Johann Hugo Worzischek, 1791–1825), who showed particular promise as a symphonist, in Smaczny's estimation,[10] waited until he was settled in Vienna before making his one and only contribution to the genre in 1821, and the most prolific Bohemian composer of symphonies in the early nineteenth century, Jan Václav Kalivoda (Johann Wenzel Kalliwoda, 1801–66), wrote all seven of his symphonies (1825–43) after he had relocated to Donaueschingen. Kalivoda's Symphony No. 1 (1825) provides an interesting sample of his approach to the genre, since it was among his most successful works; his first three symphonies were the ones to receive critical attention and were performed regularly until mid-century. The First Symphony is comparatively brief, if judged by the standard of Beethoven. In spite of the work's dramatic gestures and moments of experimentation – including some rather unpredictable modulations, particularly in the second movement, and a tendency to recapitulate only the secondary theme, which Kalivoda does in both of the outer movements – it is quite Classical in style, reflecting Alena Němcová's and John Daverio's description of the composer as one "whose allegiance to late eighteenth-century ideals was tinged by an incipient Romantic spirit."[11] Though active primarily in German circles, composers like Kalivoda should not be excluded from a history of the Czech symphony, and Smaczny makes a strong case for this:

To see the work of these composers, many of whom left their native land in childhood, from a purely Czech point of view would be to deny them their full role in a history which belongs more properly to a broader consideration of the

[9] Jan Smaczny, "The Czech Symphony," in *A Companion to the Symphony*, ed. Robert Layton (London: Simon and Schuster, 1993), 223–31.

[10] Smaczny, "The Czech Symphony," 227–28.

[11] John Daverio and Alena Němcová, "Kalliwoda, Johann Wenzel," *Grove Music Online*, ed. D. Roote, https://www-oxfordmusiconline-com.libproxy.wlu.ca/grovemusic, accessed April 26, 2023.

European symphony ... conversely, an approach which excludes the works of [those] who lived abroad would eliminate from consideration the most renowned Czech symphony of all, Dvořák's Ninth *From the New World* ... Thus any consideration of the Czech symphony has to be something of a compromise hedged around by questions of style as much as geography.[12]

Bohemian composers of the early Romantic period who remained in the Czech lands did not tend to devote themselves extensively to the symphony. Václav Jan Tomášek (Wenzel Johann Tomaschek, 1774–1850) – the sole composer in Prague to write symphonies at the start of the nineteenth century[13] – worked in the genre for only a short time at the beginning of his career, producing three symphonies over the span of six years (1801–7); ultimately, he became far better-known for his songs and piano pieces. Likewise, Václav Jindřich (Wenzel Heinrich) Veit's (1806–64) one symphony (1859), though hailed as a significant work,[14] is quite exceptional in his oeuvre, which consists by and large of chamber and choral compositions. These symphonies stood on the periphery of musical activity in Prague, leading Vladimír Lébl and Jitka Ludvová to write that "in Czech music of the first half of the nineteenth century, the genre of the symphony nearly disappeared."[15]

What is more, the two "Czech" symphonies that were likely most familiar to audiences in Prague at mid-century had strong connections to German traditions. One of these is *Jagdsymphonie* (1837), the second of four symphonies (1836–58) to be composed by Jan Bedřich (Johann Friedrich) Kittl (1806–68), the long-time head of the Prague Conservatory.[16] In his decision to write a "hunting" symphony, Kittl places himself alongside the likes of such Austrian composers as Leopold Mozart and Joseph Haydn. The work also calls Beethoven's *Pastoral* Symphony to mind in its use of descriptive subtitles for all of its movements. With its allusions to German symphonies of the past, Kittl's *Jagdsymphonie* enjoyed remarkable success in German-speaking

---

[12] Smaczny, "The Czech Symphony," 223.

[13] Jarmila Gabrielová, preface to Václav Jan Tomášek, *Thesaurus Musicae Bohemiae: Seria B – Sinfonia Grande, Op. 17*, ed. Šárka Jedličková (Prague: Supraphon, 1989), x.

[14] Veit stood out in Prague for his criticism of Wagner and Berlioz and for his stance in favor of absolute genres, though Karl Stapleton argues that Veit's role in this regard has been overstated; Stapleton, "Veit, Václav," *Grove Music Online*, www.oxfordmusiconline-com.libproxy.wlu.ca/grovemusic, accessed April 26, 2023.

[15] Vladimír Lébl and Jitka Ludvová, "Nová doba (1860–1938)," in *Hudba v českých dějinách: Od středověku do nové doby*, ed. Vladimír Lébl (Prague: Supraphon, 1983), 391.

[16] Kittl wrote his *Jagdsymphonie* before assuming directorship of the Prague Conservatory in 1843 – a post that he would hold until 1864.

Europe, garnering the interest of Mendelssohn, Schumann, and Spohr. The other symphonic work that concertgoers in Prague encountered in the 1850s was Smetana's lone contribution to the genre, which too has German associations. Composed early in his career, in 1853, the *Triumph-Sinfonie*[17] was meant to celebrate the engagement between Emperor Franz Joseph I and Princess Elisabeth of Bavaria.[18] In keeping with its imperial tone, the Symphony incorporates quotations of the Austrian anthem in three of its four movements. The anthem's appearance is brief and subtle in the first movement; it is treated as thematic material in the second; and its most obvious and full statement is reserved for the closing measures of the finale, where the reference is unmistakable (see Example 15.2). Curiously, Smetana's younger contemporary František Zdeněk Skuherský (1830–92) wrote a symphony in honor of the imperial couple as well. It is striking that both composers chose the "German" symphony as their vehicle. Together with Kittl's *Jagdsymphonie*, these pieces demonstrate that Czech composers of the early to mid-nineteenth century approached the symphony with a German frame of reference.

An "Outmoded" Genre: Theorizing the Symphony in the Czech Lands

Intense proselytization on behalf of the "more progressive" symphonic poem added another layer of complication for the symphony in the latter half of the nineteenth century in the Czech lands and abroad. Richard Taruskin characterizes the 1850s and 60s as the leanest years of the symphony's existence, when the genre was under threat of being circumvented by the symphonic poem.[19] Many Czech critics jumped readily on the programmatic "band wagon"; among them were Václav Juda Novotný (1849–1922) and Otakar Hostinský (1847–1910), both of whom wrote extensively on this topic for the music journal *Dalibor* in 1873. In a series of articles, Novotný traces the symphony from its ancient Greek roots through to Haydn, Mozart, Beethoven, and the early Romantics; Czech

---

[17] The full title on Smetana's autograph score is "Triumph-Sinfonie mit Benützung der österreich. Volkshymne für große Orchester."

[18] Brian Large, *Smetana* (London: Duckworth, 1970), 58.

[19] Richard Taruskin, *Oxford History of Western Music*, vol. 3, *Music in the Nineteenth Century* (Oxford: Oxford University Press, 2010), 675–76.

Example 15.2: Bedřich Smetana, *Triumph-Sinfonie*, fourth movement, coda, opening, mm. 695–98.

symphonic works are conspicuously absent from his discussion.[20] Taking
his cues from Friedrich Hegel and Franz Brendel, Novotný presents an
unabashedly teleological view of music history and demonstrates how the
older genre of the symphony led to the more complex and sophisticated
symphonic poem; just as the suite gave way to the symphony, so too was the
symphony destined to be "replaced" by the symphonic poem in Novotný's
historical narrative. The same volume of *Dalibor* also carried a lengthy
series by Hostinský, seeking to explain the aesthetic intent behind the
symphonic poem and in so doing, to dispel certain misconceptions that
audiences might have about the new genre.[21] Taking a page from Wagner's
playbook, Hostinský claims that one of the central aims of modern music is
the unification of the arts, which would exclude the symphony with its lack
of extra-musical content. Looking beyond aesthetics, Novotný takes an
overtly political approach, as observed by Kelly St. Pierre: "according to
Novotný, the symphonic poem was a means for Czechs to advertise their
relevance and eminence to the rest of Europe."[22] By implication, clinging to
the symphony would hinder Czechs from achieving this goal.

While Hostinský and Novotný frame their studies differently, they take
a similar attitude toward the Czech audience in two distinct ways. Firstly,
both critics operate under the basic assumption that the symphonic poem
will be met with some resistance on the part of the average listener, suggesting perhaps that, during the 1870s, audiences in Prague were still more at
home with the "traditional" symphony. In his opening article, Novotný urges
readers repeatedly to give new music a chance, counseling against hasty
conclusions and reminding readers that all novelties of the past struggled to
gain acceptance.[23] Hostinský addresses the audience as well, claiming that
any reluctance to accept that which is new ultimately stems from a faulty
understanding of the novelty and a misplaced reverence for tradition.
Secondly, both critics believe firmly in audience perspicacity, and it is this
discernment on the part of the concert audience – along with a sense of
historical inevitability – that makes Novotný and Hostinský confident that

---

[20] Václav Juda Novotný, "Sonata a symfonie – symfonická báseň: nástin historického vývinu
těchto forem," *Dalibor* 1 (1873): 117–21, 127–29, 135–36, 145–48, 153–56, 161–64, 169–71,
177–79, 193–96, 201–3, 209–12.

[21] Otakar Hostinský, "O hudbě programní," *Dalibor* 1 (1873): 281–83, 289–91, 297–300, 305–9,
333–36, 341–43, 349–51, 357–59, 381–84.

[22] Kelly St. Pierre, *Smetana: Myth, Music, and Propaganda* (Rochester: University of Rochester
Press, 2017), 34.

[23] Novotný, "Sonata a symfonie," 120. He views music history as a kind of Darwinian struggle
between winners and losers, citing several examples (including Haydn's triumph over Pleyel,
Mozart's over Salieri, etc.).

the symphonic poem will eventually win the day. "In the concert hall, we never have to take the widest circle of listeners into account, as in the theater or church," asserts Novotný; "with concert audiences, we always assume a higher degree of education and an ability to make [sound] judgments" ("V koncertu nemusíme nikdy bráti ohledu na nejširší kruhy posluchačstva tak jako v divadle či v kostele; neboť u koncertního obecenstva předpokládáme vždy vyšší vzdělání a schopnost k posuzování").[24] Hostinský makes a similar point in another of his opinion pieces for *Dalibor*, distinguishing between the Prague audience at large and a core group of enthusiasts with genuine interest in music.[25] At the same time, concert audiences – especially those in attendance at performances of the Prague Conservatory – were the most wedded to the Austro-German canon and thereby most likely to favor the symphony.[26]

Although these critics acted mainly as apologists for the symphonic poem, there are important implications here for the symphony. Novotný surveys the work of past symphonists, if only to show that the genre had outlived its usefulness, and while acknowledging its historical significance, he characterizes the symphony as an overly formulaic and inflexible genre:

A person can somehow paste a "symphony" together because he has exact forms before his eyes; he need only proceed following an ordinary template and will bring the well-known four movements of the "grand symphony for large orchestra" into God's light. What, however, is one to do with the "symphonic poem," where there is no template, where there are no prescribed forms and paragraphs, where the wretched person does not even know "what is and is not allowed?" He who wishes to compose a "symphonic poem" must know how to do more than a mere musician; he must know more than those who belong to the so-called "old school."

'Symfonii' dovede takovýto člověk předc nějak slepiti, poněvadž má předepsané formy před sebou; potřebuje jen dle obyčejné šablony si počínati a známé čtyry věty 'velké symfonie pro velký orkestr' přivede předc s pílí a namáháním na světlo boží. Co však počíti si má se 'symfonickou básní,' kde není žádná šablona, kde nejsou předepsané formy a paragrafy, kde člověk ubožec ani neví 'co je a co není dovoleno?' Kdo chce komponovati 'symfonickou báseň,' musí uměti něco více než pouhý muzikant, musí více věděti než ti, které počítáme k tak zvané 'staré škole.'[27]

[24] Novotný, "Sonata a symfonie," 194.
[25] O. H., "Feuilleton: Koncerty u nás a jinde," *Dalibor* 1 (1879): 101–2.
[26] From its inception in 1811, the Prague Conservatory had privileged Austro-German repertoire; Jan Branberger, *Konservatoř hudby v Praze: pamětní spis k stoletému jubileu založení ústavu* (Prague: Konservatoř hudby, 1911), 195–237.
[27] Novotný, "Sonata a symfonie," 179.

Novotný is more conciliatory in other parts of his study; when defining the symphony, he notes that the genre has the potential to be autobiographical. In his view, the outer movements reflect the external world and the slow movement gives voice to the composer's "inner life" and feelings. Of particular significance are Novotný's thoughts on the genre's perceived national associations, which he locates in the minuet or scherzo. Otherwise, it is clear from Novotný's writing that he sees the symphony as a manifestly German medium, and his stance is not unlike that of A. B. Marx, whom he cites on several occasions. Even so, Novotný does not consider "Germanness" to be an obstacle; in fact, he explicitly encourages Czechs, albeit in his discussion of the symphonic poem, not to shy away from a genre simply because it is German. These contemporary critical discussions of genre serve as a helpful lens through which to view Czech symphonic output in the late nineteenth century.

A Born Symphonist?

Symphonic output in the Czech lands at this time was virtually synonymous with Dvořák. "They regard me as a symphonist, yet I demonstrated a long time ago my preponderant inclination towards dramatic creation;" these were Dvořák's words in an interview with the Austrian newspaper *Die Reichswehr*, uttered just a few months before his death in 1904.[28] Indeed, the symphony was repeatedly demarcated as Dvořák's domain, much to the composer's chagrin. The writing of critic Emanuel Chvála (1851–1924) from 1912 illustrates this trend:

That Dvořák is, at the core of his talent, *a symphonist*, that his personality and way of working gravitate toward symphonic creation is a fact that is not denied by his old love for the opera, his abundant work in the realm of vocal music, nor in the least by his inclination at a ripe age toward programmatic music ... The whole method of musical thought for Dvořák, when creating instrumental music, is *symphonic*.

Že Dvořák v podstatě svého nadání jest symfonikem, že svojí povahou i způsobem práce tíhne ku tvorbě symfonické, jest faktum, které nepopře ani jeho stará láska k opeře, ani jeho vydatná práce v oboru skladby vokální, nejméně pak v zralém jeho

---

[28] H. Alan Houtchens, "A Critical Study of Antonín Dvořák's *Vanda*," (PhD diss., University of California, Santa Barbara, 1987), 32. Original in "Bei Meister Dvorzak," *Die Reichswehr* no. 3612 (1904): 7.

věku vzniklá náklonnost k hudbě programní … Celý způsob hudebního myšlení při tvorbě instrumentální jest u Dvořáka symfonický.[29]

In some ways, it is easy to see why Dvořák gained this reputation. From among the Czechs of his generation, he was the only composer to engage with the genre over an extended time – a near thirty-year period, having completed his first two symphonies in 1865 and his last in 1893. In turning to the symphony, he was definitely going against the grain during the 1860s – a decade that saw the opening of the Provisional Theater in Prague and an attendant preoccupation with opera.[30] Dvořák was also the first Czech composer to gain international exposure for his symphonies, beginning with performances of his Sixth in London in the spring of 1882. In light of these successes, the "symphonist" label seems appropriate. A less charitable explanation for why the label was repeatedly applied to Dvořák is that it was meant to downplay or perhaps denigrate his achievement in other genres. At the very least, it pigeon-holed him, failing to reflect the nature and scope of his work. Whatever the intent behind the designation, Dvořák was universally viewed as a "born symphonist" in his homeland, placing his contributions at the centre of the Czech symphonic tradition.

A striking feature of Dvořák's nine symphonies is their great variety. To some degree, Dvořák is conventional in his approach, conforming to nineteenth-century expectations; for instance, he aligns himself with many other symphonists in choosing to write a "pastoral" symphony, his Fifth, where the idyllic mood alternates with more dramatic passages, or by enacting the well-worn "heroic narrative," in his Seventh and Ninth Symphonies, both of which are cast in the minor mode and finish in the tonic major. Dvořák, however, also went against the mold, implicitly questioning the symphony's structural non-negotiables. His Third Symphony, for example, has a three-movement construction – though Beckerman suggests that the middle movement could be interpreted as "two in one"[31] – and some of Dvořák's other symphonies may have been originally conceived in three movements as well. Based on a study of the composer's sketches, Smaczny further observes that Dvořák grappled conceptually with his finales at times, seeking to find a solution to a problem that essentially all late nineteenth-century symphonists faced: namely, "how to create sufficient weight in a conclusion without inflating the

[29] Emanuel Chvála, "Symfonické skladby Dvořákovy," in *Antonín Dvořák: Sborník statí o jeho díle a životě*, ed. Boleslav Kalenský (Prague: Umělecká beseda, 1912), 129. (Emphasis mine.)
[30] Smaczny, "The Czech Symphony," 232.   [31] Beckerman, "Dvořák," 276.

structure unduly," as Smaczny puts it.[32] Dvořák's Eighth Symphony illustrates this grappling, as the sketches contain no fewer than ten variants for
the finale's main theme. Such thoughtful struggle and experimentation
hardly accords with the kind of "paint-by-numbers" approach that
Novotný imagined for symphonists.

Also noteworthy is Dvořák's penchant for cyclical procedures. Although
this was something that he tended to do more in the later part of his career,
he used cyclical techniques already in the early 1870s in his Fourth
Symphony, where the opening measures of the piece reappear in the
coda of the scherzo, serving as a kind of reminiscence. Dvořák took
a similar approach in his next symphony, the Fifth – once again bringing
about a return of the work's first few measures, but this time reinserting
them closer to the end of the piece – in the last movement, after an
attenuated recapitulation. The most obvious instance of cyclical form
occurs in the Ninth Symphony. In the development section of the finale,
Dvořák reintroduces several themes from previous movements, à la
Beethoven, creating a kind of potpourri. Not only did Dvořák recycle
themes across movements, but his symphonies are more broadly self-
referential – that is, they occasionally contain quotations from the composer's other output.[33] This is especially the case in the Eighth Symphony,
where the slow movement recalls two passages – No. 3 *Na starém hradě* "In
the Old Castle" and No. 9 *Serenáda* "Serenade" – from Dvořák's *Poetické
nálady Poetic Tone Pictures* (1889) for solo piano. Another distinct instance
of self-quotation can be heard in the scherzo of the same symphony,
though this time the pre-existing material comes from opera. Buried in
the middle of the movement, in the trio section, is a fleeting reference to
Toník's aria from *Tvrdé palice* ("The Stubborn Lovers," 1874) – a little-
known one-act comedy that Dvořák had written some fifteen years earlier.
In addition to referencing his own works, Dvořák alludes to the oft-quoted
Hussite chorale *Ktož jsú boží bojovníci* ("You Who Are the Warriors of
God")in the Fourth, Seventh, and Eighth Symphonies, and he occasionally
incorporates personal experiences into his symphonies as well; this is
evident in the First Symphony (*Zlonické zvony*, "Bells of Zlonice"), meant
to pay tribute to the town in which the composer had studied in his youth,
and in the Seventh, the opening theme of which occurred to Dvořák when
he witnessed a train of Czech nationalists pull into Prague station.

[32] Smaczny, "The Czech Symphony," 248–49.
[33] For example, Dvořák's Cello Concerto contains a quotation from his earlier song *Lasst mich
allein*, likely in honor of his sister-in-law Josefina; Michael Beckerman, *New Worlds of Dvořák:
Searching in America for the Composer's Inner Life* (New York: Norton, 2003) 192–208.

All of this raises questions of meaning. Both the cyclical procedures and the subtle references that Dvořák often embedded into his symphonies have led to speculations about some secret poetic intent. The Adagio of the Eighth Symphony, for instance, prompted one reviewer to write: "There is a story connected with it, which, however, the composer keeps to himself, and his audience would gladly know, since it is impossible not to feel that the music tries hard to speak intelligibly of events outside itself."[34] By keeping possible extra-musical content ambiguous, Dvořák cemented his reputation as "absolute music" composer,[35] even as his symphonic works moved progressively closer toward the programmatic. In the absence of explicit extra-musical material, Dvořák also lay himself open to having a program manufactured for him, as was the case with his Sixth Symphony – a piece that was written with Viennese audiences in mind and owes much to Beethoven and Brahms, but was nevertheless immediately called the "Czech Spring Symphony" in the Prague press in an effort to dispel any notion that the work might be construed as "German."[36] Similar national and programmatic issues were broached in discussions of the *New World* Symphony, which sparked vigorous debate about Dvořák's success in creating an "American" sound and the extent of its connections to Longfellow's *Song of Hiawatha*. In short, the example of Dvořák shows that, in a climate where program music was heavily promoted and where virtually every musical gesture could potentially be interpreted as having deep meaning – national or otherwise, it was impossible for symphonies to remain "unmarked" or neutral.

After Dvořák: Rethinking the Symphony's Connotations

Much like Beethoven, Dvořák set the standard for Czech symphonic composition, and many of the trends observed in his work can be seen in the output of subsequent composers. Cyclicity remained an aim during the *fin-de-siècle*. Zdeněk Fibich (1850–1900) takes a cyclical approach in both his Second (1892–93) and Third (1898) Symphonies, with the opening rhythm of the latter work reappearing in its slow movement and scherzo. Composers also continued to experiment with programmatic elements, as demonstrated by

---

[34] *The Musical Times* 31, no. 567 (1890): 279.

[35] Christopher Campo-Bowen shows that Dvořák did this even in some of his program music; "Bohemian Rhapsodist: Antonín Dvořák's Píseň bohatýrská and the Historiography of Czech Music," *19th-Century Music* 40 (2016): 181.

[36] Eva Branda, "Speaking German, Hearing Czech, Claiming Dvořák," *Journal of the Royal Musical Association* 142 (2017): 109–36.

Example 15.3: "Death motive" from Josef Suk's *Asrael* Symphony.

Josef Bohuslav Foerster (1859–1951) in his Fourth Symphony (1905) subtitled *Easter*, which explicitly enacts the death and resurrection of Christ. Moreover, by century's end, the symphony had become a deeply personal genre, which too harkens back to Dvořák. Beckerman characterizes Dvořák's Seventh Symphony as intensely personal,[37] and the same can be said of Josef Suk's (1874–1935) *Asrael* Symphony for Large Orchestra (1905–6), which provided an effective outlet for grief. Suk began writing the symphony as a tribute to the recently deceased Dvořák, his father-in-law, but it became a memorial piece for his wife Otilie as well, since she died while he was composing it. A five-movement work of massive proportions, the symphony introduces a "death motive" almost immediately, consisting of paired ascending and descending tritones, meant to represent the angel of death invoked in its title (see Example 15.3). Having been born out of tragedy, Suk's *Asrael* Symphony "provides one of the most disturbing and rewarding experiences of the late-Romantic repertoire," according to Smaczny.[38]

Meanwhile, it was precisely at this time that some of the symphony's previously held associations started to break down. As noted by Karen Painter, Germans "harbored an imaginary proprietary claim to the symphony" well into the early twentieth century, even after the death of Mahler.[39] However, such claims became increasingly tenuous, at a time when the genre was dwindling in German-speaking Europe, while thriving elsewhere. In the end, the symphonic poem also proved to be a rather short-lived genre. For all of its "progressive" promise, it no longer incited the same level of excitement at the turn of the century, since its aesthetic agenda had been set decades earlier and the most committed modernists tended to favor absolute genres. Given his relentless cultivation of the symphony, Dvořák could, at last, shed his "traditionalist" reputation and be recast as a proto-modernist, though, as Christopher Campo-Bowen points out, this simultaneously "helped to tie Dvořák to a canonical set of German composers and their symphonies."[40] These shifting connotations once again draw attention to the symphony's malleability, exposing the many challenges and contradictions that Czech composers faced when pursuing the genre in the nineteenth century.

---

[37] Beckerman, "Dvořák," 284.   [38] Smaczny, "The Czech Symphony," 254.

[39] Karen Painter, *Symphonic Aspirations: German Music and Politics, 1900–1945* (Cambridge, MA: Harvard University Press, 2007), 3–5.

[40] Campo-Bowen, "Bohemian Rhapsodist," 181.

16 | Bohemian Music Criticism and Historiography from the Late Eighteenth to the Late Twentieth Century

MARTIN NEDBAL AND KELLY ST. PIERRE

Czech-language music criticism first became prominent with the general growth of Czech journalism after the lifting of governmental restrictions on public life in the 1860s, and its authors, most prominently critics and historians Jan Ludevít Procházka, Otakar Hostinský, and Zdeněk Nejedlý, often used their musical discussions to explore then-emerging political conversations, especially ethnocentric concepts of identity. Still, they drew their models from earlier, predominantly Germanophone music critics, historiographers, and aestheticians – writers who did not subscribe to ethnocentric views yet. It is these Germanophone writers, specifically Franz Xaver Niemetschek, Anton Müller, and August Wilhelm Ambros, who are the main subjects of this chapter – late nineteenth-century Czech-language criticism and historiography are discussed in Chapter 18 (and to some extent also in Chapters 10, 13, and 23). Adding to the complexity of these critics' ideas, twentieth-century scholars, such as Mirko Očadlík and Tomislav Volek, later reinterpreted their writings to reflect still new political goals. The result is that most writings on Bohemian music and music history can engage with up to three centuries of political impulses, leaving eighteenth- and early nineteenth-century nuances perhaps the most overlooked and distorted.

One of the root causes of the ever-changing ambiguity embedded in Bohemian music criticism and historiography has to do with ever-shifting understandings of the words "Bohemia" and "Bohemian."[1] Prior to the 1830s, the words "Bohemians" and "Czechs" were synonymous in the German language, expressed in the word Böhmen. And within the geographic space of Bohemia there lived, among other groups, both *Deutsche* (Germans) and *Böhmen* (Bohemians, Czechs). Historian Jeremy King thoughtfully explores the nuances and consequences of these conflations in his 2002 book *Budweisers into Czechs and Germans*. Here, it is most useful to explore the changes from 1830s onwards, which King also outlines in his study.[2] In response to the rise of Czech nationalist sentiment, Germans living

---

[1] This and the following discussion is indebted to Jeremy King, *Budweisers into Czechs and Germans* (Princeton, NJ: Princeton University Press, 2002), 24–25.

[2] King, *Budweisers into Czechs and Germans*, 24–25.

in Bohemia abandoned using Böhmen to describe both Bohemians and Czechs and adopted the word *Tschechen*, so that they could reclaim the word *Böhmen* to specifically mean (German-)Bohemian. Contributing an additional layer of ambiguity: the Czech language never made a similar change, so still today, it does not distinguish between "Czech" and "Bohemian," relying on the single word *český* (see also Chapter 32).[3]

As a lens onto these ambiguities and the ways they impacted both past music criticism and recent music scholarship, this chapter explores an intricate web of disparities beginning from the late eighteenth century that was then recast in still-new ways during both the nineteenth and twentieth centuries. Beyond illuminating the instability of "Bohemia," such a discussion also reveals a process of canonization especially in musicological thought. Notably, the discourse surrounding Gluck and Mozart serves as a pivotal reference point, reflecting the evolving identities of past thinkers and mirroring ongoing dialogues about musical values.

Niemetschek and Mozart

A crucial figure for musical thought in Prague, Franz Xaver Niemetschek (the modern Czech version of his name, often printed, but which he never used in his writings, is František Petr Němeček) wrote the first book-length Mozart biography (first published in 1798 and again, in a revised version, in 1808).[4] He also likely authored several influential works of early Bohemian music criticism (published in the journals *Allgemeines europäisches Journal* and *Allgemeine musikalische Zeitung*). Throughout his career, Niemetschek embraced an ethnically ambiguous, Germanophone, Bohemian identity, but he was also closely linked to the Czech population. He was born in 1766 in the central Bohemian village of Sadská, a region that remained predominantly Czech-speaking even during a period of intense Germanization aimed at centralizing Habsburg power in the late eighteenth century.[5] In keeping with his immersion within a Czech population, Niemetschek – four years before completing his Mozart biography – wrote a lengthy biographical article about František Vavák (Franz Wawak), a patriotic Czech farmer,

---

[3] King, *Budweisers into Czechs and Germans*, 24–25.

[4] On the transformation of the name Niemetschek into Němeček, see Martin Nedbal, *Mozart's Operas and National Politics: Canon Formation in Prague from 1791 to the Present* (New York: Cambridge University Press, 2023), 69.

[5] The history of the Niemetschek family in Sadská is discussed in Jaroslav Čeleda, "Mozarteana: W. A. Mozart a prof. Dr. Fr. Němeček," *Za hudebním vzděláním* 3 (1928): 148–51, 153–62.

village councilor, and chronicler from the neighboring village of Milčice (Miltschitz).[6] The article shows that Niemetschek was in close contact with the exclusively Czech-speaking rural class in Bohemia. Niemetschek claims that Vavák liked Bohemian history and studied everything that was written about it "in our mother tongue" ("in unserer Muttersprache"). At the same time, Niemetschek's enthusiasm for Czech culture and language was mixed with a pessimistic outlook about its future. In his 1794 essay on Bohemian history, titled "Züge aus der Geschichte der Wissenchaften und des Geschmackes in Böhmen," Niemetschek claims that notwithstanding Czech culture's glorious past, literate Czech culture was dead in the present, no attempts at reviving it could help, and the future of Bohemia was connected to the use of German as the official language.[7]

Niemetschek's music-specific writings expressed similarly complicated relationships to notions of Bohemia. When Niemetschek talks about the first production of *Die Zauberflöte* in Czech, for example, he writes that the opera was given in "böhmisch" as opposed to German. But when he writes that after getting to know *Die Entführung aus dem Serail* in 1783, Bohemians ("die Böhmen") started to follow Mozart's compositions enthusiastically, Niemetschek is certainly not referring to a group of Czech speakers but to Prague opera lovers no matter whether they identified as Czechs and spoke Czech.[8] Some passages in his 1798 Mozart biography also clearly link Bohemia and its inhabitants specifically to Germany and Germanness. His reference to *Die Zauberflöte* as "our national work" ("unser Nationalstück") immediately after asking whether there is anyone in Germany who does not know this opera points to the possibility that he viewed himself and his fellow Bohemians as increasingly German-aligned.[9] But Germanness is often overshadowed by a Bohemian geographical identity in other examples of Niemetschek's musical writing. He downplays the widely accepted notion that Christoph Willibald Gluck was a German composer, for example, when he claimed that Gluck was "born

---

[6] Franz Xaver Niemetschek, "Einige Nachrichten von einem merkwürdigen Bauer in Böhmen. Nebst einer kurzen Übersicht des bösen und ungerechten Krieges des französischen Volkes, in böhmische Reime gebracht," *Für Böhmen von Böhmen* 3 (1794): 85–93.

[7] Franz Xaver Niemetschek, "Züge aus der Geschichte der Wissenschaften und des Geschmackes in Böhmen. Geschrieben im Jahre 1794," in *Libussa: Eine vaterländische Vierteljahrsschrift*, ed. Joseph Georg Meinert (Prague: Calve, 1804), 18–58 (42).

[8] Franz Xaver Niemetschek, *Leben des k. k. Kapellmeisters Wolfgang Gottlieb Mozart, nach Originalquellen beschrieben* (Prague: Herrlische Buchhandlung, 1798), 23; and Franz Xaver Niemetschek, *Lebensbeschreibung des k. k. Kapellmeisters Wolfgang Amadeus Mozart, aus Originalquellen*, 2nd expanded ed. (Prague: Herrlische Buchhandlung, 1808), 35.

[9] Niemetschek, *Leben des k. k. Kapellmeisters Wolfgang Gottlieb Mozart*, 74; Niemetschek, *Lebensbeschreibung des k. k. Kapellmeisters Wolfgang Amadeus Mozart*, 113.

a Bohemian" ("ein Böhme von Geburt"). In this case, Niemetschek is not suggesting that Gluck was an ethnically and linguistically Czech composer, but simply that he was born and reared within the borders of Bohemia.[10]

Even when Niemetschek seems to focus on strictly musical components in his writings, he still often links them back to notions of identity. For example, in the 1798 Mozart biography Niemetschek introduces the idea of musical classicism within the frame of a patriotic argument. He claims that Mozart's operas have "classical worth" ("klassischen Wert"), and that just as in the case of Greco-Roman artworks, this worth can be appreciated only with repeated listening. This passage has led some historians to claim that it was Niemetschek who first introduced the concept of classical music into Western culture.[11] Niemetschek's idea is conditioned both by his Bohemian patriotism and by a critical stance to Vienna, which appears frequently in his writings. Before he explains the classical value of Mozart's masterworks, Niemetschek compares them to fashionable and merely entertaining musical works, exemplified by two Viennese *Singspiele*: Wenzel Müller's *Die Schwestern von Prag* and Jakob Haibel's and Emanuel Schikaneder's *Der Tyroler Wastel*.[12] Thus, for Niemetschek, the concept of musical classics and canonicity was tied to his need to express his belonging to Bohemia – musical classicism and the concept of the canon were therefore tied to questions of identity.[13]

Anton Müller's Patriotic Aesthetics

The views Niemetschek articulated in the 1790s influenced Bohemian music criticism for decades to come. Like Niemetschek, Anton Müller, important Prague music critic from the late 1820s to the early 1840s and professor of aesthetics at the Prague university, sometimes fused aesthetic

---

[10] Niemetschek, *Leben des k. k. Kapellmeisters Wolfgang Gottlieb Mozart*, 22; Niemetschek, *Lebensbeschreibung des k. k. Kapellmeisters Wolfgang Amadeus Mozart*, 32–33.

[11] According to Magnus Tessing Schneider, Niemetschek, in his 1798 biography, was the first to introduce the concept of classical music. Magnus Tessing Schneider, *The Original Portrayal of Mozart's Don Giovanni* (New York: Routledge, 2021), 218. The idea, however, appears at least as early as a 1791 review of a commemorative performance for Mozart in Prague a week after the composer's death.

[12] Niemetschek, *Leben des k. k. Kapellmeisters Wolfgang Gottlieb Mozart*, 46.

[13] Even before Niemetschek's biography, Bohemian writers linked patriotic sentiments to canonicity. For example, the anonymous review in the *Prager Oberpostamtszeitung* of the commemoration for Mozart in Prague's St. Nicholas Church in the Lesser Town on December 14, 1791, claimed that Mozart's music "carried the stamp of classical beauty" ("das Gepräge des klassischen Schönen") and emphasized that the appreciation of that beauty was particularly strong in Prague. See Nedbal, *Mozart's Operas and National Politics*, 18–19.

and patriotic viewpoints. In a review of a *Don Giovanni* performance in
Prague on November 5, 1829, he claimed, for example, that "no capital city
in the world can compare to Prague in the well-deserved admiration of
[Mozart's] immortal works" ("[Prag] steht … in der gerechten
Bewunderung der unsterblichen Werke Mozarts keiner Hauptstadt der
Welt nach").[14] Müller was also a proponent of an early nineteenth-
century form of the historical performance movement, which aimed at
preserving a composer's presumed intentions as closely as possible. In
a review of a *La clemenza di Tito* performance in Prague on June 13,
1838, for example, Müller complained that the opera was not performed
with original recitatives as had been presumably promised prior to the
performance (throughout most of the nineteenth century Mozart's Italian
operas were performed in German adaptations with spoken dialogues
instead of recitatives).[15] Müller also proposed that the theater staff go to
a library or an archive to study the original score and copy the recitatives,
thus prefiguring the work of modern music historians and editors.

Müller's writings continue to reflect the shifting, unstable concepts of
Bohemian identity, particularly in his discussions about Czech opera
adaptations. In 1831, Müller praises the Czech opera company in Prague
for frequently offering "musical delights" ("musikalische Genüsse") such as
Così fan tutte to "the Czech-speaking public" ("dem böhmischredenden
Publikum") and "thus following one trait of our nationality" ("er folgt
hierin einem Zuge unserer Nationalität").[16] By connecting the Czech
company's interest in musically satisfying repertoire to "our nationality,"
the German-writing Müller links himself to the Czech community in
Prague. Müller therefore revives the ambiguous conceptualization of
nationality in Bohemia that had already been used in references to Czech
opera performances in the 1790s. For Müller, Czech culture was clearly
distinct from Prague's German culture, yet both belonged to the same
nationality.

The rise of Czech national culture and the Czech national elite's increasingly negative view of the predominance of German-language culture in
Bohemia also sometimes elicited negative reactions from Müller, as illustrated by his view of the famous Czech musical play *Fidlovačka*, with a text
by Czech playwright Josef Kajetán Tyl and music by František Škroup. The
play is particularly notable because it contains the song that eventually
became the Czech national anthem – *Kde domov můj* ("Where Is My
Home"). In an 1834 German-language review of the play, Müller takes

---

[14] *Bohemia*, November 10, 1829.   [15] *Bohemia*, June 7, 1838.   [16] *Bohemia*, November 1, 1831.

issue with the fact that Tyl's characters present the idea that it is shameful when Bohemians do not speak Czech.[17] Müller may have felt personally affected by Tyl's criticism of German-speaking Bohemians: he was born in Bohemia and wrote only in German, although his mother tongue may have been Czech. This becomes clear from his 1828 review of a Czech performance of *Don Giovanni* at the Estates Theater (*Bohemia*, October 7, 1828), in which he claims that listening to sung Czech is a pleasure for those who understand it and a nostalgic reminder of childhood. In his *Fidlovačka* review, Müller criticizes those who oppose the idea of a multicultural Bohemia, but at the same time praises certain poetic texts by Tyl, citing them in Czech on the pages of the German-language newspaper (this also includes the future national anthem). Throughout his career, furthermore, Müller reviewed Czech performances at the Estates Theater, studied Czech folksongs, and frequented Czech salons.

August Wilhelm Ambros and the Twilight of Bohemianism

One of the last and most important Bohemian music critics and historians to embrace the pre-ethnocentric view of identity was August Wilhelm Ambros. He was born to a predominantly German-speaking family in western Bohemia but could understand, read, and speak Czech. Although he was the nephew of the famous Viennese music historian Raphael Georg Kiesewetter and had shown an early interest in music, Ambros was forced by his parents to become a lawyer. His artistic interests, however, helped him become a prominent music critic in Prague, starting in the early 1840s. His friendship with Prague native Eduard Hanslick did not stop him from publishing, in 1856, his treatise *Die Grenzen der Poesie und der Musik*, an insightful rebuttal of Hanslick's formalistic aesthetic presented in his famous *Vom musikalischen Schönen* (1854). In the 1860s, furthermore, Ambros published three monumental volumes of an ultimately unfinished general history of music. Mainly on the basis of his historiographic work, Ambros was appointed the first "extraordinary Professor of Music History and Theory" ("ausserordentlicher Professor für Geschichte und Theorie der Musik") at the Prague university – a discipline that Ambros himself referred to as "musicology" ("Musikwissenschaft").[18] Thanks to Ambros,

---

[17] *Bohemia*, December 23, 1834.
[18] The official documents associated with the appointment are transcribed in Mirko Očadlík, "A. W. Ambros na pražské univerzitě," *Acta Universitatis Carolinae: Philosophica et Historica* 2 (1958): 131–46.

the Prague university became the second institution in the Habsburg monarchy to host the new discipline (Eduard Hanslick had already been appointed to the same position in Vienna in 1861).

Although Ambros's interests as a musicologist were quite general and did not necessarily focus on music history in Bohemia, some of his critical writings on Bohemian musical culture show that he cultivated the views initiated by Niemetschek decades earlier. In a series of articles published in the *Prager Zeitung* on the occasion of Mozart's 1856 centenary, for example, Ambros expressed both his admiration of the composer and his Pragocentric patriotism, claiming that Prague was the place where the composer "was fully understood, where the glory of his artistic existence was fully appreciated, whereas in other places the master was troubled by envy, cabals, human perversities, … petty-mindedness of publishers, [and] spiritual incompetence of critics" ("wo man ihn völlig verstand, völlig die Herrlichkeit seiner künstlerischen Erscheinung zu würdigen wusste, während anderwärts noch Neid, Kabale, die Verkehrtheit der Menschen, … der Krämergeist der Verleger, die geistige Unfähigkeit der Rezensenten … dem Meister böse Stunden genug machten").[19] At the same time, Ambros further cultivated an interest in specifically Czech-language music, similar to Müller (whom he in fact praised in some of his writings).[20] This genuine interest in Czech culture becomes particularly prominent in a series of articles titled "Musikalische Briefe aus Prag," published in the late 1860s in the journal *Österreichische Revue*. At one point, for example, Ambros claims that, whereas Prague's German opera underwent a crisis in the 1860s, the operatic repertoire of the Czech Provisional Theater was refreshing and innovative because of the productions of new operas by Smetana, Šebor, and by other Slavic composers, such as Glinka and Moniuzsko.[21] Ambros concludes the paragraph with the idea that Bohemia's main cultural role and uniqueness lie precisely in mediating between the German and Slavic peoples – he refers to the two groups as "two great nationalities" ("zwei grosse Nationalitäten").[22] Similar to many later Czech critics and musicologists, moreover, Ambros thought that folk music was a crucial aspect of Bohemia's cultural identity. Unlike many later commentators, who viewed folk music as inherently linked to

---

[19] August Wilhelm Ambros, " Mozart als Künstler und Mensch, " *Prager Zeitung* (January 23, 1856): 3–4 (4).

[20] August Wilhelm Ambros, "Musikalische Briefe aus Prag III," *Österreichische Revue* 3, no. 8 (1865): 195–210 (204).

[21] August Wilhelm Ambros, "Musikalische Briefe aus Prag (Zweite Folge)—I (Schluss)," *Österreichische Revue* 5, no. 3 (March 1867): 123–34 (132).

[22] Ambros, "Musikalische Briefe aus Prag (Zweite Folge)—I (Schluss)," 132.

a single ethnicity, Ambros connected them to his understanding of Bohemia as a multicultural meeting ground:[23]

Just as for centuries the German and Slavic elements exerted substantial influence in Bohemia, and due to the region's ethnographic and geographical conditions, now in peaceful unity, now in antagonism, imprinting the land and its inhabitants with characteristic traits, so the Bohemian folksongs represent a very happy middle ground between purely German and purely Slavic folk chants.

Wie in Böhmen nach ethnographischen und geographischen Bedingungen das deutsche und slavische Element seit Jahrhunderten gründlich seine Einwirkung bethätigte, bald in friedlicher Einigung, bald im Widerstreite, beides aber dem Lande und seinen Bewohnern die charakteristische Züge aufgeprägt hat, so bildet das böhmische Volkslied eine sehr glückliche Mittelgattung zwischen rein deutschem und rein slawischem Volksgesange.

The belief in the relationship between folk music and inherent qualities of the Bohemian population also leads Ambros to look for traces of Bohemian folk tunes in the music of classical composers, specifically Gluck, whom he, similar to Niemetschek, considered a Bohemian. Ambros is reminded of Bohemian folk tunes, though he does not specify which ones, particularly in Orfeo's "Chiamo il mio ben così" from act 1 of *Orfeo ed Euridice*, in the same opera's final chorus "Trionfi amore," and in the aria "Il faut mon destin" for the eponymous heroine of *Iphigénie en Aulide*.[24]

Czech Appropriations of Gluck and Mozart

Ambros's pre-ethnocentric approaches to the musical legacy of Gluck and Mozart in Bohemia increasingly clashed with the views of specifically Czech critics. Just a year before Ambros published his opinions about the resemblance of Gluck melodies to Bohemian folksongs, the Czech Provisional Theater in Prague staged its first Gluck opera, *Orfeus a Euridika*.[25] Whereas Ambros injected Bohemian patriotic viewpoints into his evaluations of Gluck's music, Czech critics in the 1860s relied on nationalistic ideas, according to which the identity of a large part of Prague's inhabitants was

---

[23] August Wilhelm Ambros, "Musikalische Briefe aus Prag II," *Österreichische Revue* 3, no. 7 (July 1865): 168–87 (172).

[24] August Wilhelm Ambros, "Musikalische Briefe aus Prag I," *Österreichische Revue* 3, no. 6 (June 1865): 184–96 (193).

[25] On the production, see Martin Nedbal, "Christoph Willibald Gluck and National Politics in Nineteenth-Century Prague," *Divadelní revue* (2023), no. 2: 59–82.

based on ethnic (Czech) as opposed to regional/pre-ethnic (Bohemian) identity. These Czech commentators also claimed that Gluck's creative mind was influenced by Czech, not Bohemian, folk music; that melodies in operas such as *Orfeus* exhibited similarities to specifically Czech national songs; and that the character of Gluck was more Czech than German. An early expression of such views appears in the introductory essay about Gluck's *Orfeus*, published in *Národní listy* two days before the opera's premiere. The critic is one of the first commentators to point out the connections between Gluck's music and Czech folk music:[26]

We are certain that Gluck's music with its original beauty and nobility will find its way to the hearts of our art loving audience, particularly because in its foundations we find so many similarities with our national music and can boldly claim that Czech national songs have found a mighty sounding board in Gluck's impression-able soul and that their influence was never lost.

Jsme přesvědčeni, že hudba Gluckova vůbec původní svou krásou a vznešeností, dramatickou silou a nevýslovnou ušlechtilostí výrazu k srdci našeho umění milovného obecenstva cestu najde a to tím více, an skutečně v základech svých tak mnoho příbuzného s naší hudbou národní jeví, že směle tvrditi můžeme, že český národní zpěv mocného ohlasu ve vnímavé jeho duši nalezl, a že známky jeho nikdy se nesetřely.

Unlike Ambros and Niemetschek, furthermore, the 1864 Czech commentator points out that the composer may have been of Czech origin because his family name was often spelled "Klukh," which resembles the Czech word for boy, *kluk*.[27] The Bohemian appropriations of famous composers thus acquired an ethnocentric hue.

These nationalistic ideas were further expanded by Ladislav Emanuel Labler-Daskovský.[28] In one of his essays about the 1864 Czech *Orfeus*, Labler-Daskovský went as far as to deny that Gluck's music contained any German qualities and pointed out specific connections to Czech folk music:

...we are resolutely opposed to the idea proclaimed by German musicians that Gluck was a German composer and Gluck's music was German. Although we

---

[26] *Národní listy*, December 15, 1864.

[27] *Národní listy*, December 15, 1864. The view that Gluck's name was etymologically Czech has been refuted by Rudolf Pečman, "Gluck und Böhmen: Anmerkungen zur Biographie des Meisters und zu seiner Stellung in der tschechischen Musikwissenschaft," in *Das mitteldeutsche Musikleben vor Händel; Christoph Willibald Gluck (1714–1787)*, ed. Berndt Baselt and Walther Siegmund-Schulze (Halle-Wittenberg: Martin-Luther-Universität, 1988), 93–94.

[28] Late nineteenth-century Bohemian German commentators embraced similar views of eighteenth-century composers, see Nedbal, "Christoph Willibald Gluck," 73–78; and Nedbal, *Mozart's Operas and National Politics*, 48–56.

dutifully studied the score [of *Orfeus*], we were unable to find the so-called German character … We have a greater right to claim that Gluck's music bears prominent Czech traits. Not only in the natural shortness of periods, which is typical for Czech music and Czech language, but also the remarkable similarity to Czech national songs (compare the main motive of recitative No. 24 to "horo vysoká jsi").

…opíráme [se] rozhodně proti tomu, že němečtí hudebníci vesměs vyhlašují Glucka za skladatele německého a hudbu Gluckovu za německou. Ač jsme svědomitě partituru studovali, nebyli jsme s to, nikde najíti tak zvaný německý ráz … Větším právem bychom mohli tvrditi, že hudba Gluckova nese na sobě mnoho rázu českého. Nejen Čechům jako v hudbě tak i v mluvě přirozená krátkost periodiky ale i nápadné podobenství s českými národními zpěvy (srovnej číslo 24 recitativ, hlavní motiv s 'horo vysoká jsi').[29]

Czech critics' search for Czech folksongs in the earlier music, including not only Gluck but also Mozart, continued until the middle of the twentieth century.[30] The most prominent Czech musicologist of the late nineteenth century, Otakar Hostinský, also took part. In an 1892 essay, he claimed that Czech folksongs could be traced both to Haydn's symphonies (due to the composer's stay in western Bohemia in the service of Count Morzin) and Gluck's ballets.[31] At the same time, Hostinský warned that the influence of Czech folksongs on Mozart's music is a more complex matter. Mozart's melodies that sound like Czech folksongs may have in fact been inspired by these folksongs, but this cannot be proven because Czech folk melodies were first collected only in the early nineteenth century. Another possibility is, according to Hostinský, that it was Mozart's music that inspired Czech folksongs. The option that Hostinský views as the most probable, however, is that a group of Czech folksongs similar to Mozart's melodies may have existed before Mozart composed his works, and that the similarity between these folksongs and Mozart's music was mostly coincidental. Yet, it was this similarity that ultimately made Mozart's operas so popular among the Czechs. Hostinský's explanation thus operates with the possibility that a special, though mostly coincidental, spiritual bond existed between Mozart's music and Czech folksongs.

---

[29] *Hlas*, December 17, 1864.   [30] See Nedbal, *Mozart's Operas and National Politics*, 71–78.
[31] Otakar Hostinský, "O naší světské písni lidové. (Dokončení.) V.," *Český lid* 1 (1892): 351–70, esp. 359–60. At the same time, in his 1879 essay on Gluck, Hostinský carefully avoided linking Gluck to Czechness. See Otakar Hostinský, *Krištof Vilibald Gluck* (Prague: Urbánek, 1884). The study was first published in installments in the journal *Květy* in 1879. On Hostinský and Gluck, see Pečman, 96–98.

Očadlík vs. Ambros

Ethnocentric views also dominated twentieth-century Czech discussions of nineteenth-century critics and music historians. One mid-twentieth-century example is a 1958 article on Ambros by Mirko Očadlík.[32] Očadlík, who chaired the musicology department at Charles University in Prague in the 1950s, suggests that although Ambros initially supported the Czech national movement in the 1860s, in 1869, he accepted the Prague professorship offered by oppressive Austrian authorities to entice him to join an anti-Czech, German-Austrian camp. According to Očadlík, Ambros afterwards abandoned his high-minded ideals and succumbed to servile obedience to German and Austrian elites out of fear for his lucrative position. Očadlík's interpretation is based on murky evidence. For example, he compares two essays Ambros wrote for Beethoven's centennial in 1870 – the Czech essay appeared in the progressive music journal *Hudební revue*; the German was published in an 1872 volume dedicated to Beethoven.[33] Očadlík claims that although the two versions are "identical thematically" ("tematicky zcela shodné"), the Czech version has "progressive, democratic tendencies" ("pokrokové tendence demokratické"), whereas the German version is "formulated with heightened carefulness and with hidden irony and stylistic artificiality" ("formulován svrchovaně opatrně a se zakrývanou ironií a stylistickou umělostí").[34] The lack of any examples makes it impossible to understand what precisely Očadlík saw as democratic in the Czech version and ironic in the German version. What makes Očadlík's reading suspect is that he connects the alleged ideological differences between the two versions to a simplistic nationalist binarism: the "progressive and democratic tendencies" are seen as corresponding to the Czech national movement of the 1860s, and the irony and artificiality supposedly somehow reflect Ambros's attitudes to the German nationalist camp at the Prague philosophical faculty. Ambros is therefore presented as someone who sympathized with the inherently democratic spirit of the Czechs but was not strong enough to withstand the pressure of the conservative and nationalistic Germans.

[32] Očadlík, "A. W. Ambros na pražské univerzitě."
[33] August Wilhelm Ambros, "Beethoven: Pamětní list k stoletým narozeninám Beethovenovým," *Hudební listy* 1 (1870–71): 337–38; 345–48; 353–55; 364–66; and August Wilhelm Ambros, "Beethoven, Göthe, und Michel Angelo," in *Erstes poetisches Beethoven Album*, ed. Hermann Joseph Landau (Prague: Landau, 1872), 85–95.
[34] Očadlík, "A. W. Ambros na pražské univerzitě," 142.

A similar ideological tendentiousness can be detected in Očadlík's confused reading of Ambros's 1869 application for the Prague professorship to the Austrian authorities.[35] One of the main reasons Prague needs a professorship in musicology, according to Ambros, was that as a particularly musical land, Bohemia was in need of an institution that would focus on "the scientific aspect of music" ("die wissenschaftliche Seite der Musik") and thus prevent the artform from becoming a "*luxuriae ministra*" ("a handmaiden of luxury").[36] Očadlík understood *luxuriae ministra* as referring to socially engaged music, one that represented progressive and anti-Austrian ideals – thus, according to Očadlík, by saying that his university professorship would counter the tendencies for music to be socially engaged, Ambros was pandering to the supposedly conservative Austrian government.[37] But Ambros's concept of *luxuriae ministra* is in fact linked to the nineteenth-century aesthetic idea, promulgated with special vehemence by German critics, that truly artistic music needed to be intellectual (just as most German music ostensibly was) and not simply sensual and pleasing (as Italian opera); the concept also comes forth in many of Ambros's writings, for example, when he, on numerous occasions, compares the intellectual and dramatic qualities of Gluck's and Mozart's operas to what he viewed as purely sensual music by Rossini and Donizetti.[38] Očadlík is therefore misinterpreting Ambros's ideas to construct a simplistic, binary image of music-critical thought in mid-nineteenth-century Bohemia. His views that the purportedly conservative Austrian authorities used the musicology professorship to bribe Ambros and persuade him to abandon his interest in the allegedly democratic Czech culture also smacks of what commonly happened to intellectuals in twentieth-century totalitarian regimes, such as the one in Czechoslovakia in the 1950s.

Late Twentieth-Century Musicological Nationalism

Simplistic nationalist binarisms continued to influence certain Czech musicological approaches to late eighteenth- and nineteenth-century

---

[35] The document is preserved in the Prague, Národní archiv, ČM 1856–1883, karton 926, fasc. 25, č. 9/34; it is transcribed in Očadlík, "A. W. Ambros na pražské univerzitě," 132–34.

[36] Očadlík, "A. W. Ambros na pražské univerzitě," 133.

[37] Očadlík, "A. W. Ambros na pražské univerzitě," 138.

[38] See, for example, August Wilhelm Ambros, "Die böhmische Oper in Prag," *Österreichische Revue* 3, no. 1 (1865): 173–84 (184); and Ambros, "Musikalische Briefe aus Prag III," 195 and 198.

criticism and historiography even after the end of communism, as illustrated in the writings of Očadlík's student and a noted Mozart specialist
Tomislav Volek. In the 1990s, for example, Volek criticized what he called
"relics of prejudiced thought" ("Relikte der Voreingenommenheit") in
Austrian musicologist Gernot Gruber's 1985 *Mozart und die Nachwelt*.
Gruber had written of "the great enthusiasm that the citizens of Prague felt
for Mozart and which reconciled him to his Viennese disappointments
certainly reflects well on the culture and the openness of the citizens of that
town but also on the patriotism of the Germans in Prague" ("Selbst die
große Begeisterung, mit der die Prager Mozart über seine Wiener
Enttäuschungen versöhnten, spricht wohl für den Kunstverstand und die
Aufgeschlossenheit der Bürger dieser Stadt, aber auch für den Patriotismus
der Deutschen in Prag").[39] Volek responded by claiming that "both
Germans and Czechs participated in the Prague Mozart reception, as
illustrated by the names of Dušek, Kuchař, Mašek, Vitásek, and the
Mozart biographer Němeček" ("an der Mozart-Rezeption in Prag nahmen
deutsche und tschechische Musiker teil, was die Namen Dušek, Kuchař,
Mašek, Vitásek und der Mozart-Biograph Němeček bezeugen").[40] Though
Volek acknowledges that eighteenth-century Prague was inhabited by both
Czechs and Germans in the eighteenth century, he exclusively uses modern
Czech spellings to refer to prominent Bohemian Mozart admirers. This
choice frames their identities within a modern Czech context, implying
a retrospective nationalization of figures whose historical affiliations were
more complex. In a later essay on a similar subject, Volek is even more
explicit, claiming that "the Prague Mozart cult was predominantly initiated
by purely Czech musicians, such as Dušek (Duschek), Kuchař (Kucharž),
Mašek (Maschek), Vitásek (Witassek), among others" ("Am Prager
Mozart-Kult waren in bedeutender Art und Weise rein tschechischer
Musiker beteiligt wie Dušek [Duschek], Kuchař [Kucharž], Mašek
[Maschek], Vitásek [Witassek] u. a.").[41] In viewing late eighteenth-
century Bohemians as either "Czechs" or "Germans," both Volek and
Gruber subscribe to the idea that, as King puts it, "the forebear to nation-
hood was not nonnational politics but nonpolitical ethnicity" – Volek and
Gruber do not take into account the nonnational Bohemianism that

---

[39] Gernot Gruber, *Mozart und die Nachwelt* (Vienna: Residenz Verlag, 1985), 48.
[40] Tomislav Volek, "Mozart-Rezeption in Böhmen," *Musikgeschichte in Mittel- und Osteuropa* 1
(1997): 85–86.
[41] Originally published as Tomislav Volek, "Od italské opery k německému singspielu: proměny
pražského publika," in *Mezi časy ... kultura a umění v českých zemích kolem roku 1800*, ed.
Zdeněk Hojda and Roman Prahl (Prague: KLP, 2000), 287.

characterizes the writings of Niemetschek and focus on either his nonpolitical Czechness (Volek) or nonpolitical Germanness (Gruber).[42] Volek and Gruber take for granted the common belief among some historians of Habsburg Central Europe that "ethnic groups are not national antecedents but national products," which leads them to project ethnicity "ahistorically yet with history-making effect into the past."[43]

Conclusion

The evolving and multifaceted conceptions of "Bohemia" across the eighteenth, nineteenth, and twentieth centuries shed light on the enduring discourse surrounding identity in Bohemian music criticism and historiography. Instead of merely mirroring their contemporary contexts, Bohemian music criticism and historiography reveal an ongoing dialogue about the meanings of "Czechness," "Germanness," and "Bohemianness." Niemetschek's reflections in the 1790s, while firmly situated in his time, laid the groundwork for later thought. In contrast, Volek's work serves as an example of recent scholarly research that underscores the persistence of these questions. His writings remind us that even in contemporary discourse, these issues remain as relevant as ever. Embracing the fluidity of these constructs, rather than cementing them as rigid identities, not only enriches our understanding of historical music criticism, but also offers fertile ground for scholarly explorations.

[42] King, *Budweisers into Czechs and Germans*, 7.
[43] King, *Budweisers into Czechs and Germans*, 8.

17 | Public Music Education and the Prague Conservatory

LENKA KŘUPKOVÁ

A dense network of private teachers and private music schools provided music education to the public in the nineteenth-century Czech lands. These private institutions responded to a growing demand for art education among the bourgeoisie that started to gain economic and social significance in the 1820s. The subjects offered to the predominantly middle-class students included singing, music theory, and piano playing. Some of the most well-known private piano educators were Václav Jan Tomášek (Johann Wenzel Tomaschek), who opened his school in Prague in 1824,[1] and Joseph Proksch, who established a music educational institute in 1831, offering comprehensive music education.[2] Following Proksch's example, Bedřich Smetana opened his music institute in 1848, quickly gaining significant interest from students and a good reputation in Prague circles.[3] Pivoda's singing school, founded by František Pivoda in 1866, also became renowned, educating many singers who became successful in opera houses in Prague and abroad.[4]

In the 1850s, the number of private music institutions in Prague sharply increased. When Smetana returned from his stay in Göteborg, Sweden, in 1863, he faced much greater competition than before when reopening his music school.[5] However, private music institutes were economically viable, and even those who could not rival Smetana in terms of quality engaged in this form of entrepreneurship. In 1882, music writer Josef Srb-Debrnov commented on the quality of existing music schools in the magazine

---

This chapter was translated from Czech to English by Martin Nedbal.

[1] His students included composer and pianist Jan Václav Hugo Voříšek, music critic Eduard Hanslick, and music historian August Wilhelm Ambros.

[2] Proksch's piano pedagogy followed the method of German teacher Bernhard Logier, outlined in his six-volume *Versuch einer rationellen Lehrmethode im Pianofortespiel* (1841–61). See Jarmila Gabrielová, "Výuka klavírní hry a klavírní školy v 19. století," in *Vzdělání a osvěta v české kultuře 19. století*, ed. Kateřina Bláhová and Václav Petrbok (Prague: AVČR, 2004), 420–21.

[3] Besides piano, Smetana also taught piano ensembles, music theory, and history.

[4] Forty-five graduates of Pivoda's school were members of the Provisional and National Theater ensembles, and forty-six were employed abroad. See Vladimír Horák, *František Pivoda. Pěvecký pedagog* (Brno: Purkyně University, 1970), 135–42.

[5] Marta Ottlová and Milan Pospíšil, "Soukromé hudební školy v Praze 19. století a otázka české školy operní," in *Vzdělání a osvěta v české kultuře 19. století*, 430.

Dalibor.[6] He claimed there were twenty-three piano institutes in Prague, some of which also taught singing, and five purely vocal schools. Srb-Debrnov remarked that the proliferation of music institutes in Prague was disproportionate to the actual need, with many resembling commercial enterprises rather than arts education institutions. This unfortunate situation was facilitated by the legal regulations of the time, which did not require conservatory education from teachers in private schools. Music schools continued to generate significant profits at the beginning of the twentieth century, judging by the staggering numbers as reported in *Urbánkův kalendář českých hudebníků na rok 1910* ("Urbánek's Calendar of Czech Musicians for 1910").[7] At that time, with around 300,000 inhabitants, Prague boasted fifty-nine private music schools, twenty-five singing schools, and four special singing schools for children.

Some public music societies, such as the (Archduchess) Sophia Academy (Sophien-Akademie) (an organization focused on promoting and performing Bohemian and European classical music in Prague between 1840 and 1899) and the Cecilian Union (a choral society, active in Prague between 1840 and 1865), established their own music schools, and the Union for the Improvement of Military Music also educated musicians for the Austrian military. At the same time, the education of music professionals was gradually overtaken by a handful of institutions, including the Prague Organ School, founded in 1830 and later merged with the Prague Conservatory, and the Brno Organ School, founded by Leoš Janáček and eventually transformed into the state Brno Conservatory. The most important public music education institution was the Prague Conservatory, and this chapter is dedicated to its history from its inception to the end of the Austro-Hungarian monarchy.

The Beginnings of the Prague Conservatory

The Prague Conservatory was founded in 1811 and is the second oldest institution of its kind in Europe outside of Italy (after the Paris Conservatory established in 1795). Thus, Prague surpassed even the capital

---

[6] Josef Srb-Debrnov, "Naše hudební ústavy," *Dalibor* 4 (1882), no. 8: 57–59 (57), no. 9: 67–68, no. 10: 74–75, no. 17: 130–31, no. 19: 150–51.

[7] See Vladimír Lébl and Oldřich Pukl, "Hudební školství," in *Dějiny české hudební kultury 1890 – 1945*, vol. 1 *(1890–1918)*, ed. Robert Smetana (Prague: Academia, 1972), 103.

of the Austrian Empire.[8] The immediate impetus for its establishment was the proclamation of several representatives of patriotic nobility published on April 25, 1808, in which they informed about their intention to elevate music in Bohemia, which they found to be in deep decline (see also Chapter 7).[9] The Napoleonic Wars had a significant impact on the decline of cultural and social life in Europe, and there was a shortage of musicians in Prague's concert and theater venues. To improve Prague's musical culture, the Society for Musicians' Widows and Orphans (Tonkünstler Witwen- und Waisen-Societät) was founded in 1803 and started organizing concert life in Prague. However, the society could not find enough musicians and singers, highlighting the need for an institution dedicated to training talents for musical life. The patriotic aristocracy did not just resort to symbolic support and verbal proclamations; the signatories of the declaration pledged financial support for six years and called on other music enthusiasts to subscribe with at least 100 gulden. In response, fifty-five personalities contributed, and a sum of 12,000 gulden was raised.[10] Following this proclamation, the Association for the Promotion of Music in Bohemia (Verein zur Beförderung der Tonkunst in Böhmen) was established on March 31, 1810. The Association managed the conservatory financially and administratively until the creation of independent Czechoslovakia in 1918.

Friedrich Dionys Weber and Curriculum Development

Instruction began on April 24, 1811, but due to the lack of space, students were initially taught at their teachers' homes.[11] The conservatory, however, soon managed to acquire premises in the Dominican Monastery in the Old Town, where it remained until 1884. During his thirty-one years in office, the first director, Friedrich Dionys Weber, developed curricula that, in broad outlines, remained valid until 1918. The appointed directors acted mostly as executors of the association's decisions.[12] However, they could contribute to the content of the curriculum and were responsible for the

---

[8] In Vienna, the first public music school, the Conservatorium der Gesellschaft der Musikfreunde, opened its first singing class, under the direction of Antonio Salieri, in 1817.

[9] Jan Branberger, *Konservatoř hudby v Praze: pamětní spis k stoletému jubileu založení ústavu* (Prague: nákladem Konservatoře, 1911), 12.

[10] The subscriber list is in the Prague, Archiv Pražské konzervatoře, shelfmark 2C626.

[11] Branberger, *Konservatoř hudby*, 24.

[12] For the association's statutes, see Branberger, *Konservatoř hudby*, 15.

artistic quality of public orchestral productions, which became a significant enrichment of Prague's musical life. The numbers of these stabilized at four per year. Already in 1815, the conservatory was able to present its students to the public, a fact that was commendably noted by Carl Maria von Weber, then the conductor of Prague's German opera.[13] After a theatrical stage was set up in the conservatory, it occasionally ventured into public opera productions.[14]

The conservatory initially admitted students every three years into two classes: a lower department for students in the first three years and a higher department for advanced students in the fourth to sixth year. Each contributing member of the Association had the right to propose students for admission, whom they financially supported during their studies. In the first year of the conservatory's existence, only classes for violin, cello, double bass, and wind instruments were opened, with the teaching obligation for teachers set at twelve hours per week.[15] In 1811, thirty-nine students were admitted, and the same numbers of students was to be admitted after the next three years. In 1815, a singing class was introduced, followed by harp and organ classes in 1830, and only in 1888 was a piano class created. The school was open to admitting girls from the start, and the number of female students increased with the 1815 establishment of the singing class. According to the founding document, male students were not to be older than twenty and younger than ten, whereas female students were to be at least twelve and no older than eighteen. Students were expected to be physically healthy and demonstrate vocal and musical aptitude. In addition to instrumental instruction and singing, students were to be taught in German and Italian, basic arithmetic, and later, history, geography, aesthetics, and declamation.[16] Students had no choice

---

[13] Carl Maria von Weber, *Hinterlassene Schriften*, vol. 2 (Dresden: Arnold, 1928), 131.

[14] First to be produced was *Die Zauberflöte* in 1828, followed by *Die Entführung aus dem Serail* in 1829. See Branberger, *Konservatoř hudby*, 38–39.

[15] The 1811 salaries of the first teachers varied according to instrument and the extent of teaching responsibilities. The violin and viola teacher (and the concertmaster of Prague's theater orchestra), Friedrich Pixis, had an annual salary of 900 gulden for teaching three hours a day. Teachers of cello, double bass, flute, oboe, bassoon, and French horn, with two hours of daily teaching, received 600 gulden per year, while the trumpet teacher, with a salary of 300 gulden, taught only one hour a day. The teacher of elementary education had a salary of 600 gulden for teaching four hours a day, and the catechist with a salary of 100 gulden had two hours of teaching a day. The director, whose duties also included teaching theoretical subjects, received 1,200 gulden, in addition to twelve cubic fathoms of softwood for heating. The assistant, who taught ear training and basic piano, received a salary of 600 gulden, along with accommodation and heating. See Branberger, *Konservatoř hudby*, 22.

[16] Branberger, *Konservatoř hudby*, 27–28.

of musical instruments; the conservatory's administration determined which instrument best suited their physical build. In some cases, however, they were willing to accommodate the parents' wishes. The primary goal of the institution was to assemble a fully occupied and well-functioning orchestra. Students could dedicate themselves to other instruments in exceptional circumstances, and they were publicly examined in all subjects at the end of the semester. They were prohibited from performing in public productions outside the conservatory, such as churches, theaters, concert and dance halls, processions, academies, and night entertainment venues. This ban remained in effect until 1918 and was frequently criticized but also violated, leading to expulsions. During personnel shortages in Prague's opera, however, students were occasionally permitted to assist in minor roles, which had to be studies within the conservatory's curriculum. Teachers were expected to interact with the students strictly but also gently and persuasively, keep records of student behavior and progress, and regularly report them to the director.

Weber emphasized systematic methods of instrumental instruction, often adopting those from the Paris Conservatory. However, Prague Conservatory teachers, mostly leading musicians, began to develop their own methodological textbooks.[17] Subjects were to be arranged in accordance with "the urgent development of the human spirit." Conservatory students had their entire day filled with school obligations, leaving little room for free time. According to the school regulations of 1816, the daily schedule was as follows:[18] Music theory classes were held every day from 11 am to 12 noon, and every day from 10 am and 11 am, all students were required to participate in choral singing. Time for instrumental instruction was reserved daily from 4 pm to 6 pm, but students of violin and viola continued until 7 pm. Trumpet and trombone were taught only as secondary instruments until 1826, from 1 pm and 2 pm. The curriculum also included general subjects taught at so-called normal schools and gymnasiums but excluded Latin, which was replaced by Italian. Additionally, practical logic and musical aesthetics were taught. Four hours each day were dedicated to these more general subjects. Religion was taught for one hour on Thursdays and Sundays.

Under Weber's leadership, the conservatory statutes were amended several times. In particular, the number of admitted students gradually

---

[17] Weber, too, wrote textbooks of basic music theory and notation.
[18] For excerpts from the 1816 school regulations, see Branberger, *Konservatoř hudby*, 30–32.

increased, and the curriculum was further developed.[19] In the early 1840s, the rules for vocal education were further adjusted. The duration was reduced to four years, and new applicants were admitted biennially. In the lower two years, students learned concert singing, while in the higher stage, they focused on opera singing.

International Prestige and the Directorships of Johann Friedrich Kittl and Josef Krejčí

In 1843, a conservatory was established in Leipzig under the leadership of Felix Mendelssohn-Bartholdy, adopting the organizational system based on the Prague model. The Prague Conservatory thus lost its uniqueness in the German-speaking area and gained a significant competitor in the Leipzig Conservatory, also due to the renowned personalities who worked there, such as Robert Schumann, Niels Gade, Ignaz Moscheles, Joseph Joachim, and Max Reger. Similar conservatories were soon founded in other regions. A new director, Johann Friedrich Kittl, took office in July 1843 and aimed to cope with this competition and enhance the institution's reputation by organizing concerts with contemporary programming, inspired by the Leipzig Gewandhausorchester. Kittl had numerous contacts in the European musical world, often inviting composers personally. For instance, Hector Berlioz visited the Prague Conservatory in 1846. Kittl was also a close friend of Richard Wagner, and conservatory students participated in the Prague premiere of Wagner's *Tannhäuser* in November 1854, as the orchestra of the Estates Theater was insufficient in capacity.[20] Conservatory students also performed Liszt's symphonic poem *Die Ideale* and *Dante Symphony* under the composer's direction in 1858, and a year later, they presented Liszt's works under the baton of Hans von Bülow.[21] Under Kittl's leadership, grand celebrations took place for the institution's fiftieth anniversary in 1858, attracting prominent figures from the European musical world and highlighting the institution's international prestige.

Kittl developed a comprehensive curriculum for the teaching of music theory, specifying that the first three years should be dedicated to the study of

---

[19] For the 1836 regulations, see Branberger, *Konservatoř hudby*, 43–44.
[20] Branberger, *Konservatoř hudby*, 60–61.   [21] Branberger, *Konservatoř hudby*, 70.

harmony, the next three years to counterpoint.[22] Additionally, instruction in instrumentation was included, ensuring that all students could adjust their compositions for the orchestra. During Kittl's directorship, discussions began about introducing Czech into the curriculum because many talented students had a weak command of German. In a letter to the conservatory's management from May 21, 1845, Count Lev Thun, the future Austrian Minister of Culture and Education (1849–60), considered it "incorrect and ineffective" ("nesprávné a neúčelné") to educate Czech students in a way that estranged them from their native tongue and also pointed out that without an education in Czech, "the poetry of the nation" ("poezie národa") from which these musicians came would remain unknown and inaccessible, rendering its intellectual currents inaccessible.[23] Although students came to the conservatory from various parts of the Austrian and later Austro-Hungarian Empire, most students and teachers identified with Czech nationality.[24] In 1846, however, the Association for the Promotion of Music in Bohemia opposed the possibility of teaching in Czech, instead introducing mandatory French instruction.

The revolutionary year of 1848 had significant consequences for the financing of the school as many members withdrew from the Association, and others reduced or failed to pay their contributions. Due to the dire financial situation, non-musical subjects were abolished the following year, and students had to enroll in them at other schools.[25] Teachers were dismissed, and a new requirement was introduced for new students to pay a deposit of fifty gulden for instrumental and seventy for vocal studies upon admission.[26] The deposit was refunded upon graduation but forfeited to the institution if a student had to leave the school prematurely due to poor academic performance or disciplinary offenses. The removal of general subjects damaged the institution's reputation, which had prided itself on maintaining high standards not only in music but also in general education. Additionally, dissatisfaction among teachers grew due to low

---

[22] The 1850 curriculum plan is reprinted in Ernst Rychnovsky, *Johann Friedrich Kittl: Ein Beitrag zur Musikgeschichte Prags*, 2 vols. (Prague: Verein für Geschichte der Deutschen in Böhmen, 1904), 66–72.

[23] See Branberger, *Konservatoř hudby*, 53.

[24] Markéta Hallová, "Pražská konzervatoř," in *Český hudební slovník osob a institucí*, Masaryk University, published on October 22, 2019, https://slovnik.ceskyhudebnislovnik.cz/component/mdictionary/?task=record.record_detail&id=8059, accessed December 8, 2023.

[25] See Jan Linhart, "Všeobecně vzdělávací předměty na pražské konzervatoři v letech 1811–1961," in *150 let pražské konzervatoře. Sborník k výročí ústavu*, ed. Václav Holzknecht (Prague: Státní hudební nakladatelství, 1961), 263–72.

[26] Branberger, *Konservatoř hudby*, 56.

salaries. Consequently, the association sought subsidies, which were granted by the Ministry of the Interior in 1855, amounting to 4,000 guldens. Thanks to this support, general studies were reintroduced, starting in the 1855/56 school year, albeit in a reformed format.

In 1865, Kittl ended his tenure due to a dissolute lifestyle resulting in financial debts and health issues. Composer and organist Josef Krejčí, the former director of the Prague Organ School, known for his efforts to integrate it into the conservatory, took over the institution. Although considered a conservative, he maintained connections with important musicians of his time.[27] He significantly increased the pension fund by establishing a regular concert series, with proceeds benefiting the fund. However, he faced criticism for almost excluding Czech composers and contemporary music from conservatory concerts.[28] As an educator, he was praised for elevating the teaching of music theory, delivered in both German and Czech.[29] The quality of music history education improved under August Wilhelm Ambros, who had been teaching it since Kittl's directorship. Ambros was the first professor of musicology at the Prague university and a prominent member of the Association. From the beginning of his directorship, Krejčí advocated for introducing piano lessons, but the Association rejected the proposal for financial reasons. His request to introduce composition classes was also denied, with the explanation that the primary goal of the institution was to educate orchestral players and singers.

In the late 1860s, the Bohemian Savings Bank (mainly known under the German name Böhmische Sparkasse), led by Wenzel Ritter von Bohusch, became a significant sponsor of the school.[30] Bohusch served as the secretary of the Association for twenty-five years starting in 1850. It was thanks to funds provided by the Savings Bank and individual donors that the living conditions of poor students improved, contingent only on their academic performance. Despite these contributions, the financial situation of the conservatory did not improve, preventing the realization of Krejčí's plan

---

[27] Franz Liszt praised Krejčí's Fourth Mass in A minor, Op. 25 (1854), which Krejčí dedicated to Liszt. See Markéta Hallová, "200 let Pražské konzervatoře IX. Lisztovo nadšení ze skladby ředitele Josefa Krejčího," *Hudební rozhledy* 61, no. 9 (2008): 52–53.

[28] Kittl ignored the music of Smetana and performed only the *Slavonic Dances* by Dvořák.

[29] See Branberger, *Konservatoř hudby*, 114–15. Krejčí also authored the first Czech harmony textbook, *Nauka o romonu čili harmonii pro hudebníky* (Prague: Amerling, 1850); see also Viktor Hruška, "Opětovný nález jedné z nejstarších učebnic harmonie v češtině," *Musicologica Brunensia* 50 (2015): 195–203.

[30] The Sparkasse was not a national but a regional institution, hence the title "Bohemian" as opposed to "Czech."

to establish a piano school and elevate the Prague Conservatory to a higher musical institution. Moreover, the salary conditions were not attractive enough for any internationally renowned artists.[31]

The "Golden" Era under Bennewitz and Dvořák

In 1874, the Bohemian Savings Bank took the decision to construct the Rudolfinum at its expense (see also Chapter 9). This building aimed not only to house a concert hall and an art gallery but also to provide space for the conservatory, which was previously housed in inadequate premises. The construction of the new building intended to showcase the economic success of the Savings Bank. The educational activities in the new building commenced in 1884 under the directorship of the violinist, violin pedagogue, and graduate of the conservatory, Antonín Bennewitz, who served in the position from 1881 to 1901.[32] Bennewitz's tenure is often referred to as the "golden era" in the history of the conservatory due to the outstanding level of teachers and artistic development of their students. In 1890, the previously independent Prague Organ School, established in 1830 and led by František Zdeněk Skuherský from 1866, was integrated into the conservatory.[33] Among its graduates were Czech composers, such as Dvořák, Foerster, and Janáček. In the same year, the piano school of the Prague Conservatory was finally established, with Jindřich Kàan z Albestů appointed as professor of advanced piano studies. To implement the institution's reforms and engage new educators, the Association decided to abolish the rule of free education that had been in place for the previous seventy-seven years and introduced tuition fees. In addition to the returnable deposit, accepted students with Austrian citizenship had to pay an annual tuition fee of twenty gulden and foreigners were charged forty

---

[31] Branberger, *Konservatoř hudby*, 104.

[32] As a pedagogue, Bennewitz is celebrated for teaching numerous famous violinists. See Bohumír Štědroň, "Bennewitz, Antonín," in *Československý hudební slovník osob a institucí*, vol. 1, ed. Bohumír Štědroň, Zdenko Nováček, and Gracián Černušák (Prague: Státní hudební vydavatelství, 1963), 82.

[33] Skuherský was also an important music theorist, and his *Nauka o harmonii na základě vědeckém* (Prague: F. A. Urbánek, 1885), in which he deals with the possibility of a free understanding of tonal relations, became the starting point for later generations of composers. For example, the founder of quarter- and micro-tone music, Alois Hába, claimed to have been influenced by Skuherský.

gulden per year. However, tuition fees were reduced or waived for financially disadvantaged students.[34]

In 1890, the conservatory leadership implemented another crucial innovation by establishing a separate composition department. Like instrumental disciplines, the study in this department was divided into three two-year courses. While the content of the first course focused on homophonic composition, the second delved into counterpoint, imitation, canon, fugue, the study of forms and instruments, and score reading. In the third course, students engaged in "applied study of forms," composition, and orchestration.[35] All organ-school students were required to attend the composition department, along with those who directly enrolled in composition and others who showed an aptitude for composition. The leadership of the conservatory and the organ school made significant efforts to secure Dvořák for a teaching position. However, the composer initially declined the offer for the 1889/90 school year, feeling overwhelmed by his compositional duties and international engagements.[36] After further negotiations, Dvořák was eventually persuaded to join the faculty on January 1, 1891, with a fee of 1,200 gulden and the condition that his teaching obligations in orchestration, the study of form, and practical composition would only take place from October to May.[37] Dvořák took over the third course of study and insisted that only exceptionally talented students, selected by the interim head of the composition department Karel Stecker, be admitted to the class.[38]

At the time of assuming his teaching position, Dvořák was a renowned composer with significant international acclaim, and the conservatory leadership and colleagues tolerated his non-conformity to the established organizational rules, such as disregarding the class schedule and extending his lessons at the expense of his colleagues' teaching time. Dvořák also had a somewhat unconventional pedagogical approach, as recalled by Vítězslav Novák: "He avoided any kind of theorizing. He was only a practitioner, showing how things were done or pointing out how they should not be

---

[34] Branberger, *Konservatoř hudby*, 134.

[35] Otakar Šourek, *Život a dílo Antonína Dvořáka*, 2nd ed., vol. 3 (Prague: SNKLHU, 1956), 17.

[36] Dvořák explains this in his letter to Josef Tragy from September 13, 1889. See Branberger, *Konservatoř hudby*, 136.

[37] Branberger, *Konservatoř hudby*, 138.

[38] Dvořák's students in the 1890/91 academic year included Josef Suk, Oskar Nedbal, Otto Berger, Julius Fučík, Karel Honsa, Vojtěch Kuchynka, Vojtěch Mádlo, Rudolf Reissig, Richard Schid, Ludwig Püschel, Wilhelm Riepel, and Adolf Lotter. In the following year, Suk, Berger, Nedbal, and Honsa continued studying with Dvořák, and Vítězslav Novák, Ondřej Horník, and Arnošt Praus joined the studio. See Šourek, *Život a dílo Antonína Dvořáka*, 17.

done" ("Vyhýbal se jakémukoli teoretizování. Byl jen a jen praktik, ukazující, jak se co dělá, nebo upozorňující, jak se to dělat nemá").[39] The composer gave those he believed to be talented space to express their individuality and quickly parted ways with less talented students.[40] In late November 1892, Dvořák received permission from the school leadership for a two-year leave for his activities in the USA. During his absence, Karel Stecker, Karel Knittl, and Josef Klička acted as substitutes in this composition course.

During this period, the conservatory's violin department also achieved its greatest success, especially after engaging Otakar Ševčík.[41] His studio trained renowned violinists, such as Jan Kubelík, Emanuel Ondříček, and Jaroslav Kocian.

Dvořák became the conservatory's director in 1901, at the peak of his artistic career. His appointment to this position further increased the institution's prestige. Another positive consequence was that the composer remained in Prague and did not pursue foreign engagements or move to Vienna. As the conservatory's director, Dvořák enjoyed more favorable conditions than his predecessors, allowing him to continue his creative work. His role was primarily artistic, and the administrative responsibilities were delegated to Karel Knittl, who took on the duties of the previous directors to conduct four public concerts of the student orchestra each year.[42] However, it does not mean that Dvořák was exempt from all administrative tasks. Alongside Knittl, he participated in the meetings of the Association, signed certificates, addressed student requests, and attended school events. After Dvořák's sudden death on May 1, 1904, Karel Knittl became the sole director of the conservatory for the following three years.[43]

---

[39] Vítězslav Novák, *O sobě a o jiných* (Prague: Supraphon, 1970), 43.

[40] Šourek, *Život a dílo Antonína Dvořáka*, 20.

[41] Before joining the Prague Conservatory, Ševčík worked as a professor of violin at the Kyiv Conservatory. Later, he worked in Vienna (1909–18), before returning to Prague. In the 1920s and 1930s, he also taught in the United States, in Ithaca, Chicago, New York, and Boston. He also developed his own violin method.

[42] Before Dvořák's appointment in 1891, Knittl also taught composition, choir conducting, and orchestration. When Dvořák became the director, a portion of his teaching responsibilities was returned to Knittl, who also taught music theory and score reading. Knittl believed in the necessity of solid music theory foundation for instrumentalists, urging them not to limit themselves to technical instrumental virtuosity alone. He was also the author of theoretical works used in education, among which his most significant was his *Nauka o skladbě homofonní*, 2 vols. (Prague: Urbánek, 1898–1910).

[43] Markéta Hallová, "200 let Pražské konzervatoře II. Éra Dvořákova a Knittlova," *Hudební rozhledy* 62, no. 3 (2009): 44–45.

In the Twilight of the Monarchy

After Knittl's death in 1907, Jindřich Kàan assumed directorship. In comparison to the late nineteenth century, there was a considerable economic upturn, as state subsidies tripled.[44] A notable contribution to the development of the institution was Kàan's opening of the master class in composition in 1909, where he engaged Vítězslav Novák, a student of Dvořák and a prominent composer of the early twentieth century. Another conceptual innovation was the introduction of a dramatic school. Kàan also increased the number of students who received individual lessons in their main instrument.[45]

In 1909, the Association sent a request to the Austrian Ministry of Culture and Education for the nationalizing of the conservatory, also seeking the construction of a new building. However, during the existence of the Austro-Hungarian monarchy, neither of these requests materialized. Shortly before submitting this request, the New Vienna Conservatory (Neues Wiener Konservatorium) had already been nationalized at great financial cost. Therefore, the Austrian Ministry of Finance was unwilling to undertake a similar act in Prague, although the Prague institution was the oldest and, according to some, the most important institution of its kind in the monarchy.[46] In the last decade before the monarchy's fall, the conflict over the school's linguistic character escalated. Many of Kàan's subsidy requests faced resistance from Viennese authorities due to concerns about the growing influence of Czechs and the increasing complaints from Germans about oppression at the conservatory.[47] The transfer of the conservatory to the state occurred in 1920, in the new Czechoslovak Republic. The Association also ceased its activities at that time. Kàan had to abdicate, having been criticized for his non-Czech and aristocratic

---

[44] Branberger, *Konservatoř hudby*, 162.

[45] Kàan also expanded the mandatory piano instruction from three to four years, introduced lessons in the cor anglais, bass clarinet, contrabassoon, viola d'amore, and sight reading for orchestral players. Moreover, he included liturgy for organists, practical pedagogy, and philosophy for advanced students. See Markéta Hallová, "Zestátnění pražské konzervatoře a osud ředitele Jindřicha Kàana z Albestu," *Clavibus unitis* 7 (2018): 44; www.acecs.cz/media/cu_2018_07_01_hallova.pdf, accessed December 17, 2023.

[46] See Jindřich Kàan, "Z mých vzpomínek—část druhá: Třicet let na pražské konzervatoři," typescript, 11 and 21; discussed in Hallová, "Zestátnění pražské konzervatoře," 48–49.

[47] According to Kàan, for example, the Germans demanded an equal number of Czech and German teachers at the institution, despite a significant majority of Czech students attending throughout its existence. It was not within the financial means of the Association to maintain so many teachers. Additionally, most Czech educators were proficient in German. Hallová, "Zestátnění pražské konzervatoře," 49.

background (his father was a Hungarian nobleman), excessive pedantry, and efforts to maintain the conservatory as an institution associated with both Czechs and German Bohemians (see also Chapter 18).[48] The merits of his thirty years of service in the institution were forgotten in the revolutionary turmoil of the 1918 state coup. Despite this turbulent period, the Prague Conservatory retained its status as one of the most prominent public music institutions in the Czech lands, which continues to the present day. Between 1811 and 1918 alone, the conservatory enrolled nearly 30,000 students.[49]

[48] See Hallová, "Zestátnění pražské konzervatoře," 52.

[49] This number was mentioned in a speech delivered by Karel Jonáš, member of the Czechoslovak Parliament, on December 4, 1918, on the conservatory's nationalization. The speech was published in Vladimír Blažek, ed., *Sborník na paměť 125 let konservatoře hudby v Praze* (Prague: Vyšehrad, 1936), 182–84.

PART III

The Twentieth Century and Beyond

18 | The Mutual Exclusion Society: Musicology and Criticism in Early Twentieth-Century Prague

BRIAN S. LOCKE

The atmosphere surrounding music scholarship and criticism in Prague closely mirrored the socio-political shifts of its time. Music criticism in the city had been contentious since the 1860s, bolstered by competing interests of Czech nationalism and Bohemian/Austrian/German identity in the region, and the intensification of rhetoric after 1900 shadows the collapse of Austria-Hungary and the emergence of the Czechoslovak Republic. The ever-widening Czech/German linguistic chasm shaped the experience of music in Prague, as did countless other rifts on all sides. Amid the fray, perhaps no voice caused more controversy than that of the music historian and critic, Zdeněk Nejedlý (1879–1962).[1]

The manifold divisions of musical society in the Czech lands described in this chapter are, as individual and cumulative acts, exclusions of Others from the definitions of Self. While some phases in this process of separation appear more like interpersonal disputes or grudge matches (between Nejedlý and Janáček, for instance), it is important to remember how vast segments of the population were thus excluded. Since music served so well as an ineffable marker of identity, the question of who *should* represent it, to whom, and by what means bore the responsibility of demarcating the boundaries of the collective, be it a nation, a religious group, a linguistic community, an urban location, a political allegiance, an educational institution, or a sphere of like-minded colleagues. Inherent in all nationalisms is a negative definition of Self ("who we are not"), which in this case transferred to its corollary: excluding the Other ("who is not us"). Its inevitable result was a sort of vanishing point of collective culture.

---

[1] For a more complete discussion of Nejedlý's life and career, see Brian S. Locke, *Opera and Ideology in Prague: Polemics and Practice at the National Theatre, 1900–1938* (Rochester, NY: University of Rochester Press, 2006); and Jiří Křesťan, *Zdeněk Nejedlý: politik a vědec v osamění* (Prague: Paseka, 2012). Křesťan's substantial tome treats his subject through a tragic (and occasionally ironic) lens, seeking to balance the often monolithic assumptions about Nejedlý's personal character with a careful examination of his private papers.

Musical Tensions in the Czech Lands of the Late Nineteenth Century

Any discussion of the scholarship and criticism in the Czech lands after 1900 requires a brief preamble through the previous generation, as it provided both the role models and the prototypical methodologies for the polemic debates of later decades. What we find in the nineteenth century is a gradual process of formation and reformulation, paralleling the socio-political aspirations of Bohemians into self-sufficient, Czech- and German-speaking societies, where all the tensions over inclusion and exclusion appear *in nuce*, but only latterly as factions defined by the institutions they inhabited. The separation of these cultural institutions mirrors the increasing complexity of musical factions, with Prague emerging as the main battleground for its rapid urbanization, modernization, and Czechification. And as the accomplishments of the musical community, be they compositional, performative, or scholarly, grew from local concerns to participation in a pan-European context, so too did the anxiety over cultural representation.

The end of the Alexander Bach era in 1859 and the increased freedom of cultural expression for the Czech community also proved the catalyst for cracks and fissures in musical life. "Provisional" though it may have been, the establishment of a permanent theater for Czech opera fed a discourse that was wholly distinct from the German-speaking cultural sphere. As with any emerging middle-class society, the music criticism of the capital served to advertise performances and educate the audiences aesthetically, and the proliferation of journals reflected the increasing literacy and social mobility of their Czech readers. Various short-lived music journals cropped up at this time (for example *Dalibor* and *Hudební listy*), while German-speaking audiences relied upon steady representation in the Prague dailies *Bohemia* and *Prager Tagblatt*.

No sooner had Czech-speaking Prague established a permanent cultural voice, than it bifurcated along political lines in the 1860s and 70s, between Old Czech and Young Czech parties, each with their own beliefs regarding the role of arts in society. Smetana and his supporters Otakar Hostinský and Zdeněk Fibich sided with the cosmopolitan Young Czech ideology and accordingly distanced themselves from the Old Czech establishment. The Old Czechs espoused a more parochial nationalism, exemplified by the politician František Rieger and the critic František Pivoda, who championed Dvořák's music over Smetana's. This rivalry – largely manufactured by ideologues – continued in the decades after Smetana's death in 1884 as a struggle of which faction might claim authority over Smetana's legacy and his representation of the imagined Czech nation. Hostinský and Fibich embraced their idol as a disciple of Wagnerian musico-dramatic aesthetics, while the conservative stronghold over the National Theater promoted V. J. Novotný's de-Wagnerized editions of Smetana's operas. These editions infuriated Hostinský and Fibich: indeed, the question of Smetana's Wagnerianism dominated their criticism and negatively affected the reception of Fibich's own operatic premieres in the 1880s and 90s.

Although German musical life in Prague was proportionately shrinking in comparison with the burgeoning Czech scene, German cultural institutions acquitted themselves well within their pan-Germanic musical world, undaunted by the 1882 separation of Charles-Ferdinand University into Czech and German institutions. Shortly thereafter, each university appointed a musicologist to a professorial position – Otakar Hostinský for the Czechs (1883), and Guido Adler for the Germans (1885). That same year, Adler inaugurated his journal, *Vierteljahresschrift für Musikwissenschaft*; by the time Adler left Prague for Vienna in 1898, he had made his name virtually synonymous with the first generation of musicology. Among German music critics, the great Wagnerian Richard Batka held sway at *Bohemia* and would soon publish his *Die Musik in Böhmen*, a Germano-centric history of the region's music.[2] Its final chapter focused on Czech music, which quickly proved contentious with his Czech counterpart, Nejedlý.[3]

Nejedlý and the Institutionalization of Czech Critical Rhetoric, 1900–1918

1900 signals an important shift in Prague's musical life with Zdeněk Nejedlý's entrance into the professional sphere as both a music critic and musicologist. Nejedlý sought to transform old aesthetic debates into multi-generational struggles that ultimately cleft deep, irreconcilable divisions between artistic communities. It is impossible to overestimate the effect that Nejedlý had on Czech music across the entire twentieth century. The topography of these debates – particularly in the shifting allegiances of his followers and his ever-expanding legion of foes – reflects the very history of

---

[2] Richard Batka, *Die Musik in Böhmen* (Berlin: Bard, Marquardt, & Co., 1906).
[3] Zdeněk Nejedlý, "Richard Batka über die čechische Musik," *Česká revue* 2 (1908): 305–16.

modern Czech music. At times the endless arguments, pontifications, and screeds in the Czech musical and daily press seem to treat musical works as secondary to the human drama of personal attacks. Nevertheless, what was at stake on Nejedlý's battleground was nothing less than the contestation of musical meaning, the question of the artist's right or duty to represent this meaning for Czech listeners and the outside world, and above all, the manipulation of power in the halls and institutions of art.

Born in the east Bohemian town of Litomyšl – where Smetana had been born fifty-five years earlier – Nejedlý's educational path in Prague began with positivistic historical studies at the National Museum. He soon gravitated, however, toward the more dynamic world of music, studying not at the Prague Conservatory but at Charles-Ferdinand University, where he explored musicology and aesthetics under Hostinský. Coupled with his private studies in music theory with Fibich, Nejedlý's academic and intellectual foundations were thus secured by two of the self-appointed standard-bearers of Smetana's legacy.

Fibich's death in 1900 at the age of forty-nine prompted the twenty-one-year-old Nejedlý into action on behalf of his slighted mentor.[4] His first salvo aimed at no less a target than Dvořák's *Rusalka* in a review essay published after the opera's 1901 premiere.[5] As is typical for Nejedlý's critical style, he eschewed analysis of musical detail for broad historiographical trajectories. Invoking Hostinský's Wagnerian teachings on music and drama, the young critic declared that Dvořák's Czech declamation was faulty in both melodic contour and rhythmic placement, and his inclusion of "realist" folksong melodies was trivial, undramatic, and in direct opposition to Smetana's "idealism." Nejedlý then recounted Smetana and Fibich's suffering at the hands of their conservative opponents who had failed to recognize the dramatic necessity of modern opera, and who still refused to speak the truth about Dvořák to the Czech public.

Nejedlý soon turned to a broader landscape: his 1903 *Dějiny české hudby* ("History of Czech Music") represented material from the pre-Hussite era up to the most recent operas and concerts as a highly intentional and unbroken continuum of Czech musical identity.[6] He divided the latter

---

[4] Nejedlý's four years of private study with Fibich (1896–1900) sufficed to indoctrinate the student with his mentor's grievances against the (allegedly) anti-Smetanian, Old Czech establishment; one of Nejedlý's first book-length publications concerned Fibich. Cf. Zdeněk Nejedlý, *Zdenko Fibich, zakladatel scénického melodrama* (Prague: Hejda & Tuček, 1901).

[5] Zdeněk Nejedlý, "Dvořákova *Rusalka*," *Rozhledy* 11/8 (May 25, 1901): 205.

[6] Zdeněk Nejedlý, *Dějiny české hudby* (Prague: Hejda & Tuček, 1903). Nejedlý also published a three-volume history of pre-Hussite and Hussite-era chant that was saturated with a similarly teleological nationalism, culminating in a purported state of perfection during the Hussite era.

half of the book into two large chapters: "The Era of Smetana" (that is, the mid-nineteenth century to 1884) and "The Era of Fibich" (since 1884), which Nejedlý had experienced firsthand. In these pages he lays out his system of compositional and aesthetic lineages that would shape critical discourse for his entire career and throughout the communist period, dividing Czech music history between irreconcilable factions of *Smetanovci* ("Smetanians") and *Dvořákovci* ("Dvořákians"). The latter consisted of Dvořák, his colleagues at the Prague Conservatory, and its recent students, namely Vítězslav Novák, Josef Suk, Oskar Nedbal, and Rudolf Karel. These individuals also formed the core of the musical estab- lishment at the Umělecká beseda (Artists' Union, hereafter UB). The Smetanians represented composers and critics whom Nejedlý admired or whose careers lay outside the Prague Conservatory: Smetana, Fibich, Hostinský, Josef Bohuslav Foerster, Otakar Ostrčil, and Otakar Zich, con- nected by a vague spiritual descent rather than institutional affiliation (though both Ostrčil and Nejedlý had studied with Fibich privately). Leoš Janáček, who was yet to make his name in Prague, was notably absent from any lineage.

In the early years of the twentieth century, it seems that any significant event could cause conflict: the deaths of Dvořák (1904) and his colleague Karel Knittl (1907) prompted Nejedlý to question the legitimacy of the Prague Conservatory as a cultural institution. Meanwhile, artists and scholars of the conservatory/UB faction established *Hudební revue* ("Musical Review," 1908–20), a platform for celebrating their own achieve- ments while mounting a defense against the growing Nejedlý contingent. Edited by two conservatory professors, its other regular contributors included younger composers (Jaroslav Křička, Ladislav Vycpálek), music- ologists (Jan Löwenbach and Dvořák's biographer Otakar Šourek), and the arch-conservative critic Antonín Šilhan. Articles and reviews focused on all the major Czech premieres, new opera productions, and interrelationships between Czech music and the broader European sphere: the German- Bohemian community, however, is almost entirely absent from the pages of *Hudební revue*. Indeed, reports from abroad (including German and Austrian cities) received substantially greater attention than "Prague's German Theaters," which garnered at most three brief reviews – of foreign works – per annum.

See Hana Vlhová-Wörner, "Zdeněk Nejedlý's Historical Narrative and Ideological Construction of Czech Medieval Music History," in *Nationality and Universality: Musical Historiographies in Central and Eastern Europe,* ed. Sławomira Żerańska-Kominek (Newcastle upon Tyne: Cambridge Scholars Publishing, 2016), 175–95.

Meanwhile Nejedlý had been steadily gaining ground at the Czech university in Prague and publishing criticism in various daily newspapers. He was promoted to a professorial position in 1908 and created the first full musicology curriculum during the 1910/11 academic year. But the turbulence of Nejedlý's early music criticism prompted his sudden departure from established Czech newspapers and music journals: this closed all remaining avenues for voicing his vision of a modern, Czech musical culture in the image of Smetana and Fibich. And so, under the aegis of his new university home, Nejedlý and his associates created their own platform, the bi-weekly journal *Smetana*, a name chosen to reflect their shared conceit of the exclusive and fundamentalist interpretation of Smetana's music. The journal's main contributors were Nejedlý, Zich, and their recent university graduates Josef Bartoš and Vladimír Helfert. The same group of intellectuals formed a quasi-public lecture series, known as Hudební klub (Music Club).

Possibly the fiercest polemic between the university and conservatory factions unfolded in the years 1911–14, infamous in Czech music history as the "Dvořák Affair." It started with Bartoš's public lecture on Dvořák's chamber music, in which he sought to marginalize the late master's contribution to Czech music as that of a decidedly undramatic composer.[7] Nejedlý, meanwhile, published his monograph *Česká moderní zpěvohra po Smetanovi* ("Czech Modern Opera since Smetana") in late 1911, six lectures devoted to Fibich, Foerster, and Ostrčil, with Karel Kovařovic castigated as a former Fibich student who had dishonored Smetana's legacy, and Dvořák's nine operas ostentatiously excluded from the history.[8] Soon it was Zich's turn to bring down Dvořák's symphonic music; meanwhile, *Hudební revue* fired back, with Löwenbach and Vycpálek attacking the musical credentials of the university faculty and students – as represented in the infrequency and inaccuracy of Nejedlý and Zich's musical examples. For while the conservatory's alleged pan-Austro-German cosmopolitanism might imply a lack of Czech nationalist credentials, the intellectualism of the university contingent could just as easily showcase a lack of musicality, and through it their inability to comprehend Czech musical culture.

Under Nejedlý's command, the discourse turned quickly to contemporary composers on both sides. Zich, by now a professor of aesthetics at the university, paid dearly for his early tirade against Dvořák's legacy, and his

[7] Published as Josef Bartoš, "Dvořákova hudba komorní," *Smetana: Hudební list* 2/5 (November 17, 1911) through 4/18 (May 22, 1914).
[8] Zdeněk Nejedlý, *Česká moderní zpěvohra po Smetana* (Prague: Otto, 1911).

compositions would never gain acceptance outside the Nejedlý circle. But the greater impact fell on graduates of the conservatory, who till now had been merely hapless victims of their elders' purported irresponsibility toward Czech musical culture. In 1912, members of the Hudební klub went so far as to court Vítězslav Novák, star pupil of Dvořák and newly minted composition professor at the conservatory. They only partially succeeded in broaching the institutional walls, however, fostering the discontent of young graduates Emil Axman and Karel Boleslav Jirák against their older contemporaries, Křička and Vycpálek, and bringing them temporarily into Hudební klub. The stakes were rising.

The climax of the Dvořák Affair arrived on November 18, 1912, with Helfert's scathing report of an otherwise innocuous music festival in the German spa town of Pyrmont to commemorate Dvořák's seventieth birthday.[9] For the Nejedlý circle, this event was proof of the un-Czech quality of Dvořák's music, celebrated abroad while the true (Smetanian) representatives of Czech music languished at home. A month later, almost all of Prague's dailies carried a protest signed by thirty-one of the city's most respected musical leaders, including Kovařovic from the National Theater, Czech Philharmonic director Vilém Zemánek, Suk and Nedbal from the Czech Quartet, and Novák among the leading composers of the conservatory. The protest decried the insulting tone of Bartoš, Helfert, and Nejedlý, concluding thus: "It is our duty to object publicly to these expressions of fanatic prejudice, and we protest against their crude and base tone, in which immature and uneducated people presume to speak about a master of world renown."[10]

This public drama only served to pour accelerant on a fire well out of control. By January 1913, Nejedlý was openly targeting the individual signatories of the protest with the intent of derailing their careers. Novák was first to bear the brunt of Nejedlý's ire and the effective transfer of historical grudges to contemporary ones: virtually every Novák premiere henceforth met with scorn and derision in *Smetana*. Kovařovic was regularly excoriated until his death in 1920. Meanwhile, Janáček – no friend of Kovařovic and the grand institutions of the capital – also became the recipient of Nejedlý's personal attacks after the Prague premiere of *Jenůfa* (see Chapter 19). Nejedlý's main cause for the musical and moral rejection

---

[9] Vladimír Helfert, "Více Dvořáka!" *Česká kultura* 1/4 (November 15, 1912): 114–18.

[10] "Protest 15.12.1912," *Národní listy*, December 15, 1912. "Máme za svoji povinnost ohraditi se veřejně proti těmto projevům fanatické zaujatosti a protestujeme proti jich hrubého a nízkému tónu, jímž dovolují si mluviti lidé nezralí a nevychovaní o mistru významu světového." Translated in Locke, *Opera and Ideology*, 58.

of Janáček lay in the latter's alleged sympathy for Smetana's detractors thirty years before, though from a wider vantage point, the critic's rampant jealousy of any artist's success, beyond that of his protégés, is easily apparent here. In Nejedlý's continuous belligerence, the broadly historiographical and the bitterly personal were forever intertwined.

"Our Music and the Czech State": Musical Identities in the First Czechoslovak Republic, 1918–1924

After nearly 300 years of subordinate status under the Austrian monarchy, Czech-speaking critics and scholars met the arrival of independent statehood with near universal jubilation. This celebratory mood soon merged with a more sinister strain, however, for the term "De-Germanification" entered the acceptable public lexicon, virulently hurled at any institution previously favored under the old regime. Not only were even more cultural institutions segregated on linguistic lines, but several prominent individuals were effectively purged from Czech musical life over suspicions of their national origins, pro-Austrian collaboration, or the particularly Czech charge of cultural "utraquism": participation in both cultures equally.

The Czech Philharmonic, Prague Conservatory, and the National Theater found themselves on the fault-lines of this upheaval, even before World War I had ended. In his February 1918 essay *Naše hudba a český stát* ("Our Music and the Czech State"), Vladimír Helfert asserted that any institution serving both linguistic communities had created an "unintelligible and unnatural dualism" that was categorically "un-Czech."[11] The first to fall was the Czech Philharmonic's conductor, Vilém Zemánek; born to a German-speaking Jewish family in Prague, he had received his education at German institutions. Despite sixteen years of loyal and steadfast leadership, the orchestra members rose against him in April 1918 – prompted by Helfert's inflammatory rhetoric questioning his Czechness – and his career was effectively terminated. Nejedlý, for his part, attempted to cast aspersions on the loyalties of Suk, whose tone poem *Zrání* had premiered at the first post-independence Czech Philharmonic concert; Suk's supposed crime had been to accept an Austrian Imperial award as a member of the Czech Quartet. Unlike Zemánek, though, Suk had many supporters to speak up for his patriotism, particularly at his alma mater, the Prague Conservatory.

---

[11] Vladimír Helfert, *Naše hudba a český stát* (Prague: B. Kočí, 1918).

By November 1918, however, it was the turn of the Prague Conservatory to endure a far broader purge, again prompted by Helfert's essay (see Chapter 17). Its controversial directors were two Bohemian nobles, Jindřich Kàan z Albestů and Rudolf Freiherr von Procházka, whose social rank, aesthetic leanings, and the overall utraquism of their administration became insupportable under the new regime. Both resigned from the conservatory leadership on November 18, 1918, along with the entire German-speaking faculty, who opened their own Deutsche Akademie für Musik und darstellende Kunst in Prag just four days later. The new Akademie faculty included the Viennese-born composer/conductor Alexander Zemlinsky, who had directed the New German Theater since 1910, and the musicologist/critic Erich Steinhard, soon to inaugurate Prague's most important German-language music journal, *Der Auftakt* (1920–38). Back at the Czech-only conservatory, Novák worked to democratize the administration with the help of Foerster, who returned to Prague after a quarter-century residency in Germany and Austria. Unsurprisingly – since he had long occupied a place in Nejedlý's pantheon – Foerster's national credentials were never called into question.

The fallout as regards the National Theater represented a continuation of the Nejedlý contingent's inroads on the programming choices of Kovařovic, allegedly too susceptible to German tastes at the expense of Czech operas. Kovařovic quickly changed his repertoire to exclude all German operas except those by Gluck, Mozart, and Beethoven, composers favored by Czech nationalists as part of their cultural patrimony. In November 1919, Kovařovic assuaged the Nejedlians by hiring Ostrčil as his dramaturge – who soon became Kovařovic's successor after the latter's death in late 1920, thus further altering the factional landscape of opera in the capital. By coincidence that very week, on November 16, 1920, a mob of Czech-speaking Prague citizens broke into the historic Deutsches Landestheater (also known as the Estates Theater) and claimed it as a Czech institution, mounting a hasty production of *Prodaná nevěsta* the same evening. It was clearly a chauvinist and vengeful act, for Prague's oldest theater had always been a German-owned one, however much the Czech populace might envy its pride of place.

German scholars and critics, recently deprived of empire and regional power, did their best to restrain public reactions to the loss of their historic theater: just one small paragraph in the very first issue of *Der Auftakt* coolly remarked that "The Theater in the Fruit Market has changed its proprietors. ... It is not yet foreseeable how the conditions will be cleared up."[12] Most likely

---

[12] "Prager Musikleben," *Der Auftakt* 1/1–2 (1920): 14. "Das Theater auf dem Obstmarkt hat seinen Besitzer gewechselt. . . . Noch ist nicht abzusehen, wie sich die Verhältnisse klären werden." The

the work of its editor Steinhard, the neutral text reflects his subject position as a Prague-born, German-speaking Jew who viewed Czech-German cultural interaction to great advantage. But at the German University, the staunchly nationalist musicology professor Heinrich Rietsch (Adler's replacement since 1900) expressed his hatred of the new Czechoslovak regime and a strong desire to return to Vienna. To this end, Rietsch persuaded his former student Paul Nettl to move back to Prague with the vague promise of Nettl eventually replacing Rietsch. Although Nettl joined the university as an unsalaried *Privatdozent* in 1920, Rietsch stayed on until his death in 1927. Both men hailed from families of Jewish origin in what was now the Sudeten region, and their scholarly careers proceeded as though the Austro-Hungarian Empire had never fallen: Nettl distinguished himself as one of the foremost scholars of his generation on the Classical period in the Habsburg lands.[13]

Meanwhile, Steinhard continued his efforts to bring the linguistic communities together, reporting regularly on Czech musical life as early as *Der Auftakt*'s third issue without any trace of rancor. To be sure, its pages reflect the priorities of Germans in Prague, with Steinhard's penchant for the modernism of his younger contemporaries given priority over historical essays. Zemlinsky was a clear favorite, his every move carefully tracked with the promise of increased international relevance for the now isolated German-Bohemians: significantly, he too crossed the linguistic divide on many occasions to collaborate with his Czech counterpart, Ostrčil from the National Theater. All these threads came together with their joint participation in the second annual meeting of the International Society for Contemporary Music (ISCM) in 1924, which coincided handily with Smetana's centenary. Though the Czechoslovak section of ISCM maintained a strictly divided representation from Czechs and Germans, the cooperation between Steinhard and the microtonal composer Alois Hába was among the most cordial in interwar Czechoslovakia.

Modernisms and Anti-Modernisms, 1924–1938

The arrival of international avant-gardists like Schoenberg and Ravel in Prague for the 1924 ISCM produced a sensation among all echelons of musical life. While the Czechs' and Germans' world-class performances

---

"Fruit Market" refers to the urban square adjacent to the theater, now known as Ovocný trh. Translated in Locke, *Opera and Ideology*, 142.

[13] Martin Nedbal, "Music History and Ethnicity from Prague to Indiana: Paul Nettl, Eighteenth-century Bohemia, and Germanness," *Hudební věda* 16 (2019): 391–92.

before a cosmopolitan crowd generated an undeniable sense of pride, the musical results prompted a new, generational rift over the aesthetics of modernism. This irony was embodied in the dual structure of the festival itself, wherein the National Theater's cycle of Smetana's operas (conducted by Ostrčil but closely curated by Nejedlý) was meant to showcase Smetana's perennial modernism as a model for contemporary Czech music. Czechoslovak audiences experienced Schoenberg's *Erwartung* (its world premiere) and Ravel's *L'heure espagnole* alongside recent Czech and German-Bohemian compositions. But Nejedlý, for once, wasn't the problem – for he at least supported any public access to the avant-garde as a social responsibility; rather, it was the old guard of UB-based critics, Antonín Šilhan foremost among them, who balked at what the wide world was now calling music. Šilhan had already repudiated much of what Ostrčil had premiered since 1920, particularly Zich's polytonal opera *Vina* ("Guilt"), and both the 1924 festival and its 1925 successor gave him ammunition for further attacks on modern music.

The youngest generation of composers and critics, meanwhile, exulted in the new cosmopolitanism that this exposure afforded them (see Chapter 20). Hába had recently opened a quarter-tone masterclass at the Prague Conservatory and his protégés Emil František Burian, Iša Krejčí, and Jaroslav Ježek all took to music journalism early in their careers, championing Stravinsky, Martinů, and *Les Six*. Nejedlý's young student Mirko Očadlík, given to attending all repeat performances of new works in Prague, was especially prolific in representing his generation's aesthetics.[14] And so it was that Očadlík became the sole critic to witness the notorious "*Wozzeck* Affair" as it unfolded on November 16, 1926, when a crowd of hired agitators interrupted Berg's opera on the third night of its Czech-language production under Ostrčil at the National Theater (see also Chapter 20). Surviving documents demonstrate that the plot had hatched as early as the Berlin world-premiere of *Wozzeck* in 1925, and that Šilhan had deliberately stirred up municipal authorities: indeed, the police were on hand in the theater that night, allowing the demonstration to go forward before canceling not only the evening, but the rest of the run. The ban on *Wozzeck* stirred the entire generation of young artists to action, decrying Šilhan's incitement and the stranglehold of the bourgeois subscribers on the National Theater's programming choices. Even Novák lent his support to the protest against Šilhan, whose honorary lifetime membership in the

---

[14] Brian S. Locke, "The *Wozzeck* Affair: Modernism and the Crisis of Audience in Prague," *Journal of Musicological Research* 27/1 (2008): 63–93.

UB was revoked. Ostrčil's production of *Wozzeck* went on to receive a state award for its contribution to culture in 1927.

For all this apparent artistic unity against the forces of anti-modernism, even the Nejedlý circle experienced fissures that would ultimately have dire consequences. Zich, who had left Prague in 1919 to teach at the newly established Masaryk University in Brno, recommended that Helfert relocate also, who established his own musicology program in the university's Faculty of Arts in 1921. Away from Nejedlý's overbearing influence, Helfert made peace with Leoš Janáček and his many supporters in Brno, arranging for the composer to receive an honorary doctorate from Masaryk University in 1925. Helfert's curriculum would influence a generation of subsequent musicologists. For Nejedlý, of course, this path meant the betrayal of his ideals: Janáček's alleged antipathy to Smetana – and his recent success beyond that of Foerster, Ostrčil, and Zich – were unforgiveable. But Helfert pressed on undaunted, his interwar scholarship culminating in the broadly historiographical *Česká moderní hudba* ("Czech Modern Music") of 1936, a thorough and balanced assessment of music from the pre-Smetana generation to his contemporaries.[15] Outlandish as it may seem, Helfert treated all his subjects fairly or even generously, often describing composers of all factions as "heroic." His epilogue issued a warning against historians who sought to stifle creativity through the overuse of ideological bias. Helfert had effectively overturned his mentor's *History of Czech Music* from thirty-three years earlier, and no greater condemnation of Nejedlý's historiography was necessary in interwar Czechoslovakia. Any who sided with Helfert would henceforth be anathema – had the storms of European politics not intervened (see Chapter 23).

Helfert and Steinhard tried one last time to bridge the linguistic gap between Czech and German speakers in the final years of democratic Czechoslovakia. In 1936, they co-authored the volume *Geschichte der Musik in der Tschechoslovakischen Republik*, which appeared simultaneously in French as *Histoire de la Musique dans la République Tchécoslovaque*; following in the spirit of the 1935 ISCM festival in Prague, it represents their communities' combined musical efforts to a European readership.[16] That festival, however, had already brought to

---

[15] Vladimír Helfert, *Česká moderní hudba*, reprinted in *Vybrané studie I.: O hudební tvořivosti* (Prague: Supraphon, 1970), 163–312.

[16] Vladimír Helfert and Erich Steinhard, *Geschichte der Musik in der Tschechoslovakischen Republik* (Prague: Orbis, 1936) (later reprinted as *Die Musik in der Tschechoslovakischen Republik*, 1938); and *Histoire de la Musique dans la République Tchécoslovaque* (Prague: Orbis, 1938).

light the country's increasingly racialized cultural politics, whose boycott paralleled the rise of Konrad Henlein's *Sudetendeutsche Partei* and the split between right-wing conservatives identifying as Aryan Sudeten-Germans, and German-speaking Jews, whose identities and allegiances were increasingly fraught. Possibly for antisemitic reasons, Nettl's application to replace Rietsch as chair of musicology at the German University was passed over for that of the German-born Gustav Becking (see Chapter 23).[17] Soon after his arrival in 1930, Becking changed his political allegiances from socialism to National Socialism, and his lectures became a rallying point for like-minded university students. A follower of Henlein after 1935, Becking nevertheless used his influence to shield his Jewish colleagues and students from some of the antisemitic threats they endured before their expulsion in 1939. For Nettl and Steinhard both, their deep commitment to the music history of the Czech lands and the nuances of their respective historiographical viewpoints receded before the elementary question of personal survival.

To the Exclusion of All Else: Beyond 1939 and 1948

By 1939, several of the early protagonists in the debates over culture and representation had died, among them Rietsch, Zich, Suk, and Ostrčil. Between the Munich Agreement and the start of World War II, many more fled Central Europe: Löwenbach, Ježek, Zemlinsky, and Nettl all gained passage to the United States (see Chapter 22), whereas Nejedlý – an ardent communist since the early 1920s – received Soviet citizenship and went east. Those who remained were segregated into three ethnic camps: Germans, Czechs, and Jews, based on Nazi racial laws. Czech universities being closed, there were no occasions for historiographical debate, and Jews were excluded from public intellectual life. Erich Steinhard was transported to the Łódź ghetto on October 26, 1941, and was murdered shortly thereafter. Helfert and Burian were all arrested, tortured, and interned for their resistance activities but survived to liberation; however, Helfert succumbed just days later to typhus. Becking, who had risen in the German University administration to the post of dean of the academic senate, was arrested and shot on May 8, 1945, by Czech revolutionaries.

---

[17] Nedbal, "Music History and Ethnicity from Prague to Indiana," 401–3.

With the return of the Czechoslovak State came the expulsion of the remaining German Bohemians, and with them most traces of the German University, the Akademie, and the German theaters. It also brought the return of Nejedlý from the Soviet Union, ready to participate in political affairs and settle old scores. By this time, his perennial enemies were few: Novák was elderly, though still bitter enough to pen a tell-all autobiography before his death in 1949. And so, it only remained for Nejedlý to turn his wrath upon his own student, Josef Hutter, ostensibly for involvement in non-communist resistance activities, but more likely for having applauded Helfert's historiography in 1936.[18] As Minister of Education and National Culture, Nejedlý had Hutter fired from his professorship in March 1948, then arrested and convicted without trial on January 7, 1950, with a sentence of fifteen years imprisonment. Amnestied in 1956, Hutter died just three years later.

With none of his prewar opponents left, Nejedlý could remake the history of his country's music in his own image, instituting a curriculum that stayed largely in place until 1989. The vanishing point of collective culture had arrived: a dystopian society in which all were excluded.

[18] Milan Kuna, "Hutter, Josef," in *Český hudební slovník osob a institucí*, https://slovnik.ceskyhudebnislovnik.cz/component/mdictionary/?task=record.record_detail&id=1279, accessed April 10, 2024.

JIŘÍ ZAHRÁDKA

Leoš Janáček is considered one of the most original composers of twentieth-century operatic modernism, yet his mature works from the 1920s – *Káťa Kabanová*, *Příhody lišky Bystroušky* ("The Cunning Little Vixen"), *Věc Makropulos* ("The Makropulos Case"), and *Z mrtvého domu* ("From the House of the Dead") – are based on principles and techniques developed already in his third opera *Jenůfa* – original Czech title: *Její pastorkyňa* ("Her Foster-Daughter") – composed between 1894 and 1903.[1] The main concept that Janáček pursued in *Jenůfa* was realism, which inspired his choice of subject matter, his use of a prose text, and a compositional style rooted in spoken language. Janáček's unique innovations in *Jenůfa*, nevertheless, faced stiff resistance in Czech music circles, and it took more than a decade before they found at least partial appreciation.

When Janáček began to work on *Jenůfa* in 1894, he already had some experience as an opera composer: in the late 1880s and early 1890s he created two other works, *Šárka* and *Počátek románu* ("The Beginning of a Romance"). *Šárka* is based on a libretto about mythological Czech warrior women by Czech playwright Julius Zeyer. In *Šárka*, Janáček followed the tradition of Czech mythological operas, exemplified most importantly by Smetana's *Libuše*. There are a few links between *Šárka* and Smetana's work, particularly in terms of recurring motives and instrumentation. At the same time, in 1886 Janáček wrote an essay that was critical of Smetana, which meant that many Smetana fans later considered Janáček an opponent of Smetana.[2] Among Smetana supporters was Zeyer, who in turn withdrew his consent for Janáček to set

---

This chapter was translated from Czech to English by Martin Nedbal.

[1] The literal translation of the opera's Czech title, *Její pastorkyňa*, is "Her foster daughter," but outside the Czech lands, the opera is usually titled after its main protagonist, *Jenůfa*. This is the title used in this chapter, and it distinguishes the opera from the play on which it is based.

[2] Particularly significant is the 1886 exchange between V. V. Zelený (who published in the journal *Dalibor*) and Janáček (who published in the journal *Hudební listy*). For an English translation of Janáček's 1886 essay, see Martin Nedbal, trans and ed., *The Published Theoretical Works of Leoš Janáček* (Brno: Editio Janáček, 2020), 59–64. See also John Tyrell, *Janáček: Years of a Life* (London: Faber and Faber, 2006), 260.

his text.[3] Because of this conflict, *Šárka* was not performed until 1925, but already at the time of its first inception in the 1880s, Janáček's friend and mentor Antonín Dvořák had good things to say about its music. There are elements in *Šárka* that would become characteristic of Janáček's later works – the use of short motives and the reduction of the original text (so that the resulting opera lasts only about an hour). In this opera, shortening the text keeps focus on the relationship between Šárka, one of the warrior women, and Ctirad, the man she seduces.

Janáček's second opera, *Počátek románu*, is a folksy comedy inspired by a short story by Czech writer Gabriela Preissová, whose work also became the basis of *Jenůfa*. Janáček did not like *Počátek románu* very much; as he wrote in his 1924 autobiography, he could not understand how he could have composed it immediately after *Šárka*, which he considered more advanced.[4] Janáček disliked the subject, which he later considered naive; the rhymed libretto; and his own musical setting, which he found too closely tied to his study of folk music. Furthermore, the work was not completely original because Janáček borrowed music from his earlier ballet *Rákoš Rakoczy* as well as from his suite *Lašské tance* ("Lachian Dances"), which was first called *Valašské tance* ("Wallachian Dances"). *Počátek románu* premiered in 1894 and was well received, but it was not performed outside of Brno.

Janáček's third opera, *Jenůfa*, is an adaptation of Preissová's play *Její pastorkyňa* ("Her Foster-Daughter"), which premiered in Prague's National Theater in 1890. The play developed from Czech debates about literary realism and naturalism, initiated by Czech translations of authors such as Gogol, Ostrovsky, and Ibsen in the 1880s. In reaction to these foreign works, Czech authors accentuated social criticism and rural environments. Preissová's *Její pastorkyňa* premiered on November 9, 1890, and immediately caused controversy. Critics were troubled by what they considered the play's excessive naturalism and brutality. Even Preissová's colleagues from the realistic camp, who published in the journal *Čas*, criticized her work. Tomáš Garrigue Masaryk, later the first Czechoslovak president, was possibly among these colleagues; one of the negative critiques is sometimes attributed to him.[5] Another production of

---

[3] Václav Němec, "Osud Janáčkovy opery *Šárka* ve světle dosud neznámé korespondence Julia Zeyera," *Opus musicum* 60, no. 6 (2009): 17–20.

[4] See Jiří Zahrádka, *"Pravdu, první věcí, ne krásu." Příběh Janáčkovy Její patrokyně / "Truth, the first thing is truth, not beauty." The Story of Janáček's Jenůfa* (Brno: Moravské zemské muzeum, 2021), 19.

[5] Anonymous [possibly Tomáš Garrigue Masaryk], "Její pastorkyňa: Drama z venkovského života o 3 jednáních Gabriely Preissové," *Čas* 4, nos. 47 and 48 (November 22 and 29, 1890): 746–47 and 760–63.

Preissová's play opened the following year in Brno and was received more positively.

It is unclear whether Janáček attended the Brno production of Preissová's play, but he was clearly interested in setting it to music. In a letter to Janáček from November 6, 1893, the playwright wrote: "I think that the subject of P. [*Její pastorkyňa*] is certainly not fit for musical treatment – but we will find something more appropriate eventually."[6] It is possible that one of the impulses for Janáček to start setting the play to music was an earlier letter from Preissová (from November 1, 1893), in which she wrote that the composer Josef Bohuslav Foerster (who was slightly younger but becoming better known than Janáček in the early 1890s) wanted to set her earlier realist play *Gazdina roba* ("The Farm Mistress"). Foerster's opera *Eva*, named after the heroine of *Gazdina roba*, premiered in Prague's National Theater on January 1, 1899. Foerster's approach to Preissová's text was quite different from Janáček's: Foerster wrote his own libretto in verse, and his lyrical musical setting undermined the realistic bent of the original play.

Janáček's interest in *Její pastorkyňa* must have been related to its realist subject. His sensitivity to the idea of incorporating realist principles to musical theater is obvious in his earlier opera reviews.[7] As a folk-music researcher, Janáček had undertaken many ethnographic field trips, making him aware of the social conditions of common people in the Moravian countryside, which is the setting of *Její pastorkyňa*. Janáček's interest in Russian realist literature must have also contributed to his decision to compose *Jenůfa*.

Janáček began studying *Její pastorkyňa* intensely in 1894, as illustrated in his personal copy of the 1891 edition.[8] The book contains numerous notes about dramaturgy and music, and at the end of each act there are dates, which likely mark when Janáček finished his close analysis of the work. (The end of the first act is marked March 18, 1894, the second, February 11, 1895.) Janáček eventually created his own libretto by significantly shortening Preissová's text. His revisions intensified the main psychological and dramatic elements of *Její pastorkyňa* while keeping

---

[6] Gabriela Preissová's letter to Leoš Janáček (November 6, 1893), Brno, Archiv Leoše Janáčka Moravského zemského muzea (henceforth JA MZM), shelfmark A 3384. "Myslím, že látka P. rozhodně se nehodí k hudebnímu zpracování—ale najdeme snad časem něco vhodnějšího." See also John Tyrrell, *Janáček's Operas: A Documentary Account* (London: Faber and Faber, 1992), 43.

[7] See, for example, Leoš Janáček, "Eugen Oněgin," *Moravské listy* 3, no. 25 (February 28, 1891).

[8] The book is in JA MZM, shelfmark I. 6.

the intense, clear, and gripping narrative and, unlike Foerster, retaining Preissová's prose. Because he was familiar with Moravian ethnography, he replaced the songs originally chosen by Preissová with more authentic ones.[9]

Janáček was also concerned with how to translate the realist elements of *Její pastorkyňa* to music. He started setting his new text in 1895, but invented a new, realist musical language only after 1897, the year he started to study and record human speech.[10] In his innovative approach to the prose text, Janáček drew on both his long-term interest in folk music and his study of how people of different social backgrounds, regions, and ages expressed different psychological states. Janáček recorded the intonation of spoken phrases in conventional notation and referred to these notated segments as "nápěvky mluvy" ("speech tunelets").[11] Janáček's speech transcriptions also contained information about the places in which they were recorded; descriptions of the speakers; notes about the circumstances in which they were spoken; and later also the length of the speech, measured by the Hipp chronoscope. Janáček recorded several thousand speech tunelets, and he often used them in his theoretical and literary essays.[12] He considered this approach a scientific method and thought it was related to both psychology and the study of the Czech language and its dialects. Although Janáček studied "speech tunelets," he did not use them in his compositions, instead merely drawing inspiration from them. "Speech tunelets" allowed Janáček to decide how to represent the intonation and rhythm of his characters' speech in various situations. He explained his reservations about using pre-existing "speech tunelets" in his compositions in a 1904 notebook entry:

To fetch a tunelet, to take a tunelet – [to use] someone else's words [to express] my own words – is [like] not having enough of one's own blood sensitivity, one's own physical and spiritual life – to appropriate only partially: to be incomplete. Some exceptions: motives from nature, from [musical] instruments . . . Word tunelets are images, expressions of moods, circumstances, intentions, dislikes, likes, etc., that accompany the word. When the word falls off and all that is left is the tunelet – we have the expression, the image of the mood – but we no longer have what these

---

[9] See Zahrádka, *Pravdu, první věcí, ne krásu*, 49.

[10] See Zahrádka, *Pravdu, první věcí, ne krásu*, 67–73.

[11] This term is sometimes translated as "speech melodies," but I follow the translation of Michael Beckerman, *Janáček as Theorist* (Stuyvesant, NY: Pendragon, 1994), viii; this translation is also used in *The Published Theoretical Works of Leoš Janáček*.

[12] Janáček pays attention to tunelets in most of his essays after 1903. See Teodora Straková and Eva Drlíková, eds., *Leoš Janáček, Literární dílo*, vol. 1 (Brno: Editio Janáček, 2003).

[images and moods] are connected to; everyone can deduce this, but everyone deduces it in a different way!

Jít si tudíž jen pro nápěv, vzít si tudíž jen nápěv – cizí na svá slova jest: nemíti vlastní krve citu, vlastního tělesného i duševního života – bráti částečně: nemíti s dostatek toho. Zvláštní případy: motivy z přírody, z nástrojů. [...] Nápěv slova – jest obrazem, výrazem nálady, okolností, vůle, nechutí, chutí atd. jež doprovází slovo. Když slovo odpadne a zůstane jen nápěv – máme výraz, obraz nálady – ale ne toho na co se váže: to si může každý domyslit a sice každý jinak domyslit![13]

Although Janáček does not use pre-existing "speech tunelets," he relies on them heavily in his own compositions. These motives also penetrate orchestral layers – sometimes in fragments, sometimes in more complex structures – as ostinatos or in diminutions and augmentations, to name a few possibilities. Janáček also notated animal sounds, natural phenomena, and other noises. In the first act of *Jenůfa*, for example, he uses the xylophone to represent the clatter of the mill.[14]

Janáček's approach to operatic realism in *Jenůfa* differed from and was more radical than the contemporaneous experiments of French operatic realists, such as Gustave Charpentier and Alfred Bruneau. Although as he worked on *Jenůfa*, Janáček was unaware of the realistic experiments of these French composers, he was later quite taken with them. Charpentier's and Bruneau's realist leanings and interest in setting prose rather than rhymed texts were discussed in a 1901 article by Foerster.[15] In the following year, Foerster published a series of articles on Charpentier and his most famous opera *Louise* (1900).[16] While there are no indications that Janáček knew of or read these articles, he must have been aware of the debates about *Louise* that appeared in connection to the first production of the work in Prague's National Theater, which opened on February 13, 1903. Czech critical reactions to *Louise* were split. Some critics were concerned about the plot, particularly about the fact that Charpentier supposedly sympathized more with the morally depraved bohemians than with Louise's hard-working parents. Apart from the subject, the

---

[13] Janáček's notebook, 1904, JA MZM, shelfmark Z 26.

[14] For an analytical discussion of Janáček's style, see Tiina Vainiomäki, *The Musical Realism of Leoš Janáček: From Speech Melodies to a Theory of Composition* (Helsinki: University of Helsinki, 2012).

[15] Josef Bohuslav Foerster, "Z hudební Francie," *Dalibor* 33, no. 29 and 30 (July 13 and 20, 1901): 230, 239–40.

[16] Josef Bohuslav Foerster, "Gustave Charpentier I–IV," *Dalibor* 34, nos. 20, 22–23, 25, 26–27, and 33 (May 10, 31, June 14, July 5, and August 9, 1902): 159, 176–77, 195–6, 206–7, 260–61. On Charpentier, realism, and *Louise*, see Flora Willson "Listening for Realism in Charpentier's *Louise*," *Journal of the Royal Musical Association* 146 (2021): 397–424.

music of *Louise* was received enthusiastically. For example, Czech critics welcomed the opera's motivic structure as an outgrowth of Wagnerian approaches.

Janáček saw *Louise* in the National Theater on May 21, 1903, shortly after the theater's directorship rejected *Jenůfa*. Immediately after the performance, he wrote enthusiastically to his cousin's widow, Josefa Janáčková: "Dear sister-in-law! Ah, I had to escape before the last act; it was after ten! The plot speaks to my soul; it paints with music perfectly!" ("Milá švakrová! Ach musel jsem před posledním jednáním již – utéct; bylo přes 10 hod! Ten děj mluví do mé duše; ideálně kreslí hudbou!").[17] After returning to Brno, Janáček again expressed his excitement about *Louise* to Janáčková: "I am working again. The ingenious Charpentier has anticipated many of my own ideas! Some moments are – breathtaking! I had to escape from the theater – I did not even hear the last act, but I can imagine it is excellent" ("Tož jsem zase při práci. Ten geniální Charpentier mne s mnohou myšlenkou předešel! Některé okamžiky jsou – až k utajení dechu! Bylo mi třeba utíkat z divadla – poslední jednání jsem již neslyšel, ale mohu si představit, že bude stejně výtečné").[18] Janáček found a kindred soul in Charpentier. *Louise* took place in contemporaneous Paris, dealt with social questions, and featured the working class, vagabonds, and bohemians. Charpentier's musical language was filled with elements that Janáček pursued in his own work, such as occasional short motives that resembled Janáček's tunelets. Janáček returned to *Louise* many times in the following years as Charpentier's work helped him articulate his own compositional innovations in a larger context. Soon after seeing *Louise*, Janáček published several theoretical essays that discuss realism in *Jenůfa*.

At the time Janáček started composing *Jenůfa*, realism was established in Czech visual arts, literature, and drama, but Czech music critics and musicologists either did not deal with the concept in opera or understood it differently from Janáček. Early twentieth-century Czech music critics and musicologists understood *verismo*, which they associated with a specific type of Italian opera from the turn of the twentieth century, as an operatic movement that relied on realistic techniques. In his 1908 book about Smetana's operas, Zdeněk Nejedlý, then a musicology professor at Prague's Czech university, claimed that Wagner's works had a realist core because Wagner returned

---

[17] Leoš Janáček's postcard to Josefa Janáčková, May 22, 1903, JA MZM, shelfmark A 6325.
[18] Leoš Janáček's postcard to Josefa Janáčkova, May 22, 1903, JA MZM, shelfmark A 6328.

...truthfulness to the operatic stage when he declared that drama should once again be the highest principle of music-dramatic works ... The principle of truthfulness in music dramas parallels the principle of truthfulness in realist literature of the second half of the nineteenth century.

...na operní scénu zase pravdivost, prohlásiv dramatičnost zase za nejvyšší zákon celé hudebně-dramatické tvorby ... Princip pravdivosti v hudebním dramatě je však parallelní zjev v principu pravdivosti v realistické literatuře v druhé polovici 19. století.[19]

In Nejedlý's view, Smetana, presumably a Wagnerian composer, was also a realist, and Nejedlý saw in his works "the style for people of the real life" ("sloh pro lidi reálného života").[20] When discussing works of Bruneau and Charpentier, Czech critics also used the term "naturalism." This concept was often used in connection to the literary works of Émile Zola and had a slightly pejorative connotation.[21] In discussions of operatic works, furthermore, "naturalism" was often interchangeable with "verismo." This style of opera was sometimes criticized for depicting extreme psychological states and featuring music that was considered primitive. Nejedlý would soon find and criticize these elements in *Jenůfa*, which, moreover, he faulted for using actual folksongs and imitations of speech patterns.

Prior to the first performance of *Jenůfa* in Brno on January 21, 1904, Janáček hoped his contemporaries would notice the uniqueness of musical innovations, as is clear from the essay that was published in the program of the first Brno production. The essay is anonymous but there is no doubt that Janáček was the author:

On the Significance of "Jenůfa."

The work presented on our stage today is unusually important not only for dramatic music but also specifically for Moravian music. [For dramatic music, this opera is significant] in that it uses prose and musical principles that lie at its core, [for Moravian music] in that it is the first work that explicitly aims at becoming a Moravian opera. The first composer to use prose in an operatic work was Alfred Bruneau in 1897. In his history, Karel Stecker writes: "His works are crucial for the history of opera because they represent the first and certainly interesting attempts at operatic works in prose." The same needs to be said about the work of Janáček, the first Czech composer to do so – not under the influence of the French, but from his own initiative, set in this direction by the principle of truth in notated speech tunelets. Since a clean copy of [the finished] orchestral score of "Jenůfa" was

[19] Zdeněk Nejedlý, *Zpěvohry Smetanovy* (Prague: Otto, 1908), 46.
[20] Nejedlý, *Zpěvohry Smetanovy*, 67.
[21] Emanuel Žák, "Z domácího světa hudebního," *Vlasť* 19, no. 7 (April 1903): 658–59.

created in 1897, the French composers forewent Janáček only in terms of first performance. The principle that guided the creation of "Jenůfa" is as follows: Janáček realized that intonational little motives of speech reflect the most truthful image of the soul. That is why instead of arias, he used these tunelets. Thus, he achieved a truthful image in those places where it matters the most. In his effort to achieve truthful expression not only in the mood but also the situation, he also aimed at a realistic depiction of the environment, particularly in the choruses. In this characterization, he abandoned typical leitmotifs; it is his orchestra that characterizes the moods of entire scenes.

Speech motives and appropriately applied elements of folk music stamp his work with national spirit.

O významu 'Její pastorkyně.'

Dílo, jež ztělesňuje se dnes na naší scéně, má neobyčejný význam nejen pro hudbu dramatickou vůbec, ale pro specielně moravskou zvlášť. Pro první užití prosy a principy, na nichž vytvořeno, pro druhou tím, že je to prvé dílo, které vědomě chce býti moravským na tomto poli. Prosy poprvé užil v opeře francouzský skladatel Alfred Bruneau – 1897. Karel Stecker píše o tom ve svých dějinách: 'Jeho opery stávají se dějinách zjevy stěžejnými, jsouce prvními a dojista zajímavými pokusy komposice operní na text prosou psaný.' Totéž nutno nyní říci o práci Janáčkově, který první z českých skladatelů tak učinil, a to ne po příkladě Francouzů, nýbrž ze své vlastní iniciativy, přiveden na tuto dráhu principem pravdy v zachyceném nápěvku mluvy. Francouzští skladatelé předešli ho jen provedením, neboť roku 1897 partitura 'Její pastorkyně' byla již opisována na čisto. Princip, na němž 'Pastorkyňa' tvořena, je tento: Janáček poznal, že v nápěvných motivcích mluvy leží nejpravdivější obraz duše. Proto na místě árií užil těchto nápěvků. Tím dosáhl pravdivého obrazu tam, kde jistě je jednou z nejdůležitějších věcí. Snahou po pravdivém výrazu nejen v náladě, ale i situaci, veden byl, že sáhl i k realistickému znázornění okolí, zejména ve sborech. V charakteristice odchýlil se od obvyklých příznačných motivů; jeho orchestr charakterisuje náladu celé scény.

Motivky mluvy a vhodně užitý způsob lidové hudby vtiskují dílu jeho pečeť národního ducha.[22]

Janáček's text is not entirely trustworthy; for example, his claim about copying the orchestral score in 1897 is misleading. When, after finishing *Jenůfa*, he learned that French composers used prose in their works from the same period, he decided to claim precedence and scratched out the dates in the manuscript copies of his opera's first act that showed they were created only in 1900; and in 1910, he even burnt the autograph score of the opera. Janáček was mostly overlooked prior to the late 1910s and wanted to

---

[22] Program booklet, January 21, 1904, JA MZM, shelfmark D. 139.

add significance to his third and up-to-then most innovative opera. After he completed *Jenůfa* in early 1903, it took Janáček nearly a year to articulate the significance of his innovative approach and to connect it to realism. On January 12, 1904, an anonymous author published an interview with Janáček, titled "Její pastorkyňa," in the Brno newspaper *Lidové noviny*, in which the composer emphasized the uniqueness of the prose text and his use of "speech tunelets" as the main building blocks.[23] Thanks to the tunelets, Janáček claimed, "the music grows from the word" ("hudba jeho roste na slově"). This was also the first time that Janáček defined his musical style in terms of realism:

> What were the reasons that brought Janáček to compose this opera in one way and not the other? He himself defined these reasons with the words: realism in music. Truth, truth in the first place, not beauty. But the truth should bring beauty along.

> Které jsou příčiny, jež Janáčka přiměly, že tak a ne jinak operu komponoval? On sám definoval je slovy: Realismus v hudbě. Pravdu, první věcí pravdu, ne krásu. Pravda ovšem ať přinese krásu s sebou.

Following the 1904 Brno premiere of *Jenůfa*, reviews published in Brno were predominantly celebratory while the few published in Prague were more critical. The most negative was by Prague musicologist and critic Jan Branberger, who did not find the work all that innovative. He criticized the frequent repetition of motives without development as well as the imitations of speech.[24] He also thought that the orchestra merely accentuated the mood and declamation and lacked symphonic qualities, leading to monotony, lengthiness, and scarcity. Branberger also disliked what he thought were extreme ranges in the vocal lines. Many other Czech musicologists, critics, and musicians did not know how to understand *Jenůfa*. They considered Janáček a regional composer whose music was mainly performed in Brno and who had anti-Smetana attitudes. This lack of understanding did not change even after the piano reduction of the opera was published in Brno in 1908, not by a music publisher but as a membership bonus by the Friends of the Arts Club (Klub přátel umění).[25] Even in Brno, interest in the opera was not particularly strong – between the second production in 1906 and the 1916 Prague premiere, the opera received only eleven performances.

Despite being largely unknown, *Jenůfa* found vocal critics in Zdeněk Nejedlý and his circle. Together with musicologist Vladimír Helfert,

---

[23] "Fejeton. Její pastorkyňa," *Lidové noviny* (January 12, 1904): 3–4.

[24] Jan Branberger, "Nové dráhy pro budoucí opery? II," *Čas* 18, no. 26 (January 26, 1904): 1–2.

[25] Leoš Janáček, *Její pastorkyňa* (Brno: Klub přátel umění, 1908).

Nejedlý conceptualized the development of Czech music as an opposition between progressive and regressive composers. The progressives drew on the works of Bedřich Smetana, whom Nejedlý considered a perfect composer. Smetana's heirs, according to Nejedlý, were Zdeněk Fibich, Foerster, Otakar Ostrčil, Otakar Zich, and Otakar Jeremiáš. The main representative of the regressive group was Dvořák, whom Nejedlý found superficial, eclectic, and uninventive.[26] Nejedlý and his circle also had a negative view of Janáček. Nejedlý first presented his opinions about *Jenůfa* in a public lecture, titled "Problém moravské opery: Leoš Janáček, Její pastorkyňa" ("The Problems of Moravian Opera: Leoš Janáček, Její pastorkyňa"), given in Prague on May 27, 1910. Janáček attended the lecture and later complained to Prague music critic Artuš Rektorys:

I attended a lecture by Dr. Nejedlý today, and I have received similar information from his university lectures. Believe me, I have never been more upset as by what this gentleman ascribes to me! The way he speaks is his choice; but [I can't believe] what he says.

Byl jsem v Praze na Dr. Nejedlého přednášce, mám též informace z jeho přednášek universitních. Věřte, že v životě svém nebyl jsem více roztrpčen jako tím, co mi ten pán přisuzuje! Způsob, jaký si vybral, je jeho věcí; ale co mluví.[27]

Nejedlý expanded his criticism of Janáček in his 1911 book *Česká moderní zpěvohra po Smetanovi* ("Czech Modern Opera after Smetana"), where he compares *Jenůfa* to Foerster's *Eva*. Nejedlý claims the characters in *Jenůfa* have no inner dimension and the work's dramatic interest is based on external means only. He sees the opera's heroine as a mere plaything without an individual will, as opposed to the main protagonist of *Eva*, who is supposedly more active and follows her emotions. Nejedlý also accused Janáček of formalism, which he viewed as regressive, especially in comparison to Smetana. One characteristic that Nejedlý labeled "formalist" was Janáček's emphasis on vocal lines as opposed to the orchestra and his imitation of not only folksongs but also folk speech:

Janáček based his theory of national and folk music on so-called tunelets, which for him are musical motives derived from certain shapes of human speech. This opinion represents one of the most recent outgrowths of the scientific romanticism in the study of folksongs, music, and speech ... Both here and elsewhere, this primitivism threatens precisely that at which the work's author aims: the sense of

---

[26] Vladimír Lébl, ed., *Hudba v českých dějinách: od středověku do nové doby*, 2nd ed. (Prague: Supraphon, 1989), 347–48.

[27] Leoš Janáček's letter to Artuš Rektorys, June 2, 1910, JA MZM, shelfmark B 1507.

naturalness and simplicity leads to a contrived theoretical fabrication. *Jenůfa* in particular is more an experiment than a creative deed.

Janáček svou theorii národní a lidové hudby buduje na tzv. nápěvku, jenž mu jest hudebním motivem určitého tvaru lidové řeči. Jest to názor, jenž jest z posledních výběžků vědeckého romantismu ve studiu lidové písně, hudby i řeči. . . . Jako jinde, tak i zde primitivismus ohrožuje právě to, po čem tvůrce takového díla nejvíce touží: dojem přirozenosti a prostoty vede k nepřirozenosti theoretického výmyslu. *Její pastorkyňa* jest právě spíše experimentem než tvůrčím činem.[28]

Nejedlý published many similar diatribes against Janáček's opera. As a result, and somewhat paradoxically, for twelve years following *Jenůfa*'s first production in Brno, the opera was known only thanks to Nejedlý's critical commentaries. Prague's National Theater was not interested in the work although it did stage many other works by contemporaneous composers.

Despite this criticism, Janáček continued to pursue his innovative compositional techniques. In his fourth opera, *Osud* ("Fate"), he again applied his theory of speech tunelets, this time to a story from an urban environment and partially inspired by Charpentier's *Louise*.[29] One prominent innovative aspect of *Osud* is its autobiographical bent. Janáček's own libretto depicts a composer, Janáček's alter ego Živný, trying to complete an opera about his lover Míla, which was inspired by Janáček's encounter with Kamila Urválková, an unhappily married middle-class woman, in the Moravian spa Luhačovice in the summer of 1903. The idea of injecting autobiographical elements into a fictious work was widespread in literature but less prominent in opera. Janáček's depiction of the process of composing an opera in *Osud* was unique. Janáček's libretto was put into verse by young poet and teacher Fedora Bartošová, and Janáček's musical setting is a gem. Janáček draws on his study of human speech; for example, Janáček's observations of the speech of patients with mental disorders influenced his approach to the character of Míla's mother, who ultimately dies by suicide. In the musical setting, Janáček also uses layering, polymetric passages, monothematicism, and fourth-based melodies and harmonies. He worked on the opera in 1904–5 and originally offered it to Prague's Municipal Theater in Vinohrady, which opened in 1907. But the opera was never produced there or anywhere else during Janáček's lifetime. (The first staged production took place only in 1958.)

---

[28] Zdeněk Nejedlý, *Česká moderní zpěvohra po Smetanovi* (Prague: Otto, 1911): 189–90.
[29] The influence of *Louise* on Janáček's *Osud* is discussed in John Tyrrell, *Janáček: Years of a Life*, vol. 1 (London: Faber and Faber, 2006), 583–89.

Janáček's fortunes changed radically after the celebrated premiere of *Jenůfa* in Prague's National Theater in May 1916. After being an overlooked outsider, he became an admired and internationally respected composer. His international fame was largely initiated by Max Brod, the opera's translator into German, and the publication of the orchestral score by Universal Edition in 1918. As *Jenůfa* became internationally known, Janáček no longer discussed the work's connections to realism – he may have felt that it was no longer necessary to explicitly point out the work's historical uniqueness. Janáček's later works, nevertheless, continue to rely on realism, as is the case with his fifth opera, *Výlety páně Broučkovy* ("The Excursions of Mr. Brouček"), which he started before the success of *Jenůfa*, in 1908 and completed in 1917. Janáček again explored the ways in which music could reflect spoken language, although the opera's subject was radically different from his previous works. The plot features an egocentric landlord in Prague who, partially due to excessive drinking, is swept away first to the moon and then to fifteenth-century Prague during the Hussite revolution. Janáček's next four operas (*Káťa Kabanová*, *Příhody lišky Bystroušky*, *Věc Makropulos*, and *Z mrtvého domu*), composed in quick succession between 1920 and 1928, demonstrate a similar need to find untrodden paths. After his initial search for concepts through which he could frame the compositional and dramaturgical procedures in his operas, Janáček successfully combined musical modernism with deeply humanistic and expressive approaches to intimate personal tragedies.

20 | Avant-garde Aspects of Czech Interwar Music

MILOŠ ZAPLETAL

The term "avant-garde" is often used in connection to those currents in early twentieth-century music that self-consciously and explicitly called for "progress," which usually meant radical departures from aesthetic norms of the "long" nineteenth century and a thorough transformation of social contexts for the arts. The term, however, should be used with care when discussing Czech interwar music because only a few artists explicitly called for, and even fewer pursued, radical departures from local traditions. This was the case with two generations of so-called Czech "modernists," such as Josef Suk, Otakar Ostrčil, and Ladislav Vycpálek, who produced their most mature compositions and dominated Czech musical culture of the period. Leoš Janáček was not only recognized as the leader of the Czech musical avant-garde in the 1920s but also as an official composer of the First Czechoslovak Republic. Similarly, Bohuslav Martinů, a prominent representative of avant-garde currents in European interwar music, noted in 1935: "I have never been an avant-gardist."[1]

It is therefore more appropriate to look for avant-garde tendencies in the works of those composers who used techniques and procedures that went against generally accepted conventions of nineteenth-century music and who collaborated with avant-garde groups that predominantly focused on non-musical artforms, such as theater and literature. Tracing these avant-garde tendencies, this chapter will discuss the search for a modernist musical culture in the newly created Czechoslovakia after 1918 and the underpinnings of this search, before focusing on three specific modernist tendencies: neoclassicism, neofolklorism, and a set of musical trends that I have termed *civilism* and that runs parallel to the German New Objectivity movement.

This chapter was translated from Czech to English by Martin Nedbal.

[1] Cited in Miloš Šafránek, *Bohuslav Martinů: život a dílo* (Prague: Státní hudební vydavatelství, 1961), 117.

The Search for New Czech Music

Although the music produced immediately after 1918 was not radically progressive nor "avant-garde," its social and political contexts have changed fundamentally. Between 1918 and 1938, the former Bohemian crownlands with their multiethnic population (including Czechs, Germans, and Jews) were incorporated into Czechoslovakia, which was dominated by the political and cultural interests of what was referred to as the "Czechoslovak" nation. At the same time, however, the Czechs and Slovaks developed independent national cultures, which they hoped would become dominant within the multiethnic territories of the Czechoslovak Republic. In the confusing period of the 1920s, Czech composers sought to define and articulate their views of modernist styles emanating from France (Stravinsky and *Les Six*) and from Austria and Germany (Krenek and Hindemith). The process of negotiating a Czech response to German modernism led to debates about "physiological music." The term was originally used by German critic Paul Bekker to refer to general explorations of autonomous sounds detached from commonly accepted aesthetic norms, and later Czech critics used it (often disregarding Bekker's initial definition) to criticize specific styles of German and Czech modernist music, including that by Krenek, Hindemith, and Alois Hába.[2] The debate about "physiological music" was as influential and polarizing for the Czech music scene as the conflicted reactions to the Prague premiere of Berg's *Wozzeck* in 1926 (on the "*Wozzeck* Affair," see also Chapter 18). Many Czech critics viewed the work as representing radically leftist ideas, and the opera's production therefore contributed to escalating tensions between the political left and right.[3]

The search for new musical expression was marked by several radical proclamations that called both for revolutionary transformations of artistic approaches and total, or totalitarian, "liberation" of humankind. Many of these proclamations were influenced by French avant-garde movements, including neoclassicism.[4] Partially in tandem with these proclamations, some composers (especially Janáček and Hába) developed

---

[2] Miloš Zapletal, "Fysiologická hudba: z českých bojů o Novou hudbu let dvacátých," *Hudební věda* 56 (2020): 22–51.

[3] See Brian S. Locke, "The '*Wozzeck* Affair': Modernism and the Crisis of Audience in Prague," *Journal of Musicological Research* 27 (2008): 63–93; and Vladimír Lébl, "Případ Vojcek," *Hudební věda* 14 (1977): 195–229.

[4] See, for example, G. Delibré and T. T. Garell [a.k.a. Jiří Svoboda and Karel Teige], "Musica a Muzika," *Život: list pro výtvarnou práci a uměleckou kulturu* 2 (1922): 86–89; an expression of Czech neoclassical thought can be found in Iša Krejčí, "Ponětí modernosti v dnešní hudbě," *Rozpravy Aventina* 3 (1928): 97.

highly individualistic aesthetic viewpoints. One of the most prominent and influential theoreticians of the Czech avant-garde was Emil František Burian, who claimed that new music should be radically different from nineteenth-century idioms, which came to be considered esoteric and psychologizing, in that it would be concise, easily understandable, appealing to modern sensibilities, and physiologically stimulating. Burian rejected both the concept of "a listener's immersion" ("posluchačovo vciťování") in music and the search for "psychological relationships between intervals" ("psychologické vztahy intervalů").[5] At the same time, Burian was opposed to what he termed the "new formalism" of Schoenberg's school. As an antithesis of these German tendencies, Burian pointed to jazz which he viewed as filled with "naturalism and sentiment" ("naturalismus a sentiment").[6]

Czech Responses to Expressionism and Futurism

One particularly influential avant-garde style of the first half of the twentieth century was expressionism, closely associated with the music of the Second Viennese School. Expressionist tendencies have been detected in many other artworks, particularly those seeking to express inner truths believed to be associated with "apocalyptic" states, as well as with shocking, ecstatic, and subconscious experiences. In terms of specific techniques, expressionism was connected to morphological, syntactic, and semantic deformations. Jaroslav Novotný was one of the first Czech composers to enthusiastically accept the work of Schoenberg, starting to explore expressionist idioms before 1918.[7] Expressionist tendencies became more prominent in the interwar period, though Czech composers explored them only occasionally. One reason for the lukewarm reception of expressionism among Czech composers was that its focus on shocking and distorted depictions of subconscious visions and nightmares did not align with the need of the new Czechoslovak music to promote national optimism. Also problematic was expressionism's association with German culture and mentality, which clashed with the Czech interwar culture's orientation toward France. As a result, most Czechoslovak composers who experimented with musical expressionism came from German and Jewish

---

[5] Emil František Burian, "Estetika v pokračováních," *Tam-tam* 1, no. 2 ([n.d.] 1925): 15.
[6] Emil František Burian, *Jazz* (Prague: Aventinum, 1928), 18 and 81–82.
[7] Jaroslav Novotný, "Nová díla Arnolda Schönberga," *Hudební revue* 4 (1911): 325–26.

backgrounds, most prominently Erwin Schulhoff, who was nevertheless also an accomplished practitioner of musical neoclassicism.

Czech interwar composers also largely overlooked atonal techniques, possibly because they viewed them as tainted with expressionist connotations. Some compositions of Pavel Bořkovec involved atonal practices but mostly relied on polytonality and extended tonality. Otakar Ostrčil, too, developed an individualistic approach to the concept of chromatic saturation. Atonality also appears in two piano cycles from the early 1920s: Václav Kaprál's *Miniatury* ("Miniatures") and Karel Boleslav Jirák's *Na rozhraní* ("At the Dividing Line").

Other prominent Czech composers had a more ambiguous attitude to expressionism. Although Janáček categorically rejected atonality,[8] his works have expressionist tendencies, particularly in their focus on extreme psychological states and social criticism. In terms of musical techniques that could be related to expressionism, Janáček often stretches musical parameters to the extremes and uses sharp contrasts. Another musical technique in Janáček's operas and other works that resembles expressionist procedures is the reliance on arioso in the vocal line. These ariosos draw on so-called "speech tunelets" ("nápěvky mluvy" – musical renditions of actual speech that Janáček noted down in real-life situations) and sometimes also short fragments of Moravian folk melodies. The most prominent example of these techniques is the opera *Z mrtvého domu* ("From the House of the Dead"), which Miloš Štědroň has viewed as a parallel to Berg's *Wozzeck*.[9]

Another Czech avant-garde composer who was born in Moravia and gained international recognition was Alois Hába. Although he was in close contact with German and Austrian expressionists, Hába went in a different direction. In response to Schoenberg's, Berg's, and Webern's serial music, Hába developed an individualistic idiom that uses all twelve tones of the chromatic scale but freely and on the principle of tonal centrality and athematicism. Hába referred to this new idiom as "twelve-tone composition" ("dvanáctitónová skladba")[10] and first explored it in his 1932 Fantasy for Nonet No. 1, Op. 40. In compositions from 1921–47, Hába also claimed to have used what he referred to as "athematic style," which in his case means avoiding traditional motivic and thematic procedures and the

---

[8] Miloš Štědroň, *Leoš Janáček a hudba 20. století: paralely, sondy, dokumenty* (Brno: Nadace Universitas Masarykiana, 1998), esp. 104.

[9] Štědroň, *Leoš Janáček a hudba 20. století*, 114.

[10] Alois Hába, "Harmonické základy dvanáctitónového systému: tématický a netématický hudební sloh," *Tempo* 17 (1938): 141.

attendant traditional forms, though he does not avoid musical themes completely. The "athematic style" was prominently influenced by some aspects of east Moravian musical folklore, as well as by various musical styles of the past (such as Gregorian chant) and some non-European (such as Arabic) musical traditions.[11] In 1929, Hába started to refer to athematic and microtonal music as "liberated music" ("Musik der Freiheit").[12] "Liberated music" aimed at the use of sound materials without regard to conventions, which paralleled Bekker's concept of "physiological music." Like Janáček, Hába understood his music in terms of musical realism. Hába claimed that "liberated music" is realistic in that it reflects the practice of musical improvisation and, more broadly, can express the music that musicians clearly hear in their imagination.[13] There are also parallels between Hába's athematic and fantasia-like melodic procedures and Schoenberg's concept of "musical prose" ("musikalische Prose"), that is, "the direct and straightforward presentation of [melodic] ideas, without any patchwork, without mere padding and empty repetitions,"[14] as well as between Hába's "liberated music" and the expressionist dissolution of form.

Neither Hába nor Janáček were pure expressionists due to their strong roots in Moravian folklore, which was quite distant from expressionist modes. Nevertheless, the two composers managed to combine expressionist impulses with neo-folkloric styles and modal organization. As Miloš Schnierer has shown, this synthesis can be observed particularly well in Hába's opera *Matka* ("Mother") and Janáček's *Věc Makropulos* ("The Macropulos Case").[15]

It would be equally futile to look for pure examples of futurism in Czech interwar music. Although futurism resembled expressionism in rejecting nineteenth-century traditions, it focused on external aspects of the objects it sought to depict, as opposed to expressionist interest in the human psyche. This futurist emphasis on the external also appears in some music by Czech interwar authors. E. F. Burian resembled futurists in his interest in radically new sounds, which he explored in his concept

---

[11] Hába discussed "athematic style" in his "Harmonické základy dvanáctitónového systému."

[12] Alois Hába, "Casellas Scarlattiana – Vierteltonmusik und Musikstil der Freiheit," *Anbruch* 11 (1929): 331–34.

[13] Hába cited in Vlasta Reittererová, "Hudební umění jako realizovaná pravdivost," *Hudební věda* 45 (2008): 167.

[14] Arnold Schoenberg, "Brahms the Progressive [1947]," in Arnold Schoenberg, *Style and Idea* (Berkeley: University of California Press, 1975), 415.

[15] Miloš Schnierer, *Český a východoevropský neofolklorismus: v artificiální hudbě 20. století* (Brno: Editio Moravia, 2007), 48–57 and 237.

of the so-called "voiceband," developed beginning in 1927 under the influence of Soviet avant-garde. "Voiceband" refers to a mode of reciting poetic texts in which there are precise specifications about timbre and rhythm; the juxtaposition of the recited text with instrumental accompaniment imbues the text with new meanings and creates emotional tension. For example, Burian organized a "voiceband" performance of the famous Czech romantic poem *Máj* ("May") by Karel Hynek Mácha to commemorate the poem's 1936 centennial. Futuristic tendencies can also be observed in some Czechoslovak composers' experiments with synesthesia, such as Miroslav Ponc's 1920s project called "colorful music" ("barevná hudba"), in which colors were assigned to various sounds on the basis of a complex set of rules. As part of the project, Ponc created visual objects that were supposed to function as a kind of score that could be used either to produce music or allow the observers to imagine it. Ponc also produced more complex artworks for the stage, such as the 1925 chamber opera *Abstraktní erotika* ("Abstract Erotica"), which brought together poems based on free combinations of syllables, quarter-tone music, modern dance, colors, and lighting.

Leftist and Religious Leanings

Most of the Czech musical modernists had a leftist political orientation, which was reflected in their music in various ways, from tempered social criticism to explicit adoration of Stalin's Soviet Union. A prominent example of explicitly political approaches in interwar Czechoslovak music is Schulhoff's 1932 oratorio *Das Manifest*, which sets to music Marx and Engels' *Manifesto of the Communist Party*. The composers planned to present the piece at a massive open-air multimedia event that would resemble a religious ceremony.[16] During the Great Depression, furthermore, Czech composers produced many works that were socially critical, embraced revolutionary themes, and set poetry by communist writers, such as Jiří Wolker, Josef Hora, and Vladimir Mayakovsky. In the 1930s, socially engaged music reacted to the rise of fascism and Nazism, for example Hába's symphonic fantasy *Cesta života* ("A Life's Journey") and Ostrčil's opera *Honzovo království* ("Jack's Kingdom"), both from 1933.

Not all avant-garde composers sympathized with radical political movements. In the 1920s, Janáček still empathized with social outcasts – who

---

[16] Josef Bek, *Erwin Schulhoff: Leben und Werk* (Hamburg: Bockel, 1994), 126ff.

represent the collective protagonist of his last opera *Z mrtvého domu* – although he supported the political right, and his Sinfonietta (1926) was understood as an apotheosis of values and institutions associated with the First Republic.[17]

Some composers used avant-garde techniques to express either their inclinations toward Christian spirituality and Catholic religiosity or their interest in combining Christianity with leftist ideas. During the First Republic, Czech composers both continued the tendency to secularize Church styles and forms initiated by Dvořák and Janáček and produced music that was religiously inclined but not necessarily bound to Catholic traditions. For example, Vycpálek's 1922 *Kantáta o posledních věcech člověka* ("Cantata about the Last Things of Man") explores texts and intonation procedures of Moravian folksongs about death and dying in the form of a fugue.[18] Another cantata by Vycpálek, his 1933 *Blahoslavený ten člověk* ("Blessed Is the Man"), sets psalm texts from the *Bible kralická* ("Bible of Kralice"), the first complete translation of the Bible from the original languages into Czech, to music to celebrate the ethical and religious values of T. G. Masaryk, the first Czechoslovak president. Ostrčil's 1928 orchestral variations *Křížová cesta* ("Stations of the Cross") represents its subject with fourteen variations of a theme that contains all twelve chromatic tones. Although at the end of his life Janáček claimed he was not a believer,[19] he still composed his *Mša glagolskaja* ("The Glagolitic Mass") in 1926, an emphatic and earnest setting of five texts that correspond to the Ordinary of the Mass in Old Church Slavonic translation.

The interest in synthesizing Christian spirituality with the radical humanism of the communist movement achieved a powerful expression in numerous musical settings of Jiří Wolker's poetry. Wolker was an avant-garde poet who became venerated by the Czech middle class of the First Republic after his premature death in 1924. One of the most fascinating settings of Wolker's texts is Vilém Petrželka's 1927 song cycle *Štafeta* ("The Relay") for voice and string quartet that combines three separate poems by Wolker with a text by Jules Romains. Petrželka expressed Wolker's depiction of natural phenomena, moods, and sexual fantasies by combining late Romantic idioms with many modernist techniques, some of which he learned from his teacher Janáček, especially

[17] Miloš Zapletal, "Apoteóza Sokola, armády a nového člověka: rané recepce Janáčkovy Sinfonietty," *Hudební věda* 53 (2016): 257–87.

[18] Jaroslav Smolka, *Ladislav Vycpálek: tvůrčí vývoj* (Prague: Státní nakladatelství krásné literatury, 1960), 127.

[19] Bohumír Štědroň, *Leoš Janáček: k jeho lidskému a uměleckému profilu* (Prague: Panton, 1976), 160.

the older composer's use of so-called "sčasovky" ("rhythmic units"), that is, rhythmic and melodic ostinato patterns, and speech-like melodies;[20] the cycle also makes use of polytonality and extended instrumental techniques.

Another composer who combined leftist viewpoints with Christian sensibilities was Hába. In Hába's view, the Bolshevik Revolution represented the completion of Salvation History, and twentieth-century music, particularly opera, was supposed to reflect that idea and actively contribute to the revolution.[21] A shocking example of Hába's ideological persuasions is his opera *Nová země* ("New Land"), which celebrated the transformation of Ukraine into a "new land" in the 1930s and was banned by the Czechoslovak Ministry of Education and National Edification in 1937.[22] The opera does not overlook the horrors associated with the enforced collectivization and genocide but presents them as labor pains leading to the creation of a paradise on earth. Hába was also influenced by Anthroposophy – an esoteric teaching based on the belief that salvation, that is, the liberation of the soul from the shackles of materiality, can be achieved through one's own efforts. The teaching also influenced Bohemian-Jewish-German composer Viktor Ullmann, whose apocalyptic atonal opera in the form of a symphony *Der Sturz des Antikrist* ("The Fall of the Antichrist"), based on a drama by Albert Steffen, president of the General Anthroposophical Society, depicts an artist who manages to free his soul from the shackles of modern civilization abused by the Antichrist and thus initiates the Antichrist's downfall.

Neoclassicism

In the 1920s and 30s, many European artists rejected Romantic aesthetics, including expressionism, sometimes viewed as the most extreme form of Romanticism, and embraced objectivity and dispassionateness. These tendencies are often associated with the concept of neoclassicism. The term "novo-/neoklasicismus," however, was used in connection with interwar Czech music only retrospectively. Czechoslovak composers who pursued the ideals eventually associated with neoclassicism sought to find a balance

---

[20] See also Martin Čurda, *The Music of Pavel Haas: Analytical and Hermeneutical Studies* (New York: Routledge, 2020), 117–20.

[21] See Alois Hába, "Zvukový film a opera," *Klíč* 2 (1931/32): 60.

[22] Vlasta Reittererová and Lubomír Spurný, *Alois Hába (1893–1973): mezi tradicí a inovací* (Prague: KLP, 2014), 161–72.

between radical anti-Romanticism and the need to produce music that would be comprehensible to broad audiences. Neoclassical art found inspiration in French models, which resonated with the international orientation of the First Republic. Musical idioms, techniques, forms, genres, and instruments (such as the cembalo, used by Martinů and Burian) of pre-Romantic music were updated, presented in new settings and contexts, and combined with modernist techniques and procedures. Idioms connected to neoclassical views started to appear in Czech music in the early 1920s, such as in Karel Boleslav Jirák's 1920 piano piece *Suita ve starém slohu* ("Suite in Old Style"). In later years, Czech composers synthesized neoclassical approaches with other modernist styles, such as avant-garde approaches to folk idioms, often referred to as neofolklorism. One of the most famous examples of the synthesis of neoclassicism with neofolklorism is Martinů's 1932 ballet with songs *Špalíček* ("The Chapbook"). The work is a collection of folk sayings, ritual games, and narrations and combines action with narration. The music of *Špalíček* synthesizes melodic and rhythmic folk idioms from Bohemia and Moravia with references to classical styles from the Renaissance to the nineteenth century (including Renaissance harmonic procedures, Baroque sequences and *concertato* styles, eighteenth-century forms, and the polka). At the same time, *Špalíček* makes use of modernist diatonic polytonality. The work is also exemplary of the 1930s musical trends in that it turns to traditional values of Czech culture, possibly in reaction to the increasing tensions and insecurity ushered in by the Great Depression.

Neoclassical sensibilities avoided the anxieties and extreme subjectivity of prewar culture and exuded happiness and health by balancing form and expression, using clear forms and diatonicism, and replacing programmatic and psychological themes with playfulness. This meant that neoclassicism was particularly well suited to abstract instrumental genres, such as the string quartet (for example, Martinů's String Quartets Nos. 2–5). The "classical" in neoclassicism had to do with its reliance on seventeenth- and eighteenth-century music. Some of these tendencies can be understood as neo-Baroque and include the use of the *concertato* principle and ritornello form, such as in Martinů's Concerto grosso (1937), and Vycpálek's 1929–30 suites for solo violin and viola. Neoclassicism's "classical" qualities are also associated with the choice of Greco-Roman themes in some compositions. This is the case with Iša Krejčí's 1933 opera *Antigona*, based on Sophocles, and Martinů's first opera *Voják a tanečnice* ("The Soldier and the Dancer") from 1927, based on a comedy by Plautus. Some compositions that use neoclassical procedures do engage with intense emotional expression that can be connected to autobiographical and historical events, similar to Romantic music. This is the case of Martinů's Double Concerto and String Quartet No. 5 from 1938, both of which express the composer's anxiety in view of Nazi Germany's aggressive expansion. Whereas Martinů's interwar output embraced a multiplicity of styles although it had strong neoclassical leanings, the music of Iša Krejčí can be considered exclusively neoclassical, starting with his 1925 *Divertimento (Kasace)*.

Neofolklorism

Neofolklorism represents another important, and similarly broad, tendency in interwar Czech music that, like neoclassicism, continued to thrive in the second half of the twentieth century, particularly in Central and Eastern Europe. The prefix "neo" reflects the difference between nineteenth-century and interwar approaches to folk music. Nineteenth-century folkloristic composers focused on adapting folksongs in Lieder-like settings for consumption by urban middle classes and incorporating folk-like elements into orchestral, chamber, and operatic works. By the early twentieth century, some composers aimed at being authentic, which was often connected to their ethnomusicological activities. The interwar period also introduces the synthesis of folkloric idioms with modernist techniques.

Janáček's works operate with different aspects of neofolklorism. The basic concept of Janáček's style is an inventive and individualistic use of folk elements, which often undermines both nineteenth-century conventions and the original characteristics of folk music styles. Janáček transformed stylized speech patterns, melodic models, and rhythmic patterns of folk dances into instrumental motives and ostinato-like rhythmic-melodic patterns (which he called "sčasovky" – see above). Folk music also affected Janáček's instrumentation, which often avoided middle registers and used unusual instrumental colors. Instead of conventional forms, Janáček's mature works rely on vertical and horizontal bundling of heterogeneous material, marked by frequent repetitions and occasional sharp cuts. Like Bartók, Janáček used modal procedures and "flexible diatonicism" (that is, diatonicism in which some diatonic tones are "flexible" and can be represented by two different pitches, half a step apart) to construct his melodic and harmonic material, which allowed him to create a compositional alternative to serialism.

Hába, too, explored various neofolklorist approaches. Growing up in the family of a folk musician and possessing absolute pitch, Hába transformed inspirations from east Moravian microtonal folk heterophony into his own microtonal music, most notably in his quarter-tone works. Hába did not discover quarter tones and was not the first Western composer to use them in musical works, but he was a pioneer in searching for ways to use microtones systematically in vertical and horizontal structures of vocal and instrumental music. With his first attempts at using a "bichromatic" tonal system, in which the octave is divided into twenty-four equal intervals, and which can be found as early as in his 1920 String Quartet No. 2, Hába aligned himself with the German avant-garde. His later works explore more differentiated approaches to microtones. Besides quarter tones, he used quintuple and sextuple tones, and used them to enrich major, minor, and modal diatonic systems. These experiments peaked in Hába's works for quarter-tone piano, his string quartets from 1922–27, and his 1928 opera *Matka*, all premiered in Munich in 1931. The opera is composed with quarter tones and combines traditional instruments with quarter-tone instruments that were constructed at Hába's instigation.

Many other composers pursued neofolklorist goals in the interwar period. Among them were the composers of the so-called "Janáček school," such as Pavel Haas, Václav Kaprál, Vilém Petrželka, and Jaroslav Kvapil.[23] One internationally known example of these composers' approaches to neofolklorism is Kaprál's 1933 *Uspávanky* ("Lullabies"), an orchestral song cycle based on Slovak folk poetry, which was performed at the 1936 ISCM festival in Barcelona to great acclaim.

Civilism

Another type of modernist approach in interwar Czech music involved the selection of contemporaneous subjects for compositions. Similar tendencies were prominent in the visual arts and literature, and Czech art and literary historians often refer to them by the term *civilism*, which, as I have suggested elsewhere, can be applied to Czech interwar music that tries to represent elements associated with modern (particularly urban) lifestyles, both real and imagined.[24] Composers made use of a variety of musical styles to represent modernity, and the resulting compositions were often radically different from nineteenth-century music.

[23] Miloš Zapletal, "'Always Seeking Truth both in Life and Art.' The Janáček School of Composition," *Czech Music Quarterly* 2014: 28–34; 35–41.

[24] Miloš Zapletal, "Civilist Tendencies in the Inter-war Czech Music: At the Beginning of a Research," *Musicologica Brunensia* 54 (2019): 237–51.

One of the most prominent aspects of *civilism* was connected to representations and celebrations of everyday modernity, exemplified in three works by Jan Evangelista Zelinka: his 1927 ballet-pantomime *Skleněná panna* ("The Glass Doll"), which depicts a metropolitan street and a bar, two typical phenomena of modern (urban) lifestyle; 1933 wind sextet *Vzduch zdarma* ("Free Air"), based on a novel by Sinclair Lewis and depicting everyday life in America in the 1920s; and 1939 orchestral suite *Weekend*, focusing on the phenomenon of the two-day period away from work, which was introduced in the interwar period and became widespread. The same subject also appears in Emil Hlobil's orchestral suite *Weekend* from 1933.

Civilism also aims at representing and addressing "new men" – individuals unburdened by traditional religious views, individualism, idealism, and approaches to everyday life. *Civilist* artworks were supposed to combine high aesthetic value, contemporaneous perspectives, and accessibility to broad segments of society (this aim makes *civilist* music akin to so-called *Gebrauchsmusik* in Germany). *Civilism* also reflected a new kind of unsentimental heroism that celebrated collectives as opposed to individuals. Martinů's 1927 "mechanical ballet" *Le Raid merveilleux* is a good example of these aesthetic goals. The work, a modern tragedy of sorts, depicts an unsuccessful flight over the Atlantic Ocean with an un-romantic approach that relies on motoric pulsations, syncopations, and polyrhythms both to express the drama and illustrate the movements of the propeller and the air engine. One of the ballet's innovations was that it replaced live dancers with moving props, light and shadow play, and the use of photography and intertitles, similar to silent films. Czech musical *civilism* also references sport, as is the case with two 1929 compositions by Bořkovec: the symphonic Allegro *Start* and the song cycle *Stadion* ("The Stadium").[25] The works employ musical techniques that were typical for most contemporaneous compositions inspired by sporting activities: mechanical and repetitive musical processes, based on rhythmic and melodic ostinatos, pulsations, agitated tempos (reflecting accelerated heart beat and breath that accompany physical activities), enhanced linearity of musical structures, which at times borders on atonality, and, in *Stadion*, instrumental treatment of vocal lines.

An important aspect of what I understand as Czech interwar *civilism* in music is the interest in jazz. References to jazz were often connected to representations of modern civilization and urbanity – this, for example, is

---

[25] Miloš Zapletal, "Playful but Animalistically Serious: Czech Interwar Music and Sport," *Czech Music Quarterly* (2018): 15–25.

the case of Otakar Zítek's 1925 symphonic poem *Město* ("The City"). In the 1920s, the term "jazz" referred to multiple types and styles of popular music, including ragtime and tango, the instrumentation associated with these styles, and to the styles' social connotations, particularly their anti-romantic, modern, and provocative symbolism. The connection between jazz references and avant-garde poetics is exemplified in Schulhoff's 1919 piano cycle *Fünf Pittoresken*, consisting of four stylized jazz dances and a movement titled "In futurum," which is exclusively based on pauses and agogic markings.

Czech interwar compositions with jazz elements oscillate between two main tendencies. On the one hand, there are compositions that view jazz as an abstract musical idiom, which can be used as a "neutral" element in a search for innovative sounds. On the other hand, jazz can be viewed as an extramusical element and a reference to modern civilization, which imbues the use of jazz in musical works with programmatic tendencies, similar to musical depictions of sport and modern industrial technologies. This second tendency is not dissimilar from how the composers associated with *Les Six* understood jazz.[26] Many compositions from the interwar period work with both tendencies, and many Czech interwar composers try to make use of jazz references. One exception is Janáček, who hated jazz.

Conclusion

Civilism, neofolklorism, and neoclassicism represent the dominant tendencies in Czech interwar avant-garde music. Although based on radically different sets of techniques and viewpoints, the three tendencies are also marked by internal similarities that are not immediately obvious. All three approaches to modern composition aim at abandoning romantic sensibilities and rejecting what Stefan Zweig termed "the world of yesterday" ("die Welt von Gestern"), the social and cultural order that dominated European civilization during the so-called *belle époque* prior to World War I and that came to be viewed as hypocritical and internally rotten after the cataclysms of the war. All three tendencies aimed at avoiding romanticism through different means: neoclassicism by a recourse to pre-Romantic music; neofolklorism in an exploration of musical traditions of the common people from different ethnic groups; and *civilism* in a reliance on jazz.

---

[26] On this understanding, see Jean Cocteau, *Cock and Harlequin: Notes concerning Music* (London: Egoist Press, 1921), 23.

21 | An Evolving Dance with a Tragic Ending and a Tentative Revival: The Jewish Musical Experience in the Czech Lands

MICHAEL BECKERMAN

Introduction

Observing the history of Jews and music in the Czech lands is a bit like watching the Czech movie *Všichni moji blízcí* ("All My Loved Ones"), which takes place mostly in 1939 just before the Nazi invasion. We see the Jewish characters proceeding with their worthy lives, but we, the audience, know there can be no happy ending. So, while there may be some joy in the fact that one of the characters remains alive after the war, and surely there is joy in aspects of contemporary Jewish life in the Czech Republic, the subject itself can never escape a veil of tragedy. That this distorts both the past and the present is certain, and while it is regrettable, it is not clear that we can do much about that. Another legacy of the Nazis is forcing us to write bad history, because the losses here are simply too great.

Ideally, this chapter would try to corral music both heard and unheard over many centuries; famous composers and performers; anonymous cantors in small Moravian shuls and celebrity cantors in Prague; it would shed light on the development of local liturgies over centuries, and encompass snippets of songs heard by camp survivors. It would also engage the many films about the Jewish experience in Czechoslovakia, the tragic Jewish inflections of the film *Musíme si pomáhat* ("Divided We Fall") and the awful ballad, "Don't buy sugar, coffee, flour from the Jews, they killed our blue-eyed girl, Anežka" heard in the film *Zločin v Polné* ("Murder in Polná"); and of course, the inquiry would have to embrace thousands of songs echoing and resounding across many borders. Thus, many things must be left out, actually almost everything.

Some Thoughts on Nomenclature and History

Like many other languages, Czech does not happen to have a specific word for someone who is a citizen of the country but is not of its leading ethnic group (see also Chapter 16). Thus, the word "Czech," when applied to a person, tends to mean "ethnic Czech," unlike, say, the word "American," which does not specify ethnicity. Lacking such a word for its "other" citizens, it turns them all, even those earnestly wishing to buy into the Czech enterprise, into hyphenated Czechs, whether they happen to be Vietnamese, Romani, or Jewish. That Pavel Haas was born into a "Moravian Jewish family," while neither Smetana, Dvořák, nor Janáček have their religion routinely mentioned in biographical summaries, showcases the obvious reality that Christianity was so normative in the Czech lands, it did not even have to be mentioned. But even the expression, "born into a Jewish family" doesn't necessarily mean anything, especially if we do not know whether the family was secular or religious, whether they might have spoken German or Czech, or even Yiddish, and whether, in the end, being Jewish meant anything to them at all.

Škroup's *L'cha Dodi* and his Little Jewish Kids

If you go into the Maisel Synagogue in Prague, you may see an astonishing video. It is a kind of "flying" trip through the old Jewish district, Josefov, courtesy of the fantastically detailed Langweil model of Prague constructed between 1826 and 1837 and containing virtually every structure from that time. This is especially valuable because much of the Jewish district was leveled at the end of the nineteenth century as part of urban renewal, and several old synagogues were destroyed along with more than 250 other buildings. One of the synagogues you can see in the model was on Dušní Street, today the site of the famous Spanish Synagogue, and it was in that place that František Škroup served as organist between 1836 and 1845 (as we shall see, there is evidence of organs in Prague synagogues as early as the fifteenth century). Though not a Jew, rather a Catholic, he wrote some lovely choral music for the liturgy that has survived. His *L'cha dodi* ("Come, My Beloved") would have fit nicely in the Masonic sections of Mozart's *Die Zauberflöte*, with its stately waltz-like rhythm and close harmony, with even a chromatic darkening on the text, "Liqrat Shabbat" ("To meet the Sabbath"). Veronika Seidlová makes the point, in her important article about Škroup, about the way this "Enlightenment" movement actively sought to purge Jewish music of its "orientalisms," to create a modern version of the liturgy.[1]

---

[1] Veronika Seidlová, "K působení Františka Škroupa v synagoze v Dušní ulici aneb Vyjednávání pražských Židů s modernitou a jinakostí," in *Víra, kultura a společnost: náboženské kultury v českých*

Example 21.1: František Škroup, *Fidlovačka*, "Sbor žíďátek" ("Chorus of Little Jews"), mm. 35–40.

Of course, Škroup's fame did not derive from his work in the synagogue, but rather as the composer of one of the first Czech operas, *Dráteník* ("The Tinker") in 1826, and the even more important incidental music to Josef Kajetan Tyl's *Fidlovačka*, which contains the famous song *Kde domov můj* ("Where Is My Home" – see also Chapter 10). Beginning its life as a kind of "show tune," it quickly became a patriotic song, then the first half of the Czechoslovak national anthem, and is now the anthem of the Czech Republic. But it is neither this song from act 4 of *Fidlovačka* nor the *L'cha Dodi* which interests us most at this point. Nothing could illustrate the complex relationship between Czechs and Jews better than the juxta-position of *Kde domov můj* with the beginning of act 3 of the same work, a caricature "Sbor žíďátek" ("Chorus of Little Jews" – Example 21.1). With its A minor tonality, featuring the fall of a diminished seventh, cries of "wai, wai" ("oy, oy") and then mincing repeated notes on the text, "pomalinku kroky, nedělejte skoky" ("take small steps, don't jump"), the chorus of little Jews is the quintessence of musical difference.

Kde domov můj, on the other hand, is a classic nationalist fable, begin-ning as a pastoral extolling the landscape, and moving to its rousing conclusion on the words, "země česká, domov můj" ("Czech land, my homeland"). But the real climax comes not on the words "land," "Czech," or "homeland," as one might expect, but on the word "můj," *my*, suggesting

zemích 19. a 20. Století, ed. Miloš Havelka (Červený Kostelec: Pavel Mervart, 2012), 439–70. I am extremely grateful to Dr. Seidlová for her assistance in this project, for sending me recordings of Škroup's synagogue music, and of course for her deeply thoughtful work on the subject.

that the most important thing is possessing the land as one's own. The little Jews then, whatever else they might do, raise the question of whether they can ever also be "little Czechs," or whether they must forever exist in a "special category."

In his recent article on *Fidlovačka*, Milan Pospíšil discusses the updating or excising of such scenes in post-war productions due to the fact that, after the Nazi persecution and extermination, everything about the Jews "appeared in unsuspected contexts" ("vystupovalo v netušených souvislostech").[2] Of course, the idea that you needed Hitler to suggest that the "Jewish portraits" in *Fidlovačka* could be offensive is part of the problem. First, it should have been noted far earlier, and second, as late as 1952, with the publication of the piano vocal score the problematic chorus is left intact.[3] Josef Plavec, author of a Škroup biography, blithely claims in his notes to the score that although Tyl did not omit the figure of the Jew Šiveles with a bunch of Jews ("s kupou žíďat"), he in no way mocks or despises them but presents them as lifelike as other figures; Šiveles, according to Plavec, is simply a creditor of the indebted "Baron" Dudek.[4] While we cannot impose our contemporary views of the Holocaust on the past, one would think, only eight years after Auschwitz, there would be greater understanding around the dangers of Jewish caricature.

Some Music by Non-Jewish Jews

If you do a search for "most popular Czech children's songs" you are sure to come across *Já mám koně* ("I Have a Horse") a kind of proto-polka. It was on this charming tune that Isaac (Ignaz) Moscheles, a German-speaking Bohemian Jew, composed a charming series of variations for piano, violin, cello and clarinet, Op. 46. While it is true that Moscheles eventually converted to Christianity, we could argue that his relationship to the Czech lands means that this work ought to be considered a piece of Czech or Bohemian Jewish music, although many might be more tempted, considering the tune and Moscheles' birthplace and childhood in Prague, to include it as part of a putative field of "Czech music," or Czech music by a German-speaker. Of course, we would then have to ask if the fact that Moscheles settled in Vienna ultimately made him less

[2] Milan Pospíšil, "Fidlovačka," in *Fidlowačka nebo cokoli chcete*, ed. Jitka Ludvová (Prague: Divadelní ústav, 2014), 57–110 (105).

[3] *Fidlovačka aneb Žádný hněv a žádná rvačka* (Prague: Národní hudební vydavatelství, 1952).

[4] *Fidlovačka aneb Žádný hněv a žádná rvačka*, iii.

a participant in Czech music history, or comparatively, his conversion to Christianity made him less of a Jew.

The same is true, more or less, for Gustav Mahler, who, if he was to be considered a "Czech Jew," would be the most important Czech Jewish composer of all. Of course, this is somewhat sticky territory. After all, if we treat converts *to* Judaism as fully and completely Jewish, shouldn't we respect the choices made by Mahler and Moscheles, who both chose to become Roman Catholic, and stop considering them as Jews at all? On the other hand, if being a Jew is considered by a large enough part of the surrounding population to be something like an ineradicable mark of Cain, one must struggle with the question of how much self-ascription ultimately matters in our historical reckoning.

We may also recall a "Jewish" composer who ended his days in a concentration camp, not because he was Jewish, but because he was a communist. I am speaking here of Erwin Schulhoff, a brilliant composer and pianist whose stylistic legacy involves everything from jazz and avant-garde Dada (including such works as his sonatas *Erotica* and *Germanica* and his *Bass Nightingale* for contrabassoon) to socialist realist symphonies (his final symphony, unfinished, has the chorus declaiming "Marx! Lenin! Stalin!" – see Chapter 20). His relationship to things "Czech" is one of a certain ambivalence, as can be heard in his semi-caricature, the "Alla Czeca" movement from his Five Pieces for String Quartet, WV68. But there is also a curious composition titled *The Czech Worker* written in 1936, combining the socialist realist aesthetic, with jazzy references over a jagged ostinato, gradually increasing in intensity to a powerful climax.

It is often forgotten that there were a substantial number of Christians in Terezín (Theresienstadt), and in addition to this, many people who might not have been the least bit religious and did not consider themselves Jews. Among these was certainly Viktor Ullmann, among the most productive personalities in Terezín, as an organizer, critic, composer, and poet. Described on the Ullmann website as an "Austrian composer of Jewish descent," he was baptized Catholic, and then abandoned that religion for Anthroposophy and the ideas of Rudolf Steiner (see Chapter 20).[5] One could argue, with some bitterness, that through Nazi race ideology and geography he ended his life as a Czech Jew. From this vantage point, then, his music cannot be separated from the

---

[5] For a brief biography, see Jacqueline Cole, "Viktor Ullmann," The Viktor Ullmann Foundation, https://viktorullmannfoundation.com/viktor/, accessed March 21, 2024.

Czech Jewish experience, particularly in the blindingly original "signature" moment of the final movement of his final piano sonata where he combines into a quodlibet the name of Bach (B-A-C-H), a German chorale, the Czech Hussite song, *Ktož jsú boží bojovníci* ("You Who Are the Warriors of God"), and a Hebrew song. Rather than any one of these dominating, they orbit each other like identities in constant motion.

Three Examples of Jewish Music Vanished, Unheard, or Fragmented

One of the "problems" with documents is that they may blind us to those things for which we have no documents. In musical terms this means thinking about missing sounds; things we know must have taken place, but for which we have no scores or recordings.

A classic example of this is the miniature *Music of Jews in the House of God* found in the Lobkowitz Breviary from 1494 (Figure 21.1). From the viewpoint of later orthodoxies, the presence of instruments is startling: we have a portative organ (a more permanent instrument was not installed in Prague synagogues for another century), with someone standing behind to pump; in the foreground a kind of double drum; and then a wind instrument, possibly something like a shawm. While it is impossible to tell whether the participants are meant to be singing, there seem to be two figures in front of the torah ark clapping. While this illustration could simply be a fantasy, it does line up with later sources which document the presence of instruments in Prague synagogues, though never during services. The image captures a moment crying out to be heard, even as, once again, it possibly presents Jewish music as cacophonous noise in the sense discussed by Ruth HaCohen in her monograph, *The Music Libel Against the Jews*.[6]

One of the most searing texts written in Terezín is Petr Kien's five-part poem titled *The Plague*.[7] Kien, a German-speaking Czech Jew, was one of the exceptional personalities in the ghetto, making profound contributions as a poet, librettist, and a graphic artist. Among the *less* grotesque passages in the poem is the following:

---

[6] Ruth HaCohen, *The Music Libel Against the Jews* (New Haven: Yale University Press, 2013).

[7] The poem, and information about the poet can be found in an extraordinary volume *Franz Peter Kien* produced by the Terezín Music Foundation. Elena Makarova and Ira Rabin, eds., *Franz Peter Kien* (Prague: Oswald, 2009), 197.

Figure 21.1: *Music of Jews in the House of God.* Miniature from the breviary of Count Lobkowitz, Prague, 1494. Prague, Národní knihovna České republiky, shelfmark XXIII F 202, fol. 110v. Reproduced by permission.

Durch die Strassen rollt der Leichenkarren, von vermummten Knechten stumm begleitet, über morsche Knochen hingebreitet.	Through the streets rolls the plague cart, accompanied by masked and silent drones, boiling over weakened bones.

Filled with horror, fear, and visceral images of Terezín, this poem served as the basis for Gideon Klein's song cycle of the same name, set for alto and piano. We know this composition existed because there is a poster announcing it in the second concert of the Studio für neue Musik dedicated to the "Young Authors in Theresienstadt," but it has never surfaced and is presumed lost.

How might Klein have set the poem's last lines:

Das Schlachthaus Pest dampft von verwesten Leibern, dort zwischen Knaben, Greisen, schamlos aufgedeckten Weibern, dort arbeitet der letzte Arzt.	The slaughterhouse, plague, steams from bodies, decomposed. There – between youth, the aged, and women shamelessly exposed – practices the last physician.

Would he have used the atonal language of his piano sonata, the aching dissonance of his German madrigals, or some variant of Janáček's Moravianisms? Imagining such things is also part of gathering together the shards of Czech Jewish music experience.

Some works exist, but only in the tiniest fragments. Viktor Ullmann's comments on Pavel Haas's lost *Partita in the Old Style* appear in the eighth of the numerous concert reviews he wrote in Terezín. He begins his discussion by saying that Haas "introduces new sounds into the tonal system – one could describe it as tonal twelve-tone music. The *Partita in the Old Style* preserves the forms, or at least the original archetype phenomena of suite movements. In this aspect as well, Haas's music is certainly praiseworthy – it is playfully powerful, effortlessly polyphonic, transparent in the piano part, interesting and graceful."[8]

And if that was all there was, one could just leave it with all the other unheard music, but there is this, two fugal entries from the last movement of the piece (Figure 21.2).[9]

---

[8] Mark Ludwig, *Our Will to Live: The Terezín Music Critiques of Viktor Ullmann* (Göttingen: Steidl, 2021), 127. This volume, published by the Terezín Music Foundation and Steidl Publishers in 2021, is one of the most important recent books dealing with music in the Ghetto. With hundreds of illustrations and translations of all of Viktor Ullmann's concert reviews, it makes available to the English reader a wealth of material.

[9] Composers frequently give incipits of works or fragments to friends as souvenirs and memorials. Of course, in most cases, the complete works survive, but in this case, only the fragmentary

Figure 21.2: Pavel Haas, *Partita in the Old Style*, fourth movement, autograph. Památník Terezín. Reproduced by permission.

Terezín

We have noted that, told as a narrative, the story of Jews in the Czech lands is infused with tragedy. Nothing captures the Shakespearean nature of this, with its elements of normalcy and farce coupled with the darkest possible deeds, more forcefully than the Terezín Ghetto.

A discussion of music and musical life in Terezín is significant for several reasons. It could be reasonably argued that, strange as it might

dedication. The facsimile is reproduced as image 35 in Lubomír Peduzzi, *Pavel Haas* (Brno, Muzejní a vlastivědná společnost, 1993).

seem, Terezín was actually one of the most dynamic cultural centers anywhere in Europe during World War II. But beyond that, Terezín is a place where one is forced to ask and try to answer knotty questions about ethnicity, culture, and such things as the limits of musical expression.

Some of the difficulties in teasing out the nature of the place can be found in Anna Hájková's recent monograph on everyday life in the ghetto. This passage alone spells out a kind of unreal world:

> In Terezín, Eastern Jews were construed as the ultimate other. Eastern Jews consti-
> tuted the "real" Jews, the marked part of the binary: assimilated Jew (unmarked,
> normal) versus Eastern Jew (marked, negative). Antisemitic prejudice fed the nega-
> tive image. By using the Eastern Jews as a counter-group, the Central or Western
> European Jews could appear non-Jewish, or Jewish in a good, unmarked way.[10]

To amplify, religious Jews in Terezín were something like "Jews" in Czechoslovak society. In other words, Czech culture divided the world into Czechs (us), Germans (them), and Jews (really, really "them" – who of course were sometimes included among the Germans). In Terezín, composed mostly of Jews, *Czech* Jews were the "normal" or "unmarked" ones, German Jews were Germans (marked somewhat problematically), and then orthodox, "Eastern" Jews were marked as real Jews, "Jews."

When we try to make sense of the cultural life of this place, we encounter three primary narratives. First, the dominant narrative, that in keeping up a semblance of public cultural life, with concerts and reviews in a God-awful place like Terezín, the artists and composers, pianists and set design-ers were brave and noble, showing the world that as long as human beings had breath they would be concerned with the higher things in life. The most oft-quoted and powerful testimonial to this are these words at the end of Viktor Ullmann's essay "Goethe and Ghetto":

> I would only like to emphasize that my musical work was fostered and not
> inhibited by Theresienstadt, and that we in no way merely sat around lamenting
> by the banks of Babylon's rivers, and that our desire for culture was equal to our
> will to live.[11]

The second, somewhat opposing view would be to turn those very words on their head, arguing that Terezín, like many other such places during the war, was what Primo Levi called a "Gray Zone," a place in which nothing was normal, no one knew which end was up, and where ethics and

---

[10] Anna Hájková, *The Last Ghetto* (New York: Oxford University Press, 2020), 91.
[11] Translation in Ludwig, *Our Will to Live*, 289.

aesthetics were horribly skewed.[12] Performers in a concert one evening might be on a train to Auschwitz the following morning. Thus, behaving in a "normal way" under such circumstances might be considered absurd. The most powerful articulation of this comes from the former prisoner H. G. Adler, author of the massive *Theresienstadt 1941–1945: The Face of a Coerced Community*:

The cultural activities that initially had fulfilled a real need, with diligence and devotion, lost all sense of proportion and reflection. The behavior of a large number of prisoners, particularly the more influential groups, created the conditions that fueled this curse's corrupting influence. Many young, still immature musicians and theater people lost all restraint, putting on airs and nearly forgetting about the camp and the SS. A gifted conductor thoughtlessly led the life of a star, a darling of the muses, celebrated by his audiences.[13]

As an antidote to this harsh judgment, we may offer something more sanguine, a third view. In this approach, more equivocal than either of the preceding two, it is understood that we are simply not in any position to judge the choices individuals made in such places, that at the very least, those involved were simply doing their very best in unprecedented circumstances and deserve the benefit of the doubt.

However, no matter how one construes it, some remarkable compositions were created, and from Ullmann's careful reviews, we can assume that certain performances were memorable. What follows are just two "Terezín case studies."

Haas's *Al S'fod*

Pavel Haas was born in Brno in 1899 into a literate and artistic Czech-speaking family. His brother, Hugo, became a successful actor, and even managed to resurrect his career in Hollywood after he emigrated in the 1930s. Pavel's works, such as the string quartet "From the Monkey Mountains," incorporated elements of jazz, Moravian music, and a range of avant-garde approaches. His opera, *Šarlatán* ("The Charlatan"), had

---

[12]   Levi explores the term in his chapter of the same name in *The Drowned and the Saved* (New York: Vintage Books, 1989), 36–69. I have explored this theme in my "Listening in the Gray Zone," in *The Routledge Handbook to Music under German Occupation, 1938–1945: Propaganda, Myth, and Reality*, ed. David Fanning and Erik Levi (New York: Routledge, 2019), 451–58.

[13]   H. G. Adler, *Theresienstadt 1941–1945: The Face of a Coerced Community*, trans. Belinda Cooper (New York: Cambridge University Press, 2017), 525.

a successful premiere in Brno in 1938, but political events (the Munich Agreement, the invasion of Czechoslovakia) shut it down.

His first Terezín work, *Al S'fod* ("Do Not Lament") is marked November 30, 1942, a year after Haas's arrival. It is a male choir setting of a Labor-Zionist poem by David Shimoni, exhorting the reader/listener not to hang their head, to work, to plow and sow, to pave the path to light and liberty, and when "the blood cries out to the soul of the people," it is labor that is the source of redemption.

It is noteworthy for its title page alone (Figure 21.3). Things that look like musical notes are Hebrew letters spelling out the message: "Mazkeret leyom hashana harishon vehu acharon begalut Terezín" ("Memento of the first, and may it be the last anniversary in the Terezín Exile") to which someone has added with a lighter stroke the Hebrew word *Sof* (using a treble clef for the final "f") meaning "the end."[14] The text-setting itself undercuts its strongest lines with markings like *dolce*, revealing a level of ambivalence that only is amplified in the composer's masterpiece, the *Four Songs on Chinese Poetry*, passionate laments for home and loved ones.

Klein's Last Line

The final major composition written in Terezín was Gideon Klein's string trio, completed, according to dating on the manuscript, only nine days before the composer's transport to Auschwitz on October 16, 1944. Klein was a wunderkind, gifted as a composer, scholar, pianist, and organizer. His final piece raises questions that fall both within the sphere of a putative "Czech Jewish" music, and outside it as well. A composition written by a Jew who is about to be transported to a death camp for being a Jew cannot be considered somehow outside of the Jewish experience. But the external signs of the composition are firmly Moravian. The core of the work is the second movement, a series of variations on the beautiful folksong, *Ta kněždubská věž* ("The Kněždub Tower"). But the surface is not everything in this trio; there are hidden things. The song text itself has a young man shooting a wild goose, the symbol of freedom. There is an allusion to Mahler's *Kindertotenlieder*, a quote from Schubert's *Gretchen am Spinnrade*, a dark shadow of Josef Suk's angel of death from the *Asrael* Symphony, and most bitingly, a mysterious

---

[14] A photocopy of the score is in Židovské muzeum v Praze, shelfmark i nv. no. 319a.

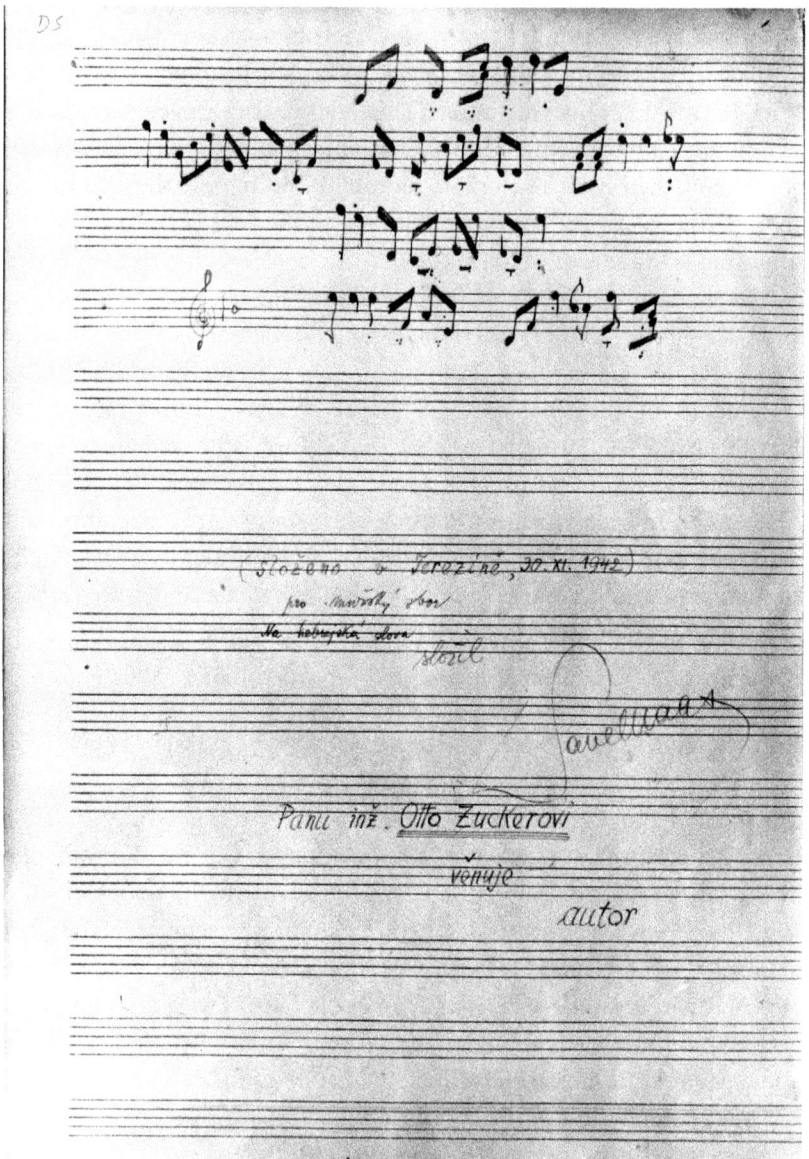

Figure 21.3: Pavel Haas, *Al S'fod*, title page, autograph, copy. Prague, Židovské muzeum. Reproduced by permission.

interruption by the muted cello descending two octaves to the depths before rising for a final funereal chromatic descent.[15]

---

[15] I have dealt with this composition more fully in Michael Beckerman, "Gideon Klein at 100, His Cello Scream at 75," in *Torso eines Lebens. Der Komponist und Pianist Gideon Klein (1919–1945). Symposium 13./14. Dezember 2019*, ed. Albrecht Dümling (Neumünster: Bockel, 2020), 195–210.

In parsing this work, we encounter a classic problem: if Klein is combining these materials to create an important work in the Western tradition of abstraction, who are we to burden it with such dark backstories? But if Klein is using instrumental music, most specifically the cello solo, to tell us a searing tale of his experience, who are we to look away?

Abnormalization

Jewish communities and Jews as individuals suffered the cruel double indemnity of World War II and three years later the ascendence of communism. The vastly reduced Jewish population was in no way encouraged by the state, and at various times there were "anti-Zionist" persecutions. While the Jewish Museum in Prague, and its famous synagogues and cemetery, remained tourist attractions, they were not attached to any thriving community. By the time I arrived in Brno for a year in the late 1970s, the only "Jewish music" I heard was in synagogues in Brno and Prague. Although colleagues took me to see Jewish architectural remnants in Holešov, Mikulov, Břeclav, and Velké Meziříčí there was no music in these places. There may have been klezmer concerts somewhere, or memorials to Terezín composers in Czechoslovakia during that year, but I never heard about them, nor did I see them advertised. In fact, during the entire year of my stay, not a single musician identified themselves to me as Jewish, with the exception of the Russian musicologist and composer Vladimir Blok who came up to me and said, "I am Jew. Are you Jew too?" And then when I was identified by the dean to the faculty of the university in Brno as a "Zionist spy," the Vice-Dean, by way of apology said: "some of my father's best friends were Jewish." This was clearly not an atmosphere where music associated in any way with Jews could safely thrive.

Contemporary Revivals

Before World War II, there were about 350,000 Jews in Czechoslovakia, comprising about two and a half percent of the total population. Now, according to online data, Jews make up less than one tenth of one percent of the population of the Czech Republic. It would be impossible for Jewish life, or the life of those who identify as Jews to have the same kind of impact as in the past, which embraced secular and sacred worlds with vibrancy and variety.

There are further complications. The eminent composer and scholar Milan Slavický once said that the Nazis did not only destroy Jewish culture in the Czech lands, they destroyed Czech culture, German culture, *and* Jewish culture. Yet Tomáš Kraus, former head of the Prague Jewish Community sees the prewar period somewhat differently:

> The time is said to be marked with a unique and glorious coexistence of three cultures – Czech, German, and Jewish. However, this nice projection does not work. There was a Czech culture, and there was a German culture. And the Jews were on either side, or on both, sometimes in the middle.[16]

In his essay, Kraus also points out that there was a kind of clash of Jewish cultures after the war, since a majority of survivors from the Czechoslovak Jewish community were from Ruthenia and the Carpathians, many of whom moved to Prague. They brought with them their traditions, an approach to Judaism radically different from the world of Kafka, the Haas brothers, and Max Brod.

When, after the fall of communism, it became possible to freely engage with aspects of Jewish culture, much of the effort, naturally considering the history, turned either to memorialization, or the creation of a kind of hybrid Jewish culture. In terms of the former, a recent celebration in Terezín in May 2023 drew thousands, including survivors, the Czech president, diplomats from all over Europe, rabbis and priests, and the heads of the Jewish community. While there was some music associated with the main ceremony, it mostly consisted of a military band and a girl's chorus. A sparsely attended concert afterward presented some music composed in Terezín.

On the other hand, attempts to create a sense of Jewish cultural life through various festivals sometimes rely on a mix of elements not traditionally associated with any Czech Jewish traditions or cultural patterns. For example, the very name of the "ŠTETL FEST," a new festival of Jewish music and culture in Brno, recalls an aspect of Jewish culture, the shtetl, that never existed in the Czech lands. And the mixture of klezmer, Hasidic culture, memorialization, and references to secular Jewish activities, may or may not come together in the coming years to create something dynamic.

---

[16] Thomas Kraus, "Thirty Years After. The Yesterday, Today, and Tomorrow of the Czech Jewish Community," in *Being Jewish in 21ˢᵗ Century Central Europe*, ed. Haim Fireberg, Olaf Glöckner, and Marcela Menachem Zoufalá (Berlin: De Gruyter, 2020), 314.

More Little Jews, This Time in the Window

During normalization, some of the most common Czech souvenirs were little dolls of The Good Soldier Švejk (the hero of a satirical novel by Jaroslav Hašek), some with backpacks filled with tiny photos of Prague. After 1989, with the country no longer under the thumb of a great power that needed to be manipulated, Švejk began to take a back seat to the Golem, a perfect symbol for the varied mythologies of the Czech Jewish community. Today though, there is another sight that will greet visitors. In several shop windows in downtown Prague, you can see vast hordes of little Jews, and many of them are musicians (Figure 21.4). Some are playing cellos and others violins. We can find accordions, bagpipes, and clarinets to go along with the torah scrolls and menorahs. The absurdity of these little orthodox *klezmerim* bears as much real relationship to any Czech tradition as does the ever-present sweet treat known as the "Trdelník," giving evidence of what Tomáš Kraus calls "American *Fiddler-on-the-Roof* culture, based on roots of Carpathian *shtetls*."[17] By this, of course, he means Jewishness as a kind of performance in costume, but in this case, one without roots in the Czech lands.

The documented history of Prague begins with the writing of the Jewish traveler Abraham Ibn Yaqub in the second half of the tenth century. Before

Figure 21.4: Little Jews on sale in a Prague tourist shop (summer 2022). Photo by the author.

---

[17] Kraus, "Thirty Years After," 314.

that, things are shrouded in myth and legend. The future of Jewish communities and anything like Jewish music in the Czech lands also swirls into the world of conjecture. Will new liturgies emerge in the Jewish community? Will hip hop, Romani music, Moravian folksong, and klezmer fuse into some powerful local sound? These things possibly remain for the next edition of this volume.

22 | Czechoslovak Musicians in North American Exile

BRIAN S. LOCKE AND MARTIN NEDBAL

While many Czech (or Bohemian) musicians had come to the United States and Canada prior to the Munich Agreement,[1] those whose emigration fell between September 1938 and the fall of communism in 1989 bear the distinction of having fled racial persecution or political authoritarianism. Unlike the performers and composers before 1938, whose residence in North America depended upon the duration of employment, the mid- to late twentieth-century exiles were bound by politics and legal status, since in most cases their Czechoslovak citizenship had been revoked.

In the case of the émigrés of 1938/39, their citizenship was invalidated by the erasure of Czechoslovakia itself. Among the musicians of this wave of migration we can count both Czech and German-Bohemian Jews (Jan Löwenbach, Oskar Morawetz, Paul Nettl, Jaromír Weinberger) and non-Jews (Jaroslav Ježek, Rudolf Firkušný, Jiří Voskovec, Jan Werich) who fled precipitously in the months surrounding the Nazi invasion.[2] To these we can add Czech-born musicians already abroad (Bohuslav Martinů, Walter Susskind). Regardless of the means of escape to North America, their biographies are shaped by narratives of trauma, loss, and moral strength, though in the coming months the uniqueness of the Czech experience would be eclipsed by the sheer volume of human displacement during World War II.

This chapter focuses on several notable musicians who came to the United States and Canada after 1939. Their experiences were widely divergent and depended on their musical activities, means of employment, and duration of stay. Though these musicians' encounters with their new places of residence and unfamiliar cultures were individualistic, they each explored the new environment through the lens of the musical traditions

---

[1] For two recent studies on nineteenth- and early twentieth-century musical émigrés, see Matěj Kratochvíl, "Music as an Adaptation Strategy: The Hruby Family Voyage from Cehnice to Cleveland," *Journal of Austrian American History* 6, no. 1 (2022): 1–13; and Martin Nedbal, "Czech-German Collaborations at the Metropolitan Opera in the Early Twentieth Century," *Journal of Austrian American History* 6, no. 1 (2022): 14–43.

[2] On Paul Nettl's escape from Nazi-occupied Czechoslovakia, see Martin Nedbal, "Music History and Ethnicity from Prague to Indiana: Paul Nettl, Eighteenth-Century Bohemia, and Germanness," *Hudební věda* 56 (2019): 386–508.

they brought with them. Conversely (as shown in this chapter's penultimate case study on *Finian's Rainbow*), the exposure of Czech musicians to American culture also had long-lasting effects in their homeland.

Jaroslav Ježek's American Tragedy

Jaroslav Ježek and his colleagues from the Liberated Theater (Osvobozené divadlo, see Chapter 27) were among the first to depart from Prague in early 1939.[3] After a brief stop in Paris, they boarded the SS *Aquitania* and disembarked in New York City on January 20. Ironically, despite Ježek's hopes, the most iconic of Czech popular musicians would remain unknown – beyond the modestly sized Czech expatriate community – in the land whose music and culture he idolized.

Ježek's barriers in the New World were many: his English was not conversationally functional, he had no professional network, and his blindness and generally declining health impeded him. Voskovec and Werich, on the other hand, mastered English in six months and established professional contacts within and beyond the Czech émigré community. At first, their American success seemed assured among the Czechs of New York City, and within weeks they mounted a successful series of cabaret performances at the Sokol Club of Manhattan based on their Liberated Theater repertoire, lasting until April; engagements in Chicago followed in May.

In late 1939, Voskovec and Werich translated *Těžká Barbora* as *Heavy Barbara* for the Cleveland Play House, opening in March 1940 with Ježek's original music and continuing for a modestly successful thirty-five performances. Their second offering, a translation of *Osel a stín* ("The Donkey and the Shadow"), this time with new music by the American Harold Rome, did not fare as well in November. For Ježek, its poor reception reflected the disparity between avant-garde Czech artists and their American counterparts: "It seems to me that Americans can never understand our entire style, because they are immensely conservative and don't like to accept anything a little new and different" ("Zdá se mi, že Američané stále nemohou celý ten náš styl pochopit, protože jsou nesmírně konzervativní a neradi připouštějí něco, co je jim trochu nové

---

[3] Two heavily anecdotal biographies relate Ježek's final years: Václav Holzknecht, *Jaroslav Ježek a Osvobozené divadlo*, 2nd ed. with corrections by Petr Lachmann (Prague: ARSCI, 2007); and František Cinger, *Šťastné blues, aneb Z deníku Jaroslava Ježka* (Prague: BVD, 2006).

a jiné").[4] Adrift from his theatrical partnership, Ježek tried to subsist on work with a men's choir at the Czechoslovak Workers' House (Československý dělnický dům, 347 East 72nd Street) in 1940–41. A full-evening concert followed in April 1941; a women's choir concert became Ježek's final performance that December. Earning only 30 dollars per week, he was living off handouts from Voskovec, Werich, and other generous émigrés.

Two contentious anecdotes dominate the historiography of Ježek's declining career in 1941, both emblematic of the alleged heartlessness of his would-be competitors: that is, from Czechs in America. The first involves the Prague-born operetta composer Rudolf Friml, who had emigrated to the United States in 1906, and who might have opened doors to publishing and recording opportunities. Sometime in early 1941, Voskovec and Werich arranged for Ježek to play his work for Friml, who is said to have made rude remarks about Ježek's visual impairment and improvisational ability. (Friml denied that the meeting ever took place.)[5]

The second anecdote concerns a rumor that either Martinů or Paul Nettl sidelined Ježek's attempts to establish a career in concert music. Ježek's Piano Sonata, completed in early March 1941, was submitted to the jury of the International Society for Contemporary Music, and it was initially accepted for a performance in May. By the time of the concert, however, Ježek received word that the jury had substituted another work, possibly Martinů's *Tre ricercari* or one of Viktor Ullmann's piano sonatas.[6] Martinů vehemently denied any accusation of jury tampering when the anecdote was published in Holzknecht's 1954 biography of Ježek.

For all these hindrances – intentional or coincidental – it was Ježek's health that controlled the longevity of his American career. Shortly after the December 1941 concert, he was hospitalized, and on Christmas day, his new girlfriend, the émigré Frances (Františka) Bečáková, noted that he had lost his sight completely.[7] As a final wish, Ježek married Frances from the hospital bed on December 29, where he died from kidney failure three days later.

---

[4] Jaroslav Ježek to Zdena Werichová, November 10, 1940, reprinted in Cinger, *Šťastné blues*, 165.

[5] See Petr Lachmann, "Nad reedicí Holzknechtovy monografie," in Holzknecht, *Jaroslav Ježek*, 382–83.

[6] Regarding Martinů's alleged role, see discussion in Holzknecht, *Jaroslav Ježek*, 383–86; and Michael Beckerman, "The Dark Blue Exile of Jaroslav Ježek," *Music and Politics* 2/2 (2008): 1–14. Beckerman posits the theory that Paul Nettl lobbied for his wife's performance of an Ullmann piano sonata, a more likely substitute for a chamber concert setting than Martinů's orchestral work.

[7] Cinger, *Šťastné blues*, 190.

Bohuslav Martinů's American Triumphs

Bohuslav Martinů was a recent immigrant to the United States at the time of the above anecdote, having arrived on March 31, 1941, after an arduous nine-month-long journey from Paris with only four scores from his immense œuvre. Unlike Ježek, Martinů had already lived abroad in Paris for some time; his last visit to Czechoslovakia was in the summer of 1938. His views toward Czech cultural and musical identity were complicated by his polemical relationship with the music institutions and critics of Prague. Thus, his period of exile in the United States was characterized not only by a nostalgia for a lost nation, but also bitter memories of his place in it.

More significant than the *Tre ricercari* performance in May, the premiere of Martinů's Concerto Grosso took place on December 14, 1941, with the Boston Symphony Orchestra under Serge Koussevitzky, who had championed Martinů's music since the 1920s.[8] This pivotal occasion led to a commission for more orchestral work, and Martinů responded by composing five symphonies in five consecutive years (1942–46), alongside works in many other genres. This period also witnessed the expansion of Martinů's professorial career at Tanglewood, Princeton University, the Mannes School of Music, and the Curtis Institute of Music.

Martinů not only composed, but wrote extensive essays, autobiographical sketches, and diary entries that reveal the complexity of his thinking during and immediately following the war.[9] Unpacking the problem of critical interpretation, he questions whether a composer's music ever mirrors their own biographical experiences and feelings. However, the historiography of Martinů's works in American exile – in part influenced by the composer's own comments – supports the notion that some pieces reflect the vicissitudes of the Czechoslovak nation, for example his Double Concerto, which he acknowledged reflected a sense of desperation after the Munich Agreement.[10] An even greater connection between collective experience and music appears in his *Memorial to Lidice* of 1943 and Symphony No. 3 (completed just after D-Day).[11] Martinů's hopes of returning to a free and liberated Czechoslovakia, and his despair at the rise of communism in 1948, are often ascribed to the music of his post-war career. It is important to mention, however, that he composed many more

---

[8] Michael Crump, *Martinů and the Symphony* (Rochester, NY: Boydell & Brewer, 2010), 177.

[9] These are translated and analyzed in Thomas D. Svatos, *Martinů's Subliminal States: A Study of the Composer's Writings and Reception, with a Translation of His American Diaries* (Rochester, NY: University of Rochester Press, 2018).

[10] Svatos, *Martinů's Subliminal States*, 35.   [11] Crump, *Martinů and the Symphony*, 263–67.

works in these years that carry no evident markers of biographical or collective identity, such as the Symphony No. 2 (1942–43), commissioned by the same Cleveland Czechs that welcomed Voskovec, Werich, and Ježek in 1940. Such conflicting interpretations reflect the upheaval experienced by émigré artists in transition between multiple totalitarian regimes.

Jan Löwenbach's Fight for Czech Music in America

Among the most active figures in the Czech émigré musical scene in the United States was Jan Löwenbach, Czech-Jewish musicologist and lawyer. Löwenbach authored numerous articles and books about Czech music and musicians, served as one of the editors of the journal *Hudební revue*, wrote opera librettos for Martinů and Jaroslav Křička, and became a respected authority on copyright law. Löwenbach arrived in New York in 1941, worked for the cultural department of the Czech consulate, and relentlessly raised the awareness of Czech culture in numerous articles published in American journals. Löwenbach's 1943 *The Musical Quarterly* article on Czech musicians in America, for example, claimed that Ježek, Martinů, and Weinberger were "sufficiently characteristic for certain [Czech] national and artistic tendencies to claim the attention of musical America."[12]

In America, Löwenbach also promoted the music of Smetana and Dvořák, campaigns that illustrate the cultural politics of Czech musical activities in exile. For example, in the 1940s Löwenbach worked indefatigably to introduce Dvořák's *Rusalka* to America, bringing together several American institutions and Czech émigré communities. Dvořák's most frequently performed opera in the Czech lands had yet to be performed on a professional American stage – it had only been performed by a Czech amateur troupe in Chicago in 1935. Löwenbach first mentions the possibility of producing *Rusalka* in his April 13, 1942, letter to Frank Kubina, Chicago-based music director of Czech origin, asking whether Kubina owns the orchestral score and performing materials, as the opera had not yet been published in full score and acquiring musical materials from Prague was impossible.[13] A few days later, on April 24, 1942, Löwenbach wrote to his friend Olin Downes, music critic for the *New York Times*,

---

[12] Jan Löwenbach, "Czechoslovak Composers and Musicians in America," *The Musical Quarterly* 29 (1943): 328.
[13] San Diego, San Diego State University, Special Collections, Jan Löwenbach Papers, Box 1, Folder 11.

asking about a translator for *Rusalka*.[14] Downes recommended Ruth and Thomas Martin, who had translated Mozart's *Die Zauberflöte* for the Met's 1941 production and were to become prominent translators of operatic texts into English.[15] The Martins eventually did complete the first English translation of *Rusalka*, though they did not speak Czech and relied on an earlier German-language text and a rough English translation by Löwenbach's wife Vilma.[16]

The initial stages of the project were highly politicized – the Czechoslovak government in exile funded the translation, Löwenbach asked the Met's prima donna Jarmila Novotná to participate, and Czech politicians, most notably Czechoslovak foreign minister in exile Jan Masaryk, lobbied influential New Yorkers to support the opera's production in the city.[17] But this approach failed in the end. Most significantly, *Rusalka* was rejected for artistic and political reasons by the Met's music director Bruno Walter:

The libretto, a diluted version of the Undine story, seems weak to me, its dramatic life insufficient, and not even the creative power of a genius could have overcome the textual weakness through musical-dramatic strength!

We would be doing a disservice to Dvorak and the Czech cultural cause if *Rusalka* had to disappear from the Met's repertoire after a short out-of-courtesy success, and thus after conscientious consideration of the matter I have to advise against pursuing it any further.

Das Buch, eine Verdünnung des Undine Stoffes, erscheint mir schwach, sein dramatisches Leben ungenügend, und wie hätte die Schöpferkraft auch eines Genies die textliche Schwache durch musikalisch-dramatische Kraft verdecken können!

Wir würden aber Dvorak und der Sache der tschechischen Kultur keinen Dienst erweisen, wenn "Rusalka" nach kurzem Achtungserfolg wieder vom Spielplan der Metropolitan verschwinden müsste, und somit glaube ich nach gewissenhafter Prüfung der Angelegenheit von ihrer weiteren Verfolgung abraten zu müssen.[18]

Yet, *Rusalka* did reach an American stage in the end. While conducting in Cincinnati in the summer of 1944, Thomas Martin brought his *Rusalka*

---

[14] Löwenbach Papers, Box 1, Folder 12.

[15] Löwenbach discusses Downes's recommendation in his letter to Czechoslovak diplomat Ján Papánek from May 31, 1942. Löwenbach Papers, Box 1, Folder 15.

[16] Jan Löwenbach to Mrs. and Mr. Thomas Martin, May 12, 1942, Löwenbach Papers, Box 1, Folder 14.

[17] The cost of the translation was $250. See the letter to Löwenbach from September 21, 1942, Löwenbach Papers, Box 1, Folder 20. Löwenbach instructed Jan Masaryk about how to lobby for *Rusalka* in New York in a letter from June 12, 1942. Löwenbach Papers, Box 1, Folder 17.

[18] Bruno Walter to Jan Löwenbach, July 20, 1942. Löwenbach Papers, Box 1, Folder 20.

translation to the attention of the Detroit Friends of Opera.[19] The cultural and political representatives of Czechoslovakia in America therefore shifted their attention from New York to Detroit, as shown in a letter draft Löwenbach wrote for the Czechoslovak minister in exile Ján Papánek to send to the Detroit Opera president Fred Butzel.[20] In the letter, Löwenbach skillfully elaborates on how *Rusalka* would appeal to American audiences: he stresses that Dvořák, the composer of the *New World* Symphony, wrote *Rusalka* after his return from America; that the premiere of an opera by Dvořák, so well liked in the United States, would certainly prove to be an artistic event; and that as "a tuneful fairy tale with effective solo-parts and delightful ensembles" it would easily win the audience. Completely missing from Löwenbach's draft is any discussion of the opera's national and political significance. The reviews of the Detroit production, too, mostly overlook *Rusalka*'s Czechness. In the *Detroit Free Press*, J. D. Callaghan points out that the Detroit production was the first in English, but does not mention anything about the language from which it was translated – nor does the advertisement in the same newspaper on May 27, 1945.[21] Similarly, in *The Detroit Evening Times*, Charles Gentry viewed the production from a purely local perspective, claiming that it was "an interesting experiment, particularly since the opera had never been given in this country before and because all of the singers were Detroiters."[22] Gentry did not comment on the national background of the work or its composer either. Thus, although Löwenbach and his Czechoslovak colleagues managed to get *Rusalka* onto the stage of one regional opera company in the United States, the political and national significance of their efforts was much less visible than what they had likely hoped for. The opera's depoliticization may have also been connected to the fact that by the time Löwenbach and his colleagues succeeded in having *Rusalka* performed in English, the war in Europe was over.

Post-1948 Émigrés

The "generation of 1948" encapsulates the Czechs and Slovaks who emigrated to the West just before or after the Communist Coup in February of

---

[19] That Martin initiated the Detroit production is clear from Löwenbach's letter to Martin from June 28, 1944. Löwenbach Papers, Box 1, Folder 24.

[20] The proposal is dated October 26, 1944. Löwenbach Papers, Box 1, Folder 28.

[21] J. D. Callaghan, "Rusalka English Premiere Is Staged by All-City Cast," *Detroit Free Press*, May 28, 1945.

[22] Charles Gentry, "'Rusalka' Premiere," *Detroit Evening Times*, May 29, 1945.

that year. Their experiences differ from those of wartime refugees, since the cause of their departure was not only a foreign power (the USSR), but also their own compatriots, Czech communists who sought to inhibit their personal and artistic freedom. Their sense of isolation was now often compounded by professional animosity and feelings of betrayal, not to mention the sheer determination to outlive the regime. The generation of 1948 also had ready-made contacts in the West, since many earlier émigrés (for example Voskovec, Firkušný, and Löwenbach) resumed their North American exile after the coup.

The list of new immigrants reveals artists at various stages of their careers. Karel Boleslav Jirák, accused in 1945 of wartime anti-communist agitation (and, baselessly, of having denounced Martinů), relinquished his decades-long career in Prague and accepted a position at Chicago's Roosevelt College in 1947. Rafael Kubelík, performing in Amsterdam when news of the coup reached him, decided to stay in the West, for a time conducting the Chicago Symphony Orchestra (1950–53). The young Karel Husa was also abroad, studying with Honegger and Boulanger in Paris since 1947. As early as 1948, Martinů invited Husa to Tanglewood, proposing that he apply for the "Ježek Fund" established by Löwenbach (the trip came to naught).[23] Six years later, Husa was hired as professor of music theory and composition at Cornell University (where Weinberger had taught briefly in the 1920s), and he arrived in the United States in 1954.

It would be a full thirty-five years before Husa returned to Czechoslovakia. His time in the United States was productive and professionally rewarding; his ever-expanding network prompted artistic collaborations and new commissions. Yet he struggled over separation from his homeland and family, particularly after his mother's death in 1955. Husa's personal connection to Czechoslovakia and its identity unfolds as a continuum of self-referential works. His *Évocations de Slovaquie* for clarinet, viola, and cello (1951), *Four Little Pieces* for amateur string ensemble (1955), *Eight Czech Duets* for piano (1955), and the *Twelve Moravian Songs* (1956), many of them derived from folksong sources, form a kernel of musical material that Husa revisited frequently over the next six decades.[24]

---

[23] The creation of the Memorial Fund of Jaroslav Ježek is documented in Libuše Márová to Ministerstvo školství v Praze, October 12, 1945, in Löwenbach Papers, Box 1, Folder 38; see also Bohuslav Martinů to Karel Husa, April 8, 1948, translation reprinted in Mark A. Radice, ed., *Karel Husa – A Composer's Life in Essays and Documents* (Lewiston, NY: Edwin Mellen Press, 2002), 173–74.

[24] For analysis of these works, see Jiří Vysloužil, *Karel Husa: Skladatel mezi Evropou a Amerikou* (Prague: AMU, 2011), 27–44.

It is perhaps for his broadly programmatic works, however, that Husa is known internationally, particularly for *Music for Prague, 1968* and the *American Te Deum*. Famously, Husa began *Music for Prague* as events of the Warsaw Pact invasion were still unfolding, and its score thematizes both aggression and resistance. Although otherwise a twelve-tone work, it features quotations from the fifteenth-century Hussite chorale, *Ktož jsú boží bojovníci* ("You Who Are the Warriors of God"), tapping into a recognizable code of Czech identity (see also Chapter 2). *Music for Prague*'s remarkable appeal hinges on Husa's use of the wind ensemble, integral to the North American music education system, allowing for its rapid dissemination among band directors. The *American Te Deum* for mixed chorus, baritone solo, and wind ensemble (1976) reflects not a political event, but rather the multi-faceted voices of American immigrants: Husa's portrayal of collective identity includes, but is not limited to, his Czech identity. Various international texts are sung in English translation alongside liturgical Latin and American-born authors such as Thoreau. Husa's Czech material includes a chorale from the Moravian Church (sung in German), his own translation of Otokar Březina's poem *Je to Zem?*, and a quotation from Dvořák's "American" String Quartet.

Finian's Rainbow into *Divotvorný Hrnec*

One example of how the American experiences of Czechoslovak musical émigrés have influenced, and still influence, cultural life in their homeland, is the history of Voskovec and Werich's 1948 adaptation of *Finian's Rainbow*, the first, and also for many years the only, Broadway musical performed in Czechoslovakia. Voskovec got to know *Finian's Rainbow* on Broadway during his 1947 trip to America, partially because he was friends with Yip Harburg, the co-bookwriter.[25] Similar to *Rusalka*, *Finian's Rainbow* underwent a transformation on its transatlantic journey, but one that was much more substantial. Voskovec and Werich did not merely translate the book and the lyrics but revised them completely, starting with the Czech title *Divotvorný hrnec* ("The Magic Pot"). Whereas the original title emphasizes the idea of following one's dream, expressed in the song "Look to the Rainbow," and thus relates to the concept of American individualism, the Czech title draws attention to the supernatural aspects

---

[25] Pavel Bár, *Od operety k muzikálu: Zábavněhudební divadlo v Československu po roce 1945* (Prague: KANT, 2013), 81.

of the work, thus connecting it to the world of Czech fairy tales and the popular tradition of Central European theater works based on magic (including *Rusalka*). Voskovec and Werich also changed the plot substantially, inserting several specifically Czech elements. Most importantly, all the main characters acquire a Czech background. Irish immigrants Finian and Sharon McLonergan become Josef and Káča Maršálek from the south Bohemian Třeboň region. Woody and Susan Mahoney are transformed into the Rychtariks, descendants of Czech immigrants (possibly a reference to Richard Rychtarik, Czech-born stage designer at the Met and author of the sets for the 1945 Detroit *Rusalka*). Radical transformation also affected Og the leprechaun, who became Čochtan, a south Bohemian water goblin. The ending of the Czech adaptation, too, changed significantly. The two couples that formed throughout the original show (Woody and Sharon; Og and Susan) remain in the Rainbow Valley, Missitucky, and Finian goes in search of his own rainbow. In the Czech version, Maršálek, Čochtan, and Susan return to Bohemia to use their American experience in improving agricultural productivity and thus transform their native land into an earthly paradise. The adaptation for the Prague stage also affected the sound of the show: Voskovec did not purchase the musical's score in New York, and composer Zdeněk Petr therefore recreated it from a recording, though in an orchestration adjusted to fit the Karel Vlach Orchestra, a Prague jazz band.

The show premiered in Prague on March 6, 1948, just a few days after the February Communist Coup. As Pavel Bár points out, the show did not fit the ideological doctrines of Czechoslovak culture because it failed to depict America as an evil imperialist empire.[26] Despite strong objections by the critics and Voskovec's emigration to the United States, the show became enormously popular with Czech audiences and was soon performed in regional theaters as well.[27] *Divotvorný hrnec* was also for a long time the only Broadway musical to make it to the Czech stage – more than a decade later, in 1963, did *Kiss Me Kate* manage to cross the borders of communist Czechoslovakia.

Voskovec and Werich's unique approach to *Finian's Rainbow*, drawn from their exile experience, combined American popular culture with Czech sensibilities so effectively that the show became a Czech cultural classic. Numerous popular singers covered its songs in the following

---

[26] Bár, *Od operety k muzikálu*, 89–90.

[27] Soňa Červená, the original Káča Maršálková, discusses the show's initial popularity in her memoir *Stýskání zakázáno: Kousek mého divadelního děje-spisu a země-spisu* (Prague: Opus musicum, 2014), 34.

decades, several new adaptations updated Voskovec and Werich's original, and the musical continues to be performed regularly in the Czech Republic until the present day.[28] The Czech adaptation of *Finian's Rainbow* also complicates the show's ambiguous message on race. Although the musical promoted the progressive and anti-racist viewpoints of its day, its attempt to advocate for racial equality by using blackface (for example the Southern segregationist senator Billboard Rawkins magically transforms into a Black man) has since become politically and culturally unacceptable in the United States.[29] Even the most recent Czech productions of *Divotvorný hrnec*, however, continue to rely on blackface not only in the figure of the villainous senator, but also in the depiction of African Americans in the plot, suggesting that its Czechification has insulated *Divotvorný hrnec* from American discourses of racial equality.

Czech Musicians in Canada

The history of Czech émigré musicians in Canada parallels that of the United States; though smaller in number, their significance within the Czech-Canadian community stands comparatively high. Here, too, we see the relative success of art music composers and performers in a country with strong ties to European cultural institutions, and conversely a more difficult path faced by popular musicians in exile. Composer Oskar Morawetz (1917–2007) fled to Canada in 1940, remaining active as a leading composer and educator for over fifty years. The conductor Walter Susskind (or Süsskind, 1913–80), resided in the United Kingdom before leading the Toronto Symphony Orchestra, 1956–65. Throughout his time in Toronto, Susskind represented a wide variety of Czech, European, and Canadian works, premiering Morawetz's Symphony No. 2 and his own *Nine Slovak Sketches*; notably, both his first and final concerts with the TSO featured Dvořák's music.[30]

The swing composer, lyricist, and pianist Jiří Traxler (1912–2011) also contributed to Czech identity in Canada, albeit somewhat indirectly. After a successful career in Czech popular music during the Protectorate, Traxler

---

[28] For example, Liberec Theater, 2019, and Ústí nad Labem Theater, 2023.

[29] For a recent exploration of the show's ambiguous message on race, see Chase Brindgardner, "'A Rainbow in Ev'ry Pot': Southern Excess, Racial Liberalism, and Living Large in Harburg and Lane's *Finian's Rainbow*," *Studies in Musical Theater* 10 (2016): 117–32.

[30] Richard S. Warren, *Begins with the Oboe: A History of the Toronto Symphony Orchestra* (Toronto: University of Toronto Press, 2002), 61–80.

saw his prospects radically diminish under communism, with its ideological opposition to Western capitalist culture.[31] He defected to West
Germany in late 1949 and received an immigration visa to Canada in
1951. Though initially employed as a jazz pianist in Ottawa, Traxler soon
settled in Montréal, realistic about the dim future of Czech swing in the
New World.

For a time, Traxler wrote musical satires for Czech-language programming at CBC Radio, material broadcast to young Czech emigrants – and
possibly his compatriots still under communism. But his repeated assaults
on Zápotocký and Nejedlý during the first, critical years of the Cold War
prompted his show to be canceled.[32] Except for musical events at the
Montréal Sokol, Traxler relinquished his first career to embark on
a second: as a technical illustrator for an airplane parts manufacturer.
Only with the arrival of the novelist Josef Škvorecký in 1969 and his
establishment of 68 Publishers in Toronto did Traxler's musical career
enter a revival phase: Škvorecký, who had idolized Traxler since his teenage
years in the Protectorate, commissioned his autobiography. When the
memoir *Já nic, já muzikant* ("I'm Just a Musician") was published in
1980, Traxler's name became central to the nostalgia of his exiled generation, and his lifespan beyond the fall of communism assured him a place
in new historiographies of Czech jazz.

Like Škvorecký, Karel Ančerl (1908–73) belonged to the "generation of
1968." The conductor had been abroad at the time of the Warsaw Pact
invasion and entered into contract negotiations with the Toronto
Symphony Orchestra while residing temporarily in Zurich.[33] Ančerl,
whose career had begun under Ježek at the Liberated Theater and who
had survived internment in Terezín and Auschwitz, achieved international
fame conducting the Czech Philharmonic over twenty years (as successor
to the departed Kubelík, 1948–68). Prior to his defection, Ančerl had
performed in Canada on two occasions: the first visit to Montréal, on
tour with the Czech Philharmonic in 1965, resulted in a critical débâcle
in which the Czechs of Montréal – including Jiří Traxler – rallied to
Ančerl's support.[34] Ančerl's more successful appearance in Toronto

---

[31] See Jiří Traxler, *Já nic, já muzikant* (Toronto: 68 Publishers, 1980), 260–320.
[32] "Tryskem komunistickým tiskem" ("A gallop through the communist press"), typescripts,
Traxler estate papers (private archive, Ontario, Canada); see also Traxler, Já nic, já muzikant,
400–40.
[33] Warren, *Begins with the Oboe*, 93–107.
[34] The catalyst for controversy was a negative review: Joan Irwin, "Dvorak by Czech Orchestra,"
The Montreal Star, October 26, 1965; debate spilled over in the Montréal newspapers for several
weeks thereafter.

(1967) led to his final conductorship, replacing Seiji Ozawa at the end of the 1968–69 season.

Ančerl's time in Toronto was tragically brief, but significant for both the musical and Czech communities of Canada. Like Susskind before him, he made no secret of his ambassadorial role for Czech music, with Smetana, Dvořák, and Firkušný represented at his opening concert, and works by various Czech exiles over the next three seasons. The 1972 season, Ančerl's fourth as director, saw a resurgence of the hepatitis and diabetes he had battled since Terezín, and his death on July 3, 1973, came as a shock. Never interred in Toronto, Ančerl's ashes were kept by his widow until her passing in 1986, at which point the family secured permission to inter them at the Slavín cemetery at Vyšehrad.

The emotional impact of return from exile cannot be overstated, whether it be near the end of a long life (Firkušný, Husa, Kubelík, and Traxler) or after death (Ježek, Martinů, and Ančerl). Certain episodes of "return" have become iconic: the ceremonial burial of Ježek at Olšanský Cemetery, Kubelík's post-communist performance of *Má vlast* in Old Town Square, or the Czech Philharmonic premiere of Husa's *Music for Prague, 1968*. Each of these milestones – and countless private ones for Czech émigré families – has been transformative for the relationship between musical life in the modern Czech Republic and the diasporic communities of composers, performers, and listeners worldwide.

23 | Categorizing Music, Classifying People: Music Research and Race Studies in the Czech Lands

KELLY ST. PIERRE

The 1895 Czechoslavic Exhibition, held just outside of Prague, remains well recognized for its spectacle. The elaborate and detailed reconstructions of cultural artifacts including clothes, food, music, dance, arts and crafts, buildings, and even whole villages attracted over two million visitors. More than spectacle, however, the exhibition also reflected a confluence of thinking about the roles of ethnographic research, including folksong research, within notions of ethnicity and ethnonationalism. Researcher František Bartoš, together with Leoš Janáček, for example, presented their famous Moravian music demonstration alongside exhibits dedicated to Czechoslavic anthropology, statistics, geography, language, psychology, physiology, and sociology. The exhibition's music section similarly incorporated ethnographic analyses in the forms of topographical maps, and the event's tome of a program – a spectacle unto itself at over 600 oversized and intricately illustrated pages – positioned musicologist Otakar Hostinský's folk-music scholarship alongside chapters discussing skull and facial dimensions.[1] That is, more than an expression of nationalism, the Czechoslavic Exhibition participated within larger, then-unfolding conversations about the potential for science to *prove* the existence of a kind of ethnonation. And within this framework, music research, participated within the newly emerging fields of cultural studies, race studies, and physical anthropology – fields that, at the turn of the twentieth century, were especially interested in categorizing humans.[2]

This chapter explores the ways folksong research in the Czech lands emerged both within and alongside race and ethnicity studies during the

Funding for this project was provided by the Czech Science Foundation (GAČR) under the research project "The Second Sense: Sound, Hearing and Nature in Czech Modernity" (20-30516Y). All translations are my own unless otherwise indicated. When the translation is mine, the original Czech will appear following the citation.

[1] Karel Klusáček et al., eds., *Národopisná výstava českoslovanská v Praze 1895* (Prague: Otto, 1895), 153–56.

[2] For more, see Filip Herza's "Anthropologists and their Monsters: Ethnicity, Body, and Ab/Normality in Early Czech Anthropology," *East Central Europe* 43 (2016): 64–98; and Filip Herza, "Sombre Faces: Race and Nation-Building in the Institutionalization of Czech Physical Anthropology (1890s–1920s)," *History and Anthropology* 31 (2020): 371–92.

first half of the twentieth century.[3] That folksong research was deeply political during this era will come as no surprise. Scholars like Pamela Potter, Ronald Radano, Philip Bohlman, Celia Applegate, Klára Móricz, and Julie Brown have all thoughtfully exposed interrelationships between folksong research with German nationalism, specimen culture, and Darwinian assumptions.[4] Within Czech music research, however – and in no small part likely due to the discomfort of comparing Czech researchers with German nationalists – examinations of these same inter-relationships have only recently begun to emerge.[5] In the field of anthropology, too, scholars including Peter Skaník, Chris Hann, Mihály Sárkány, and Filip Herza have brought into focus the political roles of ethnographic studies in twentieth-century history, especially in defining the Czech and Slovak nations, but the role of folksong research as an important tool within this discipline remains unstudied.[6] Examining the ways music research in the Czech lands participated alongside and sometimes over-lapped with German nationalist race and ethnicity research, however, illuminates early Czech folk-music studies as an instrument of ethnona-tionalism; a tool not merely descriptive of a repertoire, but also delineative of who belonged and who did not.

Early Assumptions in Folksong Research

As it did elsewhere, folksong collection in the Czech lands began as a nineteenth-century nationalist project but shifted to reflect ethnonationalist

---

[3] A larger version of this project is forthcoming in the journal *Music & Politics*.

[4] These scholars' publications include a number of landmark studies, among them: Pamela Potter, *Most German of the Arts: Musicology and Society from the Weimar Republic to the End of Hitler's Reich* (New Haven: Yale University Press, 1998); Ronald Radano and Philip Bohlman, eds., *Music and the Racial Imagination* (Chicago: University of Chicago Press, 2000); Celia Applegate and Pamela Potter, eds., *Music and German National Identity* (Chicago: University of Chicago Press, 2002); Julie Brown, ed., *Western Music and Race* (New York: Cambridge University Press, 2007); and Klára Móricz, *Jewish Identities: Nationalism, Racism, and Utopianism in Twentieth-Century Music* (Berkeley: University of California Press, 2008).

[5] Mirjam Moravcová begins to take on race studies in Czech research in her "Politický národopis v pojetí Lubora Niederla a Karla Chotka," in *Od lidové písně k evropské etnologii: 100 let Etnologického ústavu Akademie věd České republiky*, ed. Jana Pospíšilová and Jana Nosková (Brno: Etnologický ústav AV ČR, 2006), 101–12.

[6] See Peter Skalník, ed., *A Post-Communist Millennium: The Struggles for Sociocultural Anthropology in Western and Eastern Europe* (Prague: Charles University, 2002); and Chris Hann, Mihály Sárkány, and Peter Skalník, eds., *Studying Peoples in the People's Democracies* (Münster: Lit, 2005). See also Herza, "Anthropologists and their Monsters," and Herza, "Sombre Faces."

thinking by the turn of the twentieth century. This conflation of scholarship and politics also met with shifts in period legislature, so that folksong collection by the turn of the twentieth century became part of a larger mission to teach an imagined Czech "people" – usually rural and lower-income communities – how to *be* Czech.

Rural communities at the end of the nineteenth century would have expected members to be bilingual; children were sent on summer- or year-long student exchanges ("Kindertausch-handl") between Czech- and German-speaking families to facilitate fluency.[7] Marriages were often "mixed"; individuals deliberately avoided ethnic alignment; and still others – labeled "amphibians" by Czech nationalists and, later, Nazi administrators – moved easily between the Czech and German languages.[8] But from as early as the 1880s, nationalist policy makers and researchers moved to draw supposedly clear boundaries between Czech and German ethnicities, an impulse eventually codified in the 1905 Moravian Compromise.[9] Under this legislation, Moravia's 2.5 million inhabitants were required to register exclusively with either Czech or German political parties, rather than moving freely within an open political landscape. A particular clause within this legislature also granted school boards the right to "reclaim" Czech students from German schools, should students' German language skills be deemed insufficient; bilingual children and children of mixed parents were "claimed" and "reclaimed" by Czech and German school boards through the beginning of the twentieth century as a consequence. A 1910 update further determined that students might attend German schools regardless of their language proficiency, as long as they were, in fact, German – at least according to supposedly objective third parties. Rather than proficiency exams or parents' self-identification, nationality in these instances would be determined through investigations of parents' social lives, political affiliations, language use, reading habits, and ancestry – modes of investigation aligned with then-emerging ethnological research, including folksong research.

Matěj Kratochvíl outlines the beginnings of folksong collection more thoroughly in his own contribution to this volume (see Chapter 24). Here,

---

[7] This and much of the following discussion of public policy in Moravia is indebted to Tara Zahra, "Reclaiming Children for the Nation: Germanization, National Ascription, and Democracy in the Bohemian Lands, 1900–1945," *Central European History* 37 (2004): 501–43, esp. 510–19.

[8] Chad Bryant, "Either German or Czech: Fixing Nationality in Bohemia and Moravia, 1939–46," *Slavic Review* 61 (2002): 683–706 (684). See also Gary Cohen, *Politics of Ethnic Survival: Germans in Prague, 1861–1914* (Lafayette: Purdue University Press, 2006), 206.

[9] Zahra, "Reclaiming Children for the Nation," 510–15, 519.

it is important to acknowledge that early folksong research was more attentive to witnessing cultural richness through quantity than by scientifically proving the existence of an ethnicity. Karel Jaromír Erben's two volumes of *Písně národní v Čechách* ("National Songs in Bohemia," 1842–43) together with his *Prostonárodní české písně a říkadla* ("Czech Folksongs and Nursery Rhymes," 1862–64), for example, together totaled 811 melodies and over 2,200 texts. František Sušil's *Moravské národní písně* ("Moravian National Songs," 1869) similarly included 1,890 melodies and 2,361 texts.[10] But into the twentieth century, folksong research increasingly invested in notions of scientific rigor and notions of ethnicity. A landmark publication by František Bartoš, *Lid a národ* ("The People and the Nation," 1883), for example, presented data-driven ethnographic essays describing the communities in Zlín (Bartoš's birthplace) and Moravské Valašsko in eastern Moravia. In it, the author called on eclectic bodies of evidence to support this discussion including folksong texts, extensive inventories of these regions' produce, their histories of serfdom, detailed analyses of familial relationships, and descriptions of their holiday rituals. That is, Bartoš's study, though including folksong research, actually participated in much larger discussions aimed at defining communities by their specific biological landscapes, cultures, and social systems – to explore emerging notions of race and ethnicity.

Like Bartoš, founding practices in musicology also engaged with notions of ethnicity, although, with sometimes greater consequences, especially in the subdisciplines of comparative musicology (later, ethnomusicology) and systematic musicology. Albrecht Schneider explains that comparative musicology's then-focus on discovering and mapping "ethnographic parallels," or musical traces, across nations and through time combined with systematic musicology's attention to the physical measurement of subjective listening experience had the potential to be (and did sometimes become) dangerous.[11] If the morphology of ethnographic parallels made it possible to identify "progressive" communities, for example, then it was also possible to identify "primitive" ones. And if measurable listening experience is a part of an individual's psychology, then those of limited hearing (among other possibilities) might be rendered less psychologically able, or, at its most extreme, less human. In either case, music research was not necessarily a study unto itself during much of the nineteenth century,

---

[10] Both statistics according to Barbara Krader, "Bohemia, Moravia, and Slovakia," in *Ethnomusicology: Historical and Regional Studies*, ed. Helen Meyers (New York: Norton, 1992), 178–79.

[11] Albrecht Schneider, "Comparative and Systematic Musicology in Relation to Ethnomusicology: A Historical and Methodological Survey," *Ethnomusicology* 50 (2006): 236–58 (247–50).

but one of several interdisciplinary methods toward classifying humans – their ethnicity, biology, and possibly even worthiness.

Prague's Charles University (then Charles-Ferdinand University) was exceptionally well positioned to facilitate ethnonationalist and separatist research, especially in music. Aesthetician August Wilhelm Ambros established a tradition of music criticism and research from his appointment at the university in 1869 (see also Chapter 16). In 1882, the university divided into separate German and Czech institutions (the Deutsche Karl-Ferdinands-Universität and the Česká universita Karlo-Ferdinandova), and in 1885 Guido Adler was appointed to the German half of the university – the same year of his landmark "Umfang, Methode und Ziel der Musikwissenschaft" ("Scope, Method, and Aim of Musicology"). Otakar Hostinský, student of Ambros, was appointed to a professorial position in the Czech half of the university in 1883.

Hostinský's research, and especially his collaborations with Charles University's first Professor of Archaeology and Ethnology Lubor Niederle, often reflected the political work embedded in early musicology, including its ethnonationalist impulses. He published a groundbreaking study in Czech musicology in 1892, for example, titled *36 nápěvů světských písní českého lidu z XVI. století* ("36 Melodies of Czech Secular Folksong from the Sixteenth Century") that became a cornerstone for all future musicological studies in Czech music, especially in comparative musicology.[12] In it, Hostinský extensively annotated each melody, tracing their supposed ethnogenesis, especially with the aim of protecting the Czech repertoire from possible moments of German-inspired transmission. He argued, for example, that although similarities between *Ach mlynářko, mlynářko* ("Oh Mill Maiden, Mill Maiden") invited comparison with the German *Ich weiss ein hübsche Müllerin* ("There Was a Lovely Mill Maiden"), the melody most likely came from a Latin source from 1601, rather than the German song. The author also granted, however, that this relationship was actually impossible to prove (see also Chapter 16).[13] Niederle's research also regularly made use of comparative musicological methods, especially toward tracing supposed "ethnographic parallels" between nations and across time.[14] But

---

[12] The study was printed in Prague by F. Šimáček.

[13] Hostinský, *36 nápěvů*, 9–10. Martin Nedbal explores a similar, folksong-related example of confirmation bias or, in the case of his discussion, (politically) motivated reasoning in the second chapter of his *Mozart's Operas and National Politics: Canon Formation in Prague from 1791 to the Present* (New York: Cambridge University Press, 2023), 73–78.

[14] See, for example, Lubor Niederle, "Počátky slovanské hudby," *Národopisný věstník českoslovanský* 9 (1915): 49–74.

he also harnessed such tools toward pioneering the field of "politically engaged ethnography" ("politicky angažované etnologie"). This field called on research in early human history to comment on the current political moment, requiring scholars to reach out to politicians and make their expertise accessible to the "people."[15] Niederle's research significantly impacted understandings of ethnicity at the time: though others had previously identified eight or nine Slavic ethnicities, Niederle determined the existence of anywhere between eleven to fourteen Slavic ethnonations. He published his findings in his 1909 *Slovanský svět* ("The Slavic World"), which provided some of the foundational philosophies for redrawing maps in Central Europe after World War I.

If Hostinský and Niederle already produced scholarship in dialogue with one another, their collaborations yielded important consequences for future musicological and ethnological research. In 1891 the pair founded an organization called the Czechoslavic Ethnographic Society (Národopisná společnost Českoslovanská), which helped host the famous 1895 Czechoslavic Exhibition that opened this chapter. By the time of the exhibition, too, the Society boasted 154 departments in regions across Bohemia, forty-seven in Moravia, and four in Silesia. Between 1892 and 1895 these individual departments also staged 175 of their own exhibitions: 118 in Bohemia, fifty-four in Moravia, and two in Silesia.[16] That is, the Ethnographic Society's demonstrations effectively asserted the "otherness" of 205 ethno-localities within relatively close quarters, today's Czech Republic comparable in area to the US state of South Carolina.

Folksong, Ethnicity, and Race Studies

Folksong research became state-funded at the start of the twentieth century, especially upon the founding of the *Folksong in Austria* ("Das Volkslied in Österreich") project. Though first imagined as early as 1902 by Viennese publishing house Universal Edition, by 1905 the project yielded several committees and working groups that I will collectively refer to as the Ethnological Institute, of which Hostinský was named head of a Czech Department, and Adolf Hauffen a German.[17] These halves were also divided into smaller departments, including subdivisions for

---

[15] The following discussion is indebted to Moravcová, "Politický národopis," 101–12.

[16] Klusáček, *Národopisná výstava českoslovanská*, 23–24 and 31–34.

[17] In a speech celebrating the one-hundred-year anniversary of the Ethnological Institute, today part of the Czech Academy of Sciences, Lubomír Tyllner identified its beginning as the Organizational Committee for Czech Song in Moravia and Silesia (Pracovní výbor pro českou

"German Song in Bohemia" based in Prague; "German Song in Moravia and Silesia," seated in Brno; "Czech Folksong in Bohemia" based in Prague; and "Czech Song in Moravia and Silesia," also seated in Brno, with Janáček its head. Within this framework, the Czech half of the Ethnological Institute actively worked to assert its "otherness" and independence from its parent project. In one of the organization's first public announcements, for example, members explained that, though its organization under the *Folksong in Austria* project might imply "central – naturally German – management" ("ústřední – přirozeně německé – vedení"), its committees were actually "completely autonomous" ("úplně autonomní").[18] They were also dedicated to forming new research methods to suit their repertoire's supposedly Czech (and not German) sounds. They rejected the possibility of organizing their work according to Josef Pommer's *Grundzüge für die Sammlung* ("Guidelines for Collection," 1905), for example, and created their own guide, *Sbíráme českou národní píseň na Moravě a ve Slezsku* ("Collecting Czech National Song in Moravia and Silesia"), its methods modeled from Hostinský's 1906 *Česká světská píseň lidová* ("Czech Secular Folksong"), an updated version of his 1892 study. Within the Moravian department, Janáček also worked to further meet the nuances specific to its repertoire.[19] He continued developing methods of transcription and made some of the first recordings of folksongs on wax cylinders. The combination of such rigorous methods alongside the assumption that the quantity of folksongs evidenced the supposed ethnic richness of any particular region allowed the organization to boast nearly 15,000 folksongs in its catalogue for each of the Bohemian and Moravian-Silesian Departments by World War I, and 10,000 folksongs in its German Department.[20] At a time of instability, then, folksong seemed to bear witness to the scientific validity and implicit independence of ethnic states within the empire.

The Ethnological Institute was reorganized to reflect new understandings of both the state and research methods after World War I. Most fundamentally, the organization's re-founding in 1919 as the State

píseň na Moravě a ve Slezku) as part of the *Folksong in Austria* project. Lubomír Tyllner, "Jubilejní ohlédnutí," in *Od lidové písně k evropské etnologii*, 9.

[18] Otakar Zich, "O sbírání lidových písní," *Smetana: Hudební revue* 1/21 (December 1, 1906): 275–77 (276).

[19] For more on Janáček's early work in the organization, see Jarmila Procházková, "Janáčkova koncepce činnosti Pracovního výboru pro českou národní píseň na Moravě a ve Slezsku," in *Od lidové písně k evropské etnologii*, 42–49; and Jiří Vysloužil, "Brněnský Pracovní výbor, Ústav a Kabinet pro lidovou píseň," in *Od lidové písně k evropské etnologii*, 133–36.

[20] Věra Thořová, "Vznik Státního ústavu pro lidovou píseň a první léta jeho existence," in *Od lidové písně k evropské etnologii*, 53.

Institute for Folksong (Statní ústav pro lidovou píseň) included new sub-divisions designed to reflect the demographics understood to exist in the then-new Czechoslovak Republic. A Slovak Department was headed by Karol Medvecký, a German Department by Adolf Hauffen, a Moravian-Silesian Department still under Janáček, and the Czech Department under looming political figure Zdeněk Nejedlý. Nejedlý would later serve as Minister of Culture and Education under the Czechoslovak communist administration from 1948–62, but he had trained as a musicologist with Hostinský and joined Charles University's faculty in 1905 (see Chapter 18). In keeping with the interdisciplinarity of folksong research, too, the first leader of the Institute upon its re-founding in 1919 was not a professor of musicology, but Slavic folklorist and friend of Niederle, Jiří Polívka.

Within this new structure, the Institute's projects also became increasingly and more explicitly in dialogue with German nationalist projects. Most fundamentally, Niederle's protégé, Karel Chotek, became a particularly visible member of the Institute. Chotek had radicalized Niederle's politically engaged ethnography within the framework of his own "political ethnography" ("politický národopis"), which he taught and promoted in his Seminar for General Ethnography (Semiář pro všeobecný národopis) at Charles University from 1932 and in which he presented methods increasingly aligned with Nazi scholarship.[21] Additionally, Institute members from the 1920s onwards called for a compendium of source materials in folksong research to be organized under Nejedlý's editorship. More than collection for collection's sake, the proposed project was in dialogue with the Berlin-based German Folklore Union's launch of its *Landschaftliche Volkslieder* project – also a type of compendium – in 1924. As Philip Bohlman shows us, this project was actually part of research to support Germany's philosophy of *Lebensraum*, anticipating its future territorial moves.[22] To that end, several volumes explore folksong in Czechoslovakia's Sudetenland – the region Hitler would first occupy following the 1938 Munich Agreement. A 1938 volume focuses on Czechoslovak Egerland, and a 1934 volume explores Czechoslovak Silesia. Additionally, the collection's forty-third volume, though not published until 1971, was collected during "Song Weeks" held by its committee from 1929–39 in southern Moravia.

---

[21] Moravcová, "Politický národopis," 101–12.

[22] This and the following discussion of the project is indebted to Philip Bohlman's close analysis in "Landscape – Region – Nation – Reich: German Folksong in the Nexus of National Identity," in *Music and German National Identity*, 105–27.

Ethnological Institute members never did complete their compendium. They did, however, insert their work into then-emerging conversations on music and race, as modeled by Richard Eichenauer's landmark *Musik und Rasse* (1932).[23] In particular, three of the organization's leading members – Niederle, Chotek, and Jiří Horák, secretary of the Czech Department – contributed to a collection of essays, *Rovnocennost evropských plemen a cesty k jejich ušlechťování* ("The Equality of European Races and Means for Their Refinement"), published in 1934. The book's introduction explained that the loss of life during World War I had affected the "genetic foundation" ("dědičnostní základ") of all nations involved, and that it was necessary to "repair all of the damage to national health" ("napraviti všecky škody na národním zdraví").[24] These Institute members' contributions, in turn, demonstrated the ways interdisciplinary bodies of evidence could be used to describe "The Racial Composition of Slavs" (in the case of Niederle) or examine relationships between "Race and Culture" (Chotek). Horák's contribution on "Race in Slavic Folktales" discussed the usefulness specifically of ethnographic parallels. While these essays were primarily theoretical, other studies within the book demonstrated the application of their methodologies. An essay by Vladislav Růžička on "The Improvement of the State of the Nation by Racial Hygiene or Eugenics," for example, listed forty characteristics of the "Nordic Man" ("nordický člověk") – an "ideal of German, racial hygiene" ("ideál německé plemenné hygieny"). According to the author, the Nordic Man is tall, has a slender cranium, has light blue or gray eyes, has light skin, is "enterprising" ("podnikavý") and "stubborn" ("tvrdošíjný"), has a "strong will" ("silnou vůli") that borders on "ruthlessness" ("bezohlednost") and gives "preference to metaphysics" ("přednost metafysice").[25] Race, then, was not merely biological or political, but also philosophical and psychological.

It is within this increasingly radicalized framework that Ethnological Institute member Vladimír Helfert and musicologist Gustav Becking were killed. Bruno Nettl has situated these scholars' deaths as resulting in part, if not primarily from their 1936 public scholarly debates, much of which concerned ethnogenesis in supposed Western art music.[26] More

---

[23] Projects dedicated to race in imperial Austria and even before World War I in anthropology supported by the empire were not unique. For more on this topic especially the uses and theorizations of skull dimensions and craniology by Niederle and Chotek, see Herza, "Sombre Faces," 371–92.

[24] Karel Weigner, ed., *Rovnocennost evropských plemen a cesty k jejich ušlechťování* (Prague: České akademie věd a umění, 1934), 1.

[25] Weigner, *Rovnocennost evropských plemen*, 78.

[26] Bruno Nettl, "Ethnicity and Musical Identity in the Czech Lands: A Group of Vignettes," in *Music and German National Identity*, 282.

specifically, Helfert and Becking analyzed the musical scores of Bohemian composers like Johann Stamitz, Heinrich Biber, František Benda, and Johann Schobert – Franz Schubert even fell into the discussion – to determine their supposedly scientific, biological races. Outside of these debates, however, Helfert's activities had also positioned him to become an enemy of the state moving into World War II. In his professional life, he chaired a newly founded musicology department at Komenský (now Masaryk) University from 1919, but in his political life, Helfert had also collaborated with the Czech resistance group Maffie against Austria-Hungary during World War I; given increasingly political and eventually anti-Nazi lectures in his professorial work; and, just before the Nazi takeover of the university, smuggled the Brno collection of Ethnological Institute sound recordings into the care of the editorial board of Czech Radio (Český rozhlas).[27] All recordings were returned after the war, only ten wax cylinders damaged.[28] Helfert's political background, then, at least as much as his conversations with Becking poised him to receive extra scrutiny under the Protectorate. He was called in for Gestapo questioning in November 1939 and eventually sent to the Nazi camp Terezín. He lived to see the camp's liberation but died only a few days later of spotted fever on May 18, 1945. In contrast, Becking worked at Prague's Charles University between 1930 and 1945; promoted Nazi ideologies during the 1930s, while still advising the doctoral work of Jewish students; and joined the Nazi Party in 1939. He was killed on May 8, 1945, during the Prague uprising against Nazi Germany (the days of May 5–9). He was reported to have been executed on the street alongside thirty other prominent Germans.[29]

The careers and deaths of Helfert and Becking remind us that Czechs and Germans shared in the same scholarly projects through the twentieth century, worked within the same political systems, and even fell victim to mutual acts of violence. A brief overview of folksong research during the first half of the twentieth century also shows that Czech and German scholars were immersed in the same radicalized political discourses of the

[27] Rudolf Pečman, *Vladimír Helfert* (Brno: Universitas Masarykiana: 2003), 29, 47–55, 223–24.

[28] For more, see Jiří Vysloužil's "Brno's Organizational Committee," in *Od lidové písně k evropské etnologii*, 133–36.

[29] Bruno Nettl reports that Becking might well have intervened with the Gestapo to allow him and his family, including his musicologist father Paul Nettl, to escape during the Nazi occupation. See Martin Nedbal's "Music History and Ethnicity from Prague to Indiana: Paul Nettl, Eighteenth-Century Bohemia, and Germanness," *Hudební věda* 56 (2019): 386–416 (401, 418–19). See also Kurt Stangl, "In Memoriam Gustav Becking," *Die Musikforschung* 2 (1949): 126–31.

era and that their scholarship was not separate but instead informed by, interacted with, and responded to one another.

Conclusion

Rachel Mundy has shown that even outside of folksong research, the positivist methods foundational to musicology, especially its search for supposed musical "styles," were also entrenched in a process of "categorizing culture as a form of essential, biologized difference." Interrogating its assumptions, she writes, therefore has the potential to illuminate "music's power to classify human cultures" and "define human beings."[30] This exploration of early folksong scholarship in the Czech lands similarly illuminates the political roles this scholarship played. For these researchers, the existence of some sort of Czechoslavic nation did not just warrant its own borders, it was a scientifically measurable fact. And if it was possible to measure some sort of imagined Czechness, it was also possible to measure not-Czechness, or "otherness." That is, folksong researchers in the Czech lands made the same types of musico-political moves as their German nationalist colleagues. They operated within the same political landscapes, scholarly conversations, and research organizations. And their radicalism yielded a unique set of paradoxical assumptions: the nation was united precisely because it could be broken into (possibly even 205) ethnicities, and its folksong repertoires were empirically as rich, if not richer than Germany's precisely because its richness could not be described by contemporary (German) musicological methods. That is, more than sound, folksong research concerned the taxonomy of a People – their ethnicity, their race, and perhaps most importantly, their hierarchy.

---

[30] Rachel Mundy, "Evolutionary Categories and Musical Style from Adler to America," *Journal of the American Musicological Society* 67 (2014): 735–68 (761).

The Nation's Image in Songs: Folk Music
Research and Revival in the Twentieth Century

MATĚJ KRATOCHVÍL

The Birth of National Collections

In the past two centuries, folk music acquired prominent political and
national symbolism in the Czech lands. This chapter explores the ways in
which folk music and dance were linked to science and politics in the
twentieth century. To understand these relationships, one needs to start
with nineteenth-century collections of folksongs, which determined the
canon of Bohemian and Moravian folk music up to the present day.
Furthermore, during the nineteenth century, folk music and dance ceased
to function as organic aspects of communal life. The advancements in
urbanization and industrialization suppressed opportunities for communal
singing and dancing, and large portions of the folk repertoire disappeared.

Until the early nineteenth century, only amateur enthusiasts from different backgrounds collected folksongs, and the results of their work were
usually not presented to the broader public.[1] The next generation of collectors, which included Karel Jaromír Erben and František Sušil, was interested
in preserving and promoting music that they felt illustrated Czech culture's
distinctiveness from other ethnic groups within the Habsburg monarchy and
was falling victim to social modernization and urbanization. What drove
Erben's and Sušil's efforts more generally was the idea that musical folklore
was important for the construction of collective identities.

During the national revival, the interest in folk music was associated with
patriotism and could be understood as a political endorsement of the
attempts to increase the Czech nation's autonomy within the Habsburg
monarchy. And yet, two distinct fundamental projects focused on documenting musical folklore were initiated in Vienna, the imperial capital. In
1819, the Viennese Society of Music Friends (Gesellschaft der

---

This chapter was translated from Czech to English by Martin Nedbal.

[1] An example can be found in the activities of Jan Jeník z Bratřic (1756–1845), soldier and
aristocrat, who transcribed many songs for his and his friends' use.

Musikfreunde), specifically its co-founder Joseph Sonnleithner called for the collection of folksongs in all the Habsburg crownlands. This led to collecting activities in Bohemia, Moravia, and Austrian Silesia. Although most of the collected material was either lost or remained unknown until the late twentieth century, it represents a significant sample of the body of Czech folk music.[2] Less than a century later, in 1905 another ambitious collecting endeavor took place, this time focused on the musical folklore of Austria-Hungary. The project *Folksong in Austria* ("Das Volkslied in Österreich"), officially started in 1902, was initiated by Universal Edition, and, starting in 1904, was supervised by the imperial Ministry of Cultural Affairs and Education (Ministerium des Kultus und Unterrichts). This project was organized more systematically than its early nineteenth-century predecessor, and the collecting activities in the individual crownlands were supervised by committees of experts. The main imperial committee in Vienna included Czech aesthetician Otakar Hostinský, who also led the Bohemian committee. Within the Bohemian crownlands, there were also the Moravian committee, led by Leoš Janáček, and a separate committee for German songs in Bohemia and Moravia, led by Adolf Hauffen, professor of ethnography at Prague's German University. The goal of the project was to collect not only purely folk repertoire, but also any music that was used by the people, including "art" music that became widespread in folk settings. The instructions to the collectors asked for detailed descriptions of the interpreters, and places and times of transcription. The collecting activities were interrupted by World War I. Although the collected materials were supposed to be sent to Vienna, neither the Bohemian nor the Moravian committees did so, and the songs therefore remained in Prague and Brno, forming the basis for the State Institute for Folksong (Státní ústav pro lidovou píseň), founded in 1919. The project made explicit the diverging interests of various national and ethnic groups, as illustrated by the tense relationship between the representatives of the Czech and German committees in Bohemia and Moravia.

Folksong in Austria introduced music-recording technologies to the Bohemian crownlands. In 1909, composer and aesthetician Otakar Zich used Edison's phonograph to record south Bohemian bagpiper František Kopšík in the village of Klenovice and an anonymous instrumental trio (consisting of a bagpipe, violin, and clarinet) in the same region. The recordings were published digitally together with the project's history by

---

[2] See Jaroslav Markl, *Nejstarší sbírky českých lidových písní* (Prague: Supraphon, 1987); and Karel Vetterl and Olga Hrabalová, eds., *Guberniální sbírka písní a instrumentální hudby z Moravy a Slezska z roku 1819* (Strážnice: NULK, 1994).

Lubomír Tyllner.[3] A few months later, the phonograph was also used to collect folksongs in Moravia, after being introduced by *Folksong in Austria*. The recording was initiated by Janáček and executed by Hynek Bím and Františka Kyselková. Although the recording took place in Brno and other Moravian locales, most of the recorded songs were from Slovakia because Janáček and his collaborators focused on Slovak workers who came to Moravia for work. Moravian folk music was recorded only in the village of Vnorovy near Hodonín.[4]

Recording technology was also widely used by the so-called Phonographic Committee, founded after the creation of independent Czechoslovakia and with similar personnel to the *Folksong in Austria* committee. The Phonographic Committee was initiated by linguists interested in documenting disappearing dialects. Instead of phonographs and wax cylinders, the committee made use of gramophone records, which provided better sound quality, but made it necessary to bring performers to a recording studio due to the size of the recording equipment, which prevented field recordings. The committee sought to create a sound map of the new republic, which was to include not only folk music but also regional dialects, classical music, and speeches by important people. Folk music still represented most of the collection, taking up 291 sides of vinyl records, each with a playing time of about three minutes. The recording started in collaboration with the French company Pathé in the Národní dům (National House) in Prague's Vinohrady in 1929. Pathé's technology provided a better sound quality but prolonged the recording process: whereas with Edison's phonograph it was possible to listen to the recordings immediately, the Prague recordings had to first be inscribed on a shellac record in France and then sent back to Czechoslovakia. Records in the committee's archive show that the French company was slow in returning the recordings to Czechoslovakia. The committee later fired Pathé and entrusted the recording first to the Czechoslovak Radio and then to the newly founded company Esta. Although the recording process was often delayed due to personal conflicts and attempts to replace the technological provider, a lot of recordings were made by 1937. The recordings had a relatively widespread coverage in Slovakia and Carpathian Ruthenia (which was then a part of Czechoslovakia) but were made only sporadically in Bohemia; a larger number of recordings were made of south Bohemian bagpipe music, while other regions were largely ignored.

---

[3] Lubomír Tyllner, *Dudy a dudácká muzika* (Prague: Etnologicky ústav AVČR, 2001).

[4] Jarmila Procházková et al., *As Recorded by the Phonograph: Slovak and Moravian Songs Recorded by Hynek Bím, Leoš Janáček and Františka Kyselková in 1909–1912* (Brno: Etnologicky ústav AVČR, 2012).

At the beginning of the recording project, the committee issued a proclamation that explains that the people to be recorded should be preferably men who spoke "their dialect" ("své nářečí"), were "fearless" ("nebojácní"), had voices that were "neither too high, nor too low (preferably a baritone)" ("ani příliš vysoký, ani nízký (nejraději baryton)"), and were "willing to speak into the phonograph" ("ochotni do fonografu promluviti"); particularly desirable were those who could sing.[5]

The committee also planned to issue select recordings and distribute them publicly; the main buyers of the records were expected to be state schools. The letters that some school directors wrote in response to the committee's offers show, however, that these institutions could not afford to buy the recordings because of their strained finances, which became particularly acute during the financial crisis in the 1930s. The attempt to sell the records commercially was likewise unsuccessful.

The Phonographic Committee project illustrates that folk-music research reflected the conditions of the times in which it was initiated. The collections were supposed to construct an image of Czechoslovakia as a state of ethnic Slavs, despite the country's multiethnic character. The collectors ignored the music of the roughly three million German-speaking inhabitants, Hungarians in Slovakia, Jews, and Roma. At the same time, the collectors included recordings of female singers from Upper and Lower Lusatia, linguistically Slavic regions in Germany, close to the border of Bohemia.[6] The choice of a French recording company to produce the records had political connotations, as illustrated in the committee's archival records:[7]

The committee also welcomes that the matter will be in the hands of our French friends and specialists and the company will not be dependent on the Germans. The promotion of our songs abroad, which the company Pathé in Paris will undertake, merits our attention.

Akademii také přichází vhod, že věc bude v rukou našich přátel a odborníků francouzských a podnik nebude závislý na Němcích. Také propaganda naší písně v cizině, kterou provede závod Pathé v Paříži, je věc zasluhující pozornosti.

Independent of the committee's project, musicologist Mieczyslaw Kolinski recorded the songs of German-speaking communities in Czechoslovakia

---

[5] Prague, Masarykův ústav AVČR, fond ČAVU, uncatalogued and undated.

[6] Matěj Kratochvíl, "Presence and Absence of Minorities in Folk Music Research Projects in the 20th-Century Czech Lands," in *Music – Memory – Minorities: Between Archive and Activism*, ed. Zuzana Jurková and Veronika Seidlová (Prague: Karolinum, 2020), 36–48.

[7] Prague, Masarykův ústav AVČR, fond ČAVU, uncatalogued and undated.

for the German Academy in Munich in 1931–34. Kolinski used a phonograph and wax cylinders, and his recordings were later deposited in the Berlin Phonogramm-Archiv. According to the inventory from the Berlin archive, Kolinski recorded eighty-three wax cylinders in the Šumava (Böhmerwald) region – specifically the villages of Chroboly (Chrobold), Nýrsko (Neuern), Lenora (Eleonorenhain), and Prachatice (Prachatitz) – and another eleven in the Krkonoše (Riesengebirge) region – specifically in Poříčí u Turnova (Parschnitz). Most of the recordings were likely destroyed at the end of World War II, when a part of the Phonogramm-Archiv was confiscated by the Soviet Red Army.[8]

Searching for a New People

Following World War II, and particularly after the establishment of the communist regime in Czechoslovakia in 1948, ideological views and functions of folk culture changed significantly. Czech and Slovak national sentiments were replaced with so-called socialist patriotism. Party ideologues, led by musicologist Zdeněk Nejedlý, attempted to construct a new, teleological understanding of Czech history, which pointed to the formation of the Czechoslovak Communist Party and its assumption of power. At the same time, however, the party ideologues allowed the institutions and personnel from earlier periods to continue their collection and study of folk music.

In the first half of the 1950s, Czechoslovak scientific endeavors were reorganized according to communist ideology, which also led to the establishment of the Czechoslovak Academy of Sciences in 1953. In 1954, the Academy combined the Department of Folksong, which succeeded the State Institute of Folksong and was led by literary scientist and folklorist Jiří Horák, with the Department of Ethnography into the Institute of Ethnography and Folkloric Research. The first important research project of the new institute focused on the Kladno region in central Bohemia, which was considered significant due to coal mining and its status as a nineteenth-century center of the workers' movement. The communist regime considered workers, together with village people, the most important segment of society, and their culture was supposed to become central in the new socialist order. The project was led by Olga Skalníková and was supposed to map various aspects of workers' and miners' communities in

---

[8] Artur Simon, ed., *Das Berliner Phonogramm-Archiv 1900–2000* (Berlin: VWB, 2000), 32–33.

the Kladno region, including folk music. The project team was later joined by musicologist and folklorist Vladimír Karbusický, who significantly contributed to the chapter on musical culture in the monograph that was to be the outcome of the project. Karbusický claimed that the main goal of the project was "to outline the specific culture of the working class" ("aby byla vytčena specifická kultura dělnické třídy"), as opposed to describing "the legends, types of central Bohemian dances, children's folklore … which … are not specific to the Kladno region" ("pověry, typy středočeských tanců, dětský folklor … které … nejsou pro Kladensko typické").[9] The exploration of the general culture of the working class was, according to Karbusický, crucial for understanding the character of the entire nation, would be received positively by the public, and was innovative in the international context of ethnographic research.[10]

Although the collected materials contained a varied mixture of genres from different backgrounds, including contemporaneous urban popular music, the published material featured only three types of musical culture. Irena Janáčková's chapter focused on traditional village folklore, related to the content of earlier collections;[11] Bohumír Nušl's chapter discussed workers' wind bands and their repertoire;[12] and Karbusický wrote both a theoretical discussion about folk music in the Kladno region and a disquisition about what he viewed as workers' songs, that is, songs that were connected to the political aspects of the workers' movement, including songs about strikes and strikebreakers, mining disasters, social injustice, and songs against mine owners.[13] Karbusický ignored songs reflecting everyday realities of the communities under scrutiny, including humorous and erotic songs, many of which are preserved in the collected materials.[14] Thus, the Kladno project resembled modern ethnomusicological procedures and methods in that it focused on details from the lives of the informants and varied musical activities, but the final presentation of the research was strongly distorted by the ideological need to present workers and miners as a specific political force.

[9] Vladimír Karbusický, "Nové cesty naší folkloristiky," *Česká literatura* 8 (1960): 165.
[10] Karbusický, "Nové cesty naší folkloristiky," 165.
[11] Irena Janáčková, "Lidová tradice a umělá tvorba v kladenské písni," in Olga Skalníková, ed., *Kladensko. Život a kultura lidu průmyslové oblasti* (Prague: Československá akademie věd, 1959), 487–583.
[12] Bohumír Nušl, "Hornické hudby na Kladensku", in Skalníková, *Kladensko*, 447–86.
[13] Vladimír Karbusický, "Dělnické písně na Kladensku", in Skalníková, *Kladensko*, 283–446.
[14] The complete collected material is preserved in Prague, Archiv Etnologického ústavu Akademie věd České republiky. See Matěj Kratochvíl, *Vy havíři umouněný, co vy z toho máte … Výzkum hornických písní na Kladensku v letech 1953–1959 v kontextu dobové vědy a politiky* (Prague: Etnologický ústav AVČR, 2022).

From Field to Stage

Folk music in the forms recorded by nineteenth-century collectors nearly disappeared in the twentieth century. This process occurred gradually and can be understood as part of society's natural transformation, though some researchers viewed it as a sign of decay. Biologist and ethnographer Vladimír Úlehla associated these changes with the "ugly tonics and dominants" ("hnusná tónika a dominanta") that were produced by a combination of the blare of brass bands and the tones of the accordion that soldiers often brought home from service. These "ugly" sounds overpowered old tonalities, peculiar wind harmonies, the violins, and the clarinets, which peasants had used previously, and thus "impoverished" ("ochudily") folk rituals and customs such as harvest festivals and weddings, depriving them of "the most beautiful decoration" ("nejkrásnější ozdoba").[15] Instead of old songs, Úlehla continued, village taverns were filled with "suburban trash" ("předměstské odpadky"), and Sunday dances were dominated by "popular hits" ("šlágry").

Parallel to the disappearance of old forms was the emergence of "the second existence of folk culture" or "a folk culture revival." The roots of this phenomenon can be found in the nineteenth century, when folksongs and dances were sometimes transferred from their original environment to the stage, wherein they were presented to an audience as reified artifacts. An example of this process is the National Ethnographic Exhibition, which took place in Prague in 1895 and featured performances of singers, musicians, and dancers from different regions of Bohemia and Moravia. One year after this event, people from the region of Moravian Slovakia living in Prague established the Moravian Slovakia Association. Similar associations were founded in other cities with people who migrated from the countryside for work or education. The goal of these associations was to preserve the culture of individual regions and allow the migrants to keep in touch with their compatriots. These associations represented a fertile ground for the later folkloric movement, that is, the system of ensembles, festivals, and other institutions focused on staged presentations of folk music and dance in arranged and choreographed forms.

After World War II, and particularly after the communist takeover, folkloric ensembles appeared all over Czechoslovakia. They operated as leisure-time activities for children and adults and reflected the communist view of the people's culture as the basis for the new socialist society. The communist view was presented in numerous articles in the press and was

---

[15] Vladimír Úlehla, *Živá píseň* (Prague: František Borový, 1949), 176.

the subject of discussions among the Communist Party officials and state institutions. For example, the minutes from a 1960 meeting of the Central Advisory Committee for Folk Dance (Ústřední poradní sbor lidového tance) claims, in a convoluted style typical for communist newspeak, that the Communist Party supports folk-art creativity and amateur artistic endeavors in various forms because they represent "one of the means that enriches the satiation of people's needs, the enrichment and beautification of their lives, the improvement of their personalities and communist moral values."[16]

The post-war boom of amateur folklore collectives was complemented by the establishment of professional ensembles. In 1947, the Czechoslovak State Company of Songs and Dances (Československý soubor písní a tanců) was created to promote folk traditions on local and international stages. In 1952, the Brno branch of the Czechoslovak radio sponsored the establishment of the Brno Orchestra of Folk Instruments (Brněnský orchestr lidových nástrojů). These ensembles presented folk music as it was preserved in nineteenth- and twentieth-century collections, but their performances were highly stylized, and the musicians were increasingly professionalized.

Besides reviving musical folklore of the past, the early communist period also witnessed attempts at the creation of folklore that would reflect the new age. This new repertoire was supposed to reflect what people sang in the countryside, which was quickly changing due to collectivization and the attendant violent confiscation of land. The less savory aspects of the new village life were naturally absent from the new repertoire. Instead, the texts celebrated the use of modern agricultural technologies and the fact that the land no longer belonged to the "lords" but to "the people." In the 1950s, a new wave of songwriters came of age; one of the most productive songwriters, of both texts and melodies, was Anežka Gorlová from Boršice in Moravia. Gorlová's work is filled with optimism, which reflects both communist propaganda and genuine enthusiasm about the improvement in the quality of life after the war. In the song *Teprú sa slunéčko* ("The sun has just begun [to rise]"), for example, Gorlová sings: "A nice day awaits us, my love, we will go to the field with two harvesting machines, hey" ("Čeká nás má milá velice pěkný den, dvůma vazačkama do žita pojedem, ej").[17] The inspiration for the lyrics, however, did not come only from communist ideology: Gorlová's older brother left for the

---

[16] Prague, Národní archiv České republiky, fond ÚKVČ, karton 42, "Oblastní výběrové přehlídky; Schůze Ústředního poradního sboru lidového tance 1957–1960; Ze zasedání ÚPS dne 5. 12. 1960 v Domě strojírenství."

[17] Anežka Gorlová, *Nech sa dobre darí* (Prague: Osvěta, 1951), 28.

United States before the war, became a farmer, and informed the song-writer how helpful harvesting machines could be in the field.

Zítra se bude tančit všude as an Illustration of the Uses of Folklore

Following World War II, film became an important instrument of propaganda, and the communist regime therefore subjected the film industry to strict control. The doctrine of socialist realism both made folk culture the main source of inspiration and demanded that it be depicted in films. The 1952 film *Zítra se bude tančit všude* ("Tomorrow, People Will Be Dancing Everywhere") is both an epic film featuring many rising stars and a model example of film propaganda in the time of early socialism. Director Vladimír Vlček wrote the script together with Božena Šochová, a member of the Josef Vycpálek Ensemble of Folksongs and Dances (Soubor lidových písní a tanců Josefa Vycpálka) and political supervisor in the Czechoslovak Youth Union (Československý svaz mládeže). Vlček together with Pavel Kohout, a writer and later also a dissident, based the film script on Šochová's diary. The film focuses on the story of one Prague company and reflects contemporaneous thought about the activities of these ensembles. The company is initially focused mainly on "correct" matching of music and dance, which the film presents as an unacceptable, formalist approach. In the next part of the film, the company departs for the field, illustrated by picturesque images of Moravian Wallachia, where they recognize the "authentic" forms of regional folksongs and dances. The film-makers used real amateur dancers and singers from Wallachia to appear as local villagers. The film also presents staged performances, most prominently one at the 1951 World Festival of Youth and Students in Berlin, where the company performs a choreography that goes beyond mere correct phrasing of rhythmic figures and dance steps, one which becomes a demonstration of collective energy, and projects an ideological message. The local materials collected in the countryside become part of an eclectic mix, and the performance's main idea is that local traditions should serve as inspiration but need to be synthesized into a new, universal idiom. This idea is also represented visually in that the performance makes use of a variety of folk costumes from various regions of Bohemia and Moravia together with modern civil and work clothes. The music is a collage of melodies of different origins (folksongs are mixed with new works, including non-folkloric material), unified by the orchestral accompaniment. The title song (text Pavel Kohout, music Ludvík Podéšť), for example, is in the style of so-called "mass songs," that is, songs expressing optimism about the building of a new communist society. The Vycpálek Company, founded in 1947, contributed to the film significantly. The company's founder František Bonuš collaborated with the film-makers as dancer and choreographer. The final scene was created by dancer and choreographer Alena Skálová in the form of a folk carnival, in which traditional masks are complemented by activist youth, a tractor driver, and a wealthy fop (a symbol of the youth corrupted by Western lifestyles) and his father, a village landowner. The tractor driver and the young communists chase the fop and the landowner away from the carnival, but the two return, hidden behind a traditional death mask, symbolizing the atomic bomb. Once recognized, the father and son are denounced as "obstinate enemies of the peace and the happiness of the village" ("zavilí nepřátelé míru a štěstí vesnice") and are expelled permanently. Although the film is filled with propaganda and eclecticism, it also features some accurate presentations of the Vycpálek Company's repertoire.

"Weight of the Folklore"

In the first half of the 1950s, folk music played a key role in the communist state's culture and was supposed to become the main inspiration for classical music and mass songs. Folk music became prominent in radio programming and in the output of state-controlled recording companies. Gradually, this approach became unsustainable, as illustrated in the short text "Tíha folkloru" ("Weight of the Folklore") by Slovak writer Vladimír Mináč, published in *Literární noviny* ("The Literary Journal") in 1958. In the text, he criticized the overuse of folklore and the generally accepted view that folklore "is progressive, progressive everywhere and forever" ("je pokrokové, pokrokové vždy a všude"); claimed that "among many other stupidities of recent years, we mistreated folk art" ("kromě mnohých jiných hloupostí v minulých letech naložili jsme špatně i s lidovým uměním"); and that "our literature and art want to be liberated from the unbearably pleasant burden of folklore" ("naše literatura a umění se chtějí osvobodit od nesnesitelně příjemné tíhy folklóru").[18] Mináč's text summarized the sentiments of many and contributed to discussions about reforming the

---

[18] Vladimír Mináč, "Tíha folkloru," *Literární noviny. Týdeník pro kulturně politické a umělecké otázky* 7, no. 12 (March 22, 1958): 1.

approaches to folk culture. In reaction to Mináč's article, for example, Josef Raban wrote in the same journal:[19]

Instead of a true folk culture that would organically infuse and enrich our lives, we cultivate folklore as an empty mask, a clown's act, a superficial and denigrating show for sentimental townies, who try to cover their pettiness with ideological phrases about the national and the folkish.

Místo opravdové lidové kultury organicky prostupující a obohacující život pěstujeme pouhý folklor jako prázdnou masku, šaškovské gesto, povrchní a ponižující podívanou pro sentimentálního měšťáka, zastírajícího svou malost idealistickými frázemi o národním a lidovém.

With the easing of restrictions following the deaths of Stalin and the first Czechoslovak communist president Klement Gottwald in 1953, more varied approaches to culture became possible including those affected by Western popular music, and as a result folk music started to lose its prominence. The network of folkloric ensembles did not disappear, however, and continued to operate as a state-controlled and supported portion of artistic representation and leisurely activities.

The decreasing social and political prominence of folklore made it possible for new, artistically more adventurous people to become involved with the folk ensembles and shift focus from propagandistic optimism to either more substantial reconstructions of original forms of folk music and dance or more original theatrical stylizations. Among the most prominent was composer and dramatist Emil František Burian, who incorporated elements of folklore into avant-garde theatrical productions as early as the 1930s, such as in his 1935 show *Vojna*, which used song texts from Erben's collections and choral recitations called "voiceband." Post-war revivals of *Vojna* inspired the search for alternatives to socialist realist approaches to folklore.

The more adventurous solutions are exemplified in the activities of the ensemble Chorea Bohemica, founded in 1967 by choreographer Alena Skálová and composer Jaroslav Krček. Their productions engaged previously banned themes, such as religion. The music reflects Krček's compositional training and his interest in unusual instrumental combinations, such as the inclusion of the *niněra* (hurdy-gurdy) and various percussion instruments.

Throughout the entire communist period, however, the activities of the folklore movement were, at least officially, always in line with the

---

[19] Josef Raban, "Skoncujme s diletantismem," *Literární noviny. Týdeník pro kulturně politické a umělecké otázky* 7, no. 17 (April 26, 1958): 9.

Communist Party's politics and remained intensely propagandistic. Even in the 1960s, folklore ensembles continued to participate in various communist celebrations, although the content of the performance had little in common with the subjects of these festivities.

Folklore ensembles also became communities in which members and their children spent free time and found life partners. Besides official stylized performances, ensemble members met informally in pubs, private homes, and at weddings. In 2017–19, the Ethnological Institute of the Czech Academy of Sciences conducted interviews with several generations of ensemble members as part of the project "The Heaviness and Weightlessness of Folklore: Folklore Movement in the Czech Lands in the Second Half of the Twentieth Century" ("Tíha a beztíže folkloru: Folklorní hnutí druhé poloviny 20. století v českých zemích"). The interviews, led by Daniela Světlová, showed that folkloric activities became a significant component of the members' lives and a form of escape from the gray reality of their restricted existence under communism, particularly during the so-called normalization period in the early 1970s. The opportunity to spend time with a community of like-minded individuals and be creatively engaged while also keeping in touch with local traditions was highly motivational for thousands of people.[20]

The state continued to control folk music and used it as an export material for presentations abroad, which made it more attractive for potential participants who otherwise could not travel freely, particularly to the West. The folklore movement was therefore under the constant supervision of state police and its informants, which created an environment of fear and suspicion. The possibility that some ensemble members could report to state authorities about private views of others undermined the sense of security and sociability.

Folklore in a Crossroads of Influences

In the late twentieth century, social functions of folk music continued to transform. In the 1960s, a network of People's Art Schools (Lidové školy umění), later called Basic Art Schools (Základní umělecké školy), was created and served generations of children. The schools taught basic

---

[20] See Daniela Světlová and Theresa Jill Buckland, eds., *Folklore Revival Movements in Europe post 1950: Shifting Contexts and Perspectives* (Prague: Ethnology Institute, Czech Academy of Sciences, 2018).

performance skills and the foundations of the European classical music theory. Children trained in these schools who also participated in folk-music ensembles had a different set of skills from earlier practitioners of folk music. Instead of oral transmission of the folk repertoire, they relied on notation. As a result, folk ensembles used larger instrumentation and more complicated arrangements.

The radio, which was under the complete control of the state until 1989, played an important role in the transformation of musical folklore and represented a key channel for the dissemination of recordings and therefore also the knowledge of regional styles and repertoire. The radio also shaped the styles of folk music. Various studios sponsored ensembles, such as the Brno Orchestra of Folk Instruments and the dulcimer band Technik, which was associated with the Ostrava studio. Prominent folk-music specialists were linked to these radio ensembles. Folklorist, educator, composer, and folk-music collector Albert Pek worked for the Prague studio before World War II and designed a new thematic program that combined music with the spoken word (the format has been used up to the present day). Other prominent people associated with the radio include Vladimír Klusák, collector, arranger, and impresario of a dulcimer band; Jaromír Nečas, musicologist; and Zdeněk Bláha, bagpiper, composer, and conductor who was associated with the Plzeň radio and contributed to the construction of the conventions of how folksongs from Bohemia are expected to sound. Bláha was also the head of the Plzeň Folk Ensemble, which included members of the radio symphony orchestra. Professional composers Zdeněk Lukáš and Jaroslav Krček also collaborated with the Plzeň Folk Ensemble, and produced recordings of high technical quality and professionalism that were aired on the radio and thus influenced several generations of amateur musicians. Although the ensemble's repertoire was based on folksongs from historical collections, the performing styles, harmonization, and arrangements pushed this music closer to classical idioms. Because of the widespread media coverage, however, many listeners got accustomed to the style, and it in turn came to be considered folk-like.

Folk music not only absorbed elements of classical music but also influenced other genres. Whereas classical composers drew inspiration from folk music in the early twentieth century, such as Leoš Janáček and Vítězslav Novák, popular musicians turned to this musical style in the century's second half. In the 1960s, folklore was no longer strongly associated with propaganda, and younger artists became interested in it. Among the first were Ostrava's Bukanýři (Buccaneers), who combined rock rhythms with jazz elements and melodies from Moravian and Slovak songs. Whereas in their first single, containing two songs and released by Supraphon in 1970, Bukanýři accompanied the vocals with the guitar, violin, and flute, in the 1974 album *Bukanýři*, folksongs featured jazzy rhythms and a vibraphone accompaniment by Karel Velebný. One of the most influential achievements was the 1974 album *Nikola Šuhaj loupežník* ("Nikola Šuhaj the Robber" – released by Panton), with songs by Petr Ulrych inspired by a famous book by Czech writer Ivan Olbracht. The album was recorded by Hana and Petr Ulrych, who had been considered mostly rock musicians until then, accompanied by Gustav Brom's orchestra and a section of the Brno Orchestra of Folk Instruments with the impresario Jindřich Hovorka. Folk elements also entered the singer-songwriter community, where they crosspollinated with American artists, such as music by Bob Dylan. An early example is Vladimír Merta's album *Ballades de Prague*, recorded in Paris in 1968, which contained both original music and four folksongs. In 1975, singer-songwriter Jaroslav Hutka included recordings of several ballades from František Sušil's nineteenth-century folksong collection in his album *Stůj, břízo zelená* ("Stop, Green Birch Tree"). Hutka therefore introduced nineteenth-century folk music to listeners who had considered the genre politically suspect kitsch until then. Folk influences gradually appear in the output of mainstream pop stars, such as Karel Gott and Waldemar Matuška; jazz musicians, such as Emil Viklický and Jiří Stivín; and occasionally rock bands. In the late twentieth century, the band Čechomor gained mass attention with arrangements of folksongs using electric guitars and rock drums.

Until the fall of communism, it seemed that folk music would become a marginal brand, interesting mainly to older generations and specialists. However, folk music managed to adapt and continues to gain varied audiences in the twenty-first century. In the present, folk music can be heard in such diverse venues as restaurants, where it is presented for foreign tourists, and informal parties, where it operates in modes similar to those that characterized folk musicianship before it became a collectible, archival ware.

25 | Romani Music in the Czech Republic

ZUZANA JURKOVÁ

Romani people are the largest ethnic minority in the Czech Republic, making up about 2.4 percent of the population. Romani presence in the Bohemian crownlands is first documented in the fourteenth and fifteenth centuries,[1] though most of these Roma were murdered during World War II.[2] Present-day Czech Roma came from Slovakia after World War II and belong to the Servika Romani group. They traditionally worked as blacksmiths and performed music for the majority population for centuries. That is why music is so important in present-day Czech Romani culture and represents one of the few aspects of this culture that is appreciated by the majority population. Approximately a quarter of the Roma in the Czech Republic come from the Vlach Roma group, which practiced an itinerant lifestyle until it was prohibited by law in 1959. The itinerant lifestyle prevented professional musicianship, and the music of this group will be discussed only briefly in the following essay.

Sources

Although Romani (or "Gypsy") music was a source of fascination for the majority population for a long time, studies and collections of this music appear relatively late. In 1916, music folklorist Jožka Černík published *Cikánské písničky* ("Gypsy Songs"), a short collection of Romani songs from Moravia, some of which were published with new texts derived from the folksongs of the majority population.[3] The first sound recordings of Romani music performances were made in the 1950s by Eva Davidová (1932–2018), who later (in 1991) cofounded the Museum of Romani Culture. In the 1960s, Milena Hübschmannová (1933–2005), the founder

---

This chapter was translated from Czech to English by Martin Nedbal.

[1] Ctibor Nečas, *Špalíček romských miniature* (Brno: Centrum pro stadium demokracie a kultury 2008), 7.

[2] See Jana Horváthová, ed., *. . .to jsou těžké vzpomínky* (Brno: Větrné mlýny, 2021); for musical aspects, see Dušan Holý and Ctibor Nečas, *Žalující píseň* (Strážnice: Ústav lidové kultury, 1993).

[3] Jožka Černík, "Cikánské písničky," *Hudební revue* 9, no. 5 (February 1916): 162–69.

of Czech Romani studies, started collecting Romani music systematically.[4] Others followed (including the author of this chapter), and the field recordings were later used for various publications – songbooks, popular LPs, and scholarly studies.[5]

These materials illustrate the rich musical culture of the Roma in the Czech lands after World War II. Some genres of Romani musical folklore clearly originated in prewar Romani culture in Slovakia. These include csardas dances and slow songs with Romani texts, called *halgató* in Hungarian, *čorikane giľa* ("songs of misery") in Romanes.[6] These genres temporarily disappeared with the deaths of the female singers who had learned them in Slovakia and reappeared only in recent decades. Other important aspects of Romani musical culture, reflected in the canonic collections of Davidová and Hübschmannová, are genre crosspollination, absorption and transformation of new influences, and recontextualization of older elements.

Romani Music at the Beginning of the Twenty-First Century

In 2008, I mapped out the ideas Praguers associated with the term "Gypsy / Romani" music.[7] These included live music events, concerts, open-air events, restaurant music, and commercial recordings. I used Kay Kaufman Shelemay's concept of soundscapes, which I briefly defined as "worlds of people who listen to certain types of music," to organize the collected materials into four aurally and conceptually distinct groups,

---

[4] Most of Davidová's and Hübschmannová's recordings are today in the Vienna Phonogrammarchiv, together with the collection of recordings of Romani folklore by Mozes Heinschink.

[5] For songbooks, see, for example, Ivan Havlů and Harry Macourek, *Aven Roma* (Prague: Panton, 1985); Eva Davidová and Jan Žižka, *Folk Music of the Sedentary Gypsies of Czechoslovakia* (Budapest: Institute for Musicology of the Hungarian Academy of Sciences, 1991); for LPs, see Eva Davidová and Jaromír Gelnar, *Romane giľa. Antologie cikánského písňového folklóru* (Prague: Supraphon, 1971).

[6] See, for example, Jana Belišová, *Phurikane giľa, starodávne rómske piesne* (Bratislava: Žudro, 2002); Zuzana Jurková, "Archetypální zpěvačka," *Romano Džaniben* 1998, nos. 1–2: 19–28; Zusana Jurková, "Co víme a nevíme o hudbě 'našich' Romů," *Romano Džaniben* 2003, no. 2: 96–114. Most Roma in the Czech Republic speak the north-central dialect of Romanes, and the transcriptions of Romani words and phrases in this text therefore follow orthographic rules approved by the Gypsy-Romani Union in the 1970s. See Milena Hübschmannová, Hana Šebková, and Edita Žigová, *Romsko-český and česko-romský slovník* (Prague: Fortuna, 1988).

[7] Zuzana Jurková, "Myth of Romani Music in Prague," *Lidé města / Urban People* 11 (2009): 351–77.

defined by the relationship between performers and listeners.[8] The first group, for *gadje* (that is, non-Romani people) about Roma, is exemplified by composers such as Antonín Dvořák, who in his *Cikánské písně* ("Gypsy Songs") communicates his views of the Roma with the means of classical music; the second, Roma for *gadje*, originated with professional Romani musicians playing for non-Romani listeners in coffee shops and restaurants; the third, Roma (not only) for themselves, is represented by *rompop*; and the fourth, Romani hip hop, was at that time exemplified by the popular formation Gypsy.cz and its frontman Radek Banga.

The situation in Prague has changed in the last decade: in the 2010s, the old *halgató* songs reappeared as symbols of ethnic identity, although in the previous decades they had been presented only by the oldest generations and a few enthusiasts.[9] The re-emergence of these songs illustrates Aleida Assmann's concept of a link between "cultural reference memory: the archive" (which resonates with the attempts by Romani studies scholars to record and preserve the older generations' performances of *halgató* songs) and "cultural working memory: the canon" (which parallels present-day Romani activists' attempts to connect the songs to Romani identity).[10] Romani hip hop has recently transformed from the more decorous style of Banga into a less polished and more socially critical idiom. *Rompop* remains the most popular Romani style. Both as recorded and actively performed music, *rompop* has the classical function of *bashaviben* ("music-making"), played and sung for the entertainment of Romani audiences, accompanying social gatherings, often connected to dance.[11] At the same time, out of all the genres associated with the Roma / Gypsies, *rompop* is the most popular among non-Romani audiences.

The following pages use recordings, interviews, and other primary materials to outline the development of *rompop* from the 1970s on, to define its characteristic features, and to explore the meanings it carries for the Czech Republic's Roma. By focusing on this unique and distinct style,

[8] Kay Kaufman Shelemay, *Soundscapes: Exploring Music in a Changing World* (New York: Norton, 2006), XXXV; Jurková, "Co víme a nevíme o hudbě 'našich' Romů," 8; Jurková, "Myth of Romani Music in Prague."

[9] Zuzana Jurková, "Romani Musical Remembering," in Zuzana Jurková and Veronika Seidlová, eds., *Music – Memory – Minorities. Between Archive and Activism* (Prague: Karolinum, 2020), 138–59.

[10] Aleida Assmann, "Canon and Archive," in Astrid Erll and Ansgar Nünning, eds., *A Companion to Cultural Memory Studies* (Berlin: De Gruyter, 2010), 97–109.

[11] Zuzana Jurková, "The Czech Rompop Scene: (Un?)surprising Continuity," in Rosemary Statelova et al., eds., *The Human World and Musical Diversity* (Sofia: Bulgarian Musicology Studies, 2008), 77.

I do not want to create the impression that it is the only popular music style of the Romani community. One could also discuss the pop stars who are extremely popular with the Romani youth, such as singers Jan Bendig, Moika Bagárová, and Jan "Áčo" Slepčík (1954–2008), the once extremely popular Brno funk group Gulo čar, and the stylistically diverse musicians of the Fečo family.[12]

The Origins of *Rompop*

As far as I am aware, the term *rompop* (originally *Rom-pop*) first appeared in the 1985 songbook *Kali zpívá* ("Kali Sings") by singer Věra Bílá and in the title of the first album that Bílá recorded with the group Kale (The Blacks) from 1995. According to Jan Dužda, frontman of the band Le čhavendar and the son of Kale's guitarist, the album's title was suggested by Zuzana Navarová (1959–2004), accomplished folk singer and composer who discovered several prominent musicians, including Bílá.[13] I use this term to refer to the style of Czech Romani groups, which relies on a common musical language, texts, and social references. Besides Bílá and Kale, the style has also been practiced by the groups Točkolotoč, Terne čhave, Bengas, and most recently Le čhavendar. Most of these groups have at some point been well known among the Roma and had non-Romani fans.

The development of *rompop* prior to the fall of communism in 1989 is not well known. One reason is that the regime pursued assimilation policies that aimed at erasing the cultural voices of ethnic minorities, and the Roma were therefore mostly ignored in public discourse. Matěj Kratochvíl's study about the ethnographic research project of the Czechoslovak Academy of Sciences in the Kladno region of central Bohemia in the 1950s illustrates this persuasively (see also Chapter 24): although the region was inhabited by a large Romani community, the community was completely ignored in the collected materials.[14] The situation changed briefly in response to the Prague Spring liberalization in the late 1960s and early 1970s, when the

---

[12] On Gulo čar, see Zuzana Jurková, *Romští hudebníci v 21. století. Rozhovory s Olgou Fečovou, Josefem Fečem, Pavlem Dirdou a Janem Duždou. / Romani Musicians in the 21st Century. Interviews with Olga Fečová, Josef Fečo, Pavel Dirda and Jan Dužda* (Prague: FHS, 2018); for the Fečo family, see Olga Fečová, "Muzeum Olgy Fečové: Rodinné hudební světy romského primáše," https://muzeumolgyfecove.cz, accessed March 21, 2024.

[13] Interview with Jan Dužda, November 13, 2017.

[14] Matěj Kratochvíl, "Presence and Absence of Minorities in Folk Music Research Projects in the 20th Century Czech Lands," in *Music – Memory – Minorities*, 36–48.

existence of the Romani-Gypsy Union (Svaz Cikánů-Romů) was briefly allowed. This liberalization also produced the 1971 film *Rom zpívá, hraje, tančí* ("A Rom Sings, Plays, Dances"), produced by Czechoslovak Television.[15] Besides the stereotypical dulcimer bands with csardas and *halgató* songs, the film also showed young bands that played in styles of current pop music but with Romani texts. The lead singers of these bands (Anička Fečová from Roma štar and Květa Halušková from Terne čhave) clearly emulated pop stars of the majority in their facial expressions, movements, and modulations of voice.[16] Another reason for the relative obscurity of *rompop*'s origins is paradoxically the work of Romani studies researchers, such as Davidová and Hübschmannová, who tried to resist the assimilation pressure by recording music and taking photographs focused mainly on what they viewed as "old" genres.[17] In the extensive, and largely uncatalogued, recording collection of Hübschmannová, however, there are some 1980s *rompop* recordings from the west Bohemian town of Rokycany, which became one of the centers of the emerging *rompop* style.

Rokycany is also where a 1978 video was made of the twenty-four-year-old Bílá performing one of her later hits – *O poštaris avel* ("A Mailman Is Coming") – with guitar accompaniment by Emil "Bišu" Miko, a future member of Kale.[18] Although the recording was made nine years before Bílá was discovered by Navarová at a concert for a non-Roma audience in Prague's Lucerna Hall and seventeen years before she released her first album, the singer showcases all the qualities that later made her a world-famous star of *rompop*.

The video features a surprising contradiction between the lyrics and the performance style. The text has *halgató* characteristics: "O poštaris avel, / Telegramos anel. / Nič ma nane ča kada gat / Ča gada gat so pre mange, / Paš mire čhavore" ("The mailman comes, / Bringing a telegram. / I am wearing but a shirt, / The shirt I am wearing / Because of my children"). There is nothing cheerful about the lyrics: the text depicts a woman who lives in poverty (as suggested by the line that she is wearing only a shirt) with her children, which implies that she has been abandoned by her husband or lover; in *čorikane giľa* texts, furthermore, telegrams usually

[15] *Rom zpívá, hraje, tančí*, dir. Jiří Hanibal (Brno: Czechoslovak Television, 1971).

[16] The film received renewed attention in 2013, when it was shown in Prague and Brno in connection to a discussion with the original protagonists.

[17] See Eva Davidová and Jaromír Gelnar, "Tradiční i současný romský (cikánský) písňový folklór," *Český lid* 1989, no. 1: 39–46; and Jurková, "Co víme a nevíme o hudbě 'našich' Romů."

[18] "Věra Bílá – O poštaris avel (1978) + Mamo, dado (1998)," www.youtube.com/watch?v=s711VXltd1E, accessed March 21, 2024.

bring bad news. And yet, Bílá smiles, occasionally looks at the guitarist, slightly rocks in rhythm, and, most importantly, sings without reservation, cheerfully, and full of temperament. Many European musical traditions use nuanced changes in dynamics and tempo to display emotion, but these are absent from Bílá's performance. Whereas the text hints at a tragic story, the musicians mainly express their excitement at performing the music. Some could understand this style as based on a separation between the meaning of the sung material and the musical performance, but as Jan "Jenda" Dužda, a member of the youngest *rompop* generation, explains, the meaning is "inside" ("uvnitř" – see the interview below); inside the voice, inside the music; all the other means of interpretation are useless; those with enculturated ears can hear it clearly.

The First Lady of *Rompop*

Bílá was born in 1954 to a family of a famous band leader who moved with two or three other Romani families of musicians from Slovakia to Rokycany after World War II.[19] The family spoke Romanes, did not receive formal music education, and could not read music. The father was illiterate, yet Bílá, together with her father and siblings, composed music and could play several instruments. Bílá showed an aptitude for music, and her father often took her to his performances at weddings and other celebrations, where she became familiar with Romani repertoire and performance style.[20] She was also attracted to popular music, and because Rokycany was full of Romani musicians, it was not difficult to put together ad hoc bands. After graduating from elementary school, Bílá took care of her siblings and an adopted son. In the 1970s, she performed in two films directed by Dušan Hanák, member of so-called Czech new-wave cinema. These films helped her become known, so that she started to appear on TV, which was then completely exceptional for Roma. Even today, Czech Roma are grateful to Bílá for promoting a positive image of their community. In 1995, Bílá released her first album (*Rom-pop*) with her new group Kale, consisting of Rokycany musicians. The second album – *Kale kalore* ("Black

[19] I base this biographical overview on the interview with Bílá, published in Marie Formáčková, *Věra Bílá: Nahoru a zase dolů* (Prague: Hidoval, 2011).

[20] Bílá can be heard singing with a dulcimer band in which her father plays an accompaniment part on the violin on a recording of unknown origin, which supposedly dates from 1978. See "Giňovci z Opavy a Věra Bílá rok. 1978," www.youtube.com/watch?v=9Qeh_ATzx_A, accessed April 19, 2023.

Blackish") – followed in 1998 and initiated her international career. Kale was represented by the France-based manager Jiří Smetana, who negotiated a contract with BMG, which published and distributed the albums *Rovava* (2001) and *C'est comme ça* (2005). Bílá gave concerts in all continents and became the only Czech musician to ever sell out the Hollywood Bowl.

Even at the time of her greatest success, Bílá was rumored to have a gambling addiction and stopped paying her rent, a common problem of Czech Roma. In 2005, Bílá canceled fifteen concerts abroad, including one in Carnegie Hall, and moved to Slovakia, where she sang with local musicians in clubs and pubs. She soon returned to Rokycany, formed a family band, occasionally performed, and released two CDs, but her international career was finished. Although her voice was affected by her unhealthy lifestyle, she still received huge applause at the 2015 Khamoro Roma Festival. After her unexpected death in 2019, Bílá was honored by many Romani musicians and a predominantly Romani audience at a remembrance concert. As Timothy Rice put it, she was "the iconic performer . . . who was shaped by the society . . . that she in turn reshaped in innovative ways."[21]

The Formation of *Rompop*

Bílá, and later her group Kale, often crossed genre boundaries, which was typical for *rompop* in general. Stylistic diversity and crosspollination were characteristic of the Rokycany Romani music scene in the late 1980s. At the time of Kale's formation, several fascinating music groups were active in Rokycany: the dulcimer band of Bílá's father Karol Giňa; the older women choir Amare neni (Our Aunts), focused on performing the *halgató*;[22] the band Rytmus 84, specializing in well-known older Romani songs in updated arrangements for saxophones, guitars, and percussion;[23] and the group Čercheň (Star), which performed "traditional" Romani songs for a children's dance group of the same name and original repertoire, often filled with social criticism, such as songs with texts against language assimilation and songs commemorating the Roma Holocaust.[24] Many of

[21] Timothy Rice, *Modeling Ethnomusicology* (New York: Oxford University Press, 2016), 216.

[22] Some of their repertoire was transcribed in Milena Hübschmannová and Zuzana Jurková, *Romane giľa. Zpěvník romských písní* (Prague: Fortuna, 1999), 42–51.

[23] See video of a performance by Rytmus 84, "Zábava Rokycany," www.youtube.com/watch?v=SRTkRWcjq6M, accessed May 9, 2023.

[24] See Hübschmannová and Jurková, *Romane giľa*, 52–55.

these groups collaborated with Emil Miko and Jan Dužda, the founding members of Kale.

Bass player and bass guitarist Miko reminisces about how the musical styles that influenced him reflect the stylistic variety that gave rise to *rompop*. Miko points to The Beatles; Stevie Wonder, who was enormously popular among Romani musicians; the Gipsy Kings, whose thick guitar accompaniment and parallel polyphonic singing became the basis of Czech *rompop*; and Točkolotoč, another Romani band from a small Czech town (east Bohemian Svitavy).

Točkolotoč formed around the Pešta family and became famous after appearing at the open-air music festival Porta in Plzeň in 1985. Točkolotoč released their first album, *Čhave Svitavendar* ("The Boys from Svitavy"), in 1989 – it was this album that Miko considered particularly influential. Apart from two later albums, 1990's *Kakle bala, kale jakha* ("Black Hair, Black Eyes") and 2005's *So has oda has* ("Let Bygones Be Bygones"), the group also became renowned thanks to its appearance at the 1990 mega-concert SOS Against Racism, featuring performers such as Paul Simon, and as the warm-up band at R.E.M.'s first concert in the Czech Republic in 1995. Recently, Točkolotoč has been performing irregularly, which is quite common for Roma bands – for most Romani musicians, music is not the main source of income, and they perform only when their principal employment allows it. At the same time, the relative success of Točkolotoč has been an inspiration for many young Romani musicians, who struggle with constant rejection by the majority. Another band from eastern Bohemia, Terne čhave (Young Boys), has repeatedly professed their admiration for and indebtedness to Točkolotoč.[25]

Terne čhave is one of the most active Romani bands in the Czech Republic today, and its development also reflects the stylistic diversity typical for *rompop*. In their first album, 2004's *Kaj džas* ("Where Are You Going"), Romani musicians, guitarists, and percussionist were accompanied by a non-Romani violinist; in later albums – 2015's *Bo Me Som Rom* ("As I'm A Rom") and 2018's *Balvaj* ("The Wind") – the violinist was replaced by non-Romani wind and accordion players. The style of the group is sometimes reminiscent of funk, sometimes of swing, and the musicians themselves have called it "Rom'n'Roll."[26]

[25] This group is not identical with the one that appeared in the 1971 film *Rom zpívá, hraje, tančí* discussed above.
[26] See the official website of the band: www.ternechave.com/, accessed March 21, 2024.

Another popular *rompop* group is Bengas (The Devils) from Prague, which consists of musicians from the related families Horvát, Sivák, and Kurej. Bengas claim to be closely linked to the Gipsy Kings, whose 2004 Prague concert they opened. At the same time, Bengas view Kale as a major source of inspiration. Their two albums – 2003's *Dža* ("Come") and 2005's *Amen Phiras* ("We Are Going") – and live performances combine original songs with songs by other Romani groups and songs that they refer to as traditional.

One of the younger groups of Czech *rompop* is Le čhavendar (From Boys), which also formed in the Rokycany Romani community, particularly from descendants of the Kale musicians. One of the group's founders, Jan "Jenda" Dužda, explains that the group started during meetings with his teenage friends in a railway underpass to practice part singing.[27] Some of the musicians associated with Le čhavendar are university educated and connected to various Romani and pro-Roma social and cultural organizations. As a result, the group's musical language is more sophisticated than that of the earlier groups.

Texts

The stylistic diversity of Rokycany musicians, who seamlessly switched from folklore to jazz to *rompop*, can also be seen in the song texts they used. The groups with Roma folklore and older popular songs in their repertory, particularly Bílá and Kale or Bengas, often appropriate phrases and themes from older songs. Thus, just as traditional songs of the *halgató* group, also referred to as *phurikane* ("ancient") and *čorikane* ("songs of adversity"), feature the phrase "Marel o Del, marel" ("God punishes, punishes") followed by a list of disasters (an unfaithful wife, a mother's death, hunger), in "Te kerel" ("What can we do") from the album *Rovava* ("I'm Gonna Cry"), Bílá sings: "Amare terne čhave / Pro forocis našťi džan. / . . . So čore jon kerena. / Našťi nikaj phiraha. / . . . Sar khere avenna, / Pre dajori, pro dadori rovena. / Imar na kamel / Bari bida. / Te kerel . . ." ("They won't let / Our little ones out. / . . . What are they supposed to do now. / When they can't go anywhere. / . . . When they come back home, / They have tears in their eyes. / Their parents tell them / Not to worry about it. / What can we do . . ."). Similarly, the songs of the *phurikane giľa* genre often present relationships between men and women as the main source of trouble (the

---

[27] Jurková, *Romští hudebníci v 21. století*, 103.

word "lubňi" ("bitch") is used frequently), and the Bengas, too, sing in their song "Romňori" ("My Wife") from the album *Dža*: "Romňori ma na kamel / Andro svetos me džava" ("My wife doesn't want me / I'll go to the world").

Rompop texts are not entirely depressing, however. In "Ma dara" ("Don't be afraid") from *Rom-pop*, Kale sing: "Ma dara, me avava, / Užar čhaje, / Me pal tute avava" ("Don´t be afraid, I´ll come, / Just wait, / I'll come to you") and "Nič vaš oda / Jak čoro som / . . . Dživaha, buťi keraha, / Le čhaven peske bararaha" ("It doesn´t matter / That I´m poor / . . . We´ll live, we´ll work, / We'll bring our kids up"). Točkolotoč offers even more optimistic lyrics. Women are no longer the source of suffering but appear in cheerful visions of the world: "Lačhi kedva te kerel, / Le čhajence me tekhelav, / Manca mri čhaj te bešel, / So mro jilo kamel" ("We know how to have fun, / We want to dance with girls, / Let my darling sit next to me, / The one I love with all my heart").

Many *rompop* songs, furthermore, express spontaneous feelings of happiness. In the song "Bachtale" ("Happy"), the youngest of the groups under discussion, Le čhevandar, sing: "Amen sam, sam bachtale / Hoj pes džanas rado pes dikhas" ("We are happy / That we know and like each other"). Similar emotion appears in the song "Šunen Roma" ("Listen, Roma") from *Kaj džas* by Terne čhave: "Kala svetos / But lačho hin, / Ča the kelel te bašavel, / Le romenge le čhajenge / Šukar giľa te bašavel" ("This world / Is so beautiful, / You can dance and sing here, / Give joy to the old and the young, / Sing nice songs"). Although *rompop* musicians think the world is beautiful, many of their songs claim that what makes it particularly beautiful is the ability to sing, play, and dance.

Understanding *Rompop*

Although it is possible to describe various aspects of *rompop*, I find it too presumptuous to attempt to understand what this musical style means for Romani performers and listeners. I can understand the discomfort of Spanish anthropologist Paloma Gay y Blasco, who has studied the experience of Romani women from the Spanish Gitanos group. Although she has spent a lot of time and formed close relationships with them, she was unable to share her observations and conclusions with the women because she was tied to a scholarly discourse that used expressions and theories that were hard to understand. She also thought it unacceptable that the women could not control how they were represented in the pages of academic publications. That is why she and her main informant Liria Hernández, who has become a close friend after a twenty-seven-year collaboration, made the decision to collaborate on anthropological texts: they write them together, avoid theories that are too sophisticated, and are jointly responsible for each formulation.[28]

Although I still write my texts myself, I believe it is necessary to allow my native informants to enter my studies and explain their musical practices in their own words.[29] As a result, I conclude with an interview with one of the protagonists of the above text, Jan "Jenda" Dužda, to offer a deeper introspective into *rompop*. Readers will find a lot of important themes in the interview: the complex linguistic situations in Romani families, the sensitivity (at least on Jenda's part) to certain expressions and to the evaluation of one's own language skills, and the functions that Jenda ascribes to the Romani language in *rompop*. These themes clarify the importance of *rompop*, at least for one young, but in many ways typical, performer.

Readers who would insist that I interpret the music-anthropological discourse presented should consider the words of British cultural theorist Stuart Hall: "Perhaps instead of thinking of identity as an already accomplished fact, which . . . cultural practices then represent, we should think . . . of identity as a 'production,' which is never complete, always in process, and always constituted within, not outside, representation."[30] Hall's ideas have been adapted for the study of musical performance by ethnomusicologist Thomas Solomon: ". . .anthropologists and ethnomusicologists have recognized that . . . interactive performances are also key sites where identities are actively negotiated. Performance thus becomes an arena for experimenting . . . with new identities in situations where the social relations at stake in identity formation are made the center of attention."[31] From this point of view, *rompop*, as the main performance style of Czech Roma, appears as a perfect tool for negotiating "productions" and "reproductions" of individual and group identities that they can be proud of.

---

[28] Liria Hernández and Pamela Gay y Blasco, "Životní zkušenosti romských žen: kolaborativní přístup k jejich studiu," *Romano Džaniben* 2018, no. 2: 39–46.

[29] Jurková, *Romští hudebníci v 21. století*.

[30] Stuart Hall, "Cultural Identity and Diaspora," in Jonathan Rutherford, ed., *Identity: Community, Culture, Difference* (London: Lawrence & Wishart, 1990), 222–37 (222).

[31] Thomas Solomon, "Performing Indigeneity: Poetics and Politics of Music Festivals in Highland Bolivia," in Donna A. Buchanan, ed., *Soundscapes from the Americas* (Farnham: Ashgate, 2014), 143–65 (144).

An Interview with Jan "Jenda" Dužda[32]

zj: We begin our conversation with my observation that Czech Roma write their texts in Romanes although they primarily speak Czech. In our last interview, I noted two significant points: first, that your parents spoke Romanes to each other but spoke Czech to you, and second, that you write music first and add text only later, as you pointed out at a workshop. At what age did you start writing?

jd: I wrote my first piece when I was thirteen.

zj: And how was your Romanes at that time?

jd: I could speak it then but used it little. In fact, I started [to speak it more] only when I started to perform. I simply had no choice; when I started to make music, I was thinking in that language.

zj: That is what puzzles me.

jd: We were always surrounded by it although we did not use it actively very often, [at least] not as much as our parents – and we perceived music as something in the [Romani] language.

zj: And did you ever speak Romanes to your older sisters?

jd: We go back and forth a lot. We say a sentence [in Romanes], then we switch to Czech, or simply use a few Czech words. But in most cases, we use Czech. In our family, it was more complicated, my father's side spoke only Romanes. Including to us. Our grandmother in particular spoke Romanes a lot. All of us understood her but responded in Czech because on my mother's side everyone tried to speak Czech a lot.

zj: To have it easier in life?

jd: Maybe. But today I think they were trying to be like the Czechs. It was really quite intense then, everyone spoke Romanes, even young people. Only our generation became afraid to speak the language [that is, Romanes]; they were either not secure in it, or they were trying to hide something. But it is interesting that when our generation met outside and switched from the then current pop music to Roma songs, various songs by Kale and later, when we started doing our own songs, we did not hesitate to switch to Romanes.

zj: And how do you approach composing, where do you begin?

jd: I talked to my father about it, and it is quite similar for us. He said: "Whenever I started composing, I already had a song in my head." He knew beforehand what he was going to play.

zj: But what did he know? The melody? The harmony?

jd: He knew the melody, the harmony, but he also knew what text would fit the melody, the harmony, and the mood they evoked. He knew what it would be about. And it is the same for me, but I hear the sound more than anything

---

[32] Recorded in Prague, November 13, 2017.

else – a harmony, a single chord is enough for me; I can start with that. When the music is finished, I think about what would fit with it, but it is mostly about intuition. Usually, it comes to me with the mood, the emotion that it invokes in me.

zj: And now you are no longer worried about incorrect declinations because you know you can speak it. But what about at the beginning?

jd: It was always the same – it is in the music. When I started to compose songs, I knew what they were going to be about and was not afraid although I could not yet speak it very well. I think that Romanes is important for us because we can use it to express ourselves at over one hundred percent. I miss that in Czech, I simply cannot use it in the same way. I think I cannot speak Czech well. I decline correctly, I don't have a problem with the accent and such, but we don't know all the Czech words and their exact meanings. Our vocabulary is limited in Czech, which limits my opportunities compared to Romanes. Although Romanes is not as widespread, thinking in it takes me further. It opens more doors for me.

zj: For example?

jd: For example: We have the word *paťiv*, which means "to respect, to revere" in Czech. But the Czech equivalents are insufficient from the Romani point of view.

zj: And *paťiv* means something else?

jd: *Paťiv* in itself means "respect," "reverence," but it is also a combination of values and moral behavior. "Respect" and "reverence" do not express its full meaning. When I say "paťivalo Rom" or "paťivali Romni," I understand it as referring to people who are respectful but also know how to behave in certain situations, know how to behave when someone comes to visit, know how to behave when something goes wrong, it is really an extensive collection of actions and behaviors. [Jenda provides other examples, some of which even the members of his band don't understand.] Or some old phrases that are not often used anymore and appear only in the *phurikane*.

zj: And you use them?

jd: I try to when I can. But I also try to find new paths. To start with what we know but to use what is no longer used very often although it is truly Romani. At the same time, because the Romani language is not evolving in many domains in which it should evolve, I try to, when possible, to create new phrases and achieve what I am after. . . . Earlier I did it intuitively, I had the need to represent Romani culture, especially the language, because that is the only thing that is left to us.

zj: So you tend to present it to other Roma?

jd: To everyone. I don't care that non-Roma don't understand it. I don't find the text inferior to the music, but the text and music are so interconnected, and the way you sing it should evoke the sentiment I am experiencing. The word becomes so emotionally charged in the sound, in singing, that it

Figure 25.1: Le čhavendar, Jenda Dužda in the middle. Photo by Zuzana Jurková.

should be clear, at least subconsciously. . . . I never know who will listen, but I tried to practice Romanes in a way that Roma realize what a great language it is and that it is a pity that fewer and fewer in the younger generations speak it. . . . Just as Roma should be visible everywhere in the present, in [a variety of] positions, the language should be heard everywhere. And the way to achieve this is through music, which is the main thing. I think it really is not about the language, the language is not important, it is about what an artist wants from himself, from the world, from the music. So when I think of myself and my career, I will do what many Romani musicians do. And great Romani musicians. But I think I am losing time because it is already here. But to do things in Romanes, to support the language, the culture, and the ethnic group itself, and to represent the culture to some extent in the bad times is important, and I think it is a means to become someone special in terms of the music scene and to find the sound that we all are looking for and to spread the music as much as possible, and because not everyone understands Romanes, it is also something that can help one break through.

26 | Decolonial Resonances in Czech Opera after 1948

TEREZA HAVELKOVÁ

Czech contemporary classical music after the Communist Coup of 1948 has generally been approached in terms of the political pressures of the new regime on the one hand and the resistance to these pressures on the other. In the 1950s, these pressures were strongly felt at the levels of both aesthetics – with the imposed doctrine of socialist realism – and communist ideology more generally. In the 1970s and 1980s, during the period of "normalization" after the Soviet-led invasion of Czechoslovakia by the Warsaw Pact armies, the pressure mainly concerned composers' compliance with the forcefully re-established political order, with lesser attention to compositional style. The 1960s have then been perceived as a period of relative artistic freedom, which coincided with the political thaw that culminated in the liberal reforms of the so-called Prague Spring of 1968, quashed by the invasion.

In this chapter, I offer an alternative perspective on classical composition, particularly opera, in post-war Czechoslovakia, utilizing postcolonial and decolonial theory as it has been developed since the 1990s for the study of socialist and post-socialist East Central Europe. Within this context, the region has been characterized as off-center and in-between, a (semi)periphery that is "on the one hand, founded on the strong identification with Europe, and, on the other, driven by the anxiety of incomplete belonging."[1] The experience of modernity as global coloniality of power arguably manifested itself here as the condition of "intermittent dependence" on Prussian/German, Austro-Hungarian, or Russian empires, and later Soviet Russia, lasting until the collapse of state socialism in the years 1989–91.[2] In

---

[1] Dorota Kołodziejczyk and Siegfried Huigen, "East Central Europe Between the Colonial and the Postcolonial: A Critical Introduction," in *East Central Europe Between the Colonial and the Postcolonial in the Twentieth Century*, ed. Siegfried Huigen and Dorota Kołodziejczyk (Cham: Palgrave Macmillan, 2023), 2.

[2] The experiences of the individual East Central European nations and societies cannot be homogenized. There is a marked difference, for example, between the former Soviet republics and Central European countries, such as the Czech Republic, Slovakia, Poland, and Hungary. In this chapter, I only concentrate on what is now the Czech Republic. In this way, I bypass the complex dynamics of power between the Czech and Slovak parts of the former Czechoslovakia.

fact, as Kołodziejczyk and Huigen suggest, the post-World War II order that turned East Central Europe into the Eastern Bloc may be understood as a consequence of the coloniality of power, as it was decided without the participation of the interested nations.[3] At the same time, it has increasingly been recognized that the region cannot claim colonial innocence or "colonial exceptionalism," as it participated, in various ways, in both intra-European domination and the overseas colonial project.[4]

I find this theoretical framework productive in approaching opera as a crucial cultural site for (re)negotiating the relationship with "the West," Soviet hegemony, and the Global South after 1948. It helps understand the importance of the Western operatic canon, which continued to dominate Czech opera houses for most of State Socialism, as a way of confirming the Czechs' lasting participation in (Western) European culture at large. This interpretation, which also pertains to the recourse to Western canonic literature in newly composed operas,[5] aligns with the self-fashioning of Central Europe under State Socialism as "The Kidnapped West."[6] A (post)colonial perspective is also useful for interpreting the centrally enforced programing of Soviet opera (and operetta) in Czech theaters in the 1950s, and again in the 1970s, as a – largely unsuccessful – attempt at cultural colonization.[7] This perspective also explains the mobilization of Czech national classics such as Smetana's *Libuše* in times of threat to Czech nationhood and state sovereignty, particularly during the 1968 Warsaw Pact invasion and the preceding experience with German occupation during World War II. The interpretation of Czech history in terms of a fight against German domination more generally, exploited by the official nationalist discourse, was also

---

[3] Kołodziejczyk and Huigen, "East Central Europe," 3–7.

[4] Filip Herza, "Colonial Exceptionalism: Post-colonial Scholarship and Race in Czech and Slovak Historiography," *Slovenský národopis* 68 (2020): 175–87. See also Matthew Rampley, "Decolonizing Central Europe: Czech Art and the Question of 'Colonial Innocence,'" *Visual Resources* 37 (March 2021): 1–30. On the perspective of whiteness and the politics of race in relation to Czech music, see Michael Beckerman, "Is Czech Music White?" *Czech Music Quarterly* 2021, no. 4: 26–30.

[5] Such as in two television operas: Iša Krejčí's *Antigona* (1964) and Luboš Fišer's *Věčný Faust* (*Eternal Faust*) (1985).

[6] Milan Kundera, "The Tragedy of Central Europe," trans. Edmund White, *New York Review of Books* (April 26, 1984): 33–38.

[7] For a discussion of Soviet opera in Prague's National Theater after 1968, see Tereza Havelková, "Dokumentární gesamtkunstwerk aneb Může Lenin zpívat? Opera Deset dnů, které otřásly světem v pražském Národním divadle," *Divadelní revue* 33, no. 1 (2022): 31–53. For a discussion of Soviet operetta on Czech stages, see Vojtěch Frank, "Musical Theatre as an Object of Transnational Political Exchange," *Historical Studies on Central Europe* 2 (2022): 219–36.

reflected in new operas on themes from Czech history, especially those related to the Hussite Wars.[8]

A decolonial approach also helps recognize the ambivalence in representations of the racialized Other in Czech opera, which highlights the specific, lateral relationship between what was formally known as the Second and Third worlds.[9] In what follows, I offer a close reading of a work that effectively illustrates the double-bind of the Czech postcolonial condition – the opera *Jezero Ukereve* ("Lake Ukerewe") by the composer Otmar Mácha (1922–2006), premiered at Prague's National Theater in 1966. The opera explores the search for a cure for malaria in German East Africa at the beginning of the twentieth century, featuring Black and mixed-race characters and depicting a violent conflict between Africans and the colonizers. While it generally expresses empathy for and solidarity with the colonized populations, informed by the Czechs' own experience with German oppression, it unavoidably reproduces the colonial ideology of a civilizational mission.

The opera was based on a theatrical play (originally written as a film script) by the Czech left-wing author and playwright Vladislav Vančura (1891–1942). The opera's libretto closely follows the play, and there are important similarities between the play's 1936 production by the National Theater, featuring music by Jaroslav Ježek (1906–42), and the opera's production thirty years later, which is why I will first discuss the play and its music in some detail before turning to the opera.

Jezero Ukereve 1936

The play was written in 1935 and was clearly intended as a critique of the rise of Nazism in Germany. Vančura, a vocal anti-fascist, had repeatedly protested Nazism publicly since 1934. After the Munich Agreement of 1938 and the following Nazi occupation of the Czech lands, Vančura became an active member of the Czech resistance movement, leading to his arrest and execution in Prague in 1942. *Jezero Ukereve* takes place on the shores of the eponymous lake – better known as Lake Victoria – and it is situated in

---

[8] Tereza Havelková, "From Crisis to Stasis: Depicting History in Czech Opera after 1948," *Hudební věda* 60 (2023): 49–68.

[9] The specific relationship of Czech artists to non-European Others may be traced back to the nineteenth century. On how it is reflected in Antonín Dvořák's last opera *Armida* (1904), see Martin Nedbal, "Dvořák's *Armida* and the Czech Oriental 'Self,'" *Current Musicology* 84 (2007), https://doi.org/10.7916/cm.v0i84.5097.

Uganda. (It should be noted that Uganda was a British rather than a German colony; German East Africa in the Great Lake region included present-day Tanzania, Rwanda, and Burundi, and Germany lost the colony after its defeat in World War I).

The play's opening scene takes place in the German Reichstag, and it may be read as a direct critique of German colonial politics. It features the famed German bacteriologist Robert Koch, who seeks to secure funding for malaria research and treatment in German East Africa and warns against a humanitarian catastrophe. Instead of heeding Koch's warnings, the members of the ruling party dismiss his request and choose to support German economic and military interests in the colony. These interests, and German expansionism more generally, are expressed by the member of parliament named Tümpl:

The German spirit, German civilization is making [literally pushing] its way through all parts of the world. We are bringing sustenance and education to the colored peoples, but if we ourselves are to derive any benefit from the labor and capital that has been invested there ... [w]e must build our trade on the understructure of canals, roads, and iron railways, not only in the Reich, but wherever German order prevails. To be German is to be a conqueror of civilization.

Německý duch, německá civilisace si razí cestu všemi díly světa. Přinášíme obživu a vzdělanost barevným pronárodům, avšak máme-li sami míti nějaký užitek z práce a kapitálu, který tam byl investován, ... Musíme postavit svůj obchod na základnu průplavů, silnic a železných drah nejen v říši, ale všude tam, kde vládne německý pořádek. Být Němcem znamená být dobyvatelem civilizace.[10]

The rest of the play takes place in the African colony, and I am particularly interested in the depiction of the Black and mixed-race characters. (I acknowledge the offensive nature of the images and some of the language quoted in what follows.) The main female character, called Lee, is the biracial daughter of the local ruler Goan, who is described in the play as a "noble Ugandan." Lee is the common-law wife of the play's main male character, the French malaria researcher Dr. Forde. Apart from Lee and her father Goan, there is also her biracial younger brother Majáné, and her Black older brother Kara-Kara. (In the course of the play, it is revealed that Lee and Majáné were fathered by a white trader.)

Lee, depicted as Europeanized, educated, and well-traveled, is admired and respected by the white colonizers for her grace and manners. The play

---

[10] Vladislav Vančura, *Jezero Ukereve* (Prague: Orbis, 1958), 6. All translations from Czech are mine.

Figure 26.1: Jiřina Šejbalová as Lee and Eduard Kohout as Dr. Forde in the 1936 National Theater production of Vladimír Vančura's play *Jezero Ukereve*. Prague, Archiv Národního divadla. Reproduced by permission.

indicates that she wears a European-style dress, which is how she was depicted in the 1936 production. The production used dark makeup for the Black and mixed-race characters but the actress Jiřina Šejbalová, who portrayed Lee, wore a relatively light makeup, what appears to be a simple European-style dress, and a Western hairstyle (Figure 26.1). The list of costumes also mentions an evening dress.[11] Yet, Lee is very much aware of her precarious position as a biracial person, not belonging to either world. This is how she explains to Dr. Forde that she cannot join him in Europe: "I would follow you as a maid, as a colored dog, but they would not accept me," although "my skin is only a little darker than yours" ("Šla bych za tebou jako služka, jako barevný pes, ale nepřijali by mě . . . má kůže je jen o poznání tmavší než tvá").[12] And when Goan temporarily rejects her for being mixed-race, calling her "mulatto" ("míšenka"), "unclean" ("nečistá"), and "white and black" ("bílá a černá"), she describes herself as someone who has "no place on any land" ("na žádné zemi místa").[13]

The oppression felt by the Africans and their mistrust or direct hostility toward Dr. Forde and the white colonizers are expressed most vocally

---

[11] "Rozpočet na výpravu hry Vladislava Vančury Jezero Ukereve." Prague, Archiv Národního divadla, shelfmark Č 360 a.
[12] Vančura, *Jezero Ukereve*, 53.   [13] Vančura, *Jezero Ukereve*, 59.

Figure 26.2: The National Theater's 1936 production of Vladimír Vančura's play *Jezero Ukereve* used dark makeup to depict the local ruler Goan (Václav Vydra) and his Black son Kara-Kara (Jaroslav Průcha). Prague, Archiv Národního divadla. Reproduced by permission.

by Goan and his older son Kara-Kara (Figure 26.2). Racial tensions gradually rise and ultimately lead to an uprising, partially incited by a white sailor Charpeau, who is in love with Lee and tries to get rid of Forde (here we have the future opera's obligatory love triangle). Faced with the threat of violence, Dr. Forde panics and orders shooting into the crowd, with fatal consequences. Throughout the play, Vančura expresses his sympathy for the plight of his African characters. Lee is by far the most sympathetic, especially in comparison with the men around her, who are all depicted as flawed, with the exception of Majáné, portrayed as a gentle soul.

Apart from repeated references to African drumming in the play's stage directions, the main means of exoticizing the African characters is their stylized, metaphorical mode of speaking, which contrasts with the terse and, at times, vulgar dialogue of the white colonizers. As the famed Czech literary theorist Jan Mukařovský observed, however, the Africans' metaphorical mode of expression comes close to Vančura's own use of language in his other literary work and thus may not have been intended as a means

Figure 26.3: The scenography for the 1936 National Theater production of Vladimír Vančura's play *Jezero Ukereve* (directed by Jiří Frejka). Prague, Archiv Národního divadla. Reproduced by permission.

of exoticism.[14] Following this line of reasoning, it may be better understood as an expression of the playwright's empathy with the colonized. Mukařovský also praises Vančura for attempting to avoid the then common form of exoticism primarily focused on the depiction of the tropical locale. Indeed, the playwright's stage instructions were simple, and so was the scenography for the 1936 Prague production (Figure 26.3).

The music for the play was composed by Jaroslav Ježek, a visually impaired Czech composer and pianist best known for his jazz-style songs, and associated with the Liberated Theater, a left-wing company that was vocal about its anti-fascist stance (see Chapter 27). The play's director, Jiří Frejka, specifically requested Ježek "for his special qualities and knowledge of Black music, and in line with the author's wishes" ("jednak pro své zvláštní kvality a znalosti v černošské hudbě, jednak na přání autorovo").[15] I believe this formulation reflects the discursive framing of jazz by Czech left-wing music critics from the

---

[14] Jan Mukařovský, "Dramatik Vančura v boji za rovnoprávnost a solidaritu národů," in Vladislav Vančura, *Jezero Ukereve* (Prague: Orbis, 1958), 72–3.

[15] A duplicate of a letter from Jiří Frejka to the National Theater drama administration dated January 7, 1936, Prague, Archiv Národního divadla, shelfmark Č 360 a.

1930s onwards as the "music of the oppressed Black people" ("hudba utlačovaného černošského lidu").[16]

In *Jezero Ukereve*, all the musical numbers were used to represent the African local community and featured quasi-African drumming (per the playwright's instructions), except for a song written for Lee. None of the white characters sang or expressed themselves musically. (It is worth noting that while women sang melodically, men chanted.) Of special interest are two extensive chorus scenes that highlight the plight of the African population, with contrasting spoken interjections by the white characters and the use of drumming in both. While the association of drums and singing or chanting may be understood as an exoticizing feature, it also allowed for establishing an affective connection with the represented Africans. Moreover, drums were used in the play not only as a local mode of expression but also to highlight oppression – they accompanied the forced labor (ordered by Forde) that prompts the uprising. The play concluded with a musical number that merged a triumphant motive in the trumpet, an instrument hitherto used as a sign of colonial oppression, with (quasi-African) drumming, in what may be read as a musical gesture of (potential) unity.[17]

Lee's Song markedly differs from these numbers. It is self-standing and allegedly based on an "original South-African text."[18] It was scored for clarinet, guitar, and double bass, in Tempo di blues. In 1936, the song was recorded in a piano version (and in transposition) by the play's Lee, Jiřina Šejbalová, under the title "Když se usmívala" (When She Smiled).[19] The song's melodic inflections and Šejbalová's sensuous interpretation suggest eroticized exoticism. Yet, the text was written from a man's point of view that Lee appropriates, creating a distance between herself and the song's poetic descriptions. Moreover, the song was not directly used as a means of seduction in the production, and from its placement in the play, it appears that Lee might have sung it as if to herself.

The song took on a life of its own, and while it is not as popular as some of Ježek's other songs, it has been reinterpreted and re-recorded in almost every decade since (most recently in 2015).[20] I would argue that, within the

---

[16] For a detailed analysis of how this perspective was elaborated by the influential music critic Emanuel Uggé, see Petr Vidomus, "Music with a Revolutionary Purpose: Jazz Journalist Emanuel Uggé," *Hudební věda* 59 (2022): 246–314.

[17] My observations are based on a manuscript score of Ježek's music for the play preserved in Archiv Národního divadla.

[18] Inscription on the front page of a manuscript of the piano version of the song, Prague, Czech Music Museum, shelfmark S224/753a.

[19] *Osvobozené divadlo 1929–1938* (Supraphon 2020).

[20] The piano version of the song was published in 1959 by Panton. The same year, it was recorded in an orchestral version by Jiří Vašíček and the Karel Vlach Orchestra (issued by Supraphon in

general cultural context, the song loses its more complex undertones and is mostly appreciated for its simple exotic connotations. In any case, when the opera was first performed thirty years later, the play, and to some extent also Lee and her song, were arguably already part of Czech cultural consciousness.

Jezero Ukereve 1966

Otmar Mácha started composing his opera in 1960, dubbed the Year of Africa, as seventeen African nations gained independence. By the time the opera was finished in 1963, the nations around Lake Victoria had also become independent. The opera follows the play closely, and it also bears some similarities with Ježek's approach to the music, although Mácha stays squarely within the tradition of classical composition, mostly leaning on extended tonality.[21]

The opera starts with a trumpet, associated, as in the play, with colonial oppression. The opening Reichstag scene is spoken, including Tümpl's monologue about German colonial expansion; the only character that sings is Dr. Koch. This is a similar strategy as in the play, where music is used to invite affective identification with the plight of the colonized. Like the playwright Vančura, the composer Mácha was praised for largely avoiding exoticism, especially the possibility to draw on "African" or "Black" folklore.[22] The chief means of musical exoticism is, again, the use of quasi-African drumming associated with the Ugandans. As in the play, there are also military drums to accompany forced labor and signal colonial oppression.

Another exoticizing means is a flute motive that runs through the whole opera and works as a kind of leitmotif associated with the African locale and people, especially the female characters. Here again, Mácha's approach is not dissimilar from Ježek's in "Když se usmívala," with the melody revolving around ascending and descending fourths and minor second embellishments. Through repetition, this motive becomes the opera's "natural environment," and it is the music used to characterize the

---

1960). Of note is also the 1976 recording by Panton with Miloš Ježil, which uses the original instrumentation of clarinet, guitar, and double bass.

[21] A typewritten libretto and a manuscript of the opera's vocal score are in Archiv Národního divadla, an orchestral score is in Prague, Dilia Archive. A recording of the opera from June 22, 1966, is in Prague, Archiv Českého rozhlasu, shelfmark CR.HKV.1990.1179 (MAC 21-4).

[22] Bohumil Karásek, "Nová česká opera," *Rudé právo*, June 7, 1966. Cf. Vladimí Bor, "O českou soudobou operu," in *Operní večery* (Prague: Panton, 1981), 127–55.

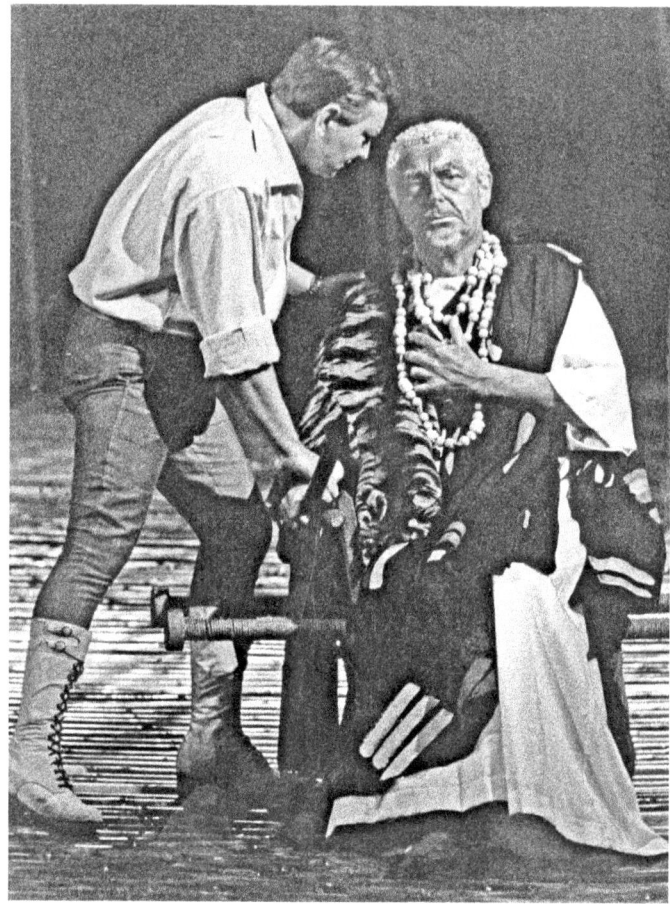

Figure 26.4: Eduard Haken as Goan and Zdeněk Švehla as Dr. Forde in the National Theater's 1966 production of Otmar Mácha's opera *Jezero Ukereve*, which used dark makeup for Black and mixed-race characters. Prague, Archiv Národního divadla. Reproduced by permission.

German colonizers that ultimately stands out as strange, bordering on caricature due to its military connotations. At some point, there is also a waltz, the conventional musical sign of bourgeois decadence. The two chorus scenes dedicated to the oppressed Africans that were highlighted by music in the play were apparently also the most impressive numbers in the opera, judging by the reviews.[23] Goan was again perceived as "noble" – one reviewer speaks of his "royal dignity" (Figure 26.4).[24] And the opera's

[23] Karásek, "Nová česká opera."   [24] Karásek, "Nová česká opera."

Figure 26.5: Oldřich Šimáček's simple scenography in the National Theater's 1966 production of Otmar Mácha's opera *Jezero Ukereve* (directed by Hanuš Thein). Photo by Jaromír Svoboda. Prague, Archiv Národního divadla. Reproduced by permission.

scenography, too, wasn't dissimilar in approach from that of the play (Figure 26.5).

Yet, there is a shift in the depiction of Lee in the opera. She no longer wears a Western-style dress, and thus visually blends with the other African women (Figure 26.6). Moreover, some of the more explicit lines where she reflects on her precarious position as a biracial woman were cut. While still being the opera's main female character, she thus loses some of her complexity. As one reviewer observed, the operatic Lee "only appears to be an impetus for the actions of the other [and I should add male] characters and does not have enough space to express herself" ("působí stále jen jako impuls k jednání ostatních postav a nemá dost prostoru k vyjádření sebe").[25]

Nevertheless, Lee is essential to the opera's message. Toward the end of his life, Mácha planned to rework the opera, with the intention of turning Lee into a "Black Libuše," in whose prophecy the opera would culminate, promoting "the idea of white and Black people living together across the

---

[25] Jaroslav Volek, "Jezero Ukereve," *Kulturní tvorba*, June 2, 1966.

Figure 26.6: The National Theater's 1966 production of Otmar Mácha's opera *Jezero Ukereve*. Eva Zikmundová as Lee. Photo by Jaromír Svoboda. Prague, Archiv Národního divadla. Reproduced by permission.

planet" ("myšlenku na společný příští život bílých a černých na celé planetě").[26] This statement foregrounds the suggestion, only implicitly present in the performed version of the opera, that it is the female, biracial character that carries the hope for the future of Africa. Indeed, unlike in the play, Lee has the last word in the opera, declaring that "The time is now" ("Teď nastal čas"). Mácha's reference to Bedřich Smetana's opera *Libuše* is also telling. *Libuše* was used to open the National Theater in 1881 and has since served as the operatic symbol of Czech nationhood. It draws on Slavic mythology to tell the story of the eponymous Czech legendary female ruler and culminates in a lengthy prophecy where Libuše dramatically declares that the Czech nation will never perish. Mácha's understanding of Lee as a "Black Libuše" highlights the perceived parallels between the historical experience of the Czech nation and the colonization of Africa.

Yet, the ending of *Jezero Ukereve*, as well as its overall message, are ambivalent. The opera ends optimistically, with Robert Koch announcing the discovery of a safe cure for malaria, and Dr. Forde reaffirming his belief

---

[26] Marie Kulijevičová, "Ještě něco chci," *Reflex* 13, no. 48 (2002): 58–59.

in science as the foundation of solidarity, brotherhood, and peace between nations. But while the opera is overtly critical of the German economic interests in the colony, it does not shy away from imposing the civilizing process in the name of presumably universal humanity, personified by Dr. Koch. Moreover, the depiction of biracial characters and the foregrounding of Lee suggests a problematic racial hierarchy and possible colorism (which, however, is downplayed in the opera's production). And if it is indeed Lee, rather than the failing Dr. Forde, who is supposed to represent the hope for Africa, it is because she adopts his (Western) ideals. As she puts it, "You said that everything is changing to come back in a higher sense. I can't renounce your words, I hope, I believe, I will protect you" ("Říkal jsi, že se všecko mění, aby se vrátilo ve vyšším smyslu. Nemohu se zříci tvých slov, doufám, věřím, budu tě chránit").

Music and State Politics

In the play, Forde's idealism is confronted with the reality of colonial exploitation (and put to the test by the uprising). This reality is acknowledged by the character Sergeant:

SERGEANT: You say health, but why should they be healthy? So that they can labor for the whites! You don't have to be crazy to understand that.
FORDE: Sergeant, you think we've found ourselves on the side of...
SERGEANT: On the side of money and guns.
SERŽÁN: Vy říkáte zdraví, ale proč mají být zdraví? Aby mohli dřít na bělochy! Člověk nemusí bejt ani blázen, aby tomu rozuměl.
FORDE: Seržáne, myslíš, že jsme se ocitli na straně...
SERŽÁN: Na straně peněz a ručnic.[27]

In the opera's libretto, these lines were omitted. Indeed, it would have sounded most ironic within the context of the 1960s Czechoslovak foreign policy in Africa. During the interwar period, Czechoslovakia mainly had economic interests on the continent, most famously represented by the Baťa shoe company in Nigeria. In the late 1950s and 1960s, the socialist state built on these connections to spearhead the Soviet Bloc's political and economic relations with the newly decolonized Africa. While Czechoslovakia "pursued numerous humanitarian efforts across the continent such as providing clean drinking water, education, and medical services," it also supplied military aid

---

[27] Vančura, *Jezero Ukereve*, 48.

and benefited from extensive arms exports.[28] In this way, it did find itself "on the side of money and guns." These observations open the way for questioning the opera's position in relation to Czechoslovakia's official Africa policy.

While its subject matter was unique within the Czech operatic context, *Jezero Ukereve* was not the only composition with an African theme at the time. There were others, most notably Jan Rychlík's *Africký cyklus* ("African Cycle") (1961–62), and according to Geoffrey Chew, these compositions may be connected to the Congo crisis after the assassination of Patrice Lumumba in early 1961.[29] As Chew points out, the Union of Czechoslovak Composers was involved in "an orchestrated Soviet propaganda campaign" after Lumumba's death, sending telegrams to the UN Secretariat and to UNESCO. Given the extent of the campaign, Chew is convinced that "no composition invoking an African motif, publicly produced in Czechoslovakia during 1961 or 1962, could possibly have escaped associations with the Congo crisis."[30] Yet, he also recognizes that it would be reductive to understand these works simply as tools of political propaganda, and I believe the same goes for *Jezero Ukereve*. Mácha's interest in Africa when he first started composing the opera could have been inspired by the extensive media coverage of the ongoing decolonization of the continent, including high-profile visits by dignitaries from various African nations.[31] Finished in 1963, the opera waited for its premiere for three years, by which time the more explicit associations could have faded. Moreover, when the opera was staged in 1966, there was no mention of recent political events in either the program booklet or its critical reception, beyond the general "protest against capitalist colonialism and racial hatred" ("protest proti kapitalistickému kolonizátorství a rasové nenávisti") already expressed in Vančura's play and still deemed relevant.[32] It seems

[28] Philip Muehlenbeck, *Czechoslovakia in Africa, 1945–1968* (Basingstoke: Palgrave Macmillan, 2016), 4. See also Petr Zídek and Karel Sieber, *Československo a subsaharská Afrika v letech 1948–1989* (Prague: Ústav mezinárndních vztahů, 2007); and Jakub Vít, "V roli exportéra 'věci komunismu': Československo a subsaharská Afrika 1948–1962," *Soudobé dějiny* 10 (2003): 29–57.

[29] Geoffrey Chew, "'Always Something New from Africa': Jan Rychlík's *Africký Cyklus* and Czech Experimental Music in the Early 1960s," *Central Europe* 1, no. 2 (November 2003): 115–32.

[30] Chew, "Always Something New," 117.

[31] According to Muehlenbeck, "Nearly every month a visiting dignitary from Africa visited Prague to thank Czechoslovakia for its friendship with his country." (Muehlenbeck, *Czechoslovakia in Africa*, 3.) Thus, for example, representatives of Uganda visited Czechoslovakia prior to independence: Benedicto Kiwankuka (Catholic Democratic Party) in 1960, and Milton Obote (Ugandan People's Congress) in 1961 (Muehlenbeck, *Czechoslovakia in Africa*, 41).

[32] P. E. [Pavel Eckstein], "Jezero Ukereve," in *Jezero Ukereve* [Program Booklet] (Prague: National Theater, 1966), 244.

that both the composer and the reviewers sought to highlight the "general validity" ("obecná platnost") of the opera's themes.[33]

In the case of Rychlík's *Africký cyklus*, Chew suggests the Congo crisis "offered a safe pretext for pursuing other agendas," namely, to promote a specific vision of musical modernism.[34] *Africký cyklus* has been considered one of the key works of the Czech New Music of the 1960s and has been interpreted as an early Central European parallel to American minimalism.[35] As the local response to the Western avant-garde, the Czech New Music has generally been viewed as a way of "catching up" with the West. It was mainly characterized by recourse to the techniques of (post)serialism and aleatoric music, of which Rychlík also made use. Yet, his understanding of what he called "nonconformist" compositional techniques was broader, and it was arguably based on "negation of the untenable cultural Eurocentrism" ("negaci neudržitelného kulturního evropocentrismu").[36] Apart from his interest in African rhythm reflected in *Africký cyklus* and fueled by his long-standing engagement with jazz, it also included aspects of other non-Western traditions as well as some features of European early music and folk music.[37] A similar interest in non-Western musics bound up with exploration of new compositional techniques was also significant for Miloslav Kabeláč, one of the leading figures in Czech post-war modernism.[38]

Mácha and Rychlík were friends, and when Rychlík died prematurely in 1964, Mácha wrote what is probably his best-known work, *Variace na téma a smrt Jana Rychlíka* ("Variations on the Theme and Death of Jan Rychlík," 1965), which use a theme from *Africký cyklus*. Compared to Rychlík, however, Mácha's approach in *Jezero Ukereve* was more traditional, both in the sense of standing closer to what Ralph Locke terms "overt exoticism,"[39] and in its relation to the Western avant-garde. In fact, *Jezero Ukereve* was praised by critics for avoiding the techniques of new music with their "complicated constructions and calculations" ("složitých

---

[33] Jiří Bajer, "Druhá sklizeň jarní operní úrody," *Divadelní a filmové noviny*, June 29, 1966.

[34] Chew, "Always Something New," 115.

[35] Petr Kofroň, *Třináct analýz* (Jinočany: H & H, 1993), 64–72.

[36] Milan Křížek, *Jan Rychlík: Život a dílo skladatele* (Prague: H & H, 2001), 130.

[37] Jan Rychlík, "Prvky nových skladebných technik v hudbě minulosti, v hudbě exotické a lidové," in *Nové cesty hudby*, ed. Milena Černohorská and Věra Dolanská (Prague: Státní hudební vydavatelství, 1964), 54–73.

[38] On Kabeláč's explicitly exotic works, see Tereza Havelková, "When the Morgenland looks East," in *New Music in the "New" Europe 1918–1938: Ideology, Theory, and Practice*, ed. Geoffrey Chew (Prague: KLP, 2007), 71–76.

[39] Ralph P. Locke, *Musical Exoticism: Images and Reflections* (New York: Cambridge University Press, 2009), 6 and 217.

konstrukcí a výpočtů");[40] and as such it was univocally hailed as a great success. These reviews testify to the ongoing "battle" for new music and the perceived need to defend the composer's approach in times of radical innovation in Czech contemporary composition when, as Otmar Mácha allegedly put it, "the major fifth chord has become cursed" ("durový kvintakord se stal prokletým").[41] While the Czech New Music experimentation mainly focused on chamber and orchestral compositions, it did not completely bypass the realm of opera. Indeed, it was the 1959 National Theater production of Alban Berg's *Wozzeck* that helped incite renewed interest in the European avant-garde, and some new operas produced by the National Theater in the same period as *Jezero Ukereve*, such as Václav Kašlík's *Krakatit* and Jarmil Burghauser's *Most* ("The Bridge"), took a more daring approach.

To conclude, *Jezero Ukereve* marks a special moment in the history of Czech post-war classical composition, primarily defined by negotiations of its relationship with the Western avant-garde. As works such as *Africký cyklus* and *Jezero Ukereve* help recognize, however, the Czechs' relationship to the Global South and its musical traditions was equally at stake. Moreover, apart from their participation in debates concerning the politics of aesthetics, which were focused on issues of compositional technique, these works also testify to the way music continued to be entangled in official politics, even in the comparatively liberal 1960s. If instrumental works such as Rychlík's *Africký cyklus* cannot be detached from political associations, in the case of opera they become even more explicit. While *Jezero Ukereve* strived for a generalized perspective, it ultimately offered a view of (post)colonialism that was in line with Czechoslovak Africa policy and propaganda, which emphasized the country's own quasi-colonial experience due to Austro-Hungarian domination and German occupation to further its political and economic interests on the continent.[42]

As Pavel Barša has recently argued, the heavy-handed anticolonial discourse of state socialism, together with Central Europe's self-perception as victims of Soviet colonization (expressed in Kundera's conception of the kidnapped West), may be to blame for what he calls the "zero degree of decolonization" ("nulový stupeň dekolonizace") in today's Czech society.[43] As he puts it, based on his own experience with anti-communist sentiments during late socialism, "for many of us, Western colonialism was

[40] Vilém Pospíšil, "Jezero Ukereve," *Hudební rozhledy* 19, no. 13 (1966): 12–13.
[41] Pavel Eckstein, "O autoru opery," in *Jezero Ukereve* [Program Booklet], 251.
[42] Muehlenbeck, *Czechoslovakia in Africa*, 62.
[43] Pavel Barša, "Nulový stupeň dekolonizace," *Artalk Revue* 4 (Winter 2020): 1–4.

propaganda invented by the Soviet Union to draw attention away from its own colonialism and its victims (us)," a view that continues to inform (East) Central Europe's approach to non-European refugees and the Global South more generally. A close analysis of works such as *Jezero Ukereve* contributes to a more nuanced understanding of the global colonial past and its present ramifications beyond the binary of metropolis and (post) colony. It helps to illuminate the Czechs' own participation in ideologies of colonial modernity, including the ideology of whiteness. And the comparison between the 1936 production of Vančura's play and the 1966 staging of Mácha's opera makes it possible to recognize the continuity of the visual, and to some extent also acoustic discourses between pre-World War II democracy and post-war state socialism.

27 | Jazz as Sound for the Stage: The Liberated Theater and its Progeny

DAVID VONDRÁČEK

Theater as an artform sensitively responds to societal developments and can reflect them in a timely fashion. This is particularly true for those forms that can be brought out with little effort, such as cabaret and small-scale theater. Thus, the societal liberalization of the decade that culminated in the Prague Spring in 1968 coincided with a wave of newly emerging small-scale theater companies: in 1958, Rokoko and Divadlo Na zábradlí; in 1959, Večerní Brno, Semafor, and many more. This wave reached both larger and smaller cities (Studio Ypsilon in Liberec; Skumafka in Olomouc; Kladivadlo in Broumov, later relocated to Kadaň; and Ústí nad Labem). These new ensembles were concentrated around Prague's Wenceslas Square and represented a revival of a tradition from the First Czechoslovak Republic, disrupted by World War II and centralization following the Communist Coup of 1948. The main model for these ensembles, especially for Semafor, was the Liberated Theater (Osvobozené divadlo) of the interwar period (1926–38), which earned a legendary reputation thanks to the comedy duo Jiří Voskovec and Jan Werich.

Equally legendary was the music of the nearly blind, in-house composer and bandleader of the Liberated Theater, Jaroslav Ježek (1906–42). Music played a special role in the Liberated Theater, as the following pages illustrate. Ježek offered his audience the latest musical styles, which in the interwar years (1920s–1930s) was mainly represented by American jazz. Thus, the company took on a pioneering role in the dissemination of jazz in Czechoslovakia. The ensemble's popularity was further fueled by the historical contexts and its personnel. As National Socialism rose in neighboring Germany, the ensemble presented works with leftist viewpoints and did not hesitate to mock the Führer. This became untenable after Nazi Germany invaded the First Czechoslovak Republic, and Ježek, Voskovec, and Werich had to flee to the United States in 1939. After the end of the war, Werich returned permanently to Czechoslovakia and served as a link between the Liberated Theater and new companies (Ježek died in New York in 1942, and Voskovec fled a second time in 1948, this time

This chapter was translated from German to English by Martin Nedbal.

from the communists). So, while this chapter will begin by exploring the place of the Liberated Theater and its music in Czech theater culture, I will conclude by pointing out the continuities with the Semafor Theater.

Between Cabaret and "High Art" – Against Clear Classifications

For the sake of historical contextualization, a brief account of the development of Prague's entertainment theater is necessary. The phenomenon I am concerned with has been referred to as "theater of cabaret type" ("divadlo kabaretního typu")[1] or "theater of small forms" ("divadlo malých forem"). The latter is the more recent term, inspired by the name of the Semafor theater company, an acronym for "sedm malých forem" ("seven small forms"). Cabaret elements or small forms such as sketches, songs, and improvisations were also used in mainstream theaters and repertoires, making a clear distinction between "high" and cabaret art impossible.[2]

A variety theater with programs inspired by French entertainment models, called Divadlo Varieté, had existed in the Prague district of Karlín since 1881. Starting in the 1890s, a popular form of entertainment was the French-influenced Café-chantant, known as *šantán* in Czech. This type of theater offered singing performances, acts by magicians, and similar entertainment, accompanied by gastronomic service. An important venue for this type of theatrical entertainment was the restaurant Bílá labuť (White Swan) on Na Poříčí Street from 1907 to 1936, where an eponymous department store stands today. The establishment was referred to as either *šantán* or cabaret, but many commentators thought that cabarets catered to a younger, more intellectual audience. When Jiří Červený founded his literary cabaret Červená sedma (Red Seven) in December 1909, his aim was to offer tasteful entertainment with artistic aspirations.[3] Červená sedma was also well known for its music. Červený composed close to 600 songs for his company. However, recordings of this music were only made after the company's dissolution in 1922, thus already carrying a nostalgic quality.[4]

---

[1] Vladimír Just, "Nebyl jen Semafor a Zábradlí aneb Malá divadla jako hnutí," in *Pódia z krabičky. Nesoustavné nahlédnutí do historie malých neprofesionálních scén 60. let 20. století* (Prague: NIPOS, 2005), 6–22 (22, n. 6).

[2] Just, "Nebyl jen Semafor," 22, n. 6.

[3] See František Černý, "Úvodem," in Jiří Červený, *Červená sedma* (Prague: Orbis, 1959), 8.

[4] *Červená sedma 1907–1922 na dobových gramodeskách*, original mono remastered recording, Radioservis, CR03632, 2007, compact disc.

As is customary in commercial theaters, the turnover of these ensembles was high and directly dependent on the support or lack thereof from the audience. The cabaret Lucerna, founded in 1910, is primarily associated with Karel Hašler, but he also temporarily directed Rokoko and served as the resident director at Divadlo Varieté in Karlín (1916–29). With his patriotic songs, also known as "old-Prague" ("staropražské") songs, Hašler himself became one of the theater's main attractions.[5]

Similarly, the beginnings of the Liberated Theater were unstable in terms of institutional organization and repertoire. As early as 1923, Jiří Frejka, together with fellow conservatory students, produced theatrical performances in locations in Prague. The first permanent venue was the Theater Na Slupi, built in 1924. The young artists were united by their membership in the artistic group Devětsil (Butterbur) and adopted the name Liberated Theater in early 1926. The term "Liberated Theater" was a translation of the term "das entfesselte Theater" ("the unshackled theater") used as the German title of a book by Soviet director Alexander Yakovlevich Tairov, originally titled *Zapiski rezhissera* ("Notes of a Director").[6]

By 1927, the Liberated Theater had become the central hub of the Czech theater avant-garde. When celebrating its tenth anniversary, Voskovec and Werich chose to overlook the company's earlier history.[7] Born in 1905, they were law students when they brought a youthful entrepreneurial spirit to the Liberated Theater with their first show, *Vest pocket revue*, which opened on April 19, 1927. They were dedicated to comedy, drawing inspiration from figures like Charlie Chaplin and Jaroslav Hašek.[8] In April 1927, Frejka left the Liberated Theater with a significant portion of its staff to establish a new ensemble, Theater Dada. It is important to note that this departure was not a protest against Voskovec and Werich. In fact, both Voskovec and Werich, along with Ježek, continued to collaborate with both theater companies because comedic performances were crucial for

---

[5] Hašler was later murdered in a Nazi concentration camp. See Milan Kuna, *Musik an der Grenze des Lebens. Musikerinnen und Musiker aus böhmischen Ländern in nationalsozialistischen Konzentrationslagern und Gefängnissen*, trans. Eliška Nováková (Frankfurt/M.: Zweitausendeins, 1993), 285–87.

[6] Alexander Tairow, *Das entfesselte Theater. Aufzeichnungen eines Regisseurs*, reprint of the 1923 edition (Berlin: Alexander, 1989). In Czech: Alexandr Tairov, *Odpoutané divadlo. Zápisky režiséra*, trans. Josef Menzel (Prague: Orbis, 1927). This edition also contains the essay "Vznik ruského moderního divadla" by the Liberated Theater's director Jindřich Honzl.

[7] See Josef Träger, ed., *10 let Osvobozeného divadla 1927–1937. V+W*, 2nd ed. (Prague: Borový, 1937), 1.

[8] Jiří Voskovec, *Klobouk ve křoví. Výbor veršů V+W (1927–1947)*, 3rd ed. [1st ed. 1965] (Prague: Mladá fronta, 1996), 78.

their financial stability.[9] Although Frejka's Theater Dada is often regarded as a more artistically ambitious ensemble, the Liberated Theater also produced some experimental, avant-garde works, such as Alfred Jarry's *Ubu Roi* in Voskovec's translation in 1928.

In the years following the ensemble split, most of Voskovec and Werich's shows were directed by Jindřich Honzl.[10] Honzl was also known as a theater theorist. Inspired by Tairov's ideas, Honzl aimed to liberate theatrical means from the dominance of the dramatic text and grant them their own rightful prominence. He regarded circus artists as ideal figures in this pursuit:[11]

Desperation, cheerfulness, resignation – cannot be embodied by any actor; for actors are merely surfaces of living costumes, faces, hands, and voices. We should admire an actor's legs instead of his "spiritual trials and tribulations." Acrobats, who walk on tightropes, how enviable your success is! Because your means are so simple, you possess the entire soul of the audience and leave no emptiness in it.

Zoufalství, veselost, rezignace – není herec; neboť herec jest jen povrch živého kostýmu, tvář, ruce a hlas. [N]eobdivovali jsme ještě hercových nohou na místo jeho "duševní prazkušenosti." Komediante, který chodíš po provaze, jak je ti možná závidět tvé úspěchy! Že tvoje prostředky jsou tak prosté, máš duši diváků celou a nenecháš v ní prázdnoty.

Honzl's emphasis on independent theatrical elements at the expense of the text parallels ideas that later became associated with *Regietheater* ("director's theater," emphasizing the director's creative interpretation in a theatrical production, often diverging from traditional interpretations).

Honzl was also the holder of the official concession required to operate the theater before it passed to Voskovec in 1929. After various interim stages, a permanent venue was only secured in 1929 in a building (Palác U Nováků) near Wenceslas Square. The company performed seven nights a week, with additional matinees on Sundays and holidays. Typically, they produced two new plays per season, with Ježek regularly providing music from the beginning of 1928. Ježek's use of jazz was partly influenced by the youthful composition of the company – he joined the troupe at the age of twenty, and Frejka founded the Liberated Theater at nineteen. Jazz was thus seen as a musical reflection of the new company's youthful

---

[9] Andrea Jochmanová and Ladislava Petišková, *Osvobozené divadlo na vlnách Devětsilu* (Brno: JAMU, 2022), 126.

[10] An overview of these productions can be found in Jarka M. Burian, "The Liberated Theater of Voskovec and Werich," *Educational Theatre Journal* 29, no. 2 (1977): 176–77.

[11] Jindřich Honzl, *Základy a praxe moderního divadla* (Prague: Orbis, 1963), 13.

rebelliousness. In more general terms, the unconventional theater company played a role in popularizing an unconventional musical style.

Theater and Jazz

The relationship between theater and jazz raises questions about historical preservation. While jazz was certainly performed elsewhere besides the theater, there are usually no sources available for these venues. The transitory nature of music was further compounded by a lack of institutional responsibility. While theaters are institutions that engage in archiving, they only represent a portion of the spectrum. Nevertheless, theaters are crucial when it comes to researching the spread of jazz on the European continent.

Until 1927, Emil František Burian, Iša Krejčí, and Ježek contributed their music to the programs of the Liberated Theater. They belonged to the same generation and shared an interest in jazz. Burian was the author of the first book on jazz in Czech, which was among the first of its kind on the European continent.[12] Ježek joined the company while still studying composition and piano. He completed his first degree in composition in the summer of 1927 with a piano concerto that combined avant-garde and jazz elements.[13] In the same year, he composed music for theaters in Prague, including the National Theater.[14] Before establishing a lasting collaboration with Werich and Voskovec, Ježek spent half a year in Paris from 1927 to 1928. Upon his return, he continued his studies with Josef Suk at the Prague Conservatory. While a comparison to George Gershwin may be tempting, particularly because both Ježek and Gershwin composed theater music, Ježek's distinct musical education sets him apart from his American counterpart.[15]

Ježek was strongly influenced by Tin Pan Alley, the center of New York's recording industry, where Gershwin had started his career. The Prague composer is believed to have owned one of the largest collections of

---

[12] Emil František Burian, *Jazz* (Prague: Aventinum, 1928).

[13] David Vondráček, *Jaroslav Ježek zwischen Avantgarde und Jazz. Mit einem Werkverzeichnis des Komponisten von Mojmír Sobotka*, Münchner Veröffentlichungen zur Musikgeschichte 81 (Munich: Allitera 2021), 170–85.

[14] Vondráček, *Jaroslav Ježek*, 279; and František Cinger, *Šťastné blues aneb Z deníku Jaroslava Ježka* (Prague: BVD, 2006), 106.

[15] See Michael Beckerman, "Ježek and Musical Bilingualism," *Czech Music Quarterly* 2022, no. 2: 33.

recordings (1,350 records) in the city.[16] His orientation toward Tin Pan Alley is reflected in his own works. The AABB form, referred to as the "popular-song-form" by Allen Forte, is prominent in Ježek's output, and this is the form of commercial music.[17] Hence, it is debatable whether Ježek's music should be considered jazz or jazz-influenced popular songs. This raises similar questions about stylistic ambiguities as those discussed above in connection to theater forms.

One of the objections against viewing Ježek's music as jazz is that improvisation is rare in his recordings.[18] This can be interpreted in various ways: the simplest explanation would be that improvisation was indeed infrequent in practice. However, we know from other sources that Ježek's early performances in the theater consisted exclusively of piano improvisations, specifically style imitations on request.[19] Therefore, it may be that improvisation occurred frequently but did not often make its way from the theater to the recording studio, perhaps due to technical limitations regarding record length.[20] An elaborately arranged big band swing in a style similar to that of Glenn Miller naturally offers fewer opportunities for improvisation, which is why some authors do not classify it as jazz. So, as a third possibility, Ježek may have avoided improvisation to match this specific style. All three possibilities are likely partially correct, but the sources do not allow us to determine the answers with certainty.

At the end of its development, Ježek's theater band consisted of four saxophones, three trumpets, and three trombones, in addition to strings and a rhythm section. As such, the band emulated the big band style. From a form of entertainment music that wanted to swing but was not quite sure how, Ježek's idiom became genuine jazz within a few years. Brian S. Locke has attributed this transformation to "one of the closest examinations of American culture in Central Europe during the interwar period."[21] Ježek's style was quite diverse, however, and jazz dances were just one of several inspirations. To make a specific point, Ježek would also turn to a ballad

---

[16] This information is based on an account by a contemporary eyewitness, however, and should therefore be read with a grain of salt. Cinger, *Šťastné blues*, 106.

[17] Ulrich Kaiser, "Babylonian confusion. Zur Terminologie der Formanalyse von Pop- und Rockmusik," *Zeitschrift der Gesellschaft für Musiktheorie* 8, no. 1 (2011): 58.

[18] One instance of improvisation can be heard in the blues *Svět na ruby* which was recorded twice. *Osvobozené divadlo V+W 1929–1938*, 7 discs, Supraphon, SU 5810–2, 2007, compact disc, disc 4, tracks 8 and 11.

[19] Cinger, *Šťastné blues*, 95.   [20] Vondráček, *Jaroslav Ježek*, 133–34 and 146.

[21] Brian S. Locke, *Opera and Ideology in Prague. Polemics and Practice at the National Theater, 1900–1938* (Rochester, NY: University of Rochester Press, 2006), 281.

(*kramářská píseň*), as in "Píseň strašlivá o Golemovi" ("A Scary Song about the Golem," 1931) or a song in the style of Czech tramping movement, as seen in "Babička Mary" ("Grandmother Mary," 1935). He was also capable of reducing his expressive means to push through a specific point, as in political songs. Perhaps the best-known example is "Proti větru" ("Against the Wind"), which was used both in *Panoptikum* (1935) and *Balada z hadrů* ("Ballad of Rags," 1935). The song clearly exhibits characteristics that differentiate it from jazz songs, including march rhythms and a simple, rhythmically pronounced melody.

Politicization, Closure, and Rebirth of the Liberated Theater

In their works, Voskovec and Werich embraced political satire – a development that is also reflected in the music. Political topics become more prominent in *Caesar* (1932), followed by *Osel a stín* ("The Ass and His Shadow") in 1933 and *Kat a blázen* ("An Executioner and a Fool") in 1934. The rumba "Evropa volá" ("Europe Is Calling") from *Caesar* surpassed all previous Ježek songs in its diverse form and the use of instrumental effects (such as chromaticism, instrumental transitions, and contrasts).[22] Whereas *Caesar* satirized Mussolini's fascism in Italy, as Ježek's biographer Václav Holzknecht argued,[23] *Osel a stín* is an early example of satire on Hitler's Germany. *Kat a blázen* is aimed against domestic nationalists and as such incited protests during performances in the theater.[24] In *Osel a stín*, the authors, with frightening foresight, have the donkey say: "The old pure Abderian race will live. Discard your brains, forget how to read and write, destroy everything that has been invented and written, and listen to the voice of the new, third Abdera" ("Jen stará čistá abderská rasa bude žít. Zahoďte mozky, zapomeňte číst a psát, spalte vše, co bylo vymyšleno a napsáno, a slyšte hlas nové, třetí Abdéry").[25] While this passage references the Nazis' book burning, later, a bilingual song text refers to the Reichstag fire: "He who wants to conquer Volk und Land / braucht manchmal einen kleinen Reichstagbrand" (Kdo ovládnout chce

---

22 *Osvobozené divadlo*, disc 2, track 8.

23 Václav Holzknecht, *Jaroslav Ježek a Osvobozené divadlo*, 2nd ed. [1st ed. 1957] (Prague: ARSCI, 2007), 108.

24 Michal Schonberg, *Osvobozené*, trans. Ivo Řezníček (Toronto: 68 Publishers, 1988 [PhD. diss., 1979]), 273–74.

25 Jiří Voskovec and Jan Werich, *Hry Osvobozeného divadla I* (Prague: Československý spisovatel, 1961), 133.

Volk und Land. . .). The title of this song is "Usměrněná píseň," and *usměrnění* is the Czech equivalent to the German term *Gleichschaltung*, which means the enforced unification of institutions, culture, and everyday life with Nazi ideology, bringing them under the regime's control.[26] It has a simple piano accompaniment so that the text can be easily understood, and at the beginning of the refrain Ježek cited "Es war einmal ein Musikus," a popular song by Friedrich Schwarz.

With programs like this, the leftist and liberal company became a thorn in the side of the Nazis. However, its downfall came at the hands of the authorities of the illiberal Second Czechoslovak Republic, which was proclaimed after the forced cession of the Sudetenland to Germany in 1938. That fall, the theater, which was seen as a troublemaker by local fascists, had its license revoked, effectively leading to a ban.[27] In January 1939, Voskovec, Werich, and Ježek fled across the ocean, just in time before the German occupation of Prague in March 1939 (see Chapter 23).[28]

Back in Prague after the end of the war, Voskovec and Werich worked to revive their theater (Ježek passed away in New York in 1942). However, following the 1948 Communist Coup, Voskovec left the country. While Werich continued his activities in communist Czechoslovakia, Voskovec's name had to be kept secret in public, and over time, Miroslav Horníček stepped into his roles in the plays. It turned out that the satire *Těžká Barbora* ("Heavy Barbora"), originally directed at the specific situation before World War II, had a timeless quality and continued to resonate with the audience under new political circumstances.[29] Thus, the productions of this and other plays originally by the Liberated Theater retained their popular appeal. In their extemporizing, Werich and Horníček could be quite critical of the new regime. However, this openness came at the cost of integrating the initially independent ensemble into the state theater administrative structures. After a temporary stay in Karlín's former Theater Varieté, the company returned to Wenceslas Square in 1956 and

---

[26] This song was a replacement for "Bůh suď," which contained a direct reference to Hitler and led to an official protest from the Third Reich.

[27] See Jiří Voskovec and Jan Werich, *Osel a stín* (Prague: Čs. spisovatel, 1965), 150–57; Karel Hodač documented the press reactions in Karel Hodač, ed., *Spadla opona Osvobozeného divadla. Tisk z let 1938–1952 o Osvobozeném divadle* (Brno: self-pub., 1995).

[28] They were helped by the dancer and member of the cabaret Pfeffermühle Lotte Goslar, who herself emigrated to Prague and performed at the Liberated Theater in the 1935 *Balada z hadrů*. Josef Träger, "Cestou k politické a sociální satiře," in Voskovec and Werich, *Hry Osvobozeného divadla I*, 529.

[29] Just, "Nebyl jen Semafor," 12.

acquired the neutral name Theater ABC.[30] Although the ensemble kept relying on "small forms," its organizational structure made it more like the regulated, mainstream theaters. Stuck in the past in terms of its repertoire, the company was now financially supported by the state. More so than before, the post-war Liberated Theater and its successor troupes oscillated between improvisation on one hand and organization on the other, between artistic innovation and mass entertainment, and between rejection and recognition by the elites. The ossification of Theater ABC in the 1950s created the opportunity and the desire for new companies operated by younger generations according to their ideals to step in.

From the Liberated Theater to the Semafor

Theater scholar Vladimír Just saw the new theater ensembles that formed in the late 1950s as driven by ideals of youthfulness, do-it-yourself approaches, a stress on improvisation, and anti-authoritarianism:[31]

Anyone can surround themselves with friends, whitewash a cellar, clear out an attic, take a bucket and a brush, and paint white stripes in a forgotten room – like [Jiří] Suchý did at the Na Zábradlí Theater. By doing so, a space can be reimagined, taken over, domesticated, while more "pragmatic" colleagues try to obtain relevant permits from the authorities. The point was not to actually play theater but to play with words. Not everyone can be Ferdinand Havlík [Semafor's bandleader], but many people can dust off a guitar or persuade a friend from the local brass band to come with a clarinet and try playing the blues together. And in five weeks, it's the premiere!

Každý se může obklopit svými přáteli, vybílit sklep, vyklidit půdu, vzít kbelík a štětku a pomalovat bílými pruhy – jako [Jiří] Suchý Na zábradlí – nějakou zapadlou místnost. Tím si, zatímco pragmatičtější kolega shání na úřadech příslušné razítko, ten prostor pro sebe znovu stvoří, osvojí, zdomácní. Ne[šlo o to] rovnou hrát divadlo, ale hrát si se slovy. Každý nemůže být Ferdinandem Havlíkem, ale může například oprášit kytaru anebo přemluvit kamaráda z místní dechovky, ať někdy dorazí s klarinetem a zkusí s nimi dohromady blues. A za pět neděl je premiéra!

Both the Semafor and Rokoko have been called "song theaters" ("divadla písniček"). Regarding the musical component, the musical numbers in the new ensembles' productions deviated from the traditional role of theater

---

[30] See Just, "Nebyl jen Semafor," 12; and Vondráček, *Jaroslav Ježek*, 249–50.
[31] Just, "Nebyl jen Semafor," 15.

music. Instead of supporting the plot, it seems to almost interrupt, which followed the model established by director Honzl at the Liberated Theater. At the same time, critics have pointed out that the audience at these theaters differed from that in established venues, and their loud reactions were reminiscent of concertgoers at rock and roll and jazz concerts.[32] Music takes center stage in the "song theaters," and the intermittent, at times unconvincing scenes serve as transitions from one musical number to the next. From the perspective of the dramatic text, the music may seem detached, but within the organization of the theatrical event it appears to be exactly in the right place.[33]

Accordingly, the Semafor's stars were primarily singers, or at the very least, singing is what brought them fame. It was founded in 1959 by Jiří Suchý, a trained advertising graphic designer, and Jiří Šlitr, a trained lawyer (just as Červený, Voskovec, and Werich). Suchý was also a founding member of the Theater Na Zábradlí in 1958 and had previously performed with Šlitr at the Reduta wine bar. The repertoire of the Semafor centered around songs with words by Suchý and music by Šlitr, most of which they had previously performed in the Reduta. Some hits gained enormous popularity outside the theater: "Pramínek vlasů" ("A Strand of Hair," 1959), "Malé kotě" ("A Small Kitten," 1961), "Co jsem měl dnes k obědu" ("What I Had for Lunch Today," 1966), to only name a few. By 1963, the Semafor had to move to no fewer than fourteen venues due to government restrictions, often citing fire-safety regulations as an excuse.[34] Finally, the company found a permanent stage in the Passage Alfa. This era ended abruptly with Šlitr's fatal poisoning from a gas leak in a heating system on December 26, 1969.[35] Under Suchý's leadership, the theater continues to operate to this day (as of 2023).

Although he initially performed exclusively as a pianist, in 1962 Šlitr began to appear in stage roles as well, first in the show *Jonáš a tingl-tangl* ("Jonáš and the Sideshow"). Suchý describes the power and success of Šlitr's first performances in a memoir as follows:[36]

Sitting at the piano came naturally to him, but when he spoke, it was almost unreal. He stood up, turned to the audience, his eyes fixed somewhere, and then he

---

[32] Just, "Nebyl jen Semafor," 14–15.   [33] Just, "Nebyl jen Semafor," 16–17.

[34] Petr Kalina, "Divadlo Semafor," *Český hudební slovník osob a institucí*, https://slovnik .ceskyhudebnislovnik.cz/component/mdictionary/?task=record.record_detail&id=2555, last modified March 14, 2020, accessed April 10, 2024.

[35] Many have speculated that Šlitr committed suicide.

[36] Suchý cited in Jiří Datel Novotný, ed., *Ďábel z Vinohrad. Vzpomínka na Jiřího Šlitra* (Prague: XYZ, 2010), 16–17.

delivered his line in such a peculiar, whimsical manner. He said the first sentence, and there was tremendous laughter. He said the second sentence, and there was applause. When he said the third sentence, I felt like the roof of the theater would fly off, it was roaring in there. They thought he was a masterful figure, and they appreciated him greatly.

Sedět u piana mu šlo, ale když promluvil, byla to věc téměř neskutečná. Vstal, obrátil se k publiku, oči upřené kamsi, a pak řekl tu svou větu takovým zvláštním, nabiflovaným způsobem. Řekl první větu a ozval se ohromnej smích. Řekl druhou větu a měl potlesk. Když řekl třetí větu, měl jsem pocit, že uletí střecha divadla, tak to tam burácelo. Mysleli si, že je to taková mistrná figura, a hrozně ho brali.

In the second half of the 1960s, Suchý and Šlitr began to act more independently. Suchý, in particular, drew strong inspiration from Werich. Together with Šlitr, Suchý performed and adapted Ježek's songs, and this practice intensified after Šlitr's death. In 1966, Šlitr performed a solo program titled *Ďábel z Vinohrad* ("The Devil from the Vinohrady District"), which was nevertheless still written by Suchý, like all his previous works. Musically, Šlitr's preference for new musical trends such as British rock becomes noticeable in this show. The new sound is also due to the fact that the previous arranger and bandleader, Jaromír Havlík, temporarily left the theater.

Šlitr's 1964 song "Golem" can be understood as both a stylistic reminiscence of The Beatles ("She Loves You") and a parody of the British band's songs. The final notes of "Golem" seamlessly transition into the opening notes of Voskovec and Werich's 1931 "Píseň strašlivá o Golemovi"; Voskovec and Werich are also mentioned in the later song. It becomes evident that some of the songs were innovative and responsive to contemporary trends in 1960s pop music, while others drew from older traditions and were adapted to the needs and sensibilities of the 1960s. "Golem" can be considered a synthesis, as it encompasses both aspects. The title and the musical style created a link between the old and the new.

The 1969 show *Jonáš a doktor Matrace* ("Jonáš and Doctor Mattress") represents a surprising turn backwards. First, it invokes the imaginary character of the cabaret artist Jonáš, who had not been used in Suchý and Šlitr's shows since 1962. Second, the show's music reflects the return of Jaromír Havlík, who continued to collaborate with the company even after Šlitr's death.[37] The music avoids new trends and returns to Dixieland jazz, particularly in the song "Mississippi." The connection with the Liberated

---

[37] On Havlík, see Petr Ch. Kalina, "Tvorba Ferdinanda Havlíka pro divadlo Semafor," *Muzikologické fórum* 11, nos. 1–2 (2022): 57–64.

Theater became unmistakable in the closing song "Proti všem" ("Against Everyone") through parallels to the Liberated Theater's "Proti větru." This song also contains skillful musical references to several other of Ježek's pieces: "Full Hand," "Pochod stoprocentních mužů" ("March of One-Hundred-Percent Men"), and "Svět patří nám" ("The World Belongs to Us").

Whereas the older "Proti větru" carries a clear message of overcoming obstacles, Suchý and Šlitr's "Proti všem" presents a detached protest that is exaggerated to the point of absurdity: "Proti autům proti jmění / Proti skautům proti bdění / Proti době proti frakům / Proti sobě proti mrakům" ("Against cars, against wealth / Against scouts, against staying awake / Against the times, against tails / Against each other, against clouds").[38] It is unclear who or what the text is directed against, and whether it should be taken seriously as a protest at all. This can be seen as one of the typical tactics for confusing the totalitarian regime. On the one hand, there are no clear references to a real situation: anyone trying to take this song seriously and attempting to censor it would appear ridiculous. At the same time, the absurdity is entertaining, and it cannot be denied that it reflects a general sense of nonconformity.

For some, the Semafor represented an amplification of the Liberated Theater under altered circumstances, while for others, it was a feeble replication. The criticism of the Semafor resembled that which had been directed at the Liberated Theater in the past. Outdated forms of avant-garde elements were served to the audience in easily digestible doses, allowing the audience to revel in a temporary state of nonconformity. It was only under the pressure exerted by the regime, which had intended the opposite effect, that the relevance of comparatively harmless shows and songs grew enormously. The question of the company's proximity to or distance from the Liberated Theater is still contested, but I would like to caution against overemphasizing this question, as the Semafor offers many more complex artistic and political matters to explore.

With *Jonáš a doktor Matrace*, the Semafor's authors, who were no longer that young themselves, distanced themselves from youth culture. In a time when new styles of popular music were becoming available, the potential of jazz to represent cultural and political provocations was wearing thin – the Semafor's use of jazz idioms could appear as nonconformist only through

---

[38] Jiří Suchý, *Encyklopedie Jiřího Suchého, svazek 10, Divadlo 1963–1969* (Prague: Karolinum and Pražská imaginace, 2002), 269. The lack of punctuation in the original Czech can be regarded as part of Suchý's avant-garde stance.

its link to the Liberated Theater. For Czech listeners, the sound of jazz is so closely associated with the sound of Voskovec and Werich that those who recognize this connection also discern its nonconformist message, which is conveyed through the music alone. The Semafor capitalized on this sound in their songs, opening up an additional layer of meaning. Thus, the Semafor ultimately continued the trend to juxtapose incongruous elements, such as "high" art and "mere" entertainment, associated with the "theaters of small forms" in general. The Semafor's references to the Liberated Theater not only play with and establish collective memory, but also highlight the Liberated Theater's pioneering role in the use of nonconformist music (jazz) for political means (political satire).

28 | Understanding Czech Rock from the Period of Normalization

JAN BLÜML

The development of rock music in the Czech lands was tied both to contemporaneous trends in Anglo-American music and the cultural policies of the Czechoslovak Communist Party. The emergence of rock and roll in the late 1950s partially overlapped with the period of Stalinist repressions in Czechoslovakia, and the regime initially tried to stop the nonconformist cultural import from the United States. In the 1960s, Czechoslovakia underwent a period of liberalization and openness to the West, and as a result, Czechoslovak citizens could experience the beginnings of Beatlemania and the differentiation of Western rock music in the late 1960s. The occupation of the country by Warsaw Pact armies in 1968 initiated the period of "normalization," which prevented the spread of pro-Western ideas and reintroduced repressive cultural policies. In music, this repression was aimed mainly at rock music due to its wide social appeal, particularly among young people.

The following chapter first explores the professionalization of Czech rock under the influence of The Beatles in the 1960s and then focuses on the distinction between official and unofficial types of popular music that emerged in the 1970s and 1980s. My discussion of select musicians during this period illustrates how rock music was politicized during normalization, and how this politicization influenced the later Czech historiography of rock.

The Origins of Czech Rock and Beatlemania

Until the mid-1960s, Czech rock developed mainly in Prague, where about 300 amateur groups formed.[1] The history of one of these groups, Olympic, exemplifies the professionalization of Czech rock. The group was co-founded by guitarist Petr Janda, who first gained experience in the rock and roll ensemble Sputnici (The Sputniks) and later in his own Big Beat Quintet,

This chapter was translated from Czech to English by Martin Nedbal.
[1] Vojtěch Lindaur and Ondřej Konrád, *Bigbít* (Prague: Plus, 2010), 20.

which specialized in instrumental music in the style of The Shadows.[2] Besides these amateur groups, Czech rock was also initially tied to small theatrical ensembles that specialized in literary and musical shows, which composer and writer Jindřich Brabec characterizes as "mixing satire, poetry, rock and roll, modern jazz, fashionable Charleston, traditional jazz revival, twist, and beat."[3] Olympic was initially connected to one such small Prague theater ensemble – Semafor (see Chapter 27). The group accompanied several Czech singers as part of Semafor's show *Ondráš podotýká* ("Ondráš Points Out"), which included several American rock and roll songs sung in English. The music from the show inspired the creation of the first Czech rock and roll recordings. In 1964, the state music publisher Supraphon issued five singles by Olympic, including the first cover of The Beatles: "From Me to You" with the Czech title *Adresát neznámý* ("Addressee Unknown").[4] The singles were released commercially in the middle of 1964 and were soon sold out. Although Supraphon usually did not release extra copies of new recordings, the first rock disks went through many reprints, and by 1965, 400,000 rock disks were sold.[5] *Adresát neznámý* was particularly successful and became the fifth-best-selling record of 1964–66.[6]

Janda reminisced that employees and technicians of professional state music institutions and recording studios smiled condescendingly when confronted with amateur rock musicians, with their long hair and shabby guitars, and without any sheet music.[7] Janda also remembers that the less-than-ideal equipment of Czechoslovak recording studios contributed to the unrefined quality of the recordings:

We were recorded on mono tape recorders, first the bass, then the singing was mixed in. The percussion was recorded with a single microphone. Errors were not considered a big deal.

Natáčelo se na monomagnetofon nejdřív band a pak na druhý přimíchaný zpěv. K bicím se dával pouze jeden mikrofon. Některé chybičky se odpouštěly.[8]

Olympic became a trailblazer for Czech rock and roll in other ways, often under the influence of The Beatles. The Liverpool foursome set the

[2] Petr Korál, *Vzpomínky plíživé, aneb Jasná zpráva o Olympiku* (Prague: Bestia, 2002), 177.
[3] Jindřich Brabec, "Beatová injekce v produkci TOČRu," in *Taneční hudba a jazz 1968–69*, ed. Lubomír Dorůžka et al. (Prague: Supraphon, 1968), 147.
[4] See Jaromír Tůma, *Čtyři hrají rock, jasná zpráva o skupině Olympic* (Prague: Panton, 1986), 51. For more discographic information about the singles, see www.discogs.com/label/467985-Big-Beat-Supraphon, accessed March 21, 2024.
[5] Lindaur and Konrád, *Bigbít*, 19.   [6] Tůma, *Čtyři hrají rock*, 51.
[7] Petr Janda, *Olympic 50* (Prague: Knižní klub, 2012), 14.   [8] Janda, *Olympic 50*, 14.

tone for the aesthetics and ideology of 1960s rock, making prominent the idea that rock could rely on individual creativity and that performers could also write songs.[9] Olympic pursued similar goals: in 1964, the group left Semafor, stopped accompanying solo singers, and in 1965, they professionalized, meaning they left their previous jobs and registered as professional musicians with state authorities.

In 1965, Czechoslovakia became enthralled with Beatlemania, following the release of *A Hard Day's Night* in Britain in July 1964. According to Dagmar Fialová, it was the film *A Hard Day's Night* rather than the album that initiated Czechoslovak Beatlemania.[10] The film was first shown in Prague as part of the "Week of English Film" festival in October 1964, a mere three months after the British premiere, but the official Czechoslovak release did not come until June 23, 1965. The song "A Hard Day's Night" – broadcast under the Czech title "Perný den" ("Busy Day") – was particularly successful; it remained number one on the Czechoslovak chart Houpačka (The Swing) for most of 1965. Olympic assumed the role of the Czech Beatles and focused on combining the style of *A Hard Day's Night* with original songs in the Czech language. A famous example of this effort is "Želva" ("The Turtle") from 1967, the introduction of which evokes "I Should Have Known Better" by using a fast tempo with the repetitive alteration of basic harmonic progressions in the identical key of G major, and the use of the harmonica.

In 1968, "Želva" was incorporated into the album of the same name, the very first Czech rock album. In his study of this album, Czech musicologist Aleš Opekar pointed out that Olympic adopted many elements from the British Merseybeat style, including the sounds and rhythm of English texts, which were imitated in Czech.[11] At the same time, the album is quite distinct, thanks to the specific poetic style of the humorous and somewhat subversive lyrics by bass guitarist Pavel Chrastina, the unique timbre of Petr Janda's voice, and his individualistic compositional approach (see below). The album references a fascinating number of different styles and genres. The style of *A Hard Day's Night*, which was somewhat outdated by 1968, is juxtaposed with psychedelic rock and elements of traditional Czech music, which are particularly prominent in the song "Línej skaut" ("Lazy Scout"). According to Opekar, the song's triple meter with an accordion accompaniment resembles a folk tune, specifically the old market song *Ku*

---

[9] Rosy Shuker, *Popular Music: The Key Concepts* (New York: Routledge, 2010), 24.

[10] Dagmar Fialová, "Perné dny na plátně," in *Beatlemánie!*, ed. Peter Balog (Prague: Národní muzeum, 2010), 24.

[11] Aleš Opekar, "K počátkům českého rocku: nad prvním profilovým albem skupiny Olympic," *Hudební věda* 30 (1993): 60–69.

Praze je cesta dlouhá ("There Is a Long Road to Prague"); the song "Dědečkův duch" ("Grandpa's Ghost"), by contrast, references the sentiments of Czech tramping songs, associated with Czech tramping recreational activities and blending country and folk styles.[12]

Czech Adaptations of British Progressive Rock and American Underground

In the late 1960s, Czech rock music, following trends elsewhere, started to differentiate into multiple subgenres. This process was reflected in the first Czechoslovak Beat Festival, which took place in Prague's Lucerna Hall in 1967. Official critics, associated with the main Czech popular music magazine *Melodie*, especially appreciated the groups that emulated The Beatles and British rhythm and blues, represented by Cream. The festival's main prize was awarded to the Slovak group The Soulmen. Not everyone, however, followed the official doctrine of popular music criticism. For example, Ivan Martin Jirous, then a recent graduate in art history from Charles University in Prague and later the leader of the Czech underground, contradicted the views of Jaromír Tůma and others when he appreciated the happening of The Primitives Group from Prague, which was inspired by the American avant-garde, combined elements of theater, performance, and plastics arts, and which one official critic referred to as "a clown show."[13]

The second Beat Festival took place in December 1968 and incited similarly polarized reactions. Official critics were drawn mainly to The Nice, a British progressive rock group that fused rock, classical music, and jazz in the late style of The Beatles. According to Tůma, The Nice impressed the Czechoslovak audience and showed that there was still a significant distance between local groups and top performers abroad.[14] Jirous had a different view: he did not care for most of what was performed at the festival, except for The Primitives Group, who based their program on the American underground, specifically the work of The Mothers of Invention (led by Frank Zappa).[15]

---

[12] Opekar, "K počátkům českého rocku," 62.
[13] Ivan Martin Jirous, *Magorův zápisník*, ed. M. Špirit (Prague: Torst, 1997), 154. For the negative review, see Miloslav Langer, "19.–28. 3. 1967, Music F Club Praha. Přehlídka beatových skupin," *Melodie* 5, no. 9 (March 1967): 211.
[14] Jaromír Tůma, "Vánoční beat," *Melodie* 7, no. 2 (February 1969): 49.
[15] Jirous, *Magorův zápisník*, 156–57.

In 1968 and 1969, Czech musicologist Josef Kotek studied the phenomenon of the underground. In 1968, Kotek reviewed the Internationale Essener Songtage (Essen International Song Days) for *Hudební rozhledy* ("Musical Horizons"), the journal of the Union of Czechoslovak Composers. The festival featured American avant-garde groups, including The Mothers of Invention with Zappa, as well as German Krautrock, and the Czech band Olympic, whose performance was not very successful. Kotek discussed the nature of the underground and claimed that its political proclamations represented mere provocations and whims of "the children of the economic boom."[16] In a later article, Kotek explored the question of whether underground music could be transferred in its authentic form from its original social environment in the capitalist West to socialist Czechoslovakia. He concluded that such a transfer was theoretically possible because the economic (and other) difficulties in 1969 Czechoslovakia shared similar social consequences to the economic prosperity in West Germany and other Western countries: "Undernourishment and satiety – both produce the sentiments of emptiness, desolation, a scene from Kafka's *The Castle* in young people" ("Nenasycení i přesycení – obojí jako by v mladém člověku vyvolávalo pocit marnosti, bezútěšnosti, scenérii Kafkova *Zámku*").[17] At the end of the article, Kotek rejected the possibility that the underground could become as socially disruptive and shocking in Czechoslovakia as it was in West Germany because social criticism featured prominently in mainstream Czechoslovak rock:

Our worries and sorrows are quite different from those in the USA and West Germany – especially after [the occupation of Czechoslovakia in] August 1968. And the songs that react, and hopefully will keep reacting, to our domestic situation could be moved "to the underground" only against the will of thousands and hundreds of thousands of listeners who eagerly await them.

Naše starosti, potíže a smutky jsou od oněch v USA a NSR přece jen hodně daleko – alespoň od srpna 1968. A písničky, jež na naši domácí situaci reagují a snad ani nadále reagovat nepřestanou, by mohly být odsunuty "do podzemí" leda proti vůli tisíců a statisíců posluchačů, kteří na ně u nás doma tak dychtivě čekají.[18]

This situation did not last long, however, and throughout the early 1970s, mainstream Czechoslovak rock became primarily apolitical. Contrary to Kotek's views, moreover, the strengthening of cultural restrictions during

---

[16] Josef Kotek, "Paradoxy z Essenu," *Hudební rozhledy* 21 (1968): 630–31.
[17] Josef Kotek, "Underground Music a její sociální otazníky," *Melodie* 7, no. 2 (February 1969): 37–40.
[18] Kotek, "Underground Music a její sociální otazníky," 37.

normalization affected nonconformist currents in rock and stamped them with specific political meanings. Whereas in the West, the mechanisms of a market economy transformed the sentiments of revolt that the "over-satiated" youth associated with the underground into a fashion, in the Czech lands, the same musical style came to be associated with true political dissent and was commercialized only after the fall of communism in 1989.

Official and Unofficial Styles: Blue Effect and The Plastic People of the Universe

The process by which the underground transformed into an unofficial, dissident style during normalization was connected to the administrative system of "requalification" introduced in the early 1970s.[19] The system relied on continual political reviews of potential popular music artists. It became illegal for unsuccessful requalification seekers to be active artists. These cultural policies split the progressive rock scene, one of the main types of popular music of the period, into official and unofficial segments, each of which drew inspiration from different foreign models. Official rock musicians predominantly emulated British groups, such as The Beatles, The Nice, and others. Their music emphasized instrumental elements, clarity of form, apolitical and abstract subjects, and virtuosity, often connected to the musicians' conservatory training. These official groups were allowed to record albums with state music publishers, appear in media, give concerts abroad, and reach a wider audience. Unofficial rock musicians, by contrast, who could not benefit from the support of the state, were drawn to the American avant-garde, specifically to groups and artists associated with the Fluxus, The Velvet Underground, and The Mothers of Invention. The attraction to these artists was not necessarily based on a natural inclination to one of many models, but rather a deeper psychological identification with the extravagant and provocative yet playful and entertaining aesthetics of the American avant-garde, which did not accentuate instrumental virtuosity but paid attention to conceptual art and the form of the "happening." Music that incorporated social criticism prominently, such as the work of Frank Zappa, made a deep social and intellectual impact in Czechoslovakia's unofficial culture.[20]

[19] Miroslav Vaněk, *Byl to jenom rock'n'roll? Hudební alternativa v komunistickém Československu 1956–1989* (Prague: Academia, 2010), 386–404.

[20] Jan Blüml, *Progresivní rock: světová a československá scéna ve vybraných reflexích* (Prague: Togga, 2017), 266–67.

The differences between the official and unofficial types of Czech rock are illustrated in the histories of the groups Blue Effect (also known under the Czech names Modrý efekt and M efekt during normalization) and The Plastic People of the Universe. Both bands were established in 1968 and disbanded in the late 1980s but developed different kinds of refined aesthetics under different conditions and for different audiences. The main representative of Blue Effect was Radim Hladík, who studied at the Prague Conservatory, became the first Czech rock guitar virtuoso, and found inspiration in both British progressive rock and classical music. Hladík also claimed that although it may seem paradoxical, he was never interested in Zappa.[21] Blue Effect recordings from the early 1970s were based on the fusion of rock and jazz. One example is the album *Coniunctio* that Blue Effect recorded together with the Jazz Q Praha ensemble in 1970. Whereas the compositions by the collaborating jazz musicians point to the influence of free jazz, Hladík's "Návštěva u tety Markéty a vypití šálku čaje" ("Visiting Aunt Margaret and Drinking a Cup of Tea") resembles the style of the British band Jethro Tull. Another example of Blue Effect's interest in fusion was the acclaimed 1971 album *Nová syntéza* ("New Synthesis") that attempted to combine rock with big band jazz. Thanks to this collaborative project, Blue Effect was invited to the prestigious Prague International Jazz Festival and other prominent public forums. In fall 1971, the group appeared in the successful program produced by Prague's Theater of Music (Divadlo hudby) about contemporaneous types of music fusion. Later, Blue Effect collaborated with the Socialist Youth Union in an educational program that tied together various forms of popular and classical music. Because of these ties to jazz and classical music, Czech critics in the early 1970s often used Blue Effect as an example of how popular music could have positive effects on the education of young people.[22] In the mid-1970s, Blue Effect embraced symphonic rock in the style of the British group Yes. In his 1976 review of the first concert with repertoire in their new style, Czech music critic Josef Vlček claimed that, to the unsuspecting audience, the group offered music not previously performed in Czechoslovakia – it was modern, new, inspired by the harmonic inventions of the English symphonic-rock group, yet was also "essentially unique and original" ("bytostně vlastní a původní").[23] This new musical approach informed

---

[21] Richard Müller, "Verím hudbe, kterú hrám. Radim Hladík," *Populár* 12, no. 5 (May 1980): 17.
[22] See, for example, Leo Jehne, "Kde a co jsou hodnoty v pop music," *Melodie* 10, no. 2 (February 1972): 38.
[23] Josef Vlček, "Zbytečná skromnost M. Efektu," *Jazz* 5, no. 16 (1976): 30.

the albums *Svět hledačů* ("The World of Seekers"), released in 1979, and *33*, released in 1981. The songs on these albums were based on the predominantly abstract poetic texts by Pavel Vrba. In the later 1980s, the group went through several personnel changes and could not compete with new styles and genres, leading to its disbandment in 1990.

The Plastic People of the Universe developed the aesthetics of the American underground, initially introduced to the Czech public by The Primitives Group. Like The Primitives Group, The Plastic People explored elaborated staging collaborations with Jirous, who became the group's artistic leader, similar to Andy Warhol's collaborations with The Velvet Underground. In the late 1960s, The Plastic People could still perform in official venues; after one such concert they even received an award from the magazine *Mladý svět* ("Youthful World") for their large-scale psychedelic song "The Universe Symphony and Melody about Plastic Doctor," with English sung texts, Czech recitatives, and quotes from famous rock groups that illustrated the genre's history. In the early 1970s, however, the non-conformist group lost its official status. The group became more politically subversive after the illegal festival of "second" (that is, unofficial) culture in the village of Bojanovice in 1976. Most of the participants, including the group's members, were imprisoned soon after the festival's end, and Jirous received the longest sentence of eighteen months (based on the law regarding disorderly conduct). The trial of the underground caught the attention of Czech dissident intellectuals including the later president Václav Havel and contributed to the formation of a public anti-communist resistance platform, called Charta 77 (Charter 77).[24]

In 1974, The Plastic People used makeshift equipment to record their first "studio" album, *Egon Bondy's Happy Hearts Club Banned*, the title of which imitated Zappa's parodistic reference to The Beatles in his album *We're Only in It for the Money*. Egon Bondy was an eccentric Czech poet and philosopher who also wrote many of the texts used by the band. The recording combined Bondy's provocative poetry with Milan Hlavsa's individualistic singing style and music and the experimental use of the theremin. The album was imbued with the spirit of the American underground; Czech music historian Jaroslav Riedel noted that the recording combined hypnotic ostinatos that evoked The Velvet Underground, bizarre humor and sound diversity reminiscent of Zappa, an intermingling of heavy rock with eruptive free-jazz entrances in the saxophone resembling the radical aspects of Captain Beefheart's

---

[24] See Ladislav Kudrna, *Kapela: pozadí akce, která stvořila Chartu 77* (Prague: Academia, 2017).

music, and a humorous vocal cacophony that was typical of The Fugs.[25] The album was first released in France in 1978 and was available in Czechoslovakia only unofficially.

Like Blue Effect, The Plastic People followed late 1970s progressive rock trends to maximalize forms, which is reflected in their ambitious theatrical work *Pašijové hry velikonoční* ("Easter Passion Plays"). The complex work, with music by Hlavsa and a libretto by Vratislav Brabenec derived from biblical texts, took half a year to complete and was premiered in a concert setting with an enlarged ten-member ensemble in front of several hundred spectators in the barn of Václav Havel's eastern Bohemian country estate Hrádeček. Hlavsa may have been partially inspired by Krzysztof Penderecki's *St. Luke Passion*, but Riedel claims that Hlavsa mostly listened to "the Gothic recordings" ("gotické nahrávky") by the German singer Nico.[26] A recording was released under the title *Passion Play* by the Canadian firm Boží Mlýn Productions.

In the 1980s, The Plastic People went through many personnel changes – which were often induced under political pressure – and disbanded in 1988. During their last years, The Plastic People collaborated more closely with Václav Havel, who chose texts by domestic and foreign poets for the band and wrote the liner notes for the 1984 album *Hovězí porážka* ("The Beef Slaughter"). Havel explained the importance of the group in the history of Czech rock:

. . .one could even say that it was the Plastics who first – and in isolation – took the road that is nowadays followed by all Czechoslovak rock music that is worth anything. It is as if they were the first Czechoslovak rock musicians who started to map out some prominent sentiments and experiences of today's people and tried to express them in ways that were appropriate for the local environment, traditions, and language.

. . .snad by bylo možné dokonce říct, že to byli právě Plastici, kdo začal – osaměle – klestit před lety cestu, po níž se dnes ubírá téměř všechna československá rocková hudba, která za něco stojí. Jako by to byli prostě oni, kdo první začal v československé rockové hudbě mapovat některé dominantní pocity a zkušenosti člověka této chvíle a hledat zdejšímu prostředí, tradici i jazyku přiměřený způsob jejich vyjádření.[27]

---

[25] Jaroslav Riedel, *Plastic People a český underground* (Prague: Galén, 2016), 123.

[26] Riedel, *Plastic People a český underground*, 226.

[27] Václav Havel, *Do různých stran. Eseje a články z let 1983–1989*, ed. V. Prečan (Prague: Lidové noviny, 1990), 240–44.

The Reception of Czech Rock from the Normalization Period

The positions of Blue Effect and The Plastic People within Czechoslovak normalization culture were radically different although both were formed in the late 1960s, the period that John Covach associated with the concept of "hippie aesthetic."[28] Whereas Blue Effect was part of the official culture and participated in various types of public events, including educational programs in schools, The Plastic People became the subject of negative propaganda in films, TV series, and newspaper articles that showed them as socially pathological, criminal, and ideologically subversive. The two groups' positions within state cultural policies also affected the views of Czech critics and rock historians, who tended to defend and favor dissident phenomena and be skeptical toward official culture. These views also prompted many Czech critics to value political content and social commentary over musical precision. In a 1979 manifesto of Czech alternative rock, Josef Vlček claimed, for example, that whether a group had something to say to people was more important than whether a singer had perfect intonation and a drummer could keep the rhythm; in his view, "technical prowess, perfection, and the closeness to modern jazz and classical music [were] the most useless measures of criticism" ("nejzbytečnějšími kritickými měřítky jsou technická zdatnost, perfektnost a blízkost k modernímu jazzu nebo klasické hudbě").[29] Vlček's viewpoints were derived from Anglo-American criticism that admired punk rock and also reflected experience of the repression of rock music by state authorities and with the original ideology of the 1960s underground. These views also represented a major reason why anti-communist Czech intellectuals and critics adored The Plastic People. This adoration is prominent in both Havel's activities and Vlček's essay about Czech rock, published in 1989 (before the end of communism).[30] Vlček views The Plastic People as the creators of "the first Czech rock style" ("prvního českého rockového stylu") that could not be imitated anywhere else in the world. Vlček does not provide a clear definition of this "rock style," but it is clear he associates it with the literary aspect of their songs and the

---

[28] John Covach, "The Hippie Aesthetic: Cultural Positioning and Musical Ambition in Early Progressive Rock," in *The Ashgate Library of Essays on Popular Music: Rock*, ed. Mark Spicer (Burlington, VT: Ashgate, 2012), 65–75.

[29] Josef Vlček cited in Petr Hrabalík, "Úkoly české alternativní hudby," www.ceskatelevize.cz/specialy/bigbit/ceskoslovensko/clanky/193-ukoly-ceske-alternativni-hudby/, accessed March 21, 2024.

[30] Josef Vlček, "Nová vlna v Čechách – příběh dušičkový," in *Excentrici v přízemí*, ed. Aleš Opekar and Josef Vlček (Prague: Panton, 1989), 27.

ways in which The Plastic People set moral examples and embraced anti-commercialism. In particular, he appreciated that the songs showed realistic images from life at the fringes of society, talking about sex, youth drug abuse, and other problems that state authorities puritanically overlooked.

The narrative of The Plastic People's exceptionalism became even more prominent in the post-communist era when Czech commentators turned away from the formerly official culture and fully embraced dissident countercultures. In the last thirty years, Czech historians have paid more attention to these countercultures than any other current of Czech popular music. The official rock music of communist Czechoslovakia, including Czech adaptations of British progressive rock and 1970s jazz rock, was viewed through a political prism as a desperate way out of the quagmire of the normalization era.[31] In 2018, Czech musician Mikoláš Chadima went so far as to refer to the continual focus of post-communist historians and critics on the pre-revolutionary Czech underground and The Plastic People's legacy as a new type of mythology that resembled the celebratory narratives about the heroes of the communist period.[32]

Conclusion

Czech rock music emerged in the mid-1960s in reaction to the British invasion spearheaded by The Beatles. In the late 1960s, several different rock subgenres appeared. The first Czechoslovak Beat Festivals of 1967 and 1968 illustrated a differentiation of the Czechoslovak rock scene into groups that drew inspiration from British models and those that identified with the ideas of the underground mediated through American music. The two groups reflected a more general duality in the aesthetics of rock: the first group of rock musicians and critics valued traditional virtuosity and formal perfection, whereas the second group focused on social commentary. As the examples of Blue Effect and The Plastic People illustrate, both approaches were politicized. Blue Effect initially benefited from the conservative cultural policies of the communist authorities but was later criticized as "governmental" and "corrupt."[33] The other approach became associated with Czech dissent and was therefore privileged over other cultural forms of the communist era and considered a part of elite intellectual culture after 1989.

---

[31] See, for example, Jan Rejžek, "Krátká jasná stopa Mahagonu," in *Československý jazzrock* [CD booklet] (Prague: Indies Happy Trails, 2008), 15.

[32] Mikoláš Chadima, *Alternativa 2* (Prague: Galén, 2018), 650.

[33] Mikoláš Chadima, *Alternativa 1* (Prague: Galén, 2015), 12–13.

It is clear, nevertheless, that the view, outlined by Havel and Vlček, of The Plastic People as a central phenomenon of Czech rock history and as representative of "the first Czech rock style," is one-sided because it overlooks the long-term contributions of groups such as Olympic in the 1960s and Blue Effect in the 1970s and 1980s. The tendentiousness of this approach is illustrated by Vlček's claims that The Plastic People's *Egon Bondy's Happy Hearts Club Banned*, which he sees as the "most famous album of the Czech underground," was based on "radical musical structures," without acknowledging that, similar to the work of Blue Effect and other official Czechoslovak groups (particularly Collegium Musicum), it was also strongly influenced by foreign models.[34]

It is also significant that the exceptionalism of The Plastic People in the Czech critical discourse on rock music does not correlate to how current global platforms, such as Progarchives.com, discuss this group. The American author of the group's profile on Progarchives.com characterizes the band as "a rather innovative but otherwise unexceptional post-psychedelic band" that would not tower in the history of modern rock music had they not been active behind the Iron Curtain and had they not become a symbol of anti-totalitarian resistance.[35] On the same platform, a Canadian author writes that Blue Effect was "one of the major progressive bands in Czechoslovakia; they were to their own country what OMEGA were to Hungary, or SBB to Poland."[36] The artistic viability of Blue Effect's works from the 1970s, which Tůma has called "somewhat detached jazz-rock fusion" ("poněkud odtažitá jazzrocková fúze"), is also illustrated in the fact that some of these works continued to garner attention in the following decades.[37] For example, a fragment from Blue Effect's 1971 album *Nová syntéza* was used as a sample in the 2002 European hit "The Magic Key."

The one-sided and ideological approach in the post-communist era to Czech popular music from the 1970s and 1980s was initiated by researchers without musicological training, predominantly historians

---

[34] Vlček, "Nová vlna v Čechách," 28. One example of The Plastic People's dependence on foreign models is Milan Hlavsa's song "Magické noci" ("During a magical night") that is nearly identical to the introduction to Zappa's 1966 "Help, I'm a Rock."

[35] Bob Moore (aka ClemofNazareth), "Plastic People of the Universe," in *Prog Archives: Your Ultimate Prog Rock Resource*, http://www.progarchives.com/artist.asp?id=2800, accessed March 21, 2024.

[36] Lise (HIBOU), "Blue Effect (Modrý Efekt)," in *Prog Archives: Your Ultimate Prog Rock Resource*, http://www.progarchives.com/artist.asp?id=1493, accessed March 21, 2024.

[37] Jaromír Tůma, "Blue Effect (Modrý efekt; M. efekt)," in *Český hudební slovník osob a institucí*, ed. Petr Macek, last modified March 27, 2009, accessed March 21, 2024.

and sociologists. Such approaches, however, were not unique to Czech rock studies. Similar trends also affected international discourse on rock music in the form of "rockism," an influential ideology that continually and uncritically viewed "alternative" as superior to "mainstream" productions and idolized "the authentic old legend (or underground hero)."[38]

---

[38] Kelefa Sanneh, "The Rap against Rockism," *New York Times*, October 31, 2014.

29 | Czech Film Music: From Potpourri to Sound Design

ALEŠ BŘEZINA

Across more than a century of film music's history, numerous Czech and Slovak composers have excelled in the field. However, their works have gone largely unnoticed by musicologists. This chapter sheds light on some of the major paradigms and unique aspects of Czech film music by focusing on two key figures: Bohuslav Martinů and Zdeněk Liška. Prior to World War II, Bohuslav Martinů made important contributions to the emerging medium of sound film, although film music did not represent a major part of his overall output; and in the second half of the twentieth century, Zdeněk Liška became a major figure in this domain and devoted his entire career to creating film scores. In more recent decades, several diverse composers have emerged at the forefront of the Czech film music scene.

From Silent to Sound Films

By 1920, there were 450 cinemas in Prague, and their screenings included the first Czech films.[1] The musical accompaniment of these films often relied on works by Czech composers, such as Smetana, Dvořák, and Suk. However, as Czech musicologist Mirko Očadlík has pointed out, Mozart's themes were widespread in early Prague cinemas as well.[2] For example, themes from *Le nozze di Figaro* accompanied images of horse rides and chases of robbers in many cinemas, although the musical style often did not match the on-screen action. In small cinema halls, pre-existing music was performed in arrangements for piano or accordion, and in larger halls, by small orchestras consisting of a string trio or quartet, flute, clarinet, trumpet, trombone, and harmonium. Original film music was an exception until the 1920s. The first Czech original film score was composed by

This chapter was translated from Czech to English by Martin Nedbal.
Funding for this project was provided by the Czech Science Foundation (GAČR) under the project "Bohuslav Martinů's Music Theater 1913–1937" (GA21-21228S).

[1] See Antonín Matzner and Jiří Pilka, *Česká filmová hudba* (Prague: Dauphin, 2022), 17; and Luboš Bartošek, *Náš film. Kapitoly z dějin (1896–1945)* (Prague: Mladá fronta, 1985), 59.
[2] Mirko Očadlík, "Hudba v biografu," *Kino* 1, no. 4 (September 26, 1931): 50.

internationally renowned opera composer Karel Weis for the 1921 motion picture *Magdalena* directed by Vladimír Majer.

The first Czech sound films were based on purely commercial and sensational topics. Czech avant-garde artists and critics (the most significant being Karel Teige) responded to this trend by founding the New Film Club (Klub za nový film) in May 1927. In their program manifesto, they distanced themselves from earlier productions:[3]

Our attitude toward the existing Czech cinema is uncompromisingly rejecting and unyielding ... We will intervene in the press, through lectures and other successful forms of promotion, and boycott. A confrontation with foreign cinema shall prevent petty provincialism and the cult of local stars and finally prompt the interest in the questions of librettos [film scripts], photography, and new artistic and technological methods.

Náš poměr k dosavadnímu českému filmu je bezohledně odmítavý a nesmlouvavý ... Způsoby, jimiž zasáhneme, budou naše projevy tiskové, přednáškové a jiné úspěšné formy propagace a bojkotu. Konfrontací našeho s cizím filmem se má zabránit malichernému provincionalismu a kultu místních hvězd a postavit u nás konečně živé a aktuální otázky libreta, fotografie, jakož i nových metod uměleckých a technických.

A significant contribution to the development of many central figures in Czechoslovak cinema was the 1928 establishment of the film and photography department within the promotional section of the Baťa shoe company in the Moravian city of Zlín, which began to invest in film advertising by the end of the 1920s. The promotional films revolved primarily around various types of shoes. They were initially outsourced, but by the late 1920s, the Baťa factories began to use their own film technology. In the 1930s and 40s, the main composers for the Zlín commercials were Bedřich Kerten, Julius Kalaš, Eduard Ingriš, and František Škvor. In 1934, screenwriter and director Elmar Klos, producer Ladislav Kolda, and cameraman Alexander Hackenschmied joined the film department, and the company began producing sound commercials. Several members of this team later achieved success in their own independent work. Klos collaborated on several outstanding films with Jan Kadár, including *Obchod na korze* ("Shop on Main Street"), which won an Academy Award for Best International Feature Film in 1966. Hackenschmied later became a top documentary film-maker and photographer in the USA under the name Alexander Hammid. In 1936, the Zlín company opened a film studio with a laboratory, equipped with state-of-the-art technology

---

[3] Cited in Matzner and Pilka, *Česká filmová hudba*, 21.

purchased in the United States, where Klos and his colleagues studied the work of Hollywood studios, including Walt Disney Animation Studios. One of the early films by the Klos team was 1935's *Střevíček* ("The Slipper") with music by Bohuslav Martinů.

Martinů's Music for Silent and Sound Films

From 1923, Martinů worked in France, where it was common for leading young composers, such as Jacques Ibert, Darius Milhaud, and Georges Auric, to dedicate their efforts to film music. Martinů respected only Arthur Honegger, who composed music for thirty-six films.[4] Martinů contributed music to four shorter films and one feature-length film.[5] He received his first film commission, *Slovácké tance a obyčeje* ("Dances and Customs of Moravian Slovakia," H134), in 1922, before his departure for Paris and prior to the sound-film era. Thus, the music was not part of the film reel but was performed live during the screenings. Director Jan Antonín Palouš asked Martinů to transcribe folksongs and melodies that were performed at a folk festival in the Moravian town of Uherské Hradiště and were preserved in the National Museum in Prague. From the selected folksongs, Martinů created a three-part piano suite.[6]

Martinů also engaged with silent-film music in his 1928–29 "film opera" *Tři přání aneb Vrtkavosti života* ("Three Wishes or Inconstancy of Life," H175).[7] The first two acts of this opera, with a libretto by prominent French Dadaist Georges Ribemont-Dessaignes, follow the filming of a silent movie, and the third depicts the movie's premiere with the accompaniment of live instrumental music and the reactions of the main characters.

A few years later, in 1932, Martinů received his first commission for a sound film. It was directed by Paul Czinner and released in both a French-language version under the title *Mélo* and a German-language version under the title *Der träumende Mund* ("Dreaming Lips"). Martinů mentions the work, without specifying the title or director, in two letters from

[4] See Miloš Šafránek, ed., *Bohuslav Martinů. Domov, hudba a svět. Deníky, zápisníky, úvahy a články* (Prague: Státní hudební vydavatelství, 1966), 49.
[5] See Anna Kozáková, "Bohuslav Martinů ve filmu" (Bachelor's thesis, Palacký University, Olomouc, 2019).
[6] Only a silent version of the film with Czech intertitles was preserved in Prague, Národní filmový archiv.
[7] Ivana Rentsch, "Opernfilmmusik. Bohuslav Martinůs cineastische Kompositionen zwischen Illusion und Realismus," in *Ton-Spuren aus der alten Welt. Europäische Filmmusik bis 1945*, ed. Ivana Rentsch and Arne Stollberg (Munich: text+kritik, 2013), 152–69.

May 1932.[8] For unknown reasons, Czinner eventually used music by Beethoven and Wagner, and Martinů's score (H223) is lost.

In 1935, producer Ladislav Kolda approached Martinů with an offer to compose music for two promotional films for the Baťa shoe company. The first one, *Střevíček*, H239, has a duration of eight and a half minutes and documents the entire process of shoe production in Zlín, from design and manufacturing to sales.[9] The film represented a new type of advertising within the Zlín studios, emphasizing an equal relationship between visuals and music, no longer relegating music to a subservient role. Martinů composed the music for the film using a chamber orchestra, which included clarinet, trumpet, trombone, percussion, piano, and strings.[10] A comparison between the original manuscript and the sound recording reveals that Martinů's original finale was omitted from the film. Instead, Martinů composed a completely new piece that exists only in the film, and the score is now missing.[11] The advertisement was filmed in two versions, one in Czech and a slightly shorter one in English. Compared to other Czechoslovak advertising and promotional films of the 1930s, *Střevíček* stands out due to its well-developed script that integrates the music, so that it evolves rhythmically and melodically in accordance with the spoken text and visuals, setting it apart from the simple and endlessly repetitive melodies in other contemporary films.

The second documentary film, *Město živé vody: Mariánské Lázně* ("The City of Living Water: Mariánské Lázně"), H240, captured the panorama of the famous west Bohemian spa town and featured a car ride through it. Regrettably, the film is now lost. For the film, Martinů composed music that emulated the ambience of an outdoor spa concert and used instrumentation that was nearly identical to that used in *Střevíček*, with the exceptions of the trombone, triangle, and tam-tam. Martinů noted that he was inspired by the music of Julius Kalaš, the most sought-after composer for the Baťa company's advertisements at the time. It is possible that this note reflected a request from the client. The music in both advertisements was conducted by Václav Trojan (1907–83), who would later

---

[8] See Martinů's letter to his family in Polička, May 8, 1932; Polička, Martinů Center, shelfmark PBM Kr 77; and his letter to family, May 26, 1932; Polička, Martinů Center, shelfmark PBM Kr 80.

[9] On the title page of the orchestral score, Martinů wrote "a short history of the shoe" ("malá historie boty").

[10] The autograph was considered lost until it appeared at a Sotheby's auction in December 2001. It is presently held in the Bohuslav Martinů Center in Polička.

[11] See Martina Cechová, "Hudba v reklamě zlínských ateliérů v letech 1930–1940: Střevíček Bohuslava Martinů a jeho dobový kontext" (MA thesis, Charles University, Prague, 2011).

become known for composing music for the internationally acclaimed animated films of Jiří Trnka.

Marijka nevěrnice

Martinů's most substantial contribution to the field of film music is his score for the 1933 avant-garde film *Marijka nevěrnice* ("The Unfaithful Marijka"), H233. Film producer Ladislav Kolda commissioned the music as early as 1931, but due to funding delays, it was not composed until between November 1933 and January 1934, a time when the film was in advanced post-production stage.[12] Martinů intended to personally record the music with the National Theater orchestra during his temporary stay in Prague but later decided to return to Paris, and the recording was directed by František Škvor, conductor at the National Theater and himself a successful film-music composer at the time.[13] The film's creators and the producer were satisfied both shortly after the recording was finished and after the premiere, which took place on March 2, 1934, in Prague.

Similar to *Slovácké tance a obyčeje*, *Marijka nevěrnice* depicts simple, rural life. The film is set in the multicultural environment of Carpathian Ruthenia, which was part of interwar Czechoslovakia and is now in Ukraine. It focuses on the lives of ordinary people: Petro Birčak and his wife Marijka. After their house burns down, Petro leaves for the mountains to cut wood for the new house and hires Danilo to help rebuild it. Marijka develops a romantic relationship with Danilo. Petro confronts Danilo when he returns home, and Danilo drowns during a trip with Petro on a raft. After Danilo's death, the spouses reconcile and complete the construction of their new home. The film is innovative in several respects: the performers are non-actors from Carpathian Ruthenia who speak the local dialect as well as Czech, German, and Yiddish. Furthermore, Jiří Slavíček's editing appears to draw clear inspiration from Sergei Eisenstein's film *Battleship Potemkin*.

Martinů's music starts even before the opening credits and accompanies the film for a significant portion of its duration, especially during wordless sequences. Some portions of Martinů's music resemble the composer's most ambitious compositions from the mid-1930s. For example, the opening title music recalls the 1937 cantata *Kytice* ("A Bouquet"), H260,

---

[12] This information is based on Martinů's letters from 1931–34; Polička, Martinů Center.
[13] See Martinů's letter to family in Polička, January 18, 1934; Polička, Martinů Center, shelfmark PBM Kr 122.

specifically its briefest section titled "Intráda" ("Entrance"), which introduces the most substantial and extensive concluding section, "Člověk a smrt" ("The Man and the Death"). The ostinato passages in the strings, by contrast, evoke Martinů's 1931 Partita for string orchestra, H212.

The manuscript score is lost, and only sketches survive, along with the recording. These sketches show that the composer received precise timings for individual musical sequences. This posed no problem for him, as he had previously successfully worked with exact timings in Jarmila Kröschlová's 1927 ballet *Kuchyňská revue* ("The Kitchen Revue"), H161.[14] Martinů's proficiency with precise time indications is illustrated on the first page of the continuous draft of the film score (see Figure 29.1). The page begins with a portion of the musical score, followed by a textual description of a brief section of the script, the film, and the music. This description corresponds to the content and timing of the film's final cut:

Woodworking 9 seconds – without [music]? [in the film, this occurs at 39:22ff; Martinů eventually decided to set the passage to music, which must have been on a previous, now missing, page of the draft.] Baba goes to the shop, repeated harmonica in a different key up to the detail of the letter (trombones)[,] Baba at about 1 minute 20 seconds the children from school – up to the letter[,] total 2.5 seconds (2:20)[,] still at the end Baba[.] the end sad 35 seconds.

Práce na dřevě 9vt. – bez [hudby]? Baba jde do krámu, opakuje se harmonika v jiné tónině až k detail[u] dopisu (pozouny trombony)[,] Baba – asi na 1 m 20 děti ze školy – až dopis[,] celkem 2.5vt. (2:20)[,] ještě na konec baba[.] závěr smutný 35vt.

Given the film's setting and its semi-documentary style,[15] it is not surprising that it incorporates distinct folk elements, dance rhythms, and authentic songs of the Carpathian highlanders. These elements resonate with Martinů's interest in Czech folk music at the time of the film's creation, and the soundtrack often blends music composed by Martinů with folk music. The transitions between these two musical styles are masked by pronounced sound delays and reverberation. This blending can be observed, for example, in the extensive dance party scene and the subsequent departure of the lumberjacks from the village. Another instance

---

[14] On the collaboration between Martinů and Kröschlová, see Aleš Březina, "'I changed practically nothing': Bohuslav Martinů's Collaboration on *The Kitchen Revue*," in *Martinů and His World*, ed. Aleš Březina and Michael Beckerman (Chicago: University of Chicago Press, 2025), 127–40.

[15] Vladislav Vančura, one of the three film authors, characterized the creative approach in making the film as a "selection of documents, report" ("výběr dokumentů, reportáž"). Pavel Taussig, ed., *Marijka nevěrnice* (Prague: Odeon, 1982), 232.

Figure 29.1 Bohuslav Martinů, *Marijka nevěrnice* ("The Unfaithful Marijka"), continuous draft, p. [1]. Bohuslav Martinů Center in Polička. Reproduced by permission.

is the scene where a young couple of reformed Jews reads the daily press in Yiddish, accompanied by a simple arrangement for two horns of the well-known folksong *Což se mně má milá hezká zdáš* ("You Seem Lovely to Me, My Darling").[16] A precise assessment of the use of these sound techniques

---

[16] The reason for including this song is not clear. In his 1864 collection of folksongs, Karel Jaromír Erben places it in the Prácheňsko region, which is on the border of southern and western Bohemia. Perhaps the choice of the song for this episodic scene was based on the lyrics.

and the alternation between folk and composed music would only be possible with the discovery of the film's lost score.

Discussions of *Marijka nevěrnice* often quote Martinů's statement that "it is mainly a film, and the music is subordinate to it" (je to hlavně film a hudba je při tom podřadná)[17] and interpret it as an expression of the composer's pessimism toward the medium of film.[18] However, the sentence needs to be read in context:

I would also be curious to see the film; I don't know if they will send it [to Paris], I doubt it. I also think that they covered [the music] up with the spoken word from what I saw when they were shooting it. What's the use, it's mainly a film, and the music is subordinate to it.

Také bych byl zvědav vidět ten film nevím, zdali jej sem pošlou, dost pochybuji. Myslím také že to hodně překřičeli, podle toho, jak jsem to viděl točit. Co je platno, je to hlavně film a hudba je při tom podřadná.

The composer, who had previously only worked on films where music was not interrupted by spoken dialogue, encountered the coexistence of image, music, and spoken word for the first time when working on the music for *Marijka nevěrnice*. Furthermore, for most of the film, music exists in symbiosis with the visuals. This is evident in both love scenes between Marijka and Danilo, which contain no spoken text, and where emotion is conveyed through music. An exception is the scene depicting Marijka's quarrel with her mother-in-law and Danilo. However, the dialogue is almost insignificant in that moment compared to the visuals and music. Some of the most dramatic scenes replace composed music with diegetic sounds and noises, such as the looting of the Jewish merchant's house and the revolt of the lumberjacks against their abusive employer. Also noteworthy is the use of the accordion in the scene that depicts the beginning of Marijka's and Danilo's affair, showing an affinity with the much later love scene of Manolios and Katerina in Martinů's last opera *The Greek Passion*, H372 (1954–59). The most prominent music in the whole film is in the raft scene, where dramatic trumpets and string tremolos prefigure Danilo's death.

The music for *Marijka nevěrnice* represented more than just an occasional job for Martinů, and he remembered it well even many years later

---

[17] Martinů's letter to his family in Polička, June 4, 1934; Polička, Martinů Center, shelfmark PBM Kr 131 .

[18] On Martinů's allegedly marginal interest in film music, see Jana Janulíková, "Vladislav Vančura a *Marijka nevěrnice* aneb Česká filmová avantgarda v praxi," *Opus musicum* 1 (2001): 70–88.

when he included it in his manuscript list of compositions in 1953 or 1954.[19] Furthermore, it is clear from the composer's correspondence that in the following years, he sought other similarly valuable commissions.

Zdeněk Liška: A Life for Film Music

Zdeněk Liška (1922–83) was one of the few twentieth-century composers to focus exclusively on film and TV music. His music appeared in more than 160 feature films and nearly four hundred short films. His musical style kept evolving throughout his career, and he consistently demonstrated an ability to skillfully match his music to the dramaturgy of the cinematic image in ingenious ways.

Liška's career started at the Zlín film studios in 1945 when he provided music for the Baťa company's promotional film *Dřeváčková serenáda* ("The Wooden Shoe Serenade"). Thanks to its success, he remained with the Baťa company until the 1960s and composed for puppet and animated commercials created by Karel Zeman and Hermína Týrlová, two internationally known film-makers specializing in fantasy and animated films.

Liška composed his first music for a feature film, *Pára nad hrncem* ("Steam over the Pot"), in 1950. At that time, his musical language was influenced by the styles of Janáček and Martinů. The early pinnacle of his work came with 1957's *Vynález zkázy* ("Invention for Destruction"), directed by Karel Zeman, which combined live actors with puppets and animation. In this film, based on a novel by Jules Verne, Liška demonstrated his fondness for unconventional instrumental combinations, such as an out-of-tune honky-tonk piano and a spinet which effectively illustrated the atmosphere of the nineteenth century in which Verne's story unfolds. To accentuate the artifice of the setting, Liška electronically modified natural musical sounds (for example, by adding electronically modulated sounds, such as the low-frequency oscillation of a synthesizer). Liška even participated in the final editing of the film, a practice that would become almost customary for him in subsequent years and included his involvement in the creation of sound effects (Foley), for instance in Zeman's 1961 film *Baron Prášil* ("The Fabulous Baron Munchhausen"). In later years, Liška, with the directors' and producers' consent, personally modified the films to achieve perfect harmony with his music.

---

[19] See Martinů's manuscript list of compositions from late 1953 to early 1954; Polička, Martinů Center, shelfmark PBM Na19.

The period in which Liška created his most influential scores was initiated with Ján Kadár and Elmar Klos's 1965 *Obchod na korze* (see above). In this film, Liška continued his practice of combining unusual instrumental colors and techniques by contrasting a brass band, dulcimer, and a solo violin playing double stops at the interval of a seventh. Two years later, Liška collaborated with František Vláčil on his historical epic *Marketa Lazarová*, which has been voted the best film in Czechoslovak cinema by Czech film critics. The film features a nearly uninterrupted musical component that substantially contributes to the cinematic narrative.[20] The story takes place in the thirteenth century, and Liška evokes this late medieval period with not only ahistorical references to Igor Stravinsky's style from *The Rite of Spring* but also ancient modes, homophonic blocks, and chants reminiscent of late Renaissance Italian music. These elements are contrasted with bird sounds and clusters based on the sounds of a scythe. Marketa, the film's protagonist, is characterized by solo soprano vocalization, with short segments drawn from the twelfth-century sequence *Veni sancte spiritus* and Psalm 151. One of the most fascinating purely instrumental numbers in the film is the so-called *Rajská sonáta* ("Paradise Sonata"), which accompanies a scene depicting incest, and presents the unusual combination of an alto flute and percussion (see Example 29.1).[21] The music may have been inspired by Martinů. In his technical script, Vláčil references the composer's 1955 orchestral work *The Frescoes of Piero della Francesca*, H352, and the Lento – Allegro from the Fifth Symphony (H310), written in 1946.

In the late 1960s, Liška expanded his instrumental palette with various types of percussion instruments, solo and choral vocal parts, bells, and intricately composed sound effects, such as the cawing of crows, the sound of the wind, clinking of cutlery, and rhythmic strikes. These innovative sounds form an integral part of the music for Jan Švankmajer's animated films *Rakvičkárna* ("The Coffin House") in 1966, *Don Šajn* in 1969, and *Leonardův deník* ("Leonardo's Diary") in 1972. These sounds were incorporated directly into the film score and were deployed strategically and only in certain films. By contrast, in Juraj Herz's 1968 *Spalovač mrtvol* ("The Cremator"), Liška worked with a traditional orchestra, for which he composed an impressive mix of delightful waltzes and operatic music. Liška's

[20] Peter Hames refers to the film as a "film-opera," which parallels Martinů's subtitle of his *Tři přání*: "opera-film." See "Marketa Lazarová," in *The Cinema of Central Europe*, ed. Peter Hames (London: Wallflower Press, 2004), 158–60.

[21] See Jan Černíček, "Hudba Zdeňka Lišky k filmu Marketa Lazarová" (PhD diss., Charles University, Prague, 2009), 67, n. 265.

Example 29.1: Zdeněk Liška, *Rajská sonáta* ("The Paradise Sonata") for alto flute ("altová flétna"), two grand pianos ("Klavír I., Klavír II."), Hammond organ ("Hammond"), and percussion – marimba ("Marimba"), vibraphone ("Vibrafon"), chimes ("Zvonkohra"), bongos ("Bonga"), rattles ("Chřestidla"), and timpani ("Timpani"), from *Marketa Lazarová* (reproduced by permission).

Example 29.1: (cont.)

music here does not mirror the film's dramatic narrative, which becomes increasingly dark, but stands in complete contrast to it. Liška enjoyed juxtaposing contrasting music and images in other films as well. In *Smrt si říká Engelchen* ("Death Is Called Engelchen") from 1963, Liška accompanies scenes of abduction and murder with an idyllic Christmas carol sung by a children's choir.

Liška also refined his approach to synthesized music, often in collaboration with top Czech sound engineers and under the influence of contemporary sound experimenters, such as Pierre Schaeffer. For example, in the 1961 science fiction comedy *Muž z prvního století* ("The Man from the First Century"), he created electronic music derived from the sounds of acoustic instruments. In Vláčil's *Holubice* ("The White Dove") from 1960, he manipulated combinations of loops from pre-recorded bird songs and insect buzzing. In the 1974 comedy *Jáchyme hoď ho do stroje* ("Joachim, Throw Him into the Machine"), Liška used electronically generated sounds in the opening credits.[22] He also experimented with traditional instruments through unusual compositional techniques, such as reverse audio loop playback, and extended techniques, such as the scratching sounds created by excessive pressure on a cello's bow in the 1963 science fiction film *Ikarie XB-1*. When the timbral music of the Polish School (Penderecki, Lutosławski, Górecki) arrived in Czechoslovakia in the 1970s, Liška immediately assimilated it into his scores as well.

Starting in the mid-1960s, Liška also incorporated contemporary pop music into his scores. He began to use popular-music styles even more during the period of so-called "normalization," following the occupation of Czechoslovakia by Warsaw Pact countries. An important example of this practice is Liška's music for the ideologically tainted series *30 případů majora Zemana* ("Thirty Cases of Major Zeman") from 1974–79, in which the communist regime sought to misinterpret (or revise) modern Czechoslovak history. Perhaps as an escape from the oppressive reality in communist Czechoslovakia, Liška also composed music for many children's films.

Other Prominent Czechoslovak Composers of Film Music

Among the contemporaries of Bohuslav Martinů, Jaroslav Ježek is another composer who made forays into film scoring. Although he is primarily known as the composer of theater music for the plays of Jiří Voskovec and Jan Werich Theater (see Chapter 27), Ježek also wrote music for six films

---

[22] See Jonáš Kucharský, "Elektroakustická hudba a český film," in *Ukryto v pásech – Vybrané kapitoly z české elektroakustické hudební tvorby do roku 1989*, ed. Petr Ferenc (Prague: Národní muzeum, 2022), 148.

between 1931 and 1937. Most of his film scores combined original film music with Ježek's jazz-influenced songs originally created for the Liberated Theater plays.

Jiří Srnka (1907–82) was a foundational figure in Czech film-music history, both in terms of his work and his collaborations with famous directors (particularly Jiří Weiss and Otakar Vávra). He studied with modernist composers Vítězslav Novák and Alois Hába, and, at the recommendation of Ježek, also worked as a conductor and violinist at the Liberated Theater. Srnka's work was significantly influenced by the political situation in Czechoslovakia after World War II, particularly the 1948 Communist Coup. Among his most important post-war scores are those for Otakar Vávra's ideologized portrayal of fifteenth-century Czech history in his technically brilliant "Hussite" trilogy – *Jan Hus*, 1954, *Jan Žižka*, 1955, and *Proti všem* ("Against Everyone"), 1956. Srnka was also important as a pedagogue and for a time lectured at the film department of the Prague Academy of Performing Arts (AMU), founded in 1946. After 1967, Srnka mainly composed for Czechoslovak Television.

Emil František Burian (1904–59) was an award-winning film-music composer who was also active as a theater artist, actor, scenographer, and writer. Burian was one of the signatories of the aforementioned 1927 manifesto of the New Film Club and composed more than twenty film scores. The artistic qualities of his film scores were recognized at international competitions. His music for Karel Steklý's 1947 film *Siréna* ("The Siren"), about a miners' strike in the central Bohemian city of Kladno, received an award at the Venice Film Festival. Another notable film was Karel Zeman's science fiction adventure *Cesta do pravěku* ("The Journey to the Beginning of Time"), which received a Venice Film Festival award for its visual design and sound dramaturgy in 1955.

Jiří Šust (1919–95) composed music for more than eighty feature-length films and an even greater number of short and documentary films. He is best known for his collaboration with director Jiří Menzel, with whom he created the critically acclaimed drama *Ostře sledované vlaky* ("Closely Watched Trains"), about a young train dispatcher in a rural railway station during World War II, his first sexual experiences, and his death while dropping a bomb on a Nazi ammunition train. The film won an Academy Award for Best Foreign Language Film in 1968 and received nominations, including one for Best Music, from the British Academy of Film and Television Arts (BAFTA) in 1969. A distinctive feature of Šust's music was the effective characterization of the protagonists' colorful personalities by distinct musical styles. Menzel valued Šust's ability to compose music that did not overshadow the film but instead supported it.

Similar to Šust's collaboration with Menzel, Svatopluk Havelka (1925–2009) is particularly known for his work with directors Vojtěch Jasný and Karel Kachyňa. One film Havelka created with Jasný is *Touha* ("The Desire," 1958), the music of which features clear references to Martinů's 1955 chamber cantata *Otvírání studánek* ("The Opening of the Springs"), H354. The collaboration with Kachyňa resulted in *Ucho* ("The Ear," 1970), in which Havelka utilized techniques such as sound clusters, timbral textures, aleatory elements, and artificially prolonged reverberations to illustrate the increasing paranoia of a senior official of the Communist Party and his alcoholic wife as they realize they are under surveillance by their own government.

Another collaborator of Kachyňa was Jan Novák (1921–84), who studied composition with both Aaron Copland and Martinů. Though mainly known as a composer of theater music, Novák contributed music to seven films by Kachyňa, including 1966's *Kočár do Vídně* ("The Coach to Vienna"), about two German deserters who force a Czech woman to drive them from southern Moravia to Vienna at the end of World War II. Novák, similarly to Václav Trojan (see above), also collaborated with Trnka on several animated films.

Stylistic versatility marked the output of Luboš Fišer (1935–99), such as in his music for Kachyňa's 1979 film *Lásky mezi kapkami deště* ("Loves among Rain Drops"), about the lives of common people in Prague's Žižkov neighborhood in the 1930s, which combines symphonic passages with folk melodies, references to music from Prague's dance halls, and the shrill sounds of the violins, accordion, and drums. Equally fascinating is Fišer's collaboration with Juraj Herz on two dramas from the 1970s. The first, *Petrolejové lampy* ("Oil Lamps," 1971), focuses on the leading heroine – an independent woman in a small town around 1900 who marries a dashing army officer, only to discover that he has contracted syphilis, necessitating constant care without ever consummating the marriage. Fišer's orchestral score is melodious and lyrical, featuring extensive use of a female chorus. In the subsequent project, *Morgiana* (1972), Fišer's music skillfully delineates two contrasting sisters. The good and kind sister is portrayed with the harp, strings, and flute, while the evil sister, embodying hatred and envy, is accompanied by screeching winds and percussive ostinatos. Fišer employs a wide variety of instrumental colors in this film, including solo piano, cembalo, organ, and an orchestral imitation of an out-of-tune orchestrion.

A living legend of Czech film music is Jan Klusák (b. 1934). In the 1960s, he collaborated with many directors of the so-called Czechoslovak New Wave, such as Věra Chytilová and Evald Schorm. For Schorm's 1964 film *Každý den odvahu* ("Courage for Every Day"), Klusák made use of then avant-garde serial techniques. During the normalization period, Klusák provided a more traditional soundtrack for the successful television series *Nemocnice na kraji města* ("Hospital at the Edge of the City") – a Czechoslovak socialist predecessor to *Grey's Anatomy*. After the fall of communism, Klusák became one of the first composers to provide new scores for motion pictures from the silent film era, specifically Gustav Machatý's *Erotikon* (1929).

In the 1960s, several Czech film composers started relying on popular-music styles, which are prominently represented in the works of Ferdinand Havlík, Angelo Michajlov, Karel Svoboda, Petr Hapka, Evžen Illín, William Bukový, and the creative duo Jiří Bažant and Jiří Malásek. References to popular music are also prominent in the works of Jan Hammer, who composed music for the 1968 fairy-tale musical *Šíleně smutná princezna* ("The Incredibly Sad Princess") at the age of twenty, starring Helena Vondráčková and Václav Neckář. He went on to achieve great success in America, primarily with music for the television series *Miami Vice* (1984–89).

In the present, some Czech film-makers avoid using film music altogether, drawing inspiration from the so-called Romanian New Wave cinema. Otherwise, present-day Czech film music can be seen as encompassing three main directions. The first group of composers finds inspiration in classical music of the twentieth and twenty-first centuries. Notable representatives of this direction include Elia Cmíral, Vlado Godár, Jan Jirásek, Michael Kocáb, Ondřej Soukup, Aleš Březina, and Michal Novinski. A second group of composers is deeply rooted in the popular music of the last few decades. While some of these composers (Jan P. Muchow and Petr Ostrouchov) explore more traditional forms of popular music, others are drawn to alternative styles. This group includes Květy, Katarzia, and more recently Oliver Torr, with scores drawing on hip hop and rap music. Most recently, many Czech film-music composers have also developed an interest in sound design, similar to major international representatives, such as Vangelis, Hans Zimmer, or Ben Frost. In the Czech context, they build upon the legacy of Liška, including Pjoni, Aid Kid, and Šimon Holý.

30 | Czechs in Search of Slovak Music

VLADIMÍR ZVARA

Czech and Slovak ethnic groups have lived side by side for centuries, though they were separated by various state borders, such as that between the Austrian and Hungarian parts of the Habsburg monarchy. For many nineteenth-century Bohemians and Moravians, Slovakia represented a "close Other," both familiar and alien.[1] At the same time, one could consider Slovakia a "time capsule," preserving an earlier developmental stage of the culturally and nationally more advanced Czech "older sibling."[2] Nationalistically minded nineteenth-century Slovaks drew inspiration and encouragement from the Czechs, and some of them, including poet Jan Kollár, viewed Czechs and Slovaks as a single Western Slavic tribe. Close ties between Czechs and Slovaks had existed for a much longer period, however, because Slovak Protestants of the Augsburg Confession used the Czech of the *Bible kralická* ("Bible of Kralice"), the first complete Czech translation of the Bible from the original languages, as their official language since the early seventeenth century.[3]

In the nineteenth century, Hungarian elites stopped viewing the Hungarian nationality as a supra-ethnic political concept and embraced a modern nationalist approach: Hungarians were those who identified with the *magyar* ethnicity. As a result, Slovaks and other minorities of Hungary subscribed to modern ideologies of ethnically defined nations that were increasingly at odds with the policies of the central Hungarian government.[4] Compared to the developments in the Czech lands, where the idea of a Czech nation became widespread by the

This chapter was translated from Slovak to English by Martin Nedbal.

Funding for this project was provided by the Slovak VEGA Agency under the research project No. 1/0629/22.

[1] See Lucia Kvočáková, *Cesta ke slovenskému mýtu: Konstrukce identity slovenské moderny v kontextu ideje čechoslovakismu* (Prague: Charles University, 2020), 24–26.

[2] Marta Filipová, "Peasants on Display: The Czechoslavic Ethnographic Exhibition of 1895," *Journal of Design History* 24 (2011): 32.

[3] See Elisabeth Bakke, "Czechoslovakism in Slovak History," in *Slovakia in History*, ed. Mikuláš Teich, Dušan Kováč, and Martin D. Brown (New York: Cambridge University Press, 2011), 247–68.

[4] Adam Hudek, *Najpolitickejšia veda: slovenská historiografia v rokoch 1948–1968* (Bratislava: SAV, 2010), 21.

late 1800s, the Slovak national awakening was, for a long time, driven by a relatively small group of enthusiasts. In the nineteenth century, the only highbrow artform to be established was literature. The situation changed radically after the creation of Czechoslovakia in 1918 when the formation of Slovak national culture became an important political goal in the new republic. The Czechoslovak state ideology with which Tomáš Garrigue Masaryk and Edvard Beneš won the support of the victorious powers postulated that the new country was based on the existence of a Czechoslovak nation that was larger than German and Hungarian communities living within Czechoslovak borders. This ideology also included the concept of a highbrow Slovak culture that would be both authentic and based in the value system of Czech culture.

Dobroslav Orel and the Invention of Slovak Music

Most of the institutional and financial support for Slovak musical culture was aimed at Bratislava, known as Pressburg/Pozsony prior to 1919. Although the city was proclaimed the capital of Slovakia, it was a predominantly German and Hungarian city in terms of language and culture – in contemporaneous Czechoslovak newspeak, it was "our city that is infected with foreignness" ("naše mesto nakazené cudzotou").[5] Many new institutions were established. The Prague radio station Radiojournal opened a branch in Bratislava in 1926 and established a radio orchestra there in 1929. The newly founded Slovak National Theater moved into the municipal theater in 1920, pursuing a mission similar to that of the National Theater in Prague, though in an unfriendly environment and with a state subvention that was one fifth of what the Prague institution received.[6] New educational institutions were founded as well: the Music School for Slovakia (present-day Bratislava Conservatory) was founded in 1919; and the Institute for Musicology at the newly established State (later Comenius) University was founded in 1921 and directed by Czech hymnologist and Catholic priest Dobroslav Orel.

Beside his duties at the Institute, Orel directed the Academic Choral Association (Akademické pevecké sdruženie) and initiated an influx of music by Czech composers into opera houses and concert halls in Slovakia. He also organized the celebration of Smetana's centennial in 1924 and that for

---

[5] See documents related to the founding of the Slovak National Theater, in Ladislav Lajcha, ed., *Dokumenty SND*, vol. 1 (Bratislava: Divadelný ústav, 2000), 187–88.

[6] For example, in 1931, the Prague National Theater received a subvention of 11,875,000 crowns, whereas the Slovak National Theater received only 2,300,000 crowns, the same amount that was provided for the other regional theaters in Czechoslovakia. See Lajcha, *Dokumenty SND*, vol. 1, 113.

the twenty-fifth anniversary of Dvořák's death in 1929. Both events commemorated the two heroes of Czech music as representatives of Czechoslovak culture.[7] State authorities often appointed Orel to influential positions in executive boards in various cultural and educational institutions. As I have shown elsewhere, Orel's varied activities were influenced by his "Czechness" and his religious and political links to Catholicism.[8]

Orel contributed significantly to the interwar debates about the nature of Slovak music. What was Slovak music supposed to be like? If it even could exist (Czech musicologist Zdeněk Nejedlý, for instance, thought it could not)?[9] Slovak music was supposed to express national identity, a task given to artists in all states established after World War I.[10] Slovak music was also supposed to emulate the national traditions of Czech classical music, which was constructed in the nineteenth century by Czech nationalists and gradually also accepted by the international community. In the interwar period, Czech commentators accepted the (essentially colonialist) idea that Slovaks could be successful only if they accepted Czech stewardship to catch up in areas, including music, in which they – at no fault of their own – lagged the Czechs. At the same time, Slovak music was supposed to keep up with the times and be modern. Paradoxically, furthermore, although Slovak music was in the process of being invented, it also needed a history.

This brings me to the broader subject of the narratives of Slovak history. No generally accepted understanding of Slovak history existed either in the

---

[7] Naďa Hrčková, *Tradícia, modernosť a slovenská hudobná kultúra 1918–1948* (Bratislava: Litera, 1996), 112–15. See also Miroslav Michela, "Státní oslavy a konstruování československé národní pospolitosti za první republiky," in *Čechoslovakismus*, ed. Adam Hudek, Michal Kopeček, and Jan Mervart (Prague: AVČR, 2019), 223–42.

[8] Vladimír Zvara, "Constructing the Past and the Future of Slovak Music: Dobroslav Orel in Interwar Bratislava," *Historický časopis* 69 (2021): 921–39.

[9] Nejedlý's reflection on the first concert of works by Slovak composers in Prague on March 20, 1919, echoes a widespread view: "The creation of Slovak national music would require more than a dialect, provincialism, and temporary political separatism, it would require a unique Slovak national idea that would equal the Czech national idea, and those of other nations. . . . Slovakia can acquire strength through a unity with the Czech nation, otherwise it would disappear in an alien world. This means that in music Slovakia, in order to achieve strength, needs to accept the Czech idea and abandon the chimera of Slovak music." ("K vytvoření slovenské hudby nestačí dialekt, provincialismus nebo dobový politický separatismus, k tomu by bylo třeba *zvláštní* národní ideje slovenské, již by bylo možno postaviti rovnocenně vedle takové ideje české i jiných národů jako samostatné ideje národní. . . . Slovensko může býti silné právě jednotou s českým národem, jinak by úplně propadlo ve světě cizím. To však znamená, že i v hudbě musí přijmout ideu českou, a nikoli honiti se za přeludem slovenské hudby, chce-li býti silné.") Zdeněk Nejedlý, "Slovenská hudba: K pražskému koncertu 20. března 1920," *Smetana* 10, no. 3 (March 29, 1920): 34.

[10] See Agnieszka Chmielenska, "National Art and the Theory of Nationalism," in *History of Art History in Central, Eastern and South-Eastern Europe*, ed. Jerzy Malinowski, vol. 2 (Toruń: Tako, 2012), 97–103.

nineteenth century or during the early Czechoslovak period. What were the ideologues of Slovak identity to do with the fragmentary story of so-called "Great Moravia," a predominantly Slavic state that existed in the ninth century and combined areas inhabited by both modern Czechs and Slovaks?[11] How were they to interpret the centuries during which modern Slovakia was incorporated into the Kingdom of Hungary? Should they ignore or appropriate them? How were they to present the new Czechoslovak history? And is it even possible to speak of Slovak history, or was most of it really the story of Hungarian elites, and should the development of the predecessors of modern Slovaks be studied by ethnographers rather than historians?[12]

The first conceptualization of Slovak music history I want to mention is that of Dobroslav Orel. Orel approached Slovak history from a Czechoslovak perspective. At the same time, Orel avoided then-widespread ethnocentric viewpoints – this may have been the result of his studies with Guido Adler at the University of Vienna and possibly also the reason why his approaches were ultimately overpowered by others. Thus, Orel believed that Slovak musical heritage consisted of not only folk music but also the musical practices of the elites who lived in the territory of Slovakia in the past and spoke languages other than Slovak. According to Orel, it was important to study sources that had to do with "foreign music" ("cizí hudba").[13] The goal of music historical studies in Slovakia was to be the deepening of the understanding of both musical life in Slovakia and general music history. In his cosmopolitan views, the conservative and Catholic Orel was ahead of his time. However, he was also a student of Czech musicologist Otakar Hostinský, one of the initiators of the cult of Smetana as a Czech national composer. Thus, Orel based the essence of Slovak music on important men whose work would serve as a springboard for future musical developments.

Bella and Novák as "Slovak" Composers

Orel pointed to Ján Levoslav Bella (1843–1936) and Vítězslav Novák (1870–1949) as the main heroes of Slovak music. Whereas the view of

---

[11] See Jiří Macháček, "'Velkomoravský stát' – kontroverze středoevropské medievistiky," *Archeologické rozhledy* 64 (2012): 775–87.

[12] See Hudek, *Najpolitickejšia veda*, 22–24.

[13] Dobroslav Orel, "Hudební prameny na Slovensku," in *Príspevky k praveku, dejinám a národopisu Slovenska*: Sborník archeologického a národopisného odboru Slovenského vlastivědného muzea za rok 1924 – 1931, ed. Jan Eisner, Jan Hofman, and Vilém Pražák (Bratislava: *Spoločnost vlastivědného muzea* slovenského v Bratislavě, 1931), 79.

Novák as the "most Slovak of all composers" was widespread in the early twentieth century,[14] the position of Hungarian-Slovak Bella, who created most of his works in the nineteenth century, was less clear. Although he set some Slovak texts, wrote compositions inspired by Slovak folksongs, and published articles about Slavic and Slovak music,[15] Bella spent most of his career in a German Protestant community in Transylvanian Hermannstadt/Nagyszeben (today Romanian Sibiu) and composed mostly sacred works in Latin and German. Bella's only opera, *Wieland der Schmied* (composed 1880–90, premiered as *Kováč Wieland* in the Slovak National Theater in 1926), used a German libretto by Oskar Schlemm, based on a sketch by Richard Wagner.[16]

Bella's position in the annals of Slovak music was a matter of contention. In his memoirs, Novák wrote that Bella "spent most of his life among the Saxons in Transylvania, got married there, and composed entirely in the spirit of Liszt, without any connection to Slovak music."[17] In Novák's view, the fact that Bella's work is stylistically related to the ideas of the New German School disqualified him from entering the Slovak – and therefore also the Czechoslovak – musical canon. In the communist period, another strike against Bella was that he mainly composed sacred works and his output was dominated by "cosmopolitan and anti-individualistic" ("kozmopolitným a individuálnosť vylučujúcim") aspects of church music.[18]

Some commentators also attempted to appropriate Bella, including his German opera, for the Slovak cause. For example, Miloš Ruppeldt viewed *Wieland der Schmied* as the first Slovak national opera and understood the story about a blacksmith who forges wings to escape captivity as an expression of Bella's desire for the freedom of the Slovak nation.[19] In his discussions of Bella, Orel avoided such trivializations and presented the composer as a link between the Slovak past (which was only partially Slovak

---

[14] See Otakar Zich, "O slovenské písni lidové," in *Slovenská čítanka*, ed. Jan Kabelík, 2nd rev. ed. (Prague: Šolc, 1925), 617.

[15] See Hana Urbancová, "Bella a slovenská ľudová pieseň," in *Ján Levoslav Bella, národovec a Európan (1843–1936)*, ed. Emanuel Muntág (Martin: Matica slovenská, 2004), 44–52.

[16] See Ottfried Hafner, "*Wieland der Schmied* zwischen Bella und Wagner," in *Ján Levoslav Bella v kontexte európskej hudobnej kultúry*, ed. Jana Lengová (Banská Bystrica: Nadácia Jána Levoslava Bellu, 1993), 53–56. A list of Bella's compositions can be found at: https://hc.sk/en/o-slovenskej-hudbe/osobnost-detail/993-bella-jan-levoslav/diela, accessed March 21, 2024.

[17] Vítězslav Novák, *O sobě a o jiných* (Prague: Supraphon, 1970), 311.

[18] *Dejiny slovenskej hudby*, ed. Ladislav Burlas, Zdeněk Nováček, and Ladislav Mokrý (Bratislava: SAV, 1957), 268.

[19] See Jana Lengová, "K exegéze opery Jána Levoslava Bellu Kováč Wieland," in *Ján Levoslav Bella, národovec a Európan*, 17–30.

due to circumstances) and present. Orel viewed Bella as a model for later Slovak composers because he was professional and European and at the same time clung to a Slovak ethnic and cultural identity.

Bella also fit into Orel's concept of Slovak music history because of his visits to Prague in 1871 and 1873 and his contacts with Czech musicians, including Jan Ludevít Procházka, a friend of Smetana. The search for traces of Czech-Slovak relations was an important aspect of Czechoslovak historical research, and Orel could not resist the temptation to emphasize Bella's links to Prague. In his 1924 study of Bella that was partially based on Orel's 1923 conversations with the composer, Orel's rendition of Bella's reminiscences about his relationship to Procházka and Smetana is likely idealized.[20] For example, the following passage in which Bella speaks about his meeting with Smetana seems to have been tampered with:[21]

Smetana's interest in me was greater than I liked because my friend Procházka praised me to the composer more than I deserved. ... After this visit I not only understood Smetana's greatness but also became persuaded that the new universal principles of operatic composition were reasonable, that all national traditions of music had to be built on such principles not to fall out of step with contemporary artistic production and lose in worth and effect. The best illustration of this was Smetana's work, which was so ahead of its time and simultaneously purely national.

Zajímal se [Smetana] o mne více, než mi bylo milo, poněvadž mne můj přítel [Procházka] více vychválil před Smetanou, než jsem si zasloužil. ... Po této návštěvě pochopil jsem nejen velikost Smetanovu, nýbrž nabyl jsem i přesvědčení, že oprávněny jsou nové světové zásady o operní skladbě, na nichž musí býti založena každá hudba národní, aby nezůstala v pozadí za uměleckým dílem soudobým a nepozbyla na ceně ani na účinu. Nejlepším důkazem toho bylo dílo Smetanovo, tak předbíhající dobu a při tom ryze národní.

As Ernest Zavarský has pointed out, Bella's reminiscences likely contain Orel's interpolations, particularly in the passages where Bella evaluates Smetana's music. According to Zavarský, the evaluation quoted above is based on much later Czech views of Smetana that Bella could not have been familiar with when he talked to Orel.[22] The reverence with which Bella speaks about Smetana illustrates, furthermore, the Czechcentric ideology of two unequal siblings and the internalization of the concept of Prague as the superior center that determines cultural developments in the

---

[20] Dobroslav Orel, "Ján Levoslav Bella. K 80. narozeninám seniora slovenské hudby," *Sborník Filosofickej fakulty University Komenského v Bratislave* 2 (1924): 33.

[21] Orel, "Ján Levoslav Bella," 44.

[22] Ernest Zavarský, *Ján Levoslav Bella. Život a dielo* (Bratislava: SAV, 1955), 165.

periphery.[23] The quoted passage also contains traces of Hostinský's theory of national music, developed as part of his defense of Smetana against accusations of "Wagnerism." For Hostinský, creators of national opera had to take into consideration current innovations in international music, most importantly Wagner's principle that operatic style had to be rooted in spoken forms of a composer's national language.[24]

For Orel, Czech composer Vítězslav Novák was the second founding father of Slovak music. In the interwar period, Czech musicians and musicologists viewed Novák as a pioneer of Slovak music because of his compositions inspired by Slovak folksongs and Slovakia in general. Novák visited Slovakia on numerous occasions even before the creation of Czechoslovakia.[25] He channeled his impressions of the Slovakian Tatra Mountains into his symphonic poem *V Tatrách* ("In the Tatra Mountains," 1902, revised 1907) – an analogue to Richard Strauss's *Eine Alpensinfonie*. Novák also arranged Slovak folksongs in the cycle *Slovenské spevy* ("Slovak Songs"), and melodic and rhythmic aspects of Slovak folk music influenced his musical style. However, Novák's approach to folk music was unlike the radical approaches of Stravinsky and Bartók. Instead, he used motives from Slovak folksongs in the thematic materials of his music (such as his 1900 *Sonata eroica* for piano) in the manner of Beethoven and Brahms and integrated them into late Romantic and early modernist musical language that incorporated Debussy's innovative instrumentation techniques but not his radical innovations in terms of texture and form.

Early twentieth-century commentators viewed Novák's conservative use of folk music in classical composition as ennobling and paving the way for Slovak national music. In his compositions, Novák also wanted to evoke the Slovak "national character" – naturally according to how it was understood by the Czechs. Czech stereotypes about Slovaks formed in the nineteenth and early twentieth centuries and combined patronizing attitudes – viewing the Slovaks as younger siblings and a Hungarian branch of the "Czechoslavic nation" – and a fascination with the natural beauty of the country and uniqueness of its inhabitants – a romanticizing and orientalist view not dissimilar from the representations of Scotland in British

---

[23] Kvočáková, *Cesta ke slovenskému mýtu*, 25.

[24] Marta Ottlová and Milan Pospíšil, "K motivům českého wagnerismu a antiwagnerismu," in *Povědomí tradice v novodobé české kultuře. Doba Bedřicha Smetany*, ed. Milena Freimanová (Prague: Národní galerie, 1988), 137–54 (147).

[25] See Lenka Křupková, "Folk culture as an outward source of artistic inspiration: Vítězslav Novák the tourist," in *Czech music around 1900*, ed. Lenka Křupková and Jiří Kopecký (Hillsdale, NY: Pendragon Press, 2017), 225–36.

literature.[26] Czech understanding of Slovaks often included the concepts of suffering (related to the centuries-long oppression by the Hungarians and resulting in poverty and backwardness), bravery (associated with anti-establishment rebels, such as Juraj Jánošík),[27] and emotional richness. Deep emotionality is a common feature of how Western Slavs tended to characterize themselves and was often used to emphasize the difference between the Slavs and the Germans, who were imagined as possessing a profoundness of spirit (*Tiefsinn*).[28] But in the Czech imagination, Slovaks were often so emotional as to become irrational savages of a sort.[29]

Constructing "Slovakness" in Music

Otakar Zich was a Czech aesthetician and musicologist whose writings about Slovak music shaped the master narrative of modern Slovak music, both directly and through his Slovak followers, influential critic Ivan Ballo and composer and musicologist Jozef Kresánek. Zich's recommendations to Slovak composers were explored in many studies[30] and resulted in two principal ways of approaching "Slovakness" in modern classical music. The first was to base Slovak national music on the unique qualities of the Slovak language – an approach influenced by Hostinský's theories. The second was to draw on folk music, not in the sense of direct quotations but in searching for individual unique traits that could "fertilize" modern composers' imagination.[31] Slovak composers were also supposed to keep Slovak

---

[26] See Karel Klusáček, ed., *Národopisná výstava českoslovanská v Praze 1895* (Prague: Otto, 1897), 12, 24, 511; and Jana Pátková, "Obraz Bratislavy v českých cestopisech meziválečného období," *Slovenská literatúra* 68 (2021): 241.

[27] The rebel stereotype is illustrated in Pavel Sýkora, "Vítězslav Novák 1," in *Český hudební slovník*, https://slovnik.ceskyhudebnislovnik.cz/component/mdictionary/?task=record. record_detail&id=2207, last modified January 13, 2016, accessed April 10, 2024. Sýkora claims that *V Tatrách* is "a symbol of the Slovak nation's rebellious streak, related to Jánošík" ("symbol vzdorujících jánošíkovských principů slovenského národa").

[28] This view also often appears in German criticism. In a 1912 article on Karol Szymanowski in the *Neue Zeitschrift für Music* (February 8, 1912, 75), Max Unger claimed that "the Slavs remain sensually sensitive even at their most spiritual" ("Der Slave bleibt eben bei aller Vergeistigung doch stets sinnlich sensitiv"). Cited in Stefan Keym, "Zur Bedeutung des Nationalen bei der deutschen Rezeption polnischer Musik von 1900 bis 1914 am Beispiel von Szymanowski und Paderewski," in *Nationale Musik im 20. Jahrhundert*, ed. Helmut Loos and Stefan Keym (Leipzig: Schröder, 2004), 235–64.

[29] See, for example, Zich, "O slovenské písni lidové," 615.

[30] Juraj Dóša, "Vývoj hudebně estetických názorů na fenomén národní hudby na Slovensku," *Opus musicum* 16 (1984): 265–67; Hrčková, *Tradícia, modernosť*; Slávka Kopčáková, *Vývoj hudobnoestetického myslenia na Slovensku v 20. storočí* (Prešov: Prešov University, 2013).

[31] Zich, "O slovenské písni lidové," 617–18.

listeners in mind and educate them "like good parents would educate their children."[32] Slovak composers were also reminded that the emerging tradition of Slovak music did not have a firm foundation yet, particularly when compared to Czech music, and therefore should not be subjected to "unhealthy experimentation" ("nezdravé experimentovanie").[33] In other words, Zich, Ballo, and Kresánek urged Slovak composers to be modern in the style of Novák, not decadent like Schoenberg and Stravinsky.

Although these aesthetic and ideological viewpoints influenced young Slovak composers quite a bit, their application in actual music still needed to be conditioned by specific creative endeavors that both critics and audiences would accept as "correct" and persuasive incarnations of the spirit of Slovak music. Such endeavors became possible once Novák accepted several young composers from Slovakia into his studio at the Prague Conservatory. Among Novák's most prominent Slovak students were Alexander Moyzes in 1928–30, Eugen Suchoň in 1931–33, Ján Cikker in 1935–36, and Jozef Kresánek in 1937–39. Novák was not necessarily the most influential teacher of these composers, as they also drew inspiration from the teachers they studied with before Novák. Whereas Moyzes and Cikker were influenced by Otakar Šín and Jaroslav Křička, their earlier teachers at the Prague Conservatory, Suchoň was shaped by Friedrich (Frico) Kafenda, his teacher in Bratislava.

Novák's students eventually came to be viewed as the core of the "Slovak musical modernism" – in their works the dreams of Slovak national music materialized in a way that was generally accepted and therefore historically significant.[34] The generation of Moyzes, Suchoň, and Cikker created a musical idiom that balanced "Slovakness" and modernity. A similar feat was accomplished by contemporaneous visual artists, specifically Martin Benka, Janko Alexy, and Miloš Augustín Bazovský, who constructed what Slovak art historians refer to as the "Slovak myth," by combining modernist techniques with themes from the life of common Slovaks living harmoniously with nature.[35] The three composers came up with a similar recipe for what was generally accepted as Slovak music, as illustrated in Eugen Suchoň's work discussed below.

---

[32] Jozef Kresánek, *Národný umelec Eugen Suchoň* (Bratislava: Slovenské vydavateľstvo krásnej literatúry, 1961), 71.

[33] Ivan Ballo, "Mikuláš a Alexander Moyzes," *Slovenské pohľady* 44 (1928): 816–18; and Ivan Ballo, "Bratislavské koncerty," *Slovenská politika* 10, no. 5 (1929): 2.

[34] Ladislav Burlas, *Slovenská hudobná moderna. Malá moderná encyklopédia* (Bratislava: Obzor, 1983).

[35] See *Slovenský mýtus*, ed. Aurel Hrabušický (Bratislava: Slovak National Gallery, 2006); Kvočáková, *Cesta ke slovenskému mýtu*, 10–14.

Eugen Suchoň's *Žalm zeme podkarpatskej*

Suchoň and his early works from the 1930s came to be viewed as exemplary for Slovak music. One of his most influential early works, the 1938 cantata *Žalm zeme podkarpatskej* ("Psalm of the Carpathian Land") clearly illustrates the ideological underpinning of "Slovak musical modernism." The cantata sets the poem *Podkarpatoruský žalm* ("Carpathian-Ruthenian Psalm") by Czech writer Jaroslav Zatloukal. The poem originally dealt with Carpathian Ruthenia, a region in north-eastern Upper Hungary that was incorporated into Czechoslovakia in 1919 and became an important subject of Czech romantic-orientalist imagination (it was annexed by the Soviet Union after World War II and is now part of Ukraine). Ruthenia was less developed economically and was considered more exotic than Slovakia by the Czechs.[36] Many Czech artists depicted Ruthenia in their works. Zatloukal, a Czech educator and writer in Bratislava in the 1930s, was interested in Ruthenia and its culture, and promoted them in his 1936 collection of poems *Vítr z Polonin* ("The Wind from the Poloniny Meadows").[37] In *Podkarpatoruský žalm*, Zatloukal simultaneously admires, mourns, and criticizes Ruthenia and Ruthenians, and his metaphors touch on both the region's history and its current social problems, including alcoholism, Jewish money lenders, and emigration to America.[38] The poem also engages in strong criticism of the living conditions of the common people of Ruthenia, which was affected by the Great Depression to a greater extent than other regions of Czechoslovakia.

Suchoň collaborated with his friend Ivan Ballo on adapting the poem to Slovak. Suchoň and Ballo's adaptation shifted the text's focus from Ruthenia to Slovakia by removing specifically Ruthenian references and changing the title from "Carpathian-Ruthenian Psalm" to "Psalm of the Carpathian Land" (similar to Ruthenia, Slovakia is surrounded by the Carpathian Mountains on several sides). The only person who was not too excited about the adaptation was Zatloukal.[39] The reconfiguration of Zatloukal's socially critical message, however, resonated with Slovak sensibilities in the 1930s, and continued to do so both after Slovakia

---

[36] Felix Vodička, "Český literární mýtus o Slovensku," in *Kontext české a slovenské literatury: Antologie českých a slovenských textů 1830–1989*, ed. Ludvík Patera and Rudolf Chmel (Prague: Karolinum, 1997), 218.

[37] Jaroslav Zatloukal, *Vítr z polonin* (Bratislava: Podkarpatoruské nakladatelství, 1936).

[38] Zatloukal, *Vítr z polonin*, 55–67.

[39] See Igor Vajda, "Suchoňov 'Žalm zeme podkarpatskej,'" *Musicologica Slovaca* 1 (1969): 43–91 (45).

formed an independent state allied with Nazi Germany in 1939 (when the poem could have been understood as a critique of Czech domination) and after the 1948 Communist Coup in the recreated Czechoslovakia (when it was viewed as a critique of the conditions under a capitalist government).

The music of *Žalm zeme podkarpatskej* evokes "Slovakness" mainly through its harmonic language, as illustrated in the opening measures. The dramatic opening gesture – an exclamation in the trombones and trumpets (developed by the horns starting in m. 6) that is combined with a tremolo in the strings and woodwind – is not dissimilar from the beginnings of Richard Strauss's symphonic poems. The tonal procedures are more individualistic due to modal and chromatic inflections and sonorities created from stacked thirds and seventh chords. In the opening measures (see Example 30.1), we find the sonority G-B-D-F-A-C-E♭, which in the following measures (see Example 30.2) is replaced with a sonority that contains seven of the first thirteen pitches of the harmonic series (harmonics 4, 5, 6, 7, 9, 11, 13; C-E-G-B♭-D-F♯-A) – a sonority that Suchoň calls "diatonic totality" ("diatonický totál"). Arranging the "diatonic totality" into a scale creates the Lydian-Mixolydian mode, which often appears in Slovak folk music (where it is referred to as the Podhale scale): C-D-E-F♯-G-A-B♭-C.[40] Suchoň uses this mode to form both his harmonies and melodies, which are also determined by the declamation patterns of spoken Slovak. By combining different pitches from the stacked sonorities, Suchoň can create not only diatonic major and minor chords but also dissonant sonorities, such as the combination of two tritones a major second apart, which is a preferred dissonant sonority in the cantata – its first instance in the first measure being the combination of E♭-A and F-B. In the context of Suchoň's harmony, this sonority sounds dramatic and modern but not sharply dissonant and not at all bitonal. The augmented fourth can also be heard as the Lydian fourth from Slovak folksongs, which imbues it with national significance.[41]

[40]   See Naďa Hrčková, "Od reflexie k teórii: rozhovor s Eugenom Suchoňom," *Opus musicum* 10 (1978): 123–26; Markéta Štefková, "Podstata hudobnej reči Suchoňovej Krútňavy," *Slovenská hudba* 34 (2008): 239–57.

[41]   For a more extensive discussion of the search of "Slovakness" in harmony, see Branko Ladič, "Transformations of Folklorism in 20th-Century Slovak Composition," *Studia Musicologica* 56 (2015): 367–96; and Branko Ladič, "Music by František Škvor for the Karol Plicka's Film *The Earth Sings* – the Beginning of Slovak National Music?," *Musicologica Brunensia* 51 (2017): 79–87.

Example 30.1: Eugen Suchoň, *Žalm zeme podkarpatskej*, mm. 1–10.

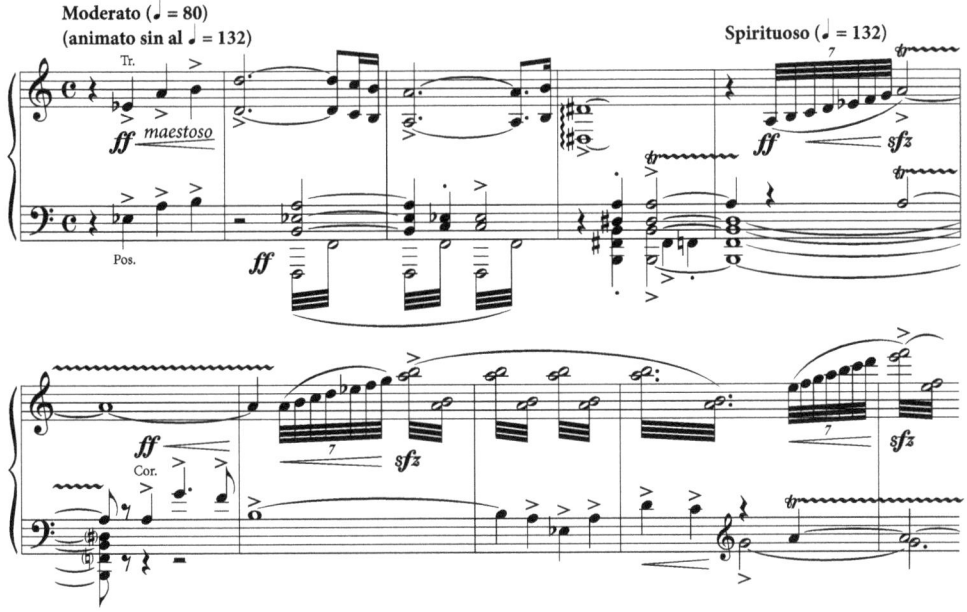

Example 30.2: Eugen Suchoň, *Žalm zeme podkarpatskej*, mm. 19–24.

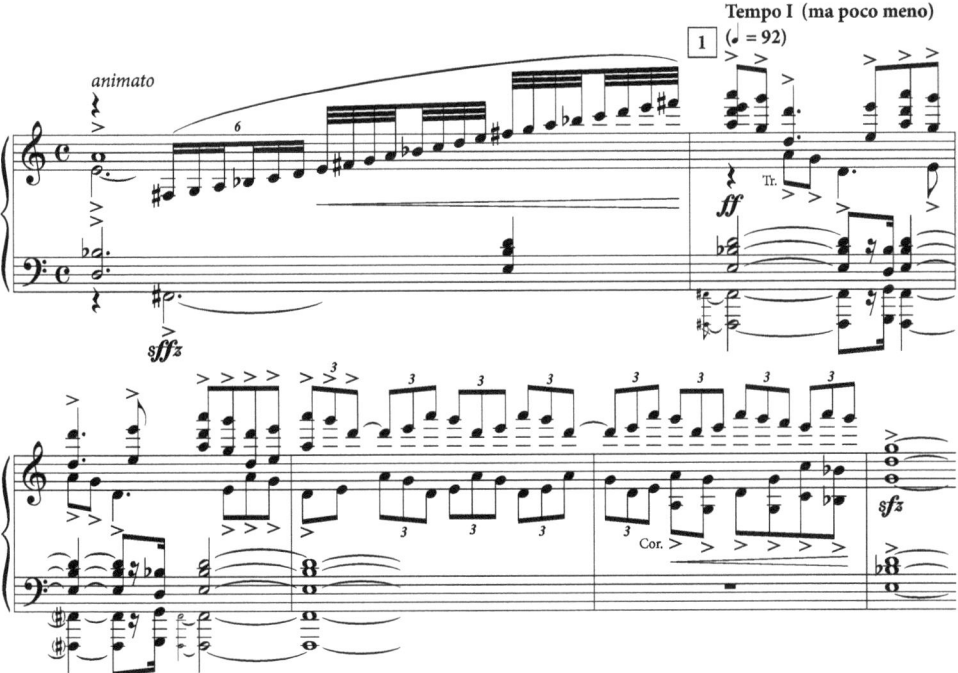

Žalm zeme podkarpatskej's Musicological Reception

Most twentieth-century Slovak musicologists have viewed Suchoň's music (both *Žalm zeme podkarpatskej* and other of his canonic works) as combining, on the one hand, Slovak emotionality and temperament and, on the other hand, intricate inner structures. Igor Vajda, for example, claimed that in his music Suchoň achieved an admirable balance between "immediate inspiration and subsequent rational completion of that inspiration" ("obdivuhodnú rovnováhu medzi bezprostrednou inšpiráciou a jej racionálnym dotváraním").[42] To illustrate Suchoň's uniqueness, Slovak commentators looked for parallels with how the most famous European modernists approached harmony and motivic integration.[43] None of these studies explored the connections between Suchoň's music, including *Žalm zeme podkarpatskej*, and nineteenth-century traditions. This musicological paradigm started to change in 1998 when composer Peter Zagar published an article that compares *Žalm zeme podkarpatskej* to Zoltán Kodály's 1923 cantata *Psalmus hungaricus*, a national elegy for tenor, mixed chorus, and orchestra, from which Suchoň drew inspiration.[44] As Zagar points out, Kodály's composition is clearly linked to contemporaneous modernist techniques and tendencies, whereas Suchoň's music is rooted in premodernist conventions. The fact that Zagar started exploring the conservative aspects of Suchoň's music only in the late 1990s had to do with the prominence of a generally accepted narrative, according to which modern Slovak music did not and should not have anything to do with nineteenth-century practices. Kresánek, Vajda, and other musicologists managed to construct a nationalist myth that Suchoň and his colleagues were modernist artists who created an original form of musical "Slovakness" by drawing on modal inflections of Slovak folk music and the plebeian spirit that the Slovak people held on to through conflicts and subjugation. Such views created a grand conceptual arch connecting the present with the mythical past while steering clear of what was viewed as centuries of oppression. The same imagined, quasi-historical trajectory of the Slovaks also represents the

---

[42] Igor Vajda, "Eugen Suchoň," in *100 slovenských skladateľov*, ed. Marián Jurík and Peter Zagar (Bratislava: Národné hudobné centrum, 1998), 263.

[43] Suchoň's approach to harmony, for example, has been compared to the harmonic innovations of Olivier Messiaen; see Ľubomír Chalupka, "Eugen Suchoň a 12 tónov v oktáve," *Slovenská hudba* 24 (1998): 15. For a discussion of Suchoň's treatment of motives, see Vajda, "Suchoňov 'Žalm zeme podkarpatskej,'" 51–72.

[44] Peter Zagar, "Žalmové kantáty Eugena Suchoňa a Zoltána Kodálya," *Slovenská hudba* 24 (1998): 73–81.

main idea of Suchoň's second opera *Svätopluk* (1960), which draws on the mythology of the Great Moravian period.

Suchoň's *Žalm zeme podkarpatskej* features many moments that evoke stereotypical images of Slovaks – and Ruthenians. Most of these images originated in the Czech imagination but became an important part of the Slovaks' self-image as depicted in the arts. Compared to Zatloukal's poem, Suchoň's cantata presents a predominantly monumentalizing and affirmative depiction of the Slovaks (and Ruthenians) and oscillates between two basic positions – a heroic and a tragic one. Suchoň's musical language grows out of the traditions that also reared Novák. Similar to Moyzes and Cikker, Suchoň listened to the teachings of his Czech mentors, friends, and advisors and was rooted in the identity politics embraced by the Czechs, and at the same time he constructed his own musical concept of Slovak authenticity.

But the ideological and practical relationship between Czechs and Slovaks in classical music was gradually changing. Whereas Czech audiences knew hardly any Slovak music in the interwar period, following World War II, some Slovak composers became respected in the Czech lands, partially due to the new, asymmetrical organization of the Czechoslovak state, in which the Slovaks achieved, at least symbolically, some level of autonomy (this new organization is illustrated in the establishment of two different composer unions in post-1948 Czechoslovakia – a Czechoslovak one and an exclusively Slovak one). The Czechs also started to admire the work of Slovak composers, particularly the operas of Suchoň and Cikker, which made use of an accessible style of modernism. The story of Suchoň's first opera *Krútňava* ("Whirlpool") will serve as a concluding example of the complex relationship between Slovak music and the Czechs. The work was based on a 1920s literary model, a psychological story about a crime of passion that takes place in a village.[45] The plot was an individualistic representation of the "Slovak myth." The opera was composed in the early 1940s, the period of the independent, Nazi-supported Slovak state, but was premiered only in 1949, after the Communist Coup in Czechoslovakia. At first, most Marxist critics doubted whether the opera was ideologically acceptable, and the work became the canonic Slovak national opera only after Czech musicologist and communist minister of culture Zdeněk Nejedlý claimed that it presented "the proper understanding of socialist realism."[46]

---

[45] Milo Urban, *Za vyšným mlynom* (Bratislava: Knihy Slovenského národa, 1926).

[46] Danica Štilichová-Suchoňová, *Život plný hudby. Hudobný skladateľ Eugen Suchoň 1908–1993 v spomienkach* (Bratislava: Mladé letá, 2005), 151–52.

31 | Twentieth-Century Czech Female Composers in Cultural and Political Context: The Pre-1989 Music of Ivana Loudová and Sylvie Bodorová

MIRIAM BLÜMLOVÁ

This chapter focuses on the careers of Ivana Loudová (1941–2017) and Sylvie Bodorová (born 1954), two prominent Czech female composers who embarked on their careers in different historical phases of communist Czechoslovakia, dealt with specific cultural-political circumstances, and reacted to distinct domestic and global music styles. Whereas Loudová began her career in the liberal 1960s, a time when Czech artists started to embrace Western avant-garde styles, Bodorová's work took shape during the normalization era following the 1968 occupation of Czechoslovakia by Warsaw Pact countries. This period officially rejected the reforms of the previous decade and sought to reinstate the aesthetics of socialist realism, which had dominated Czech culture after the communists initially came to power in Czechoslovakia in 1948. The following paragraphs also explore the context of cultural and political developments in post-war Czechoslovakia and examine generationally conditioned artistic programs that were mostly independent of local politics. Although the two composers were significantly influenced by prominent music institutions, such as the Union of Czechoslovak Composers (Svaz československých skladatelů (henceforth SČS), 1949–70) and the Union of Czechoslovak Composers and Concert Artists (Svaz československých skladatelů a koncertních umělců (henceforth SČSKU), 1970–90), they also developed unique compositional styles. The following essay captures the initial, but decisive phase of the composers' careers before 1989, while also touching on the period after the fall of communism.

Czech Music in Cultural and Political Context between 1948 and 1989

To understand the origins of the two composers' musical styles, it is necessary to explore the development of Czech musical culture and its

This chapter was translated from Czech to English by Martin Nedbal.

institutional background in communist Czechoslovakia. The initial period was characterized by Sovietization tendencies of the early 1950s Stalinist era. Authoritative views of Soviet theorists were introduced into the Czech environment through translations and emulations of works by Andrei Zhdanov and V. M. Gorodinsky.[1] Domestic articulations of the principles of socialist realism first appear in Antonín Sychra's 1951 study *Stranická hudební kritika spolutvůrce nové hudby* ("Party Music Criticism as a Co-Creator of New Music").[2] According to Sychra, socialist realist music should be consciously realistic and deeply national, with a significant influence of domestic folk music and without any Western musical influences. In the late 1940s, following the example of the Union of Soviet Composers, the SČS was established as a selective organization of composers, musicologists, critics, and concert artists. Their goal was the comprehensive management of musical life and cultural-political work with composers in accordance with the reigning ideology.

Whereas in the 1950s, the SČS staunchly adhered to socialist realism and categorically rejected any manifestations of Western new music, in the 1960s, a time of political thaw, it gradually opened to new influences from the West, much like the rest of the domestic musical culture. The SČS's journal *Hudební rozhledy* ("Musical Horizons") started to publish reports on premieres in Paris, London, and Dresden. Simultaneously, Czech translations of leading Western composers and musicologists, such as Boulez and Stuckenschmidt, were undertaken.[3] Among original Czech publications, Ivan Vojtěch's anthology *Skladatelé o hudební poetice 20. století* ("Composers on the Musical Poetics of the Twentieth Century") from the 1960s and Ctirad Kohoutek's *Novodobé skladebné teorie západoevropské hudby* ("Modern Composition Theories of Western European Music") from 1962 discussed dodecaphony, serialism, and musique concrète – styles that were condemned as "formalist" just a few years earlier.[4] In 1963, an unprecedented conference on Franz Kafka took place in Liblice, where Czech researchers discussed ideas influenced by Western neo-Marxism and its theory of "alienation."[5] Similar concepts were introduced

---

[1] Miroslav Nový, "Kniha bojující," *Hudební rozhledy* 6 (1953): 506.

[2] Antonín Sychra, *Stranická hudební kritika spolutvůrce nové hudby* (Prague: Za novou hudbu, 1951).

[3] H. H. Stuckenschmidt, "Premiéry a poloprázdné sály," *Hudební rozhledy* 17 (1965): 523; and Pierre Boulez, "Úvahy o dnešní hudbě," *Hudební rozhledy* 18 (1965): 5.

[4] Ivan Vojtěch, *Skladatelé o hudební poetice 20. století* (Prague: Československý spisovatel, 1960); and Ctirad Kohoutek, *Novodobé skladebné teorie západoevropské hudby* (Prague: Státní hudební nakladatelství, 1962).

[5] Eduard Goldstücker, *Vzpomínky 1945–1968* (Prague: G&G, 2005), 128–31.

into the Czech discourse through the texts of Theodor W. Adorno, whom
Czech musicologists rediscovered through the 1964 translation of the study
"On the Fetish Character in Music and the Regression of Listening."[6] Two
years later, Adorno visited Czechoslovakia at the invitation of the Prague
Sociological Society and, in an interview with Vladimír Karbusický,
expressed surprise at the relaxed development of the local music scene.[7]

The period of political thaw and cultural opening to the West in the
1960s came to an end with the onset of the normalization period. The 1970s
and 1980s were characterized by the reinstatement of censorship, the
closure of borders with Western countries, and widespread institutional
reorganization and purges. The SČS ceased to exist in 1970, and in its place,
the SČSKU was established. This organization largely attempted to update
socialist realism as the leading creative principle,[8] along with Marxist
musicologists, such as Jaroslav Jiránek, the author of one of the last
significant publications on the subject.[9] However, there was no return to
the artistic or political atmosphere of the 1950s. Despite the official rhetoric
of state institutions, including the SČSKU, new influences from the West
were so deeply rooted in the work of Czech composers that ideologically
motivated appeals largely remained confined to the realm of formal congress declarations and manifestos.

In the 1970s and 1980s, the SČSKU became the main creative milieu for
several generations of Czech composers, placing a particular emphasis on
the youngest artists. In 1972, a committee for the support of new and older
styles in music was established within the SČSKU. The initiative brought
together young concert artists, music critics, and musicologists under the
age of thirty-five. A prototype of this committee existed in the late 1960s; it
was initiated by Ivana Loudová and was titled Young Composers Group
(Skupina mladých skladatelů). In 1973, the Young Stage (Mladé podium)
festival was established in Karlovy Vary, where, in addition to concerts,
intense discussions and clashes between supporters of both neoclassical
and avant-garde concepts took place. In the 1970s, modern artistic
approaches intertwined with cultural and political appeals for the broadest
social impact of music. Jan Vičar referred to these approaches as "an

[6] Antonín Sychra, "Odcizení, fetišismus v hudbě, regrese sluchu a jak dál," *Hudební rozhledy* 17 (1964): 731.

[7] Vladimír Karbusický, "Půlhodinka s Adornem," *Hudební rozhledy* 11 (1966): 323–24.

[8] "Programová část sjezdového referátu předneseného Lubomírem Železným," *Hudební rozhledy* 26 (1973): 3.

[9] Jaroslav Jiránek, *Socialistický realismus jako vůdčí ideově estetický princip naší současné hudební tvorby* (Prague: Divadelní ústav, 1980).

integrative stylistic process" ("integrační stylový proces"), marked by respect for the pluralism of individual compositional syntheses and experiments and demands for the increased societal functionality of creative works, reintroduced by the newly established SČSKU.[10]

It was under these general conditions that the works of Loudová and Bodorová took shape. Loudová drew from the aesthetics of the 1960s, emphasizing experimental elements of the Western avant-garde. Bodorová, by contrast, rehabilitated traditional expressive means during the normalization era. Paradoxically, Bodorová's turn to traditionalism did not stem primarily from ideological demands for universal comprehensibility but rather from international trends, particularly the rediscovery of tonal procedures. Similar approaches were undertaken by composers from other socialist countries, including Poland and Estonia.

Loudová's Growth as an Artist

Loudová studied composition during high school under the supervision of Jaroslav Řídký (1857–1956). Although she intended to enroll at the Academy of Performing Arts (AMU) in Prague, she was advised to first study at the conservatory. Thus, in 1958, Loudová entered the Prague Conservatory in the composition class of Miloslav Kabeláč (1908–79). Despite being silenced for most of his life in his own country, first by the Nazis and then by the communists, Kabeláč's music was performed in many international venues, and his name was inseparably linked with the Swiss ensemble Les Percussions de Strasbourg.[11] Fascinated by Uday Shankar's Indian dance and instrumental ensemble during its 1935 visit to Prague, Kabeláč was the first Czech composer to elevate percussion instruments to a status equal to other orchestral instruments.[12] Kabeláč's passion for percussion instruments, especially as used in Japanese music, and modality influenced the compositional style of Loudová.

In the 1960s, Loudová developed a musical language characterized by stylistic polarity – her output included both easy-going, melodious tonal compositions and weighty pieces inspired by the musical avant-garde. Loudová could produce both children's choral compositions and complex symphonic works. The enormous scope and breadth of her work during

---

[10] Jan Vičar, "Skladatelská generace sedmdesátých let, názory, orientace (výňatky)," *Opus musicum* 15 (1983): 101–9.

[11] Paul Nardi, "A un ami très cher," *Hudební věda* 36 (1999): 169–78.

[12] Zdeněk Nouza, *Miloslav Kabeláč: Tvůrčí profil skladatele* (Prague: AVČR, 2010), 359.

this period is also reflected in the stage music that Loudová wrote in collaboration with students from Prague's drama and film schools (DAMU and FAMU), including music for puppet performances and films – she wrote the score for Juraj Jakubisko's film *Mlčení* ("The Silence") and Jiří Fréhar's *Svatá Jana* ("St. Jane") and *Tabáková cesta* ("The Tobacco Road"). She also wrote music for documentaries, such as *Krnov – město varhan* ("Krnov – City of Organs").

A fusion of Loudová's lighter and more serious musical styles can be found in her Symphony No. 2 (1965), based on Jacques Prévert's poem "Cet amour" and Michelangelo Buonarroti's love sonnet "Fuggite, amanti, Amor," with which she graduated from the AMU. The Symphony's fourth movement features vocal lines that range from recitation through lyrical and dramatic singing to *Sprechgesang* and voiceband style. The movement's texture is also highly varied, transforming from monophony to complex twelve-part harmonies. In a theoretical essay Loudová wrote in the same year, she explained, likely referring to the fourth movement, that her main consideration was expression, not the comprehensibility of each word.[13] Although the Symphony had to adhere to contemporary conventions, it also demonstrated the composer's compositional and aesthetic autonomy, as noted by the chairman of SČS, Jiří Dvořáček, in 1966:[14]

There are indeed few composition students who could match Ivana Loudová in having traversed the path from naively amateur beginnings to a serious artistic profession during the regular course of study. I consider Loudová an artist well-prepared for life and fulfilling the most significant tasks in the musical-creative field. I recommend she be admitted to the SČS.

Skutečně je málo adeptů studia kompozice, kteří by se mohli měřit s Ivanou Loudovou v tom, že za dobu normálního studia dokázali urazit cestu od naivně amatérských začátků k vážné umělecké profesi. Loudovou pokládám za umělkyni dobře připravenou pro život a plnění nejzávažnějších úkolů v hudebně-tvůrčí oblasti. Doporučuji, aby byla přijata do SČS.

In addition to Symphony No. 2, Loudová submitted other compositions for evaluation to the AMU faculty. In her Sonata for Clarinet and Piano, one reviewer noted the composition was marked by "an effort toward 'modernity' (harmonic sharpness, bitonality, causality)" ("úsilí o 'modernost'

---

[13] Ivana Loudová, "Vokální složka v symfonii" (MA thesis, AMU, Prague, 1965).

[14] Prague, Czech Music Museum, Loudová's personal file, critical evaluation, June 22, 1966. The process of accepting new members to the SČS is discussed in Jan Blüml, "Svaz československých skladatelů a jeho vliv na populární hudbu šedesátých let a kariéru Bohuslava Ondráčka," *Musicologica Brunensia* 58 (2023): 25–39.

(harmonická ostrost, bitonalita, příčinnost)") and was "a likeable attempt" ("sympatická snaha") to make the most of the chosen thematic material. The reviewer also made some negative comments, claiming that the piece lacked refined melodic invention.[15] In her *Pražské sonety* ("Prague Sonnets"), the reviewers complained about Loudová's "verbosity," and in her First String Quartet, they noted that she managed to liberate herself "from the unpleasant pressures brought by the incessant demand for 'modernity'" ("od nepříjemně pociťovaného tlaku v úzkostlivém požadavku 'modernosti'") and thus in many places achieved "spontaneous, youthful musicianship" ("spontánního, mladého muzicírování").[16]

Loudová wrote many notable compositions during this period, some of which won prizes and brought in financial rewards. These include the 1967 cantata for children's choir *Malý princ* ("The Little Prince"), which won the Prix Italia, and the 1966 cycle of three-part children's choruses *Mámo...* ("Mummy..."). The more serious category of Loudová's output is exemplified by *Rhapsody in Black* (1966), ballet music with prominent percussion, which won a competition in Mannheim. Her 1966 *Stabat Mater* for two male choirs received an honorable mention and a financial reward of 1,200 Czechoslovak crowns.[17] For the commission of the full-length ballet *Pouta* ("The Bonds"), Loudová was to be paid a fee of 10,000 crowns, divided over ten months, corresponding to the submission deadline.[18] The average gross monthly salary in Czechoslovakia at that time was 1,453 crowns.[19]

Loudová's career was significantly influenced by her studies with André Jolivet and Olivier Messiaen in Paris in the early 1970s. She first encountered Messiaen's music when she heard his *Oiseaux exotiques* on the radio sometime around 1960. In a later autobiographical comment, she reminisced: "It was a strong experience during which I realized that I, too, had loved bird songs since childhood. I used to write them down, but they supposedly didn't belong to compositions because it was the cheapest musical effect, as they taught us at the conservatory" ("Byl to silný

---

[15] Prague, Czech Music Museum, Loudová's personal file, anonymous review.

[16] Prague, Czech Music Museum, Loudová's personal file, anonymous review.

[17] Prague, Czech Museum of Music, Loudová's personal file, Loudová's letter, December 2, 1968.

[18] Prague, Czech Museum of Music, Loudová's personal file, signed contract, October 7, 1966. Loudová never finished the ballet and returned the funds.

[19] For information about average salaries in Czechoslovakia between 1955 and 1992, see: www .google.com/url?sa=t&rct=j&q=&esrc=s&source=web&cd=&ved=2ahUKEwiO8_i54qKDA xUU3QIHHcXlAssQFnoECA0QAQ&url=https%3A%2F%2Fwww.czso.cz%2Fdocuments% 2F10180%2F35067255%2F1100251539.pdf%2Fafd4b303-aa1d-42f6-a1e8-8bab1b3f58ae% 3Fversion%3D1.1&usg=AOvVaw3C1rA_RYIyyzXFE-Js1tFD&opi=89978449, accessed March 21, 2024.

zážitek, při kterém jsem si uvědomila, že i já jsem od dětství milovala ptačí zpěv. Zapisovala jsem si ho, ale do kompozice nepatřil, protože, jak nás učili na konzervatoři, jde o nejlacinější tónový efekt").[20] During that period, no textbooks and conservatory lectures mentioned Messiaen. Nevertheless, in the 1960s, Loudová increased her international contacts by traveling to the Gaudeamus Festival in Darmstadt and the Gedok Festival in Mannheim, where she achieved great success with her *Rhapsody in Black*. In 1970, Loudová won a postgraduate scholarship from the French government. In connection to the award, Loudová talked to Henri Ehret, the former cultural attaché in Prague, who was very impressed by Loudová's *Stabat Mater*. In the conversation, Ehret mentioned he knew Messiaen well, and on January 21, 1971, Loudová entered Messiaen's composition class at the Paris Conservatory. Loudová later recalled that her arrival was complicated due to the restrictions Czechoslovak citizens faced when crossing borders and that at one point, it seemed the trip might not even take place. The main reason why Loudová was eventually allowed to travel to France was that unlike other Eastern European communist states, Czechoslovakia never severed diplomatic ties with Washington, London, and Paris, and the French state bureaucracy insisted that the scholarship be utilized.[21]

During her six-month stay in Paris, Loudová worked on the symphonic composition *Spleen: Hommage à Charles Baudelaire*. Messiaen appreciated the work's thoughtful form, instrumentation, and melodic material. Loudová noted that he "smiled a bit" ("se trochu usmál") at the work's specific "'modal technique' (a combination of a basic four-tone mode – F, B, C♭, E – with a twelve-tone row)" ("'modální techniku' (kombinace čtyřtónového základního modu, f, b, ces, e, s dvanáctitónovou řadou)"); the idea was allegedly "too primitive" ("příliš primitivní") for him, but he no longer objected when she wrote it in the score.[22] Messiaen thought that the composition, structured as a sequence of contrasting color patches juxtaposed against a solo instrument, would bring a moment of surprise, based most prominently on the melodic lines of the alto flute and the timpani. Individual segments are separated by specific timbres, such as by the sound of the tam-tam. The tam-tam's second occurrence at the end of the sixth segment plays a particularly crucial role in terms of not only

---

[20] Miloš Haase's private archive, Loudová's lecture "Meine Begegnungen mit Olivier Messiaen," delivered at the Symposium "La Cité celeste," Dresdner Zentrum für zeitgenössische Musik, June 13–14, 1998.

[21] Jindřich Dejmek, ed., *Československo, dějiny státu* (Prague: Libri, 2018), 469.

[22] Loudová's lecture "Meine Begegnungen mit Olivier Messiaen."

color but also structure – in a consultation with Loudová, André Jolivet calculated that the tam-tam strike occurs precisely at the golden ratio, that is, six minutes and ten seconds into the piece (see Figure 31.1).[23]

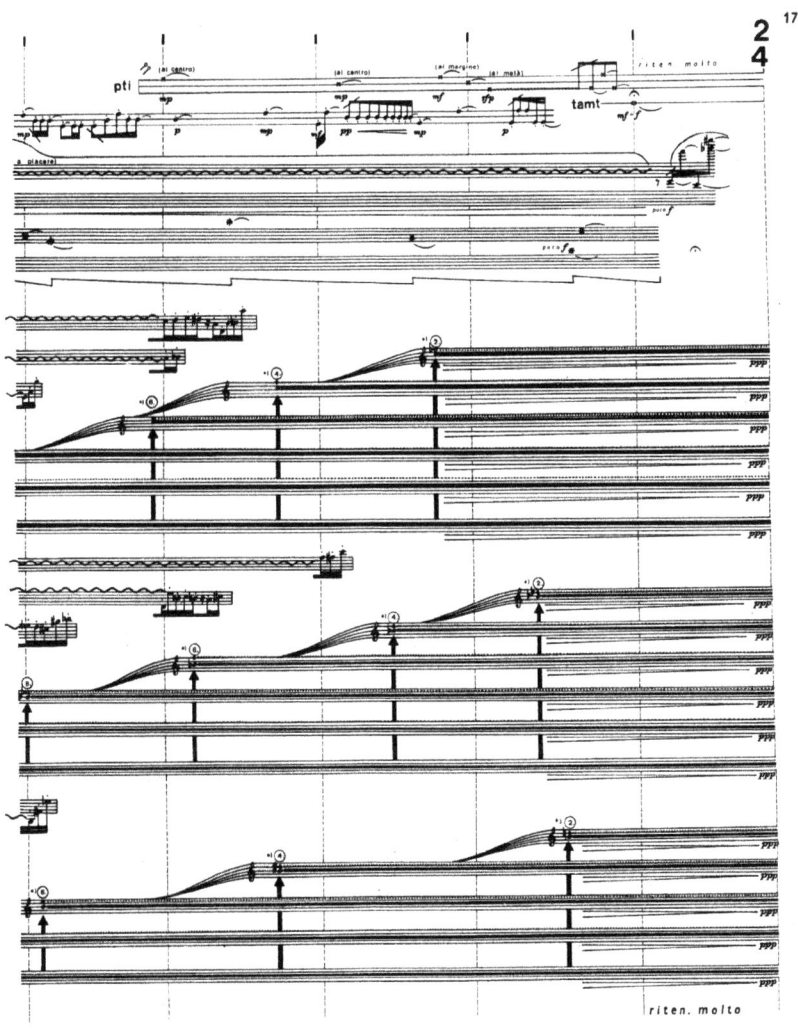

Figure 31.1: Tam-tam strike at 6'11", in Ivana Loudová, *Spleen: Hommage à Charles Baudelaire* (Prague: Panton, 1974), 17. Courtesy of Schott Music International and Miloš Haase.

[23] Ivana Loudová, "Témbrová a aleatorní technika v hudbě" (doctoral diss., AMU, Prague, 1971), 40.

During her stay in France, Loudová's international contacts intensified. She began collaborating with the American Wind Symphony Orchestra, to which, in the following decade, she dedicated many compositions featuring an original use of the percussion. After the 1973 suite for solo percussion, *Agamemnon*, and the 1974 Concerto for Percussion, Organ, and Wind Instruments, she was included among twelve other composers from around the world in a competition to write a concerto for solo percussion and wind orchestra. The result was the *Dramatic Concerto* in 1980, premiered by soloist Steven Schick, earning the award for the most successful competition piece at the First International Interpretation Competition for Percussion Instruments in Pittsburgh.[24] However, as she later recalled, due to the closing of the borders during the "normalization" period, it was the ties to Soviet musicians that became particularly strong:[25]

I eventually got to America with the ninth scholarship; eight earlier ones had fallen through. When I was supposed to go to Pittsburgh in 1972 for the premiere of my composition *Hymnos*, the ministry told me that I had to go to the Soviet Union first. They sent me there to lecture about Czech music . . . The journey through the Soviet Union at that time was unforgettable. In Moscow, I had an "official" presentation at the Union of Composers with Tikhon Chrennikov. There was also the sympathetic Tajik composer Firous Bakhor from Dushanbe, who immediately realized that he could trust me and introduced me to the "Soviet underground" of the time, consisting of banned composers, such as Andrey Volkonsky, Alfred Schnittke, and Sofia Gubaidulina. I established contact and long-term friendships with them.

Do Ameriky jsem se nakonec dostala na deváté stipendium, osm jich před tím propadlo. Když jsem měla jet v roce 1972 na pozvání do Pittsburghu na premiéru své skladby Hymnos, na ministerstvu mi řekli, že musím jet dřív do Sovětského svazu, poslali mě tam přednášet o české hudbě [. . .] To putování po tehdejším Sovětském svazu bylo nezapomenutelné. V Moskvě jsem měla ,oficiální' přehrávku ve Svazu skladatelů u Tichona Chrennikova. Byl tam i sympatický tádžický skladatel Firus Bachor z Dušanbe, který okamžitě poznal, že mi lze věřit, a zavedl mě to tehdejšího ,sovětského podzemí' zakázaných skladatelů jako byli Andrej Volkonskij, Alfred Schnittke a Sofia Gubajdulina, s nimiž jsem navázala kontakt a dlouholeté přátelství.

Several compositions by Loudová achieved great success abroad but did not get the chance to be performed in Czechoslovakia during the period in question due to the decision of the Union. For example, Loudová's 1972

---

[24] Prague, Czech Music Museum, Loudová's personal file, music director Robert Austin Boudreau's letter to the Union of Composers, August 18, 1980.

[25] Martin Franc, ed., *Dějiny Akademie múzických umění v Praze* (Prague: AMU, 2017), 236.

Hymnos for wind and percussion instruments and her 1970 trio *Gnómai* for soprano, flute, and harp did not receive a single performance in Czech venues.[26] By contrast, compositions inspired by Czech musical traditions garnered significant success, including String Quartet No. 2 ("In Memory of Bedřich Smetana") from 1976, *Hukvaldy Suite* for string quartet from 1984, and *Variations on a Stamitz Theme* for string quartet from 1989.

Bodorová's Artistic Career

Sylvie Bodorová underwent an artistic and compositional emancipation at the end of her studies. Despite reverence for the contemporary canon and avant-garde styles during her time at the Bratislava Conservatory and later at the Brno Janáček Academy (JAMU), where she studied under Ctirad Kohoutek, a student of Jaroslav Kvapil and a graduate of courses by Lutosławski, Boulez, and Ligeti, she surprisingly graduated in 1978 with the tonal composition *Ladno, kdykoli pohladím zemi* ("Easy, Whenever I Stroke the Earth"). This caused significant consternation among the faculty, as she recalled: "It was like a bomb exploded in the school. She must have gone mad!" ("Jako by ve škole vybuchla bomba. Ona se musela zbláznit!").[27] Kohoutek and especially Alois Piňos, the founder of the so-called Czech New Music that gained prominence in Czechoslovakia in the 1960s, could not come to terms with the turn to simplicity. Miloslav Ištván, another representative of the Brno school and advocate of New Music inspired by total serialism and mathematical methods in music, also distanced himself from Bodorová. Like Bodorová, however, Ištván later incorporated pop, jazz, and early music into his compositions and was one of the first Czech composers to work with postmodern musical elements. Reflecting on her compositional approach in 1980, Bodorová stated: "My generation is moving away from incomprehensible modernity, modernity at any cost, and is turning to simplicity and melody instead" ("moje generace se vzdaluje nesrozumitelné modernosti, modernosti za každou cenu a spíše se navrací k prostotě a melodice").[28] Bodorová adopted this

---

[26] Prague, Czech Music Museum, Loudová's personal file, questionnaire about music commissions, September 27, 1972, containing the note "return to the author with thanks."

[27] *Hudba je největší dar*, dir. Blažena Hončarivová, Czech Television, 2018, documentary, www .ceskatelevize.cz/porady/10637723143-sylvie-bodorova-hudba-je-nejvetsi-dar/, accessed March 21, 2024.

[28] Prague, Czech Music Museum, Sylvie Bodorová's personal file no. 153/7, "Hudba jako poslání," interview with the composer.

new style immediately after graduating from JAMU, and had to get accustomed to it by starting with simpler forms. Thus, unlike Loudová, who established herself compositionally during her studies, mature examples of Bodorová's work did not crystallize until the late 1980s.

Whereas Loudová managed to travel and thereby confirm her interest in Western new music, Bodorová came of age during the normalization period in the 1970s. Although contacts with Western culture were significantly limited, they were not non-existent. Bodorová traveled to Poland (to the Warsaw Autumn festival) and Italy (she later recalled she was not allowed to travel to Germany), and her experiences are reflected in her compositional technique. She never abandoned her fundamental "belief in melody,"[29] and in the context of European music developments, she stood alongside composers of accessible and traditionally expressive music, such as Henryk Górecki, who composed the *Symphony of Sorrowful Songs* in 1976, after the traumatic experience of visiting a Nazi prison, and Arvo Pärt, who composed his 1976 piano miniature *Für Alina* in seclusion and thought of it as having extramusical and spiritual connotations.

Discussions of Lutosławski, Górecki, and Szymanowski had regularly appeared in the pages of *Hudební rozhledy* since the late 1950s, whereas Pärt was first featured only in 1987 in connection to a festival in West Berlin. Pärt's deviation from strict avant-garde techniques elicited similar reactions to Bodorová, whose teachers also had significant doubts about the direction of her career. Stylistic plurality, a return to tradition, broadly conceived neoclassicism, the minimalization of chosen means, and the rejection of the avant-garde were typical features for an entire generation of composers studying in the 1970s. This shift, which could be understood as a slightly sycophantic surrender to the ideological pressures of normalization, had genuine qualities that persisted in the following decades.

In the 1980s, Bodorová expanded her activities significantly. In 1981, the Prague Spring Festival premiered her meditation for solo viola *Gíľa Rome*, which foreshadowed her later compositions in its use of exoticism and folk elements. Her later works *Dža more* for solo violin (1990) and *JA RA LAJ* (2009) employ "expressive positions of Gypsy temperament – from quiet melancholy to fiery outbursts."[30] Furthermore, her 1999 *Concerto de Estío* for solo guitar was inspired by Hispanic and Latin American music, and

---

[29] Zdeněk Brabec, "Interview with Sylvia Bodorová," in *Quo vadis* [program booklet to Bodorová's opera](Plzeň: Josef Kajetán Tyl Theater, 2022), 15.
[30] Prague, Czech Music Museum, Bodorová's personal file no. 225/5.

her 2003 *Mysterium druidum* for harp incorporated elements of Irish folk music.

The aesthetic ideals of the SČSKU were repeatedly articulated both in regular performances and critical reviews, clearly reflecting a large amount of opposition to the West, a fondness for expressive melodic lines, and an emphasis on listeners and interpretative comfort. These ideas also affected Bodorová's works. For example, the 1984 composition *Kovadliny* ("Anvils") used unconventional notation, and a lecturer remarked: "The opening notes mention . . . 'cluster semiminima,' that is 'half-minim cluster.' What am I supposed to understand by this term? Did the author perhaps pick it from some foreign pseudo-avant-garde scores?" ("V úvodních poznámkách se uvádí . . . 'cluster semiminima,' tedy 'polonejmenší.' Co si mám pod tím pojmem představit? Pochytila to snad autorka z nějakých zahraničních pseudoavantgardních partitur?").[31] The issue of notation also affected the 1985 composition *Tre canzoni da suonare* for guitar and orchestra, where Bodorová also grappled with simplifying her style: ". . .too much simplicity in places, the sound seems rather poor to me, inventively basically lyrical, but mostly without more distinctive originality and ingenuity" ("té prostoty nějak příliš mnoho, místy se mi zdá zvuk dosti chudý, invenčně v zásadě lyrický, většinou však bez výraznějších osobitosti a vynalézavosti").[32] In evaluating Bodorová's 1986 work *Panamody* for flute and piano, the reviewer appreciates that the author evidently abandoned some of her "overly simplifying approaches" ("příliš zjednodušující přístupy"), and the composition is "playfully grateful and accessible" ("hráčsky vděčná a přístupná").[33] In the case of *Dozvěny* ("Reverberations," 1987), she is criticized for not being original and finding too much inspiration in the work of Czech composer Luboš Fišer, whose influence later became one of the characteristic features of specific passages in her works.[34] For example, in her 1987 string quarter *Dignitas homini*, Bodorová used a distinct, yet simple melody, references to Janáček rhythmic units ("sčasovky"), and Fišer-like neo-Romantic spaces, which also often appear in lyrical, adagio sections of her compositions (such as the second movement of her 2006 piano concerto *Come d'accordo*).

---

[31] Prague, Czech Music Museum, Bodorová's personal file no. 172/20, anonymous review, June 18, 1984.

[32] Prague, Czech Music Museum, Bodorová's personal file no. 172/20, anonymous review, July 18, 1984.

[33] Prague, Czech Music Museum, Bodorová's personal file no. 172/20, anonymous reviews, November 30, 1986, and June 1987.

[34] Prague, Czech Music Museum, Bodorová's personal file no. 172/20, undated anonymous review.

Bodorová thus created a language characterized by precise formal structure, clarity, and distinctive sound color.

Loudová and Bodorová after 1989

In the post-communist era, Loudová started her academic career at Prague's AMU, becoming the first female professor of composition in 2006. In 2015, she received the State Award from the Ministry of Culture of the Czech Republic. During the award ceremony, the moderators touched upon the issue of stereotypical perceptions of composition as an exclusively male field.[35] She also mentioned the significant number of talented female composition students. The institutions SČS and SČSKU supported authors like Loudová and Bodorová not only financially (through commissions of new works) but also through concert performances and providing living spaces and studios for creative work. However, a survey of the archives of these institutions reveals that the ratio of female composers within the overall membership of music authors was minimal.

Pursuing prestigious opportunities in academia diminished Loudová's compositional activity. For Bodorová, however, the 1990s marked a significant creative upturn. She developed a distinctive style characterized by "postmodern" collage-like elements, a thematic turn to the past, and integration of seemingly incongruous elements. This period also involved a renewed search for a lost classical music audience. Successful collaborations with various international ensembles, such as the Luxembourg Sinfonietta, and interactions with notable figures set the stage for Bodorová's creative activity in the following decades, during which she could devote herself exclusively to composition. In her 1996 "neo-Baroque" *Concerto dei Fiori* for violin and string quartet, she presented herself as a member of the Quattro group. Founded in 1996 by her colleagues Otmar Mácha, Zdeněk Lukáš, and Luboš Fišer, the group pursued artistic goals based on the belief that contemporary classical music could appeal to present-day listeners and reach a broad audience. This vision, in the context of the new market economy and the general commercialization of musical culture, was quite bold, considering the diminished state subsidies. Despite her utopian views, premieres of Bodorová's compositions took place at major festivals, such as Smetana's

---

[35] The broadcast of the 2015 Ministry of Culture awards ceremony can be accessed at: www.ceskatelevize.cz/porady/15172998550-ceny-ministerstva-kultury/21554215019/, accessed March 21, 2024.

Litomyšl (oratorio *Moses* in 2008, song cycle *Lingua Angelorum* in 2021), the Prague Spring, and, most notably, the premiere of the 2002 oratorio *Judas Maccabeus* at Prague's St. Vitus's Cathedral, as well as the 2022 opera *Quo vadis*, written for the Tyl Theater in Plzeň.

Conclusion

Both Loudová and Bodorová defied the negative stereotypes traditionally associated with women composers through diverse and intellectually sophisticated works. Loudová established herself as a student of Messiaen and Kabeláč in the 1960s and gravitated toward the musical avant-garde. Bodorová, by contrast emphasized a broader stylistic integration and a desire for simplification and detachment.[36] Bodorová's career also illustrates that the simplification of musical expression in the 1970s and 1980s, often associated with official demands of the normalization cultural policy for the general comprehensibility of music with references to the original aesthetics of socialist realism, was also rooted in the international tendency to revive tonality, which occurred spontaneously and under differing conditions in various European countries. The composers' unions played an important role in the careers of both artists during normalization, such as by issuing travel bans and excluding certain compositions from concert programs. However, the examination of the two composer's careers also contradicts the notion, developed in the post-communist era, that the unions were exclusively political and had a clearly negative influence on musical culture. Both composers received commissions, financial support, and administrative services from the unions, which laid the foundation for their success.

---

[36] Sylvie Bodorová, "Tvůrčí tendence nejmladší české skladatelské generace," *Hudební věda* 22 (1985): 134–54.

ALEŠ BŘEZINA AND JAKUB HRŮŠA

Jakub Hrůša is one of the most renowned Czech classical musicians of the present day. He currently serves as the Chief Conductor of the Bamberg Symphony, Music Director of the Royal Opera House, Covent Garden, and Principal Guest Conductor of the Czech Philharmonic. Born in Brno, Hrůša studied conducting at the Academy of Performing Arts in Prague (HAMU). Throughout his career, Hrůša has collaborated with orchestras and opera companies worldwide, including the Berlin Philharmonic, the Bavarian Symphony Orchestra, Munich Philharmonic, Staatskapelle Dresden, Gewandhausorchester Leipzig, Vienna Philharmonic, Vienna State Opera, Chicago Symphony, New York Philharmonic, Cleveland Symphony, Boston Symphony, Lyric Opera of Chicago, NHK Symphony Orchestra Tokyo, Tokyo Metropolitan Symphony Orchestra, and others.

Hrůša is also active in the literary sphere and serves as a prominent advocate for the public appreciation of classical music. In 2020, he published a book of essays in Czech and English about Bohuslav Martinů.[1] In 2021, Hrůša collaborated with his friend Aleš Březina, a composer, musicologist, and the director of the Bohuslav Martinů Institute, to produce a documentary series for Czech Television popularizing the six symphonies of Bohuslav Martinů. The documentaries are set to be released on the Unitel label.

In 2022, Březina engaged in a series of email exchanges with Hrůša. The resulting conversation, translated and edited by Martin Nedbal, presents Hrůša's views on the traditions of Czech music and the place of Czech composers in the world of classical music. Hrůša explains what the term "Czech music" means to him, how he distinguishes it from Central European music, and what he thinks about the concepts of mainstream and peripheral musical traditions. He also comments on his experiences as a Czech conductor in the cosmopolitan environment of classical music and more specifically as the music director of the Bamberg Symphony, the German orchestra formed in 1946 predominantly from German musicians expelled from Czechoslovakia after World War II. Hrůša also explains his

This chapter was translated from Czech to English by Martin Nedbal.
[1] Jakub Hrůša, *Hrůša on Martinů* (Prague: International Martinů Circle, 2020).

understanding of how music conveys national meanings and the similarities and differences between Czech and German music.

BŘEZINA: How do you understand the term "Czech music"? Is it possible to limit the term to the period between the first compositions of Bedřich Smetana and the last works of Bohuslav Martinů, or do you see it differently?

HRŮŠA: I see it differently. It obviously depends on how we define the adjective "Czech." As we Czechs know, our mother tongue does not distinguish between the concepts of "Bohemian" [that is, related to anyone who lives in Bohemia or the Czech lands, whether they identify as Czech or not] and "Czech" [that is, related to self-identified ethnic Czechs]; for us the history and culture of our motherland is simply Czech. The first concept (Bohemian) focuses on the culture and society of Bohemia, and from that point of view, the musicians who lived in this region prior to Smetana, such as [Wenzel Johann/Václav Jan] Tomášek [Tomaschek], [Franz/František] Škroup [Skraup], and perhaps also the emigrant musicians who retained their ties to their homeland, were Czech. The second (ethnic and national) concept is more problematic. For example, it is debatable as to whether Smetana was clearly the first composer who consciously and steadily and despite adversity worked for the idea of a Czech national revival; it is a fact, however, that in terms of their symbolic significance, Smetana's works clearly belong to Czechness, although this significance is more subjective than objective. I personally believe, moreover, that Czech music did not end with a specific composer but continues to thrive.

BŘEZINA: What do you think about the difference between Czech music and the music of the Central European region in general?

HRŮŠA: The idea of Central European music is very dear to me, and I always aim at connecting Czech music to this context. It is probably important to consider who observes these musical traditions and from where. When someone from Austria or Germany thinks about Czech music, they necessarily distinguish it from the more general Central European tradition. When someone looks at the music from our part of the world from America or Japan, insistence on the distinctiveness of the Czech musical environment becomes nearly inappropriate. The reason is simple: Central Europe is part of a large continent, and the Czech lands are part of Central Europe. As an artist, I am always concerned about the ties between music and the broader cultural environment. It is interesting to think about Smetana, Dvořák, and Czech composers of their time (and particularly them), but also those from later generations and their relationship to a larger community of Central European composers: Smetana in the period of Liszt and Wagner, Dvořák and his links to Brahms and Tchaikovsky – to me, these links are more important than pondering the similarities and differences between Smetana and Dvořák only. With a few exceptions, this is how we usually approach concert programming and recording plans (as was the case with our monumental project of recording the symphonies of both Dvořák and Brahms with the Bamberg Symphony). I am also interested in illustrating the organic connections between Janáček and Bartók, Suk and Mahler, Novák and Strauss, and Martinů and someone like, for example, Korngold (although after his emigration and partially also beforehand, Martinů became more attuned to the non-Central European inspirations of French and other Western traditions).

BŘEZINA: What is your experience with the concepts of center and periphery in connection to Czech music, which is often viewed as an in-between tradition?

HRŮŠA: I think that to answer this question, one needs to consider the perspective. First, we could think about the role of Czech music within the European mainstream (for us, this means especially the Austro-German tradition). Second, one would focus on the principal and subsidiary tendencies in Czech music, or in the music in the Czech lands, or music somehow connected to "Czechness."

In connection to the first point of view, which I would prefer to discuss, I think once again that the perspective and background of the listeners or performers is important. Are they approaching Czech music from close-by Vienna and Leipzig? From Paris, London? Or perhaps from (Dvořák's) New York? Or from another direction – from Moscow and St. Petersburg? All these perspectives affect the way in which listeners respond to Czech music.

Personally, I have always understood Czech music – and I know I have already made this point – as essentially and organically tied to the Central European region. Although I don't want to deny anyone the right to have an opinion, it does not make sense to me to understand Smetana's music as merely a colored branch of German music, and Dvořák's work as merely "Brahmsian." I understand these artists as integral participants in a larger tradition. But I understand other approaches. For example, let's take Dvořák – his case illustrates the matter well. He himself "played" with different perspectives in his work. To a large extent he composed for specific communities and purposes. Let us compare his sixth and seventh symphonies (perhaps excluding their scherzos), his operas *Dimitrij* and *Armida*, or *Píseň bohatýrská* ("A Hero's Song"). How much exoticism do we find in them? The symphonic scherzos provide a folklore-inspired respite, but the essence of the rest of these compositions is as close to the tradition of German music (Beethoven, Brahms) as possible – I think that Dvořák wanted very much for these works to be tightly connected to the Austro-German context. I see a similar approach in Dvořák's church compositions (*Stabat Mater*, Requiem), which converse with various traditions of sacred music. But we find a completely different approach in works written for England (*Svatá Ludmila/Saint Ludmila* – a Handelian work with a specific Czech "flavor") and for America. In the case of America, Dvořák, both when he was getting excited about his trip and after he started to understand the place a little bit, wanted to compose in a way that he believed could resonate there as much as possible. Figuratively speaking, I could say that Dvořák, whom I am using as an example chosen at random, had a perfect command of at least the German language (partially – and I continue to speak figuratively – because this language was also known in his homeland), but at the same time never got rid, and never even wanted to be rid, of his Czech accent. He considered this accent an authentic and perhaps also attractive aspect of his personality – something that helped him express where he belonged and catch everyone's attention. However, and please don't take me literally, I know that Dvořák identified fully as Czech, and although he mastered German as much as he needed to, he also felt culturally and essentially distant from it (Smetana before him was a slightly different case). I am still speaking figuratively here: Dvořák simply knew how to speak, and compose, in the languages of his cultural neighbors (or – to put it differently – in the second language; of those who also settled in his homeland), and he used this language without scruples to communicate with the Germans successfully. But he never wanted to sound "like a German." A more complicated matter was Dvořák's musical "English" during his stay in the United States. There, he created a strange (and beautiful!) fusion of the Czech language with American accents. Let me bring these metaphors to a close.

Returning to the question of mainstream and periphery – to determine whether Dvořák was a peripheral composer in comparison to Brahms (symphonies) and Wagner (operas, cantatas) depends on the perspective. It is also important how broadly one defines Dvořák's cultural background. Ultimately, this is also a political matter (as it was in Dvořák's time). Did the Czech lands represent a periphery or the heart of Austria-Hungary? Whether Dvořák (and – later and more pointedly – also Janáček) was considered "ours" or an artist from the periphery in the capital of the Austrian empire depended on the personal tastes of individual reviewers (but also on the composers to whom Dvořák was compared). Even nowadays, there are people all over the world, not only in the German-speaking countries, who consider all composers outside the "canonized" German mainstream to be secondary – and for them works such as *Rusalka* will always be late derivatives of Wagner. I can understand their reasoning. But I cannot think so simplistically. For me, the strength and individualism of *Rusalka* guarantee its independent identity – and originality. It could never be created without Wagner, but it could also never come into being in its unique beauty had it not been fed by Dvořák's inherent Czechness. It is the quality of the opera that "de-peripherizes" it for me in all aspects.

And then there is Janáček. Is his inherent originality the reason why we consider his music highly exotic? Or was he a composer who in his period created a completely unique musical language that was (and still is) more substantial than many other creative currents? Let's compare Janáček to the Second Viennese School!

I can imagine an understanding of Czech music as a tradition "in between," but in between what? Personally, I think that above all it belongs to the large family of Central European creations and significantly differs from musical currents in France, Italy, and the distant Russia (although the kinship among Slavs was certainly important at least for our nineteenth-century composers).

In the case of Gustav Mahler, a composer born in the Czech lands, all possible distinctions between centers and peripheries become completely murky. As is known, he himself felt alienated from (as if on the periphery of) many cultural circles of his time, yet he was also constantly at the center of events. I would like to know what he would say about Czech music (if he hadn't been forced to follow the political realities of the time – if he hadn't been shaped by them). Did Mahler view Smetana, Dvořák, and Suk as peripheral? And if so, then why? Because they did not live in Vienna? What we know for sure is that he valued their music greatly – and I dare say he was more willing to let their music speak to him than many of his contemporaries (when compared to, say, Richard Strauss). I am constantly trying to clarify whether Czech music played or was able to play an independent role within that Central European cultural realm. For me, it is an essential part of that realm.

BŘEZINA: Have you encountered the view that as a Czech or Central European conductor you should focus on Czech or Central European music? And did you establish yourself as a conductor of all kinds of Western symphonic music?

HRŮŠA: My relationship to the Western symphonic tradition in general developed organically and naturally. I can't say I ever had to struggle to be invited to conduct anything other than just Czech or Central European repertoire. But I have always aimed to balance repertoire that is closer to my background and works that are not. Occasionally, this balancing requires a little bit of diplomacy in both directions. At times, I am concerned about being labeled merely an expert in Czech music and want to develop my knowledge and skills in the entire symphonic repertoire in both unrestrained and controlled ways (fortunately, I have been successful in that). At other times, I am more concerned about bringing out lesser-known works. That is the key strategy: not to focus on the same works the quality of which is generally accepted but that sometimes become too commonplace (for example, Smetana's *Vltava*, Dvořák's *New World* Symphony and Second Cello Concerto). And when I program these works, my plan is to do everything to make the works sound fresh and novel – not as if on autopilot.

It is natural and certainly pleasant that the introduction of lesser-known works is becoming easier as my reputation increases. But my ability to embrace adventurous programming also depends on the region and the occasion. I am currently writing these reflexions from Japan, and so I want to use a local example. The subscription series of local orchestras focus on unusual programming, and because these symphonic institutions have a devoted audience, I was able to present some unorthodox programs during my twenty-two visits to this country. Although these unusual choices were drawn predominantly from Czech music, I have also chosen other repertoire that I don't perform very often otherwise – I was particularly fond of French works by Debussy, Saint-Saëns, and Honegger, which I rarely program elsewhere. The Czech works I have presented in Japan include the complete symphonies by Martinů, his cantata *Kytice* ("A Bouquet"), some lesser-known works by Dvořák (such as his *Husitská overtura* ["Hussite Overture"]), compositions by Miloslav Kabeláč, and the entire *Má vlast*, which is not performed very often as a whole in Japan. When I visit Japan on tour with a Central European orchestra (recently with PKF–Prague Philharmonia and later with the Bamberg Symphony), I need to focus on the most marketable titles (this is the case not only in Japan), and thus (similar to other Czech conductors) I mostly perform a few works by Dvořák together with Smetana's *Vltava* and the overture to *Prodaná nevěsta* ["The Bartered Bride"]. I don't have to say I love these works. But it is difficult to perform them in any context that induces an approach that relies on autopilot. In this regard, performing these works is sometimes a real struggle, a struggle for authentic and genuine beauty.

It is possible to say that when concert programming is mainly concerned with being profitable, it is more difficult to present anything that defies expectations, be they that as a Czech I should mainly conduct (and be more accomplished than others in conducting) Czech music, or that lesser known works and composers are not as interesting as more famous ones (the most typical and excellent example is Suk and his *Asrael* Symphony). Nevertheless, in my experience, the audience derives great pleasure from performances that are persuasive, no matter what the repertoire is (and I personally am inspired and motivated by less common works). The most important task is to bring listeners into the concert hall in the first place!

It is naturally more difficult to promote lesser-known Czech works in opera, mainly because the entire enterprise is more costly. Strangely enough, I have never been explicitly labeled an expert in Czech music in the opera world – except when the epithet was used ex post (during a production) and in a positive sense (as a token of appreciation). I will gladly admit, however, that in the complex world of opera, where conductors must explore not only the musical aspects but also the broader cultural environment in which a work was created, it is enormously advantageous when musicians are culturally related, even essentially linked to the work's place of origin. Many of us speak foreign languages adequately (and sometimes also in surprising and inspiring ways), but when we speak about issues of beauty in our mother tongue, we are able to go further and deeper. It is unavoidable, and it is similar to when Czech music is performed by Czech musicians.

Still, I believe that presenting Czech music in international contexts is extremely advantageous. Performing Suk's *Asrael* Symphony and Foerster's Fourth Symphony next to Mahler and Strauss (as I did in my recent concerts with the Bamberg Symphony in Vienna and Prague), Janáček next to Puccini and Wagner, Smetana next to Beethoven's symphonies, Martinů next to Roussel and Stravinsky, Kabeláč next to Britten and Shostakovich (I am using examples from my own programs), shows most clearly the quality of Czech music even in terms of the highest standards. And through such comparisons, we can also separate the wheat from the chaff.

BŘEZINA: Do you think that compositions, and specifically nationalistic compositions, contain an inherent meaning, or is that meaning created only through the context in which a particular work is created and later performed? (I am referring, for example, to performances in tense or elated times, such as the 1939 performance of *Má vlast* under Talich following the Nazi occupation, the same piece under Kubelík after the fall of communism in 1990, and your own performance of that work in Dortmund in 2022, immediately following Russia's invasion of Ukraine. And also performances of Kabeláč's orchestral passacaglia *Mysterium času* ("Mystery of Time") and Eben's [*sinfonia concertante*] *Noční hodiny* ("Night Hours").

HRŮŠA: In my view, compositions contain, on the one hand, undeniable forms, or perhaps tectonics (because when we consider musical forms as rigidly set, it is significant what terminology we use in our analysis), and on the other hand, the ability to incite through moods certain directions in which listeners experience their content. The ability to affect listeners' experiences is greater when composers incorporate specific themes into their works or their works' titles. Unless we want to complicate the matter, it is clear that a composition titled *Karneval* will not have the ability to create the impression of a meditation or a commemoration of the dead (I am excluding the possibility of intentional irony). When we assume that listeners whom a composer addresses have at least a basic understanding of their inherited cultural tradition (I am here omitting the cases, such as one I have unfortunately encountered, when a certain unenlightened listener claimed that the problem of classical music was that unlike rock or pop it all sounds the same) and, in an ideal case, that they have at least some training in basic music analysis, it is certain that the moods experienced by the composer during a work's inception will be at least somewhat transferable to the listener, albeit not completely and explicitly. In terms of clear-cut attributes, the meaning of a composition is understandably more vague than its formal properties. What you are asking about is, in my opinion, a question of type and profundity, the breadth of appeal, the depth of the impact on listeners in a particular historical moment and at a particular public occasion. I also think that during the performances you mentioned in your question, the great compositions such as *Má vlast* and *Mysterium času* acquired meanings that not even the composer could foresee and even less plan for. As long as such acquired meanings are not contrary to the spirit of the work, they represent an enrichment of that composition.

BŘEZINA: Did your views of music in the Czech lands change after the start of your tenure with the Bamberg Symphony? If so, how?

HRŮŠA: Yes, I would say that my understanding has deepened. It is an ideal situation to work with music that I have naturally related to since my youth, if not since my childhood, in the company of (and in cooperation with) people who love it as much as I do. In some ways, Czech music is part of the orchestra's cultural identity, and yet it may not be the core of their authentic experience. In Bamberg, I have, simply put, encountered musicians and music administrators who deeply treasure and appreciate music from the Czech lands – often more intensely and with greater personal engagement than, say, most Americans (with obvious exceptions) – and who do not find it too exotic, unlike the more geographically distant French and Italians. For the Bamberg musicians, the Czech lands are basically in the neighborhood and are also their country of origin since the orchestra is the successor of Prague's former German Philharmonic. However, they do not think of Czech music as their core musical activity. The orchestra's core repertoire certainly includes the music of, to name a few, Bach, Mozart, Beethoven, Brahms, Wagner, Mahler, and Strauss. I often liken my relationship with the Bambergers to a family relation: not to a sibling, but to a cousin. It is common, however, that people often get along better with more distant relatives than with siblings. To continue this metaphor, I think that encounters that are not commonplace help us better understand the nature of behavior, development, problem-solving, and the similarities and differences within large families or village and city communities. Parents and siblings often overlook how their closest relatives develop over time, but various aunts and uncles notice changes immediately and from a different perspective during their visits. Maybe I have stretched this metaphor too far, but I wanted to say this: my German (and other international) musicians in the Bavarian (or, more accurately, Franconian) orchestra can place the music from our lands into a broad context in a more objective way. This becomes apparent when we perform Czech music – the works by Smetana, Dvořák, Suk, and to a lesser extent, the more individualistic Janáček and Martinů. My musicians leisurely and naturally point out similarities to and differences from many German (and other non-Czech) composers. They not only reference Schumann, Wagner, Brahms, Bruckner, Mahler, and Strauss, but also the Second

Viennese School and composers whom I would never connect with our
music as strongly, given my grounding in our composers. This does not
mean that we should consider German music in any way superior to ours.
While our nineteenth-century composers certainly looked to German
music, later generations, particularly Janáček and Martinů, rebelled
against it. It is understandable that some visionaries, such as Beethoven,
Schumann, Wagner, and Schubert in his Lieder, set trends for the following decades, which later also influenced our music, especially nineteenth-
century orchestral music. But since our composers were somewhat distant
from these trends, they could selectively adopt the best from established
values or synthesize different cultural flavors without losing their own
identity. Dvořák exemplified this approach in his best works, which combine classical traditions from Beethoven and Brahms, inspirations from the
New German School (Wagner and Bruckner), Slavic elements derived
from Tchaikovsky and others, and touches of village musicianship and
folk music in general. From a musical point of view, the border between
Germany and the Czech lands plays a rather positive role: it clarifies the
sense of belonging to one's own group without creating any real barrier.
The best expression of this interconnectedness was our blessed time with
Smetana's *Má vlast*; I never felt that the Bamberg musicians found it
difficult to identify with the more broadly defined Bohemian homeland
because they did not speak Czech. I have had similarly fruitful experiences
with the composers of the troubled period around World War II, such as
Haas, Ullmann, and Schulhoff. With their music, I have learned to honor
problematic periods of our own history.

BŘEZINA: What do you think about the similarities and differences between
    Czech and German (including Austrian) music, particularly in the nine-
    teenth and twentieth centuries?

HRŮŠA: To define similarities and differences in such a large field is quite
    difficult for me. I would like to avoid platitudes.

    I think that at the time when authentic Czech national culture first crystal-
lized, basically in the time of Smetana, the artistic orientation of both traditions was quite intertwined. In its inspiration, German music was naturally
drawn to its historical sources (as far back as Bach for example) and dealt with
subjects that essentially reflected its traditions. The Romantic generation
(Weber in opera, Schubert in the Lieder and chamber music, Schumann in
instrumental programmatic music) tended to deepen these trends; one could
say that the Germans were satisfied with making use of what was indigenous
to their broader culture. The Czech situation was more complex because the
natural growth of a rich literary culture and other arts had been disrupted for
several centuries, and the generation of revivalists had to basically rekindle
and reinvent national culture. I think that the main task for composers such as
Smetana was to help Czech music find its footing and become independent of

the crutches borrowed from the other nations; he accomplished this by making use of and innovating the best and most advanced aspects of our neighbors' cultures according to our own tastes. He did this at the highest level in the context of his own time, and I am not surprised that some see his musical language as corresponding closely with then-modern trends in the German lands. In other words, I don't see any substantial differences between Smetana's musical language and originality, and the compositional procedures of his German contemporaries. In no way does this mean, however, that Smetana imitated or directly copied from anyone (he was too great a creator for that), but that his music is clearly and organically wedged in the compositional traditions of the larger Central European region, which was dominated by the music of the German-speaking lands.

The situation changes in the time of Dvořák and Janáček. Members of their generation worked with substantially more-varied subjects and intonations. It is not surprising that starting in this period, our music sounds more exotic to our western and southern neighbors. It depends on what their point of view is. Smetana's *Má vlast* (regardless of his earlier works, such as his Swedish symphonic poems) belongs almost equally to the musical language of both Germans and Czechs. Germans do not have the slightest problem understanding this work as their own musical language. This is clearly an advantage, which means that they have come to appreciate this music more easily because it sounds more universal. They don't think of it as completely original, unique – more as a branch of their own culture. I, too, don't find it difficult to find a lot of Beethoven and Wagner in *Má vlast*; I think that the strength of Smetana's music is not in the endless originality of his language as such, but in the originality of his conception (form, overall design), invention, inspiration; and, to speak in a lofty manner, in the glowing of the heart, in emotion. This is what makes Smetana a fantastic composer. I believe that *Má vlast* is amazing musically although it also works well in concert programs because the message of the work can be understood long before the music itself starts (as such, even today *Má vlast* has great PR potential). Smetana's music in *Má vlast* can succeed even when no one knows the story behind it. Smetana would have certainly become an outstanding composer even if he hadn't taken the path of absolute devotion to his own country and its spirit. Compositions such as *Vltava* could be performed under any circumstances and everywhere, even if their creators did not claim any nationality. In the case of Dvořák and his themes (starting with the *Moravian Duets* and the *Slavonic Dances*), exoticism became more important. I believe, for example, that the Germans perceive the *Slavonic Dances* as more Eastern and Slavic than Smetana's polkas. This generation of composers was influenced by a larger number of ideas, the most important of which were those from Russia, which had practically very little impact in Germany. These ideas eventually prevailed in the works of Janáček. Our neighbors have learned to appreciate these tendencies as long as they did not become excessive. The limit of what is considered excessive is Leoš Janáček, starting approximately with *Jenůfa*. Dvořák sounds exotic, but not foreign, which is also the case with Fibich, Foerster, Novák, and Suk. But Janáček speaks the language of a cultural alien – one who is loved and admired at times, misunderstood and denigrated at others, depending perhaps on the level of familiarity with a foreign language (which is the case with human approach to languages in the general, non-metaphorical sense: the knowledge of languages deepens the appreciation of the cultures they represent). In sum, I think that Germans view Czech music before the generation of Dvořák and his pupils as closer to their own tradition (they also identify, at times justifiably, at others inappropriately, those elements that our composers appropriated from German music). This is no longer possible with Janáček. We could say the same about Martinů, whose works represent a special, compelling synthesis of his country's folk elements with French (and other cosmopolitan) and later also American influences.

In the previous sentence, I articulated a crucial aspect of our music that has always self-consciously differentiated it from German music: folk inspirations. I think authentic folk elements are also present in German music, but perhaps they have been applied in less obvious (more hidden) ways – and, significantly, much earlier. There is a difference between how Mozart and Beethoven use folk music and how Smetana and Janáček do so. In this regard, we have experienced an organic turn to folk music later – at a time when in the German realm local culture was being refreshed by Wagner with different kinds of probes into the greatest depths thanks to the myths he used in his operas. Our *Libuše* (and, with great historical delay, also *Rusalka*) corresponds closely to the German spirit of the time, which aims at the greatest possible timelessness of expression, whereas works such as *Prodaná nevěsta* and *Jakobín* ["Kate and the Devil"], to name a few examples, correspond to the needs of the local circumstances and times in which they were created. Janáček has synthesized universal emotional messages with highly idiosyncratic settings: *Jenůfa* and *Káťa Kabanová*, for example. We can see that German audiences experience his operas as if despite the musical language. The artistic statements of these works are so strong that they force listeners from all over the world to accept the musical language with the greatest seriousness, although it is occasionally – in the spirit of Zdeněk Nejedlý's biased criticism – somewhat suspect. Janáček is an artist who benefited from an uncompromising and non-ingratiating approach, which was the main reason he gained respect and even popularity.

Another way to put this would be: our best composers created their compositions with an awareness of regional conditions at a time that demanded the greatest interconnectedness with and the greatest possible sublimation of local traditions. That is why Dvořák set the poetry of

K. J. Erben. In the German lands, the best composers of the period were more often focused on more universal themes (usually represented in myths) because the need to express local traditions had already been accomplished and experienced, so they did not feel the need to justify the natural strengths of their own musical culture.

Selected Bibliography

Archives

Archiv Českého rozhlasu / Czech Radio Archive

Archiv Dilia / Dilia Archive

Archiv Etnologického ústavu Akademie věd České republiky / Archive of the Ethnological Institute of the Czech Academy of Sciences

Archiv hlavního města Prahy / Prague City Archives

Archiv Leoše Janáčka Moravského zemského muzea / Leoš Janáček Archive of the Moravian Museum

Archiv Narodního divadla / National Theater Archive

Archiv Pražského hradu / Archive of the Prague Castle

Archiv Umělecké besedy / Archive of the Artists' Union

Archiv zpěváckého spolku Hlahol / Archive of the Hlahol Singing Society

Archivum Romanum Societatis Iesu / Roman Archives of the Society of Jesus

Bayerische Staatsbibliothek / Bavarian State Library

Centrum Bohuslava Martinů / Bohuslav Martinů Center

České muzeum hudby / Czech Museum of Music

Fales Library, New York University

Historisches Archiv der Sächsischen Staatstheater / Historical Archive of the Saxon State Theater

Knihovna cisterciáckého kláštera ve Vyšším Brodě / Library of the Cistercian Monastery in Vyšší Brod

Masarykův ústav Akademie věd České republiky / Masaryk Institute and Archives of the Czech Academy of Sciences

Narodní archiv České republiky / National Archives of the Czech Republic

Národní knihovna / National Library

Niedersächsische Staats- und Universitätsbibliothek Göttingen / Göttingen State and University Library

Památník Terezín / Terezín Memorial

Phonogrammarchiv der Österreichischen Akademie der Wissenschaften / Phonogram archive of the Austrian Academy of Sciences

Sächsische Landesbibliothek – Staats- und Universitätsbibliothek Dresden / Saxon State University and Library Dresden

San Diego State University, Special Collections

Staatsbibliothek zu Berlin – Stiftung Preußischer Kulturbesitz / Berlin State Library, Prussian Cultural Heritage Foundation
Státní oblastní archiv Plzeň / State Regional Archive Plzeň
Státní okresní archiv Teplice / State District Archive Teplice
Traxler Estate Papers (Private Archive)
Židovské muzeum v Praze / The Jewish Museum in Prague

Historical Journals

Allgemeine Theaterzeitung und Originalblatt für Kunst, Literatur, Musik, Mode und geselliges Leben
Berliner allgemeine musikalische Zeitung
Čas
Česká kultura
Dalibor
Hudební listy
Hudební revue
Lumír
Moravské listy
The Musical Times
Národní listy
Smetana: Hudební list
Teplitz-Schönauer
Teplitzer Zeitung
Vlasť
Zeitung für die elegante Welt

Published Sources

Abraham, Gerald. *Slavonic and Romantic Music: Essays and Studies*. New York: St. Martin's Press, 1968.

Adler, H. G. *Theresienstadt 1941–1945: The Face of a Coerced Community*. Translated by Belinda Cooper. New York: Cambridge University Press, 2017.

Agnew, Hugh. "Ambiguities of Ritual: Dynastic Loyalty, Patriotism and Nationalism in the Last Three Royal Coronations in Bohemia." *Bohemia* 4 (2000): 3–22.

Applegate, Celia, and Pamela Potter, eds. *Music and German National Identity*. Chicago: University of Chicago Press, 2002.

Ágústsson, Jóhannes. "Joseph Johann Adam of Liechtenstein, Patron of Vivaldi." *Studi Vivaldiani* 17 (2017): 3–77.

Ágústsson, Jóhannes, and Janice B. Stockigt. "Records of Catholic Musicians, Actors and Dancers at the Court of Augustus II, 1723–32: The Establishment of a Catholic Cemetery in Dresden." *Royal Musical Association Research Chronicle* 45 (2014): 26–73.

Allgemeine Deutsche Biographie. Leipzig: Duncker & Humblot, 1891.

Allmanach für die Badegäste zu Teplitz, auf das Jahr 1802. Prague: Gerzabek, [1802].

Ambros, August Wilhelm. *Geschichte der Music,* 3 vols. Breslau: Leuckart, 1868–82.

Ardesi, Carlo. *Il Primo Libro de Madrigal a quattro voci.* Venice: 1597.

Augustinová, Božena. *Marie Červinková-Riegrová, Životopisný nástin.* Prague: Bursík & Kohout, 1897.

Bachtík, Jakub, Lukáš Duchek, and Jakub Jareš, eds. *Chrám umění Rudolfinum.* Prague: Česká filharmonie, 2020.

Bajer, Jiří. "Druhá sklizeň jarní operní úrody." *Divadelní a filmové noviny,* June 29, 1966.

Ballo, Ivan. "Mikuláš a Alexander Moyzes." *Slovenské pohľady* 44 (1928): 816–18.

Balog, Peter, ed. *Beatlemánie!* Prague: Národní muzeum, 2010.

Bár, Pavel. *Od operety k muzikálu: Zábavněhudební divadlo v Československu po roce 1945.* Prague: KANT, 2013.

Barša, Pavel. "Nulový stupeň dekolonizace." *Artalk Revue* 4 (Winter 2020): 1–4.

Bartlová, Milena, and Michal Šroněk, eds. *Public Communication in European Reformation. Artistic and other Media in Central Europe 1380–1620.* Prague: Artefactum, 2007.

Bartoš, František, ed. *Bedřich Smetana: Letters and Reminiscences.* Translated by Daphne Rusbridge. Prague: Artia, 1955.

Bartošek, Luboš. *Náš film. Kapitoly z dějin (1896–1945).* Prague: Mladá fronta, 1985.

Baselt, Berndt, and Walther Siegmund-Schulze, eds. *Das mitteldeutsche Musikleben vor Händel; Christoph Willibald Gluck (1714–1787).* Halle-Wittenberg: Martin-Luther-Universität, 1988.

Bastlová(-Šedivá), Eliška. *Collectio operum musicalium quae in bibliotheca Kinsky adservantur.* Prague: Národní knihovna, 2013.

Baťa, Jan. "Ferdinand of Tyrol and the Music Culture in Renaissance Prague." *Wissenschaftliches Jahrbuch der Tiroler Landesmuseen* 5 (2012): 16–23.

   "Hudba a hudební kultura na Starém Městě pražském 1526–1620." PhD diss., Charles University, Prague, 2011.

   "Praga festivans: Music Played during the Prague Festivities of 1527 and 1558." *Historie-Otázky-Problémy* 2 (2015): 247–59.

   "Remarks on the Festivities of the Order of the Golden Fleece in Prague (1585)." *Musicologia Brunensia* 51 (2016): 25–35.

Baťa, Jan, Jiří Kroupa, and Lenka Mráčková, eds. *Littera Nigro Scripta Manet: In honorem Jaromír Černý*. Prague: KLP, 2009.

Batka, Richard. *Die Musik in Böhmen*. Berlin: Bard, Marquardt, & Co., 1906.

Baťová, Eliška. *Kolínský kancionál z roku 1517 a bratrský zpěv na počátku 16. století*. Prague: KLP, 2011.

———. "Opomíjený pramen husitského zpěvu doby poděbradské a repertoár cantiones hebdomadae sanctae." *Hudební věda* 51 (2014): 229–76.

Beckerman, Michael. "The Dark Blue Exile of Jaroslav Ježek." *Music and Politics* 2 (2008): 1–14.

———. "Ježek and Musical Bilingualism." *Czech Music Quarterly* 23 (2022): 32–36.

———. "In Search of Czechness in Music." *19th-Century Music* 10 (1986): 61–73.

———. "Is Czech Music White?" *Czech Music Quarterly* 2021, no. 4: 26–30.

———. *New Worlds of Dvořák: Searching in America for the Composer's Inner Life*. New York: Norton, 2003.

Bek, Josef. *Erwin Schulhoff: Leben und Werk*. Hamburg: Bockel, 1994.

Bek, Mikuláš. *Konzervatoř Evropy?: K sociologii české hudebnosti*. Prague: KLP, 2003.

Bělina, Pavel, Jiří Kaše, and Jan P. Kučera. *Velké dějiny zemí koruny české*, 8 vols. Prague: Paseka, 2001.

Belišová, Jana. *Phurikane giľa, starodávne rómske piesne*. Bratislava: Žudro, 2002.

Benda, Václav. *Noční kádrový dotazník a jiné boje*. Prague: Agite, 2009.

Beránek, Jiří. "K otázce hudební složky českých korunovačních slavností v roce 1791." *Miscellanea Musicologica* 30 (1983): 81–110.

Berger, Christian. "Musikalische Formbildung im Spannungsfeld nationaler Traditionen des 17. Jahrhunderts." *Acta Musicologica* 64 (1992): 17–29.

Berkovec, Jiří. *České pastorely*. Prague: Supraphon, 1987.

Biba, Otto, and David Wyn Jones, eds. *Studies in Music History Presented to H. C. Robbins Landon on His Seventieth Birthday*. London: Thames and Hudson, 1996.

Bilwachs, Jan. "Die Konkordanzen der Carl Luythons Motetten *Bellum insigne* und *Festa dies hodie*." *Musicologica Brunensia* 51 (2016): 37–45.

Black, David. "Mozart and the Practice of Sacred Music." PhD diss., Harvard University, 2007.

Bláhová, Kateřina, and Václav Petrbok, eds. *Vzdělání a osvěta v české kultuře 19. století*. Prague: AVČR, 2004.

Blažek, Vladimír, ed. *Sborník na paměť 125 let konservatoře hudby v Praze*. Prague: Vyšehrad, 1936.

Blüml, Jan. *Progresivní rock: světová a československá scéna ve vybraných reflexích*. Prague: Togga, 2017.

———. "Svaz československých skladatelů a jeho vliv na populární hudbu šedesátých let a kariéru Bohuslava Ondráčka." *Musicologica Brunensia* 58 (2023): 25–39.

Blüml, Jan, and Jana Spáčilová, eds. *Carl Ditters von Dittersdorf – Contexts and Perspectives*, special issue *Musicologica Olomucensia* 30 (December 2019).

Bodorová, Sylvie. "Tvůrčí tendence nejmladší české skladatelské generace." *Hudební věda* 22 (1985): 134–54.

Bohadlo, Stanislav. "Questenberg a Sporck – oddělené a nezávislé barokní hudební subkultury na Moravě a v Čechách?" *Musicologica Brunensia* 46 (2011): 15–34.

Bonds, Mark Evan. *Music as Thought*. Princeton, NJ: Princeton University Press, 2006.

Bor, Vladimír. *Operní večery*. Prague: Panton, 1981.

Boulez, Pierre. "Úvahy o dnešní hudbě." Translated by Vladimír Štěpánek. *Hudební rozhledy* 18 (1965): 5–6.

Bowring, John, ed. *Cheskian Anthology: being a history of the poetical literature of Bohemia with translated specimens*. London: Rowland Hunter, 1832.

Branberger, Jan. *Konservatoř hudby v Praze: pamětní spis k stoletému jubileu založení ústavu*. Prague: Konservatoř hudby, 1911.

 "Nové dráhy pro budoucí opery? II." *Čas* 18 (January 1904): 1–2.

Branda, Eva. "Speaking German, Hearing Czech, Claiming Dvořák." *Journal of the Royal Musical Association* 142 (2017): 109–36.

Brázdová, Lucie. *Hudba a kardinál Dietrichstein 1599–1636*. Olomouc: Univerzita Palackého, 2012.

Brewer, Charles E. *The Instrumental Music of Schmeltzer, Biber, Muffat and Their Contemporaries*. New York: Routledge, 2016.

Brindgardner, Chase. "'A Rainbow in Ev'ry Pot': Southern Excess, Racial Liberalism, and Living Large in Harburg and Lane's *Finian's Rainbow*." *Studies in Musical Theater* 10 (2016): 117–32.

Brown, Julie, ed. *Western Music and Race*. New York: Cambridge University Press, 2007.

Bryant, Chad. "Either German or Czech: Fixing Nationality in Bohemia and Moravia, 1939–46." *Slavic Review* 61 (2002): 683–706.

Buchanan, Donna A., ed. *Soundscapes from the Americas*. Farnham: Ashgate, 2014.

Bunzel, Anja. "František Palacký's (Musical) Life with the 'Aristocrats': Private and Semi-Private Musical Sociability in Prague during the First Half of the Nineteenth Century." *Musicologica Austriaca* (2023). Accessed February 8, 2024. https://musau.org/parts/neue-article-page/view/158.

Bunzel, Anja, and Christopher Campo-Bowen, eds. *Women in Nineteenth-Century Czech Musical Culture*. New York: Routledge, 2024.

Bunzel, Anja, and Natasha Loges, eds. *Musical Salon Culture in the Long Nineteenth Century*. Woodbridge: Boydell, 2019.

Burian, Emil František. "Estetika v pokračováních." *Tam-tam* 1 (1925): 11–16.

 Jazz. Prague: Aventinum, 1928.

Burian, Jarka M. "The Liberated Theater of Voskovec and Werich." *Educational Theatre Journal* 29 (1977): 153–77.

Burlas, Ladislav. *Slovenská hudobná moderna. Malá moderná encyklopédia.* Bratislava: Obzor, 1983.

Burlas, Ladislav, Zdeněk Nováček, and Ladislav Mokrý, eds. *Dejiny slovenskej hudby.* Bratislava: SAV, 1957.

Burney, Charles. *The Present State of Music in Germany, the Netherlands, and United Provinces*, 2nd ed. London: T. Becket and others, 1775.

Buš, Marek, ed. *Haugwitzové a hudba.* Náměšt nad Oslavou: Národní památkový ústav, 2003.

Butt, John, and Tim Carter, eds. *The Cambridge History of Seventeenth-Century Music.* New York: Cambridge University Press, 2005.

Callaghan, J. D. "Rusalka English Premiere Is Staged by All-City Cast." *Detroit Free Press*, May 28, 1945.

Campo-Bowen, Christopher. "Bohemian Rhapsodist: Antonín Dvořák's *Píseň bohatýrská* and the Historiography of Czech Music." *19th-Century Music* 40 (2016): 159–81.

Carolides, Jiří. *Farrago Symbolica Sententiosa.* Prague, 1597.

Cechová, Martina. "Hudba v reklamě zlínských ateliérů v letech 1930–1940: *Střevíček* Bohuslava Martinů a jeho dobový context." MA thesis, Charles University, Prague, 2011.

Čeleda, Jaroslav. "Mozarteana: W. A. Mozart a prof. Dr. Fr. Němeček." *Za hudebním vzděláním* 3 (1928): 148–51, 153–62.

Čemus, Petronilla, and Richard Čemus, eds. *Bohemia Jesuitica*, 2 vols. Prague: Karolinum, 2010.

Čermák, Marek. "Anton Neumann. Nové poznatky k životním osudům a tvorbě zapomenutého skladatele, houslisty a kapelníka." *Musicologica Olomucensia* 30 (2019): 131–52.

Černíček, Jan. "Hudba Zdeňka Lišky k filmu Marketa Lazarová." PhD diss., Charles University, Prague, 2009.

Černík, Jožka. "Cikánské písničky." *Hudební revue* 9 (February 1916): 162–69.

Černohorská, Milena, and Věra Dolanská, eds. *Nové cesty hudby.* Prague: Státní hudební vydavatelství, 1964.

Černý, Jaromír. "Středověký vícehlas v českých zemích." *Miscellanea musicologica* 27–28 (1975): 9–116.

Černý, Jaromír, ed. *Historical Anthology of Music in the Bohemian Lands (up to ca 1530).* Prague: KLP, 2005.

Černý, Jaromír, ed. *Hudba české renesance.* Prague: SNTL, 1982.

Červená sedma 1907–1922 na dobových gramodeskách. Original mono remastered recording, 2007 by Radioservis. Compact disc.

Červená, Soňa. *Stýskání zakázáno: Kousek mého divadelního děje-spisu a země-spisu.* Prague: Opus musicum, 2014.

Červený, Jiří. *Červená sedma.* Prague: Orbis, 1959.

Chadima, Mikoláš. *Alternativa 1.* Prague: Galén, 2015.

    Alternativa 2. Prague: Galén, 2018.

Chafe, Eric Thomas. *The Church Music of Heinrich Biber*. Ann Arbor, MI: UMI Research Press, 1987.

Chaloupková, Eliška. "Lázeňský hudební život v Teplicích." BA thesis, Charles University, Prague, 2012.

Chalupka, Ľubomír. "Eugen Suchoň a 12 tónov v oktáve." *Slovenská hudba* 24 (1998): 5–35.

Charlton, David, ed. *The Cambridge Companion to Grand Opera*. New York: Cambridge University Press, 2003.

Charlton, David, ed. *E. T. A. Hoffmann's Musical Writings: Kreisleriana, The Poet and the Composer, Music Criticism*. Translated by Martyn Clarke. New York: Cambridge University Press, 2003.

Chew, Geoffrey. "'Always Something New from Africa': Jan Rychlík's *Africký Cyklus* and Czech Experimental Music in the Early 1960s." *Central Europe* 1 (November 2003): 115–32.

"The Christmas Pastorella in Austria, Bohemia, and Moravia." PhD diss., University of Manchester, 1968.

Chew, Geoffrey, ed. *New Music in the "New" Europe 1918–1938: Ideology, Theory, and Practice*. Prague: KLP, 2007.

Cinger, František. *Šťastné blues, aneb Z deníku Jaroslava Ježka*. Prague: BVD, 2006.

Čižmář, Jan, ed. *Acta Losyana: sborník příspěvků k odkazu Jana Antonína Losyho a jeho rodu*. Prague: Česká loutnová společnost, 2021.

Clapham, John. "The Smetana-Pivoda Controversy." *Music & Letters* 52 (1971): 353–64.

Cmíral, Adolf. *Staročeské zpěvy duchovní*. Prague: Blahoslav, 1953.

Cocteau, Jean. *Cock and Harlequin: Notes Concerning Music*. London: Egoist Press, 1921.

Cohen, Gary B. *The Politics of Ethnic Survival: Germans in Prague, 1861–1914*, 2nd rev. ed. West Lafayette, IN: Purdue University Press, 2006.

Cole, Jacqueline. "Viktor Ullmann." The Viktor Ullmann Foundation. Accessed March 21, 2024. https://viktorullmannfoundation.com/viktor/

Coreth, Anna. *Pietas austriaca*. Vienna: Verlag für Geschichte und Politik, 1959, 2nd ed. 1982. West Lafayette, IN: Purdue University Press, 2004.

Crump, Michael. *Martinů and the Symphony*. Rochester, NY: Boydell & Brewer, 2010.

Čurda, Martin. *The Music of Pavel Haas: Analytical and Hermeneutical Studies*. New York: Routledge, 2020.

Dacos, N., ed. *Relations artistiques entre les Pays-Bas et l'Italie dans la Renaissance: Études dédiées à Suzanne Sulzberger*. Brussels: Institut historique belge de Rome, 1980.

Daněk, Petr. "On the Fate of the Collection of Bohemian Musical Prints and Manuscripts in the Sabbateni Collection New York." *Czech Music Quarterly* 2022, no. 1: 16–19.

Historické tisky vokální polyfonie, rané monodie, hudební teorie a instrumentální hudby v českých zemích do roku 1630. Prague: KLP, 2015.

"Rudolfinian Prague as a Musical Center in Its Time." *Die Tonkunst* 6 (2012): 312–19.

Daněk, Petr, and Martin Horyna, eds. *The Double-Choir Motets of Rudolphine Prague: An Anthology of Eight-Voice Motets from Bohemian Manuscripts and Prints*, vol. 1. Prague: KLP, 2020.

Daněk, Petr, and Jiří K. Kroupa, eds. *Jan Amos Komenský, Kancyonál. Faksimile vydání z roku 1659 (Amsterdam, Christoffel Cunradus)*. Prague: KLP, 2018.

David, Zdeněk V. *Finding the Middle Way: The Utraquists' Liberal Challenge to Rome and Luther*. Washington D.C.: Woodrow Wilson Center Press, 2003.

David, Zdeněk V., and David R. Holeton, eds. *The Bohemian Reformation and Religious Practice*, vol. 6. Prague: Czech Academy of Sciences, 2007.

Davidová, Eva, and Jan Žižka. *Folk Music of the Sedentary Gypsies of Czechoslovakia*. Budapest: Institute for Musicology of the Hungarian Academy of Sciences, 1991.

Davidová, Eva, and Jaromír Gelnar. "Tradiční i současný romský (cikánský) písňový folklór." *Český lid* 76 (1989): 39–46.

Dejmek, Jindřich, ed. *Československo, dějiny státu*. Prague: Libri, 2018.

Delibré, G. [Jiří Svoboda], and T. T. Garell [ue]. "Musica a Muzika." *Život: list pro výtvarnou práci a uměleckou kulturu* 2 (1922): 86–89.

[Denzio, Antonio]. *Praga nascente da Libussa e Primislao*. Prague: Kamenitzky, 1734.

Dietz, Roman, and Lenka Přibylová. *Severočeská filharmonie Teplice: Historie a současnost* Teplice: Severočeská filharmonie Teplice, 2018.

Dlabacz, Gottfried Johann. *Allgemeines historisches Künstler-Lexikon für Böhmen und zum Theil auch für Mähren und Schlesien*, 3 vols. Prague: Haase, 1815.

Dobiáš, Dalibor. *The Forged Dvůr Králové and Zelená Hora Manuscripts*. Prague: CAS, 2019.

Dobiáš, Dalibor, ed. *Rukopisy královédvorský a zelenohorský v kultuře a umění*, 2 vols. Prague: Academia, 2019.

Doležil, Hubert. *Staročeské duchovní zpěvy 14. a 15. století. Dle transkripcí Zdenka Nejedlého pro čtyřhlasý sbor mužský*. Prague: Melantrich, 1917.

Doružka, Lubomír, et al., eds. *Taneční hudba a jazz 1968-69*. Prague: Supraphon, 1968.

Dóša, Juraj. "Vývoj hudebně estetických názorů na fenomén národní hudby na Slovensku." *Opus musicum* 16 (1984): 265–67.

Doudová, Milena, ed. *Velké ženy české*. Prague: X-Egem, 1997.

Drašarová, Eva. "Společenský život v Čechách v období neoabsolutismu." *Paginae Historiae. Sborník státního ústředního archivu v Praze* 1992: 128–69.

Dreves, Guido Maria, and Clemens Blume, eds. *Analecta hymnica medii aevi* 48. Leipzig: Reisland, 1905.

Ducreux, Marie-Elizabeth. "Emperors, Kingdoms, Territories: Multiple Versions of the 'Pietas Austriaca'?" *The Catholic Historical Review* 97 (2011): 276–304.

Dümling, Albrecht, ed. *Torso eines Lebens. Der Komponist und Pianist Gideon Klein (1919-1945)*. Verdrängte Musik, vol. 23. Neumünster: Bockel, 2020.

Durante, Sergio. "The Chronology of *La clemenza di Tito* Reconsidered." *Music & Letters* 80 (1999): 566–67.

Van Dussen, Michael. *From England to Bohemia: Heresy and Communication in the Late Middle Ages*. New York: Cambridge University Press, 2012.

Van Dussen, Michael, and Pavel Soukup, eds. *A Companion to the Hussites*. Leiden: Brill, 2020.

Edwards, Scott Lee. "'Is There No One Here Who Speaks to Me?' Performing Ethnic Encounter in Bohemia and Moravia at the Turn of the 17th Century." *Diasporas* 26 (2015): 17–34.

    "Repertory Migration in the Czech Crown Lands, 1570–1630." PhD diss., University of California, Berkeley, 2012.

Eichler, Andreas-Chrysogonus. *Teplitz und seine Umgebungen. Geschichtlich, topographisch, naturhistorisch, statistisch, medizinisch und mahlerisch. Ganz neu dargestellt*, 8th ed. Prague: Gerzabek, 1834.

Eichner, Barbara. *History in Mighty Sounds: Musical Constructions of German National Identity, 1848–1914*. Woodbridge: Boydell & Brewer, 2012.

Eisner, Jan, Jan Hofman, and Vilém Pražák, eds. *Príspevky k praveku, dejinám a národopisu Slovenska: Sborník archeologického a národopisného odboru Slovenského vlastivedného muzea za rok 1924 – 1931*. Bratislava: *Společnost vlastivědného muzea* slovenského v Bratislavě, 1931.

Erll, Astrid, and Ansgar Nünning, eds. *A Companion to Cultural Memory Studies*. Berlin: De Gruyter, 2010.

Esterlová, Tereza. "Neznámý pramen v archivu Pražské konzervatoře: Komorní hudba v domě Františka Švestky (1842-1864)." MA thesis, Charles University, Prague, 2014.

Evans, Robert James Weston. *The Making of the Habsburg Monarchy, 1550–1700*. New York: Clarendon Press, 1979.

    Rudolf II and His World: A Study in Intellectual History. New York: Clarendon Press, 1984.

Fanning, David, and Erik Levi, eds. *The Routledge Handbook to Music under German Occupation, 1938–1945: Propaganda, Myth and Reality*. New York: Routledge, 2019.

Fečová, Olga. "Muzeum Olgy Fečové: Rodinné hudební světy romského primase." Muzeum Olgy Fečové. Accessed March 21, 2024. https://muzeumolgyfecove.cz

Fejtová, Olga, ed. *Barokní Praha – Barokní Čechie*. Prague: Scriptorium, 2004.

Fend, Michael, and Michael Noiray, eds. *Musical Education in Europe (1770–1914): Compositional, Institutional, and Political Challenges*, 2 vols. Berlin: Berlin Wissenschafts-Verlag, 2005.

Ferenc, Petr, ed. *Ukryto v pásech – Vybrané kapitoly z české elektroakustické hudební tvorby do roku 1989*. Prague: Národní muzeum, 2022.

Fifield, Christopher. "Smetana and *The Devil's Wall*." *The Musical Times* 128 (February 1987): 78–80.

Filipová, Marta. "Peasants on Display: The Czechoslavic Ethnographic Exhibition of 1895." *Journal of Design History* 24 (2011): 15–36.

Finscher, Ludwig. *Die Musik in Geschichte und Gegenwart*, vol. 8. Kassel: Bärenreiter, 1998.

Fireberg, Haim, Olaf Glöckner, and Marcela Menachem, eds. *Being Jewish in 21st Century Central Europe*. Europäisch-jüdische Studien – Beiträge, vol. 43. Berlin: De Gruyter, 2020.

Fisher, Alexander J. *Music, Piety, and Propaganda*. New York: Oxford University Press, 2014.

Foerster, Josef. *Katolický varhaník/Der katholische Organist*. Prague: Jana Hoffmanna vdova, 1860.

Forkel, Johann Nikolaus. *Über Johann Sebastian Bachs Leben, Kunst und Kunstwerke*. Leipzig: Hoffmeister und Kühnel, 1802.

Formáčková, Marie. *Věra Bílá: Nahoru a zase dolů*. Prague: Hidoval, 2011.

Franc, Martin, ed. *Dějiny Akademie múzických umění v Praze*. Prague: AMU, 2017.

Frank, Vojtěch. "Musical Theatre as an Object of Transnational Political Exchange." *Historical Studies on Central Europe* 2 (2022): 219–36.

Freeman, Daniel E. *The Opera Theater of Count Franz Anton von Sporck in Prague*. New York: Pendragon Press, 1992.

Freemanová, Michaela. "Bohemia in the Early 19th century. The Second Life of Wolfgang Amadeus Mozart." *Hudební věda* 50 (2013): 83–102.

"In the Shadow of the Conservatoire: The Prague Organists College (1830–1889/1890)." *Hudební věda* 48 (2011): 369–92.

Freimanová, Milena, ed. *Povědomí tradice v novodobé české kultuře. Doba Bedřicha Smetany*. Prague: Národní galerie, 1988.

Fukač, Jiří, and Jiří Vysloužil, eds. *Slovník České hudební kultury*. Prague: Supraphon, 1997.

Fürstenau, Moritz. *Zur Geschichte der Musik und des Theaters am Hofe zu Dresden*. Dresden: Kuntze, 1862 and Hildesheim: Georg Olms, 1971.

Gabrielli, Giulia. "*Cantus fractus* in South Tyrolean Medieval Manuscripts." *Journal of the Alamire Foundation* 15 (2023): 53–66.

Gancarczyk, Paweł. "The Dating and Chronology of the Strahov Codex." *Hudební věda* 43 (2006): 135–45.

García, Miguel Ángel Asiain. "Calasanz y Nikolsburg." *Analecta calasanctiana* 61 (2020): 11–232.

Gats, Oleksandra Gorbina. "Eliška Krásnohorská a její zápas o ženskou emancipaci." BA thesis, Charles University, Prague, 2010.

Gatterman, Günther, and Wolfgang Reich, eds. *Zelenka-Studien II: Referate und Materialien der 2. Internationalen Fachkonferenz Jan Dismas Zelenka (Dresden und Prague 1995).* Deutsche Musik im Osten 12. Berlin: Academia, 1997.

Gelbart, Matthew. *The Invention of "Folk Music" and "Art Music": Emerging Categories from Ossian to Wagner.* New York: Cambridge University Press, 2007.

Van Gelder, Klaas, ed. *More than Mere Spectacles: Coronations and Inaugurations in the Habsburg Monarchy during the Eighteenth and Nineteenth Centuries.* New York: Berghahn, 2021.

Gentry, Charles. "'Rusalka's Premiere." *Detroit Evening Times,* May 29, 1945.

Glück, Helmut, Holger Klatte, Libuše Spáčilová, and Vladimír Spáčil, eds. *Deutsche Sprachbücher in Böhmen und Mähren vom 15. Jahrhundert bis 1918: Eine teilkommentierte Bibliographie.* Berlin: De Gruyter, 2011.

Goldstücker, Eduard. *Vzpomínky 1945–1968.* Prague: G&G, 2005.

Gorlová, Anežka. *Nech sa dobre darí.* Prague: Osvěta, 1951.

Graham, Barry. *Bohemian and Moravian Graduals (1420–1620).* Turnhout: Brepols, 2007.

Gratzer, Wolfgang, and Andrea Lindmayr, eds. *De editione musices: Festschrift Gerhard Croll zum 65. Geburtstag.* Laaber: Laaber, 1992.

Greene, Thomas M. *The Light in Troy: Imitation and Discovery in Renaissance Poetry.* New Haven: Yale University Press, 1982.

Gregor, Vladimír. *Dělnické pěvecké spolky. Na Ostravsku a v jiných průmyslových střediscích českých zemí.* Ostrava: Krajské nakladatelství, 1961.

Gregusová, Barbora. "Reconsidering Fibich's Šárka: Myth, Gender, and the Construction of a Nation." MM thesis, University of New Mexico, 2015.

Grossegger, Elisabeth. *Theater, Feste und Feiern zur Zeit Maria Theresias. Nach den Tagebucheintragungen des Fursten Johann Joseph Khevenhuller-Metsch, Obersthofmeister der Kaiserin. Eine Dokumentation.* Vienna: Österreichische Akademie der Wissenschaften, 1987.

Gruber, Gernot. *Mozart und die Nachwelt.* Vienna: Residenz Verlag, 1985.

Gruber, Gerold, ed. *Zur Geschichte und Aufführungspraxis der Musik des 16.–18. Jahrhunderts in Mittel- und Osteuropa.* Bratislava: Accentus Musicalis, 2013.

Günther, Josef. "Die Entwicklung des geistigen Lebens in Teplitz." *Sudetendeutsche Heimatgaue* 1924, no. 36: 22–33.

Guzy-Pasiak, Jolanta, and Aneta Markuszewska, eds. *Music Migration in the Early Modern Age: Centres and Peripheries – People, Works, Styles, Paths of Dissemination and Influence.* Warsaw: Liber Pro Arte, 2016.

De Haan, Francisca, Krassimira Daskalová, and Anna Loutfi, eds. *Biographical Dictionary of Women's Movements and Feminisms: Central, Eastern, and*

South Eastern Europe, 19th and 20th Centuries. Budapest: Central European University Press, 2006.

Hába, Alois. "Casellas Scarlattiana – Vierteltonmusik und Musikstil der Freiheit." *Anbruch* 11 (1929): 331–34.

   "Harmonické základy dvanáctitónového systému: tématický a netématický hudební sloh." *Tempo* 17 (1938): 129–30, 141–43.

   "Zvukový film a opera." *Klíč* 2 (1931/32): 57–63.

HaCohen, Ruth. *The Music Libel Against the Jews*. New Haven: Yale University Press, 2013.

Hájková, Anna. *The Last Ghetto*. New York: Oxford University Press, 2020.

Hallas, Rhianydd. "Two Rhymed Offices Composed for the Feast of the Visitation of the Blessed Virgin Mary: Comparative Study and Critical Edition." PhD diss., Bangor University and Charles University, Prague, 2021.

Hallová, Markéta. "200 let Pražské konzervatoře II. Éra Dvořákova a Knittlova." *Hudební rozhledy* 62 (2009): 44–45.

   "200 let Pražské konzervatoře IX. Lisztovo nadšení ze skladby ředitele Josefa Krejčího." *Hudební rozhledy* 61 (2008): 52–53.

   "Zestátnění pražské konzervatoře a osud ředitele Jindřicha Kàana z Albestu." *Clavibus unitis* 7 (2018): 27–62.

Hames, Peter, ed. *The Cinema of Central Europe*. London: Wallflower Press, 2004.

Hanibal, Jiří. *Rom zpívá, hraje, tančí*. Brno: Czechoslovak Television, 1971.

Hann, Chris, Mihály Sárkány, and Peter Skalník, eds. *Studying Peoples in the People's Democracies*. Münster: Lit, 2005.

Hartl, Karla. "Emmy Destinn (1878–1930)." *Women in Music*. The Kapralova Society. Accessed March 27, 2024. http://kapralova.org/DESTINN.htm

Hartmann, Jan, ed. *Kardinál Tomášek. Generál bez vojska*. Prague: Vyšehrad, 2003.

Haskell, Yasmin, and Raphaële Garrod, eds. *Changing Hearts*. Leiden: Brill, 2019.

Havel, Václav. *Do různých stran. Eseje a články z let 1983–1989*. Edited by V. Prečan. Prague: Lidové noviny, 1990.

Havelka, Miloš, ed. *Víra, kultura a společnost: náboženské kultury v českých zemích 19. a 20. století*. Červený Kostelec: Mervart, 2012.

Havelková, Tereza. "From Crisis to Stasis: Depicting History in Czech Opera after 1948." *Hudební věda* 60 (2023): 49–68.

   "Dokumentární gesamtkunstwerk aneb Může Lenin zpívat? Opera Deset dnů, které otřásly světem v pražském Národním divadle." *Divadelní revue* 33 (2022): 31–53.

Havlů, Ivan, and Harry Macourek. *Aven Roma*. Prague: Panton, 1985.

Havránek, Bohuslav. *Johannis Amos Comenii Opera omnia*, vol. 11. Prague: Academia, 1973.

Heibert, Thomas. "The Horn in Early Eighteenth-Century Dresden: The Players and Their Repertory." PhD diss., University of Wisconsin-Madison, 1989.

Helfert, Vladimír. *Bedřich Smetana*. Brno: Nový lid, 1924.

Hudební barok na českých zámcích. Jaroměřice za hraběte Jana Adama z Questenberku. Prague: Česká akademie císaře Františka Josefa, 1916.

Naše hudba a český stát. Prague: Kočí, 1918.

"Více Dvořáka!" *Česká kultura* 1(1912): 114–18.

Vybrané studie I.: O hudební tvořivosti. Prague: Supraphon, 1970.

Helfert, Vladimír, and Erich Steinhard. *Geschichte der Musik in der Tschechoslovakischen Republik.* Prague: Orbis, 1936. Repr. as *Die Musik in der Tschechoslovakischen Republik*, 1938 and *Histoire de la Musique dans la République Tchécoslovaque*, 1938.

Heller, Servác. *Slavnost položení základního kamene k národnímu divadlu.* Prague: Grégr, 1869.

Hernández, Liria, and Pamela Gay y Blasco. "Životní zkušenosti romských žen: kolaborativní přístup k jejich studio." *Romano Džaniben* 2018, no. 2: 39–46.

Herza, Filip. "Anthropologists and their Monsters: Ethnicity, Body, and Ab/ Normality in Early Czech Anthropology." *East Central Europe* 43 (2016): 64–98.

"Colonial Exceptionalism: Post-colonial Scholarship and Race in Czech and Slovak Historiography." *Slovenský národopis* 68 (2020): 175–87.

"Sombre Faces: Race and Nation-Building in the Institutionalization of Czech Physical Anthropology (1890s–1920s)." *History and Anthropology* 31 (2020): 371–92.

Hiekel, Jörn Peter, and Elvira Werner, eds. *Musikkulturelle Wechselbeziehungen zwischen Böhmen und Sachsen.* Saarbrücken: Pfau, 2007.

Hlávková, Lenka. "Behind The Stage: Some Thoughts on the Codex Speciálník and the Reception of the Polyphony in Late 15th-Century Prague." *Early Music* 37 (2009): 37–48.

Hodač, Karel, ed. *Spadla opona Osvobozeného divadla. Tisk z let 1938–1952 o Osvobozeném divadle.* Brno: self-pub., 1995.

Hojda, Zdeněk, Marta Ottlová, and Roman Prahl, eds. *Slavme slavně slávu Slávóv slavných. Slovanství a česká kultura 19. století.* Prague: KLP, 2006.

Hojda, Zdeněk, and Roman Prahl, eds. *Mezi časy ... kultura a umění v českých zemích kolem roku 1800.* Prague: KLP, 2000.

Holeton, David R. "The Celebration of Jan Hus in the Life of the Churches." *Studia Liturgica* 35 (2005): 32–59.

Holeton, David R., and Hana Vlhová-Wörner, eds. *Jistebnický kancionál: MS. Prague, National Museum Library, II C 7: Critical Edition*, vol. 1, *Graduale.* Brno: Marek, 2005.

Holeton, David R., and Hana Vlhová-Wörner. "A Remarkable Witness to the Feast of Saint Jan Hus." *The Bohemian Reformation and Religious Practice* 7 (2009): 156–84.

Holoman, D. Kern. *The Nineteenth-Century Symphony.* New York: Schirmer Books, 1996.

Holý, Dušan, and Ctibor Nečas. *Žalující píseň*. Strážnice: Ústav lidové kultury, 1993.

Holzknecht, Václav, ed. *150 let pražské konzervatoře. Sborník k výročí ústavu.* Prague: Státní hudební nakladatelství, 1961.

Jaroslav Ježek a Osvobozené divadlo, 2nd ed., corrected by Petr Lachmann. Prague: ARSCI, 2007. First published 1957.

Hončarivová, Blažena. Hudba je největší dar. 2018; Czech Republic: Czech Television. Accessed March 21, 2024. www.ceskatelevize.cz/porady/10637723143-sylvie-bodorova-hudba-je-nejvetsi-dar/

Honisch, Erika Supria. "Drowning Winter, Burning Bones, Singing Songs: Representations of Popular Devotion in a Central European Motet Cycle." *Journal of Musicology* 34 (2017): 559–609.

"Encounters with Music in Rudolf II's Prague." *Austrian History Yearbook* 52 (2021): 64–80. https://doi.org/10.1017/S0067237821000126.

Honzl, Jindřich. *Základy a praxe moderního divadla*. Prague: Orbis, 1963.

Horák, Vladimír. *František Pivoda. Pěvecký pedagog*. Brno: Purkyně University, 1970.

Horn, Wolfgang. *Die Dresdner Hofkirchenmusik 1720–1745: Studien zu ihren Voraussetzungen und ihrem Repertoire*. Kassel: Bärenreiter, 1987.

Horníčková, Kateřina, and Michael Šroněk. "Staging Oriental Delegations at the Habsburg Court in Prague (1600–1610)." *Culture & History Journal* 11 (2022). https://doi.org/10.3989/chdj.2022.019.

Horová, Iva. "Operní konkursy, vypsané v souvislosti s otevřením Národního divadla v Praze." *Hudební věda* 27 (1990): 152–59.

Horváthová, Jana, ed. *. . .to jsou těžké vzpomínky*. Brno: Větrné mlýny, 2021.

Horyna, Martin. "Česká reformace a hudba. Studie o bohoslužebném zpěvu českých nekatolických církví v období 1420–1620." *Hudební věda* 48 (2011): 5–40.

"Die Kompositionen von Peter Wilhelmi von Graudenz als Teil der spätmittelalterlichen Polyfonie-Tradition in Mitteleuropa und insbesondere im Böhmen des 15. und 16. Jahrhunderts." *Hudební věda* 40 (2003): 291–328.

"Vícehlasá hudba v Čechách v 15. a 16. století a její interpreti." *Hudební věda* 43 (2006): 117–34.

Horyna, Martin, ed. *XXII hymni quatuor et quinque vocum (1540–1600)*. České Budějovice: Státní vědecká knihovna, 2000.

Jan Trojan Turnovský: Opera musica. České Budějovice: Státní vědecká knihovna, 2002.

Officium in Nativitate Domini. Prague: Národní knihovna České republiky, 2009.

Prachatický kancionál (1610): cantilenae piae 4, 5, 6 et 8 vocum. České Budějovice: Jihočeská univerzita, 2005.

Hostinský, Otakar. *36 nápěvů světských písní českého lidu z XVI. století.* Prague: F. Šimáček, 1892.

    Bedřich Smetana a jeho boj o moderní českou hudbu. Prague: Jan Laichter, 1901.

    Krištof Vilibald Gluck. Prague: Urbánek, 1884.

    "O naší světské písni lidové. (Dokončení.) V." *Český lid* 1 (1892): 351–70.

    "Musik in Böhmen." In *Die österreichisch-ungarische Monarchie in Wort und Bild. Böhmen,* vol. 2. Vienna: Kaiserlich-königliche Hof- und Staatsdruckerei, 1896.

Houtchens, H. Alan. "A Critical Study of Antonín Dvořák's Vanda." PhD diss., University of California, Santa Barbara, 1987.

Hrabalík, Petr. "Úkoly české alternativní hudby." Bigbít. Accessed March 21, 2024. www.ceskatelevize.cz/specialy/bigbit/ceskoslovensko/clanky/193-ukoly-ceske-alternativni-hudby/

Hrabušický, Aurel, ed. *Slovenský mýtus.* Bratislava: Slovak National Gallery, 2006.

Hrbek, Jiří. *České barokní korunovace.* Prague: NLN, 2010.

Hrbek, Jiří, ed. *Panovnický majestát. Habsburkové jako čeští krákové.* Prague: NLN, 2021.

Hrčková, Naďa. "Od reflexie k teórii: rozhovor s Eugenom Suchoňom." *Opus musicum* 10 (1978): 123–26.

    Tradícia, modernosť a slovenská hudobná kultúra 1918–1948. Bratislava: Litera, 1996.

Hrůša, Jakub. *Hrůša on Martinů.* Prague: International Martinů Circle, 2020.

Hruška, Viktor. "Opětovný nález jedné z nejstarších učebnic harmonie v češtině." *Musicologica Brunensia* 50 (2015): 195–203.

Hrušková, Vlasta. "Bedřich Smetana: *Dvě vdovy* – Dramaturgická analýza opery." MA thesis, Charles University, Prague, 1972.

Hübschmannová, Milena, Hana Šebková, and Edita Žigová. *Romsko-český and česko-romský slovník.* Prague: Fortuna, 1988.

Hübschmannová, Milena, and Zuzana Jurková. *Romane giľa. Zpěvník romských písní.* Prague: Fortuna, 1999.

Hudek, Adam. *Najpolitickejšia veda: slovenská historiografia v rokoch 1948 – 1968.* Bratislava: SAV, 2010.

Hudek, Adam, Michal Kopeček, and Jan Mervart, eds. *Čechoslovakismus.* Prague: AVČR, 2019.

Huigen, Siegfried, and Dorota Kołodziejczyk, eds. *East Central Europe Between the Colonial and the Postcolonial in the Twentieth Century.* Cham: Palgrave Macmillan, 2023.

Irwin, Joan. "Dvorak by Czech Orchestra." *The Montreal Star,* October 26, 1965.

Jacková, Magdaléna. "The End of School Year on the Stage of Jesuit Schools in the Bohemian Province." *Acta Universitatis Carolinae Philologica* 2 – *Graecolatina Pragensia* 2 (2016): 125–35.

"Ján Levoslav Bella: Works." Hudobné Centrum: Music Centre Slovakia. Accessed March 21, 2024. https://hc.sk/en/o-slovenskej-hudbe/osobnost-detail/993-bella-jan-levoslav/diela

Janáček, Leoš. *Její pastorkyňa*. Brno: Klub přátel umění, 1908.

Janulíková, Jana. "Vladislav Vančura a *Marijka nevěrnice* aneb Česká filmová avantgarda v praxi." *Opus musicum* 1 (2001): 70–88.

Jareš, Stanislav, and Tomislav Volek. *Dějiny české hudby v obrazech od nejstarších památek do vybudování Národního divadla*. Prague: Supraphon, 1977.

Jehne, Leo. "Kde a co jsou hodnoty v pop music." *Melodie* 10 (February 1972): 37–38.

Jeremiáš, Bohuslav. *Pobožnost jinoha studujícího. III. část, sbory*. Písek: Kopecký, 1896.

Jiránek, Jaroslav. *Socialistický realismus jako vůdčí ideově estetický princip naší současné hudební tvorby*. Prague: Divadelní ústav, 1980.

   Zdeněk Fibich. Prague: Státní hudební vydavatelství, 1963.

Jireček, Josef. *Dějiny literatury české*. Prague: Tempský, 1876.

Jirous, Ivan Martin. *Magorův zápisník*. Edited by Michael Špirit. Prague: Torst, 1997.

Jochmanová, Andrea, and Ladislava Petišková. *Osvobozené divadlo na vlnách Devětsilu*. Brno: JAMU, 2022.

Johnson, Lonnie. *Central Europe: Enemies, Neighbors, and Friends*. New York: Oxford University Press, 2011.

Jonášová, Milada. "*Semiramide riconosciuta*. Eine Oper zur Prager Krönung Maria Theresias 1743." *Studien zur Musikwissenschaft* 55 (2009): 53–120.

Jurášková, Kateřina, and Jana Spáčilová. *Italská opera na holešovském zámku v době Františka Antonína Rottala*. Holešov: Město Holešov, 2019.

Jurík, Marián, and Peter Zagar, eds. *100 slovenských skladateľov*. Bratislava: Národné hudobné centrum, 1998.

Jurková, Zuzana. "Archetypální zpěvačka." *Romano Džaniben* 1998, no. 5: 19–28.

   "Co víme a nevíme o hudbě 'našich' Romů." *Romano Džaniben* 2003, no. 10: 96–114.

   "Myth of Romani Music in Prague." *Lidé města / Urban People* 11 (2009): 351–77.

   Romští hudebníci v 21. století. Rozhovory s Olgou Fečovou, Josefem Fečem, Pavlem Dirdou a Janem Dužďou. / Romani Musicians in the 21st Century. Interviews with Olga Fečová, Josef Fečo, Pavel Dirda and Jan Dužda. Prague: FHS, 2018.

Jurková, Zuzana, and Veronika Seidlová, eds. *Music – Memory – Minorities. Between Archive and Activism*. Prague: Karolinum, 2020.

Kabelík, Jan. *Slovenská čítanka*, 2nd rev. ed. Prague: Šolc, 1925.

Kadlinský, Felix. *Zdoroslavíček*. Prague: Staropražská kolej, 1665.

Kaiser, Ulrich. "Babylonian confusion. Zur Terminologie der Formanalyse von Pop- und Rockmusik." *Zeitschrift der Gesellschaft für Musiktheorie* 8 (2011): 43–75.

Kalenský, Boleslav. *Antonín Dvořák: Sborník statí o jeho díle a životě.* Prague: Umělecká beseda, 1912.

Kalina, Petr. "Tvorba Ferdinanda Havlíka pro divadlo Semafor." *Muzikologické fórum* 11 (2022): 57–64.

Kalousek, Josef. *Obrana knížete Václava Svatého proti smyšlenkám a křivým úsudkům o jeho povaze.* Prague: Bursík a Kohout, 1872.

Kapsa, Václav. "Account Books, Names and Music: Count Wenzel von Morzin's Virtuosissima Orchestra." *Early Music* 40 (2012): 605–20.

"Hofmusici a lokajové. K postavení hudebníka na šlechtickém dvoře v Čechách první poloviny 18. století." *Theatrum historiae* 9 (2011): 241–55.

Hudebníci hraběte Morzina. Prague: Etnologický ústav AVČR, 2010.

"Šlechtické kapely v českých zemích doby baroka: staré a nové otázky jejich zkoumání." *Clavibus unitis* 3 (2014): 177–82.

Kapsa, Václav, and Claire Mádl. "Weiss, the Hartigs and the Prague Music Academy – Research into the 'Profound Silence' left by a 'Pope of Music.'" *Journal of the Lute Society of America* 33 (2000): 47–74.

Kapsa, Václav, Jana Perutková, and Jana Spáčilová. "Some Remarks on the Relationship of Bohemian Aristocracy to Italian Music at the Time of Pergolesi." *Studi pergolesiani – Pergolesi Studies* 8 (2012): 313–41.

Karásek, Bohumil. "Nová česká opera." *Rudé právo.* June 7, 1966.

Karbusický, Vladimír. "Půlhodinka s Adornem." *Hudební rozhledy* 11 (1966): 323–24.

"Nové cesty naší folkloristiky." *Česká literatura* 8 (1960): 154–66.

Karbusický, Vladimír, and Václav Pletka. *Dělnické písně,* 2 vols. Prague: SNLKHU, 1958.

Kendrick, Robert L. *Fruits of the Cross.* Oakland, CA: University of California Press, 2019.

De Kerle, Jacobus. *Selectiorum aliquot modulorum, qui in sacris templis ... decantari solent.* Prague: 1585.

Khevenhüller-Metsch, Rudolph, and Hans Schlitter, eds. *Aus der Zeit Maria Theresias. Tagebuch des Fursten Johann Josef Khevenhuller-Metsch,* vol. 1. Vienna: Holzhauser, 1907.

Khuen, Johannes. *Epithalamium marianum.* Munich: Hainrich, 1638.

King, Jeremy. *Budweisers into Czechs and Germans.* Princeton, NJ: Princeton University Press, 2002.

Kiss, Gábor. "The 'Liedhafte E-Melodik.'" *Studia Musicologica Academiae Scientiarum Hungaricae* 40 (1999): 315–24.

Klusáček, Karel, Emanuel Kovář, Lubomír Niederle, František Schlaffer, and František Adolf Šubert, eds. *Národopisná výstava českoslovanská v Praze 1895.* Prague: Otto, 1895.

Kmetz, John, ed. *Music in the German Renaissance*. New York: Cambridge University Press, 1994.

Knittl, Karel. *Nauka o skladbě homofonní*, 2 vols. Prague: Urbánek, 1898–1910.

Kofroň, Petr. *Třináct analýz*. Jinočany: H & H, 1993.

Kohoutek, Ctirad. *Novodobé skladebné teorie západoevropské hudby*. Prague: Státní hudební nakladatelství, 1962.

Königl. Polnischer und Churfürstl. Sächsischer Hof- und Staats-Calender. Leipzig: 1728–29, 1730–33, 1734–57.

Konrád, Karel. *Dějiny posvátného zpěvu staročeského od 15. věku do zrušení literátských bratrstev*, vol. 1, *XV. věk a dějiny literátských bratrstev*. Prague: Dědictví sv. Prokopa, 1893.

Kopčáková, Slávka. *Vývoj hudobnoestetického myslenia na Slovensku v 20. storočí*. Prešov: Prešov University, 2013.

Kopecký, Jiří. "Karl Goldmark and Czech National Opera." *Studia Musicologica* 57 (2016): 349–59.

Kopecký, Milan, ed. *Zdoroslavíček Felixe Kadlinského*. Brno: Universita J. E. Purkyně, Filosofická fakulta, 1971.

Korál, Petr. *Vzpomínky plíživé, aneb Jasná zpráva o Olympiku*. Prague: Bestia, 2002.

Kotek, Josef. *Dějiny české populární hudby a zpěvu*, 2 vols. Prague: Academia, 1994.

"Paradoxy z Essenu." *Hudební rozhledy* 21 (1968): 630–31.

"Underground Music a její sociální otazníky." *Melodie* 7 (February 1969): 37–40.

Kouba, Jan. "Německé vlivy v české písni 16. století." *Miscellanea musicologica* 27–28 (1975): 117–71.

Slovník staročeských hymnografů (13.–18. století). Prague: Etnologický ústav AVČR, 2017.

Koukal, Petr. "Byl v Čechách Cristoforiho klavír?" *Opus musicum* 44 (2012): 6–13.

Kovács, Andrea. *Monuments of Medieval Liturgical Poetry in Hungary: Sequences – Critical Edition of Melodies*. Musica Sacra Hungarica, 1. Budapest: Argumentum, 2017.

Kozáková, Anna. "Bohuslav Martinů ve filmu." BA thesis, Palacký University, Olomouc, 2019.

Krásnohorská, Eliška. "Český básník a hudební drama." *Hudební listy* 1 (1870): 298–301, 306–10.

Kratochvíl, Matěj. "Music as an Adaptation Strategy: The Hruby Family Voyage from Cehnice to Cleveland." *Journal of Austrian American History* 6 (2022): 1–13.

Vy havíři umouněný, co vy z toho máte … Výzkum hornických písní na Kladensku v letech 1953-1959 v kontextu dobové vědy a politiky. Prague: Etnologický ústav AVČR, 2022.

Krejčí, Iša. "Ponětí modernosti v dnešní hudbě." *Rozpravy Aventina* 3 (1928): 97.

Krejčí, Josef. *Nauka o romonu čili harmonii pro hudebníky*. Prague: Amerling, 1850.

Krejčí, Miroslav. *Čtyři staročeské písně duchovní*. Kutná Hora: Česká hudba, 1934.

Kresánek, Jozef. *Národný umelec Eugen Suchoň*. Bratislava: Slovenské vydavateľstvo krásnej literatúry, 1961.

Křesťan, Jiří. *Zdeněk Nejedlý: Politik a vědec v osamění*. Prague: Paseka, 2012.

Křiklava, Jan, ed. *Svatý Václav ve filmu českého tisku v září 1940*. Prague: Křiklava, 1940.

Křížek, Milan. *Jan Rychlík: Život a dílo skladatele*. Prague: H & H, 2001.

Krones, Hartmut, Theophil Antonicek, and Elisabeth Theresia Fritz-Hilscher, eds. *Die Wiener Hofmusikkapelle III. Gibt es einen Stil der Hofmusikkapelle?* Vienna: Böhlau, 2011.

Křupková, Lenka, and Jiří Kopecký, eds., *Czech Music Around 1900*. Hillsdale, NY: Pendragon Press, 2017.

Kubeš, Jiří. *Náročné dospívání urozených. Kavalírské cesty české a rakouské šlechty (1620–1750)*. Pelhřimov: NTP, 2013.

Kubeš, Jiří, ed. *Vyšší šlechta v českých zemích v období baroka (1650–1750). Biogramy vybraných šlechticů a edice typických pramenů*. Pardubice: Univerzita Pardubice, 2007.

Kubínová, Kateřina. *Imitatio Romae – Karel IV. a Řím*. Prague: Artefactum, 2006.

Kudrna, Ladislav. *Kapela: pozadí akce, která stvořila Chartu 77*. Prague: Academia, 2017.

Kulijevičová, Marie. "Ještě něco chci." *Reflex* 13 (2002): 58–59.

Kuna, Milan. "Dvořák's *Dimitrij*." *The Musical Times* 120 (January 1979): 23–24.

Kuna, Milan. *Musik an der Grenze des Lebens. Musikerinnen und Musiker aus böhmischen Ländern in nationalsozialistischen Konzentrationslagern und Gefängnissen*. Translated by Eliška Nováková. Frankfurt: Zweitausendeins, 1993.

Kundera, Milan. "The Tragedy of Central Europe." Translated by Edmund White. *New York Review of Books* (April 26, 1984): 33–38.

Kvočáková, Lucia. *Cesta ke slovenskému mýtu: Konstrukce identity slovenské moderny v kontextu ideje čechoslovakismu*. Prague: Charles University, 2020.

Ladič, Branko. "Music by František Škvor for the Karol Plicka's Film *The Earth Sings* – the Beginning of Slovak National Music?" *Musicologica Brunensia* 51 (2017): 79–87.

"Transformations of Folklorism in 20th-Century Slovak Composition." *Studia Musicologica* 56 (2015): 367–96.

Lajcha, Ladislav, ed. *Dokumenty SND*, 2 vols. Bratislava: Divadelný ústav, 2000.

Lajosi, Krisztina, and Andreas Stynen, eds. *Choral Societies and Nationalist Mobilization in Nineteenth-Century Europe*. Leiden: Brill, 2019.

Landau, Hermann Joseph, ed. *Erstes poetisches Beethoven Album*. Prague: Landau, 1872.

Langer, Miloslav. "19.–28. 3. 1967, Music F Club Praha. Přehlídka beatových skupin." *Melodie* 5 (1967): 211.

Large, Brian. *Smetana*. New York: Praeger Publishers, 1970.

Laubhold, Lars E., and Gerhard Walterskirchen, eds. *Klang-Quellen: Festschrift für Ernst Hintermaier zum 65. Geburtstag. Symposionsbericht.* Munich: Strube, 2010.

Layton, Robert, ed. *A Companion to the Symphony.* London: Simon and Schuster, 1993.

Lébl, Vladimír. "Případ Vojcek." *Hudební věda* 14 (1977): 195–229.
   Vítězslav Novák. Život a dílo. Prague: ČSAV, 1964.

Lébl, Vladimír, ed. *Hudba v českých dějinách: od středověku do nové doby*, 2nd ed. Prague: Supraphon, 1989.

Lébl, Vladimír, and Jitka Ludvová. "Pražské orchestrální koncerty v letech 1860–1895." *Hudební věda* 17 (1980): 99–138.

Lenderová, Milena. "Eliška hraběnka Schliková (panu profesoru Robertu Kvačkovi k 70. narozeninám)." *Listy starohradské kroniky* 25 (2002): 7–12.
   "Portrét hraběnky Elišky Šlikové." *Z Českého ráje a Podkrkonoší: vlastivědný sborník* (2010): 33–42.

Lengová, Jana, ed. *Ján Levoslav Bella v kontexte európskej hudobnej kultúry.* Banská Bystrica: Nadácia Jána Levoslava Bellu, 1993.

Leopold, Silke. "Chiabrera und die Monodie: Die Entwicklung der Arie." *Studi musicali* 10 (1981): 75–106.

Levi, Primo. *The Drowned and the Saved.* New York: Vintage Books, 1989.

Lindaur, Vojtěch, and Ondřej Konrád. *Bigbít.* Prague: Plus, 2010.

Lindell, Robert. "Marta gentil che'l cor m'ha morto: Eine unbekannte Kammermusikerin am Hof Maximilians II." *Musicologica austriaca* 7 (1987): 59–68.

Locke, Brian S. *Opera and Ideology in Prague: Polemics and Practice at the National Theater, 1900–1938.* Rochester, NY: University of Rochester Press, 2006.
   "The *Wozzeck* Affair: Modernism and the Crisis of Audience in Prague." *Journal of Musicological Research* 27 (2008): 63–93.

Locke, Ralph P. *Musical Exoticism: Images and Reflections.* New York: Cambridge University Press, 2009.

Logier, Bernhard. *Versuch einer rationellen Lehrmethode im Pianofortespiel*, 6 vols. 1841–61.

Long, Megan Kaes. "Characteristic Tonality in the 'Balletti' of Gastoldi, Morley, and Hassler." *Journal of Music Theory* 59 (2015): 235–71.
   Hearing Homophony: Tonal Expectation at the Turn of the Seventeenth Century. New York: Oxford University Press, 2020.

Loos, Helmut, and Stefan Keym, eds. *Nationale Musik im 20. Jahrhundert.* Leipzig: Schröder, 2004.

Lorenzová, Helena, and Taťána Petrasová, eds. *Salony v české kultuře 19. století.* Prague: KLP, 1999.

Lorman, Jaroslav, and Daniela Tinková, eds. *Post tenebras spero lucem. Duchovní tvář českého a moravského osvícenství.* Prague: Casablanca, 2008.

Loudová, Ivana. "Témbrová a aleatorní technika v hudbě." Doctoral diss., AMU, Prague, 1971.

"Vokální složka v symfonii." MA thesis, AMU, Prague, 1965.

Löwenbach, Jan. *Bedřich Smetana a Dr Lud. Procházka: Vzájemná correspondence.* Prague: Umělecká beseda, 1914.

"Czechoslovak Composers and Musicians in America." *The Musical Quarterly* 29 (1943): 313–28.

Ludvová, Jitka. *Až k hořkému konci: Pražské německé divadlo 1845–1945.* Prague: Divadelní ústav, 2012.

"Hankovy padělky v české hudbě." *Hudební věda* 27 (1990): 299–319.

"Hudební motivy Hankových padělků." *Hudební věda* 25 (1988): 293–309

Ludvová, Jitka, ed. *Fidlowačka aneb cokoli chcete.* Prague: Divadelní ústav, 2014.

Ludwig, Mark. *Our Will to Live: The Terezín Music Critiques of Viktor Ullmann.* Göttingen: Steidl, 2021.

Luython, Carolus. *Liber primus missarum.* Prague: 1609.

Macek, Petr, ed. *Slovník české hudební kultury.* Prague: Supraphon, 1997.

Macháček, Jiří. "'Velkomoravský stát' – kontroverze středoevropské medievistiky." *Archeologické rozhledy* 64 (2012): 775–87.

Makarova, Elena, and Ira Rabin, eds. *Franz Peter Kien.* Prague: Oswald, 2009.

Mäkinen, Timo. *Die aus frühen böhmischen Quellen überlieferten Piae cantiones-Melodien.* Jyväskylä: Jyväskylän Yliopistoyhdistys, 1964.

Malinowski, Jerzy, ed. *History of Art History in Central, Eastern and South-Eastern Europe*, 2 vols. Toruń: Tako, 2012.

Maňas, Vladimír. "Hudební aktivity náboženských korporací na Moravě v raném novověku." PhD diss., Masaryk University, Brno, 2008.

"Musik und Musiker am Hofe der Fürsten von Liechtenstein im 17. Jahrhundert." *Studia historica Brunensia* 64 (2017): 189–215.

Mann, Brian. *The Secular Madrigals of Filippo di Monte, 1521–1603.* Ann Arbor: UMI Research Press, 1983.

Markl, Jaroslav. *Nejstarší sbírky českých lidových písní.* Prague: Supraphon, 1987.

Maryks, Robert Aleksander. *Exploring Jesuit Distinctiveness: Interdisciplinary Perspectives on Ways of Proceeding within the Society of Jesus.* Leiden: Brill, 2016.

Matějčková, Helena. "Hudební produkce Žofínské akademie v letech 1841–1850." *Hudební věda* 48 (2011): 173–200.

Matzner, Antonín, and Jiří Pilka. *Česká filmová hudba.* Prague: Dauphin, 2022.

Maur, Eduard. *12. 5. 1743. Korunovace na usmířenou.* Prague: Havran, 2003.

Maýrová, Kateřina, Stephanie Schlagel, and Hana Hrachová. *Rokycanská hudební sbírka: Katalog franko-nizozemských duchovních skladeb dochovaných v nejstarší vrstvě repertoáru.* Prague: Národní Muzeum, 2016.

Melli, Pietro Paolo. *Intavolatura di liuto attiorbato*, 3 vols. Venice: 1616.

Meinert, Joseph Georg, ed. *Libussa: Eine vaterländische Vierteljahrsschrift.* Prague: Calve, 1804.

Meyers, Helen, ed. *Ethnomusicology: Historical and Regional Studies*. New York: Norton, 1992.

Michlová, Jana. *Zámecké divadlo v Teplicích: Divadelní cedule ve sbírce knihovny muzea*, 2nd rev. ed. Teplice: Regionální muzeum v Teplicích, 2014.

Mikanová, Eva. "Dvořákova hudba v Pojizeří v repertoáru místních a pražských umělců." *Z českého ráje a Podkrkonoší* 14 (2001): 162–73.

Mikuláš, Jiří. "Dožínky v Bubenči roku 1792 jako plenérová inscenace s hudbou Vinzenze Maschka." *Divadelní revue* 23 (2012): 49–73.

Mikulec, Jiří. *Barokní náboženská bratrstva v Čechách*. Prague: Lidové noviny, 2000.

Mináč, Vladimír. "Tíha folkloru." *Literární noviny. Týdeník pro kulturně politické a umělecké otázky* 7 (March 1958): 1.

Minor, Ryan. *Choral Fantasies: Music, Festivity, and Nationhood in Nineteenth-Century Germany*. New York: Cambridge University Press, 2012.

Möller, Heinrich Ferdinand. *Wladislaw II. böhmischer Herzog, dann König*. Prague: Schönfeld, 1791.

De Monte, Philippe. *Il Quintodecimo Libro de Madrigali a Cinque Voci*. Venice: 1592.

Móricz, Klára. *Jewish Identities: Nationalism, Racism, and Utopianism in Twentieth-Century Music*. Berkeley: University of California Press, 2008.

Muehlenbeck, Philip. *Czechoslovakia in Africa, 1945–1968*. Basingstoke: Palgrave Macmillan, 2016.

Müller, Richard. "Verím hudbe, kterú hrám. Radim Hladík." *Populár* 12 (May 1980): 17.

Mundy, Rachel. "Evolutionary Categories and Musical Style from Adler to America." *Journal of the American Musicological Society* 67 (2014): 735–68.

Muntág, Emanuel, ed. *Ján Levoslav Bella, národovec a Európan (1843–1936)*. Martin: Matica slovenská, 2004.

Musica Rudolphina. Accessed March 26, 2024. http://www.bibemus.org/musicarudolphina/index_en.html

Musicalischer Zeitvertreiber, das ist, Allerley seltzame lecherliche Vapores vnd Humores, ehrliche Collation vnd Schlafftruncksbossen, Quodlibet, Judenschul vnd andere kurtzweilige Liedlein, dergleichen zuvorn nie also in einen Model zusammen gegossen worden: von mehrerley fürtrefflichen Musicis mit 4. 5. 6. 7. vnd 8. stimmen componirt: vnd durch einen der Music Liebhabern an tag gegeben. Nuremberg, 1609.

Musikedition Tirol. Accessed March 26, 2024. https://musikedition.musikland-tirol.at

Mužík, František. "Christ ist erstanden – Buóh všemohúcí." *Miscellanea musicologica* 21–23 (1970): 7–45.

Myška, Milan. *Hrabě Hodic a jeho svět: zámecká kultura ve Slezsku mezi barokem a osvícenstvím*. Ostrava: Ostravská Univerzita, 2011.

Nardi, Paul. "A un ami très cher." *Hudební věda* 36 (1999): 169–78.

Nečas, Ctibor. *Špalíček romských miniature*. Brno: Centrum pro stadium demokracie a kultury, 2008.

Nedbal, Martin. "Christoph Willibald Gluck and National Politics in Nineteenth-Century Prague." *Divadelní revue* 23, no. 2 (2023): 59–82.

———. "Czech-German Collaborations at the Metropolitan Opera in the Early Twentieth Century." *Journal of Austrian-American History* 6 (2022): 14–43.

———. "Dvořák's *Armida* and the Czech Oriental 'Self.'" *Current Musicology* 84 (2007): 25–51. https://doi.org/10.7916/cm.v0i84.5097.

———. "František Šír's First Czech Translation of Mozart's Final *Opera Buffa* and the Reception of *Così fan tutte* in Prague 1791–1831." *Divadelní revue* 27, no. 2 (2016): 53–70.

———. "Heinrich Wilhelm Haugwitz and the Reception of Mozart's Operas in Early Nineteenth-Century Moravia." *Musicologica Brunensia* 56 (2021): 43–57.

———. *Morality and Viennese Opera in the Age of Mozart and Beethoven*. New York: Routledge, 2017.

———. *Mozart's Operas and National Politics: Canon Formation in Prague from 1791 to the Present*. New York: Cambridge University Press, 2023.

———. "Music History and Ethnicity from Prague to Indiana: Paul Nettl, Eighteenth-century Bohemia, and Germanness." *Hudební věda* 16 (2019): 386–416.

Nedbal, Martin, trans. and ed. *The Published Theoretical Works of Leoš Janáček*. Brno: Editio Janáček, 2020.

———. "Smetana's *The Brandenburgers in Bohemia* and Czech Nationalism: A Historical Reevaluation." *Music and Politics* 14 (Winter 2020). https://doi.org/10.3998/mp.9460447.0014.102.

Nedbal, Miloslav, ed. *Hostinský: O hudbě*. Prague: Státní hudební nakladatelství, 1961.

Nejedlý, Zdeněk. *Česká moderní zpěvohra po Smetana*. Prague: Otto, 1911.

———. *Dějiny české hudby*. Prague: Hejda & Tuček, 1903.

———. "Dvořákova *Rusalka*." *Rozhledy: revue umělecká, politická a sociální* 11 (1901): 205–9.

———. "Richard Batka über die čechische Musik." *Česká revue* 2 (1908): 305–16.

———. "Dvořákova *Rusalka*." *Rozhledy* 11 (May 1901): 205.

———. "Slovenská hudba: K pražskému koncertu 20. března 1920." *Smetana* 10 (March 1920): 33–35.

———. *Vítězslava Nováka 'Karlštejn'*. Prague: Hudební knihovna časopisu Smetana, 1916.

———. *Zdenko Fibich, zakladatel scénického melodrama*. Prague: Hejda & Tuček, 1901.

———. *Zpěvohry Smetanovy*. Prague: Otto, 1908.

Němec, Václav. "Osud Janáčkovy opery *Šárka* ve světle dosud neznámé korespondence Julia Zeyera." *Opus musicum* 60 (2009): 17–22.

Nettl, Paul. *Forgotten Musicians*. New York: Greenwood Press, 1951.

Niederle, Lubor. "Počátky slovanské hudby." *Národopisný věstník českoslovanský* 9 (1915): 49–74.

Niemetschek, Franz Xaver. "Einige Nachrichten von einem merkwürdigen Bauer in Böhmen. Nebst einer kurzen Übersicht des bösen und ungerechten Krieges des französischen Volkes, in böhmische Reime gebracht." *Für Böhmen von Böhmen* 3 (1794): 85–93.

    Leben des k. k. Kapellmeisters Wolfgang Gottlieb Mozart, nach Originalquellen beschrieben. Prague: Herrlische Buchhandlung, 1798.

    Lebensbeschreibung des k. k. Kapellmeisters Wolfgang Amadeus Mozart, aus Originalquellen, 2nd exp. ed. Prague: Herrlische Buchhandlung, 1808.

Niubo, Marc. *Italská opera v mozartovské Praze.* Prague: Karolinum, 2022.

    The People of Prague Pay Homage to Me. Prague: Národní knihovna, 2006.

Nouza, Zdeněk. *Miloslav Kabeláč: Tvůrčí profil skladatele.* Prague: AVČR, 2010.

Nováček, Vojtěch J., ed. *Františka Palackého korrespondence a zápisky*, 2 vols. Prague: Česká akademie císaře Františka Josefa, 1898–1911.

Novák, Arne. *Czech Literature.* Translated by Peter Kussi. Ann Arbor, Michigan: Slavic Publications, 1986.

Novák, Vítězslav. *O sobě a o jiných.* Prague: Supraphon, 1970.

Novák, Vladimír, and Ludmila Mašlanová. *Musicae navales pragenses.* Prague: Národní knihovna, 1993.

Novotná, Jarmila. "The Folk Song." *The Music Journal* 6 (1948): 16–18.

    My Life in Song. Edited by William V. Madison. Lexington: University Press of Kentucky, 2018.

Novotný, Jaroslav. "Nová díla Arnolda Schönberga." *Hudební revue* 4 (1911): 325–26.

Novotný, Jiří Datel, ed. *Ďábel z Vinohrad. Vzpomínka na Jiřího Šlitra.* Prague: XYZ, 2010.

Nový, Miroslav. "Kniha bojující." *Hudební rozhledy* 6 (1953): 506.

Očadlík, Mirko. "A. W. Ambros na pražské univerzitě." *Acta Universitatis Carolinae: Philosophica et Historica* 2 (1958): 131–46.

    "Hudba v biografu." *Kino* 1 (September 1931): 50.

Očadlík, Mirko, ed. *Dvě vdovy / Emanuel Züngel.* Prague: Státní hudební vydavatelství, 1962.

    Eliška Krásnohorská – Bedřich Smetana: vzájemná korespondence. Prague: Topič, 1940.

Opekar, Aleš. "K počátkům českého rocku: nad prvním profilovým albem skupiny Olympic." *Hudební věda* 30 (1993): 60–69.

Opekar, Aleš, and Josef Vlček, eds. *Excentrici v přízemí.* Prague: Panton, 1989.

Opera nuova dove si contiene Vilanelle, Canzoni, e Ciciliane. Mantua, 1590[?]. Repr. Milan, 1595.

Orologio, Alessandro. *Intradae . . . quarum in omni genere instrumentorum musicorum usus esse potest.* Helmstedt: 1597.

Ortelius, Hieronymus. *Chronologia oder Historische beschreibung aller Kriegsemporungen vnd beläegerungen der Stätt vnd Vestungen, . . . so in*

Ober vnd Vnder Vngern, auch Sibenbürgen, mit dem Türcken von Ao. 1395 biß auff gegenwertige Zeitt gedenckhwürdig geschehen. Nuremberg, 1602.

Ossi, Massimo. "Claudio Monteverdi's 'Ordine novo, bello et gustevole.'" *Journal of the American Musicological Society* 45 (1992): 261–304.

Osvobozené divadlo V+W 1929–1938. 7 discs. 2007 by Supraphon. Compact disc.

Ottlová, Marta, and Milan Pospíšil. "Italská opera v kontextu české národní opery." *Miscellanea musicologica* 23 (1992): 39–69.

Owens, Samantha, Barbara Reul, and Janice Stockigt. *Music in German Courts, 1715–1760: Changing Artistic Priorities.* Rochester, NY: Boydell & Brewer, 2011.

Painter, Karen. *Symphonic Aspirations: German Music and Politics, 1900–1945.* Cambridge, MA: Harvard University Press, 2007.

Pánek, Jaroslav, and Oldřich Tůma, eds. *A History of the Czech Lands.* Prague: Karolinum, 2009.

[Pariati, Giovanni.] *Costanza e Fortezza.* Vienna: Ghelen, 1723.

Parker, Emma Taylor. "'The Librettist Wears Skirts': Female Librettists in 19th-Century Bohemia." PhD diss., University of California, Santa Barbara, 2016.

Patera, Ludvík, and Rudolf Chmel, eds. *Kontext české a slovenské literatury: Antologie českých a slovenských textů 1830 – 1989.* Prague: Karolinum, 1997.

Pátková, Jana. "Obraz Bratislavy v českých cestopisech meziválečného období." *Slovenská literatúra* 68 (2021): 235–45.

Pavlíček, Ota, and František Šmahel, eds. *A Companion to Jan Hus.* Leiden: Brill, 2015.

Pavlis, Matouš. "Život a dílo Josefa Matyáše Wolframa se zaměřením na operu Bergmönch." BA thesis, Charles University, Prague, 2020.

Pečman, Rudolf, ed. *Colloquium Česká hudba. Problémy a metody hudební historiografie.* Brno: Mezinárodní hudební festival, 1974.

     Vladimír Helfert. Brno: Universitas Masarykiana, 2003.

Pederson, Sanna. "A. B. Marx, Berlin Concert Life, and German National Identity." *19th-Century Music* 18 (1994): 87–107.

     "On the Task of the Music Historian: The Myth of the Symphony after Beethoven." *Repercussions* 2 (1993): 5–30.

Peduzzi, Lubomír. *Pavel Haas.* Brno, Muzejní a vlastivědná společnost, 1993.

Perutková, Jana. *Der glorreiche Nahmen Adami. Johann Adam Graf von Questenberg (1678–1752) als Förderer der italienischen Oper in Mähren.* Vienna: Hollitzer, 2015.

Petiška, Eduard. Goethe v Čechách a Čechy v Goethovi. Prague: Martin, 1999.

Petr, Pithart, and Martin T. Zikmund. *Ptám se, tedy jsem. Rozhovor.* Prague: Portál, 2010.

Pigman III, G. W. "Versions of Imitation in the Renaissance." *Renaissance Quarterly* 33 (1980): 1–32.

Pilz, Wolfgang. "Die Tätigkeit des Trautenauer Männergesangvereines seit 1854 bis zu seiner Reformierung und Erweiterung zum Musik- und Gesangverein

Harmonie 1869." In *Sborníček. Příspěvky muzea Podkrkonoší v Trutnově*, 136–43. Trutnov: Muzeum Podkrkonoší v Trutnově, 2005.

Pines, Roger. "Jarmila Novotna, Adele Leigh, and Sena Jurinac." *The Opera Quarterly* 20 (Autumn 2004): 708–10.

Pivoda, František. *O hudbě Wagnerově*. Prague: Otto, 1881.

Plavec, Josef, and František Škroup. *Libušin sňatek*. Prague: Melantrich, 1941.

Polc, Jaroslav V., and Zdeňka Hledíková. *Prague Synods and Councils of the Pre-Hussite Era*. Prague: Karolinum, 2002.

Pospíchalová, Dana. *První městské divadlo v Teplicích v letech 1874-1878 aneb pýcha města a jeho obyvatel*. Ústí nad Labem: Univerzita J. E. Purkyně, 2005.

Pospíšil, Milan. *Švýcarská rodina v Praze. Opera a její libreto / Die Schweizerfamilie*, in *Prag. Die Oper und ihr Libretto*. Prague: Divadelní ústav, 2021.

Pospíšil, Vilém. "Jezero Ukereve." *Hudební rozhledy* 19 (1966): 12–13.

Pospíšilová, Jana, and Jana Nosková, eds. *Od lidové písně k evropské etnologii: 100 let Etnologického ústavu Akademie věd České republiky*. Brno: Etnologický ústav AVČR, 2006.

Potter, Pamela. *Most German of the Arts: Musicology and Society from the Weimar Republic to the End of Hitler's Reich*. New Haven: Yale University Press, 1998.

Pražák, Přemysl. *Smetanova Prodaná nevěsta*. Prague: Lidová demokracie, 1962. *Smetanovy zpěvohry*, 3 vols. Prague: Vydavatelství za svobodu, 1948.

Preis, Pavel. *František Antonín Špork a barokní kultura v Čechách*. Prague: Paseka, 2003.

Procházka, Vladimír, ed. *Národní divadlo a jeho předchůdci*. Prague: Academia, 1988.

Procházková, Jarmila, Hana Urbancová, Alžběta Lukáčová, Lucie Uhlíková, Franz Lechleitner, Milan Fügner, Václav Mach, and Michael Škopík. *As Recorded by the Phonograph: Slovak and Moravian Songs Recorded by Hynek Bím, Leoš Janáček and Františka Kyselková in 1909–1912*. Vol. 1, *Studies and Reports*. Brno: Etnologicky ústav AVČR, 2012.

Procházková, Jarmila, Marta Toncrová, and Jiří Vysloužil, eds. *Leoš Janáček. Folkloristické dílo*. Brno: Editio Janáček, 2009.

Prog Lucky (Rony) and M@X, eds. *Prog Archives: Your Ultimate Prog Rock Resource*. Accessed March 21, 2024. www.progarchives.com/artist.asp?id=2800

"Programová část sjezdového referátu predneseného Lubomírem Železným." *Hudební rozhledy* 26 (1973): 2–6.

Pynsent, Robert B. "The Baroque Continuum of Czech Literature." *The Slavonic and East European Review* 62 (1984): 321–43.

Pynsent, Robert B., ed. *The Phoney Peace: Power and Culture in Central Europe 1945-49*. London: School of Slavonic and East European Studies, University College London, 2000.

Raban, Josef. "Skoncujme s diletantismem." *Literární noviny. Týdeník pro kulturně politické a umělecké otázky* 7 (April 1958): 9.

Radano, Ronald, and Philip Bohlman, eds. *Music and the Racial Imagination*. Chicago: University of Chicago Press, 2000.

Radice, Mark A., ed. *Karel Husa – A Composer's Life in Essays and Documents*. Lewiston, NY: Edwin Mellen Press, 2002.

Rampley, Matthew. "Decolonizing Central Europe: Czech Art and the Question of 'Colonial Innocence.'" *Visual Resources* 37 (March 2021): 1–30.

Rawson, Robert G. *Bohemian Baroque*. Woodbridge: Boydell & Brewer, 2013.

Reittererová, Vlasta. "Hudební umění jako realizovaná pravdivost." *Hudební věda* 45 (2008): 125–78.

Reittererová, Vlasta, and Lubomír Spurný. *Alois Hába (1893–1973): Mezi tradicí a inovací*. Prague: KLP, 2014.

Rejžek, Jan. "Krátká jasná stopa Mahagonu." *Československý jazzrock*. 2008 by Indies Happy Trails. Compact disc and liner notes.

Rentsch, Ivana, and Arne Stollberg, eds. *Ton-Spuren aus der alten Welt. Europäische Filmmusik bis 1945*. Munich: text+kritik, 2013.

Rice, John A. *Antonio Salieri and Viennese opera*. Chicago: University of Chicago Press, 1998.

  W. A. Mozart: La clemenza di Tito. New York: Cambridge University Press, 1991.

Rice, Timothy. *Modeling Ethnomusicology*. New York: Oxford University Press, 2016.

Richard Wagner an Mathilde Wesendonk [*sic*], *Tagebuchblätter und Briefe 1853–1871*. Berlin: Alexander Duncker, 1904.

Riedel, Friedrich W. *Kirchenmusik am Hofe Karls VI: (1711–1740)*. Munich: Katzbichler, 1977.

Riedel, Jaroslav. *Plastic People a český underground*. Prague: Galén, 2016.

Rietsch, Heinrich, ed. *Georg Muffat: Florilegium primum*. Vienna: Universal Edition, 1919.

Rossi, Michaela Žáčková. *The Musicians at the Court of Rudolf II: The Musical Entourage of Rudolf II (1576–1612) Reconstructed from the Imperial Accounting Ledgers*. Prague: KLP, 2017.

Rutherford, Jonathan, ed. *Identity: Community, Culture, Difference*. London: Lawrence & Wishart, 1990.

Rychnovsky, Ernst. *Johann Friedrich Kittl: Ein Beitrag zur Musikgeschichte Prags*, 2 vols. Prague: Verein für Geschichte der Deutschen in Böhmen, 1904.

Šafránek, Miloš. *Bohuslav Martinů: život a dílo*. Prague: Státní hudební vydavatelství, 1961.

Šafránek, Miloš, ed. *Bohuslav Martinů. Domov, hudba a svět. Deníky, zápisníky, úvahy a články*. Prague: Státní hudební vydavatelství, 1966.

Saft, Franz Paul. *Der Neuaufbau der katholischen Kirche in Sachsen im 18. Jahrhundert*. Leipzig: St Benno, 1961.

St. Pierre, Kelly. *Bedřich Smetana: Myth, Music, and Propaganda*. Rochester, NY: Rochester University Press, 2017.

Sales, Franz. *Canzonette, Vilanelle et Neapolitane, per cantar' et sonare con il liuto et altri simili istromenti*. Prague: 1598.

   Patrocinium musices in Natalem Domini Jesu Christ … Mutetum quinque vocum, et Missa, ad eius imitationem composta. Munich: 1598.

   Tripartiti operis officiorum missalium, quibus introitus, alleluia et communiones, 3 vols. Prague, 1594, and 1596.

Sanneh, Kelefa. "The Rap against Rockism." *The New York Times*, October 31, 2014.

Saunders, Steven. "The Hapsburg Court of Ferdinand II and the Messa, Magnificat et Iubilate Deo a sette chori concertati con le trombe (1621) of Giovanni Valentini." *Journal of the American Musicological Society* 44 (1991): 359–403.

Sayer, Derek. *The Coasts of Bohemia*. Princeton, NJ: Princeton University Press, 1998.

Scheinpflug, Bernhard. "Joseph Wolfram: eine biographische Skizze." *Mitteilungen des Vereines für Geschichte der Deutschen in Böhmen* 9 (1871): 120–26.

Schlager, Karlheinz, ed. *Alleluia-Melodien II: ab 1100*. Monumenta monodica medii aevi 7 Kassel: Bärenreiter, 1987.

Schmid, Manfred Hermann, ed. *Rosenkranz-Sonaten, Bayerische Staatsbibliothek, Mus. Mss. 4123. Denkmäler der Musik in Salzburg*, vol. 14. Munich: Strube, 2008.

Schneider, Albrecht. "Comparative and Systematic Musicology in Relation to Ethnomusicology: A Historical and Methodological Survey." *Ethnomusicology* 50 (2006), 236–58.

Schneider, Magnus Tessing. *The Original Portrayal of Mozart's* Don Giovanni. New York: Routledge, 2021.

Schneider, Magnus Tessing, and Ruth Tatlow, eds. *Mozart's La clemenza di Tito: Reappraisal*. Stockholm: Stockholm University Press, 2018.

Schnierer, Miloš. *Český a východoevropský neofolklorismus: v artificiální hudbě 20. století*. Brno: Editio Moravia, 2007.

Schoenbaum, Camillo. *Geschichte der böhmischen Musik. Von den Anfängen bis in die Zeit der Romantik*. Regensburg: ConBrio, 2022.

Schoenberg, Arnold. *Style and Idea*. Berkeley: University of California Press, 1975.

Scholes, P. A., ed. *Dr. Burney's Musical Tours in Europe*, 2 vols. New York: Oxford University Press, 1959.

Schonberg, Michal. *Osvobozené*. Translated by Ivo Řezníček. Toronto: 68 Publishers, 1988.

Von Schönfeld, Johann Ferdinand. *Jahrbuch der Tonkunst von Wien und Prag*. Vienna, 1796.

Schubart, Ludwig, ed. *Christ. Fried. Dan. Schubart's Ideen zu einer Ästhetik der Tonkunst* [1784–85]. Vienna: J. V. Degen, 1806.

Schumann, Robert. *Music and Musicians: Essays and Criticism.* Translated by Fanny Raymond Ritter. Freeport: Books for Libraries, 1972.

Šedivá, Eliška. *Catalogus collectionis operum artis musicae comitis Clam-Gallas.* Prague: Národní knihovna, 2018.

Sehnal, Jiří. *Adam Michna of Otradovice – Composer.* Olomouc: Palacký University, 2016.

   Pavel Vejvanovský and the Kroměříž Music Collection: Perspectives on seventeenth-century Music in Moravia. Olomouc: Univerzita Palackého, 2008.

Sehnal, Jiří, ed. *Adam Václav Michna z Otradovic: Missa sancti Wenceslai.* Musica antiqua bohemica II/1. Prague: Supraphon, 1984.

Sehnal, Jiří et al., eds. *Philippus Jacobus Rittler: Requiem Claudiae imperatricis.* Olomouc: MusicOl, 1998.

Sehnal, Jiří, and Jiří Vysloužil. *Dějiny hudby na Moravě. Vlastivěda moravská.* Brno: Muzejní a vlastivědná společnost, 2001.

Seifert, Herbert. *Die Oper am Wiener Kaiserhof.* Tutzing: Schneider 1985.

   Die Oper am Wiener Kaiserhof im 17. Jahrhundert, Ergänzungen und Korrekturen des Autors zum Spielplan 1622–1705 (Stand 2010). Accessed June 12, 2023. www.donjuanarchiv.at/fileadmin/DJA/Forschung/Zentraleuropa/Opern-_und_Theaterrepertoire/Forschungsliteratur_online/Seifert/Seifert_1985_Appendix_2010.pdf

Sekyrová, Jana. "Eliška Šliková: Život neprovdané hraběnky v první polovině 19. století." MA thesis, University of České Budějovice, 2006.

Shelemay, Kay Kaufman. *Soundscapes: Exploring Music in a Changing World.* New York: Norton, 2006.

Shuker, Rosy. *Popular Music: The Key Concepts.* New York: Routledge, 2010.

Simon, Artur, ed. *Das Berliner Phonogramm-Archiv 1900–2000.* Berlin: VWB, 2000.

Skalník, Peter, ed. *A Post-Communist Millennium: The Struggles for Sociocultural Anthropology in Western and Eastern Europe.* Prague: Charles University, 2002.

Skalníková, Olga, ed. *Kladensko. Život a kultura lidu průmyslové oblasti.* Prague: Československá akademie věd, 1959.

Skuherský, František. *Nauka o harmonii na základě vědeckém.* Prague: Urbánek, 1885.

Skuherský, Zdeněk. *27 staročeských chorálů.* Prague: Urbánek, 1887.

Šlosar, Dušan, and Miloš Štědroň, eds. "František Martin Pelcl: Akademická nástupní řeč o užitečnosti a důležitosti češtiny." *Sborník prací Filozofické fakulty brněnské univerzity, H, Řada hudebněvědná* 37–38 (1988): [67]–94.

Slouka, Petr. "'Jaroměřické' monografie Vladimíra Helferta jako vzor pro výzkum opery ve střední Evropě v první polovině 18. století." *Musicologica Brunensia* 50 (2015): 87–100.

Smaczny, Jan. "Dvořák, His Librettists, and the Working Libretto for Armida." *Music & Letters* 91: 555–67.

Smetana, Robert, ed. *Dějiny české hudební kultury 1890–1945*, 2 vols. Prague: Academia, 1972.

Smolka, Jaroslav. *Ladislav Vycpálek: tvůrčí vývoj*. Prague: SNKLHU, 1960.

Sobitschka, Josef. *Geschichte des Deutschen Sängerbundes in Böhmen 1864–1884*. Tetschen an der Elbe: Deutscher Sängerbund, 1884.

Součková, Ema. *Výzdoba hudebních rukopisů Jana Táborského z Klokotské Hory*. Prague: Academia, 2019.

Šourek, Otakar. *Život a dílo Antonína Dvořáka*, 2nd ed., 3 vols. Prague: SNKLHU, 1956.

Spáčilová, Jana. *Hudba na dvoře olomouckého biskupa Schrattenbacha*. Olomouc: Univerzita Palackého, 2018.

"Počátky opery ve Slezsku – současný stav pramenů." *Musicologica Brunensia* 51 (2016): 157–70.

"Zpracování pověsti o Libuši v barokní opeře." *Musicologica Brunensia* 57 (2022): 85–113.

Spee Von Langenfeld, Friedrich. *Trutz Nachtigal*. Cologne: Wilhelm Friessem, 1649.

Spicer, Mark, ed. *The Ashgate Library of Essays on Popular Music: Rock*. Burlington, VT: Ashgate, 2012.

Srb, Josef, and Ferdinand Tadra, eds. *Památník pražského Hlaholu. Na oslavu 25leté činnosti spolku*. Prague: Hlahol, 1886.

Srba, Antonín. *Boj proti Dvořákovi*. Prague: Lidové družstvo, 1914.

Stangl, Kurt. "In Memoriam Gustav Becking." *Die Musikforschung* 2 (1949): 126–31.

Statelova, Rosemary, Angela Rodel, Lozanka Peycheva, Ivanka Vlaeva, and Ventsislav Dimov, eds. *The Human World and Musical Diversity*. Sofia: Bulgarian Musicology Studies, 2008.

Steadman, Philip. *Renaissance Fun: The Machines behind the Scenes*. London: UCL Press, 2021.

Štědroň, Bohumír. "Husitské náměty v české a světové hudbě." *Časopis Národního muzea* (1953).

Leoš Janáček: k jeho lidskému a uměleckému profilu. Prague: Panton, 1976.

Štědroň, Miloš. *Leoš Janáček a hudba 20. století: paralely, sondy, dokumenty*. Brno: Nadace Universitas Masarykiana, 1998.

Štefan, Jiří. *Ecclesia Metropolitana Pragensis Catalogus Collectionis Operum Artis Musicae*, 2 vols. Prague: Supraphon, 1983–85.

Štefková, Markéta. "Podstata hudobnej reči Suchoňovej Krútňavy." *Slovenská hudba* 34 (2008): 239–57.

Štěpka, K. V., ed. *Staročeské zpěvy duchovní*. Prague, 1953.

Štěříková, Edita. *Více sluší poslouchati Boha než lidí*. Prague: Kalich–Exulant, 2015.

Štilichová-Suchoňová, Danica. *Život plný hudby. Hudobný skladateľ Eugen Suchoň 1908–1993 v spomienkach*. Bratislava: Mladé letá, 2005.

Stockigt, Janice B. *Jan Dismas Zelenka (1679–1745): A Bohemian Musician at the Court of Dresden.* New York: Oxford University Press, 2000.

———. *Jan Dismas Zelenka (1679–1745): Český Hudebník na Drážďanském Dvoře.* Prague: Vyšehrad, 2018.

———. "The Organists of Leipzig's Royal Catholic Chapel: 1719–56." *Hudební věda* 53 (2016): 1–12.

Stockigt, Janice B., and Jóhannes Ágústsson. "Reflections and Recent Findings on the Life and Music of Jan Dismas Zelenka (1679–1745)." *Clavibus unitis* IV (2015): 7–48.

Stockigt, Janice B., and Jana Vojtešková. "Zpráva o návštěvě císaře Karla VI. s chotí v Klementinu v roce 1723." *Hudební věda* 4 (1992): 351–59.

Straková, Teodora, and Eva Drlíková, eds. *Leoš Janáček*, 2 vols. Brno: Editio Janáček, 2003.

Strasser, Ulrike. "Copies with Souls." *Journal of Jesuit Studies* 2 (2015): 558–85.

Stuckenschmidt, H. H. "Premiéry a poloprázdné sály." *Hudební rozhledy* 18 (1965): 523.

Suchý, Jiří. *Encyklopedie Jiřího Suchého, svazek 10, Divadlo 1963–1969.* Prague: Karolinum and Pražská imaginace, 2002.

Svatos, Thomas D. *Martinů's Subliminal States: A Study of the Composer's Writings and Reception, with a Translation of His American Diaries.* Rochester, NY: University of Rochester Press, 2018.

Svatošová, Hana, and Václav Ledvinka, eds. *Město a jeho dům: Kapitoly ze stoleté historie Obecního domu hlavního města Prahy (1901–2001).* Prague: Obecní dům, 2002.

Světlová, Daniela, and Theresa Jill Buckland, eds. *Folklore Revival Movements in Europe post 1950: Shifting Contexts and Perspectives.* Prague: Ethnological Institute, Czech Academy of Sciences, 2018.

Sychra, Antonín. "Odcizení, fetišismus v hudbě, regrese sluchu a jak dál." *Hudební rozhledy* 17 (1964): 731–32.

———. *Stranická hudební kritika spolutvůrce nové hudby.* Prague: Za novou hudbu, 1951.

Tairov, Alexandr. *Odpoutané divadlo. Zápisky režiséra.* Translated by Josef Menzel. Prague: Orbis, 1927.

Tairow, Alexander. *Das entfesselte Theater. Aufzeichnungen eines Regisseurs*, repr. 1923. Berlin: Alexander, 1989.

Tanturri, Alberto. "Ordres et congrégations enseignants à l'époque de la Contre-Réforme: Barnabites, Somasques, Scolopes." *Revue historique* 313 (2011): 811–52.

Tardonová, Veronika. "Eliška Krásnohorská a *Ženské listy* (1873-1926)." BA thesis, University of Pardubice, 2009.

Taruskin, Richard. *Oxford History of Western Music*, 6 vols. New York: Oxford University Press, 2005.

Taussig, Pavel, ed. *Marijka nevěrnice.* Prague: Odeon, 1982.

Teich, Mikuláš, Dušan Kováč, and Martin D. Brown, eds. *Slovakia in History*. New York: Cambridge University Press, 2011.

Teige, Karel, ed. *Dopisy Smetanovy*. Prague: Urbánek, 1896.

Teplitz im Jahre 1830 oder: Almanach für die Teplitzer Kurgäste auf das Jahr 1831. Prague: Gerzabek, 1831.

Teplitzer Kur- und Badegästeliste für das Jahr 1823. Prague: Gerzabek, 1823.

Teuber, Oscar. *Geschichte des Prager Theaters*, 3 vols. Prague: Haase, 1883–88.

Tomášek, Václav Jan. *Thesaurus Musicae Bohemiae: Seria B – Sinfonia Grande, Op. 17*. Edited by Šárka Jedličková. Prague: Supraphon, 1989.

Tomaštík, Eduard. "Giovanni Battista Alouisi – život a dílo." PhD diss., Masaryk University, Brno, 2013.

Träger, Josef, ed. *10 let Osvobozeného divadla 1927–1937. V+W*, 2nd ed. Prague: Borový, 1937.

Tranovský, Jiří. *Sborník k 300. výročí kancionálu Cithara Sanctorum*. Bratislava: Učená společnost Šafaříkova, 1936.

Traxler, Jiří. *Já nic, já muzikant*. Toronto: 68 Publishers, 1980.

Trolda, Emilian. "Jesuité a Hudba." *Cyril* 66 (1940).

Tůma, Jaromír. *Čtyři hrají rock, jasná zpráva o skupině Olympic*. Prague: Panton, 1986.

"Vánoční beat." *Melodie* 7 (February 1969): 49.

Tyl, Josef Kajetán. *Fidlovačka aneb Žádný hněv a žádná rvačka*. Prague: Narodní hudební vydavatelství, 1952.

Tyllner, Lubomír. *Dudy a dudácká muzika*. Prague: Etnologicky ústav AVČR, 2001.

Tyrrell, John. *Czech Opera*. New York: Cambridge University Press, 1988.

Janáček's Operas: A Documentary Account. London: Faber and Faber, 1992.

Janáček: Years of a Life, vol. 1. London: Faber and Faber, 2006.

Úlehla, Vladimír. *Živá píseň*. Prague: Borový, 1949.

Urban, Milo. *Za vyšným mlynom*. Bratislava: Knihy Slovenského národa, 1926.

Vácha, Štěpán, Alžběta Veselá, Vít Vlnas, and Petra Vokáčová, *Karel VI. & Alžběta Kristýna: Česká korunovace 1723*. Prague: Paseka, 2009.

Václavek, Bedřich, and Robert Smetana. *Český národní zpěvník. Písně české společnosti 19. století*. Prague: Svoboda, 1949.

Vaculínová, Marta, and Petr Daněk. "*Vita ceu harmonia*. Jiří Carolides: A Poet and Composer between the Imperial Court and the New Town of Prague." *Musicalia* 1–2 (2022): 6–32.

Vainiomäki, Tiina. *The Musical Realism of Leoš Janáček: From Speech Melodies to a Theory of Composition*. Helsinki: University of Helsinki, 2012.

Vajda, Igor. "Suchoňov 'Žalm zeme podkarpatskej.'" *Musicologica Slovaca* 1 (1969): 43–91.

Valový, Evžen. *Sborový zpěv v Čechách a na Moravě*. Brno: Univerzita J. E. Purkyně, 1972.

Vančura, Vladislav. *Jezero Ukereve*. Prague: Orbis, 1958.

Vaněk, Miroslav. *Byl to jenom rock'n'roll? Hudební alternativa v komunistickém Československu 1956–1989*. Prague: Academia, 2010.

Varnhagen Von Ense, Karl August. *Blätter aus der preußischen Geschichte*, 5 vols. Edited by Ludmilla Assing. Leipzig: Brockhaus, 1868.

Vejvodová, Veronika. "'Jsem šťasten, že po tak dlouhém odpočinku opět mohu pracovati na tom, co já chci a ne, co chtějí jiní.' Ke genezi Dvořákovy Armidy." *Opus musicum* 47 (2015): 36–57.

Velek, Viktor. "Die St. Wenzelsche Musiktradition von ihrem Anfang bis 1848." PhD diss., University of Vienna, 2008.

"The Saint Wenceslas Tradition during the Time of the Swastika." *Czech Music Quarterly* 2015, no. 1: 29–39.

"Searching for a Programme, Searching for an Identity, or the Association and the Struggle between the Saint Wenceslas and Hus-Hussite Traditions in Czech Music of the Second Half of the 19th Century." *Musicologica Olomucensia* 33 (2021): 374–408.

"V záři rudého kalicha aneb Jan Hus a husitství v hudbě 50. let 20. století." *Opus Musicum* 55 (2022): 6–19.

Veleslavína, Daniel Adam z. *Nomenclator Quadrilinguis, BoemicoLatino GraecoGermanicus* Prague: 1598.

Veselý, Zdeněk. *Dějiny českého státu v dokumentech*. Prague: Harvardské fondy, 1994.

Vetterl, Karel, and Olga Hrabalová, eds. *Guberniální sbírka písní a instrumentální hudby z Moravy a Slezska z roku 1819*. Strážnice: NULK, 1994.

Vičar, Jan. "Skladatelská generace sedmdesátých let, názory, orientace (výňatky)." *Opus musicum* 15 (1983): 101–9.

Vídenová, Martina. "Cecilská jednota a Antonín Dvořák." *Hudební věda* 55 (2018): 321–34.

Vidomus, Petr. "Music with a Revolutionary Purpose: Jazz Journalist Emanuel Uggé." *Hudební věda* 59 (2022): 246–314.

Vít, Jakub. "V roli exportéra 'věci komunismu': Československo a subsaharská Afrika 1948–1962." *Soudobé dějiny* 10 (2003): 29–57.

Vítová, Eva. *Petr Eben. Sedm zamyšlení nad životem a dílem*. Prague: Baronet, 2004.

Vlček, Josef. "Zbytečná skromnost M. Efektu," *Jazz* 5 (1976): 30.

Vlhová, Hana. "Die Fronleichnamsmesse in Böhmen: ein Beitrag zur spätmittelalterlichen Choraltradition." *Schweizer Jahrbuch für Musikwissenschaft. Neue Folge* 16 (1996): 13–36.

"Cantus fractus in Pre-Hussite Bohemia: Lost Repertories and Reconstruction Challenges." *Journal of the Alamire Foundation* 15 (2023): 11–31.

Repertorium troporum Bohemiae medii aevi 2. Tropi ad Kyrie eleison et Gloria in excelsis deo. Prague: Bärenreiter, 2006.

"Záviš, autor liturgické poezie 14. století." *Hudební věda* 3–4 (2007): 229–60.

Vlhová-Wörner, Hana, Eva Čapková, Štefánia Demská, Rhianydd Hallas, Eduard Lazorík, Jakub Pavlík, and Jana Vozková, eds. *Codicologica et Hymnologica*

Bohemica – Index Sequentiarum Bohemiae Medii Aevi. Accessed November 21, 2023. www.hymnologica.cz

Vlhová-Wörner, Hana, ed. *Jistebnice Kancionál: MS. Prague, National Museum Library II C 7. Critical edition. Vol. 2, Cantionale.* Monumenta liturgica Bohemica, vol. 3. Chomutov: Marek, 2019.

Vogl, Emil. "Lautenisten der böhmischen Spätrenaissance." *Die Musikforschung* 18 (1965): 281–90.

Vojtěch, Ivan. *Skladatelé o hudební poetice 20. století.* Prague: Československý spisovatel, 1960.

Volek, Jaroslav. "Jezero Ukereve." *Kulturní tvorba.* June 2, 1966.

Volek, Tomislav. "Antonio Vivaldi a česká šlechta." *Opus musicum* 40 (2008): 4–9.

Mozart, die italienische Oper und das Musikleben im Königreich Böhmen, 2 vols. Edited by Milada Jonášová and Matthias Pernerstorfer. Vienna: Hollitzer, 2016.

"Mozart-Rezeption in Böhmen." *Musikgeschichte in Mittel- und Osteuropa* 1 (1997): 85–93.

Vondráček, David. *Jaroslav Ježek zwischen Avantgarde und Jazz. Mit einem Werkverzeichnis des Komponisten von Mojmír Sobotka.* Münchner Veröffentlichungen zur Musikgeschichte 81. Munich: Allitera, 2021.

Voříšek, Martin. "Kapela schwarzenberské gardy v Českém Krumlově." PhD diss., Masaryk University, 2008.

Voskovec, Jiří. *Klobouk ve křoví. Výbor veršů V+W (1927–1947),* 3rd edition. Prague: Mladá fronta, 1996. First published 1965.

Voskovec, Jiří, and Jan Werich. *Hry Osvobozeného divadla I.* Prague: Československý spisovatel, 1961.

Osel a stín. Edice hry. Prague: Československý spisovatel, 1965.

Vycpálek, Ladislav. *Vzhůru srdce. Dvě variační fantasie na chrámové písně doby: Jesu Kriste, ščedrý kněže – Buóh všemohúcí.* Prague: Hudební matice, 1950.

Vysloužil, Jiří. *Karel Husa: Skladatel mezi Evropou a Amerikou.* Prague: AMU, 2011.

Wandruzska, Adam. *Leopold II: Erzherzog von Österreich, Grossherzog von Toskana, König von Ungarn und Böhmen, Römischer Kaiser,* 2 vols. Vienna: Herold, 1963–65.

Warren, Richard S. *Begins with the Oboe: A History of the Toronto Symphony Orchestra.* Toronto: University of Toronto Press, 2002.

Weber, Carl Maria von. *Hinterlassene Schriften,* 2 vols. Dresden: Arnold, 1928.

Weigner, Karel, ed. *Rovnocennost evropských plemen a cesty k jejich ušlechťování.* Prague: České akademie věd a umění, 1934.

Wiering, Frans. *The Language of the Modes: Studies in the History of Polyphonic Modality.* London: Taylor and Francis, 2015.

Willson, Flora. "Listening for Realism in Charpentier's *Louise.*" *Journal of the Royal Musical Association* 146 (2021): 397–424.

Wilson, William A. "Herder, Folklore and Romantic Nationalism." *Journal of Popular Culture* 6 (March 1973): 819–35.

Wistreich, Richard. "Philippe de Monte: New Autobiographical Documents." *Early Music History* 25 (2006): 257–308.

Wolfram, Joseph. *Kurze Notizen über Teplitz*. Teplice: Gerzabek, 1828.

Woodfield, Ian. *Performing Operas for Mozart*. New York: Cambridge University Press, 2012.

Zagar, Peter. "Žalmové kantáty Eugena Suchoňa a Zoltána Kodálya." *Slovenská hudba* 24 (1998): 73–81.

Zahra, Tara. "Reclaiming Children for the Nation: Germanization, National Ascription, and Democracy in the Bohemian Lands, 1900–1945." *Central European History* 37 (2004): 501–43.

Zahrádka, Jiří. *"Truth, the first thing is truth, not beauty." The Story of Janáček's Jenůfa*. Brno: Moravské zemské muzeum, 2021.

Žák, Emanuel. "Z domácího světa hudebního." *Vlasť* 19 (April 1903): 658–59.

Zapletal, Miloš. "'Always Seeking Truth both in Life and Art.' The Janáček School of Composition." *Czech Music Quarterly* 2014, nos. 1–2: 28–34, 35–41.

"Apoteóza Sokola, armády a nového člověka: rané recepce Janáčkovy Sinfonietty." *Hudební věda* 53 (2016): 257–87.

"Civilist Tendencies in the Interwar Czech Music: At the Beginning of a Research." *Musicologica Brunensia* 54 (2019): 237–51.

"Fysiologická hudba: z českých bojů o Novou hudbu let dvacátých." *Hudební věda* 56 (2020): 22–51.

"Playful but Animalistically Serious: Czech Interwar Music and Sport." *Czech Music Quarterly* 2018, no. 1: 15–25.

Zara, Vasco, and Marco Gurrieri, eds. *Renaissance Music in the Slavic World*. Turnhout: Brepols, 2019.

Zatloukal, Jaroslav. *Vítr z polonin*. Bratislava: Podkarpatoruské nakladatelství, 1936.

Zavarský, Ernest. *Ján Levoslav Bella. Život a dielo*. Bratislava: SAV, 1955.

Von Zehendtgrub, Paul Zehendtner. *Ordentliche Beschreibung mit was stattlichen Ceremonien und Zierlichheiten, die Röm[ische] Kay[serliche] May[estät], . . . sampt etlich andern Ertzherzogen, Fürsten und Herrn den Ordens deß Guldin Flüß . . . empfangen und angenommen*. Dillingen: 1587.

Zelenka-Lerando, Lev. *B. Smetana a E. Züngl Listy B. Smetany E. Zünglovi*. Nymburk: Pospíšil, 1903.

"Ženský výrobní spolek český (1871–1972)." *Knihy znovunalezené*. Published September 14, 2016. Accessed March 16, 2024. www.knihyznovunalezene.eu/cs/vlastnici/zensky-vyrobni-spolek.html

Żerańska-Kominek, Sławomira. *Nationality and Universality: Musical Historiographies in Central and Eastern Europe*. Newcastle upon Tyne: Cambridge Scholars Publishing, 2016.

Zich, Otakar. "O sbírání lidových písní." *Smetana: Hudební revue* 1 (1906): 275–77.

Zídek, Petr, and Karel Sieber. *Československo a subsaharská Afrika v letech 1948–1989*. Prague: Ústav mezinárndních vztahů, 2007.

Židek, Tomáš. "Polyfonie v dílech J. B. Foerstera a jeho současníků." PhD diss., HAMU, 2014.

Żórawska-Witkowska, Alina. *Muzyka na polskim dworze Augusta III*. Lublin: Wydawnictwo Muzyczne Polihymnia, 2012.

Žůrek, Jiří, ed., *Graduale Bohemorum. Proprium sanctorum*. Prague: Krystal OP, 2011.

Zvara, Vladimír. "Constructing the Past and the Future of Slovak Music: Dobroslav Orel in Interwar Bratislava." *Historický časopis* 69 (2021): 921–39.

Zvonař, Josef Leopold, ed. *Hudební památky české. Výbor krásných zpěvů českých, církevních i světských pro smíšený i mužský sbor v původní skladbě i v novém upravění s průvodem piana i bez průvodu z rozličných zpěvníků staročeských*, 4 vols. Prague: Kober, 1862–64.

Index

For EU product safety concerns, contact us at Calle de José Abascal, 56–1°, 28003 Madrid, Spain or eugpsr@cambridge.org.

www.ingramcontent.com/pod-product-compliance
Ingram Content Group UK Ltd.
Pitfield, Milton Keynes, MK11 3LW, UK
UKHW051613101025

463821UK00010B/223